Recent Developments in Historical Phonology

Trends in Linguistics
Studies and Monographs 4

Editor

Werner Winter

Mouton Publishers
The Hague · Paris · New York

Recent Developments in Historical Phonology

edited by

Jacek Fisiak

Mouton Publishers
The Hague · Paris · New York

Professor Jacek Fisiak
Institute of English
Adam Mickiewicz University
Poznań, Poland

Papers prepared for the
International Conference on Historical Phonology
held at Ustronie, Poland, 17–20 March 1976.

ISBN 90 279 7706 2

Preface

The present collection of essays on historical phonology contains twenty-four of the twenty-eight papers submitted for presentation at the International Conference on Historical Phonology held at Ustronie (Poland) between 17th and 20th March 1976 under the auspices of the Institute of English at Adam Mickiewicz University, Poznań. Of the twenty-four papers, two were not delivered at the conference, as their authors could not attend in person.

The aim of the conference was to bring together a number of scholars working in the field of historical phonology, thus facilitating the presentation of the most recent achievements in this area of linguistic research. The intention of the organizers was not to limit the theoretical bias of the conference to one particular paradigm but rather to open a forum to the presentation of ideas within any framework. Hence the present volume contains both generative phonological works, forming the majority, as well as contributions representing other theoretical views.

The papers presented at Ustronie and included in this collection seem to represent fairly well the present state of historical phonology. The central point of interest is still, as could be expected, phonological change. As in earlier days, many questions still remain unanswered and many answers are far from being definite. Thus, the need for more research is given support and leads one to expect a further rise of interest in historical linguistics.

Although the majority of papers are general and theoretically oriented, several valuable language-specific descriptive and data-oriented contributions have also been offered. The languages analyzed or used for illustrations were not limited exclusively to the Indo-European family. Some aspects of historical phonology of Japanese, Korean, and Finnish, among other languages, have been discussed. An attempt has also been made to formalize one type of phonological change.

The conference has not settled any particular issue or solved any major controversy. After all, that was not its aim. It is hoped, however, that it brought about a better understanding of some phonological problems in a historical perspective, and has helped to indicate areas awaiting further investigation. It has also revealed some of the weaknesses of existing linguistic theories, encouraging linguists to look for improvements and to search for more powerful explanatory tools.

The conference could not succeed without the active participation of its members and therefore we would like to thank them all for what they did to make it as successful as it was.

Thanks are also due to the Rector of Adam Mickiewicz University for providing more than adequate funding and all his help, to the administration of the Ustronie conference centre for making our stay pleasant, and thus inspiring scholarly efforts, and last but not least to Ms. Ewa Siarkiewicz for her patience and skill in handling all the administrative details, so very important for an efficiently organized meeting.

Poznań, July 1976   Jacek Fisiak

Table of contents

Preface   v

List of Conference Participants   ix

Henning Andersen
Perceptual and conceptual factors in abductive innovations.   1

Stephen R. Anderson
Historical change and rule ordering in phonology.   23

Raimo Anttila
The acceptance of sound change by linguistic structure.   43

Jerzy Bańczerowski
A formal approach to the theory of fortition-lenition: a preliminary
study 57

Xavier Dekeyser
Some considerations on voicing with special reference to spirants in
English and Dutch: a diachronic-contrastive approach   99

Gaberell Drachman
Child language and language change: a conjecture and some refutations.   123

Wolfgang Dressler
How much does performance contribute to phonological change?. . .   145

Martin B. Harris
The inter-relationship between phonological and grammatical
change. 159

Henry M. Hoenigswald
Secondary split, typology and universals   173

Joan B. Hooper
Constraints on schwa-deletion in American English   183

David Huntley
Phonological models and Slavic palatalizations 209

Robert J. Jeffers
Restructuring, relexicalization, and reversion in historical
phonology 213

Chin-W. Kim
"Diagonal" vowel harmony?: Some implications for historical
phonology 221

Frederik Kortlandt
I.-E. palatovelars before resonants in Balto-Slavic. 237

Roger Lass
Mapping constraints in phonological reconstruction: on climbing
down trees without falling out of them 245

James D. McCawley
Notes on the history of accent in Japanese 287

Witold Mańczak
Irregular sound change due to frequency in German 309

Jerzy Rubach
Phonostylistics and sound change 321

Robert P. Stockwell
Perseverance in the English vowel shift 337

Guy A. J. Tops
The origin of the Germanic dental preterit: Von Friesen
revisited. 349

Paul Valentin
The simplification of the unstressed vowel systems in Old High
German 373

Theo Vennemann
Rule inversion and lexical storage: the case of Sanskrit visarga 391

Nigel Vincent
Is sound change teleological? 409

Werner Winter
The distribution of short and long vowels in stems of the type
Lith. *ĕsti*: *vèsti*: *mèsti* and OCS *jasti*: *vesti*: *mesti* in Baltic and
Slavic languages. 431

Frederik Kortlandt
Comment on W. Winter's paper 447

Index of names 449

List of participants

at the International Conference on Historical Phonology held at Ustronie,
Poland, March 17–20, 1976

Director

Professor Jacek Fisiak — Institute of English,
Adam Mickiewicz University

Participants

Professor Henning Andersen	Slavic Institute, University of Copenhagen
Professor Stephen R. Anderson	Department of Linguistics, U.C.L.A.
Professor Raimo Anttila	Department of Indo-European Studies, U.C.L.A.
Docent Wiesław Awedyk	Institute of English, Adam Mickiewicz University, Poznań
Professor Jerzy Bańczerowski	Institute of Linguistics, Adam Mickiewicz University, Poznań
Professor Broder Carstensen	Gesamthochschule Paderborn
Docent Jan Cygan	Institute of English, Wrocław University
Professor Xavier Dekeyser	Department of English, University of Antwerp
Mr James Dingley	Department of German, University of Reading
Mr Grzegorz Dogil	Institute of English, Adam Mickiewicz University
Professor Gaberell Drachman	Institute of Linguistics, University of Salzburg
Professor Wolfgang Dressler	Institute of Linguistics, University of Vienna
Professor James Foley	Department of Modern Languages, Simon Fraser University

Dr Edmund Gussmann — Institute of English, Maria Curie-Skłodowska University, Lublin

Professor Martin B. Harris — Department of Modern Languages, Salford University

Professor Henry M. Hoenigswald — Department of Linguistics, University of Pennsylvania

Professor Joan B. Hooper — Department of Linguistics, SUNY – Buffalo

Professor David Huntley — Department of Slavic, University of Toronto

Professor John Hutcheson — Institute of English, University of Silesia, Katowice

Professor George Horn — Institute of English, Adam Mickiewicz University, Poznań

Professor Frederik H. H. Kortlandt — University of Leiden

Docent Roman Laskowski — Institute of Polish Language, Polish Academy of Sciences, Cracow

Dr Roger Lass — Department of Linguistics, University of Edinburgh

Professor James D. McCawley — Department of Linguistics, University of Chicago

Professor Witold Mańczak — Institute of Romance Studies, University of Cracow

Dr Bogusław Marek — Institute of English, Maria Curie-Skłodowska University, Lublin

Docent Ruta Nagucka — Institute of English, University of Cracow

Dr Jadwiga Nawrocka-Fisiak — Institute of Linguistics, Adam Mickiewicz University, Poznań

Professor Henri Niedzielski — Institute of English, University of Cracow

Dr Mirosław Nowakowski — Institute of English, Adam Mickiewicz University

Professor Wayne O'Neil — Department of Humanities, MIT

Mr Stanisław Puppel — Institute of English, Adam Mickiewicz University

Ms Teresa Retelewska — Institute of English, Adam Mickiewicz University

Dr Jerzy Rubach — Institute of English, University of Warsaw

Dr Piotr Ruszkiewicz	Institute of Foreign Languages, University of Silesia, Katowice
Professor Keith Sauer	Department of English, University of Cluj
Ms Ewa Siarkiewicz	Institute of English, Adam Mickiewicz University
Docent Albertas Steponavičius	Department of English, Vilnius State University
Professor Robert P. Stockwell	Department of Linguistics, U.C.L.A.
Docent Aleksander Szwedek	Department of English, Pedagogical University, Bydgoszcz
Professor Mary Taylor	Institute of English, University of Łódź
Professor John Taylor	Institute of English, Maria Curie-Skłodowska University, Lublin
Dr Guy A. J. Tops	Department of English, University of Antwerp
Professor Elizabeth Closs Traugott	Linguistics Program, Stanford University
Professor Paul Valentin	Institute of Germanic Studies, University of Paris-Sorbonne
Professor Theo Vennemann	Institute of German Philology, University of Munich
Mr Nigel Vincent	Department of French Studies, University of Lancaster
Dr Alicja Wegner	Institute of English, Adam Mickiewicz University
Mr Richard C. Wiest	Department of English, University of Cluj
Professor Werner Winter	Department of Linguistics, University of Kiel

HENNING ANDERSEN

Perceptual and conceptual factors
in abductive innovations

0.0 In the development of several of the West and East Slavic languages, phonological changes have occurred by which these languages and their dialects have back vowels corresponding to original front vowels, e.g. *o* for Common Slavic (CS) *e*. The changes are a good example of one of the common quandaries of the language historian, who — faced with partially similar innovations in different dialects — must decide whether the similarities are sufficient to allow him to speak of a single, shared innovation, or the differences so great that he must view the innovations as independent of each other and ascribe their similarities to inherited typological affinities or to fortuity. Indeed the Slavic changes of *e* > *o* and *ě* > *a*, as they are usually called, seem quite comparable in this respect to the textbook case of this kind, the apparently independent development of i-Umlaut in the various branches of Germanic.

The similarities between, for instance, the Polish and the Russian alternations cited in (1) tempt us to seek a single explanation for both.

(1) Pol. *bžoza* 'birch', *bžeźina* 'birch grove'; *plotka* 'false rumor', *pleść* 'to gossip'; *žona* 'wife', *žeńsk, i* 'female'; *jeźoro* 'lake', *pojeźeže* 'lake front'. Russ. *b,er,óza* 'birch', *b,er,ézn,ik* 'birch grove'; *pl,ótka* 'whip lash', *pl,ét,* 'idem'; *žóni* 'wives', *žénsk,ij* 'female'; *oz,óra* 'lakes', *zaoz,ér,je* 'area beyond a lake'.

But our tendency to generalize is checked by apparently insurmountable difficulties: the *e* > *o* change applied before all plain (non-palatalized) consonants in Russian, but only before plain dentals in Polish (2); it applied in word final position in Russian, but not in Polish (3); it applied to the *e* that developed from CS *ĭ* in Russian, but not in Polish (4); it was paralleled by a change of *ě* > *a* in Polish, but not in Russian (5); and it occurred before 900 in Polish, but apparently not before the 1300's in Russian, i.e. at a time when

the two languages had followed independent courses of development for
perhaps a thousand years.

(2) Pol. *ńebo* 'sky', *ćepłi* 'warm', *legł* 'lay down', *ćekł* 'ran'.
    Russ. *n,óbo* 'palate', *t,óplij* 'warm', *l,óg* 'lay down', *t,ók* 'ran'.

(3) Pol. *lice* 'face', *osče* 'knife edge', *moje* 'my'.
    Russ. *licó* 'face', *ostr,ijó* 'knife edge', *mojó* 'my'.

(4) CS *lĭnŭ* 'flax', *pĭsŭ* 'dog', *orĭlŭ* 'eagle'.
    Pol. *len* 'flax', *pes* 'dog', *ožeł* 'eagle'.
    Russ. *l,ón* 'flax', *p,ós* 'dog', *or,ól* 'eagle'.

(5) CS *vĕra* 'faith', *vĕriti* 'believe', *klĕtŭka* 'cage, dim.', *klĕtĭ* 'cage'.
    Pol. *vara* 'faith', *vežić* 'believe', *klatka* 'cage, dim.', *kleć* 'cage'.
    Russ. *v,éra* 'faith', *v,ér,it,* 'believe', *kl,étka* 'cage, dim.', *kl,ét,* 'cage'.

In the face of such difficulties, it seems perhaps more reasonable to treat
these similar changes as independent of each other and to try to account
for them individually. This, in fact, is the policy most investigators have
followed. So far, however, no satisfactory explanation for either of the
developments has been proposed.

0.1 In this paper, I will follow tradition in initially considering the East and
West Slavic developments separately. But I will break with tradition in my
method of analysis. All previous treatments of the *e* > *o* changes have defined
a number of areas in the East and West Slavic language areas, each with
its characteristic variant of the *e* > *o* change, and have then tried to establish
the historical development of each area on the basis of internal evidence
(relative chronology) as well as textual evidence in order to finally pose (or,
more often, leave unformulated) the question of what motivated the particular developments. One cannot say that this method is unsound. But it can and
should be supplemented with the use of a complementary method, which
does not focus on individual linguistic systems and ask how they developed
through time, but instead focuses on isoglosses and asks how they arose.
    In the investigation of the *e* > *o* change by the traditional, area or system
oriented methods, the list of possible questions that can be put to the available data has pretty well been exhausted. To be sure, there are data pertinent
to the change which traditionally have been overlooked. But even if these
had been taken into consideration, this would merely have resulted in the

definition of a few more, smaller areas, each of which could be investigated by the traditional methods without yielding new insights. But the moment attention is turned instead to the contrasts between different areas, to the divergent developments of contiguous dialects reflected in the isoglosses that separate them, the very same data suggest a fresh set of questions to be considered.

Isoglosses are by their origin of different types. An isogloss separating two dialects may reflect the contrast between the presence of an innovation in one and the absence of the same innovation in the other (diagram A in Figure 1); I call this the simplex type. It may reflect two logically alternative innovations in the neighboring dialects (diagram B); I call this the duplex type. Or it may reflect a shared innovation which had different consequences in the two dialects because of some previous structural difference between them (diagrams Ca and Cb); I call this the complex type. Any attempt to interpret an isogloss must begin by posing the question to which of these basic types it belongs.

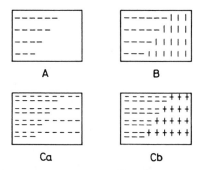

Fig. 1.   Simplex (A), duplex (B), and two kinds of complex isoglosses (Ca, Cb).

In answering this question, it is important to keep in mind that dialect differences are correspondences and that a correspondence may be the result of a single innovation or a series of innovations (cf. Andersen 1972), and furthermore that a strict distinction must be observed between abductive and deductive innovations (cf. Andersen 1973).

Finally, as has long been recognized, the spatial contiguity (bundling) or similarity (parallelism, symmetry) of isoglosses may reflect significant structural or chronological connections between the innovations that gave rise to them. Consequently the interpretation of isoglosses requires consistent attention to relations among isoglosses.

0.2 In the following pages I will try to illustrate this approach to historical dialectology by surveying the major isoglosses that the *e* > *o* change has given rise to in the East Slavic languages (section 1). All the particulars which a definitive account must explain cannot be mentioned here, but enough of the details will be discussed to show how the kinds of questions the interpretation of isoglosses may raise can contribute to a precise formulation of what needs to be explained in historical phonology.

Next I will propose a skeleton explanation of the *e* > *o* change, based on a likely parallel change outside the Slavic language family, and will show how this hypothetical account can be elaborated to cover the specifics of the East Slavic dialects (section 2).

I will then turn to the similar change in Polish and show that it, too, can be accounted for by the same skeleton explanation (section 3).

The account to be proposed explains the similarity among the various East and West Slavic *e* > *o* changes as the result of a shared deductive innovation and the differences among them as the results of different abductive innovations, in part motivated by structural differences among the dialects, in part merely made possible by the inherent perceptual complexity of the speech signal.

1.0 The isoglosses to be discussed are shown on the map below (on p. 5) with numbers corresponding to the subsections of this section.

1.1 Isogloss 1. This is the geographically most complex isogloss to be considered. It defines a few large enclaves and several dozen smaller pockets in the Russian language area — fewer near the center than around the periphery. Outside these enclaves, CS *e* has changed to *o* if followed by a plain consonant or if word final. In the enclaves, the *e* > *o* change appears not to have taken place as a phonological development; cf. (6). Dialects in the enclaves do have *o* for CS *e*, but have enough examples of unchanged *e* — largely different from dialect to dialect — to indicate that *e* is the regular reflex, and the occurrence of *o* is due to analogical leveling (curtailment or loss of an *o* → *e* rule applying to suffixes) or to contact motivated lexical substitution (cf. Orlova 1970:22—28 with detailed map; Filin 1972:196f.).

(6) Isogloss 1

kl,én	*r,év*	*b,er,éza*	*kot,énok*	*žĕlud,*
kl,ón	*r,óv*	*b,er,óza*	*kot,ónok*	*žólud,*

CS *klenŭ* 'maple', *revŭ* 'roar', *berza* 'birch', *kotenŭkŭ* 'kitten', *želǫdĭ* 'acorn'.

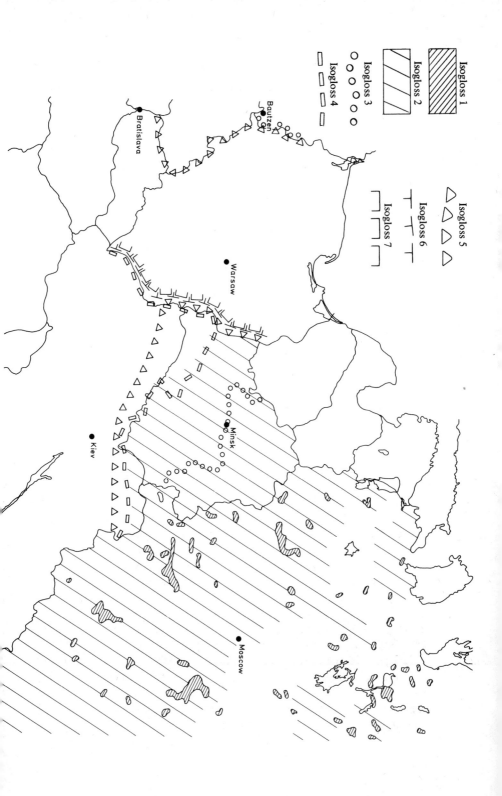

Isogloss 1

Isogloss 2

Isogloss 3

Isogloss 4 ○ ○ ○ ○ ○

Isogloss 5 ▷ ▷ ▷ ▷

Isogloss 6 ⊤ ⊤ ⊤

Isogloss 7

Bautzen

Bratislava

Warsaw

Minsk

Kiev

Moscow

Discussion. The geographical structure of the isogloss can be understood only on the background of the settlement history of Russia and cannot be discussed here. Most likely, though, Isogloss 1 at an earlier time circumscribed fewer, larger areas with *e* for CS *e*.

Isogloss 1 appears at first blush to be of the simplex type, reflecting the contrast between the absence and the presence of the $e > o$ change. Just as likely, however, it is of the duplex type, as will be shown below.

1.2 Isogloss 2. The isogloss defines a large area in the center of the modern East Slavic language area, embracing Russian as well as Belorussian dialects. Outside this area, the $e > o$ change clearly applied to accented as well as unaccented *e*. In the dialects inside Isogloss 2, *o* for CS *e* occurs only in stressed syllables; cf. (7). In some dialects inside Isogloss 2 — most of Belorussia and much of the central and south Russian dialect area — this is evidently due to secondary changes (called vowel reduction), by which the number of vowel distinctions in unstressed syllables has been reduced, the earlier *o* (for CS *e*) having changed to *a, e.* or *i*. But for the core area inside Isogloss 2 it is strictly impossible to determine whether the $e > o$ change was limited to stressed syllables, as is traditionally assumed, or its effects have merely been obscured by later developments (cf. Orlova 1970:152—158 with maps and passim; Avanesaw 1964:56—76 with maps; Filin 1972: 194ff.).

(7) Isogloss 2

s,oló	óz,oro	nos,it,o
s,eló	óz,ero	nos,ít,e

CS *selo* 'village', *jezero* 'lake', *nosite* 'carry; 2nd pl. imperative'.

Discussion. In the latter case, Isogloss 2 is of the simplex type and reflects the contrast between the absence and the presence of an innovation (vowel reduction) which is later than, and therefore unlikely to be relevant for the explanation of the $e > o$ change.

But if in the core area inside Isogloss 2 the $e > o$ change was limited to accented syllables, then the isogloss which originally defined this area must have been of the complex type, reflecting the different ways in which the $e > o$ change impinged on different systems, systems that apparently differed with respect to some aspect of word prosody.

This is potentially an interesting finding. One can imagine, for example, that this isogloss originally reflected a difference in the pronunciation rules that specified the relative duration of stressed and unstressed vowels at the time of the $e > o$ change. But it may also have reflected a deeper structural difference at the time of this innovation, a difference between dialects with phonemic stress – and a marked difference in duration between stressed and unstressed vowels – and dialects which did not have stress, but another phonemic prosodic feature. This is a possibility which must be taken seriously, for it is certain that early East Slavic had a pitch accent, inherited from the Common Slavic period, which probably at different times in different areas was reinterpreted as a force accent.

It is possible, then, that Isogloss 2 originally – i.e. before the spread of vowel reduction – reflected a difference in relative chronology: where the $e > o$ change occurred before stress became phonemic, it affected accented and unaccented e alike; where the $e > o$ change occurred after the shift from pitch accent to force accent, it may have affected only accented e (thus in the core area inside Isogloss 2).

It should be emphasized that this is only one of several possible interpretations, and that it finds no more direct support in the data than do its alternatives, mentioned above. However, we will see more connections between the $e > o$ change and prosodic innovations below, which lend it considerable support.

1.3 Isogloss 3. In the north-of-3 dialects, the $e > o$ change applied to word final e; in the south-of-3 dialects, it did not. Most occurrences of word final o for CS e are found in desinences where e originally alternated with o, and the modern o may be due to analogical levelling. But the shape of the 2nd person plural desinence in the present tense and imperative can be taken at face value, for in this morpheme analogical change is excluded; cf. (8) (cf. Avanesaw 1964:267f., map p. 240).

(8) Isogloss 3

$n,as,ic,ó$	$iʒ,ic,ó$	$s,aʒ,ic,ó$	$hl,aʒ,ic,ó$
$n,es,ac,é$	$iʒ,ac,é$	$s,aʒ,ic,é$	$hl,aʒ,ic,é$

CS *nesete* 'carry', *idete* 'walk', *sědite* 'sit', *ględite* 'look' (2nd pl. pres.).

Discussion. This isogloss must be of the complex type, just as Isogloss 2. It reflects a difference between the north-of-3 dialects and the south-of-3 dialects which existed when the $e > o$ change occurred. Viewed in isolation, this isogloss is enigmatic. But if it is compared to Isogloss 2, it suggests a hypothesis: if the $e > o$ change inside the original Isogloss 2 area depended on the relative duration of stressed and unstressed vowels, then the absence of the $e > o$ change in word final position south of Isogloss 3 may reflect a pronunciation rule which specified word final vowels as relatively short.

As it happens, there is ample evidence of just such a pronunciation rule in those South and West Slavic languages which have preserved reflexes of the innovations in quantity that took place in the late Common Slavic period. No evidence of this Common Slavic innovation has been known from the East Slavic languages, and no evidence from the other Slavic languages has suggested that this innovation was geographically limited. But it is plausible that it did take place in East Slavic, and if it did, one could reasonably expect that it occurred in an area definable as central among the Slavic dialects at that time. In fact, Isogloss 3, which seems to define the north-eastern limit of this area, correlates with an isogloss separating Sorbian from Polish, for in Sorbian, the $e > o$ change affected word-final e just as in northern East Slavic; cf. (9).

(9) Isogloss 3

Lower Sorbian	*lico*	*zbóžo*	*buźo*	*buźośo*
Polish	*lice*	*zboże*	*beńže*	*beńžeće*

CS *lice* 'face', *sŭbožije* 'grain', *bǫde, bǫdete* 'will be; 3rd sg. and 2nd pl. pres.'.

Isogloss 3, then, can provisionally be interpreted as reflecting the difference between dialects (north of Isogloss 3 in East Slavic, west of it in West Slavic) which had not introduced the central Slavic innovation by which word final vowels came to be pronounced shorter than word internal vowels, and dialects (inside Isogloss 3) which had introduced this innovation by the time of the $e > o$ change.

1.4 The last two isoglosses to be discussed cut through the southern part of the East Slavic language area in which CS e (parallel with CS o) was subject to compensatory lengthening when the following syllabic was a lax high vowel (CS $ĭ$ or $ŭ$) which was elided and eventually lost. In this environment — termed strong position — the "normal" reflexes of CS e are $\widehat{ie}$ and, where the $e > o$ change has applied, $\widehat{uo}$; in southern Ukraine, $\widehat{ie}$ and $\widehat{uo}$ have later changed to i. In other environments — termed weak position — the corresponding reflexes are e and o (Filin 1972:221ff.); cf. (10).

(10)

	Strong position		Weak position	
CS	*pečĭ*	*ščeku*	*pečĭ*	*ščeka*
NUkr.	*pĭềč*	*ščừòk*	*pečĭ*	*ščoka*
SUkr.	*pĭč*	*ščik*	*pečĭ*	*ščoka*

'stove; nom.sg.', 'cheek; gen.pl.', 'stove; gen.sg.', 'cheek; nom.sg.'.

Isogloss 4. In the north-of-4 dialects, the $e > o$ change applied to e in weak position regardless of the nature of the preceding consonant. In the south-of-4 dialects, *e* in weak position changed to *o* only after *č, š, ž,* or *j*: (Filin 1972:199f.); cf. (11).

(11) Isogloss 4

s,óli	c,ópli	dal,óka	učora	žonati
séla	téplyj	daléko	učora	žonatyj

CS *sela* 'villages', *teplŭjĭ* 'warm', *daleko* 'far', *vĭčera* 'yesterday', *ženatŭjĭ* 'married'.

Discussion. The interpretation of this isogloss must take as its point of departure the fact, long recognized, but not satisfactorily explained, that it not only defines the contrast between dialects with different reflexes of CS *e*, but at the same time is the boundary between dialects (north of Isogloss 4) with sharped consonants before the reflexes of CS *e* in weak position and dialects (south of Isogloss 4) with plain consonants before these reflexes. The origin of this latter difference between the dialects north and south of Isogloss 4 has been explained by Jakobson as follows.

In Old Russian, consonants were adjusted for tonality to following vowels, being sharped before front vowels and plain (and likely labialized and/or velarized) before back vowels. The lax high vowels, *ĭ* and *ŭ,* tended to be elided in certain environments, among them word final position, and at some point ceased to be recognized as segments. At this point, sharping became phonemic. This meant that all positional variants of consonants before vowels must be evaluated categorially as either sharped or plain. In the north-of-4 dialects, dentals and labials before weak *e* were evaluated as phonemically sharped, whereas in the south-of-4 dialects, they were evaluated as phonemically plain (Jakobson 1929/1962:71f.).

This account of the sharped/plain difference between the dialects north and south of Isogloss 4 is quite satisfactory (cf. Andersen 1974:30ff.). The task that remains is to explain the connection between this bifurcation and the *e* > *o* change. Most accounts of the change merely assume that sharping in the preceding consonant was a prerequisite for the *e* > *o* change. This is undoubtedly correct, but as it happens, there is firm evidence that the *e* > *o* change (or some phase of it) occurred earlier than the sharp/plain bifurcation. The evidence is the following.

In the south-of-4 dialects, *e* in strong position has undergone the *e* > *o* change (cf. (13)). Before sharped consonants, where the *e* > *o* change did not apply, strong *e* has merged with the reflex of CS *ě* (the tense mid front vowel of Old Russian, cf. Fig. 2), e.g. NUkr. *píeč* 'oven', *kys,íel,* 'fruit jelly' (CS *pečĭ, kyseljĭ*), *d,íed* 'grandfather', *l,íes* 'forest' (CS *dědŭ, lěsŭ*). This merger is attested in the very first texts that show evidence of the loss of

ORuss. *ĭ, ŭ* as separate phonemes (namely their identification with weak *e, o* in the environments where they were not elided). Since the reflex of CS *ě* has not been subject to the *e > o* change (cf. *d,ĭed, l,ĭes*, not *d,ŭod, l,ŭos*), the *e > o* change (or some phase of it) must have taken place before the partial merger of strong *e* with *ě*, hence before *ĭ, ŭ* were lost or identified with weak *e* and *o*.

Conclusion. The interpretation of Isogloss *4* has to account for the intimate connection between the *e > o* change and the different treatment of consonants before weak *e* north and south of the isogloss, that is, it has to explain a bifurcation that can be written schematically as in (12):

(12)   ORuss. *s,ela* $<$ $\dfrac{s,ola}{sela}$ Isogloss 4

Furthermore, it must resolve a paradox, explaining how the *e > o* change could take place earlier than this bifurcation, be reflected after *č, š, ž, and j,* and still not be reflected in south-of-4 forms of the type *séla*.

1.5 Isogloss 5. The dialects in the Ukraine differ from the South Belorussian dialects in the treatment of CS *e* in strong position. All these dialects have *ĭe* (or a secondary reflex of *ĭe*) for strong *e* before sharped consonants. But before original plain consonants, the north-of-5 dialects have *ŭo* for strong *e* without any restrictions, whereas the south-of-5 dialects show *ŭo* (in southern Ukrainian, *i*) only in original pretonic syllables (traditionally called neoacute), but *e* in syllables that were not pretonic (cf. Bulaxovs'kyj 1956:52ff.).

(13)
Isogloss 5	*m,ŭod*	*kl,ŭon*	*s,ŭol*	*n,ŭos*
	med	*klen*	*s,ŭol*	*n,ŭos*

CS *m'edŭ* 'honey', *kl'enŭ* 'maple', *sel'ŭ* 'village; gen.pl.', *nesl'ŭ* 'carry; resultative participle, m.sg.'.

Discussion. A connection between the *e > o* change and prosodic relations was suggested twice above, in the discussion of Isoglosses 2 and 3. The prosodic conditions for the treatment of strong *e* in Ukrainian have been known for some time, but have not previously been understood. It seems that once Isoglosses 2, 3, and 5 are considered together, a common denominator becomes evident. The restriction of the *e > o* change in the Isogloss 2 area to accented syllables may be due to the shorter duration of unaccented vowels after stress became phonemic. The restriction of the *e > o* change to non-final *e* in the south-of-3 dialects may be due to the short duration of final vowels in a large central Slavic area in the period before stress became phonemic. The restriction of the strong $e > \tilde{u}o$ change to pretonic position in the south-of-5 dialects can be explained in a similar fashion if one can hypothesize that in these dialects, at the time of the $e > o$ change, pretonic vowels were longer than vowels in other positions relative to the accent. Such a hypothesis has never been proposed for Ukrainian before, but it is a reasonable hypothesis. In fact, it merely posits for an early stage of southern East Slavic a pronunciation rule governing the relative duration of syllables within a phonological word which must be posited for the neighboring West Slavic dialects from which Slovak and Polish have developed: in these languages, only the pretonic long vowels of Common Slavic were preserved as long, whereas original tonic and atonic long vowels were reinterpreted as short.

As in the case of Isogloss 3, for which a counterpart was found in the West Slavic language area, so in this case: Isogloss 5 is of the complex type, reflecting an innovation which has given somewhat different results in neighboring dialects due to earlier differences between them; Isogloss 5 has a counterpart in the West Slavic language area, an isogloss which separates Slovak and Polish from Czech and Sorbian; the difference between the East Slavic dialects north and south of Isogloss 5 is the result of a central Slavic innovation by which tonic and atonic vowels came to be pronounced appreciably shorter than pretonic vowels.

But this is only the first step towards an explanation. It remains to be shown what was the nature of the $e > o$ change, and how this change — which was a change in vowel quality — could be dependent on the duration of vowels. Let us turn to a possible parallel outside the Slavic language family.

2.0 In the history of Roumanian, consonants have become palatalized before original front vowels, just as in Early Slavic. At a later time, perhaps, the lax vowels ε and $\mathfrak{o}$ (distinct from the tense e and o) have been diphthongized to *ea* and *oa*. As a consequence of these two innovations, words with original ε — and these are the ones that are of interest here — are pronounced with sound sequences that present the investigator with a problem of segmentation. The first syllable in, for instance, *seară* 'evening' [s,earə] can be analysed in two ways:

A. /s,a/. The [s,] is interpreted as a realization of /s,/; [ea] is interpreted as a positionally conditioned realization of /a/, the [e] portion in particular as a transition from a sharped consonant.

B. /s,ε/. The [s,] is interpreted as a realization of /s,/; this interpretation implies the existence of a diphthongization rule applying to /ε/ (and /ɔ/).

Roumanian phonologists have discussed these different possible phonemic resolutions of the same surface phonetics and have disagreed strongly on which of them should be considered the right one (cf. Rosetti 1959:47–54, Petrovici 1957). There is no need to rehearse this discussion here, but I would like to emphasize that there is a lesson to be learnt from cases such as this, where the linguist's methods of analysis do not yield a unique solution. The lesson is not that we must strive to develop more reliable criteria in the hope that some time in the future we will be able to settle all such issues confidently. It is rather that language data present real ambiguities for analysis.

In a synchronic description, such ambiguities should not be resolved by the mechanical application of criteria assumed to be infallible, but should be reflected in alternative hypotheses about the structure of the language in question – with the understanding that the ambiguities may exist also for the learners of the language and may lead to different interpretations of the surface forms by different speakers of the language. For the historical linguist such ambiguities are particularly interesting, for it stands to reason that where real ambiguities exist, at some juncture in the historical development of a language, they may give rise to dialect differences; for learners in different parts of a language area may resolve a phonetic ambiguity in different ways. Here is an area where the descriptivist and the historical linguist – and in particular the historical dialectologist – can profit by pooling their experience. Cases of non-unique solutions in synchronic analysis can shed light on the conditions of historical change. And, on the other hand, a meticulous analysis of the conditions of attested changes can sharpen our understanding of the difficulties of analysis with which learners of a language actually have to cope, and help us identify the factors that guide their decisions.

2.1 Let us assume for Old Russian the existence of two pronunciation rules, closely analogous to the Roumanian ones just discussed:

Rule 1. Consonants are sharped before front vowels, plain before back vowels.

Rule 2. /e/ is pronounced as a diphthong, its second portion being grave and flat, except before sharped consonants.

With the application of these two rules, an underlying representation like /sela/ would be realized approximately as [s‚εɔla].

Let us further distinguish explicitly between two phases in the *e* > *o* change, a deductive innovation consisting in the introduction of Rule 2, with the overt consequence that /e/ was realized with an [ɔ] off-glide before plain consonants and in word final position; and an abductive innovation consisting in

the interpretation of [ɛ ɔ] as a realization of the phoneme /o/ in some environ-
ment(s).

We can now reexamine the five isoglosses.

2.2 Isogloss 4. Following Jakobson, we may view surface forms with sharped
consonants as ambiguous at the time when sharping became phonemic. An
[ɛ]-colored consonant before [ɛɔ] could be interpreted as a contextual
variant of, for instance /s/ or /s,/. If it was interpreted as /s/, its sharping
would tend to be lost through a remedial adjustment (cf. Andersen 1974:26
and passim). If it was interpreted as /s,/, its sharping would tend to be correspondingly increased. In the south-of-4 dialects, the former alternative was
chosen, e.g. /sela/; in the north-of-4 dialects, the latter, i.e. /s,ela/.

A direct consequence of this bifurcation was that in the south-of-4 dialects,
a phonemic interpretation of [ɛɔ] as /o/ was precluded after phonemically
plain consonants: once labials and dentals were interpreted as phonemically
plain before [ɛɔ], there was no possibility of analysing the [ɛ]-element of
[ɛɔ] as a transition from a preceding sharped consonant. In position after
the palatal consonants /č š ž j/, however, such an interpretation was still possible, indeed favored by the general tendency for palatal glides to be "absorbed"
by preceding palatal consonants.

The posited diphthongization of /e/ to [ɛɔ], in short, is compatible with
Jakobson's account of the origin of Isogloss 4 and, at the same time, with a
plausible explanation for the change of weak *e > o* only after palatals in the
south-of-4 dialects. The tendency for the initial portion of the [ɛɔ] diphthong
to be absorbed by preceding palatals may well have been active over a long
period (cf. the similar change of Engl. /iu/ > /u/ in examples like *chew, jew*),
proceeding on a lexeme by lexeme basis. It is well attested already in the 1100's
(Filin 1972:190f.) and may well have begun already before the sharp/plain
bifurcation.

Isogloss 1. For the north-of-4 dialects which identified, for instance, [s,]
before [ɛɔ] as a realization of /s,/, there remained the ambiguity typified by
the Roumanian example discussed above: [ɛɔ] could be interpreted as a
variant of /e/, realized with an [ɔ] off-glide unless followed by a sharped consonant, e.g. [s,ɛɔla] could be interpreted as /s,ela/; or it could be interpreted
as a variant of /o/ occurring after sharped consonants, i.e. [s,ɛɔla] as /s,ola/.
Any dialect which chose the former alternative *eo ipso* preserved the ambiguity
and might at a later point interpret such sequences as sharped consonant
+ /o/.

In the preliminary discussion of Isogloss 1 (sec. 1.1), I noted that this has
the appearance of a simplex isogloss. Now that the change of *e > o* has been
analysed into a sequence of a deductive and an abductive innovation, it can

be seen that the isogloss admits of another interpretation. It may be that the deductive innovation did not occur in the enclave dialects; in this case, the isogloss does reflect the contrast between an innovation and the absence of that innovation, and is of the simplex type. But it is possible, and perhaps likely, that the deductive innovation took place in all Russian dialects, and only the subsequent abductive innovations differentiated them; in that case, Isogloss 1 reflects a bifurcation, i.e. is of the duplex type.

2.3 Isogloss 2. The difference between the dialects outside the original Isogloss 2 area, in which the *e* > *o* change applied both to accented and to unaccented syllables, and the dialects inside Isogloss 2, in which it applied only to accented syllables, was provisionally explained as due to a difference in phonemic prosodic features: the dialects outside Isogloss 2 had a pitch accent at the time of the change, whereas the dialects inside Isogloss 2 had a force accent and a concomitant marked differentiation of stressed and unstressed syllables with respect to duration. This explanation fits well with the proposed account of the *e* > *o* change. It seems reasonable to suppose that the deductive innovation, by which /e/ was diphthongized, was independent of the nature of the accent. But one would expect diphthongized vowels to be more markedly diphthongal when long than when short and therefore more susceptible to that metanalysis which is the essence of the abductive phase of the *e* > *o* change.

If one assumes, then, that inside the original Isogloss 2 area the shift from phonemic pitch to phonemic stress occurred before the abductive innovation in the *e* > *o* change, it is clear why only stressed [ɛɔ] might be interpreted as /o/.

Isogloss 3. Very similar considerations account for Isogloss 3. This isogloss traverses an area in which the *e* > *o* change applied both to accented and to unaccented syllables (cf. the examples in Karskij 1955: 171ff.). We may assume that dialects on both sides of the isogloss had a pitch accent at the time of the abductive innovation. But if we assume that the south-of-3 dialects had a pronunciation rule by which word final vowels were pronounced perceptibly shorter than word internal vowels, then it is clear why only word internal [ɛɔ] would be interpreted as /o/.

Isogloss 5. Similarly in the case of the contrast between the north-of-5 dialects, in which the *e* > *o* change applied to any strong *e* followed by a plain consonant, and the south-of-5 dialects, where only pretonic strong *e* changed to *ủo*. Here the circumstances are a little different, inasmuch as we are dealing with compensatorily lengthened vowels which were shortened unless pretonic. But we may still assume that the deductive innovation expressed in Rule 2 (sec. 2.1) took place with perfect generality in all the dialects,

creating two positional variants of /e/, [ɛ] and [ɛɔ]. By the compensatory
lengthening, these were further differentiated with the addition of two new
variants, likely both longer and tenser, perhaps [e·] and [eo]. The shortening
of all but pretonic vowels must have produced vowel variants of different
duration depending on their position relative to the place of accent and on
the number of syllables in the word – to mention but the most important
factors. But for our purposes it is enough to distinguish normal and shortened
variants of the compensatorily lengthened /e/, the normal ones being the
ones just mentioned, the shortened ones being laxer, and therefore sufficiently similar to /e/ in weak position to be identified with this; cf. (14).
Note that labials and dentals before weak /e/ were interpreted as
phonemically plain, but before the lengthened, tense variants, they were
evaluated as sharped. /ê/,/ô/ in the examples in (14) correspond to the
modern [îe] [ûo].

(14)

Common Slavic	/m'edŭ/	/m'edu/	/sel'ŭ/	/sel'o/	/sem'ĭ/	/sem'i/	/d'ĕdŭ/
Rules 1 and 2: sharping and diphthongization	[m,ɛɔdʊ	m,ɛɔdu	s,ɛɔlʊ	s,ɛɔlo	s,ɛm,ɹ	s,ɛm,i	d,iedʊ]
Compensatory lengthening	[m,eod(ʊ)	m,ɛɔdu	s,eol(ʊ)	s,ɛɔlo	s,e·m,(ɪ)	s,ɛm,i	d,ie·d(ʊ)]
Shortening	[m,ɛɔd(ʊ)	m,ɛɔdu	s,eol(ʊ)	s,ɛɔlo	s,e m,(ɪ)	s,ɛm,i	d,ied(ʊ)]
Early Ukrainian	/med/	/medu/	/s,ôl/	/selo/	/s,êm,/	/semi/	/d,êd/
	'honey;	'honey;	'village;	'village;	'seven;	'seven;	'grand-
	nom.sg.'	gen.sg.'	gen.pl.'	nom.sg.'	nom.'	gen.'	father'

2.4 From the remarks about relative chronology in sec. 1.4 and the preceding
discussion of Isogloss 5, it is evident that the deductive innovation that made
the abductive reinterpretations of /e/ as /o/ and /ô/ possible must have taken
place before the sharp/plain bifurcation that attended the loss of the lax high
vowels in the 1100's. This dating is at variance with the traditional view that
the *e* > *o* change began in the 1100's.

The traditional dating of the change is based in part on textual evidence,
in part on the fact that the *e* > *o* change affected not only CS *e*, but also CS
ĭ in those environments – termed strong position – where this was not elided,
e.g. in syllables preceding a final *i* or *u* (which was elided). The parallelism
between the reflexes of CS weak *e* and strong *ĭ* is complete; cf. (15). In an
approach that does not distinguish between deductive and abductive innova-

(15) | ORuss. | | Ukr. | | Russ. | |
|---|---|---|---|---|---|
| dĭnĭ | peči | den, | peči | d,en, | peči |
| pĭsŭ | sela | pes | sela | p,os | s,ola |
| šĭlŭ | žena(tŭjĭ) | šov | žonatyj | šol | žoni |

tions, it may seem reasonable to take the textual evidence at face value. But if this distinction is made, the earliest secure examples of written *o* for *e* must be taken as evidence only for the abductive reanalysis of /e/ variants as realizations of /o/. The diphthongization of /e/, which made this reinterpretation possible, must have occurred at an earlier time.

This means that the formulation given in Rule 2 (sec. 2.1) must be modified: the diphthongization affected not just CS *e*, but *e* and *ĭ*. This modification is a boon for our explanation, for *e* and *ĭ* constituted a "natural class" — they were the lax front vowels — for which the kind of diphthongization posited here is a commonplace (cf. Andersen 1972:31f.). One may wonder if perhaps all lax vowels were subject to diphthongization in Early East Slavic, as is usual in cases of laxness diphthongization (cf. the Roumanian examples in sec. 2.0, or the American "southern drawl"). But this question cannot be discussed here.

3.0 The account that has been developed in the preceding pages has made use of a method of analysis, applied in the interpretation of isoglosses, a model of phonological change, some specific hypotheses regarding the innovations that have been identified, and a number of assumptions concerning the kinds of motivation involved in these innovations. The account offers a way of resolving the quandary that was formulated in the introduction by analysing the different *e > o* changes in the various East Slavic dialects into sequences of two different kinds of innovation. The deductive innovation — the diphthongization of lax front vowels — was likely shared by all East Slavic dialects. But the extent to which this deductive innovation gave rise to abductive reinterpretations of /e/-variants as /o/-realizations depended on a number of different factors, which we will return to in sec. 4. In this section we will consider again the contrast that was drawn in the introduction between the *e > o* changes in Russian and Polish, which differ maximally, to see whether the explanatory apparatus needed for the East Slavic changes is adequate to explain the particulars of the Polish change.

One of the differences between Russian and Polish has already been accounted for in the discussion of the East Slavic isoglosses: the apparent preservation of *e* in word final position was explained as a consequence of the shortening of final vowels, a change which is well known to have taken place in the Slavic dialects from which Polish has developed.

But there are other differences that remain to be explained. First, in East Slavic the *e > o* change applied to both CS *e* and *ĭ*; in Polish, *ĭ* has not been affected; cf. the examples in (4). Secondly, the change of *e > o* was paralleled by a change of *ě > a* in Polish, but did not affect *ě* in East Slavic; cf. (5). Thirdly, the change applied before all plain consonants in East Slavic; but in

Polish it affected *e* and *ě* only before plain dentals; cf. (2). These differences are reflected in isoglosses in the dense bundle of isoglosses separating Polish from East Slavic. And each of these isoglosses must be analysed and interpreted along the lines followed in sec. 2.

3.0 Isogloss 6. The first and second of the differences just mentioned are obviously inseparable. They provide an interesting comment on the notion of "natural class", for when one compares the vowel systems of early East Slavic and of the dialects from which Polish has developed, it appears that *e* was a member of different "natural classes" east and west of Isogloss 6; cf. Fig. 2.

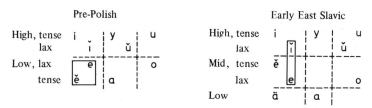

Fig. 2.   The pre-Polish and early East Slavic vowel systems. The boxes indicate the "natural classes" of vowels apparently subject to diphthongization.

Assuming that the *e* > *o* change can be explained analogously in Polish and East Slavic, Isogloss 6 must be of the complex type: the deductive innovation by which front vowels were diphthongized affected different vowels on the two sides of the isogloss, because the respective vowel systems were differently constituted. The difference between the two vowel systems is not a difference in the distinctive features they involve, but rather in the way in which the distinctive features are hierarchized: tenseness/laxness seems to have had a higher rank in the distinctive feature hierarchy of early East Slavic than in the pre-Polish dialects, where it apparently was subordinate to the features defining open front vowels.

Isogloss 7. The fact that the Polish change of *e* > *o* and *ě* > *a* was restricted to the position before plain dentals has hitherto lacked a satisfactory explanation. Traditionally the reflexes have been taken at face value, and it has seemed difficult to explain a change of front vowels to back vowels only before apical consonants (cf. Klemensiewicz et al. 1964:77f., Koneczna 1965:49f., 61f.). If we apply the model of change used above, however, we are impelled to analyse the diachronic correspondences *e* > *o* and *ě* > *a* into a sequence of deductive plus abductive innovations and thus to seek the relevant conditioning factors not only in articulatory phonetics, but also in the perceptual phase of the transmission of the speech signal.

If we assume that in the pre-Polish dialects, open front vowels were diphthongized, just as lax front vowels were in early East Slavic, and that this diphthongization applied with the same generality as the similar deductive innovation in East Slavic, then we can seek the reason for the restriction of the Polish change in its abductive phase.

Our experience with the East Slavic *e > o* change suggests that the interpretation of an [ɛɔ] diphthong as /o/ depends on the tonality of the preceding consonant, for it is after a sharped or an acute compact consonant that the initial portion of the diphthong may be interpreted as a mere transition. If we apply this experience to the relation between an [ɛɔ] diphthong and a following plain consonant, we can explain the limitations of the Polish *e > o* and *ě > a* change. Before the low tonality (plain grave) labials and velars, the final portion of an [ɛɔ] diphthong could be interpreted as a transition. Before the high tonality (acute) dentals, the final portion of an [ɛɔ] diphthong could not be analysed as a transition. In this way, the tonality of the following consonant had a seemingly paradoxical influence on the abductive evaluation of the diphthongal realizations of low front vowels: they were evaluated as grave before non-grave consonants, but as non-grave before grave consonants.

Isogloss 7 is evidently of the complex type. It reflects a shared deductive innovation, the diphthongization of a class of front vowels, which took place on both sides of the isogloss, but affected different vowels east and west of Isogloss 6. In the subsequent abductive interpretation of the diphthongs, the eastern and the western dialects went their separate ways again — giving rise to Isogloss 7 — the East Slavic dialects analysing the diphthongs only in relation to preceding consonants, the West Slavic dialects analysing them in relation to following consonants.

4.0 In the preceding pages, some old problems in Slavic historical phonology have been put in a new light by the use of a new way of analysing isoglosses and by the application of a theory of change which explicitly views the historical development of a language as an interplay between overt and covert innovations, between observable deductive innovations, which have their motivation in the grammar whose constitutive relations they make manifest, and unobservable abductive innovations — inferrable only from their deductive consequences — which arise in the process of grammar acquisition and are motivated primarily by the difficulties of analysis with which the learner has to cope.

The hypothetical account of the *e > o* change given here contains a number of points which it would be interesting for the Slavist to have discussed in greater detail. The gradual displacement of the centers of innovation from the central Slavic area (Isoglosses 3 and 5) to the central East Slavic area (Isogloss 2) to the central Russian area (the fragmentation of Isogloss 1) is one.

The connections that have been posited between the $e > o$ change and the central Slavic innovations in quantity (Isoglosses 3 and 5) and the East Slavic shift from phonemic pitch to phonemic stress (Isogloss 2) is another. Still others are the relations between the innovations discussed here and other innovations in the same languages and in other Slavic languages. But questions like these are better discussed in a different context, for they require reference to a wider, specifically Slavistic body of knowledge.

As the title of this paper indicates, the aim of the paper was of a more general nature. The $e > o$ change was chosen as a particularly good illustration of the need for historical phonology to liberate itself from the long tradition of exclusive reference to articulatory phonetics in attempts to explain phonological change.

4.1 We have here examined seven isoglosses, not one of which can be understood as motivated by articulatory factors.

The origin of Isoglosses 1, 4, and 7 seems to have been determined exclusively by conceptual factors. The question whether an [ɛ]-colored realization of a consonant before [ɛ] is to be interpreted as phonemically plain or sharped (Isogloss 4) apparently depends entirely on a mental operation. Similarly whether a diphthong is to be analysed as "center + off-glide" or "onglide + center" (Isoglosses 1 and 7) is a decision which, in principle, may be independent of the physical reality of the speech signal. These are typical examples of bifurcation with respect to valuation and segmentation (cf. Andersen 1974).

It is clear that the interpretation of an [ɛɔ] as a realization of /o/ rather than /e/ can be viewed as perceptually motivated: *ceteris paribus* the grave portion of such a diphthong is more likely to be perceived as the center of the diphthong than is the acute portion, for the grave portion's lower Formant 2 entails a greater concentration of acoustic energy within a relatively narrow frequency range and, hence, a greater perceptual intensity. This is the perceptual basis for what has been called "intensity shift" in diphthongs (Andersen 1972:23f.). But the different interpretations of [ɛɔ] before dentals and before labials or velars in Polish shows that whether "all other things are equal" may depend in part on the purely mental operation of segmenting the acoustic signal. In other words, the distinctive feature valuation of the perceived vowel sounds presupposes a segmentation.

The interpretation of Isoglosses 2, 3, and 5 made appeal to a perceptual factor by assuming that long diphthongs are more susceptible to metanalysis than short diphthongs. Here it is all too easy to point to the fact of articulatory phonetics that diphthongs tend to be pronounced more fully in slow speech than in rapid speech, more markedly heterogeneous when long than when short. But the fact remains that the abductive innovations that gave rise to these isoglosses — assuming the validity of the account proposed above — consisted in a categorial valuation as /o/ or /e/ of vowel sounds containing various amounts of [ɛ] resonance and [ɔ] resonance, occurring in an infinite variety of overall durations depending on a host of factors — the complexity of the syllable, the duration of neighboring syllables, the number of syllables in the word, position relative to the accent, position of the word in the utterance, rate of delivery, style of diction, etc. But the decision to identify vowel sounds in a given environment as realizations of /o/ or /e/ is first and foremost a mental operation performed on percepts. As such it will be influenced by the perceptual complexity of the speech signal, but it seems that what motivated the reinterpretation of certain /e/-variants as realizations of /o/ cannot so much have been their perceptual complexity as the amount of variability itself, which put the continued identification of all /e/-variants in jeopardy. The motivation for the innovations reflected in Isoglosses 2, 3, and 5, then, is to be found in the conceptual plane.

Of all the seven innovations we have examined, only one appears amenable to articulatory explanation, viz. the deductive one, the diphthongization that is ultimately responsible for isoglosses 1, 2, 3, 4, 5, and 7. The diphthongization has been explained as a dissimilatory change in vowel quality conditioned by a preceding sharped consonant (cf. Klemensiewicz et al. 1964:77ff., Koneczna 1965:61f.). But this kind of explanation at best answers the question How? It does not provide an answer to the question Why? or To what end?, to which historical explanations should be addressed. No articulatory account of the diphthongization will explain the other, abductive innovations that ensued. Indeed an articulatory account of the diphthongization must needs leave Isogloss 6 unexplained. The different "natural classes" constituted by the vowel systems west and east of the isogloss are a clear example of how also deductive innovations are governed by the conceptual structure of language. The decision to assign a higher rank to one phonemic opposition than to another is — just like the segmentation of the sound continuum and the categorial valuation in terms of binary distinctive features — not motivated by the sounds themselves, but determined by the conceptual apparatus with which the speakers analyse speech.

4.2 It seems that historical dialectology, which sets for itself the task of accounting for the origin of dialect differences — for the fact that a single linguistic system manifested in one set of overt norms of usage can develop in divergent ways in different parts of a speech community — perhaps more than other linguistic disciplines comes face to face with the principles of linguistic form (in the Saussurean sense). In synchronic phonology, it may seem unimportant whether distinctive features are defined and labeled with reference to articulatory gestures or acoustic parameters, or in metaphorical terms. The descriptivist may employ such notions as "binary opposition" or "segment" or "distinctive feature matrix" as mere convenient ways of "handling the data". Nothing prevents the historical phonologist or the dialectologist from adopting this detached attitude to the descriptive framework he needs to present his data.

But any attempt to interpret isoglosses and to understand linguistic divergence in explicit, realistic terms forces us to acknowledge that conceptual factors take precedence over perceptual or articulatory ones in determining how a phonological system may be changed as it is transmitted from generation to generation and to recognize that it is the structuring principles of linguistic form — the fact that the speech signal must be segmented, that distinctive features are binary, and that they must be ranked — and not the articulatory or acoustic or perceptual substance that shape its historical development. We are led to conclude that the ultimate source of dialect divergence — and of linguistic change in general — is the process of language acquisition, in which the speakers of a language impose form on the fluctuating and amorphous substance of speech.

References

Andersen, H.
    1972   "Diphthongization", *Language* 48: 11—50.
    1973   "Abductive and deductive change", *Language* 49: 567—593.
    1974   "Towards a typology of linguistic change: Bifurcating changes and binary relations", in: *Historical Linguistics. Proceedings of the First International Conference on Historical Linguistics* 2 (Eds: J. M. Anderson – C. Jones) (Amsterdam: North-Holland), pp. 17—60.
Avanesaw, R. I.
    1964   *Narysy pa belaruskaj dyjalektalohii* (Minsk: Navuka i texnika).
Bulaxovs'kyj, L. A.
    1956   *Pytannja poxodžennja ukrajins 'koji movy* (Kyjiv: Vyd-vo AN).
Filin, F. P.
    1972   *Proisxoždenie russkogo, ukrainskogo i belorusskogo jazykov. Istoriko-dialektologičeskij očerk* (Leningrad: Nauka).
Jakobson, R.
    1929   *Remarques sur l'évolution phonologique du russe comparée à celle des autres langues slaves* (= *TCLP* 2) (Prague). [Reprinted in *Selected Writings* 1 (The Hague: Mouton, 1962).]
Karskij, E. F.
    1955   *Belorusy. Jazyk belorusskogo naroda* 1 (Moskva: Izd. AN SSSR).
Klemensiewicz, Z. – T. Lehr-Spławiński – S. Urbańczyk.
    1964   *Gramatyka historyczna języka polskiego* (Warszawa: PWN).
Koneczna, H.
    1965   *Charakterystyka fonetyczna języka polskiego* (Warszawa: PWN).

Orlova, V. G.
   1970   *Obrazovanie severnorusskogo narečija i srednerusskix govorov* (Moskva: Nauka).
Petrovici, E.
   1957   *Kann das Phonemsystem einer Sprache durch fremden Einfluss umgestaltet werden?* (The Hague: Mouton).
Rosetti, A.
   1959   *Recherches sur les diphtongues roumaines* (København: Munksgaard).

STEPHEN R. ANDERSON

Historical change and rule ordering in phonology

During the course of the development of recent phonological theory, much
attention has been concentrated on the interactions of individual rules within
a grammar. Where rules interact in significant ways, this is usually formalized
by having them apply in a sequence, and it is usually assumed that this
sequence has much the same properties as those of other ordering relations
with which we are familiar: the ordering relation among the real numbers, for
example. Examples have sometimes appeared, however, in which the apparent
ordering relations among the rules of a grammar violate some of the formal
properties of such linear orderings: for example, two rules A and B may
appear to apply in the order A < B in the derivation of some forms, but in
the order B < A in others. Another such situation arises when rules A and B
appear to apply in that order, rules B and C in that order, but in forms where
only A and C apply, it is in the order C < A, rather than A < C. In either of
these cases (and others that can also be defined) the phonologist is confronted
with a *prime facie* case against the analogy between rule interactions and the
ordering of sets such as the real numbers.

There are several possible reactions to such a problem. Perhaps the commonest has been to assume that where such a situation appears to obtain,
some detail of the analysis must be incorrect, and that a proper formulation
of the rules involved will make them conform to the principles of linear orderings. Especially in early work in generative phonology, in fact, we find the
procedure of demonstrating that a particular formulation of the rules of the
language involves such an 'ordering paradox' used as a sort of *reductio ad
absurdum* of the analysis; and the attitude still persists that an analysis with
such 'paradoxical' consequences must involve a basic error somewhere.

Perhaps the most extreme form of this position is that taken by Newton
(1971), who demonstrates several examples of this sort from Modern Greek
dialects, concluding that they cast doubt on the plausibility of the entire
enterprise of synchronic phonology. Assuming that the phonological system of

modern Greek is to be described in terms of a set of rules applying in a sequence leads to the conclusion that the ordering relations among these rules must be non-linear. From this Newton concludes that a synchronic account of the system is impossible: only a historical account of the sequence of sound changes that gave rise to the system can be adequate.

Other linguists, however, have responded to the appearance of such ordering paradoxes by attempting to create a theoretical framework which will accommodate them. Perhaps the first such attempt was that of Chafe (1967), who distinguishes between a set of 'persistent' rules which may give rise to apparent paradoxes and the main bulk of rules whose orderings are well-behaved. An alternative view, which will be noted further below, is that of Anderson (1969, 1974), in which the ordering relation among rules is explicitly a 'local' one, relating pairs of rules with reference to classes of forms, and not entailing any of the defining properties of linear orderings. Another theoretical position for which the existence of orderings with non-linear properties is important (though this is not always recognized in the literature) is that of, e.g., Koutsoudas, Sanders & Noll (1974), and others[2] who would like to eliminate all explicit ('extrinsic') ordering statements from the grammars of particular languages. The significance of paradoxes for such a theory is that, in order to demonstrate the necessity (not merely the possibility) of eliminating ordering statements from grammars, it is necessary to show that some situations arise in which it would not be possible to describe the facts by listing the rules in a simple language-particular order. Where the observed interactions among rules are inconsistent with any possible linear ordering, a case of this sort can be argued to have been made. This point has been appreciated in recent papers by Koutsoudas, but not all of those who have proposed such theories have noted the importance of ordering paradoxes for distinguishing empirically between conventional theories and those in which (at least some of) the ordering restrictions are derived from language-independent principles.

Despite the existence of theories which explicitly allow for non-linear orderings, the majority of linguists still seem to feel that there is something not quite right about analyses which involve them. There are several possible explanations for this feeling. One of these is the feeling that a theory involving only linear orderings is in some pre-theoretical sense simpler than one allowing for other possibilities. The occasionally heard claim that a linear ordering theory is 'more restrictive' and hence to be preferred as making a stronger claim about the nature of language is often in fact quite similar to this view. Actual theories of non-linear ordering generally involve other properties and conditions such that the class of possible grammars allowed under them is different from that allowed under an assumption of strict linearity, not simply larger. In any case, the issue is surely to discover what situations actually arise in natural languages, not to decree before the fact that certain empirical possibilities are to be excluded because of the greater mental effort that might be involved in coming to understand them. In order to determine the correct set of principles governing the interactions of rules in natural languages, it is surely appropriate to go to the facts, construct descriptions of them in terms of apparently well-motivated rules, and then ask how these rules are to be related to one another. It is surely incorrect to require that an otherwise well-motivated analysis be reconstructed so as to conform to a particular view of the way rules should interact. Indeed, the methodological utility of the assumption of linear interaction becomes moot as soon as the first such instance arises: whenever an apparently valid rule must be reformulated so as to conform to this assumption, the possibility arises that it may well be the assumption of linearity, rather than the original formulation of the rule that was incorrect.

A second possible bias toward linearity no doubt comes from the often remarked resemblance between synchronic rule interactions and the historical sequence of antecedent sound changes. Many sound-changes can be viewed in terms of the addition of rules at the end of the grammar of a previous stage of the language. As a result, many of the orderings we find synchronically recapitulate in a direct way the sequence of changes by which the relevant rules entered the language. To some extent, we may say that diachrony established through internal reconstruction has a built-in tendency in this direction, for of course the method by which synchronic interactions are established is virtually the same as the method of internal reconstruction. But in cases in which the chronology can be established externally, the same resemblance can often be found, and this leads one to assume that, ceteris paribus, synchrony recapitulates diachrony. But the course of history is presumably linear: if we identify sound changes with points in time, the sound changes will be ordered in a strictly linear way: and if further we expect synchronic interactions to resemble the history, we would expect these also to be linear in nature.

It is the purpose of this paper to argue that both of these biases toward synchronic linearity are mistaken. On the one hand, the relation between history and synchronic phonological systems is far from being as simple as suggested above. As Newton (1971) emphasizes, historical changes do not take place at *points* in time, but rather through periods of time. A rule, that is, does not simply arise one day tout court, but rather evolves through an extended period of greater or lesser 'activity'. Such periods, unlike points, may overlap in complex ways, and thus even if rule addition at the end of the grammar were the only possible mechanism of change there would be no reason to expect the resultant systems to have a simple strictly linear character. In fact, we will argue that the attested mechanisms of linguistic change are such that we would expect non-linear or paradoxical interactions to develop from them. We could only expect such non-linearities to be absent, therefore, if we believed there were some other compelling constraint against them.

We might imagine that such a constraint does in fact exist, in the structure of the language-learning system. It is certainly the case that humans show a definite preference, in certain sorts of cognitive activity, for linear ordering relations. It might be the case, then, that human cognitive capacities are limited in this area, and that non-linear relationships are essentially unlearnable. In that event, whatever ordering paradoxes might arise through historical change would inevitably be eliminated through restructurings imposed in the learning process by the next generation of speakers.

In fact, however, no such constraint on human cognitive capacities appears to exist. As we will note below, closely similar problems have been faced in other disciplines, and it appears that there are circumstances interestingly analogous to those involved in human language use under which non-linear orderings are perfectly well tolerated. On the other hand, in circumstances more analogous to the reflective, scientific activity of linguists analysing language, a very definite predilection for linear relationships is found. We thus have an explanation not only for the fact that humans can learn systems involving non-linear relations, but also for the strong bias of linguists against such theories: the enterprises of learning and speaking a language on the one hand, and of describing and theorizing about it on the other, are essentially different and thus subject to different cognitive limitations.

We should at this point give an example of the sort of situation we have in mind, and describe the way in which it could arise historically on the simplest set of assumptions. Consider one of the examples presented by Newton (1971) from the Modern Greek dialect of Lesbos. In this dialect, the derivations of 'they have' and 'he has' are given as follows:

(1) /éxun/   /éxi/
                   éx'i   (palatalization)
     éxn   éx'   (loss of unstressed high vowels)
     éxin   (epenthesis in final clusters)
     [éx'in]   [éx']   (palatalization)

Now it will be immediately noted that the appearance of palatalization at two distinct points in the rule sequence in (1) is essential. Palatalization must precede the loss of high vowels, for it is the /i/ which is lost that gives rise to the palatalization in [ex']. Further, the loss of these vowels must precede the insertion of epenthetic /i/, for it is only after the impermissible final cluster /xn/ has been created that epenthesis is possible in [ex'in]. But, again, it is only after epenthetic /i/ has been inserted in the latter form that it can provoke palatalization. We see, therefore, that the total set of ordering relations observed involves an essential violation of the condition of transitivity, a condition fundamental to the definition of linear orderings.

Historically, the source of this situation is not hard to find. The rule of palatalization is and has been for some time an active part of the grammar of this dialect (and also, of course, of many others). Thus, when the sound change by which unstressed high vowels were lost originally took place, velars preceding original /i/ were presumably palatalized, and the sound change of high-vowel loss in no way changed that fact. That is, in the absence of an additional sound change of depalatalization, there is no reason to expect that the forms which were originally palatalized would lose this feature. Subsequently, epenthetic vowels were inserted to break up certain impermissible final clusters. At this point, new instances of the sequence velar plus high front vowel came into existence. Since palatalization was apparently still an active part of the (synchronic) grammar of the dialect, there is no reason not to expect these new sequences to provoke palatalization as well. Thus, the deviations given above result, in which from a synchronic point of view there is a violation of linearity. From the historical point of view, however, this is completely unproblematic: it results simply from the fact that palatalization was a rule of the grammar not just at a single point in time, but rather over a stretch of time extending from before the change reflected in the grammar by the rule of high-vowel loss until after the change reflected as the rule of epenthesis (and still further, perhaps).

The point of this example is that, while sound changes may or may not be properly viewed as taking place at points of time, the rules which can be added to grammars as a result exist in the synchronic system over an extended period. Thus, where rule R is present in synchronic grammars over a given period, we would expect that when other rules enter the grammar during that period, as a result of other sound changes, rule R would give the appearance of applying both to the inputs and to the outputs of these later rules. Given that R is a part of the grammar at the time some new change occurs, it would require a special restriction on R to keep it from applying to the forms that result from a new sound change, assuming they meet the structural description of R. Thus, the simplest view of the effects of sound change on synchronic grammars, the view that they invariably result in the addition of a new rule to the grammar, can be seen to give rise to the expectation that paradoxical situations such as in (1) above should exist in the grammars of natural languages. One reaction to this might be to throw in the synchronic towel, as it were, and to limit discussion of phonological systems to their history, but it would seem more constructive to attempt to construct a view of rule interaction that can accommodate them.

The point that rules exist in a grammar over an extended time, and follow a (partially predictable) evolutionary course, is hardly a new one. It was made quite well by Baudouin de Courtenay (1895), whose description of the course followed by a rule has not been substantially improved on since. When rules first enter a language, they appear as essentially phonetic generalizations: exceptionless (though perhaps highly specific) effects on surface forms. They may retain this character indefinitely, as is often the case with highly natural phonetic processes such as palatalization of velars before front vowels. They may subsequently become morphophonemic rules, however, by having their scope restricted in various ways. A common development which leads to this is a further sound change which creates new inputs for the rule. The rule may, of course apply to these new forms as well as to those originally within its scope, as was the case for palatalization in the discussion of Modern Greek above. It may be, however, that the applicability of the rule is limited to those forms which underwent it prior to the new sound change. In that case, the interaction of the old rule and the new can be expressed by saying that the grammar has incorporated an ordering restriction, requiring that the old rule not apply to the outputs of the new one. Recall that the motivation for such a restriction is simply that the original rule continues to apply to exactly the class of cases to which it applied before; but as a result of the presence of the new rule this result can only be obtained by restricting the rule in its application. As a result, it may no longer be a true generalization about surface forms in the language, and is thus on its way to further restriction and eventual loss.

As an example of this situation, we can take the history of the rules that gave rise to the Verschärfung alternation in Modern Faroese (cf. Anderson 1972b, 1974 for further details). Consider the following pair of derivations for *spýggja* "to spit" and *strýða* "to struggle":

2.   /spui̯+a/   /strui̯d+a/
       spui̯ + ia   (insertion of glide at hiatus)
       spuǰ + ia   (dissimilation of geminate glide)
                         strui̯+a   (loss of intervocalic single *g, d*)
                         strui̯+ ia   (insertion of glide at hiatus)
       [spUǰa]   [strUi̯ia]   (phonetic rules)

Faroese has apparently had a rule which breaks up hiatus through the insertion of a glide for most of its history. The interest of this rule is that it provides the source for the development of long glides in certain forms, where an original falling diphthong was followed by a vocalic ending. In the older Germanic languages the conditions for the development of these long glides (an essential precondition for the Verschärfung) may be quite problematic, but this is not the case in Faroese: the glide insertion rule is and has long been a live, phonetically motivated part of the language, quite independent of the Verschärfung alternation. It was undoubtedly present in the language before the development of the dissimilation process that leads to the affricate in [spUȷ̌a].

At some point after the process of dissimilation applied, single intervocalic voice stops *d* and *g* (then phonetically [ð] and [γ]) were lost. This loss gave rise to new instances of vowel hiatus, of course. However, the rule of glide insertion was still a productive rule of the synchronic phonology, and this fact resulted in the insertion of new glides in forms like [strUiia]. Now notice that the conditions for the dissimilation process are satisfied in these forms, but it does not apply: the rule has been limited in its applicability to those forms to which it applied before. This limitation (formalized in the grammar as a statement of extrinsic ordering) does not at all entail that the rule of dissimilation is no longer a part of the grammar of Faroese, but only that its applicability has been restricted. We see that the rules of glide insertion and dissimilation are at different stages of evolution: glide insertion (though probably the older of the two) is still a productive phonetic rule, while dissimilation has become a limited, morphophonemic rule. Both are present in the grammar, but only glide insertion is still a true generalization about surface forms. The derivation in (2) displays an ordering paradox synchronically, but again the historical explanation is clear: the rules involved remain part of the grammar of the language over a period of time, during which other sound changes may take place, giving rise to interactions among the rules which cannot be adequately modeled in terms of the points on the real line. The mechanisms involved are still the elementary ones of historical change, however, and our synchronic theory of rule orderings should reflect the fact that these mechanisms can be expected to give rise to such situations.

In the course of a rule's life in the grammar of a language, it is most 'active' during the period when it is phonetic in character. As it becomes phonologized, and hence restricted, its capacity to enter into new relations with other rules becomes more limited. It may also be the case that the rule goes a step further: it may be that, as it becomes less of a generalization about surface forms, its conditioning is reanalyzed as non-phonological. When a rule is thus morphologized, its capacity to interact with other rules is again seriously altered. It may also be the case that subsequent change leads to the restriction of the rule to a semi-productive or fossilized relation within the lexicon, or to its complete loss. These later stages of change in a rule's character are of little interest to the point at issue here, for a rule which has reached them has already become a 'traditional alternation', and is thus unlikely to lead to any further synchronic non-linearities. During the early, phonetic stages of a rule's life, however, we have seen that there is every reason to expect the mechanism of sound change through rule addition to give rise to 'paradoxes' such as those we have examined above.

We can now ask whether change through rule addition is the only mechanism which might yield such a situation. Among other attested sorts of change, it seems clear that a rule can be lost (perhaps through an intermediate stage of morphologization), restricted, or generalized, but it is not clear that any of these changes would be likely to alter the rule's interactions with other rules in the grammar in relevant way. There is one other mechanism of linguistic change, however, which we would certainly expect to affect rule interactions: this is the class of changes describable as re-orderings of existing rules.

Among the first to point out this possibility was Kiparsky (1968), who suggested further that there are significant constraints on the sort of re-orderings that can be effected. He suggested, in particular, that rule re-orderings frequently have the effect of increasing the generality of a given rule, in one of two ways. Suppose that rule A creates new forms for the application of rule B: then we say that A can *feed* B. Suppose, on the other hand, that A removes certain forms from the domain of rule B. Then we say that A can *bleed* B. Kiparsky's original observation about re-ordering, then, was that rules can be re-ordered to establish a feeding relationship, or to eliminate a bleeding relationship, but that the opposite changes are unattested. We can thus establish a hierarchy of relationships between rules: feeding relations are more natural (in the sense "more likely to be established through historical change") than neutral (neither feeding nor bleeding), and both feeding and neutral relations are more natural than bleeding relations. We could then suggest that rule re-ordering always consists in replacing a less natural relation between two rules by a more natural one.

Subsequent work has shown that this principle is not sufficient to deal with all cases of rule re-ordering, and other proposals have been made concerning the factors which contribute to the naturalness of a given interaction between rules. A complete discussion of rule re-ordering, then, would have to take these additional factors into account. For the present, however, let us look a little more closely at the principle just cited, that of re-ordering rules into an order in which their applicability is maximized. We have presented this notion as if it were possible to define, for any given pair of rules, the 'naturalness' (on the above hierarchy) of a given interaction between them. Consider, however, the following derivations of "package (dat.sg.)" and "kettle (dat.pl)" in Modern Icelandic[3].

3. /bagg+ul+e/   /katil+um/
    bögg+ul+e   (u-umlaut: a → ö/ – C u)
    bögg+1+e   katl+um   (syncope before vocalic endings)
                    kötl+um   (u-umlaut)
    [böggli]   [kötlüm]   (phonetic rules)

Consider the interaction of the two rules u-umlaut and syncope. Note that in the derivation of *kötlum*, the application of syncope establishes the conditions for u-umlaut, since it is not until after the operation of syncope that the /a/ of the first syllable is followed by an/u/. Syncope thus feeds umlaut here, while the opposite order would be neutral (sometimes called 'counterfeeding' in these circumstances). From forms like this, then, we might conclude that the order syncope > u-umlaut is the natural one, in the sense of maximizing the applicability of the rules in question. When we consider derivations such as that of *böggli*, however, we see that this conclusion would be too hasty. In this form, syncope has the effect of removing the /u/ which conditions umlaut, and hence of bleeding the latter rule. For this form, then, we see that it is the opposite order (u-umlaut < syncope) which is more natural: it is neutral as opposed to bleeding.

The point of this example is to show that the notion of maximal rule applicability cannot be defined simply and directly for a pair of rules in isolation. The notion is definable only for a pair of rules in relation to a class of forms. We must stress the point that the classes of forms involved are defined in terms of their phonological structure. Thus, for forms containing the structure /...aC VC$_0$ u.../, the order syncope < umlaut is feeding, and hence natural. For forms containing the structure /...aC$_0$ uCV.../, however, it is the opposite order, u-umlaut < syncope, a non-bleeding order, which is natural, since for these forms this is a neutral as opposed to bleeding order. The classes of forms involved thus are implicitly defined by their structure in relation to the definitions of feeding and bleeding orders, and are in no way arbitrary subdivisions of the lexicon. It has occasionally been suggested that arbitrary lexical items or classes of lexical items might be associated with a particular ordering of rules, but we should like to avoid that possibility if we can. In any case, no such arbitrary lexical classes are involved in the present discussion, which is directed towards the point that "maximal applicability" must be defined for rules relative to (phonological) classes of forms.

Kiparsky and other scholars writing since his original paper dealing with historical changes describable as rule re-ordering have adduced a number of examples which can be accounted for in terms of the notion of maximizing the applicability of the rules involved. We can thus accept this principle as a reasonably well established mechanism of linguistic change, corresponding to many cases traditionally described as generalization or phonological analogy. But we have just seen that the notion of "order which maximizes rule applicability" has a very special property: it may be the case that the order satisfying that description in one set of the forms of a language is just the opposite of the order satisfying the same description for other forms. But if this is the case, we would expect that a change which consists exactly in re-ordering the rules into a state which maximizes their applicability would sometimes have the consequence of producing, within the same language, some derivations in which the order of A and B is $A < B$, and others in which the order is $B < A$. In fact it is just this sort of violation of the principle of assymentry, fundamental to the definition of a linear ordering, which we have seen above in the Icelandic derivations in (3). We can see now that a situation of this sort is not to be rejected as simply anomalous: it is the perfectly logical outcome of a well-established mechanism of historical change, re-ordering into a relation in which applicability is maximized, once this latter notion is properly understood. Again we conclude that the mechanisms we find operating in historical change should be expected to lead to at least some cases in which the resulting synchronic system will contain nonlinear rule orderings; and thus that we should construct a model of synchronic phonology which provides for them.

We have confined our discussion of rule re-ordering here to the single principle of maximizing applicability. When other principles of natural rule ordering are considered, however, similar cases can be seen to arise in much the same way. It has also been suggested by a number of scholars (on the one hand, Kiparsky, 1973; and from a very different perspective, by Hooper 1976) that rule interactions are more natural insofar as they lead to a condition in which each rule is maximally 'transparent' (i.e., true as a generalization about the surface forms of the language). We would expect, then, that a possible historical change would consist exactly in altering a previously 'opaque' situation by applying the rules so as to maximize transparency. But again, the order which is transparent in some respects may be the opposite of that which is transparent in others, and so we would expect that such a change could lead to cases of non-assymetric ordering relations. A case of this sort is discussed by Anderson (1974:209–18), and others could also be cited to confirm the validity of this prediction.

Yet another principle which has been adduced as a motivating force in rule interactions is a tendency to paradigm regularizations: a tendency, that is, to apply the rules of a grammar in such a way that the shape of the root or stem portion of a word remains as constant as possible throughout a set of closely related forms. Harris (1972) presents an example which makes the point that, in order to maximize the degree of intra-paradigmatic regularity, it may be necessary to apply a given pair of rules in one order in some forms, and in another order in other forms. The point is that insofar as paradigmatic regularity is a significant factor in determining the naturalness of rule interactions (and linguists have long felt that this was the case), it ought to serve as a motivation for linguistic change; and insofar as this is true, the fact that paradigm regularity may only be obtainable through non-linear orderings ought to lead to such orderings as the consequence of such sound changes. Once again, we see that a traditional, well-motivated principle of historical change should be expected to lead to non-linear synchronic orderings as a natural consequence.

The weight of the evidence from the study of historical change is clearly in favor of the proposition that synchronic grammars will contain non-linear ordering relations. The suggestion made above, that the linearity of temporal sequence ought to combine with the relation between synchrony and diachrony to produce linearity in grammars can be seen to be false. In fact, unless we can establish some general principle which would prohibit such non-linearities, we must clearly provide for them in synchronic phonological theory.

Such a general prohibition against non-linear structures cannot plausibly be expected to be found from the study of language itself. After all, our information about the general properties of human languages comes just from our efforts to construct grammars (or explicit accounts) of them, and it is exactly the appropriate form of such descriptions that is in question. If we are to find a non-circular basis for a general prohibition against violations of linearity, then, it must come from more general properties of human cognitive systems, of which language is but one. We must thus ask whether it is the case that other, non-linguistic forms of human cognitive activity motivate a strong (or perhaps absolute) preference for linearly ordered structures.

When we turn to the psychological literature, it appears at first as if evidence for such a general preference for linear orderings is available. On the basis of experiments dealing with subjects' ability to internalize and reproduce correctly a description of a social structure, Desoto & Albrecht (1968) suggest that there are laws of conceptual organization which favor certain sorts of structures over others. Such 'conceptual good figures' are thus analogous to principles in perception, explored by the Gestalt psychologists, which favor the organization of perceived forms into certain basic 'well-formed' types. Henley *et al.* (1969) review several experiments in which subjects were given information about a set of social relations among members of a group of people (such as "A influences B & C, B influences C", etc.). Their task was to learn the entire set of relations so that they could reproduce it without error. It is clear from the results presented in this paper that the subjects' ability to learn such structures is inversely correlated with the degree of non-linearity they exhibit: performance on this task goes down directly as a nearly linear function of the extent of non-linearity. We might consider, then, that human cognitive capacities have a strong bias toward linear organization, and would tend to arrange any complex set of relationships into a linear scheme. Insofar as this is impossible, subjects' abilities to deal with the structures involve degrades.

Henley *et al.* make clear, however, that this result is limited to the special case in which the subject is required to cognize the entire structure at once. Subjects are not allowed, that is, to treat each of the individual relations that make up the structure as isolated from the others, but are rather required to organize them into a single coherent whole. In fact, there is abundant evidence concerning the effects of such a requirement. An extensive literature exists on the procedures involved in solving syllogistic problems (on the order of "A is bigger than B; C is smaller than B; what is the relation between A and C?"). While there are a number of proposals that have been made, one result that seems fairly well supported (cf. Huttenlocher, 1968; Handel *et al.* 1968; Huttenlocher & Higgins 1971) suggests that an essential step in this process involves the construction of a spatial representation of the structure. Subjects construct a mental image of the structure they are to learn, in which some spatial dimension represents the relationship involved in the syllogism or other complex structure (e.g., position to the right may indicate 'bigger than'), and then place the terms of the relation on this dimension. Such spatial images seem to be an essential (or at least very common) part of the mental 'computation' involved in internalizing an involved set of relations as a totality. Given that fact, of course, the bias toward linearity is easily explained: non-linear sets of relations simply cannot be represented in terms of positional relations along (linear) spatial dimensions. Insofar as this strategy of computation is essential, structures which are not amenable to representation in linear terms will naturally be disfavored.

We must ask, however, whether the tasks in which a preference for linearity can be demonstrated (and in part explained) are actually analogous to the situation with which we are primarily concerned, the interrelation of phonological rules within a synchronic grammar. Is it in fact the case that this result carries over into language, predicting that a system involving violations of linearity will be essentially (or nearly) unlearnable? In order to draw that conclusion, we would have to presume that the task faced by language learners (and users) shares the essential features of the task faced by subjects asked to internalize a set of relationships in a social structure or to solve a syllogism. It is by no means obvious, however, that this is the case.

We can outline the task of language learners and users with respect to rule interactions in the following terms. We presume that as a primary feature of this problem, our subject deduces certain regularities about the forms in his language from the data available to him, and we can represent these regularities in the form of rules of his grammar. Sometimes, of course, more than one of the rules in such a grammar will be applicable to a given form, and in some such cases it will make a difference which sequence they are applied in. Some of the forms of the language will of course provide data about some such interactions: from the fact that a given form has one shape rather than another, he may infer that the rules of relevance applied in the order $A < B$, rather that the opposite. Each such fact about rule interaction, however, is in principle a separate datum. There is no necessary reason why any such interaction should be coupled with any other interaction, provided that they are attested in distinct forms. Given simply the fact that there are rules and forms, and that the rules interact in particular ways in the derivation of particular forms, we have as yet no necessity to assume that the totality of rules and their interactions is ever cognized at once by our subject.

We might ask, though, what happens when our subject has to deal with a new form. This might be either a new morphological formation, whose elements he knows but which he has never heard directly and needs to know how to pronounce; or it might be a form he hears and needs to know whether it can be analyzed in such and such a way using rules already present in his grammar. In either case, the question arises of what interactions are possible among the rules which may be involved in the derivation of the form. Let us suppose that he has become familiar with some forms in which rules A and B apply, in the order $A < B$; and also with some forms in which rules B and C apply, in the order $B < C$. Now let us further suppose that the form with which he is presently confronted involves (potentially) rules A and C. Since he has never (ex hypothesi) encountered a form in which precisely these rules (but not B) are involved, he has no direct evidence for the correct interaction of A and C. The hypothesis that rules always apply in a linear order, of course, would allow him to deduce from the other facts at his disposal that A must precede C. But to arrive at that conclusion, it is necessary to perform a mental computation which is precisely analogous to the solution of a three-term syllogism. Is there any reason to believe that such a process is involved in language learning or use? We might well conclude that this was so, granted that our subject must make some choice about the interaction of rules A and C, provided he has no independent way of making such a choice without reference to anything beyond rules A and C and the form in question. But we have already seen above that this is not the case: he is not in fact limited to the facts which he has already incorporated into his grammar in the form of rules and observed derivations using them. There is by now a substantial body of evidence in favor of the view that there are general, substantive principles underlying and motivating rule interactions, principles which are independent of the grammars of particular languages, but which allow us to predict in a wide

range of cases the way in which a given pair of rules can be expected to interact. Such principles as the maximization of applicability, transparency, and
paradigmatic uniformity will in fact make definite predictions about many
rule interactions completely independent of any other facts about the language.

Thus, when our subject asks about the interaction of rules A and C, he is
not required to go to the rest of the grammar to arrive at an answer, but in
many cases can answer his question on the basis of a strictly local consideration of rules A and C themselves, in relation to the form in question. Notice
that this general conclusion is independent of the correctness of the specific
set of principles we have suggested above for dealing with the naturalness of
rule interactions. It is only necessary that there be some such set of principles,
providing a substantive and not merely a formal account of rule interactions.
Given such a set of principles, our subject is enabled to decide at least a great
many orderings in isolation from one another, and there is therefore no reason
to believe that the linguistic system he internalizes ever had the essential
feature that led to the preference for linear orderings in the memorization of
social structures: namely, the property of being cognized as a whole by the
speaker. As long as he can deal with rule interactions on such an individual,
piecemeal basis, there is really no necessity for suggesting that the totality of
ordering relations in a grammar are ever organized into a coherent whole in
the natural course of events. But if the system is never organized into a single
structure, there is no longer any basis for assuming a predilection for linearity.

We conclude that the ordering relations in a synchronic grammar can be
treated in such a local fashion and that the facts of one derivation need not
necessarily be employed in a sort of computational process to determine the
course of another. It is interesting to note that there is one general class of
cases in which this independence does not exist. Suppose that the grammar
contains rules A and B, and that for all forms in which they interact the principles of natural ordering would predict that they should apply in the order
$A < B$. But now suppose that, for some reason, the language actually contains
some forms which must be assumed to involve these rules in the order $B < A$.
Now in analyzing these, the language learner or user has to recognize that his
a priori prediction about the order of A and B was wrong. We might suggest
that he accordingly reorganizes his entire system of order-predicting principles, but this seems extremely unlikely even if these principles were of a
form that made this possible. Much more plausible is the supposition that he
simply records the fact that, as an idiosyncratic property of his language, the
rules A and B happen to apply in the order $B < A$. This would be exactly the
sort of idiosyncratic restriction that was involved, say, in preventing the application of dissimilation to/strUiia/in (2) above, which would have given the
incorrect output *[strUǰa] . Interestingly, it is apparently the case that wher-

ever such extrinsic or unnatural orderings arise in a language, they are quite general across the language. Thus, there do not appear to be well-established cases in which one completely arbitrary class of forms undergoes rules A and B in an unnatural order, while another equally arbitrary class displays the natural order. Where an unnatural order obtains, this seems to be internalized in grammars as a constraint applying to any other derivation which might involve the same rules.

There is much more to be said about the model of linguistic organization which emerges from these remarks, but the important point is this one: linguistic organization appears to be such that the relations between rules can be treated independently, and there is no need to assume that all of these relations are ever organized into a whole by speakers. Our question concerning whether there is any over-riding preference for linear organization, then, must be addressed to the evidence concerning systems of this type, rather than to holistic structures such as those involved in the literature referred to above.

In fact, we know that human cognitive systems are quite capable of dealing with structures involving extensive violations of linearity so long as the component relations can be treated in isolation from one another. Marschak (1964) has reported on experiments in which subjects were asked to indicate preferences among objects (such as rewards), taken two at a time. In many instances, the total set of comparisons obtained in this way will involve violations of linearity. Thus, I may prefer Mary to Joan because she is wealthy, Alice to Mary because she likes to go to football games with me, Anne to Alice because she laughs at my jokes, but Joan to Anne because she is much better looking. So long as I am confronted with one choice at a time, I may have no problem and in fact not notice that my various choices are in a sense inconsistent: it is only if I am forced to indicate a preference for one out of the entire set that I may have difficulty. In fact, it seems that whenever a number of distinct dimensions are involved in making a choice of this sort, non-linearities are quite likely to result.

Similar situations abound in the everyday networks of social interactions in which we are continuously enmeshed. An example offered by Henley *et al.* (1969) is the following: consider A, who is "old family", and thus receives deference from B, who is a self-made millionaire. B, in turn, receives deference from C, who does not have money but respects it. C in turn may receive deference from A, since C is a tough brute who does not care about "family" while A is an effete aristocrat who respects physical strength. Each of these people is quite thoroughly involved in the entire structure, but the crucial aspect of the situation is that each sees his relations to the others one at a time: it is unlikely that the entire cycle is visible to anyone. Parallel examples can be cited from many other domains: the "pecking orders." established among chickens are a particularly notorious example from a sub-human domain of a system of inter-relationships which frequently involves non-linearities.

There is thus no reason to believe that human cognitive systems are incapable of dealing with networks of interactions that violate linearity, so long as it is possible to treat each component of the network in isolation from all the others. This is just the situation, however, that we have argued is characteristic of natural language use and learning with respect to ordering relationships, considered from the point of view of the native speaker. We can thus see that there is no basis in a theory of "conceptual good figures" for the assumption that the system of language which a speaker acquires and employs is heavily biased toward linear organization.

But we can go farther than that. Just as we have seen that speakers should have no urgent requirement for linear organization, so we can see that linguists probably will. The enterprise of linguists, as opposed to that of speakers, essentially involves the cognization of the entire system of the grammar, taken as a whole. Linguists construct whole grammars (or at least inter-related parts of these), and by its very nature this activity involves looking beyond the facts obtaining locally in a given form to the way in which the system of rules fits together into a coherent whole. Thus, we should expect linguists to behave in much the same way as the subjects who were asked to internalize an entire social system as a unity rather than in the way subjects living in such a social network of inter-relationships (compare the deference relations among A, B, and C in the example just given) may act. In fact, this disparity is a problem by no means unique to the subject of linguistics. In psychology and sociology as well, when systems such as non-linear pecking orders or non-transitive sets of preferences are found, there is a strong tendency for researchers to ignore the fact, or to attempt to explain it away in some other terms. Henley *et al.* (1969:198) observe that when faced by non-linearities (called by them "cycles") in the real world, people, including researchers in particular will:

"1. avoid seeing cycles, distort their perception of them, and minimize the number of cycles perceived;
 2. tend to do things to change the actual structure so that there are fewer cycles (preferably none): and
 3. suffer cognitive strain, if they are forced to perceive cycles which they are unable to change".

All of these reactions can be documented from the literature dealing with (possibly non-linear) ordering relations in linguistics.

Knowing and using a language, then is a different enterprise from analyzing, describing, and writing a grammar of it; and in just the relevant way to account for the evident tendency of phonological systems to contain non-linear orderings as opposed to the obvious reluctance of linguists to recognize them. The same point, in essence, can be made about the difference between living in a society and doing sociology. In both cases the cognitive constraints applicable to the two sorts of enterprise may well be quite distinct.

We see thus a part of the difference between knowing and using language and doing linguistics. Much use is made in the literature of the field of individuals' judgements and intuitions about what is a "likely" or "plausible" structure for a language to have. The question is seldom asked seriously, however, of where these judgements and intuitions come from, and importantly, what relation they may bear to the facts of actual languages. The example just discussed ought to serve as a warning that our intuitions as linguists may be very unreliable indicators of the sort of properties we are likely to find in actual languages when we look without preconceptions.

We have argued above, then that the independently motivated mechanisms of linguistic change have the property that they ought to be expected to lead to synchronic systems involving non-linear ordering relations among the rules of the grammar, in at least some cases. We could only expect not to find violations of linearity if we believed in the existence of a general, not specifically linguistic, cognitive constraint disallowing such systems. We have seen that there is no reason to expect such a constraint to be found, and that in light of the essential differences between language use and linguistics, we must be especially careful not to close our mind to the possibility that such situations may arise as properties of actual languages. Given the evidence for non-linear relations that exists in the linguistic literature, we should therefore attempt to construct synchronic theories which allow for them. An attempt at such a theory, along the lines outlined in this paper, is that of Anderson (1974), though it is obvious that much more needs to be said about these issues.

Regardless of the details of the construction of such a theory, however, one aspect of it is clear: grammars of natural languages cannot be constrained to contain only such ordering relations among rules as can be organized into a single internally consistent linear arrangement. And from this, a broader conclusion follows, of the sort which it is the avowed purpose of contemporary linguistics to provide. Linguists are fond of saying that their investigations into a wide variety of natural languages will eventually provide insights into the nature of mind and of complex human mental processes. It is therefore of interest that grammars, and the internalized organizations of linguistic knowledge which they represent, provide one more piece of support for the proposition that the nature of human cognitive processes is not always accurately modeled by the sort of deductive reasoning which we generally employ in conscious, reflective problem solving.

Notes

1. I would like to thank Prof. V. Fromkin for discussion during the preparation of this paper. I would also like to thank Dr Saul Sternberg of Bell laboratories, Murray Hill, N.J., for drawing my attention to some of the relevant literature in psychology. Neither of these people is to be held accountable for my views, naturally.
2. Venneman (1971 and elsewhere) has also argued for this position.
3. For further discussion of this material from Icelandic, cf. Anderson (1972a, 1974).

References

Anderson, Stephen R.
    1969   *West Scandinavian vowel systems and the ordering of phonological rules.*
              [Doctoral dissertation, MIT, Cambridge, Mass.]
    1972a   "Icelandic u-Umlaut and breaking in a generative grammar", in: *Studies for
              Einar Haugen* (Eds.: E. S. Firchow *et al.*) (The Hague: Mouton), pp. 13–31.
    1972b   "The Faroese vowel system", in: *Contributions to generative phonology*
              (Ed.: M. Brame) (Austin: University of Texas Press), pp. 1–21.
    1974   *The organization of phonology* (New York: Academic Press).
Baudouin de Courtenay, Jan N.
    1895   "An attempt at a theory of phonetic alternations: A chapter from psycho-
              phonetics", in: *A Baudouin de Courtenay anthology* (Ed.: E. Stankiewicz)
              (Bloomington: Indiana University Press, 1972), pp. 144–213. [Translated
              from German.]
Chafe, Wallace L.
    1968   "The ordering of phonological rules", *IJAL* 34: 115–136.
DeSoto, C. B. – F. Albrecht
    1968   "Conceptual good figures", in: *Theories of cognitive consistency: A source-
              book* (Eds.: R. P. Abelson *et al.*) (Skokie, Ill.: Rand McNally), pp. 504–511.
Handel, S. – C. B. DeSoto – M. London
    1968   "Reasoning and spatial representations", *Journal of Verbal Learning and
              Verbal Behavior* 7: 351–357.
Harris, J. W.
    1972   "On the ordering of certain phonological rules in Spanish", in: *A festschrift
              for Morris Halle* (Eds.: S. Anderson – P. Kiparsky) (New York: Holt),
              pp. 54–76.
Henley, N. M. – R. B. Horsefall – C. B. DeSoto
    1969   "Goodness of figure and social structure", *Psychological Review* 76:
              194–204.
Hooper, Joan
    1976   *An introduction to natural generative phonology* (New York: Academic
              Press).
Huttenlocher, J.
    1968   "Constructing spatial images: A strategy in reasoning", *Psychological Review*
              75: 550–560.

Huttenlocher, J. – E. T. Higgins
    1971   "Adjectives, comparatives, and syllogisms", *Psychological Review* 78:
            587–604.
Kiparsky, Paul
    1968   "Linguistic universals and linguistic change", in: *Universals in linguistic
            theory* (Eds.: E. Bach, R. T. Harms) (New York: Holt), pp. 171–202.
    1973   "Phonological representations", in: *Three dimensions of linguistic theory*
            (Ed.: O. Fujimura) (Tokyo: TEC Corporation), pp. 1–136.
Koutsoudas, A. – G. Sanders – C. Noll
    1974   "On the application of phonological rules", *Language* 50: 1–28.
Marschak, J.
    1964   "Actual versus consistent decision behavior", *Behavioral Science* 9:
            103–110.
Newton, Brian
    1971   "Ordering paradoxes in phonology", *Journal of Linguistics* 7: 31–53.
Vennemann, Theo
    1971   *Natural generative phonology.* [Paper read at the annual meeting of the
            Linguistic Society of America, St. Louis, Mo.]

RAIMO ANTTILA

The acceptance of sound change
by linguistic structure

One of the enigmas of sound change is perhaps its "uselessness". There does
not seem to be any reason for its existence (except for *variatio delectat*). It is
generally (and legitimately) taken as the agent that feeds into analogical re-
modeling, including the linguistic cycle. Sound change is also the most treated
aspect of linguistic change. All this is extremely well known and needs no
comment[1]. The question that has been neglected is "Why do the irregularities
produced by sound change stay in the linguistic structure so long, often for
centuries and longer?" Low rate of change would be expected if sound change
is just a disturbing factor, but given enough time, there is always sound
change, even if here and there we have slightish parallels to the ant (no
change for fifty million years). If analogy is a regularizing force, why does it
often wait so long? This is the above question from a different angle. In other
words, there seems to be a no man's land right in the middle of Sturtevant's
paradox (sound change is regular and causes irregularity, analogy is irregular
and produces regularity). The middle ground comes here under the notion of
irregularity, and thus the Stoa is embedded in the center of Alexandria, it
would seem. Or traditionally the first part of the paradox could point to the
Stoa, the latter to Alexandria. My contention here is that the old analogy/
anomaly controversy can be overcome in a comprehensive semiotic frame, as
it was in fact solved in practice in antiquity already.

Sound is of course the normal medium of the linguistic sign, and thus it is
proper to consider phonetics a linguistic and even a "verbal" domain. Sound
is also a "parasite" of human physiology and has consequently a certain
mechanical base, even if the speech organs in their turn are controlled by the
mind. This mechanical base has often been overstated in the literature on
sound change. But it is of course absolutely real and necessary, and I want to
make use of it — for non-mechanical arguments.

Assume now, for the sake of the argument, that *the production of speech
sounds is nonverbal behavior.* This is of course an *as — if* argument, which are

so useful in science. Nonverbal behavior as a semiotic vehicle is studied very vigorously today and it has deepened our understanding of both semiotics and linguistics. I will refer only to Ekman and Friesen (1969) who map the repertoire of nonverbal behavior from the point of view of *origin* (how that behavior became part of the person's repertoire), *usage* (the circumstances of its use), and *coding* (the rules which explain how the behavior contains or conveys information). Nonverbal behavior is extensively used in addition to or instead of language, and such modes generally escape efforts to deceive. The same is true of pronunciation, this being, e.g., a well-known obstacle to social climbers. Nonverbal behavior is based on various natural bodily functions and movements which become coded in various ways. Similarly, variation in speech production is a natural bodily function which gets recoded in sound change. And in a way sounds are indeed nonverbal, since they are diacritic in essence; they treat the deeper atoms. Ekman and Friesen give five classes of nonverbal signs: emblems, illustrators, regulators, affect displays, and adaptors. Basically, emblems are *symbolic* gestures, illustrators emphasize what is being said verbally (and include batons, ideographs, deictic movements, kinetographs, and pictographs), affect displays cover facial expressions of emotional states, regulators control the back-and-forth nature of speaking and listening, and adaptors are codings of (childhood) patterns of personal grooming and the like (the most evasive category). Here emblems are intentional symbols with the awareness comparable to that of the choice of words. From here on awareness and intentionality decrease, being typically nonexistent in adaptors. What is important is that bodily "gestures" have been coded into highly intricate systems whether the users are aware of it or not. *These nonverbal aspects typically leak information.* Note further that phonetic (supra-segmental) means are used for verbal illustrators, regulators, and affect displays, and here also we might get information leakage that goes counter to the "segmental" message. Such suprasegmentals are of course analogically coded (they permit gradience), whereas "normal" words are digitally coded. Both aspects recur in nonverbal communication systems. Nonverbal behavior shows thus quite clearly that necessary biological activity is encoded for specific uses. In spite of great fluidity in the system there is a substantial shared sector in the decoding. The vagueness pertains also to the level of awareness, which is so crucial in sound change. In sound production the necessary physiological base creates variation that can be encoded for various tasks. As already Francis Bacon (*Novum organon*) noted, anything that can be perceptually discriminated provides potential material for semiotic ends. This was an important observation that has now lain dormant for over three hundred years. As for distinctions in phonetics, William Labov's more recent work has tried to document extreme cases of discrimination in which speakers deny the distinctions they actually make (see e.g. Labov-Yaeger-Steiner 1973). On the whole Labov's work does show the scale from awareness to total unawareness in the factors of sound change. While this scale is real and important it is perhaps not crucial for the definition of sound change (as e.g. Vincent here uses it).

The biological model of change (evolution) has some relevance for sound change also. Living matter is a kind of sparkle machine that sends out tentacles into the surroundings. These tendrons increase continuity and bind the structure together. Sound change is exactly such a machine. It produces qualities, feelings, chance. This fits into the universal categories of Peirce (1955:74–97; Anttila 1974:8–9), viz. firstness, secondness, and thirdness; and of course we have to do with firstness in dealing with sound change. Firstness characterized "property" in phenomenology, "perception" in cognition, and "possibility" according to the theory of modality; secondness would be correspondingly: object, experience, reality; thirdness: relation (copula), thinking, necessity. The general direction is that the first flashes of chance take on habits and become codified as laws. For sound change we have *first* the as-if-nonverbal domain of anger, annoyance, etc., the so-called non-symbolic area, but this does not figure in sound change too much and I leave it at that.

Secondly we get to the inlexical functions of sound variation. Sociolinguistics shows that this is crucial for sound change. True, we have to do with flashes provided by the mechanical base, but they get encoded for social meaning. This axis is *pragmatic*, pertaining to the users of signs (Morris). We are able to perceive idiosyncratic personal pronunciations and thereby to identify the speakers. On a larger scale this works for diagramming wider regional or social dialects. The facts are extremely well-known and need not be repeated. This is the main launching-pad for sound change, and creates no conceptual problems. But the social-index aspect reminds us of one neglected point. Sound laws are traditionally constrained by specifying their time and location; consciousness by speakers is irrelevant. This shows the human aspect behind it all. It shows that the variation has been encoded for semiotic use. We do not get sound change unless the mechanical sparkle is given direction by speakers. Sound change is thus a mental act. And the regularity of sound change is due to the fact that it is based on abductions on language as *knowledge* (cf. Coseriu 1958, Andersen 1973; Anttila 1977:§5).

But pronunciation indexes are not confined to the pragmatic axis. In a series of studies I have discussed the *syntactic* function of allomorphs (Anttila 1974, 1975b, 1976a). Here we have to do with *relative* signs, the signs in relation to other signs ('syntactics' in Morris' terminology). Allomorphic alternation is supposed to be an immediate disturbing result of sound change. But this is not true at all, since variants point to adjacent morphemes and have an important synechistic function (cf. Anttila 1975a). We have information leakage as in nonverbal communication, although this leakage is of a rather technical kind. The variant delimits the number of possible choices in the sequel, and in fact Komárek (1964) and Korhonen (1969) have calculated numerical information values for this (without drawing in the sign aspects in an overall semiotic frame). The existence of allomorphic alternation in the root morpheme diminishes the uncertainty of the following morpheme, and can in fact totally determine it, as e.g. in Komárek's example of Czech nom.pl. *vlc-i*, acc.pl. *vlk-i* <-y> 'wolves' (see also Anttila 1975b:20). In this Czech case the alternation is phonemic, but the same can be true of subtle allophonic differences, which already act as morphological indexes. Korhonen's great merit is to have given a name for this situation: a unit which is just an allophone according to its distribution but has indexical function in the linear order of morphemes is a *quasiphoneme* (1969:335). Thus the Proto-Lapp open syllable *l̄* in nom.sg. **kol̄e* 'fish' is determined by pure phonetic facts of syllable structure vs. the slightly shorter *l* in the gen.sg. **kolen*. In basic linguistic training we are taught to eliminate such allophonic alternation as fast as we can, and many of us cannot even think that we are dealing with a *syntactic index*. Arguments against this position by referring to awareness are hardly valid, since by using Bacon's criterion such differences in length are perceptible. (One can perceive up to some twelve degrees of length in Lapp, with a trained ear). Thus, even if we said that the rise of a social index does not really pertain to linguistic structure (it being just surface paint, or name-tags of users), the morphological index resides in the middle of linguistic structure. In my earlier work I have discussed, along Sapir's lines, how the characteristic mechanism for this is assimilation. And I can now add that the particular form of iconicity is adaptation (cf. 'adaptors') iconicity. Adaptation iconicity is the mechanism through which an organism becomes indexical to its environment. This is a main aspect in evolution. Iconicity leads in pronunciation to indexicality, which is normal in linguistic change, but few have noticed it on such "low levels". It is quite parallel to an iconic reproduction of an animal cry, which is of course an index of that animal.

Pike (1965), Werner (1976), and myself (1975b, 1976a), among others, have discussed the optimal features of suppletion. Pike's term for it, *ideal*, is apt, although perhaps startling to many. Allomorphic variation is a step toward suppletion, and in fact it is perhaps the normal situation. As already Sapir said, allomorphic alternation indicates the subjection of the part to the whole; it enhances the unity of the total word. In fact most conceptions of language have relied on the independence of the word. One important function of sound change is to stress this. Again we see that sound change is as-if-non-verbal, since this function is that of a "formal illustrator" or a "boundary regulator". The medieval notion of underlying form has been inimical for relevant semiotic analysis. I have argued in my recent morphological papers against constant underlying identity (in the current sense). Here I add another plea for the relevance of a semiotics of perception. In fact, I want to defend my defence of a semiotics of variants also (Wandruszka 1971) with the following statement from the psychology of perception (Vernon 1971:16–17):

> Thus although we expect the world around us to retain its constant iden-
> tity, and the objects within it to remain relatively unchanged, the percep-
> tual system is geared to understand and respond appropriately to frequent
> change. Recent experimental investigation has shown that change and
> variation of stimulation are essential to maintain the efficiency of percep-
> tion, and of the cognitive processes associated with it. If people are exposed
> to artificial conditions in which stimulation remains homogeneous and
> unvarying over a period of time, perception may even cease to function.
> Or with reduction in the natural variation there may be a decrease of
> alertness and of attention to certain features of the environment. Con-
> trasted with this are the rapid perception of and response to sudden change,
> and to novel and unfamiliar objects. Indeed, it has been established that
> certain physiological processes in the brain have the special function of
> arousing and alerting the individual to the variations in his environment.

All this is relevant for sound change/variation also. In this light sound change is after all a healing agent.

Signs grow, they get generated from icons to indexes to symbols (cf. Peirce 1955:98–119; for the best introduction to semiotics see Walther 1974). Thus it is not surprising that in language use the morphological indexes get recoded as symbols, e.g. *bake* vs. *batch*, German *sachlich* 'objective' vs. *sächlich* 'neuter', Finnish *yhtenäinen* 'uniform' vs. *yksinäinen* 'lonely' (see particularly Anttila 1975b:13–16). But this movement is now higher up in the hierarchy and does not concern sound change as such (cf. Vincent here). We have to do with the lexical-*semantic* axis, and this is far enough removed from the present topic to be left out in this context.

It might be useful to turn now to questions of awareness and teleology. Vincent suggests (here) his Principle of Speaker Control:

> According to this principle languages are hierarchies of systems, with
> semantics at the top and phonetics at the bottom, the ordering in the
> hierarchy reflecting the degree of conscious control speakers ordinarily

have over the sub-systems of their languages. In general, the phonetic system is not so controlled, and therefore teleological explanations should be ruled out in dealing with sound change.

I would hope that most linguists would feel that there is something to the notion, but as Vincent says:

> The PSC is undoubtedly in need of considerable sharpening and refinement, (...) but (...) the kind of data relevant to its establishment (and perhaps eventual disconfirmation) are sufficiently clear...

I would say that *if* the evidence is clear, the PSC gets disconfirmed in the form given by Vincent. There is a certain plausibility in the hierarchy, and it is indeed traditionally almost a truism, see the diagrams in Chafe (1962), especially the one modified in Anttila (1972:5). The crucial point is that the phonetic and semantic ends actually converge. The same situation came out independently in Andersen (1974:22), and further (again without reference to earlier suggestions) in Makkai and Makkai (1976), who name the "hierarchy" a horse-shoe shape. This is like a magnet between the points of which language is learned and used. To still maintain the PSC as suggested one would have to show why the earlier horse-shoe conceptions are invalid. This would seem to be an impossible task, since one should at the same time do justice to the semiotic character of language. Ever since the Greeks it has been accepted that the linguistic sign is an indivisible unity of the material, referential, and interpretant parts. You cannot stretch it into a straight hierarchy for *explanation*, even if analysis like that is always allowed for partial description. Then, on the other hand, if the data for PSC are not clear, the principle gets into grave doubt. But I think that the data are rather clear — and the principle is still in serious doubt.

Grammatical conditioning of sound change is facing difficulties again after having been a pet of "generative" historical linguists (e.g. Vincent here). I have myself used it (1972) in the traditional Finnish sense as in Kettunen (1962). I did recognize the essential, viz. that it might be a diachronic correspondence only (1972:79), and in this sense I did accept the basic dichotomy of sound change and analogy, and in fact I took grammatical conditioning of sound change as a form of analogy, as a handy step from sound change to analogy. I will attempt to clarify my position here. It is understandable that basic handbooks have to omit most of the theoretical arguments, and these cannot be inferred as easily as I had expected. Labov's well-accepted requirement about sound change is that it gets under way only when social meaning is attached to phonetic variation. This is correct. Thus the indexical coding is part of the sound change itself, because the phonetic sparkle machine is definitely not enough (it lacks the direction required). Whether there is speaker awareness or not is irrelevant, the fact is that various kinds of hypercorrection carry the change forward. Whatever we call this, drift, some kind of intentionality, etc., it is not only linguistically, but also philosophically a necessary notion (Itkonen 1974:307–26). In short, sound change is physical/mechanical sparkle base plus the semiotic coding of the variation it produces. My contention is that the semiotic coding should not be restricted to the pragmatic index only. In fact I have shown that the notion of the quasiphoneme provides a parallel situation for the syntactic index. Here also, the end result is often (most of the time?) proper phonemicization of the allophonic alternation (e.g. North Lapp *guolle/guole*); a "drift" that is rather ubiquitous. I have also reminded us of the fact that the starting point is "natural" articulatory (adaptation) iconicity. Now the following aspect becomes clear: in grammatical conditioning of sound change we have to deal with a new axis of encoding, viz. phonetic variation becomes an index (symbol?) of grammatical categories. Note again how this is a kind of illustrator for categorial information, which is quite parallel to the syntactic index. The syntactic index (in terms of allomorphy) tells us about the unity of the total word, the categorial index about the grammatical membership of the word. In both cases the basic semiotic process is *selection*.

The matter of the semioticity of such grammatically-conditioned sound change seems so obvious when looked at from the semiotic point view. Linguists almost invariably (except for Chomsky and perhaps some others) define language as a paragon of sign systems, but then procede to ignore the fact. Walther (1974) gives one important reason for the neglect of finer detail in this area by pointing out that generative-transformational grammar (and this approach has been prominent in the recent past) is based on degenerative semiosis and a partial selection of sign types, and that linguistics has not yet been semiotically founded. While waiting for that we should of course analyze every possible sign type in language. This is what I try to do here with sound change, even if it might sound vague speculation to some. The position of my critics can be interpreted in the following way (criticism concerns my apparent denial of the now again accepted Neogrammarian sound change/analogy dichotomy and opting for grammatically conditioned sound change when the situation is right). Rejection of grammatical conditioning implies a denial of the reality of grammatical categories. I maintain that they are indeed real and can be designated in various ways (bezeichnet) (note that I do not refer in this paper to affixal indication of the indexes). It is useful to recede here into Slagle's (1975) argument for the unity of perception and thought. More particularly to the argument that "disembodied actions and qualities are not be found in immediate experience" (188):

Instead, actions and qualities are found only as differentiating aspects of 'things'. Thus, for example, one will never encounter a 'dancing' as an entity with a segregated givenness in sensory experience although one might well see a bear dancing. Nor would one ever encounter a 'tall', but rather tall things or people. Consequently since the denotata of adjectives and verbs occur only as differentiating aspects of entities with a segregated givenness, and since entities with a segregated givenness are generally denoted by nouns, then it is clear that the restrictions in regard to which nouns can co-occur with which adjectives and which verbs, are ultimately based on whether the segregated entities denoted by the nouns can manifest the 'actions' or attributes denoted by the given verbs and adjectives. Although it might seem that only spatial entities can have a segregated givenness, this is not the case. Figure-ground differentiation is perhaps the most ubiquitous mode of perceptual organization, for some form of figure-ground differentiation is possible in all sensory modalities. As Walther Ehrenstein 1965 astutely pointed out, by focusing our attention on a given aspect of sensory experience, we can achieve a much greater degree of awareness of that particular aspect, with this aspect becoming the focal point of our consciousness, and thus being set off from the rest of the given perceptual field which then constitutes the ground. Consequently, we can focus on any aspect of our sensory consciousness in such a way as to experience it as a segregated entity.

This applies, of course, to the attributes and actions, aspects which normally do not have a segregated givenness in experience. Thus, phenomena which would normally belong to either the verbal or adjectival domain of reference can be focused on in such a way as to become the focal point in terms of figure-ground differentiation and consequently belong to the nominal domain of reference. From the forgoing, it is obvious that we believe Roger Brown (1957:3) was correct in suggesting that the part-of-speech membership of a word operates as a perceptual filter guiding our attention towards the relevant aspects of the phenomena being classified. Indeed, within this framework one can easily explain the meaning of the part-of-speech membership of words. For once one realizes the importance of figure-ground differentiation in this context, nouns constitute no problem — nouns characteristically denote phenomena with a segregated givenness in sensory experience. And verbs can be considered as characteristically denoting those temporal aspects of segregated phenomena which manifest qualitative or spatial change (or absence of change) in time; while adjectives characteristically denote attributes without regard to whether or not they are manifesting some sort of change in the process of time. Shifts in form class ... can easily be explained in terms of shifts in the sensory criteria required to correctly use a term. Needless to say, the classification of form class meaning given here is meant to be merely illustrative and not in any way exhaustive. (188–9)

I find it very plausible that parts-of-speech focus would sometimes take to sound change to create a sign. As already mentioned, this sign is a kind of illustrator. The main feature is always selection even if not exact individual pinpointing of the item referred to by the index. This comes out in more "tangible" form when we have segmental morphemes in this function: Samuels (1972:50) compares the rich redundancy in Old English morphology due to gender to the Middle English specifier (determiner) system. Thus, OE *þaere* vs. *þaes* restricted the expected possibilities of noun occurrence, whereas in Middle English the function of determiners was anaphoric/cataphoric only. These referred farther into the context, but *a* vs. *the* would still limit the range of possibilities (cf. Anttila 1975b:26–27). My position is of course not totally new (that does not exist in science). It reminds one of Varro's *res*, which represents morphological substructure, grammatical categories in fact, but also the objects signified by words. Grammatical categories are *real*, and thus also grammatically-conditioned sound change is real in the semiotic sense. I am of course aware of historical indeterminacies (Anttila 1972:79–80). The Estonian loss of final -*n* (Kettunen 1962) was a phonetically-conditioned change which was grammatically encoded before the situation was balanced off. And note that the same structural result can be secured by piling up sound changes, e.g. English *belief/believe, safe/save* or French *nœuf/nœuve*, etc. Grammatical conditioning is thus a possibility of a shortcut to a good pattern.

When one selects, i.e. when one has to use the semiotic process of selection, there must be a kind of teleology involved. I would also say that one of Andersen's merits is to have delineated teleology of function from teleology of purpose (1973). I disagree with Vincent that we can do away with the first as nonteleology. Of course these discussions are old, and about the same terms have been used, to just quote Slotty (1935:1):

Zunächst muß gesagt werden, welche Art der Teleologie in der Sprachwissenschaft angewendet wird. Die theoretische Begründung der teleologischen Sprachwissenschaft gibt Havers... . Er bezeichnet mit Sterns Terminologie als Kern der teleologischen Sprachwissenschaft die funktionelle Anlageteleologie.

Stern unterscheidet Anlage- und Absichtsteleologie. Anlage (oder Disposition) ist ein Zustand, der zur Herbeiführung eines Zieles geeignet ist, ist ein dem Träger der Anlage immanentes Verhalten und ist meist unbewußt. Absicht hingegen ist bewußtes Streben, das von aussen her auf einen bestimmten Zweck gerichtet ist. Gemäß diesen ihnen zugrunde liegenden Begriffen unterscheiden sich natürlich auch Anlage- und Absichtsteleologie. Die Absichtsteleologie kommt für die Sprache wenig in Betracht; auch hängt heute niemand mehr der sogenannten "Erfindungstheorie" an.

and (2):

> Wie haben wir uns nun die Teleologie, auf die Sprachbetrachtung angewendet, vorzustellen? Die Erklärung sprachlicher Erscheinungen erfordert eine zweifache Betrachtungsweise. Es sind an sprachlichen Veränderungen zwei Faktoren zu unterscheiden, der rein kausale und der teleologische. Beide zusammen genommen ergeben erst eine vollständige Erklärung. Die ätiologische Betrachtungsweise untersucht die "Bedingungen", die teleologische die "Triebkräfte".

Slotty has of course more to say on the topic, but I will just make one final quotation to get back to the sparkle machine (2):

> Um einem häufig begegnenden Irrtum vorzubeugen, muß ausdrücklich betont werden, daß die Teleologie durchaus nicht im Gegensatz zur Lehre von der Kausalität steht. Die Kausalität kann und soll nicht vernachläßigt oder gar geleugnet werden. Die teleologische Betrachtungsweise der Sprache steht als ideelle nur im Gegensatz zur rein kausal-mechanischen.

Since the Stoics it has been acknowledged that the sign relation is two-thirds objective, one-third mental (I have discussed this in relation to linguistic reconstruction; Anttila 1976c). Slotty thinks that the Neogrammarians' requirement of sound laws without exceptions is put to rest, since "today" (i.e. 1935) linguistics is considered a Geisteswissenschaft, not a Naturwissenschaft (4). Her assessment was wrong, because American Structuralism and generative—transformational grammar upheld the Neogrammarian principle till today in fact (i.e. 1976). But the situation is drastically changing (Anttila 1976c). It seems that Spitzer's point is finally going home (1948:1):

> it is not the humanities themselves that are at fault but only some so-called humanists who persist in imitating an obsolete approach to the natural sciences, which themselves evolved toward the humanities. ...

Slotty's general position that any kind of function entails a teleological position is well founded, and Andersen's notion of teleology of function makes

it explicit within phonology, and other areas do not come into consideration
here. One must recognize that language is based on *constant systematization*
(Coseriu [1974:236] : structure and systematization; Jakobson [1965:37] :
system of diagrammatization). In other words, speech production brings forth
diagrams of various kinds (depending on the levels of language), and diagrams
are iconic signs. This position has been well argued for and developed in
Andersen's output, and I have myself discussed it and added to it (Anttila
1977 [particularly § §2, 3.6]; and elsewhere). One of the standard notions
of linguistics has always been that there is a difference between lexical or
root morphemes vs. grammatical affixes. This is one reality that should find
diagrammatization in morphology. And, in fact, the situation is quite clear
for many reasons. Jakobson (1965) pointed out that in English the productive inflectional suffixes are represented by dental stops, dental spirants, and
their combination in *-st*. Similar situations exist in other languages; consider
particularly the Semitic pattern where consonants represent lexical meanings
and vowels grammatical (cf. further Anttila 1975a, 1975b, 1977). Again we
see that we have to do with the semiotic process of selection, which diagrammatically represents the categories. As for morphological iconicity in general,
see Shapiro (1969), and the difference between derivation and inflection in
Shapiro (1974). And now we are ready to go back to Russian *pojas* 'belt' (Vincent,
here). The fact that in the 1940s there were speech styles which did not raise
unstressed *a* to *i* after soft consonants in inflectional suffixes (but in words
like this) points to a typical diagram. If Vincent had connected the passage
with that on diagrammaticity (Anttila 1972:17, 196) the matter would have
been clearer, although I can understand the difficulties. Vincent's alternative
solution is:

> It is, however, also possible to argue that in the initial stages the sound
> change operates root-internally, but only with time expands across
> boundaries. Confirmation of this alternative account is found in Anttila's
> concluding observation that in contemporary Russian the sound change
> has spread to inflectional suffixes. If the sound change knew enough
> about the structure of Russian not to interfere with inflections in the
> 1940's, why should it decide to ignore this knowledge a quarter of a
> century later? It seems both methodologically and philosophically wiser
> not to ascribe it such knowledge in the first place.

The first part of this quotation is not really an alternative. This is of course
what happened. The earlier diagram has been broken, a typical fact of linguistic change. The second part is then also unnecessary, since the question
therein is parallel to a question of, say, "Why does not a sound change affect
the Schwarzwaldians at time X, but ignores this restriction a quarter of a century

later?" This is exactly how sound change operates. And I argue that morphological diagrams are *res*, as the Schwarzwaldians are. This is not a question of assigning some "knowledge" to sound change; the sign-users do the coding. The case is rather both methodologically and philosophically impeccable. The latest lucid instance of a treatment of inflectional diagrammaticity in this sense is Andersen's (1976) discussion of the rise of increasing regularity in the Russian peripheral cases in the plural. Here the distinctive features in the vowels diagram the degree of openness and closedness of the nominal categories. The case is very strong indeed.

What comes to mind are of course the grammatical *canons* of the Greeks, or even Varro's term for inflectional morphology: *declinatio naturalis*. Note that natural sounds (onomatopoeia in general) make use of similar diagrams in language (cf. Anttila 1976b).

As for the conspiracies, these are indeed restatements of the notion *canonical* forms. Here we have to do with selection again. Certain shapes indicate correct form, and semiotically this belongs to the signtypes representing signs in themselves (qualisigns, sinsigns, legisigns) (see Anttila 1976b). I will not treat selection here, I just repeat from my earlier work that this shows the viability of the notion of diagrammatization. The target of production is more important than an underlying invariant starting point. Canonical forms belong to the realm of real entities (*res*).

To sum up I have briefly looked at sound change from the semiotic point of view. This can be regarded as the highest theoretical or philosophical level in linguistic explanation, although many linguists disagree, especially those who take description as explanation. I did also use a philosophical as-if argument by showing that sound change is as-if-nonverbal. This brought out something not stressed enough before: *sound change has an important (semiotic) sign-producing function*. Particularly, I supplemented the well-known social factor in sound change with a parallel grammatical one, showing that grammatical structure can feed on sound change rather directly, to a degree greater than suspected. This is to be expected, if we understand the fact that signs grow (icon to index to symbol), and we get here another driving force for drift as a semiotic phenomenon. Sound change must be viewed as the mechanical/physiological base together with its semiotic coding, whether it is social, grammatical, or both. Since the mental aspect is crucial, sound change agrees with objective idealism: matter is effete mind. Thus the task of historical phonology is, among other things, to revive the mind behind it all (this is the requirement of history in general). For sound change the work has been initiated particularly by Henning Andersen. Finally, this paper can be taken as the next step in the discussion of the philosophy of change started in Anttila (1974). In particular, it shows again that evolution is the factor that mediates between mind and matter[2].

Notes

1. I will assume basic familiarity with literature on sound change, and will refer to a minimal apparatus only, particularly to the (recent) semiotic aspects. I am particularly grateful for Nigel Vincent's contribution "Is sound change teleological?". It influenced my exposition considerably.
2. The social/mental factors of sound change can be strengthened with Lyle Campbell's (1976) arguments. For semiotic coding it is of course irrelevant how the variation arises, i.e. it need not happen in the mouths of the speakers of one language only. Change is not just natural-phonetic.

References

Andersen, Henning
  1973   "Abductive and deductive change", *Language* 49: 765–793.
  1974   "Toward a typology of change: Bifurcating changes and binary relations", in: Anderson – Jones 1974, 2: 18–62.
  1976   "Toward a typology of change: Analogy" (Unpublished paper).
Anderson, J. M. – Ch. Jones (Eds.)
  1974   *Historical linguistics* (Amsterdam: North-Holland).
Anttila, Raimo
  1972   *An Introduction to historical and comparative linguistics* (New York: Macmillan).
  1974   "Formalization as degeneration in historical linguistics", in: Anderson – Jones 1974, 1: 1–32.
  1975a   "Exception as regularity in phonology", in: *Phonologica 1972* (Eds.: W. Dressler – F. V. Mareš) (München: Fink), pp. 91–99.
  1975b   "The indexical element in morphology", in: *Innsbrucker Beiträge zur Sprachwissenschaft,* Reihe Vorträge, 12.
  1976a   "The metamorphosis of allomorphs", in: *The second LACUS forum 1975* (Ed.: P. Reich) (Columbia, S.C.: Hornbeam Press), pp. 238–248.
  1976b   "Affektiivis[-deskriptiivis-onomatopoieettis]ten sanojen asema kielen merkkisysteemissä, *Virittäjä* 1: 126–133.
  1976c   "The reconstruction of Sprachgefühl", in: Christie 1976, pp. 215–234.
  1977   *Analogy* (The Hague: Mouton).
Campbell, L.
  1976   "Language contact and sound change", in: Christie 1976, pp. 181–194.
Chafe, Wallace L.
  1962   Phonetics, semantics, and language", *Language* 38: 335–344.
Christie, W. M. (Ed.)
  1976   *Current progress in historical linguistics* (Amsterdam: North-Holland).
Coseriu, Eugenio
  1974   *Synchronie, Diachronie und Geschichte* (Trsl.: H. Sohre) (München: Fink). [Translation of *Sincronía, diacronía e historia: el problema del cambio lingüístico* (Montevideo: Universidad de la Republica, 1958).]
Ekman, P. R. – W. Friesen
  1969   "The repertoire of non-verbal behavior categories, origins, usages and codes", *Semiotica* 1: 49–98.

Itkonen, Esa
    1974   *Linguistics and metascience* (= *Studia Philosophica Turkuensia* 2) (Kokemäki: Risteen kirjapaino).
Jakobson, Roman
    1965   "Quest for the essence of language", *Diogenes* 51: 21–37.
Kettunen, Lauri
    1962   *Eesti kielen äännehistoria*[2] (= *Suomalainen kirjallisuuden seuran toimituksia* 156) (Helsinki).
Komárek, Miroslav
    1964   "Sur l'appréciation fonctionelle des alternances morphologiques", *Travaux Linguistiques de Prague* 1: 145–161.
Korhonen, Mikko
    1969   "Die Entwicklung der morphologischen Methode im Lappischen", *Finnisch-Ugrische Forschungen* 37: 203–362.
Labov, W. – M. Yaeger – R. Steiner
    1973   *A quantitative study of sound change in progress* (NSF report printed and distributed by the U.S. Regional Survey) (Philadelphia: University of Pennsylvania).
Makkai, A. – V. B. Makkai
    1976   "The nature of linguistic change and modern linguistic theories", in: Christie 1976, pp. 1976, pp. 235–265.
Peirce, Charles Sanders
    1955   *Philosophical writings of Peirce* (Ed.: J. Buchler) (New York: Dover).
Pike, Kenneth L.
    1965   "Non-linear order and anti-redundancy in German morphological matrices", *Zeitschrift für Mundartforschung* 32: 193–221.
Samuels, M. L.
    1972   *Linguistic evolution with special reference to English* (Cambridge: Cambridge University Press).
Shapiro, Michael
    1969   *Aspects of Russian morphology, a semiotic investigation* (Cambridge, Mass.: Slavica Publishers).
    1974   "Morphophonemics as semiotics", *Acta Linguistica Hafniensia* 15: 29–49.
Slagle, Uhlan von
    1975   "A viable alternative to Chomskyan rationalism", in: *The first LACUS forum 1974* (Eds.: A. Makkai – V. B. Makkai) (Columbia, S.C.: Hornbeam Press), pp. 177–193.
Slotty, Ingeborg
    1935   *Zur Geschichte der Teleologie in der Sprachwissenschaft (Bopp, Humboldt, Schleicher)* (Dissertation Breslau) (Würzburg: Konrad Triltsch).
Spitzer, Leo
    1948   *Linguistics and literary history* (Princeton: Princeton University Press).
Vernon, M. D.
    1971   *The psychology of perception* (Harmondsworth: Penguin).
Walther, Elisabeth
    1974   *Allgemeine Zeichenlehre. Einführung in die Grundlagen der Semiotik* (Stuttgart: Deutsche Verlags-Anstalt).
Wandruszka, Mario
    1971   *Interlinguistik. Umriss einer neuen Sprachwissenschaft* (München: Piper).
Werner, Otmar
    1976   "Suppletivwesen durch Lautwandel" (in: *Salzburger Beiträge zur Sprachwissenschaft* 3).

JERZY BAŃCZEROWSKI

A formal approach to the theory of fortition-lenition: a preliminary study[1]

1. Informal theory of fortition-lenition

The sound processes termed fortition-lenition[2] are shared by a wide range of languages belonging to different language families and have been described by numerous authors.[3] From these descriptions similarities are emerging in the results being attained by fortition-lenition regardless of the languages on which they operate. This state of affairs makes the question about the universal (panglottal) nature of these processes pertinent.

The most comprehensive attempt towards the description and explanation of fortition-lenition phenomena was undertaken by L. Zabrocki (1951)[4]. The thorough scrutiny of the development of consonantal systems in various languages, especially in the IE ones, led him to establishing fundamental articulatory phonetic laws of a panglottal character which guide the change of sound systems being affected by fortition-lenition.

Following Zabrocki's line of approach the present author introduced, in Bańczerowski (1969)[5], the term *theory of fortition-lenition* referring to the knowledge already achieved in the field concerned and endeavored to complete this theory with available articulatory phonetic findings and extend it to Uralic languages drawing, above all, upon the evidence obtained from close examination of Finnish and Lappish. Of course, this theory was formulated informally.

Paving the way towards the formal theory of fortition-lenition it should be said that the informal theory incorporates at least five distinct components:
(i) The set of allophonic classifications of two genetically related languages taking into account the distribution of energy along certain well-chosen articulatory dimensions. Of special importance for these classifications are the relations holding between *fortes* and *lenes*. The results of articulatory experimental phonetics render service in justifying the basis for classification.
(ii) The set of sound mutations, i.e. the diachronic relation connecting certain classes of etymologically related sounds of two languages.

(iii) The set of fortition relationship and the set of lenition relationship, which, being included in the set of sound mutations, contain pairs of sound classes bound up by the relation of fortition and lenition, respectively. Both these relations are in their turn dependent upon the relations holding between fortes and lenes.

(iv) The mechanics of fortition-lenition account for the different degree of susceptibility to these processes displayed by the elements of certain articulatory rows, called susceptibility rows and erected on the basis of appropriate ordering relations. The theory of fortition-lenition is still unable to reveal the ultimate cause which triggers off these processes, but it studies their chronology and their advancement in the susceptibility rows in formulating panglottal laws. The sounds affected by fortition-lenition do not change at random but their shift, being law-governed, depends on their position in the susceptibility rows.

(v) Knowing the laws of fortition-lenition may be useful in reconstructing the antecedent allophonic systems of a given language, while limiting the uncertainty of choice among competing alternatives.

Thus the above five components, among others, make up the scope of the informal theory of fortition-lenition. This paper aims at the logical reconstruction of some aspects of the theory of fortition-lenition, denoted from now on by the symbol $\theta_{F/L}$. Carrying out this task is not easy because the informal theory $\theta_{F/L}$ often makes use of ambiguous terms and the formulations of definitions and theorems are not sufficiently clear and precise. Further on what renders a formalization of the theory $\theta_{F/L}$ difficult is that not all relevant factors are explicitly stated but often only present implicitly, or hinted at. Thus reconstructing the theory $\theta_{F/L}$ we will be forced sometimes to modify it or even change some parts of it. This will certainly go together with simplifications of the informal theory itself. No problems should arise if such simplifications do not change the spirit of this theory.

Applying a logical framework should contribute to eliminating vagueness in the theory $\theta_{F/L}$ obliging us to decide which are the primitive notions and which the defined ones, which properties of these notions should be introduced axiomatically and which theorems can be proved.

Our approach is certainly not free from formal slips but we believe that after being polished appropriately it can attain a tolerable state.

2. The language of the theory $\theta_{F/L}$

The language of the theory $\theta_{F/L}$ will comprise two kinds of notions, reflected in appropriate terms and symbols, and these are:

(i) *logical*,
(ii) *specifically linguistic*.

The former group has been borrowed from *propositional calculus, predicate calculus of first order*, and *set theory*. We are not going, however, to give a systematic and exhaustive survey of logical terms and symbols used here and will limit our introduction only to the brief presentation of some of them. Others will be explained later on in the context.

(a) *Logical terms and symbols*
The set whose elements are $x, y, z, \ldots$ will be denoted by $\{x, y, z, \ldots\}$. Thus $X = \{x, y, z, \ldots\}$ means that the set X is composed of the elements $x, y, z, \ldots$ The formula $x \in X$ reads x *belongs to X* or x *is an element of X*. The formula $x \notin X$ means that x *does not belong to X*.

If every element of a set X is an element of a set Y, then we say that X *is a subset of Y* or *the set X is contained (included) in the set Y*. This is indicated by $X \subset Y$. The symbol $\subset$ is called the *symbol of inclusion*. The common part of the sets X and Y is denoted by $X \cap Y$ and is called the *product* or *intersection* of these sets. By the *sum* or *union* of sets X and Y is meant the set composed of the elements that are in X or in Y. The *sum* of the sets X and Y is denoted by $X \cup Y$. ϕ will be empty set; it contains no elements. The symbol $P(X)$ denotes the set of all subsets of X.

The letters $x, y, z, \ldots, X, Y, Z, \ldots$ will be used as variables representing arbitrary individuals and classes (sets) of individuals, respectively.

The symbols $\sim, \wedge, \vee, \rightarrow, \leftrightarrow$ are applied as signs for *negation, conjunction, disjunction, implication*, and *equivalence*. Their meanings can be easily seen in the following:

$\sim$	— it is not the case that
$\wedge$	— and
$\vee$	— or
$\rightarrow$	— if ... then
$\leftrightarrow$	— if and only if

The universal quantifier *for every x* binding the variable x is abbreviated with the symbol $\bigwedge$. The existential quantifier *there exists an x such that* is written as $\bigvee_x$. The phrase *there exists exactly one x such that* will be replaced with the symbol $\bigvee_x$.

The signs $=$ and $\neq$ preserve here their usual meanings, i.e. the former denotes *identity* and the latter *distinctness*.

Given any two objects x, y an *ordered pair* with *antecedent x* and *successor*

y can be formed, to be denoted by $\langle x, y \rangle$. An ordered pair $\langle x, y \rangle$ ought to be held distinct from $\langle y, x \rangle$ if $x \neq y$. The set of all ordered pairs $\langle x, y \rangle$ such that $x \in X$ and $y \in Y$ is called the Cartesian product of the sets X and Y and denoted by $X \times Y$. The set of all pairs from the set X, called also Cartesian product of X, will be symbolized by $X \times X$ or simply X^2.

The concept of a subset of a given set X may be identified with the concept of a property of the elements of that set. Thus every property of elements specifies a subset of a given set. Consequently the convention will be adopted to identify properties with sets and to treat the formulations *x is an element of X* and *x has a property X* as synonymous. Under this convention the formulas $x \in X$ and $X(x)$ are read *x is an element of X* or *x has a property X* mean the same thing.

In our system we concede an important role to *binary relations* which are properties of ordered pairs, i.e. properties of elements of a Cartesian product. Thus binary relations may be identified with subsets of $X \times Y$, where X and Y are any sets. In order to indicate that R is a binary relation in $X \times Y$ we shall write $x \, R \, y$ or sometimes $\langle x, y \rangle \in R$. It is evident that $R \subset X \times Y$.

The set of all antecedents of ordered pairs $\langle x, y \rangle$ that bear the relation R is called *domain of R* and denoted by $D'R$. The set of all successors of ordered pairs $\langle x, y \rangle$ in R is called *converse domain* and denoted by $\Box'R$. The *field* of relation R is symbolized by $C'R$ and is defined as follows:

$$C'R \underset{df}{=} D'R \cup \Box'R$$

A binary relation $R \subset X \times X$ is called *reflexive* if the condition $x \, R \, x$ is satisfied for every $x \in X$. A relation $R \subset X \times X$ is called *symmetric* if the condition $x \, R \, y$ implies $y \, R \, x$ for all $x, y \in X$, in symbols:

$$x \, R \, y \rightarrow y \, R \, x \text{ for all } x, y \in X.$$

A relation $R \subset X \times X$ is called *transitive* if the conditions $x \, R \, y$ and $y \, R \, z$ imply $x \, R \, z$ for every three elements x, y, z of X. In symbolic notation:

$$(x \, R \, y \wedge y \, R \, z) \rightarrow x \, R \, z \text{ for all } x, y, z \in X.$$

If a relation R is at the same time *reflexive, symmetric* and *transitive* in a set X, then it is called an *equivalence* relation in X. The class of all equivalence relations in X will be denoted by equ(X).

A special kind of relation is represented by *functions*. The class of all functions will be denoted by the symbol fnc. A binary relation R, $(x \, R \, y)$, is a function defined on the elements of a set X with values in a set Y if and only if the following two conditions are satisfied:

(i) for every $x \in X$, there is an $y \in Y$ such that $x \mathrel{R} y$,
(ii) for every $x \in X$ and for all $y, z \in Y$, if $x \mathrel{R} y$ and $x \mathrel{R} z$, then $y = z$.
Thus, if R is a function defined on X, then it associates with every element $x \in X$ exactly one element $y \in Y$, such that $x \mathrel{R} y$; this unique y will be denoted by the symbol $R'x$.

The number of elements of a given set X i.e. its *cardinal number* or *power*, will be denoted by card (X). There are *infinite* (containing infinitely many elements) and *finite* sets. The set of all natural numbers is infinite. The cardinal number of the set of all natural numbers is denoted by the symbol $\aleph_0$. Hence the inequality card $(X) < \aleph_0$ means that the set X is always finite.

(b) *The specifically linguistic notions*
This group of notions embrace *primitive* i.e. in our system undefined as well as *defined* notions. The specifically linguistic terms and symbols will denote here various language objects, sets, and relations. In justification of the choice of specifically linguistic notions, especially primitive ones, for the theory $\theta_{F/L}$ the subsequent introductory remarks should be put forward.

The system-oriented approach to language has helped structural linguists to overcome the atomistic bias of neogrammarians while leading to the replacement of the history of isolated language facts by the history of language systems. (Cf. Jakobson 1931:247–67, 1962:1–2; van Ginneken 1956:74–81; Milewski 1957:120–36). From this point onwards the implementation of this theoretical framework has been attempted by appropriate linguistic practice in dealing with diachronic development of languages.

Under language system S we understand a set of language objects Z, and relations defined on this set:

$$2.1 \ S = \langle Z; R_1, R_2, ..., R_n \rangle$$

At the phonetic-phonological level we shall operate with phonic systems which are composed either of the set of individual sounds (phones) or the set of classes of sounds and respective relations defined on these sets.

Sound change or mutation will be conceived of here as a relation **Mt** connecting certain classes of phones of one phonic system S_i with respective classes of phones of another phonic system S_j while genetic relationship between S_i and S_j will be assumed. Before introducing the relation **Mt** which belongs to the set of our primitive notions we ought firstly to occupy ourselves with certain articulatory phonetic systems which are relevant for the theory $\theta_{F/L}$.

Speech sounds or phones are the result of simultaneous movements performed by articulatory organs which may be subdivided into *supraglottal*, *subglottal*, and *glottal* ones. The synergy of these three main articulatory sub-systems is responsible for the articulatory and acoustic diversity of speech sounds.

The set of all phones, past and future, produced by all members of all speech communities will be denoted by the symbol **Fon**. Thus the set **Fon** contains all human speech sounds. It should be obvious that the elements of **Fon** are individual objects. At a given period of time only a subset of **Fon** is available for a particular speech community. The subset of **Fon** available for a given speech community will be signified with an appropriate index, for instance, $\mathbf{Fon_{PIE}}$, $\mathbf{Fon_{PG}}$ denote the set of phones of Proto-Indo-European and Proto-Germanic, respectively. Thus:

2.2   card $(\mathbf{Fon}) < \aleph_0$

2.3 $\mathbf{Fon_{PIE}} \subset \mathbf{Fon}$

2.4 $\mathbf{Fon_{PG}} \subset \mathbf{Fon}$

For the sake of our subsequent considerations let us now assume that we have at our disposal a sample of phones which fulfill certain requirements and so may be regarded as sufficiently representative of **Fon**. If articulatory or acoustic analysis could be refined to a great extent, it would be found that no two phones produced by one or two speakers could have exactly the same parameters in all respects; they would differ at least in one respect from each other. But nevertheless hearers of a given speech community neglect certain differences between sounds as undistinguishable by ear from each other. The relation which binds such two undistinguishable phones will be called *homophony* and denoted by the symbol **Hph**. In the last resort this relation is based on certain properties of the auditory apparatus as well as on certain functions acquired by phones in a given language.

The relation **Hph** will be defined on the set **Fon**. Native speakers are supposed to know, at least subconsciously, the relation **Hph**[6] as well as other relations valid in their language. Successful language communication presupposes compliance with the relational structure imposed upon the phonic substance of a language.

The relation **Hph** divides the set **Fon** into equivalence classes called here allophones. The family of **Hph**-equivalence classes in **Fon** may be denoted by the symbol **Fon/Hph** and defined formally thus:

2.5 $\mathbf{Fon/Hph} = \{X: \bigvee_{y} [y \in \mathbf{Fon} \wedge \bigwedge_{x} (x \in X \leftrightarrow x \in \mathbf{Fon} \wedge x \, \mathbf{Hph} \, y)] \}$

In order to avoid the complex symbol **Fon/Hph** we will introduce the symbol **FON**:

2.6 $\mathbf{FON} \underset{df}{=} \mathbf{Fon/Hph}$

2.7 $\mathbf{FON} \in \text{clsf} \, (\mathbf{Fon})$

The sets of allophones may be further classified. Not all of these classifications will, however, be interesting for our purposes because we orient here ourselves, above all, on the processes of fortition-lenition. Keeping this in mind we will utilize certain articulatory dimensions as a basis for classifying allophones.

The articulation of speech sounds requires some amount of muscular energy in order to put the speech organs into motion. This energy may be distributed in different way along various dimensions in the sub-, supra-, and glottal systems during the articulation of particular sounds. We shall pay less attention to the articulatory energy expended in the glottal system because the acoustic effects of vocal cords depend on the distribution of energy in the sub- and supraglottal systems. The information on the distribution of articulatory energy should be drawn from experimental findings which sometimes are, however, ambiguous.

Thus the differences in the distribution of articulatory energy may serve as criteria for the articulatory classification of allophones. The articulatory space has various dimensions. For our purposes we will avail ourselves of four-dimensional articulatory space. This means that every allophone may be characterized with regard to four dimensions such as:

(i) the force of supraglottal aperture;
(ii) the force of sub- and supraglottal air pressure;
(iii) the mass of the movable supraglottal articulatory organ;
(iv) the duration in time.

The differences in the distribution of articulatory energy along these four dimensions will be reflected in the following four relations: $\leqslant_{ap}$, $<_{sb}^{sp}$, $\leqslant_{ma}$, $\leqslant_{t}$, which belong to our primitive notions and which we are going to deal with subsequently. These relations will be defined on the set $\mathbf{FON}$ which contains all allophones of all languages.

The system

2.8 $S_{Ar} = \langle \mathbf{FON}, \leqslant_{ap}, <_{sb}^{sp}, \leqslant_{ma}, \leqslant_{t} \rangle$

will be called articulatory structural phonetics.

The relation of force of supraglottal aperture

The relation $\leqslant_{ap}$ which reflects on the expenditure of energy required of supraglottal organs to maintain the desired degree of aperture, will be called the relation of force of the supraglottal aperture. The formula $X \leqslant_{ap} Y$ reads:

the allophone X has a not greater (i.e. less than or equal to) degree of supraglottal aperture that the allophone Y. Taking recourse to Latin this formula can be read as follows: an allophone X is *non fortior apertione quam* an allophone Y. In fact both readings are only short cuts for saying that phones in X have a not greater degree of supraglottal aperture than phones in Y. But even this formulation is a bit unprecise, because in establishing the relation $\leqslant_{ap}$, we ought to take into account the *minimum* and *maximum* value of supraglottal aperture the phones of X may acquire on the one hand, and the *minimum* and *maximum* value of supraglottal aperture available for the phones of Y on the other. And now if the minimum restricted to X is not greater than the minimum restricted to Y and the maxima behave in the same way then X bears the relation $\leqslant_{ap}$ to Y. A similar guiding principle will be implicit in formulating the relation $\leqslant_{ma}$ and $\leqslant_t$. In real language communication it may happen that a phone in X even has a greater supraglottal aperture than a phone in Y. But this will have no bearing on the relation $\leqslant_{ap}$.

The relation $\leqslant_{ap}$ has the following properties:

2.9 $\leqslant_{ap} \subset \mathbf{FON}^2$

2.10 $\bigwedge_{X \in \mathbf{FON}} (X \leqslant_{ap} X)$

2.11 $\bigwedge_X \bigwedge_Y \bigwedge_Z (X \leqslant_{ap} Y \wedge Y \leqslant_{ap} Z \rightarrow X \leqslant_{ap} Z)$

2.12 $\widehat{X \in \mathbf{FON}} \ \widehat{Y \in \mathbf{FON}} \ (X \leqslant_{ap} Y \vee Y \leqslant_{ap} X)$

Having the relation $\leqslant_{ap}$ enables us to define two other relations, i.e. $=_{ap}$ and $<_{ap}$.

2.13 $X =_{ap} Y \leftrightarrow X \leqslant_{ap} Y \wedge Y \leqslant_{ap} X$

Two allophones X and Y are in relation $=_{ap}$ if and only if they display an equal degree of supraglottal aperture. The relation $=_{ap}$ is an equivalence relation:

2.14 $=_{ap} \in \mathrm{equ}$

The family of $=_{ap}$-equivalence classes in $\mathbf{FON}$ will be denoted by $\mathbf{FON}/=_{ap}$. The set $\mathbf{FON}/=_{ap}$ contains such classes as: *stops, affricates, spirants, nasals, liquids.*

2.15 $X <_{ap} Y \leftrightarrow X \leqslant_{ap} Y \wedge \sim (Y \leqslant_{ap} X)$

The allophone X has the relation $<_{ap}$ to the allophone Y if and only if the degree of supraglottal aperture of X is less than that of Y; or in other words X is *lenior apertione quam* Y and Y is *fortior apertione quam* X.

With the purpose of arranging the elements of $\mathbf{FON}/=_{ap}$ linearly, we introduce the relation $\prec_{ap}$:

2.16 $A \prec_{ap} B \leftrightarrow A, B \in \mathbf{FON}/=_{ap} \wedge \overset{\frown}{X \in A} \overset{\frown}{Y \in B} (X <_{ap} Y)$

2.17 $\prec_{ap} \subset (\mathbf{FON}/=_{ap})^2$

The relation $\prec_{ap}$ is an ordering of the set $\mathbf{FON}/=_{ap}$. It is *antisymmetric*, *transitive* and *connected*, i.e. it satisfies the following conditions:

(i) $\overset{\frown}{A_1,A_2} [A_1, A_2 \in \mathbf{FON}/=_{ap} \wedge A_1 \neq A_2 \wedge A_1 \prec_{ap} A_2 \rightarrow \sim$

$(A_2 \prec_{ap} A_1)]$

(ii) $\overset{\frown}{A_1, A_2, A_3} (A_1, A_2, A_3 \in \mathbf{FON}/=_{ap} \wedge A_1 \prec_{ap} A_2 \wedge A_2 \prec_{ap} A_3 \rightarrow$

$A_1 \prec_{ap} A_3)$

(iii) $\overset{\frown}{A_1, A_2} (A_1, A_2 \in \mathbf{FON}/=_{ap} \wedge A_1 \neq A_2 \rightarrow A_1 \prec_{ap} A_2 \vee A_2 \prec_{ap} A_1)$

Hence the relation $\prec_{ap}$ arranges all elements of $\mathbf{FON}/=_{ap}$ in a row. The graph of the relation $\prec_{ap}$ has, among others, the following content:

$$\begin{bmatrix} [k] \\ [t] \\ [p] \\ [g] \\ [d] \\ [b] \end{bmatrix} \begin{bmatrix} \\ \\ \\ [gh] \\ [dh] \\ [bh] \end{bmatrix} \begin{bmatrix} \\ \\ [c] \\ \\ [ʒ] \end{bmatrix} \begin{bmatrix} [\chi] \\ [\theta] \\ [f] \\ [\gamma] \\ [\delta] \\ [\beta] \\ [s] \\ [z] \end{bmatrix} \begin{bmatrix} \\ \\ \\ [\eta] \\ [n] \\ [m] \end{bmatrix} \begin{bmatrix} \\ \\ \\ [l] \\ [r] \end{bmatrix}$$

From the finiteness of the set $\mathbf{FON}$ (card $(\mathbf{FON}) < \aleph_0$) follows the theorem concerning the *least* and the *greatest* element, respectively.

2.18 $\overset{\vee}{A} [A \in \mathbf{FON}/=_{ap} \wedge \hat{B} (B \in \mathbf{FON}/=_{ap} \wedge A \neq B \rightarrow A \prec_{ap} B)]$

2.19 $\overset{\vee}{A} [A \in \mathbf{FON}/=_{ap} \wedge \hat{B} (B \in \mathbf{FON}/=_{ap} \wedge A \neq B \rightarrow B \prec_{ap} A)]$

Between any two elements of two different columns of the above graph holds the relation $<_{ap}$, while between any two elements of the same column holds the relation $=_{ap}$, and finally between any more left and any more right column holds the relation $\prec_{ap}$. All the allophones of one column, i.e. the elements of a class $A_i \in \text{FON}/=_{ap}$ should be thought of as if located at one point.

There are extreme elements with respect to the relation $<_{ap}$, i.e. the *minimal* ones for which there is no element with a lesser degree of supraglottal aperture, and the *maximal* ones for which there is no element with a greater degree of supraglottal aperture.

$$2.20 \quad \underset{X}{\vee} \{X \in \text{FON} \wedge \underset{Y}{\wedge} [Y \in \text{FON} \to \sim (Y <_{ap} X)]\}$$

$$2.21 \quad \underset{X}{\vee} \{X \in \text{FON} \wedge \underset{Y}{\wedge} [Y \in \text{FON} \to \sim (X <_{ap} Y)]\}$$

The relation of sub- and supraglottal air pressure

This relation will be denoted by the symbol $<_{sb}^{sp}$. It binds two allophones X and Y such that in X the subglottal pressure is higher than the supraglottal one, while in Y the supraglottal pressure equals the subglottal one; in other words X is voiced and Y is voiceless.

The properties of the relation $<_{sb}^{sp}$ are characterized by the following axioms:

$$2.22 \quad <_{sb}^{sp} \subset \text{FON}^2$$

$$2.23 \quad \underset{X \in \text{FON}}{\wedge} \sim (X <_{sb}^{sp} X)$$

$$2.24 \quad \underset{X, Y}{\widehat{\wedge}} [X <_{sb}^{sp} Y \to \sim \underset{Z}{\vee} (Z <_{sb}^{sp} X)]$$

$$2.25 \quad \underset{X, Y}{\widehat{\wedge}} [X <_{sb}^{sp} Y \to \sim \underset{Z}{\vee} (Y <_{sb}^{sp} Z)]$$

$$2.26 \quad \underset{X \in \text{FON}}{\widehat{\wedge}} \underset{Y \in \text{FON}}{\widehat{\wedge}} (X <_{sb}^{sp} Y \vee Y <_{sb}^{sp} X)$$

From 2.24 and 2.25 follows obviously the theorem:

$$2.27 \quad \underset{X}{\wedge} \underset{Y}{\wedge} [X <_{sb}^{sp} Y \to \sim (Y <_{sb}^{sp} X)]$$

From 2.23–2.26 follows the theorem:

$$2.28 \quad \underset{X, Y}{\widehat{\wedge}} [X <_{sb}^{sp} Y \to \sim \underset{Z}{\vee} (X <_{sb}^{sp} Z \wedge Z <_{sb}^{sp} Y)]$$

In terms of the relation $\lessgtr_{sb}^{sp}$ the set of all voiced allophones (**SNR**) and the set of all voiceless allophones (**SRD**) can be defined:

2.29 $\textbf{SNR} = \{X: \bigvee_{Y} (X \lessgtr_{sb}^{sp} Y)\}$

2.30 $\textbf{SRD} = \{Y: \bigvee_{X} (X \lessgtr_{sb}^{sp} Y)\}$

2.31 $\textbf{SNR} = D' \lessgtr_{sb}^{sp}$

2.32 $\textbf{SRD} = \mho' \lessgtr_{sb}^{sp}$

The relation which connects two voiced allophones or two voiceless ones will be denoted by the symbol $=_{sb}^{sp}$.

2.33 $X =_{sb}^{sp} Y \underset{df}{\leftrightarrow} (X, Y \in \textbf{SNR}) \lor (X, Y \in \textbf{SRD})$

2.34 $\leqslant_{sb}^{sp} \underset{df}{=} \lessgtr_{sb}^{sp} \cup =_{sb}^{sp}$

From the definition 2.34 follows that the relation $\leqslant_{sb}^{sp}$ connects:

(i) a voiced and a voiceless allophone;
(ii) two voiced allophones;
(iii) two voiceless allophones.

From the set $\leqslant_{sb}^{sp}$ are excluded only such pairs the predecessor of which is a voiceless allophone and the successor a voiced allophone.

The relation of force of supraglottal closure
This relation will be denoted by $<_{cl}$ and defined in the following way:

2.35 $X <_{cl} Y \underset{df}{\leftrightarrow} (Y <_{ap} X) \lor [(X =_{ap} Y) \land (X <_{sb}^{sp} Y)]$

The relation $<_{cl}$ is not simply the converse of relation $<_{ap}$ because two allophones may have the same degree of aperture but different degree of closure, for instance, $\langle [b], [p] \rangle \in =_{ap} \land \langle [b], [p] \rangle \in <_{cl}$

2.36 $=_{cl} \neq =_{ap}$

2.37 $X =_{cl} Y \underset{df}{\leftrightarrow} X =_{ap} Y \land X =_{sb}^{sp} Y$

The relation of mass of a supraglottal movable organ

For denotation of this relation the symbol $\leqslant_{ma}$ will be used. Two allo-phones X and Y are in relation $\leqslant_{ma}$ if the mass of the organ involved in the articulation of X is not greater than the mass of the organ engaged in the articulation of Y; or in other words the allophone X is *non fortior pondere organi quam* the allophone Y. It is evident that the relation $\leqslant_{ma}$ mirrors the expenditure of energy needed to put a given organ into motion. The greater the mass of the organ the more energy will be expended. The properties dis-played by the relation $\leqslant_{ma}$ are similar to those of the relation $\leqslant_{ap}$.

2.38 $\quad \leqslant_{ma} \subset \mathbf{FON}^2$

2.39 $\quad \widehat{X \in \mathbf{FON}}\ (X \leqslant_{ma} X)$

2.40 $\quad \hat{X}\ \hat{Y}\ \hat{Z}\ (X \leqslant_{ma} Y \wedge Y \leqslant_{ma} Z \to X \leqslant_{ma} Z)$

2.41 $\quad \widehat{X \in \mathbf{FON}}\ \widehat{Y \in \mathbf{FON}}\ (X \leqslant_{ma} Y \vee Y \leqslant_{ma} X)$

The relations $=_{ma}$ and $\leqslant_{ma}$ can be defined in terms of the relation $\leqslant_{ma}$.

2.42 $\quad X =_{ma} Y \underset{df}{\leftrightarrow} X \leqslant_{ma} Y \wedge Y \leqslant_{ma} X$

2.43 $\quad =_{ma} \in \text{equ}$

The family of $=_{ma}$-equivalence classes in **FON** will be denoted by the symbol $\mathbf{FON}/=_{ma}$. This set contains, among other members, the following classes: *labials, apicals, frontals, dorsals, laryngeals.*

2.44 $\quad X <_{ma} Y \underset{df}{\leftrightarrow} X \leqslant_{ma} Y \wedge \sim (Y \leqslant_{ma} X)$

In order to arrange the elements of $\mathbf{FON}/=_{ma}$ linearly we have to define the relation $\prec_{ma}$:

2.45 $\quad A \prec_{ma} B \underset{df}{\leftrightarrow} A, B \in \mathbf{FON}/=_{ma} \wedge \widehat{X \in A}\ \widehat{Y \in B}\ (X <_{ma} Y)$

2.46 $\quad \prec_{ma} \subset (\mathbf{FON}/=_{ma})^2$

The relation $\prec_{ma}$ is an ordering of the set $\mathbf{FON}/=_{ma}$ because it is *anti-symmetric, transitive* and *connected*. It arranges all elements of $\mathbf{FON}/=_{ma}$ in a row. The graph of the relation $\prec_{ma}$ may have the following content:

[']	[t]	[p]	[k]
[h]	[d]	[b]	[g]
	[θ]	[φ]	[x]
	[δ]	[β]	[γ]
	[n]	[m]	[η]
	[l]		
	[r]		

There exist the *least* and the *greatest* elements of the set $\mathbf{FON}/=_{ma}$.

2.47 $\underset{A}{\bigvee} [A \in \mathbf{FON}/=_{ma} \wedge \underset{B}{\bigwedge} (B \in \mathbf{FON}/=_{ma} \wedge A \neq B \to A \prec_{ma} B)]$

2.48 $\underset{A}{\bigvee} [A \in \mathbf{FON}/=_{ma} \wedge \underset{B}{\bigwedge} (B \in \mathbf{FON}/=_{ma} \wedge A \neq B \to B \prec_{ma} A)]$

There are *minimal* as well as *maximal* elements as regards the relation $\prec_{ma}$:

2.49 $\underset{X}{\bigvee} \{X \in \mathbf{FON} \wedge \underset{Y}{\bigwedge} [Y \in \mathbf{FON} \to \sim (Y \prec_{ma} X)]\}$

2.50 $\underset{X}{\bigvee} \{X \in \mathbf{FON} \wedge \underset{Y}{\bigwedge} [Y \in \mathbf{FON} \to \sim (X \prec_{ma} Y)]\}$

The relation of duration in time

To denote this relation the symbol $\leqslant_t$ will be chosen. Two allophones X and Y are in relation $\leqslant_t$ if the duration in time of X is not longer than that of Y; putting it differently, allophone X is *non fortior tempore quam* allophone Y. The relation $\leqslant_t$ has similar properties to those of the relations $\leqslant_{ap}$ and $\leqslant_{ma}$.

2.51 $\leqslant_t \subset \mathbf{FON}^2$

2.52 $\underset{X \in \mathbf{FON}}{\widehat{\bigwedge}} (X \leqslant_t X)$

2.53 $\underset{X}{\bigwedge} \underset{Y}{\bigwedge} \underset{Z}{\bigwedge} (X \leqslant_t Y \wedge Y \leqslant_t Z \to X \leqslant_t Z)$

2.54 $\underset{X \in \mathbf{FON}}{\bigwedge} \underset{Y \in \mathbf{FON}}{\bigwedge} (X \leqslant_t Y \vee Y \leqslant_t X)$

In terms of the relation $\leqslant_t$ we can define the relation $=_t$ and $\prec_t$:

2.55 $X =_t Y \underset{df}{\leftrightarrow} X \leqslant_t Y \wedge Y \leqslant_t X$

2.56 $=_t \in$ equ

2.57 $X <_t Y \underset{df}{\leftrightarrow} X \leqslant_t Y \wedge \sim (Y \leqslant_t X)$

The relation of the force of subglottal articulation

The relation now in question will be denoted by $\leqslant_{sb}$ and defined as follows:

2.58 $X \leqslant_{sb} Y \underset{df}{\leftrightarrow} X \leqslant_{ap} Y \vee X \leqslant^{sp}_{sb} Y$

According to definition 2.58 the relation $\leqslant_{sb}$ holds between two allophones X and Y such that the subglottal energy expenditure displayed by X is not greater than the subglottal energy expended by Y. It is also evident from the definition that this energy is intimately connected with supraglottal aperture as well as with the sub- and supraglottal air pressure. Needless to say, a greater amount of energy expended in the subglottal system will be correlated with a higher subglottal air pressure.

The properties of the relation $\leqslant_{sb}$ emerge from the following theorems:

2.59 (i) $\leqslant_{sb} \subset \mathbf{FON}^2$

    (ii) $\widehat{X \in \mathbf{FON}} (X \leqslant_{ab} X)$

    (iii) $\hat{X} \hat{Y} \hat{Z} (X \leqslant_{sb} Y \wedge Y \leqslant_{sb} Z \to X \leqslant_{sb} Z)$

    (iv) $\widehat{X \in \mathbf{FON}} \ \widehat{Y \in \mathbf{FON}} (X \leqslant_{sb} Y \vee Y \leqslant_{sb} X)$

In terms of the relation $\leqslant_{sb}$, the relations $=_{sb}$ and $<_{sb}$ can be introduced.

2.60 $X =_{sb} Y \underset{df}{\leftrightarrow} X \leqslant_{sb} Y \wedge Y \leqslant_{sb} X$

2.61 $=_{sb} \in$ equ

2.62 $X <_{sb} Y \underset{df}{\leftrightarrow} X \leqslant_{sb} Y \wedge \sim (Y \leqslant_{sb} X)$

2.63 $X <_{sb} Y \leftrightarrow X <_{ap} Y \vee X <^{sp}_{sb} Y$

As can be inferred from 2.63 the more open allophones expend a higher amount of energy in the subglottal system than the more closed ones do; and analogously voiceless allophones have a higher energy expenditure in the subglottal system than the voiced ones.

The linear order of the elements in $\mathbf{FON}/{=}_{sb}$ can be established on the basis of the relation $\prec_{sb}$.

2.64 $A \prec_{sb} B \underset{df}{\leftrightarrow} A, B \in \mathbf{FON}/{=}_{sb} \wedge \widehat{X \in A} \; \widehat{Y \in B} \, (X <_{sb} Y)$

2.65 $\prec_{sb} \subset (\mathbf{FOM}/{=}_{sb})^2$

Being *antisymmetric, transitive* and *connected* the relation $\prec_{sb}$ is an ordering of the set $\mathbf{FON}/{=}_{sb}$ arranging all elements of this set in a row. The graph of the relation $\prec_{sb}$ may have the following content:

[b]	[bh]		[β]	[m]	[l]	[p]	[pʰ]		[f]	[m]	[l]
[d]	[dh]	[ȝ]	[δ]	[n]	[r]	[t]	[tʰ]	[c]	[ϑ]	[n]	[r]
[g]	[gh]		[γ]	[η]		[k]	[kʰ]		[x]	[ṇ]	
			[z]						[s]		

There exist the *least* and the *greatest* elements of the set $\mathbf{FON}/{=}_{sb}$.

2.66 $\bigvee_A [A \in \mathbf{FON}/{=}_{sb} \wedge \bigwedge_B (B \in \mathbf{FON}/{=}_{sb} \wedge A \neq B \rightarrow A \prec_{sb} B)]$

2.67 $\bigvee_A [A \in \mathbf{FON}/{=}_{sb} \wedge \bigwedge_B (B \in \mathbf{FON}/{=}_{sb} \wedge A \neq B \rightarrow B \prec_{sb} A)]$

There are *minimal* and *maximal* elements with respect to the relation $<_{sb}$.

2.68 $\bigvee_X \{X \in \mathbf{FON} \wedge \bigwedge_Y [Y \in \mathbf{FON} \rightarrow \sim (Y <_{sb} X)]\}$

2.69 $\bigvee_X \{X \in \mathbf{FON} \wedge \bigwedge_Y [Y \in \mathbf{FON} \rightarrow \sim (X <_{sb} Y)]\}$

The lenis/fortis relation

Two allophones X, Y are in the relation *lenis/fortis*, in symbols $X \, \mathbf{LF} \, Y$, if and only if the articulation of Y requires more energy than the articulation of X at least in one articulatory dimension, i.e. if Y is *fortior quam* X and X is *lenior quam* Y with respect to at least one of the following articulatory features: force of supraglottal aperture, force of sub- and supraglottal air pressure, mass of articulator, duration in time, force of supraglottal closure, and force of subglottal articulation. Formally:

2.70 $X \, \mathbf{LF} \, Y \leftrightarrow X, Y \in \mathbf{FON} \wedge (X <_{ap} Y \vee X <_{sb}^{sp} Y \vee X <_{ma} Y \vee X <_{cl}$
$Y \vee X <_t Y \vee X <_{sb} Y)$

And the *fortis/lenis* relation will be defined as follows:

2.71 X **FL** $Y \leftrightarrow Y$ **LF** X

2.72 **LF** $\subset$ **FON**^{2}

2.73 **FL** $\subset$ **FON**^{2}

2.74 **LF** $\cap$ **FL** $\neq \phi$

The axiom 2.74 accounts for the fact that two allophones X, Y may be bound by the relation **LF** in one articulatory dimension and the relation **FL** in another.

Example:

$\langle [p], [f] \rangle \in$ **LF** $\cap$ **FL**

Proof: (i) $[p] <_{ap} [f] \wedge [p] <_{sb} [f]$

$[p]$ **LF** $[f]$

(ii) $[f] <_{cl} [p]$

$[p]$ **FL** $[f]$

There are *extreme* elements as regards the relation **LF**, i.e. minimal element for which there is no weaker one, and maximal element for which there is no stronger one. Formally:

2.75 $\bigvee\limits_{X} \{X \in$ **FON** $\wedge \bigwedge\limits_{Y} [Y \in$ **FON** $\rightarrow \sim (X$ **LF** $Y)]\}$

2.76 $\bigvee\limits_{X} \{X \in$ **FON** $\wedge \bigwedge\limits_{Y} Y \in$ **FON** $\rightarrow \sim (X$ **FL** $Y)]\}$

It is implicit in the formulae 2.75 and 2.76 that having an allophone X which is not a maximal (minimal) element, we can produce a stronger (weaker) allophone Y by increasing (decreasing) appropriately the articulatory energy at least in one dimension while articulating the phones of Y.

Taking the above discussion further, we arrive at fundamental hypothesis that there are no extreme allophones with respect to all relations. Thus there is neither an absolute lenis nor an absolute fortis.

2.77 $\sim \bigvee\limits_{X \in \textbf{FON}} \bigwedge\limits_{Y \in \textbf{FON}} (X <_{ap} Y \wedge X <_{sb}^{sp} Y \wedge X <_{ma} Y \wedge$

$X <_{t} Y \wedge X <_{cl} Y)$

2.78 $\sim\overset{V}{\underset{X\in \mathbf{FON}}{}}\overset{\wedge}{\underset{Y\in \mathbf{FON}}{}} (Y <_{ap} X \wedge Y <^{sp}_{sb} X \wedge Y <_{ma} X \wedge$

$Y <_t X \wedge Y <_{cl} X)$

The second fundamental hypothesis which could be obtained is that there exist no two different allophones in one language which would be equal in all articulatory dimensions.

2.79 $\sim\overset{V}{\underset{X\in \mathbf{FON}_i}{}}\overset{V}{\underset{Y\in \mathbf{FON}_i}{}} (X \neq Y \wedge X =_{ap} Y \wedge X =^{sp}_{sb} Y \wedge X =_{ma} Y \wedge$

$X =_t Y \wedge ...)$

The relation of diachronic mutation

Passing now to the relation of diachronic mutation or diachronic change, denoted by the symbol **Mt**, we shall concentrate upon the objects, sets and relations of two genetically related languages. Consequently in the set **FON** two subsets will be distinguished, **FON**$_i$ and **FON**$_j$, which contain allophones of a proto-language and a descendant language, respectively. The impact of fortition-lenition manifests itself most evidently within the consonants and therefore we will restrict our investigation to the consonantal allophones.

2.80 **FON**$_i \subset$ **FON**

2.81 **FON**$_j \subset$ **FON**

The subsets in question are disjoint:

2.82 **FON**$_i \cap$ **FON**$_j = \phi$

In order to come closer to the notion of relation **Mt** let us consider the following statements:

(i)   PIE *b* changed to PG *p*;
(ii) PIE allophone [b] changed to PG allophone [p];
(iii) PIE phoneme /b/ changed to PG phoneme /p/.

In our approach the allophones are treated as classes of individual homophonic sounds (phones), and phonemes as classes of allophones. Whether an element belongs to a given class depends, of course, on the fulfillment of the appropriate requirements. Neither phones nor allophones nor phonemes of one language system can be changed to phones, allophones and phonemes, respectively, of another genetically related language system. A phone which is an individual object and exists only in the moment of speaking, cannot be changed to another phone because after this moment it escapes into the unrecoverable past (Batóg 1967:30). Consequently a phone cannot be produced once again, much less changed to another phone.

From such a point of view, the above statements (i) – (iii) if taken literally, would be absurd. They make more sense only under the condition that change or shift is understood as a relation holding between two respective allophones or phonemes of two genetically related languages (or two evolutional stages of the same language). Thus the domain of the relation **Mt** could be, for instance, $\mathbf{FON_{PIE}}$ and its converse domain $\mathbf{FON_{PG}}$.

There arise, however serious obstacles in attempting to establish the relation **Mt** between two allophones or two phonemes of two languages. It may be very often easily pointed out that relation **Mt** does affect only certain subsets of an allophone or phoneme of the languages in question.

Computing the field of relation **Mt** tacitly implies the knowledge of a relation **Etm** *sui generis* which holds between etymologically related classes of meaningful segments (such as allomorphs, morphemes, allolexes, lexemes) of two languages. Thus before stating that e.g. PIE *p bears the relation **Mt** to PG *f one must have at his disposal the field of relation **Etm**, i.e. two sets of etymologically related words or other meaningful segments, e.g.:

PIE *pɔtĕr*   –   PG   *fapĕr* "father"
PIE *pisko-* –   PG   *fiska-* "fish"
PIE *por-*   –   PG   *far-* "go"

Thus the relation **Mt** emerges on the basis of relation **Etm** which we are not going, however, to deal with here. In order to compute C'**Mt** we need a great deal of linguistic experience, or in other words the results of historical-comparative study. Empirical research is thus a decisive factor in computing appropriately C'**Mt** after having established C'**Etm**.[7]

Scanning comparative material, it can easily be shown that there exist such subsets of phones in allophones of a given language which do not go back to any subsets of phones in allophones of its proto-language, i.e. these subsets of phones cannot be linked by the relation **Mt** (cf. English words such as *form*, *graph* which do not originate from PG).

Consequently the relation **Mt** cannot hold between allophones. It could do so only under the condition that all meaningful segments of the proto-language had been preserved in the descendant language, and moreover, that the latter would not possess any loanwords. It is obvious that such cases are rather hypothetical.

If it is impossible to define the relation **Mt** either on the set of allophones or on the set of phonemes of two respective languages, we are bound to take recourse to other solutions. If the relation **Mt** presupposes the relation **Etm** which connects certain classes of etymologically related meaningful segments, then the relation **Mt** should connect certain classes of etymologically related phones which make up these segments. And the classes of phones in question should be set up taking into account their function within meaningful segments, e.g. morphs, or lexes. Let us limit our considerations to morphs only and arrive at the notion of the *allomorphone*.

The set of all concrete morphs of a given language will be denoted by **Mor**$_i$. Particular morphs are individual objects[8]. The set **Mor**$_i$ may be classified into allomorphs, i.e. classes containing all *homophonic* and *homosignificative* morphs. The set of all allomorphs will be denoted by the symbol **MOR**$_i$.

Examples of allomorphs:

Polish: [ręk-],   [ręc-],   [ręč-],   [rąč-]
English: [am],   [is],   [are],   [be],   [been]

The set **MOR**$_i$ is in its turn classifiable into morphemes which are classes of homomorphemic allomorphs. Thus the above four Polish allomorphs belong to the same morpheme /ręk-/ and similarly all English five allomorphs are contained in the morpheme /be/. Because of the fact that suppletive or quasi-suppletive allomorphs may belong to a given morpheme it is advisable to define the relation **Etm** on the set of related allomorphs of two languages rather than on morphemes.

Having arrived at the set **MOR**$_i$ which contained all allomorphs of a given language we can now introduce the notion of *allomorphone*, which is especially useful for our further discussion. Let us consider to this end two Polish allomorphs, X = [ręk-] and Y = [ręc-]. The symbols [ręk-] and [ręc-] denote sets of homophonic and homosignificative morphs, respectively:

$$[ręk-] = \{ręk_{-1}, ręk_{-2}, ..., ręk_{-n}\}$$
$$[ręc-] = \{ręc_{-1}, ręc_{-2}, ..., ręc_{-m}\}$$

An *allomorphone* has been conceived of as a set of all homophonic and homo-occurential phones which constitute the morphs contained in the same allomorph. According to this formulation the allomorphone X' will comprise all r-phones occurring in the initial position of *ręk*-morphs:

$$X' = \{r_{-1}, r_{-2}, ..., r_{-n}\}$$

And similarly

$$Y' = \{ŗ_{-1}, ŗ_{-2}, ..., ŗ_{-n}\}$$
$$U' = \{k_1, k_2, ..., k_n\}$$

It should be obvious that all r-phones occurring in the initial position of *ręc*-morphs do not belong to X' but are members of a different allomorphone Z'; and $Z' \cap X' = \phi$. If we denote by $\mathbf{Fon}_{(X)}$ the set of all phones occurring in the morphs which are elements of an allomorph X then $X' \subset \mathbf{Fon}_{([ręk-])}$, $Y' \subset \mathbf{Fon}_{([ręk-])}$, etc. We state also that $X' \subset [r]$ and $[r] \in \mathbf{FON}_{POL}$.

The set of all allomorphones of a given language will be denoted by $\mathbf{MRF}_i$. Particular allomorphones could be put into $\langle \ \rangle$ and subscript indexes indicating allomorphs in question attached, e.g. $\langle p \rangle_{[por-]} \in \mathbf{MRF}_{PIE}$. For the sake of simplification the subscript indexes could be omitted if there would be no reason for misunderstanding.

As can be easily inferred the set $\mathbf{MRF}_i$ is included in the set of all subsets in $\mathbf{Fon}_i$:

2.83 $\mathbf{MRF}_i \subset P(\mathbf{Fon}_i)$

There is a relation Φ connecting an allomorphone X with an appropriate allophone Y, which will be defined in the following way:

2.84 $X \Phi Y \underset{df}{\leftrightarrow} X \in \mathbf{MRF}_i \wedge Y \in \mathbf{FON}_i \wedge X \subset Y$

Moreover we state that

2.85 $\underset{X}{\wedge} [X \in \mathbf{MRF}_i \to \underset{Y}{\vee} (Y \in \mathbf{FON}_i \wedge X \subset Y)]$

Hence Φ is a function (i.e. $\Phi \in$ fnc) defined on the set $\mathbf{MRF}_i$ since for every X in $\mathbf{MRF}_i$ there is exactly one Y such that $X \Phi Y$; this unique Y will be denoted by the symbol $\Phi`X$.

2.86 $\Phi`X = (, Y)(X \Phi Y)$

2.87 $\Phi: \mathbf{MRF}_i \Rightarrow \mathbf{FON}_i$

The relation $\mathbf{Mt}$ will hold between two etymologically related allomorphones, i.e. those which presuppose the existence of a pair of allomorphs linked by $\mathbf{Etm}$. Therefore in the set $\mathbf{MRF}_i$ should be distinguished a set $\mathbf{MRFet}_i$ which will contain only such allomorphones for which there exist etymologically related counterparts in $\mathbf{MRF}_j$.

2.88 $\mathbf{MRFet}_i \subset \mathbf{MRF}_i$

The relation $\mathbf{Mt}$ is a function which maps a set $\mathbf{MRFet}_i$ onto a set $\mathbf{MRFet}_j$, formally:

2.89 $\mathbf{Mt}: \mathbf{MRFet}_i \Rightarrow \mathbf{MRFet}_j$

and fulfills the conditions:

(i) $\overbrace{X \in \text{MRFet}_i}\ \overset{\vee}{Y \in \text{MRFet}_j}\ (X \text{ Mt } Y)$

(ii) $\overset{\wedge}{X \in \text{MRFet}_i}\ \overbrace{Y, Z \in \text{MRFet}_j}\ (X \text{ Mt } Y \wedge X \text{ Mt } Z \rightarrow Y = Z)$

Thus following our notational convention we are entitled to use the symbol **Mt'X** to denote this unique Y for which X **Mt** Y.

2.90 $\text{Mt} \subset \text{MRFet}_i \times \text{MRFet}_j$

2.91 $\text{D'Mt} = \text{MRFet}_i \wedge \text{Cl'Mt} = \text{MRFet}_j$

Summing up, it can be said that the relation **Mt** is a set of pairs $\langle X, Y \rangle$ the predecessor of which belongs to **MRFet**$_i$ and the successor belongs to **MRFet**$_j$.

Examples:

$\langle\langle p \rangle_{PIE[\text{por-}]}, \langle f \rangle_{PG[\text{far-}]}\rangle \in \text{Mt}$

$\langle\langle k \rangle_{PIE[\text{korio-}]}, \langle h \rangle_{PG[\text{harja-}]}\rangle \in \text{Mt}$

The above considerations point to the importance of morphonic and lexophonic systems for the analysis of mutation processes. And needless to say, a deeper analysis of the function of phones within allomorphs and allolexes would be desired. In the historical process lexes may become morphs and vice versa. Further on a notation of *zero* allomorphone is indispensable.

The system

2.92 $S_{fm} = \langle \text{MRFet}_i\ \text{MRFet}_j, \text{Mt} \rangle$

will be called the algebra of phonic mutation.

The fortition and lenition relationships
   Now we are going to present the two most important definitions in our system. The first introduces the symbol **Frt** for the relation of fortition and the second introduces the symbol **Len** for the relation of lenition.

2.93 $\text{Frt} = \{X, Y: X \in \text{MRFet}_i \wedge Y \in \text{MRFet}_j \wedge X \text{ Mt } Y \wedge \Phi\text{'}X \text{ LF } \Phi\text{'}Y\}$

2.94 $\text{Len} = \{X, Y: X \in \text{MRFet}_i \wedge Y \in \text{MRFet}_j \wedge X \text{ Mt } Y \wedge \Phi\text{'}X \text{ FL } \Phi\text{'}Y\}$

For the sake of visual illustration of the above definitions let us avail ourselves of the graph A (for fortition) and graph B (for lenition):

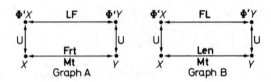

Graph A   Graph B

Thus two allomorphones X, Y bear the relation **Frt** if and only if they are in relation **Mt** and their respective allophones $\Phi^\prime X$ and $\Phi^\prime Y$ are in relation **LF**, i.e. $\Phi^\prime X$ is lenis and $\Phi^\prime Y$ is fortis. The definition of lenition is formulated in a similar way.

2.95 **Frt** $\subset$ **Mt**

2.96 **Len** $\subset$ **Mt**

According to definitions 2.93 and 2.94 fortition and lenition are diachronic relations because both are contained in **Mt**. In the face of 2.74 (**LF** $\cap$ **FL** $\neq \phi$) it may happen that a given pair $\langle X, Y \rangle$ which belongs to **Mt** may belong to **Frt** $\cap$ **Len** making it impossible to decide whether it is a result of fortition or lenition. This non-decidability grows out of the fact, and plenty of corroborating examples may be found in various languages, that in the process of mutation fortition may operate in one articulatory dimension, while lenition may operate in another. Such a phenomenon confirms the intuition of fortition and lenition as being two poles of the same process. In order to see clearly which dimension is affected by fortition and which by lenition it seems reasonable to define the relation **Frt** as well as **Len** with regard to the particular articulatory dimensions distinguished above. Thus instead of having one relation **Frt** we will arrive at six different relations of fortition and six relations of lenition.

2.97 $\mathbf{Frt}_{ap} = \{X, Y: X \in \mathbf{MRFet}_i \wedge Y \in \mathbf{MRFet}_j \wedge X \mathbf{Mt} Y \wedge \Phi^\prime X <_{ap} \Phi^\prime Y\}$

2.98 $\mathbf{Frt}_{cl} = \{X, Y: X \in \mathbf{MRFet}_i \wedge Y \in \mathbf{MRFet}_j \wedge X \mathbf{Mt} Y \wedge \Phi^\prime X <_{cl} \Phi^\prime Y\}$

2.99 $\mathbf{Frt}_{sp,sb} = \{X, Y: X \in \mathbf{MRFet}_i \wedge Y \in \mathbf{MRFet}_j \wedge X \mathbf{Mt} Y \wedge \Phi^\prime X <_{sb}^{sp} \Phi^\prime Y\}$

2.100 $\mathbf{Frt}_{ma} = \{X, Y: X \in \mathbf{MRFet}_i \wedge Y \in \mathbf{MRFet}_j \wedge X \mathbf{Mt} Y \wedge \Phi^\prime X <_{ma} \Phi^\prime Y\}$

2.101 $\mathbf{Frt}_{t} = \{X, Y: X \in \mathbf{MRFet}_i \wedge Y \in \mathbf{MRFet}_j \wedge X \mathbf{Mt} Y \wedge \Phi^\prime X <_{t} \Phi^\prime Y\}$

2.102 $\mathbf{Frt}_{sb} = \{X, Y: X \in \mathbf{MRFet}_i \wedge Y \in \mathbf{MRFet}_j \wedge X \mathbf{Mt} Y \wedge \Phi^\prime X <_{sb} \Phi^\prime Y\}$

2.103 $\mathbf{Frt}_{ap} \subset \mathbf{Frt}$

2.104 $\text{Frt}_{cl} \subset \text{Frt}$

2.105 $\text{Frt}_{sp, sb} \subset \text{Frt}$

2.106 $\text{Frt}_{ma} \subset \text{Frt}$

2.107 $\text{Frt}_{t} \subset \text{Frt}$

2.108 $\text{Frt}_{sb} \subset \text{Frt}$

2.109 $\text{Len}_{ap} = \{X, Y: X \in \text{MRFet}_i \wedge Y \in \text{MRFet}_j \wedge X \text{ Mt } Y \wedge \Phi'Y <_{ap} \Phi'X\}$

2.110 $\text{Len}_{cl} = \{X, Y: X \in \text{MRFet}_i \wedge Y \in \text{MRFet}_j \wedge X \text{ Mt } Y \wedge \Phi'Y <_{cl} \Phi'X\}$

2.111 $\text{Len}_{sp, sb} = \{X, Y: X \in \text{MRFet}_i \wedge Y \in \text{MRFet}_j \wedge X \text{ Mt } Y \wedge \Phi'Y <_{sb}^{sp}$
$\Phi'X\}$

2.112 $\text{Len}_{ma} = \{X, Y: X \in \text{MRFet}_i \wedge Y \in \text{MRFet}_j \wedge X \text{ Mt } Y \wedge \Phi'Y <_{ma} \Phi'X\}$

2.113 $\text{Len}_{t} = \{X, Y: X \in \text{MRFet}_i \wedge Y \in \text{MRFet}_j \wedge X \text{ Mt } Y \wedge \Phi'Y <_{t} \Phi'X\}$

2.114 $\text{Len}_{sb} = \{X, Y: X \in \text{MRFet}_i \wedge Y \in \text{MRFet}_j \wedge X \text{ Mt } Y \wedge \Phi'Y <_{sb} \Phi'X\}$

2.115 $\text{Len}_{ap} \subset \text{Len}$

2.116 $\text{Len}_{cl} \subset \text{Len}$

2.117 $\text{Len}_{sp, sb} \subset \text{Len}$

2.118 $\text{Len}_{ma} \subset \text{Len}$

2.119 $\text{Len}_{t} \subset \text{Len}$

2.120 $\text{Len}_{sb} \subset \text{Len}$

The following theorems show the interdependences between **Frt** and **Len**.

2.121 $\widehat{X, Y} (X \text{ Frt}_{ap} Y \to Y \text{ Len}_{ap} X)$

2.122 $\widehat{X, Y} (X \text{ Frt}_{sp, sb} Y \to Y \text{ Len}_{sp, sb} X)$

2.123 $\widehat{X, Y} (X \text{ Frt}_{ma} Y \to Y \text{ Len}_{ma} X)$

2.124 $\widehat{X, Y} (X \text{ Frt}_{t} Y \to Y \text{ Len}_{t} X)$

$$2.125 \quad \bigwedge_{X,\,Y}(X \; \mathbf{Frt}_{sb} \; Y \to Y \; \mathbf{Len}_{sb} \; X)$$

The system

$$2.126 \quad S_{F/L} = \langle \mathbf{MRFet}_i, \mathbf{MRFet}_j, \mathbf{Frt}, \mathbf{Len} \rangle$$

will be called the algebra of fortition-lenition.

3. Axioms of fortition-lenition

The axioms of our system may be subdivided into two groups: *general* and *language-specific*. The former applying to any two languages related by fortition-lenition reflect the panglottal tendencies of these processes. The latter being valid only for the two chosen languages appropriately restrict the action space of the general axioms.

In the axioms, besides the primitive notations, the defined ones will also appear. The axioms will characterize more precisely these notions. The complete list of axioms relevant to fortition-lenition will, however, be not given here because the theory developed in this paper centers only on some aspects of fortition-lenition.

General axioms

A1 $\bigwedge_X \bigwedge_Y \{[X, Y \in \mathbf{MRFet}_i \wedge \Phi'X \cdot \overset{sp}{\underset{sb}{\cdot}} \Phi'Y \wedge \bigvee_Z (Z \in \mathbf{MRFet}_j \wedge Y \; \mathbf{Frt}_{ap} Z)] \to$

$\to \bigvee_U (U \in \mathbf{MRFet}_j \wedge X \; \mathbf{Frt}_{cl} U)\}$

A2 $\bigwedge_X \bigwedge_Y \{[X, Y \in \mathbf{MRFet}_i \wedge \Phi'X <_{ma} \Phi'Y \wedge \bigvee_Z (Z \in \mathbf{MRFet}_j \wedge Y \; \mathbf{Frt}_{ap} Z)] \to$

$\to \bigvee_U (U \in \mathbf{MRFet}_j \wedge X \; \mathbf{Frt}_{ap} U)\}$

A3 $\bigwedge_X \bigwedge_Y \{[X, Y \in \mathbf{MRFet}_i \wedge \Phi'X <_{ap} \Phi'Y \wedge \bigvee_Z (Z \in \mathbf{MRFet}_j \wedge Y \; \mathbf{Frt}_{ap} Z)] \to$

$\to \bigvee_U (U \in \mathbf{MRFet}_j \wedge X \; \mathbf{Frt}_{ap} U)\}$

A4 $\bigwedge_X \bigwedge_Y \{[X, Y \in \mathbf{MRFet}_i \wedge \Phi'X <_t \Phi'Y \wedge \bigvee_Z (Z \in \mathbf{MRFet}_j \wedge Y \; \mathbf{Frt}_{ap} Z)] \to$

$\to \bigvee_U (U \in \mathbf{MRFet}_j \wedge X \; \mathbf{Frt}_{ap} U)\}$

A5 $\bigwedge_X \bigwedge_Y \{[X, Y \in \mathbf{MRFet}_i \wedge \Phi'X <_{ap} \Phi'Y \wedge \bigvee_Z (Z \in \mathbf{MRFet}_j \wedge X \, \mathbf{Len}_{sp, sb} Z)] \rightarrow$

$\rightarrow \bigvee_U (U \in \mathbf{MRFet}_j \wedge Y \, \mathbf{Len}_{sp, sb} U)\}$

A6 $\widehat{X \in \mathbf{MRFet}_i} \, \widehat{Y \in \mathbf{MRFet}_j} \, (X \, \mathbf{Frt}_{ap} Y \rightarrow \Phi'Y <_{cl} \Phi'X)$

Now we shall try to explain the intuitive sense of the above axioms:

Axiom A1 expresses the idea that if the process of fortition in the dimension of supraglottal aperture affects voiceless consonants, then the process of fortition in the dimension of supraglottal closure affects voiced consonants as well. As a matter of fact this axiom applies only to stops and therefore its range should be appropriately restricted. Axiom A1 renders the idea of a greater susceptibility of voiced consonants in comparison to that of voiceless ones with regard to the fortition process. The content of this axiom may be illustrated in the following graph:

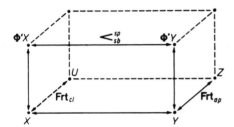

Axiom A2 states that the process of fortition in the dimension of supraglottal aperture does not skip the elements of ordering $<_{ma}$. The fortition of a consonant articulated with a speech organ having greater mass presupposes the fortition of an appropriate consonant articulated with an organ of smaller mass. Thus from the fact of fortition of *dorsal* (back tongue) consonants may be inferred the previous fortition of *labials* and *apico-frontals*. The content of this axiom may be shown in the graph as follows:

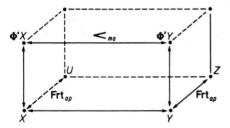

Axiom A3 states that the process of fortition in the dimension of supra-glottal aperture does not skip the elements of ordering $\prec_{ap}$. If a more open consonant is reinforced than a more closed consonant must have been reinforced previously. It follows from this statement that fortition of *spirants* presupposes fortition of *affricates* and *stops*. The graph below should facilitate the understanding of this axiom.

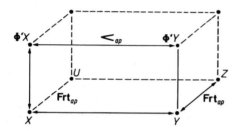

Axiom A4 renders the idea that the fortition process in the dimension of supraglottal aperture which has affected longer consonants must have affected also shorter consonants. Thus shorter consonants are more susceptible to fortition than the longer consonants. For the sake of illustration of this axiom the following graph is utilized.

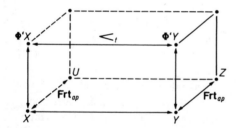

Axiom A5 concerns the process of lenition, i.e. in this case sonorisation. It follows from it that sonorisation of more closed consonants presupposes sonorisation of more open ones. Thus the latter are more susceptible to this process than the former are. In other words the voicing of voiceless stops indicates that the voicing of affricates and spirants has already happened. The graph at the top of the following page aims at illustrating the content of A5.

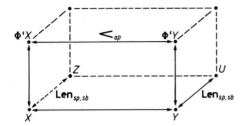

Axiom A6 states a general interdependence between two allomorphones X and Y being in relation $\mathbf{Frt}_{ap}$ and the allophones in which X and Y are included. Thus the fortition in the dimension of supraglottal aperture, $X\ \mathbf{Frt}_{ap}\ Y$, always presupposes that appropriate allophones $\Phi'Y$ and $\Phi'X$ are in the relation $<_{cl}$, i.e. $\Phi'Y <_{cl} \Phi'X$. This may be represented in the following graph:

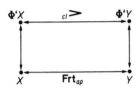

Language-specific axioms

If we want to speak of fortition-lenition in two concrete languages then we have to introduce constant symbols in the theory $\theta_{F/L}$. These symbols will denote certain objects distinguished in the model of this theory. In our system the set of the objects distinguished will contain the allophones of the languages concerned. Taking into consideration the results of genetical comparative linguistics, the following sets of consonantal allophones, among others, may be postulated for the languages we are here interested in, i.e. PIE, PG, PU(Proto-Uralic), FI(Finnish):

$\mathbf{FON}_{PIE}$ = {[p], [t], [k], [kʷ], [b], [d], [g], [gʷ], [bh], [dh], [gh], [gʷh],
[s], [m], [n], [l], [r], [u̯], [i̯]}

$\mathbf{FON}_{PG}$ = {[f], [þ], [x], [p], [t], [k], [b], [đ], [g̵], [s], [m], [n], [ŋ], [l],
[r], [w], [j]}

$\mathbf{FON}_{PU}$ = {[p], [t], [k], [kʷ], [b], [d], [g], [gʷ], [bh], [dh], [gh], [č],
[ć], [s], [š], [m], [n], [ŋ], [l], [r], [w], [j]}

$\mathbf{FON}_{FI}$ = {[pp], [tt], [kk], [p], [t], [k], [d], [s], [h], [m], [n], [ŋ], [l],
[r], [v], [j]}

Within language-specific axioms again, three groups may be distinguished. The axioms of the first group will refer to the relations **LF** and **FL**. The axioms of the second group will refer to the relation **Mt**. We are not going, however, to present all of these axioms, because they should become apparent from our articulatory classifications of allophones and from our knowledge of historical linguistics[9]. And finally the axioms of the third group state certain general dependences between allomorphones and the allophones which contain them.

I a1 $[d]_{PIE} <^{sp}_{sb} [t]_{PIE}$

    a2 $[b]_{PIE} <^{sp}_{sb} [p]_{PIE}$

    a3 $[g]_{PIE} <^{sp}_{sb} [k]_{PIE}$

    a4 $[d]_{PIE} <^{sp}_{sb} [t]_{PG}$

    a5 $[b]_{PIE} <^{sp}_{sb} [p]_{PG}$

    a6 $[g]_{PIE} <^{sp}_{sb} [k]_{PG}$

    a7 $[t]_{PIE} <_{ap} [b]_{PG}$

    a8 $[p]_{PIE} <_{ap} [f]_{PG}$

    a9 $[k]_{PIE} <_{ap} [x]_{PG}$

    a10 $[dh]_{PIE} <_{ap} [d]_{PG}$

    a11 $[bh]_{PIE} <_{ap} [b]_{PG}$

    a12 $[gh]_{PIE} <_{ap} [g]_{PG}$

$$\vdots$$

II α1 $\bigvee_{X \in \mathbf{MRF}et_{PIE}} \bigvee_{Y \in \mathbf{MRF}et_{PG}} (X \subset [d]_{PIE} \wedge Y \subset [t]_{PG} \wedge X \mathbf{Mt} Y)$

    α2 $\bigvee_{X \in \mathbf{MRF}et_{PIE}} \bigvee_{Y \in \mathbf{MRF}et_{PG}} (X \subset [b]_{PIE} \wedge Y \subset [p]_{PG} \wedge X \mathbf{Mt} Y)$

    α3 $\bigvee_{X \in \mathbf{MRF}et_{PIE}} \bigvee_{Y \in \mathbf{MRF}et_{PG}} (X \subset [g]_{PIE} \wedge Y \subset [k]_{PG} \wedge X \mathbf{Mt} Y)$

$$\vdots$$

III a1 $\widehat{X \in \mathbf{MRFet}_{PIE}}$ $\widehat{Y \in \mathbf{MRFet}_{PG}}$ $(X \mathbf{\ Frt\ } Y \to \Phi'X <_{sb} \Phi'Y)$

a2 $\widehat{X \in \mathbf{MRFet}_{PIE}}$ $\widehat{Y \in \mathbf{MRFet}_{PG}}$ $(X \mathbf{\ Frt}_{cl} Y \to \Phi'X <_{sb}^{sp} \Phi'Y)$

4. Fortition-lenition processes in Indo-European and Uralic

*Mutation of PIE *b *d *g to PG *p *t *k*

4.1 $\bigwedge_X \bigwedge_Y (X \in \mathbf{MRFet}_{PIE} \wedge Y \in \mathbf{MRFet}_{PG} \wedge \Phi'X = [b]_{PIE} \wedge \Phi'Y = [p]_{PG} \wedge$

$X \mathbf{\ Mt\ } Y \to \langle X, Y \rangle \in \mathbf{Frt}_{sb} \cap \mathbf{Frt}_{cl} \cap \mathbf{Frt}_{sp,sb})$

This theorem states a connection between a PIE allomorphone X which is included in the allophone $[b]_{PIE}$ and a PG allomorphone Y included in the allophone $[p]_{PG}$ in terms of the relation **Mt** and **Frt**. If these allomorphones are in relation **Mt** then they are also in relation **Frt** with regard to three articulatory dimensions: subglottal air pressure, force of supraglottal closure, and voicing-devoicing; or in other words X became reinforced within these three dimensions and resulted in Y.

Proof:

$\bigwedge_X (X \in \mathbf{MRF}_{PIE} \to X \subset \Phi'X)$

$\quad \Phi'X = [b]_{PIE}$

$\quad\quad X \subset [b]_{PIE}$

$\bigwedge_Y (Y \in \mathbf{MRF}_{PG} \to Y \subset \Phi'Y)$

$\quad \Phi'Y = [p]_{PG}$

$\quad\quad Y \subset [p]_{PG}$

$\langle [b]_{PIE}, [p]_{PG} \rangle \in {<_{sb}} \cap {<_{cl}} \cap {<_{sb}^{sp}}$ \hfill (Ax.)

$({<_{sb}} \cap {<_{cl}} \cap {<_{sb}^{sp}}) \subset LF$

$\bigvee_{X \in \mathbf{MRFet}_{PIE}} \bigvee_{Y \in \mathbf{MRFet}_{PG}} (X \subset [b]_{PIE} \wedge Y \subset [p]_{PG} \wedge X \mathbf{\ Mt\ } Y)$

\hfill (Ax. α2)

$\langle X, Y \rangle \in \mathbf{Frt}_{sb} \cap \mathbf{Frt}_{cl} \cap \mathbf{Frt}_{sp,sb}$

For a better understanding of theorem 4.1 and its proof let us avail ourselves of the following graph:

$$\Phi'X = [b]_{PIE} \quad <_{sb} \cap <_{cl} \cap <_{sl}^{sp} \quad \Phi'Y = [p]_{PG}$$

4.2 $\bigwedge_X \bigwedge_Y (X \in \mathbf{MRFet}_{PIE} \wedge Y \in \mathbf{MRFet}_{PG} \wedge \Phi'X = [d]_{PIE} \wedge \Phi'Y = [t]_{PG}$

$\wedge X \mathbf{Mt} Y \rightarrow \langle X, Y \rangle \in \mathbf{Frt}_{sb} \cap \mathbf{Frt}_{cl} \cap \mathbf{Frt}_{sp, sb})$

4.3 $\bigwedge_X \bigwedge_Y (X \in \mathbf{MRFet}_{PIE} \wedge Y \in \mathbf{MRFet}_{PG} \wedge \Phi'X = [g]_{PIE} \wedge \Phi'Y = [k]_{PG}$

$\wedge X \mathbf{Mt} Y \rightarrow \langle X, Y \rangle \in \mathbf{Frt}_{sb} \cap \mathbf{Frt}_{cl} \cap \mathbf{Frt}_{sp, sb})$

The proofs of the theorems 4.2 and 4.3 have been omitted for obvious reasons. The content of theorems 4.1–4.3 renders the intuition that the mutation of PIE *b *d *g to PG *p *t *k, respectively, requires:

 (i) increasing of subglottal air pressure;
 (ii) increasing of supraglottal closure;
(iii) devoicing process.

*Mutation of PIE *p *t *k to PG *f *þ *χ*

4.4 $\bigwedge_X \bigwedge_Y (X \in \mathbf{MRFet}_{PIE} \wedge Y \in \mathbf{MRFet}_{PG} \wedge \Phi'X = [p]_{PIE} \wedge \Phi'Y = [f]_{PG}$

$\wedge X \mathbf{Mt} Y \rightarrow \langle X, Y \rangle \in \mathbf{Frt}_{sb} \cap \mathbf{Frt}_{ap} \cap \mathbf{Len}_{cl})$

Proof:

$\bigwedge_X (X \in \mathbf{MRF}_{PIE} \rightarrow X \subset \Phi'X)$

$\Phi'X = [p]_{PIE}$

$X \subset [p]_{PIE}$

$\bigwedge_Y (Y \in \mathbf{MRF}_{PG} \rightarrow Y \subset \Phi'Y)$

$\Phi'Y = [f]_{PG}$

$Y \subset [f]_{PG}$

$$\langle [p]_{PIE}, [f]_{PG}\rangle \in <_{sb} \cap <_{ap}$$

$$\langle [f]_{PG}, [p]_{PIE}\rangle \in <_{cl}$$

$$(<_{sb} \cap <_{ap}) \subset \mathbf{LF}$$

$$\langle [p]_{PIE}, [f]_{PG}\rangle \in \mathbf{FL}$$

$$\underset{X \in \mathbf{MRFet}_{PIE}}{\vee} \underset{Y \in \mathbf{MRFet}_{PG}}{\vee} (X \subset [p]_{PIE} \wedge Y \subset [f]_{PG} \wedge X \mathbf{\,Mt\,} Y) \quad (\text{Ax.}\alpha)$$

$$\langle X, Y\rangle \in \mathbf{Frt}_{sb} \cap \mathbf{Frt}_{ap} \cap \mathbf{Len}_{cl}$$

The following graph serves to illustrate the above theorem and its proof:

$$4.5 \quad \underset{X}{\wedge} \underset{Y}{\wedge} (X \in \mathbf{MRFet}_{PIE} \wedge Y \in \mathbf{MRFet}_{PG} \wedge \Phi{}'X = [t]_{PIE} \wedge \Phi{}'Y = [\text{þ}]_{PG}$$

$$\wedge X \mathbf{\,Mt\,} Y \rightarrow \langle X, Y\rangle \in \mathbf{Frt}_{sb} \cap \mathbf{Frt}_{ap} \cap \mathbf{Len}_{cl})$$

$$4.6 \quad \underset{X}{\wedge} \underset{Y}{\wedge} (X \in \mathbf{MRFet}_{PIE} \wedge Y \in \mathbf{MRFet}_{PG} \wedge \Phi{}'X = [k]_{PIE} \wedge \Phi{}'Y = [\chi]_{PG}$$

$$\wedge X \mathbf{\,Mt\,} Y \rightarrow \langle X, Y\rangle \in \mathbf{Frt}_{sb} \cap \mathbf{Frt}_{ap} \cap \mathbf{Len}_{cl})$$

The proofs of theorem 4.5 and 4.6 have been omitted because they follow the same pattern as that of theorem 4.4.

The intuitive sense of theorems 4.4–4.6 is that the mutation of PIE *p *t *k to PG *f *þ *χ, respectively, presupposes:

(i) increasing of subglottal air pressure;
(ii) increasing of the force of supraglottal aperture;
(iii) weakening of the force of supraglottal closure.

*Mutation of PIE *bh *dh *gh to PG *ƀ *đ *g*

$$4.7 \quad \underset{X}{\wedge} \underset{Y}{\wedge} (X \in \mathbf{MRFet}_{PIE} \wedge Y \in \mathbf{MRFet}_{PG} \wedge \Phi{}'X = [bh]_{PIE} \wedge \Phi{}'Y = [ƀ]_{PG}$$

$$\wedge X \mathbf{\,Mt\,} Y \rightarrow \langle X, Y\rangle \in \mathbf{Frt}_{sb} \cap \mathbf{Frt}_{ap} \cap \mathbf{Len}_{cl})$$

88   Jerzy Bańczerowski

Proof:

$$\bigwedge_{X}(X \in \mathbf{MRF}_{PIE} \to X \subset \Phi'X)$$

$$\Phi'X = [\text{bh}]_{PIE}$$

$$X \subset [\text{bh}]_{PIE}$$

$$\bigwedge_{Y}(Y \in \mathbf{MRF}_{PG} \to Y \subset \Phi'Y)$$

$$\Phi'Y = [\text{ƀ}]_{PG}$$

$$Y \subset [\text{ƀ}]_{PG}$$

$$\langle[\text{bh}]_{PIE}, [\text{ƀ}]_{PG}\rangle \in <_{sb} \cap <_{ap}$$

$$\langle[\text{ƀ}]_{PG}, [\text{bh}]_{PIE}\rangle \in <_{cl}$$

$$(<_{sb} \cap <_{ap}) \subset \mathbf{LF}$$

$$\langle[\text{bh}]_{PIE}, [\text{ƀ}]_{PG}\rangle \in \mathbf{FL}$$

$$\bigvee_{X \in \mathbf{MRFet}_{PIE}} \bigvee_{Y \in \mathbf{MRFet}_{PG}} (X \subset [\text{bh}]_{PIE} \wedge Y \subset [\text{ƀ}]_{PG} \wedge X \,\mathbf{Mt}\, Y) \;\text{(Ax.)}$$

$$\langle X, Y \rangle \in \mathbf{Frt}_{sb} \cap \mathbf{Frt}_{ap} \cap \mathbf{Len}_{cl})$$

4.8 $\bigwedge_{X}\bigwedge_{Y}(X \in \mathbf{MRFet}_{PIE} \wedge Y \in \mathbf{MRFet}_{PG} \wedge \Phi'X = [\text{dh}]_{PIE} \wedge \Phi'Y = [\text{đ}]_{PG}$

$$\wedge X \,\mathbf{Mt}\, Y \to \langle X, Y \rangle \in \mathbf{Frt}_{sb} \cap \mathbf{Frt}_{ap} \cap \mathbf{Len}_{cl})$$

4.9 $\bigwedge_{X}\bigwedge_{Y}(X \in \mathbf{MRFet}_{PIE} \wedge Y \in \mathbf{MRFet}_{PG} \wedge \Phi'X = [\text{gh}]_{PIE} \wedge \Phi'Y = [\text{g}]_{PG}$

$$\wedge X \,\mathbf{Mt}\, Y \to \langle X, Y \rangle \in \mathbf{Frt}_{sb} \cap \mathbf{Frt}_{ap} \cap \mathbf{Len}_{cl})$$

The proofs of theorems 4.8 and 4.9 are obvious. The intuitive sense expressed by theorems 4.7–4.9 is that the mutation of PIE *bh *dh *gh to PG *ƀ *đ *g necessitates:

(i) increasing of supraglottal air pressure;
(ii) increasing of the force of supraglottal aperture;
(iii) weakening of the force of supraglottal closure.

Some peculiar features of fortition-lenition in PG

4.10 $\widehat{X \in \mathbf{MRFet}_{PIE}} \ \widehat{Y \in \mathbf{MRFet}_{PG}} \ (X \ \mathbf{Frt} \ Y \to X \ \mathbf{Frt}_{sb} \ Y)$

This theorem states that fortition of all three series of PIE stops to appropriate PG consonants always presupposed reinforcement in the dimension of subglottal air pressure.

Proof:

$\widehat{X \in \mathbf{MRFet}_{PIE}} \ \widehat{Y \in \mathbf{MRFet}_{PG}} \ (X \ \mathbf{Frt} \ Y \to \Phi'X <_{sb} \Phi'Y)$ (Ax. a1)

$\underset{X}{\wedge} (X \in \mathbf{MRF}_{PIE} \to X \subset \Phi'X)$

$\underset{Y}{\wedge} (Y \in \mathbf{MRF}_{PG} \to Y \subset \Phi'Y)$

$\Phi'X <_{sb} \Phi'Y \to X \ \mathbf{Frt}_{sb} \ Y$

4.11 $\widehat{X \in \mathbf{MRFet}_{PIE}} \ \widehat{Y \in \mathbf{MRFet}_{PG}} \ (X \ \mathbf{Frt}_{cl} \ Y \to X \ \mathbf{Frt}_{sp, sb} \ Y)$

The sense of this theorem is that the fortition of supraglottal closure in PG was always accompanied by a devoicing process. This applies for the shift from PIE *b *d *g to PG *p *t *k, respectively.

Susceptibility to the processes of fortition-lenition in PG

4.12 $\widehat{X \in \mathbf{MRFet}_{PIE}} \ \overset{\vee}{Y \in \mathbf{MRFet}_{PG}} \ (X \subset [\mathrm{p}]_{PIE} \wedge X \ \mathbf{Frt}_{ap} \ Y) \to \underset{U \in \mathbf{MRFet}_{PIE}}{\wedge}$

$\overset{\vee}{Z \in \mathbf{MRFet}_{PG}} \ (U \subset [\mathrm{b}]_{PIE} \wedge U \ \mathbf{Frt}_{cl}Z)$

The idea expressed in this theorem is that whenever a PIE allomorphone ⟨p⟩ is reinforced in PG in the dimension of supraglottal aperture then a PIE allomorphone ⟨b⟩ must undergo reinforcement in the dimension of supraglottal closure in PG as well.

Proof:

Let us take $X \in \mathbf{MRFet}_{PIE}$ such that $X \subset [\mathrm{p}]_{PIE}$ then $[\mathrm{p}]_{PIE} = \Phi'X$. Similarly, let $U \in \mathbf{MRFet}_{PIE}$ be such that $U \subset [\mathrm{b}]_{PIE}$. Then, of course, $[\mathrm{b}]_{PIE} = \Phi'U$. Let us assume the predecessor of our theorem, i.e. there exists $Y \in \mathbf{MRFet}_{PG}$ such that $X \ \mathbf{Frt}_{ap} \ Y$. So by A1 and A2 we obtain that there is $Z \in \mathbf{MRFet}_{PG}$ such that $U \ \mathbf{Frt}_{cl}Z$. From historical linguistics we know that $Y \subset [\mathrm{f}]_{PG}$ and $Z \subset [\mathrm{p}]_{PG}$.

90   Jerzy Bańczerowski

The graph presented below should contribute to a better understanding of the sense of theorem 4.12 and its proof.

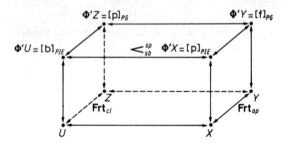

4.13 $\widehat{X \in \mathbf{MRFet}_{PIE}} \overset{\vee}{Y \in \mathbf{MRFet}_{PG}} (X \subset [\mathrm{t}]_{PIE} \wedge X \, \mathbf{Frt}_{ap} Y) \to \widehat{U \in \mathbf{MRFet}_{PIE}}$

$\overset{\vee}{Z \in \mathbf{MRFet}_{PG}} (U \subset [\mathrm{d}]_{PIE} \wedge U \, \mathbf{Frt}_{cl} Z)$

4.14 $\widehat{X \in \mathbf{MRFet}_{PIE}} \overset{\vee}{Y \in \mathbf{MRFet}_{PG}} (X \in [\mathrm{k}]_{PIE} \wedge X \, \mathbf{Frt}_{ap} Y) \to \widehat{U \in \mathbf{MRFet}_{PIE}}$

$\overset{\vee}{Z \in \mathbf{MRFet}_{PG}} (U \subset [\mathrm{g}]_{PIE} \wedge U \, \mathbf{Frt}_{cl} Z)$

The proofs of theorems 4.13 and 4.14 follow the same pattern as that of theorem 4.12.

Mutation of PU *p *t *k to FI *pp *tt *kk

Instead of *pp, tt, kk* we shall write *p:, t:, k:*, respectively.

4.15 $\hat{X} \hat{Y} (X \in \mathbf{MRFet}_{PU} \wedge Y \in \mathbf{MRFet}_{FI} \wedge \Phi'X = [\mathrm{p}]_{PU} \wedge \Phi'Y = [\mathrm{p:}]_{FI}$

$\wedge X \, \mathbf{Mt} \, Y \to \langle X, Y \rangle \in \mathbf{Frt}_{sb} \cap \mathbf{Frt}_{cl} \cap \mathbf{Frt}_{t}$

Proof:

$\hat{X} (X \in \mathbf{MRF}_{PU} \to X \subset \Phi'X)$

$\Phi'X = [\mathrm{p}]_{PU}$

$X \subset [\mathrm{p}]_{PU}$

$\hat{Y} (Y \in \mathbf{MRF}_{FI} \to Y \subset \Phi'Y)$

$\Phi'Y = [\mathrm{p:}]_{FI}$

$$Y \subset [\text{p:}]_{FI}$$

$$\langle [\text{p}]_{PU}, [\text{p:}]_{FI} \rangle \in <_{sb} \cap <_{cl} \cap <_{t}$$

$$(<_{sb} \cap <_{cl} \cap <_{t}) \subset \textbf{LF}$$

$$\underset{X \in \textbf{MRFet}_{PU}}{\vee} \ \underset{Y \in \textbf{MRFet}_{FI}}{\vee} (X \subset [\text{p}]_{PU} \wedge Y \subset [\text{p:}]_{FI} \wedge X \textbf{ Mt } Y)$$

$$\langle X, Y \rangle \in \textbf{Frt}_{sb} \cap \textbf{Frt}_{cl} \cap \textbf{Frt}_{t}$$

4.16 $\underset{X}{\wedge} \underset{Y}{\wedge} (X \in \textbf{MRFet}_{PU} \wedge Y \in \textbf{MRFet}_{FI} \wedge \Phi`X = [\text{t}]_{PU} \wedge \Phi`Y = [\text{t:}]_{FI}$

$$\wedge X \textbf{ Mt } Y \to \langle X, Y \rangle \in \textbf{Frt}_{sb} \cap \textbf{Frt}_{cl} \cap \textbf{Frt}_{t})$$

4.17 $\underset{X}{\wedge} \underset{Y}{\wedge} (X \in \textbf{MRFet}_{PU} \wedge Y \in \textbf{MRFet}_{FI} \wedge \Phi`X = [\text{k}]_{PU} \wedge \Phi`Y = [\text{k:}]_{FI}$

$$\wedge X \textbf{ Mt } Y \to \langle X, Y \rangle \in \textbf{Frt}_{sb} \cap \textbf{Frt}_{cl} \cap \textbf{Frt}_{t})$$

The intuitive sense of theorems 4.15–4.17 is that for the mutation of PU
*p *t *k to FI *pp *tt *kk, respectively, to have taken place an augmentation
of

  (i) subglottal air pressure,
 (ii) the force of supraglottal closure,
(iii) the duration in time

was necessary.

    Whether the mutation of *p t k* to *pp tt kk*, respectively, is possible through
the increase of the duration in time only without augmenting the subglottal
air pressure and the force of supraglottal closure is a problem which should be
clarified experimentally. This alternative seems, however, unlikely.

The problem of PU: two series of stops
    There are various approaches to the reconstruction of the system of PU
stops. Recapitulating it may be said that there are two solutions:

 (i) *p *t *k *pp *tt *kk
(ii) *b *d *g *p   *t   *k

In the light of the theory of fortition-lenition applied to such languages as
Finnish and Lappish the former alternative should be excluded. In the so-
called weak grade of consonants in Finnish developed voiced spirants which
caused the following alternations:

*p ~ *β, *t ~ *δ, *k ~ *γ.

The shift from $*p \ *t \ *k$ to $*\beta \ *\delta \ *\gamma$ could take place in two ways only:

(i) $*p \ *t \ *k > *b \ *d \ *g > *\beta \ *\delta \ *\gamma$

(ii) $*p \ *t \ *k > *\varphi \ *\vartheta \ *\chi > *\beta \ *\delta \ *\gamma$

But in either case we would expect that parallel to this development also the weak grade of PU $*s$ undergoes sonorisation. This, however, did not happen. Thus the existence of PU $*p \ *t \ *k$ is hardly probable at least in the light of fortition-lenition.[12] And consequently the assumption of PU $*p \ *t \ *k$ (short series) leads to an absurdity. Theorem

4.18
$$\widehat{X \in \mathbf{MRFet}_{PU}} \ \overset{V}{Y \in \mathbf{MRFet}_{FI}} \ (X \subset [\mathrm{t}]_{PU} \wedge X \, \mathbf{Len}_{sp, sb} \, Y \to \widehat{U \in \mathbf{MRFet}_{PU}}$$

$$\overset{V}{Z \in \mathbf{MRFet}_{FI}} \ [U \subset [\mathrm{s}]_{PU} \wedge \sim (U \, \mathbf{Len}_{sp, sb} \, Z)]$$

cannot, of course, be proved in our system because it runs counter to axiom A5.

15. Concluding remarks

The above formal approach to the theory $\theta_{F/L}$ does not pretend to be a comprehensive one. Our purpose was to focus attention only on some selected topics of fortition-lenition, which belong to the core of the matter, and not to exhaust the problem. We were neither able to discuss here fortition-lenition phenomena within consonant clusters nor the dependence of these processes upon the position in word and word accent. Furthermore our analysis concerned only the change of allophonic systems without touching upon the mutation of phonological (phonemic) systems. Consequently we have given up here the idea of introducing the notion of phonological mutation.

It could be argued that the formalization of the theory $\theta_{F/L}$ does not yield any new insights. Even if this were true the essential advantage of formal theory $\theta_{F/L}$ consists in indicating which primitive notions and which axioms must be *de facto* accepted in order to prove the fundamental theorems concerning the fortition-lenition processes.

The theorems of the theory $\theta_{F/L}$ may be conceived of as referring to two things:

(i) the device (mechanism) of fortition-lenition;
(ii) the output of this device, i.e. the results of fortition-lenition in particular languages.

The device is described in terms of a set of primitive and defined notions, a set of axioms, and, of course, rules of inference. The set of axioms $(Ax_{\theta_{F/L}})$ accounts for panglottally valid psycholinguistic laws of fortition-lenition as well as for language-specific limitations of these laws (cf. Milewski 1957). The rules of inference allow for a purely formal, i.e. mechanical computation (derivation) of sets of theorems based on primitive and defined notions and on axioms. Every such set of theorems being consequences of the axioms $(Csq\ (Ax_{\theta_{F/L}}))$ can be treated as a description of the output of the fortition-lenition device in a concrete language. The propositions making up such sets of theorems can undergo empirical verification, i.e. it can be empirically decided if these theorems adequately describe the results of fortition-lenition processes in particular languages.

The acceptance of a given set of theorems as an adequate description of the output of the fortition-lenition device should also involve the acceptance of the axioms, from which these theorems are derived, as well-founded. Thus, though the acceptance of axioms may be viewed as a purely conventional (arbitrary) matter, nevertheless these axioms are after all indirectly verifiable by the acceptance as adequate of the particular sets of their consequences.

Notes

1. I would like to express my warmest thanks to Prof. Dr Tadeusz Batóg (Institute of Mathematics, Adam Mickiewicz University), to Dr Jerzy Pogonowski (Institute of Linguistics, Adam Mickiewicz University) and to Dr Tadeusz Zgółka (Institute of Philosophy, Adam Mickiewicz University) for kindly reading the manuscript and making valuable suggestions and pertinent improvements. The formal slips and other inconsequences in this paper should be blamed on me for not always following their advice.
2. Instead of these terms there could also be used *reinforcement-weakening*. But in order to emphasize close connection of the processes at issue to the opposition *fortis* vs. *lenis* we decided the matter in favor of the terms *fortition-lenition*.
3. Cf. the bibliography.
4. Cf. also other publications of this author.
5. A positive attitude towards this book was expressed in the reviews by Gy. Décsy (*Ural-Altaische Jahrbücher* 42 [1970]: 221–225) and F. Grucza (*Lingua Posnaniensis* 15 [1972]: 139–143) but it called forth a negative response in the review by K. Bergsland (*Language* 47 [1971]: 954–955). The malicious critique unsupported by any piece of empirical evidence to the contrary, and unmotivated bias against the theory of fortition-lenition, pre-determined Bergsland's unscientific derisive approach revealing his relatively shallow methodological training, which prevented him from a dispassionate and competent evaluation of the theory in question. Just a regrettable incident transcending the borders of good taste and having a relative low probability of occurrence to happen in any serious field of science.
6. As a counterpart of the relation of *homophony* the relation of *homoarticulation* (=**Har**) could be distinguished. But the following equation would hold **Hph** = **Har**.
7. In the present state of affairs we have given up attempting to define the relation **Mt** in terms of the relation **Etm** because such an approach might resemble a *circulus vitiosus*. A danger of this kind arises from the fact that the assertion of the relation **Etm** is often, although not always, based on the statement of the relation **Mt**.

8. As a matter of fact morphs are strings of phones, the phones being conceived of as individual objects. For the sake of simplification we will also treat morphs as individual objects.
9. The number of the axioms of the first group can be diminished considerably by utilizing the relation $\prec$. The axioms of the second group can be virtually condensed to the axiom

$$A\alpha \bigwedge_{X\in\mathbf{FON}_{PIE}} \bigvee_{Y\in\mathbf{FON}_{PG}} \bigvee_{Z_1\in\mathbf{MRFet}_{PIE}} \bigvee_{Z_2\in\mathbf{MRFet}_{PG}} (\Phi`Z_1 = X \wedge \Phi`Z_2 = Y$$

$$\rightarrow Z_1 \text{ Mt } Z_2)$$

References

Abrahams, H.
1949   Etudes phonétiques sur les tendances évolutives des occlusives germaniques (Aarhus).
Äimä, F.
1906   "Die Hypothese von einem postkonsonantischen Wechsel $k \sim \chi$, $t \sim \theta$, $p \sim \phi$ im Urlappischen", Finnisch-Ugrische Forschungen 6: 181–211.
1914   "Eine Gruppe von Vokalwechselfällen im Inarilappischen", Finnisch-Ugrische Forschungen 14: 1–11.
1918   Phonetik und Lautlehre des Inarilappischen (= Mémoires de la Société Finno-Ougrienne 42–43).
1919   Astevaihtelututkielmia. Ensimmäinen osa. Lapin murteiden välisiä konsonanttivaihteluita (= Mémoires de la Société Finno-Ougrienne 45).
Ariste, P.
1954   Ühest eesti keele astmevahelduse küsimusest (Tallinn: Eesti NSV Teaduste Akadeemia Toimetised).
Bańczerowski, J.
1966a   "Trzy szeregi tylnojęzykowych w proto-uralskim", Sprawozdania Poznańskiego Towarzystwa Przyjaciół Nauk 1: 47–49.
1966b   "Stufenwechsel als Resultat des Lenierungs-Verstärkungsprozesses", Lingua Posnaniensis 11: 47–59.
1967   "Einige phonetische Entwicklungstendenzen des finnischen Konsonantismus", Biuletyn Fonograficzny 8: 71–78.
1968a   "A gyengülés-erösödés folyamata a finn nyelvben", Nyelvtudományi Közlemények 70: 3–21, 277–307.
1968b   "Lenierungs- und Verstärkungsprozess im Finnischen", Lingua Posnaniensis 12–13: 147–169.
1969   Konsonantenalternation im Ostlappischen unter dem Aspekt der Verstärkung-Lenierung (Poznań: Uniwersytet im. A. Mickiewicza).
1971   "Zum Problem des proto-uralischen Klusilsystems", Lingua Posnaniensis 15: 97–112.
Batóg, T.
1967   The axiomatic method in phonology (London: Routledge and Kegan Paul).
Belasco, S.
1953   "The influence of force of articulation of consonants on vowel duration", Journal of the Acoustic Society of America 25: 1015–1016.
Bleek, W. H. I.
1873-4   "Grimm's Law in South Africa", Transactions of the Philological Society.
Canonge, E. D.
1957   "Voiceless vowels in Comanche", IJAL 23: 63–67.

Chinebuah, I. K.
1970   "Consonant mutation in Nzema", *Journal of West African Languages* 7: 69–84.
Collinder, Bj.
1929   *Über den finnisch-lappischen Quantitätswechsel. Ein Beitrag zur finnisch-ugrischen Stufenwechsellehre* (Uppsala: Almqvist & Wiksell).
1937   "Uber Quantität und Intensität", *Neuphilologische Mitteilungen* 38: 97–120.
1944-8 "Az uráli fokváltakozás", *Nyelvtudományi Közlemények* 52: 15–30.
1949   *The Lappish dialect of Jukkasjärvi* (Uppsala).
1960   *Comparative grammar of the Uralic languages* (Stockholm: Almqvist & Wiksell).
1965   *An introduction to the Uralic languages* (Berkeley, Los Angeles: University of California Press).
Debrock, M.
1971   "Les corrélats physiques et physiologiques de la force articulatoire des consonnes occlusives et constrictives, initiales et intervocaliques", *Review of Applied Linguistics (ITL)* 13: 29–58.
Delattre, P. C.
1941   "La force d'articulation consonantique du français", *French Review* 14 (3).
Dieth, E.
1950   *Vademekum der Phonetik* (Bern: Francke).
Einarsson, S.
1927   *Beiträge zur Phonetik der isländischen Sprache* (Oslo).
Falc'hun, F.
1951   *Le système consonantique du breton* (Rennes: Plihon).
1965   "L'énergie articulatoire des occlusives", *Phonetica* 13: 31–36.
Fischer-Jørgensen, E.
1963   "Beobachtungen über den Zusammenhang zwischen Stimmhaftigkeit und intraoralem Luftdruck", *Zeitschrift für Phonetik, Sprachwissenschaft und Kommunikationsforschung* 16: 19–36.
Frei, H.
1948   "De la linguistique comme de la science de lois", *Lingua* 1: 25–33.
Fromkin, V. – P. Ladefoged
1966   "Electromyography in speech research", *Phonetica* 15: 219–242.
van Ginneken, J.
1956   "Roman Jakobson, pioneer of diachronic phonology", in: *For Roman Jakobson* (The Hague: Mouton), pp. 74–81.
Hajdú, P.
1962   "Die Frage des Stufenwechsels in den samojedischen Sprachen", *Ural-Altaische Jahrbücher* 34: 41–54.
Haudricourt, A. G. – A. Martinet
1947   "Propagation phonétique ou évolution phonologique. Assourdissement et sonorisation d'occlusives dans l'Asie du Sud-Est", *BSL* 43: 82–92.
Hentrich, K.
1925   Über den Einfluss der Dauer auf die Stimmhaftigkeit der Verschlusslaute", *Vox* 5.
Hintze, F.
1948   "Zum konsonantischen Anlautwechsel in einigen westafrikanischen Sprachen" *Zeitschrift für Phonetik und allgemeine Sprachwissenschaft* 2: 164–182, 322–335.
Holman, E.
1975   *Grade alternation in Baltic-Finnic* (Helsinki: Helsingin yliopiston monistuspalvelu).

96   Jerzy Bańczerowski

Itkonen, E.
1941   "Über den Charakter des ostlappischen Stufenwechselsystems", *Finnisch-Ugrische Forschungen* 27: 137–167.
1946   *Struktur und Entwicklung der ostlappischen Quantitätssysteme* (= *Mémoires de la Société Finno-Ougrienne* 88).
Jakobson, R.
1962   "The concept of the sound law and the teleological criterion", in: *Selected writings* (The Hague: Mouton), 1: 1–2.
1931   "Principes de la phonologie historique", *TCLP* 4: 247–267.
Jespersen, O.
1954   *Mankind, nation and individual* (London: Allen and Unwin).
Karlgren, B.
1949   *The Chinese language* (New York: Ronald Press).
Kert, G. M.
1961   *Obrazcy saamskoi reči* (Moskva, Leningrad: Izdatel'stvo AN SSSR).
1964   "Dolgota soglasnyx i glasnyx zvukov v kil'dinskom dialekte saamskogo jazyka", in: *Voprosy finno-ugorskogo jazykoznanija* (Moskva), pp. 44–50.
1967   "Fonetičeskie izmenenija i fonologičeskie čeredovanija", in: *Pribaltijsko-finskoe jazykoznanie. Voprosy fonetiki, grammatiki i leksikologii* (Leningrad: Nauka), pp. 20–26.
1971   *Saamskij jazyk* (Leningrad: Nauka).
Kretschmer, P.
1934   "Lautverschiebung im Griechischen", *Glotta* 23: 1–17.
Krogmann, W.
1959   "Parallelen zur ersten germanischen Lautverschiebung", *Zeitschrift für Phonetik und allgemeine Sprachwissenschaft* 12: 182–192.
Ladefoged, P.
1962   "Sub-glottal activity during speech", in: *Proceedings of the Fourth International Congress of Phonetic Sciences* (The Hague: Mouton), pp. 73–92.
Ladefoged, P. – N. P. MacKinney
1963   "Loudness, sound pressure and subglottal pressure in speech", *Journal of the Acoustic Society of America* 35: 454–460.
Lass, R.
1971   "Boundaries as obstruents: Old English voicing assimilation and universal strength hierarchies", *Journal of Linguistics* 7: 15–30.
1974   "Strategic design as the motivation for a sound shift: The rationale of Grimm's Law", *Acta Linguistica Hafniensia* 15: 51–66.
Lass, R. – J. M. Anderson
1975   *Old English phonology* (Cambridge: Cambridge University Press).
Lisker, L.
1957   "Closure duration and the intervocalic voiced-voiceless distinction in English", *Language* 33: 42–49.
MacNeilage, P. F.
1963   "Motor patterns of speech production", *Journal of the Acoustic Society of America* 35: 779 (A).
Malécot, A.
1955   "An experimental study of force of articulation", *Studia Linguistica* 9: 35–44.
Malmberg, B.
1952   "Le problème du classement des sons du langage et quelques questions connexes", *Studia Linguistica* 6: 1–56.
Marstrander, C.
1932   "Okklusiver og substrater", *Norsk Tidsskrift for Sprogvidenskap* 5: 258–315.
Martinet, A.
1952   "Celtic lenition and Western Romance consonants", *Language* 28: 192–217.

Milewski, T.
1949   "La mutation consonantique en hittite et dans les autres langues indo-
européennes", *Archiv Orientální* 17: 189–195.
1957   "Le problème des lois en linguistique générale", *Lingua Posnaniensis* 6:
120–136.
Pedersen, H.
1909-13 *Vergleichende Grammatik der keltischen Sprachen* (Göttingen: Vandenhoeck
und Ruprecht).
Pisowicz, A.
1976   *Le développement du consonantisme arménien* (Wrocław: Ossolineum).
Posti, L.
1954   "On the origin of the voiceless vowel in Lapp", in: *Scandinavica et Fenno-
Ugrica* (Stockholm), pp. 199–209.
Ravila, P.
1951   "Astevaihtelun arvoitus", *Virittäjä*, pp. 292–300.
1960   "Problems des Stufenwechsels im Lappischen", *Finnisch-Ugrische
Forschungen* 33: 285–325.
Sadalska, G.
1973   "Der Einfluss der Verstärkung-Lenierung auf die Entwicklung des Schwe-
dischen", *Studia Germanica Posnaniensia* 2: 131–154.
1976   "Die Entwicklung des isländischen Konsonantismus als Ergebnis der
Verstärkung-Lenierung", *Lingua Posnaniensis* 19: 73–92.
Setälä, E. N.
1912   "Über Art, Umfang und Alter des Stufenwechsels im Finnisch-Ugrischen
und Samojedischen", *Finnisch-Ugrische Forschungen* 12: 1–128.
Skaličková, A.
1954   "Zur Frage des Luftverbrauchs beim Sprechen", *Zeitschrift für Phonetik
und allgemeine Sprachwissenschaft* 8: 80–92.
Sommerfelt, A.
1947   " Études comparatives sur le caucasique du nord-est", *Norsk Tidsskrift for
Sprogvidenskap* 14: 141–155.
Steinitz, W.
1952   *Geschichte des finnisch-ugrischen Konsonantismus* (= *Linguistica* 1, *Acta
Instituti Hungarici Universitatis Holmiensis*, B 1) (Stockholm).
Strenger, F.
1958   "Mesure de la pression d'air sous-glottique, de la pression acoustique et de
la durée de la prononciation des différents sons du langage suédois au cours
de la phonation", *Journal français d'oto-rhino-laryngologie et chirurgie
maxillofaciale* 30, 1: 101–114.
1959   "Methods for direct and indirect measurement of the sub-glottic air pressure
in phonation", *Studia Linguistica* 13: 18–112.
Stewart, J.
1975   "Lenis stops and the origins of Volta-Comoe consonant mutation", in:
Proceedings of the Sixth Conference on African Linguistics (= *Working
Papers in Linguistics* 20) (Columbus: Ohio State University), pp. 16–31.
Ulving, T.
1953   "Consonant gradation in Eskimo", *IJAL* 19: 45–52.
Vergote, J.
1945   *Phonétique historique de l'égyptien. Les consonnes* (Louvain: Muséon).
Wagner, H.
1964   "Nordeuropäische Lautgeographie", *Zeitschrift für Celtische Philologie* 29:
225–98.
Wichmann, Y.
1911-12 "Zur Geschichte der finnisch-ugrischen anlautenden Affrikaten nebst einem

98   Jerzy Bańczerowski

Exkurs über die finnisch-ugrischen anlautenden Klusile", *Finnisch-Ugrische Forschungen* 11: 173–290.

Wiklund, K. B.
1896   *Entwurf einer urlappischen Lautlehre* (= *Mémoires de la Société Finno-Ougrienne* 10).

Zabrocki, L.
1950   Review of J. Fourquet, *Les mutations consonantiques du germanique*, *Lingua Posnaniensis* 2: 296–311.
1951   *Usilnenie i lenicja w językach indoeuropejskich i w ugrofińskim* (Poznań: Poznańskie Towarzystwo Przyjaciół Nauk).
1958   "Zagadnienia fonetyki strukturalnej", *Sprawozdania Poznańskiego Towarzystwa Przyjaciół Nauk* 2: 165–185.
1962   "Zur diachronischen strukturellen Phonetik", in: *Proceedings of the Fourth International Congress of Phonetic Sciences* (The Hague: Mouton), pp. 805–816.
1963   "Die Stimmhaftigkeit der Laute", *Zeitschrift für Phonetik, Sprachwissenschaft und Kommunikationsforschung* 16: 261–275.
1964   "Die inneren Gesetze der dänischen Lautverschiebungen", *Kwartalnik Neofilologiczny* 11: 151–169.
1965   "Die dritte Lautverschiebung im Deutschen", in: *Symbolae linguisticae in honorem Georgii Kuryłowicz* (Wrocław: Zakład Narodowy im. Ossolińskich), pp. 359–368.

XAVIER DEKEYSER

Some considerations on voicing with special reference to spirants in English and Dutch: a diachronic-contrastive approach

0.1 The present paper focuses on various voicing processes of spirants in English and Dutch along a *diachronic-contrastive line*. The facts of English are generally well-known, but are usually found scattered in many books, or chapters of books, and articles: this paper, then, purports to offer a systematic and synthetic survey of voicing in both Old and Middle English (and to some extent also in Modern English). The same holds for Dutch; in addition, this publication in English will give the Dutch data wider currency, which I hope will be welcomed by those scholars who have interests in this field. Finally, I have tried, in a tentative way, to shed light on the process of voicing in general by making use of some findings of recent experimental researches. I have discussed this matter at some length with Dr R. Collier (Antwerpen) and Dr M. Debrock (Leuven), who deserve my heartfelt thanks for their expert assistance. My thanks are also due to Prof. Dr O. Leys (Leuven), Dr J. Wełna (Warsaw), and to my friend, Dr G. Tops (Antwerpen) for their advice and critical comment. The inaccuracies and disputable points that some may find in this paper are entirely my own responsibility.

0.2 Participation in this conference on *Historical Phonology* was made possible by a grant from the Belgian *Ministerie van Nationale Opvoeding en Nederlandse Cultuur.*

1. Voicing in Old and Middle English

1.1 *Old English*[1]

1.1.1 The OE spirants *f θ s*[2] were voiced if they positioned between sonorants the first of which had to be a stressed vowel (Luick, §639):

$$\text{(F1)} \begin{bmatrix} f \\ \theta \\ s \end{bmatrix} \rightarrow \begin{bmatrix} v \\ \eth \\ z \end{bmatrix} \qquad \text{if: } [+\text{stress}] \, ([+\text{son}]) \underline{\hspace{1cm}} [+\text{son}]$$

It follows from this that voiceless fricatives were protected if they occurred in clusters with other obstruents (including geminates), in contiguity to a word-boundary (either Anlaut or Auslaut), and after an unstressed vowel.

1.1.2 I now give a set of examples illustrating (a) voicing and (b) protection of the voiceless fricative; the prosodic specification of stress invites a separate and somewhat more elaborate treatment. Since the above voicing rule was also operative in Dutch, as will be shown in § 2, modern Dutch glosses will be appended for the sake of a preliminary juxtaposition and comparison.

	Old English	*Modern English*	*Modern Dutch gloss*
v	ofen	oven	oven
	fîfe (infl.)	five	vijven (infl.)
	ceafor	chafer (with *f*)	kever
	gerêfa	reeve	_____
	scofl	shovel	schoffel (with *f*)
	wulfas (plur.)	wolves	wolven (plur.)
	twelve (infl.)	twelve	twaalven (infl.)
z	rîsen	rise	rijzen
	wesan	(be)	wezen
	cêosan	choose	kiezen
	þûsend	thousand	duizend
	bes(e)ma	besom	bezem
	bôsm	bosom	boezem
	ôsle	ousel	_____
	wesle	weasel	wezel
	gŷsl	(hostage)	gijzelaar
ð	hǽþen	heathen	heiden
	sêoþan	seethe	zieden
	fæþm	fathom	vadem
	furþor	further	verder

Note: In Dutch ð became a voiced dental stop *d* (see 2.1.1).

1.1.3 Evidence related to intersonorant voicing is not only derivable from the diachronic grammar of English, or in the case of voicing of *f* from later spellings with ⟨v⟩ (from ME on); also synchronically there are indications in OE that corroborate the voicing process: indeed, the rule is for the weak preterite morpheme to be assimilated to the final voiceless segment, if any, of the base: *cyste* (kissed) from *cyssan*, or *pyfte* (blew) from *pyffan*; but *getwǣfan* (to separate), *līesan* (to loose), *cȳþan* (to proclaim) have a non-assimilated ⟨-de⟩ in the Past Tense: *getwǣfde*, *līesde* and *cȳþde*, which testifies to ⟨f s þ⟩ representing voiced segments; if not, there would have been preterite morpheme assimilation (Luick, § 639.1).

As to the chronology of the voicing phenomenon, syncope of ⟨-i-⟩ (e.g. **lausidô → līesde*) enables us to locate voicing before the beginning of the 7th century (again Luick, § 639, Anm. 4).

1.1.4 Obviously, the intersonorant position is a preferred environment for voicing of spirants to take place in OE. Let us now turn to examples of protected environments; again Dutch glosses will be given, this time with an important caveat: the original distribution of voiceless fricatives in English is not paralleled by a similar one in Dutch owing to voicing in word-initial position; furthermore θ became *d* (in the same way as ð) (again see §2.1); Auslautsverhärtung produced *t* (often written ⟨d⟩).

Old English	*Modern English*	*Modern Dutch gloss*
(a) *f θ s*, in contiguity to a word-boundary		
#feld	field	veld
#wulf	wolf	wolf
#þank	thank	dank
âþ#	oath	eed
sûþ#	south	zuid(en)
hûs#	house	huis

(b) *f θ s*, in clusters with obstruents (including self-clusters)		
offrian	offer	offeren
æfter	after	achter (with *ft → xt*)
moþþe	moth	mot
cyssan	kiss	kussen
lǣst	least	———

Note: The Auslaut is not only characterized by the blocking of voicing of originally voiceless spirants, it also devoices voiced spirants. There are, in OE, no examples of *z* or ð since these had already shifted to *r* or *d*. Examples of γ: *genôh* (enough), *plôh – plôgas* (plough-ploughs), *dâh* (dough); for ƀ or *v*: *hlâf* (loaf), *līf* (life), etc. Inlaut devoicing in the neighbourhood of voiceless consonants can be seen in: *drîfþ* (drives) with *ƀθ → fθ*, or *cîesþ* (chooses) with $z\theta \rightarrow s\theta$, and *cwiþ* (speaks) from *cwiþeþ, with $\eth\theta \rightarrow \theta\theta$ (see Luick, § 651 and § 649).

1.1.5 I shall now take up the accent specification. The OE data reveal that a preceding unaccented vowel operated as a constraint on intersonorant voicing (or that an unaccented environment was an area of protection). "Dagegen tritt diese Entwicklung nicht ein, wenn der Spirant zwischen zwei Vokalen ausserhalb des Haupttons stand" (Luick, § 639.2).

A random selection from Luick's abundant evidence may suffice here to bring home the point. (a) Substantives in WG. ⟨*-iþu⟩ and ⟨*-isi⟩, forming abstract feminine nouns, do not show voicing of spirants: OE *trêowþ* (truth) from *triuwiþu, *hælþ* (health) from *hailiþu, *wrǣþþ(u)* (wrath), which is related to *wrâþ* and shows assimilation of ð (see 1.1.4, note); all the abstract feminines in ⟨-þ(u)⟩ are examples in point (ModE ⟨-th⟩), including *strencþ(u)* (strength), *lencþ(u)* (length), etc.; furthermore OE *blîþs* (bliss) from *blîþisi, (with assimilation of ð, the adjective being *blîþe*). (b) Verbs in WG. ⟨*-isôjan⟩: *bletsian, blessian* (bless) from *blôdisôjan (again with assimilation of the final originally voiced consonant of the base). (c) By the side of unstressed nominal and verbal suffixes ordinal numbers constitute a third source of evidence: *sêofoþa* (ME sevethe), *twentigoþa* (ME twentiethe), etc. Hence still in ModE *seventh*, etc. with θ.

Note: Moulton (1954:21–23) fully endorses Luick's view: "The voicing of medial voiceless spirants affected those following a stressed vowel, but not those following an unstressed vowel" (p. 21). Campbell (1959:180) is rather more sceptical on the ground that Luick's account "leaves isolated exceptions, each of which has to be separately explained away". Yet, he does not offer an alternative explanation apart from the null-and-void statement that "a number of formative elements seem to have escaped the voicing. . ." I think that Luick has adduced sufficient and, at the same time, satisfactory and solid evidence to accept a preceding unstressed vowel as a constraint on fricative voicing in OE.

It thus stands out that the OE voicing process of intersonorant spirants is, *ceteris paribus*, the reverse of what happened in Proto-Germanic as regards the prosodic specification of stress in Verner's Law: OE voicing is bound to [+ stress], whereas Verner's Law hinges on a feature [−stress] as far as the syllable preceding the spirant is concerned:

$$\begin{bmatrix} + \text{obstruent} \\ + \text{continuant} \end{bmatrix} \rightarrow [+ \text{voice}] \Big/ \begin{bmatrix} + \text{voice} \\ - \text{accented} \end{bmatrix} _____[+ \text{voice}]$$

(King 1969:48)

Or in words: "Fricatives become voiced in voiced surroundings following an unaccented segment". Lass and Anderson's (1975:177) statement that "the general process of intersonorant voicing is a reflex of the kind of weakening[3] that first appears in Germanic in Verner's Law" only holds as a generality; it is not supported by all the facets of the OE evidence. Even if we grant that Luick's argument is not convincing, the fact remains that OE voicing occurred, in most of the cases, in a prosodic environment quite different from the one required for Verner's Law.

1.1.6 In the southern and south-western dialects initial *f s θ* were also voiced if they were positioned before a sonorant (Luick, § 703).

$$(F2) \quad \begin{bmatrix} f \\ \theta \\ s \end{bmatrix} \rightarrow \begin{bmatrix} v \\ ð \\ z \end{bmatrix} \quad \text{if: } \# \underline{\hspace{2cm}} [+ \text{son}]$$

F3 is the formalization of the wholesale voicing process holding for these dialects:[4]

$$(F3) \quad \begin{bmatrix} f \\ \theta \\ s \end{bmatrix} \rightarrow \begin{bmatrix} v \\ ð \\ z \end{bmatrix} \quad \text{if: } \begin{Bmatrix} \# \\ [+ \text{son}] \end{Bmatrix} \underline{\hspace{1.5cm}} [+ \text{son}]$$

Voicing of initial spirants has to be seen as a systematic, but not necessarily chronological extension of the OE intersonorant voicing-rule, and is, as we shall see in § 2, also a feature of the Dutch dialects in general.

Some examples:

	LOE/EME	*Modern English*	*Modern Dutch gloss*
v	#volk	folc	volk
	#vêr	fire	vuur
	#vat	vat (from col. 1)	vat
	#vless	flesh	vlees
	#vrî	free	vrij
z	#zelf	self	zelf
	#zayl	sail	zeil
	#zuŷn	swine	zwijn
	#zuord	sword	zwaard
ð	#thêf	thief	dief
	#thing	thing	ding

Voicing in the anlaut position will be more fully highlighted when we deal with the Dutch evidence.

Note: Though we are only concerned with the principle of voicing as such, it is perhaps interesting to point out that the voicing of initial *f s θ* in Southern English raises some problems as regards chronology. Traditional historical grammars of English assume that the voicing process has to be located at some time in LOE or EME; Luick (1964: §703): "in der ausgehenden altenglischen Zeit, wahrscheinlich im elften Jahrhundert"; see also e.g. Moore (1951:115) or Brunner (1965: §192, Anm. 1). The correspondence between Low Franconian (Dutch) and Kentish-Southern initial voicing may be a matter of mere coincidence. Bennett (1955:371), however, thinks that this correspondence could be taken as evidence to date initial voicing back to the time when Jutes, Saxons and Low Franconians occupied "contiguous areas near the mouth of the Rhine". If anlaut voicing has to be imputed to inter-tribal contact, "the speech of the first Germanic settlers in southern England already possessed the initial voiced spirants [v z ð]", and "the conventional formula for determining the initial allophones of West Saxon and Kentish Old English /f s þ/ would have to be revised".

1.2 *Middle English*
Preliminary note: the data for the following sections have been culled from Dobson (1968:450–464 and 927–942), Luick (1964: §763 and §798), and Jespersen (1961:199–206).

1.2.1 *Voicing of the dental spirant θ in word-initial position*
This process is tied to (mostly monosyllabic) closed-class words that occur in unstressed positions:

(F4) $\theta \rightarrow \eth$ if: # _____ [−stress]

Examples:

the, that, this, thou, thee, thus, then, than, there, though, and *thider.*

1.2.2 *Voicing of f s θ in word-final position*
Again, potentially unstressed closed-class words provide examples: *is, was, his; with; of.*

(F5) $\begin{bmatrix} f \\ \theta \\ s \end{bmatrix} \rightarrow \begin{bmatrix} v \\ \eth \\ z \end{bmatrix}$ if: [−stress] _____ #

Sentence-stress being a variable, a great many doublets are attested: voiced spirants go with the unstressed words, while voiceless spirants go with the stressed counterparts. The phonetic contours of the unstressed words were eventually generalized in nearly all of the cases. Present-day traces of this stress-dichotomy are still discernible in *of* vs. *off*; stressed forms underlie *if* and *us*; *this* and *thus* are perhaps hybrids deriving from both a stressed form and an unstressed one. The compounds *hereof*, etc. and *herewith* may (and do) occur with voiceless spirant in the auslaut as a result of ⟨-of⟩ and ⟨-with⟩ being stressed here.

By the side of the closed-class category of words examples of voicing are rife in final unstressed syllables, albeit in a rather erratic distribution. First and foremost the morpheme of the plural of ME nouns, of the genitive singular of nouns, and of the third person singular present tense (at least for those dialects that do not have ⟨-eth⟩) should be mentioned here: *əs* or *is* → *əz* or *iz*. Examples are: ME *tîmes, lêves, gives*, etc. A rule similar to F5 could be given here, with the specification *s* instead of spirants in general.

Outside this context there are numerous other instances, such as ME *richesse*, or *trêtis*, or even ME *purpose*, but the general voicing rule, if a rule at all, is warped more than once; witness: *sickness, palace, justice*, etc. I forbear to enter into details here, but factors such as graphemic influence, or impact of the donor-language, when loans are involved, or the time of borrowing may go towards a plausible account.

Voicing of final θ is attested in the third person singular present tense of verbs, at least as far as LME and EModE are concerned. The final voiceless fricative in ordinal numbers is due to a generalization of forms like *tenth*, where the spirant occurs in the stressed syllable.

Voicing of *f* shows up in ME *hussiv* (OE *hûswîf*), and generally in ME adjectives in ⟨-if⟩ or ⟨-ive⟩: *active, pensive*, etc. There was vacillation in EModE in a few nouns, such as *plaintiff, bailiff* and *mastiff*.

1.2.3 *Voicing of intervocalic s*

Intervocalically voiceless fricatives tended to be voiced provided the preceding vowel was unstressed (and the latter stressed). This LME (or EModE) voicing process has a very limited scope, viz. *s* in some loan-words from French, there being no attestations for either *f* or θ. Furthermore the process involved manifested itself very erratically. Unmistakable cases in EModE are: *possess* (French *posséder* with *s*), *dessert* (French *dessert* with *s*), *discern*, *dissolve, philosophic* (as contrasted with *philosophy*, which has *s*). In other instances, such as *preserve* or *resign*, *z* was due to there being a voiced consonant in French, while still in others graphemics and analogy interfered with the voicing of *s*.

1.3 *In summary*

OE *f s θ* are voiced word-medially between sonorants; if, however, the preceding vowel is unstressed, the voicing tends to be blocked. The dialects of the South are also characterized by the voicing of spirants in the anlaut (see § 2 on Dutch). Clusters with other obstruents (generally geminates) and the auslaut position protect the originally voiceless spirants; particularly the auslaut has to be associated with voicelessness, as it devoices originally voiced spirants.

Unlike OE, ME voicing, which occurs initially as well as medially and finally, exhibits a striking correspondence with Verner's Law: they both share the condition of a contiguous (preceding or non-preceding) unstressed vowel.[5] ME (and EModE) voicing is marked by erraticism, so that the distribution of *v z* and *ð* is no longer predictable.

2. Voicing in Dutch

2.1 *Middle Dutch*[6]

2.1.1 *f s θ* were voiced in intersonorant positions, more particularly between vowels or between the sonorants *l, r, n, m* and a vowel, and word-initially before a sonorant (Goossens 1974:75–76):[7]

$$(F6) \quad \begin{bmatrix} f \\ \theta \\ s \end{bmatrix} \rightarrow \begin{bmatrix} v \\ ð \\ z \end{bmatrix} \quad \text{if:} \quad \left\{ \begin{matrix} \# \\ [+\text{son}] \end{matrix} \right\} \underline{\hspace{1cm}} [+\text{son}]$$

Voiceless fricatives were protected in word-final position (where also a wholesale "Auslautsverhärtung" normally operated), and if they positioned in clusters (including self-clustering or gemination). It should be added that the reflex of both *θ* and *ð* was *d* in Middle Dutch, at least from ca. 1100 (Schönfeld 1964: § 50; or Goossens 1974:75 and 95ff.).

2.1.2 *Examples of voicing*

	Middle Dutch	Modern English gloss
v	hôve (plur.)	gardens, courts
	nêve	nephew
	ic verstîve	I stiffen
	wolve (plur.)	wolves
	# vallen	to fall
	# velt	field

	Middle Dutch	Modern English gloss
v	# vloec	curse
	# vleesch	flesh
	# vrêde	peace
	# vrî	free

z	lêsen	to read
	kiesen	to choose
	reise	journey
	ganse (plur.)	geese
	alse	if, when
	# sâke	sake (thing)
	# sômer	summer
	# swack	weak

đ → d	dôdes (gen.)	death's
	vêder	feather
	heide	heath
	worden	to become
	ander	other
	# daer	there
	# dinc	thing
	# drie	three
	# dwars	thwart

2.1.3 *Examples of protected environments* (inhibition of the voicing process)

(a) *In word-final position*

Middle Dutch	Modern English gloss
hof #	garden, court
wolf #	wolf
mûs #	mouse
gans #	goose

Note about Auslautsverhärtung: Middle Dutch is marked by a wholesale devoicing of spirants as well as stops in word-final positions: *findan* (to find) — pret. *ic fant; gêven* (to give) — pret. *ic gaf; ûtganc* (exit); *calf* (calf); *lîf* (body); *weh* (way) (from WG.γ). Also in Modern Dutch voiced stops and spirants are blocked from the auslaut. See Cowan (1961:14—18); Goossens (1974:65—66).

(b) *Protection of f s θ (d) in clusters*

Middle Dutch	Modern English gloss
offeren	
(earlier: offron)	to offer
schoffel[8]	hoe (shovel)
heffen	to heave
joncfrouwe[8]	damsel
ghewisse	sure, surely
bessem[8]	besom
wespe	wasp

2.1.4 (a) Word-initially the voicing is not universal. The spirant *s* resists the voicing process when followed by *l m* or *n*; this can be seen in the clusters *sl sm* and *sn*, which remained markedly unaffected: *slaen* (to slay), *smerte* (sorrow), *snîden* (to cut).[9]

(b) Word-medially a voiceless spirant remained when it was immediately followed by one of the above-mentioned sonorants (mostly coupled with gemination of the spirant and no lengthening of the preceding vowel; see §2.1.5) *bessem* (besom) from WG. **besman-,* as compared with *bêsem* (with *z*) showing a svarabhakti vowel; *bloesem* (blossom); *wâsem* (vapour). While voiceless spirants remained voiceless, the voiced ones underwent devoicing in the environment involved: *gaffel* (fork) corresponding to German *Gabel*, *tâfel* (table), *effen* (smooth) but *êven* (smooth, even), etc. Before heterosyllabic *l* and *n* in the suffixes ⟨-lijc⟩ (later ⟨-elijc⟩) and ⟨-(e)nisse⟩ voiceless spirants were retained: *vrêselijc* (terrible) but *vrêsen* (to fear) with *z*; or the originally voiced consonant was subject to devoicing: *erfenisse* (heritage) vs. the verb *erven* (to inherit).

2.1.5 *A note on gemination*

Gemination operated in Pre-Old-Dutch before *j, r, l, m, n,* and *w,* but only if the vowel preceding the potentially affected consonant was a short one (Goossens 1974:63), while vowel-lengthening in Middle Dutch did not take place before formerly geminated consonants (Leys 1975:65): *heffen* (to heave) but the participle is *ghehêven,* or again *bessem* (nowadays dial.) vs. *bêsem* (besom). The result is that the sequences: *short vowel + voiceless fricative + vowel* and *long vowel + voiced fricative + vowel* became well-established sound patterns in Dutch to the extent of their being productive, also in the synchronic grammar of Modern Dutch.

Examples:

	VV + *voiced fric.*	*V* + *voiceless fric.*
hof (court, etc.)	hoven (plur.)	hoffelijk (courteous)
_____	even (even, smooth)	effen (even, smooth)
grof (rough)	grove (infl.)	groffe (id.)
doof (deaf)	dove (infl.)	_____
dof (dull, dim)	_____	doffe (infl.)
kaas (cheese)	kazen (plur.)	_____
kas (case)	_____	kassen (plur.)
gaas (netting)	gazen (made of ...)	_____
gas (id.)	_____	gassen (plur.)
_____	laven (to quench)	_____
laf (cowardly)	_____	laffe (infl.)
liggen (to lie)	lagen (pret.)	_____
_____	_____	lachen[10]

Mey (1968:129) captures the distribution of spirants in Modern Dutch by means of the following phonological rule:

$$\begin{bmatrix} -voc \\ +cns \\ +cnt \end{bmatrix} \rightarrow [\alpha\, vce] \;/\; \begin{bmatrix} +voc \\ -cns \\ \alpha\, tns \end{bmatrix} \underline{\qquad} \begin{bmatrix} +voc \\ -cns \end{bmatrix}$$

Or in words: "Dutch permits voiced fricatives in the environment $V-V$ only if the first vowel is a tense one; if it is lax, the intervocalic fricative has to be voiceless".

Notes: (1) This rule does not apply without exceptions; however, entering into a detailed discussion here would not be relevant at all; see Tops (1974: §2). (2) "Long" and "short" normally correlate with the features "tense" and "lax" in Dutch.

2.2 *Voicing and devoicing in Modern Dutch – Some recent trends*

2.2.1 *Voicing of s in loan-words*
Modern loan-words (from French or Latin) exhibit voicing of *s* after *n* and *r* and before a vowel:

(F7) $s \rightarrow z$ if: $\begin{bmatrix} n \\ r \end{bmatrix}$ _____ [+vowel] in loan-words

Examples: (a) con*s*ul (id.), consu*l*aat (consulate), con*s*ult (consultation), consul*t*eren (to consult), con*s*onant (id.), conc*i*lie (council), consu*m*ent (consumer), conser*v*eren (to preserve); (b) bur*saal* (grant-holder), *cur*sus (course), unive*r*se*el* (universal), unive*r*s*a*lia (universals), universi*teit* (university), etc. (De Coninck 1970).

Note: I have italicized the stressed syllable so as to bring out that the voicing process is in no way related to the distribution of stressed and unstressed syllables.

I must add (a) that the voicing of *s* is a feature of Northern Standard Dutch (roughly speaking The Netherlands), while in Flanders (Northern Belgium) this process is still in an incipient stage, if occurring at all. (b) That *s* is not universally voiced; a random selection from De Coninck (1970:87) has provided me with the following counter-examples: consa*c*reren (to consacrate), con*sor*tium (id.), con*sen*sus (id.), con*si*gne (orders), consis*tent* (id.), all of which have *s*. It is also remarkable that *f* is never affected by this voicing trend in similar environments: confe*ren*tie (conference) or con*form* (id.), etc.

2.2.2 *Devoicing of spirants in Northern Dutch*
This section devoted to voicing of spirants in Dutch would be utterly incomplete, if I did not say a few words about devoicing of *v, z* and γ, mostly coupled with strengthening, in present-day Dutch. Of these three γ seems to be the most affected: it is devoiced throughout, word-medially as well as word-initially, whereas devoicing of *v* and *z* tends to be confined to the anlaut (Goossens 1974:27).

This can be tentatively formalized as follows:

(F8) $\gamma \rightarrow x$

Examples: graf (grave, tomb), *groeien* (to grow), *gloeien* (to glow), *gaan* (to go), *goed* (good), etc.; *liegen* (to tell lies), *vliegen* (to fly) and *vlaggen* (flags).

(F9) $\begin{bmatrix} v \\ z \end{bmatrix} \rightarrow \begin{bmatrix} f \\ s \end{bmatrix}$ if: #_____

Examples: vel (skin), *voelen* (to feel), *vlak* (even), *vreemd* (foreign), *vies* (filthy), *Vlaming* (Fleming); *zijn* (to be), *zoeken* (to seek), *zeuren* (to talk twaddle).

Note: As a matter of course, *v, z* and γ never occur word-finally as a result of the Middle Dutch Auslautverhärtung: this means that *f* and *s* are universal in the anlaut and the auslaut, while *x* is no longer restricted to specific environments at all.

Devoicing of v, z, and γ is areally restricted: the most "progressive" area is the one where Standard Dutch originated a few centuries ago (and which is still largely decisive for the further development on that score), i.e. the provinces of Holland (which are not to be equated with The Netherlands at large); but also other regions of The Netherlands are increasingly affected. Belgian speakers of Dutch (Flanders), however, have generally preserved the historically voiced realizations, although I often find some speakers, including myself, using more or less devoiced variants of v, z and γ. Impressionistically I would state that there is good ground to assume that the devoicing of spirants, together with the ensuing strengthening, will be one of the most important sound features of 20th century Dutch, at least as far as the Standard varieties go. It is worth pointing out that the area where devoicing of v, z and γ takes place is, by and large, the same as the one that has voicing of s after n and r in loan-words (see § 2.2.1); Belgian speakers of Dutch, who are both geographically and socio-linguistically rather "marginal", are markedly more conservative in that they seem to be standing aloof from these two processes.

3. In summary

When contiguous to sonorant segments, mostly vowels, the spirants f, s and θ are apt to voice or sonorize. The intersonorant environment seems to be the most propitious one for this process both in English and in Dutch. While sonorization in word-initial position is areally limited in the diachronic grammar of English, it is nearly universal in Dutch, though a few phonetic constraints have to be noted. f, s and θ are protected when they collocate with another consonant (more often than not in self-clusters); the auslaut position is particularly propitious for the preservation of voiceless consonants; it should be noted that these are the very environments in which devoicing regularly shows up. Finally, the prosodic parameter of stress may come into play, albeit in a rather unpredictable way: OE as compared with Verner's Law and LME. Some varieties of Modern Dutch are marked by a cyclical development: the voicing of spirants which occurred about a millenium ago is now followed by a wave of devoicing, as yet largely restricted to anlaut positions. In these varieties s is, paradoxically, subject to voicing when it occurs in loan-words after n or r.

There is a striking discrepancy between the (seemingly) regular changes for older stages of English and Dutch on one hand, and the rather incomplete and somewhat erratic developments in more recent layers of these languages (LME, EModE, present-day Dutch). Among other things this is due to some of these changes still being in full progress (notably devoicing in Modern Dutch); or perhaps also to our having more evidence at our disposal, and above all more precise evidence. Finally, I think we can fully endorse the view of Beade (1975: 313), who states that "the very nature of literate societies, generally more stable geographically yet more complex and unstable socially, leads to the failure of sound change as a simple, general and spontaneous linguistic phenomenon".

4. The mechanism of voicing – Facts and hypotheses[11]

4.1 Lass-Anderson (1975:149ff.) have attempted to present a comprehensive and integrated model of strengthening. Articulatory strength, equated by the authors with "resistance to airflow through the vocal tract" (p. 151), is affected by two gestures: (a) weakening of closure, i.e. a supraglottal configuration, and (b) weakening through voicing, i.e. a glottal configuration. We shall look a (a) first, but only very briefly since it is not our primary concern, and then treat (b) in detail.

The hierarchical scale based on "weakening of closure", starting from the stop t, looks like this (p. 156):

4a. Aspirated   th   ts   5. Unaspirated
                        4b. Affricated
                        3. Spirantized
                        2. Dearticulated
                        1. Deleted

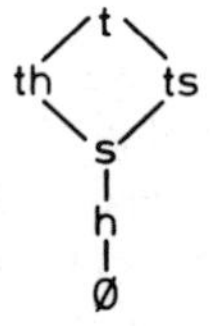

Fig. 1

There is plenty of evidence related to partial realizations of this scale, but there seem to be no attestations as to the set of hierarchies being realized all the way down.[12] A classic example is the High German consonant shift with: p, t, k becoming pf, ts, kx word-initially, after consonants, and in gemination, but the spirants f, s and x in post-vocalic position (see Prokosch 1939:81, also for illustrative material). An instance of nearly the full scale of closure is provided by English k becoming $\emptyset$ in the cluster kn: kn → xn → hn → $\emptyset$n, as shown in $knee$ or $knot$ (see Dobson 1968:976).

Lass-Anderson (1975:157) try to integrate the glottal configuration into the overall mechanism of weakening: "It seems clear that under the airflow-resistance definition, voicing must be a form of lenition (as indeed it is traditionally taken to be). That is, voiced articulations are characterized by a lessened (transglottal) resistance vis-à-vis the cognate voiceless ones". Very regrettably, this intricate process is allotted only a few lines, and the whole argument sounds rather evasive and unconvincing on that score.

Let us assume, for a while, that voicing is indeed an integrated part of an overall scale of weakening, then a scale covering both weakening by opening and by voicing or sonorization, would be something like this (again starting from the stop *t*) (see Lass–Anderson 1975:157–158):

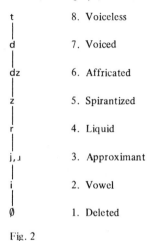

t	8. Voiceless
d	7. Voiced
dz	6. Affricated
z	5. Spirantized
r	4. Liquid
j, ɹ	3. Approximant
i	2. Vowel
∅	1. Deleted

Fig. 2

The wholesale process could be charted as follows (my own chart):

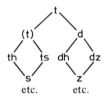

Fig. 3

From which it appears that voicing functions as a first phase in the weakening scale.

Now, the evidence provided by experimental phonetics does not support the view that voicing is a form of weakening under the airflow-resistance definition. The vocal cord separation is wider for some voiced consonants than for vowels, and again wider for voiceless consonants than for voiced ones (Halle–Stevens 1967:268–269). Evidently, airflow-resistance is inversely proportional to varying degrees of abduction, there being the least resistance with the glottis wide open (voiceless consonants). Collier (private communication) proposes the following scale for vocal cord aperture on the basis, among other things, of laryngoscopic and EMG (electromyographic) evidence:

Glottal configuration	Correlates
4. Considerably abducted_____	{ Voiceless spirants { Voiceless aspirated stops
3. Slightly abducted_____	{ Voiced spirants { Voiceless non-asp. stops
2. Loosely abducted_____	{ Voiced stops { Vowels and all other sonorants
1. Completely constricted_____	Glottal stop

Fig. 4

Note: The arrow down the scale indicates increasing airflow-resistance.

This scale shows (a) that voiceless aspirated stops rank with voiceless frica-tives, (b) that spirants are marked by less airflow-resistance (more glottal ab-duction) than their stop counterparts, and (c) that voiceless consonants involve a higher degree of opening than voiced consonants. Viewed this way, the assumption that voicing is a form of weakening is obviously not tenable, and the single weakening scale has to be replaced with two parallel ones:

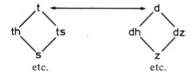

etc.   etc.

Fig. 5

4.2 By the side of glottal aperture the laryngeal configuration is subject to a second parameter: *stiffness* vs. *slackness*. Halle—Stevens (1971:203) distin-guish three possible feature combinations: [−stiff, −slack] for vowels in gen-eral and glides, [−stiff, +slack] for voiced consonants and low pitch vowels, finally, [+stiff, −slack] for voiceless consonants and high pitch vowels. As a rule slack vocal cords tend to correlate with voice, and stiff vocal cords with voicelessness. And if slackness is equated with reduced resistance to the airflow, one can readily see that voicing involves a weakening process.

However, Collier pointed out to me that the degree of laryngeal stiffness is still a moot point. Glottal opening can be observed directly by means of laryngoscopic techniques, whereas the degree of vocal cord stiffness can be derived only indirectly from electromyographic (EMG) measurements. Such EMG data are still few in number and do not always support the Halle—Stevens (1971) hypothesis. The practical moral seems to be that, at least for the time being, we have to handle this parameter with the utmost caution, if we can use it at all.

4.3 The parameters we have dealt with thus far can be schematized as follows:

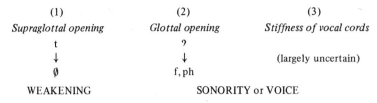

Fig. 6

We have already pointed out that voice cannot be integrated into the process of weakening. It can only be accounted for in terms of (laryngeal) assimilation to contiguous voiced segments:[13] in the case of intersonorant voicing vocal cord vibration is not interrupted, while voice in the anlaut position is due to the advancing of the VOT (voice onset time).[14]

4.4 Let us now turn to the fortis-lenis issue. This matter has been carefully probed by Debrock as regards Dutch and French, but the essentials of his findings no doubt hold for lenis and fortis consonants throughout.[15] There is a great deal of controversy among phoneticians concerning articulatory force, which is due to the absence of a physico-acoustic parameter for lenis and fortis stops and spirants; neither radiocinematographic nor electromyographic researches have so far been able to describe the phenomenon in a satisfactory way. Debrock, both in his 1971 article and his 1975 dissertation, has assembled an impressive amount of acoustic data which prove that the fortis-lenis contrast is not situated in the consonantal segments proper, but in the contiguous vowels, more precisely in the transition CV- or -VC. Vowels that pattern after fortes reach their top intensity more rapidly than do vowels after lenes, for which the amplitude envelope curve shows a more gradual contour. Conversely, vowels that position before a fortis are marked by a rather abrupt drop of intensity, as compared with a smoother drop before a lenis. As a matter of course, intervocalic consonants show the features of both -VC and CV-. So, the crucial difference between fortes and lenes is what Debrock calls the "temps de montée" (the rise time) and the "temps de descente" (the decay time) of contiguous vowels. The fortis-lenis contrast is (very coarsely) charted in Fig. 7.

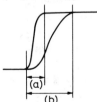

Amplitude envelope contour (rise time) for:

(a) vowel after fortis; (b) vowel after lenis.

Fig. 7

The foregoing rests on well-established acoustic facts. Now the question forces itself upon us: what is the physiological correlate of the acoustic phenomenon just described? Debrock (1971:51–2) *hypothesizes* the following: where fortes are involved, the articulation is characterized by a rapid abduction (metastasis) or adduction (catastasis) of the supraglottal articulatory organs, corresponding, acoustically, to a rapidly rising or falling amplitude of the contiguous vowel(s); on the contrary, lenes have a somewhat smoother abduction or adduction, corresponding to a less rapidly rising or falling amplitude for the contiguous vowel(s). This means that the feature of articulatory force is (largely?) reduced to the *kinetic* muscular energy needed for the metastasis or catastasis of the consonant.

Let us briefly resume the whole issue:

	FORTIS	LENIS
Acoustically:	Sharply rising (CV) or falling (VC) vowel intensity	Less sharply rising (CV) or falling (VC) vowel intensity
Physiologically: (hypothesis)	Rapid metastasis (CV) or catastasis (VC)	Less rapid metastasis (CV) or catastasis (VC)

4.5 So much for the supraglottal physiological fortis-lenis contrast. But what about voice? Can it be integrated into this theory? We know that fortes are nearly always voiceless, but not necessarily so, and that lenes mostly have voice, though voiceless and partly devoiced lenes do occur. Yet, I think we can posit the general principle that voice usually goes with lenes, and *vice versa*. This can be readily understood along the lines of Debrock's view.[16] The transition from a lenis consonant to a V-segment, or the converse, is, as we have assumed, less abrupt than for a fortis; this supraglottal configuration would be particularly conducive to the extension of vocalic voicing to contiguous lenes, but rather not to fortes: anlaut and auslaut lenes are characterized resp. by the potential advancing and prolonging of vocalic voicing, while the voicing is apt not to be broken down when intervocalic lenes are involved. Fortis consonants, on the contrary, are in a way blocked from contiguous vowels, which blocking may be underscored by aspiration of fortis stops (opening a stressed syllable), notably in English and German. This is remarkably borne out by one of Debrock's recent acoustic investigations, from which it appears that the rise time and the decay time are shorter for vowels in contiguity to geminated fortis consonants than for vowels in contiguity to a single fortis consonant. Now, gemination is the very environment which is markedly not affected by the process of voice assimilation both in English and in Dutch (see § 1 and 2), as contrasted with a single intervocalic consonant.

It must be clear by now that the supraglottal lenis configuration ideally matches glottal assimilation of voice, though a lenis articulation is not an indispensable concomitant feature of voice. In addition, the production of voice results in a lowered intra-oral air pressure, so that the realization of a voiced consonant necessitates less kinetic and static (supraglottal) energy than a voiceless consonant. For these reasons voice and lenis articulation are associative phenomena.

So far this theory has only synchronic relevance. But how to account for voicing and devoicing, coupled with articulatory force, in a diachronic grammar of a language? Vowels, and to a somewhat lesser extent the sonorants *l, r, n* and *m*, are the primary voiced segments (see also Zabrocki 1963); obstruents are either voiceless or voiced. Voiced obstruents are secondary vis-à-vis vowels and sonorants in general. Diachronically voicing involves a process of glottal assimilation,[17] which is *ideally* attended with a supraglottal lenition, i.e. the transition from a fortis to a lenis. Therefore I am inclined to believe that the glottal and supraglottal configurations are, to all intents and purposes, affected simultaneously. Devoicing may proceed rather differently: the incipient suppression of voice is not necessarily conditioned by a subsequent fortition, although this is what often happens as a normal (or natural?) corollary of devoicing.

The whole issue can be aptly schematized as follows:

(a) *An intervocalic fortis environment*

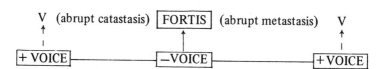

(b) *Voicing or glottal assimilation*

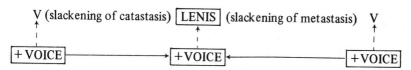

(c) *Devoicing or glottal dissimilation*

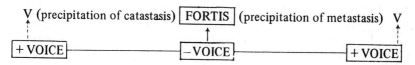

Note: Horizontal arrows indicate the direction of the assimilatory process; vertical arrows symbolize the airflow from the glottal to the supraglottal area; here the dotted line suggests a weakened flow.

Epilogue

This account of the voicing mechanism may seem unduly elaborate and rather off the point. What I wanted to bring to the fore is the following: the findings of sophisticated physiological and acoustic researches are of overriding importance for the systematic phonetics (Debrock 1975:11:"le deuxième moment phonétique") of present-day languages. Careful extrapolation of these findings to earlier stages of a given language is bound to shed light on diachronic issues, so far not or not satisfactorily clarified. Or to use Zabrocki's (1963:275) words: "Die historische Phonetik muss sich somit der synchronen statischen Lautgefügestrukturen bedienen, um Fragen der diachronen Entwicklungen verstehen und klären zu können. Beim Heranziehen von synchronen Lautgefügestrukturen sind wir imstande, gewisse allgemeine innere Gesetzmässigkeiten im Verlauf der phonetischen Prozesse auf der diachronischen Ebene festzustellen".

Notes

1. In the present paper *Old English* or OE not only covers the Old English period proper, but also the time-span which is commonly denominated Pre-Old-English.
2. WG. *x* does not feature here. Word-initially it had been weakened to *h*: e.g. *hôc* (hook), *hnutu* (nut); the same holds for the intersonorant environment: e.g. **flêohan, flêon* (to flee). *x* was preserved as a voiceless spirant in the Auslaut and, word-medially, in geminates and before another voiceless obstruent: e.g. *scôh* (shoe), *rûh* (rough); *hlehhan* (to laugh), *hleahtor* (laughter), *dohtor* (daughter). See Luick (1964: § 636).
3. More details about the concept of weakening in Lass and Anderson's book are to be found in § 4.1 of this paper.
4. For the sake of convenience I have omitted the accent specification here.
5. As far as Verner's Law is concerned, the contiguous unstressed vowel always precedes the voiced spirant, whereas in ME it may position both before and after the spirant that is subject to the voicing process.
6. The diachronic grammar of Dutch can be divided up into periods similar to those of English. However, *Old Dutch* is largely a "construct", as there are no records apart from a few proper names, some glosses of the *Lex Salica*, and 22 psalms from a Carlovingian psalter, the so-called *Wachtendonckse Psalmen* (see Goossens 1974:18–19, and Cowan 1961:1). In the present paper *Middle Dutch* is used as an overall term covering both the period before 1200 and after it. The illustrative material that will be given in the following sections reflects the language of the 13th or the 14th century.
7. Again *x* does not figure among the spirants that are liable to voicing. Word-initially it had become *h* or it had been dropped; word-finally it, of course, remained intact; *noh* (still). Intervocalically, *x* was syncopated, e.g. *flien* (to flee) from WG. **flêohan,*

or it remained unaffected in contiguity to other voiceless obstruents and in gemination, e.g. *naht* (night) and *lachen* (to laugh). Middle Dutch (and Modern Dutch) has a voiced velar spirant γ from WG. *g* or γ: *weghe* (ways), *goet* (good); this is devoiced in the auslaut: *wech* (way). See Goossens (1974:67–68).
As there are no traces of a possible operation of the stress feature in Middle Dutch, I have omitted it here. Rule (F6) does not apply unrestrictedly: see § 2.1.4.

8. *Schoffel* and *bessem* have geminated spirants before *l* and *m* (see 2.1.4); they contrast with *scûven* (to shove) and *bêsem*, with resp. *v* and *z*. *Joncfrouwe* derives from *jonc* (young) + *frouwe* (lady, woman); it should be noted that *vrouwe* has the regular voiced spirant in the anlaut.

9. There are more cases of word-initial voiceless spirants in Dutch, which have to be put down to various factors: (a) psychological intensity: *flets* (lacklustre), *foei* (fie); (b) onomatopoeia: *fluisteren* (to whisper), *flikkeren* (to flicker), *sissen* (to hiss); (c) loan-words: *fruit* (id.), *fors* (robust), *sla* (salad), *suiker* (sugar), *forel* (trout), etc. See Schönfeld (1974: § 50, Opm.1).

10. *Lachen* (to laugh) from WG. *hlahjan (OE hlehhan); the short vowel clearly points to *x* being a geminate, at least till after the completion of the lengthening process; see Leys (1975: § 5.4).

11. Dr Collier and Dr Debrock have been immensely helpful, in that they have both given generously of their time to discuss the essentials of this section. Let it be repeated once more that inaccuracies and disputable passages, if any, are my own responsibility, not theirs.

12. It should be added that the authors do not make such a claim: "What we are doing is setting up the degrees of the weakening scale, without claiming that any particular lenition must pass through all the phases" (Lass-Anderson 1975: 154).

13. Admittedly, Lass and Anderson also speak of assimilation (1975:161); let it be clear that it is second to the wholesale weakening or lenition process in the context of their book: some forms of lenition notably voicing of intervocalic spirants, *also* amount to assimilation.

14. The Auslaut is markedly a voiceless environment (Auslautverhärtung and inhibition of voicing); if voice occurs here, it has to be put down to a protraction of the voicing in the immediately preceding sonorant.

15. See Debrock's article (1971) and his unpublished dissertation, more particularly the passages related to "force articulatoire".

16. The following is my own hypothesis (prompted by Dr Debrock's views).

17. This statement implies that voiced consonants rank as secondary vis-à-vis their voiceless counterparts; the primacy of voiceless stops and spirants agrees with the Jakobsonian claim (p. 70) that a language has voiced obstruents (of some type), only if it has the cognate voiceless ones. Thus *v z ð* automatically presupposes a set *f s θ*.

References

Anttila, R.
   1972   *An introduction to historical and comparative linguistics* (New York: Macmillan).
Beade, P.
   1975   "Vowel length in Middle English: Continuity and change", *Leuvense Bijdragen* 64: 313–320.
Bennett, W. H.
   1955   "The southern English development of Germanic initial [f s þ]", *Language* 31: 367–371.

Bosworth, J. – T. N. Toller
1898-   *An Anglo-Saxon dictionary* (London: Oxford University Press).
1921
Brunner, K.
1965   *Altenglische Grammatik (nach der Angelsächsischen Grammatik von Eduard Sievers)*[3] (Tübingen: Niemeyer).
Campbell, A.
1959   *Old English grammar* (London: Oxford University Press).
Cowan, H. K. J.
1961   "Esquisse d'une grammaire fonctionelle du vieux-néerlandais (vieux bas-francique) (d'après le psautier carolingien de Wachtendonck)", *Leuvense Bijdragen* 50: 2–54.
Debrock, M.
1971   "Les corrélats physiques et physiologiques de la force articulatoire des consonnes occlusives et constrictives, initiales et intervocaliques", *ITL* 13: 29–58.
1975   *Contribution à la phonétique acoustique du français et du néerlandais.* [Unpublished doctoral dissertation, Catholic University of Leuven.]
De Coninck, R. H. B.
1970   *Groot Uitspraakwoordenboek van de Nederlandse Taal* (Antwerpen: De Nederlandsche Boekhandel).
Dobson, E. J.
1968   *English pronunciation 1500–1700*[2] (London: Oxford University Press).
Foley, J.
1973   "Assimilation of phonological strength in Germanic", in: *Festschrift for Morris Halle* (Eds.: S. R. Anderson – P. Kiparsky) (New York: Holt), pp. 51–58.
Franck
1912   *Franck's Etymologisch Woordenboek der Nederlandsche Taal*[2] (Ed.: N. van Wijk) (The Hague: Nijhoff).
Goossens, J.
1974   *Historische Phonologie des Niederländischen* (Tübingen: Niemeyer).
Halle, M. – K. N. Stevens
1967   "On the mechanism of glottal vibration for vowels and consonants", *MIT Quarterly Progress Report* 85: 267–271.
1971   "A note on laryngeal features", *MIT Quarterly Progress Report* 101: 198–213.
Jakobson, R.
1968   *Child language, aphasia and phonological universals* (The Hague: Mouton).
Jespersen, O.
1961   *A modern English grammar on historical principles* 1: *Sounds and spellings* (London: Allen and Unwin).
King, R. D.
1969   *Historical linguistics and generative grammar* (Englewood Cliffs, N.J.: Prentice-Hall).
Kurath, H.
1956   "The loss of long consonants and the rise of voiced fricatives in Middle English", *Language* 32: 435–445.
Ladefoged, P.
1962   *Elements of acoustic phonetics* (Chicago: The University of Chicago Press).
1973   *Preliminaries to linguistic phonetics*[2] (Chicago: The University of Chicago Press).
1975   *A course in phonetics* (New York: Harcourt, Brace, Jovanovich).
Lass, R.
1971   "Boundaries as obstruents: Old English voicing assimilation and universal strength hierarchies", *Journal of Linguistics* 7: 15–30.

1974   "Strategic design as the motivation for a sound shift: The rationale of
            Grimm's Law", *Acta Linguistica Hafniensia* 15: 51–66.
Lass, R. – J. M. Anderson
1975   *Old English phonology* (Cambridge: University Press).
Leys, O.
1975   "Die Dehnung von Vokalen im Niederländischen und im Deutschen",
            Leuvense Bijdragen 64: 421–449.
Luick, K.
1964   *Historische Grammatik der englischen Sprache* (Oxford: Basil Blackwell)
            [Reprint].
Mey, J.
1968   "A case of assimilation in Modern Dutch", *Acta Linguistica Hafniensia* 11:
            123–145.
Moore, S.
1951   *Historical outlines of English sounds and inflections* (Revised by A. H.
            Marckwardt) (Ann Arbor, Michigan: G. Wahr).
Moulton, W. G.
1954   "The stops and spirants of early Germanic", *Language* 30: 1–42.
1972   "The Proto-Germanic non-syllabics (consonants)", in: *Toward a grammar
            of Proto-Germanic* (Eds.: F. van Coetsem – H. L. Kufner) (Tübingen:
            Niemeyer) pp. 141–173.
Prokosch, E.
1939   *A comparative Germanic grammar* (Baltimore: Linguistic Society of America).
Schönfeld, M. – A. van Loey
1964   *Schönfelds Historische Grammatica van het Nederlands. Klankleer, vormleer,
            woordvorming*[7] (Revised by A. van Loey.) (Zutphen: N.V. W.J. Thieme &
            Cie).
Tops, G. A. J.
1974   "Assimilation of voice in Dutch. A generative approach", *Leuvense
            Bijdragen* 63: 43–51.
Van Bakel, J.
1973   *A→B/X→Y. Fonologie van het Nederlands, synchroon en diachroon*
            (Nijmegen: Nijhoff).
Van den Berg, B.
1972   *Foniek van het Nederlands*[6] (The Hague: Van Goor Zonen).
Van Loey, A.
1965   *Middelnederlandse Spraakkunst*[4], 2: *Klankleer* (Groningen: J. B. Wolters).
Zabrocki, L.
1963   "Die Stimmhaftigkeit der Láute (Versuch einer strukturell-phonetischen
            Betrachtungsweise)", *Zeitschrift für Phonetik, Sprachwissenschaft und
            Kommunikationsforschung* 16: 261–275.

Postscript: A slightly revised version of the present paper appeared in *Leuvense Bijdragen*
65(1976): 437–459.

GABERELL DRACHMAN

Child language and language change:
a conjecture and some refutations[1]

I. Introduction

1. General

From Schleicher through Paul to Saussure and later Halle and Kiparsky many
linguists have, either implicitly or explicitly, assented to the proposition that
children change language during what I shall here call primary acquisition,
i.e., during the process of learning their native language. A few, notably
Sweet and (with important reservations) Jespersen, have on the contrary held
that since children do in fact successfully learn their native language, the
instigators and sponsors of sound change must be older individuals.[2]

I shall in this paper take in earnest Popper's (1963)[3] first 'requirement
for the growth of knowledge' (ibid, Ch. 10, Section 5), viz., that (all other
things being equal) a theory should be preferred if it offers a simple, new, and
powerful idea about some connection or relation between hitherto unconnected
facts. The "hitherto unconnected facts"[4] in our case are those of the phonetic
processes in primary language acquisition, in adult language, and in language
change; and the idea connecting them is Stampe's (1969) conjecture concerning the nature and function of 'innate processes'. I shall challenge the coherency
of this conjecture, and suggest that we must perhaps for the moment rest
content with something less than a fully coherent theory of phonology.

To forestall misunderstanding, let me make it clear that I am not about to
claim that children play no role in sound change. I shall, however, try to
justify the following quite modest claim: if language learning proceeds specifically as Stampe claims it does, then *some* kinds of sound change cannot be
attributed to learning failures during primary acquisition, while other kinds
must remain ambiguous in this respect.

2. Conjecture

Briefly, Stampe holds that (1) the set of possible phonetic processes represents
inborn properties of the human speech tract, (2) the cumulative results of the

uninhibited and unordered application of these processes reduces any sequence of segments to pabulum of the *pa-pa* or *ba-ba* type, (3) the acquisition of 'correct' L-specific pronunciation requires the systematic limitation, suppression, or even (extrinsic) ordering of (certain of) these processes. For this theory, (4) phonetic change naturally results when processes are not correctly limited (etc.) during primary acquisition. Such a theory is 'coherent', in that it predicts phenomena in all three modalities, viz., the outcomes of phonetic processes in child language, adult languages, and language-change, in a homogeneous fashion.

Before going further let me first make three very general concessions, with their corresponding caveats. First, there is no doubt that individual words out of baby-talk (including hypocoristics) are sponsored by adults, and that adults often adopt a child-like pronunciation when addressing small children as also lovers, the infirm, etc. But this speech mode is hardly a model for sound change: its true importance will be hinted at below (see III).

Second, some children (e.g., twins, neglected children) retain for some time an early pronunciation (or another, equally 'primitive', of their own devising) in parallel to the (adult) norm — the so-called child secret-languages. Again, there is here no model for change.

Third, some children fail grossly to acquire the pronunciation of the parent model, whether through damage or maldevelopment of the brain, or psychosocial causes; such children are of course labelled as in need of speech therapy, and these too are hardly viable models for change.

These points granted, I shall try to show that it is not enough to point to individual child forms and show parallels; for many of the commonest types of process found in early child-language are at important points in gross non-overlap with those of adult language and language change, as regards either frequency of occurrence, function and motivation, or subtypes[5]. In suggesting that these parameters may thus prove modality-specific, I shall thus conclude that the coherency-hypothesis for phonology is not sustained in its strong (Stampean) form.

II. Refutations

1. Paradigmatic strengthening

Manner-and-place polarisation are perhaps the best known as they are the most far-reaching of child processes. But context-free (CF) process-trains such as $x \rightarrow f, f \rightarrow p$ (or $x \rightarrow k, k \rightarrow p$) have of course not the slightest chance of surviving into even late childhood, much less (normal) adult life.

Conversely a CF process $f \rightarrow p$ simply does not occur either in synchronic adult language or in diachronic change — though it will naturally occur in borrowing, as in English *fella* → Melanesian Pigin *pella* (Hall 1966) as also under *Sprachbund* influence, as in Eastern Cushitic Yaaku (private communication; H. J. Sasse).[6] Likewise, though CF *p* → *f* is well attested (e.g., within Grimm's Law), yet primary acquisition can not offer such a process.

The reason for this contrast is perhaps to be sought in the contrast between the special tract-control conditions for the child, as against the strengthening-weakening functions of processes in adult language.[7] The adult has mastered his vocal tract (at least to the extent required for his language) and can thus "use" processes to subserve style; for "ease", he "allows" a less extreme gesture to replace a stop with a spirant; but when the child does what is easiest, for a given stable output, viz., employs a ballistic rather than a continuous-control mechanism to produce obstruents, he gains a stop rather than an intended spirant. In this sense, we can characterize both child and adult as employing the parameter "gesture-strength", but though their motivations (greater "ease") are similar the results are quite opposite.

CF polarization in child language
kisses → *kitət, Loch* → *lokʰ* (Leopold)
fit → *bīʔ, food* → *būd* (Salus)

2. Weak syllable loss

2.1. *Child language*

There is general agreement in the child language literature that unstressed initial syllables[8] are lost in the earliest stages. For disyllabic words (perhaps the majority of the words attempted at such stages) this correlates fairly well with the notion that what is preserved is what is most prominent, viz., the stressed syllable, a notion explicit in the writings of Grégoire (1937) for French, or Smoczyński (cit. Pačesová 1968) for Polish, Russian, Bulgarian, and (in even more extended form) in Waterson (1971) for English.

But we may generalize this claim interestingly with reference to the psychological literature on list-learning (e.g., Neisser 1967). In list-learning, two factors interfere with memory. A novel stimulus is well remembered, as is the last stimulus before the gross stimulus-change represented by list-end, i.e., pause; call these the 'primacy' and 'recency' effects respectively. However, in tests with nonsense-syllables (Blasdell — Jensen 1970), young children recalled best syllables that were either stressed or last in their string, a result that confirms the interference of stress but also suggests that (all other things being equal) 'recency' is more important than 'primacy' in young children's auditory memory.[9]

The crucial data must clearly come not from a language with final stress like French, but from one with initial stress: there the loss of initial syllables would clearly demonstrate the overriding importance of 'recency'. Fortunately, data for one such language (Czech) are abundantly available, in Pačesová (1968). Here it is clear that the matter is more complex, for in fact we find some examples of words with retained initial (stressed) syllable. However, closer consideration of the data reveals (1) that stress controls syllable-loss up to about 16 months, (2) by 18 months only the single (early) form 'aeroplane' attests to recency, while (3) between 18 and 24 months (the end of the observation period) the overwhelming majority of cases of syllable-loss involve initial syllables.

Czech data (Pačesová):
(a) *aeroplan* → *e:lo, dekorak* → *duju~kuju*: but later
(b) *rukavički* → *kavički, trikolka* → *kolka*
   kolobeška → *beška, děkuji* → *kuju, gramofon* → *mofo:n*

It seems that (Ohnesorg 1959) memory and thus reproduction is indeed at the earliest stage controlled by pure acoustical prominence. But the grammatical relations of first importance are contained in the case-suffixes: for Czech, then, there is a natural switch of attention to word-end in association with the 'discovery' of grammatical relations, a switch strengthened by habituation to the stable nature of stress.[10]

2.2. *Adult language and history*
Hypocoristics have sources too complex for them to serve as critical data (cf. Drachman 1973); but, as first noted by Jespersen (1922) surname-contractions may serve as one type of data for syllable loss in adult language. Surnames are rarely used by very young children, but are typically contracted by older children at school, as well as by adolescents and adults. The lists in Sundén (1904) give dozens of surnames shortened by loss of end-syllables, as against a tiny handful with initial-syllable loss. This agrees well with syllable-loss in language-change, which likewise usually proceeds from word-end, despite the clear danger of loss of grammatical material.

On the other hand, the evidence for lexical shortening seems perhaps ambiguous, at least for English, where both kinds of shortening are found. Thus
1. 1st syll. (or more) lost: (a) *bus, wig, van*; (b) *car, plane, phone*; (c) *taters, baccy, varsity, chute, gater* 'alligator', *coon*; (d) *size, tend, mend, lone, live* 'alive'; *spite, stain, sport, fend*.

2. But last syll. (or more) lost: (a) *cab, extra, chap, navvy, mob, fad*; (b)
   photo, telly 'television', *auto, trolley, gent*; (c) *vet, matric, exam,
   gym, conchy* 'conscientious objector', *zep* 'zeppelin', *prop* (theatrical)
   property, *cap* 'printer's capital letter'.

Yet these examples are of vastly diverse status, e.g., those in 1/2a and b have
lost so much more than a single syllable, while those in 1 (d) may well early on
have suffered comparison with (productive) prefixes as found in *a-going*, or
de-nude. In some cases, moreover, the semantic content must be considered
in conjunction with homonymy problems; thus *-plane* and *photo-*, rather than
aero- and *-graph*. Further study is also required, to ascertain which words
are in fact known and used by very young children; thus, certainly *car* and
phone, but not *matric* or *gym*.

   One further point. It seems that loss of initial syllable(s) makes a word
more difficult to recognize in perception; as crossword fans know, words are
harder to reconstruct given only the later syllables. A *conscious* shortening
mechanism, such as is surely used by school-boys and older persons, will
reasonably guarantee dictionary access by retaining the opening syllables,
except perhaps only in the case of bi-morphemic words.

   If I am right in these conjectures, then I might tentatively conclude that
while children unavoidably waste word-beginnings, adults unavoidably *and*
intentionally waste word-endings. Then it is doubtful whether young children
are responsible for much (if any) word-shortening in language change.

3. Distant assimilation

3.1. *General*
When one compares their status in languages of the world and in historical
change with their status in child language, the processes of vowel and consonant harmony present a paradox. I first outline a deductive theory of harmony,
then contrast predictions with facts in the three modalities.

   As a starting point, I take Perkell's (1969) theory of adult speech production. Here, the ground-rhythm for speech is the ongoing vowel-gesture,
performed by the body of the tongue, on which is superposed the local
(tongue) deformations required for (many) consonant articulations. For the
child, then, inertial or anticipatory repetition of gesture through (at least) a
word program constitutes one kind of output-programming economy. In
development, however, it seems that (1) vowel-harmony, occupying the grosser
tongue musculature, progressively weakens before consonant-harmony does,

since the latter concerns the finer tongue-internal musculature, and (2) consonant-harmony should thus 'last' longer in child language. It follows that (3) if either of these is to survive and affect adult language (and thus change language) it ought to be consonant-harmony rather than vowel-harmony.[11]

3.2. *Child language*

As predicted, vowel-harmony is very strong in the earliest stages only, and that at a time when consonants are still strongly constrained by paradigmatic polarization, both for manner and place. Further, vowel-harmony is always nearly entirely suppressed by the stages when consonant-harmony is seen at its strongest, viz., when polarization processes are at least suppressed to the extent that a variety of consonants can each appear (at least under 'optimal' conditions). In Smith (1973), for instance vowel-harmony had been suppressed before 2.2 years, whereas some kinds of consonant harmony continued until at least 3 years 9 months.

Significantly enough, there is reason to believe that consonant-harmony may, at a stage when it has become optional, be used strategically[12]. In studies of Greek children (Drachman 1975) prophylactic harmony sometimes appears where a consonant would otherwise be completely lost: thus, at a stage when for him intervocalic /δ/ elsewhere semi-vocalized and was lost, one child's form *kliδí* 'key' became [lilí], rather than the otherwise inevitable [ki] (by loss of δ, then geminate vowel contraction): a segment identity was sacrificed, but syllable structure was thereby preserved.

Examples of harmony:

(1) Vowel harmony:
   little → *didi:*, *broken* → *bugu:* (Smith)
   provatáki → *povotáki*, *kókoras* → *kákaras* (Drachman)
   baguette → *bɛjɛt*, *poupée* → *pepɛj* (Grégoire)
   tire → *tere* (Bar-Adon)
(2) Consonant harmony (place)
   i. Velar harmony: *book* → *guk*, *sock* → *gok* (Menn)
   ii. Dental harmony: *meat* → *dit*, *boot* → *dot* (Menn)
       kan.ta → *tan.ta* (Chao)
       madame → *dadap* (Roussey)
   iii. Labial harmony:
       twice → *daif*, *queen* → *gi:m* (Smith)
       kapélo → *papélo* (Drachman)
       chapeau → *popo* (Roussey)
(3) Consonant harmony (manner/place)

   i. Nasal harmony: *kamm → nam, kanone → nanone* (Preyer)
    vilein → nɛn, panier → meni, nourrice → nunis (Roussey)
  ii. Lateral harmony:
    sel:ka → lel.ka (Vihman)
    kliδí → lilí   (Drachman)

    Worse, it is to be suspected that despite the apparent explanatory power
of the deductive theory of harmony (above), we have to do with altogether
mentalized rather than physiological events. For there are all too many cases
where harmonies (especially consonant harmonies) do not in fact attack words
at their debut (Moskowitz 1970) as should Stampean processes, inevitably
applicable as soon as their structural description is met. Rather, many forms
appear quite early in near-adult shapes, e.g., with consonants of dissimilar
'place' in adjacent syllables, only later to submit to harmony — or even, more
rarely, to survive the entire battle of the processes unscathed. Perhaps, then,
harmony is always (cf. Menn 1974) an information-processing strategy.
    Examples of regression (relevant stages only): [13]

  i. *yolk → u:k → jo:k → lo:k → ro:k (→jo:k)* (Smith)
   work → wə:k → və:k → wə:k
   (cf. 'apparent' regression in *sleep → li:p → ti:p (→ sli:p)*
 ii. *Brot → bro:t → gro:t (→ bro:t), drauf → grauf (→ drauf)* (Ramge)
iii. *pretty → prɪti → pѡɪti → bɪdi (→ prɪti)* (Leopold)[14]

3.3 Adult language and history

The paradox is that the adult language situation is almost the converse of
that in child language. Vowel harmony is found in not a few of the world's
languages, even language families, e.g., Finno-Ugric, Altaic, Korean, Gilyak,
Ainu, Tibetan; many West African languages (e.g., Yoruba, all Western Bantu
languages); Australian Nyangumarda; Northwest Amerindian Coeur D'Alene
and Nez Perce, etc. On the other hand, systematic consonant harmony is
comparatively rare: Grammont (1956) musters only Sanscrit retroflex harmony,
Arabic emphatic harmony, Toba (Javanese) *r*-harmony; and to these we may
add Chumash sibilant harmony (Beeler 1970), Paiute palatal harmony (Lovins
1972) and Sanscrit *s ... s̓ → s̓ ... s̓* harmony.
    Strangely enough, though vowel harmony is by far the commoner adult
language process, we find few examples of its rise in historical times.[15]
    Umlaut, though superficially similar to vowel harmony, is far less common,
and in fact operates in a radically different way[16]: vowel harmony operates
'outwards' from stems into suffixes, thus preserving (synchronic) stem shapes;
while Umlaut anticipates an unstressed suffix vowel and thus created a diver-

sity of stems across a given paradigm. For their part, the 'adult' consonant harmony types overlap poorly with those of the child — and when they do, as for example, in liquid-harmony, the Toba case shows the less natural dominance, of /r/ over /l/.

Thus, the better candidate for adult harmony, viz., consonant harmony, proves far the less widespread and less regular: it is hard to see how to coherently connect our three modalities with respect to harmony phenomena.

3.4. The problem of distant dissimilation
If harmony, i.e., consonantal distant assimilation, is common in child language and rare in adult language, almost the opposite seems to be true of systematic distant dissimilation. The latter is found in adult languages as well as in language change; but far less commonly, in child language.

3.4.1. Child language
By contrast to distant assimilation, there seem to be few cases of systematic distant dissimilation attested in child language. Cases are cited below. It is hard to agree, e.g., with Pačesová (1968) that both assimilation and dissimilation at a distance are attributable to the same principle of articulatory economy: how can we appeal to economy as creating identical successive consonants on the one hand, but diversifying them on the other? But Anttila's distinction (1972) between articulatory and neural economy takes us no further, especially in the light of the mentalistic view taken above (3.2.) on distant assimilation.

Examples for distant dissimilation:

(1) Systematic
    mimi → *mémi, quiqui* → *quéqui, fini* → *méni* (Grammont)
(2) Sporadic
    monogram → *modoglam, honem* → *holem* (Ohnesorg)
    dudlík → *budeli:k* (Pačesová)

3.4.2. Adult language and history
For synchronic distant dissimilation in adult language consider (1) Manner, Grassmann's Law, the symbolic roots in English (Bloomfield 1933:390), the $k \sim y$ alternation in Bantu-Kikuyu (Dahl's Law, cited in Guile 1972); (2) Contra Guile (1972) however, we also find place-dissimilation, though optional, in Picuris (Trager 1971). (3) Distant dissimilatory loss in the form of s-loss is common in Northern Greek dialects: the same phenomenon however, with varying degrees and directions of analogical levelling, is found systematically in the Greek of certain Chios villages (Pernot 1907).

In history we find distant dissimilation (1) of manner, e.g., the *s . . s* →
t . . s shift as between Malay and Ngaya-Dayak (Anttila 1972:74–75), (2) of
place, e.g., *k* → *č* /- . . *q* in early Cowlitz (Kinkade 1973), *k* → *k̬* /- . . . *g* in
some Mamean languages (Kaufmann 1969).

Lastly, we find distant dissimilatory blocking of processes such as Iraqi
k → *č*, but not with following *č* (Grammont 1965:365); and Ancient Chinese
initial glottals and velars → palatals, but not in words with final palatals
(Hashimoto 1970).

4. Metathesis

4.1. *General*

Three principles concerning metathesis may be found in the contemporary
literature. (1) Glide metathesis (preferably with a resonant) subserves the
unmarking of sequences of intrasyllable segments, whereby the further from
the nucleus, the stronger – thus Nucleus-Glide-Liquid-Nasal-Obstruent, and its
mirror image (Ultan 1971; Semiloff-Zelasko 1973). (2) Stop-spirant metathesis, especially strong for dentals (thus TS = → ST), in Ultan (1971) and
Silva (1973). Proneness of other stop+S sequences to metathesis is also
attested, and discussed by Bond (1971) under the rubric of perceptual confusion – in association with possibly monosegmental representations for certain
clusters (cf. later in Sigurd 1975). (3) more general is the claim in Bailey
(1970), of unmarked status, i.e., preferred 'place' sequencing, for (a) non-
apical + apical, (b) dorsal + non-dorsal.

Although these principles are in partial confrontation, especially those
under 2 and 3, there seems support for them as independent factors, so that
language-specific choices are to be expected.

4.2. *Child language*

So far, we have no coherent deductive theory of metathesis[17] and it may well
prove to be a non-entity, a cover term for diverse process types. The child
data show scattered examples of only two of the three types mentioned so
far, for glide metathesis seems not to occur. The majority of cases are of the
Bailey type, though even there contradictory cases also occur.[18] Thus,

(1) Smith (1973) gives numerous examples
     (a) apical + non-apical in *asp, desk, helping, silver*: thus *aps, deks, sivl*;
     (b) but *magnet* and *violet* also metathesize, in violation of the principle.
(2) Grammont (1902) has cases of Bailey's dorsal-non dorsal type e.g.,
     (p. 72–73) while *quépic* remains, *paquet* → *capet, beaucoup* → *cópou,
     bouquet* → *coupé.*

(3) Drachman (1975) gives cases of distant metathesis from Greek. As is common, early forms are here often very complex, later forms more straightforward. Thus
   (a) *pondikáki* → *gokabé.to*; here, the metathesis is based on bisyllabic sequences;
   (b) *tsungrána* → *gudána, mikrófono* → *konítoto*; these are of Bailey type.

Yet a fourth type of metathesis converts C-Vowel-Resonant (Stop) sequences to form CRV syllables, e.g., *milk* → *mlik, self* → *slef* (Smith).
   But there are cases of yet a fifth metathesis type, one in all likelihood only found in child language. This one is dominated by the hierarchy of strength of place of articulation; the successive consonants in a word must be successively more retracted according to the 'place' hierarchy *p-t-k*[19]. Thus Ingram (1974) gives for English

   alligator → *daeg, animal* → *maenu, coffee* → *baki.*

(cf. below 5.1, and see Karek (1975) for a Hungarian case).
   Finally, rare cases of 'unprincipled' child metathesis also appear, e.g., (cited in Anttila 1972) that of an American girl, exposed to only Finnish in the home, who 'rather consistently' between two and four years of age simply interchanged all initial and final consonants, in addition to metathesizing stop-spirant clusters (though again, in both directions!).
   The processes of contact metathesis seem 'natural' enough, given a theory of syllable-structure. However, as with consonant harmony, they are for the child not natural in the strongest (Stampean) sense, i.e., they do not necessarily apply wherever they might — that is, without exception; worse, they do not even apply whenever they might — that is, they do not necessarily apply to forms at their debut: thus (Smith 1973), we find early forms such as *whisper* → *witkə, delve* → *delv*, but later *wiktə* and *devl*.

4.3. Metathesis in adult language
Adult languages attest the first four metathesis principles mentioned though hardly the fifth. Thus,

(1) Glide metathesis towards a nucleus occurs in Zoque (Elson – Pickett 1967), Korean (Koutsoudas 1966), Classical Greek (Kiparsky 1967), and Twana[20] (Drachman 1969).
(2) S-T metathesis occurs in Classical (and Modern) Hebrew, as well as (twice in the history of) Mandaic (Malone 1971); while
(3) Bailey's principles may be illustrated from Tagalog (Bloomfield 1933) and

Sudam Colloquial Arabic (Nida 1949, citing Trimingham 1946), as well as the English data he cites.

But there is yet a sixth source for metathesis, operating in South Sierra Miwok (Broadbent 1964), whereby a two-member cluster may be created by VC metathesis, but only in order to avoid a worse evil, viz., a three-member cluster (across a morpheme-boundary), everywhere forbidden in that language. A variant of the same principle is seen in Eskimo (Pyle 1971), where VC metathesis obviates creation of word-final CC clusters — but only if a word-internal CCC cluster is not thereby created. Such cluster-avoiding metathesis seems not to occur in child language, probably because cluster-simplification is the more powerful process over the time-span when metathesis is active[21].

4.4. Metathesis in history
History attests to all the processes referred to excepting almost certainly the sonority principle, as probably also cluster-avoidance.[22] Thus,

(1) *h*-glide metathesis occurred in all dialects of classical Greek (Kiparsky 1967)
(2) Stop-spirant metathesis is seen in Irish loans from English (Silva 1973).[23] It appears in its extremest form perhaps in the comparison of Tagalog and Ilocano (Anttila 1972), where it regularly switches S and T even across an intervening consonant, provided that consonant is not S or T (cf. Jensen's 1974 'relevancy' condition on rules).
(3) Bailey's principles operate in history, but (so far as I am aware) only sporadically, as, e.g., in Old English.
(4) The type C-V-R-C → CR-V-C is of course well attested in South Slavic, though the opposite tendency is also attested in history, as in Old English (*brid* → *bird*).

4.5. Conclusion on metathesis
There is again no coherency between child language and the other two modalities; for though there are types of metathesis in common, yet other types are unique to either child language or to adult language and history.

5. Epentheses and phonetic analogy

There are process sub-types found not uncommonly in child language which seem never to occur, even sporadically, in adult systems or in language change. I confine myself here to (1) unusual types of epenthesis, and (2) phonetic analogy.

5.1. Epenthesis

Unattested outside child language is glottal epenthesis with spirants,[24] a process not to be confused (as unfortunately in Smith 1973:123, and fn.1) with the common glottal substitution as found in Cockney [lıʔl] 'little', [ðæʔ] 'that'. Relevant forms here from Smith are [ba:ʔf] 'bath', [ha:ʔf] 'half'. Similar forms from German (Chromec, project notes) are [tu.ʔfm] 'Stufen', [íʔxe] 'Igel'.

Equally unattested in adult language is the word-final epenthetic spirant (Schourrup 1973) in forms like [bɛç] 'bed', [mɛç] 'meat', [wiç] 'grape'. As Schourrup (1973, fn. 5) points out these forms have lost a final consonant, and the added segment seems to match the function (though not the shape) of the Danish *stǿd*, viz., it prevents a front vowel in a (derived) open syllable from over-lengthening. That this is a reasonable explanation (i.e., that the data are not simply freakish) is supported by parallel data from the same corpus showing ʔ-epenthesis for similar forms with back vowels, e.g., [fuʔ] 'foot', [saʔ] 'socks'.

A further case of final epenthesis is cited in Ingram (1974) from Roussey (1899–1900). A French child showed data such as: *poupée* → [pəpɛt], *buchette* → [pəkɛkə], *Paris* → [pədɛč], in which the final consonant (Ingram argues) shows completion of a Front to Back place of articulation pattern.

A most interesting case of substitution with initial epenthesis is found in Smith (1973) again; this time we have to do with a strategy for replacing diverse unstressed initial syllables by an invariant [ri:-], later [in-] when the (adult) unstressed vowel is [i, ɛ, ı, or ə]. Thus, this occurs with [rı:-] in

(a) *deserve, elastic; enjoy, estate; disturb; attack; compare* [*-in*] later for
(b) *conductor, return, expensive.*

The analogical force of this process (cf. 5.2 below) seems to have been strong enough to extend even to one or two forms with stressed initial syllables; thus *energy* is reshaped to [rinə́:dzi:], and *Nigel* even gains the ubiquitous [ri:-] prefix to give [ri:náidzəl].

The converse case, viz., final epenthesis, is seen in Menn (1971), where words with final /-ejr/ took a final [-s] for a time, e.g., in *bear, hair, pair*; and cf. Stern (1927, Ch. 8) for addition of [-ä].

5.2. Phonetic analogy

A frequent phenomenon of child language is the sudden appearance of forms in which apparently sporadic processes have occurred. Thus, while [n] was early pronounced in Smith (1973), forms such as [bú:ke*nd*] *broken*, [*ŋ*gek] *neck* suddenly appear rather later; Velten (1943) reports a similar situation with [-st] for earlier (correct) [-s]. Both authors are agreed, however, that

the anomalous forms arose at the time the children had newly mastered
certain clusters (final NC, and -st, respectively).[25] It is thus clear that we
have to do with purely phonetic analogy of a developmental origin. Needless
to say such forms did not long survive.

6. Lexical diffusion

It is well documented and agreed that the child's progress in the mastery of
the pronunciation of his native language spreads, process for process, more
or less swiftly across his vocabulary: and this point too has been held to
show how child language is a miniature working model of diachronic linguistics. But again, there are important differences between what has been
claimed for the historical situation and what is known about 'lexical diffusion' in child language.

Thus, (1) the adult vocabulary is comparatively stable, while that of the
child grows explosively (cf. Chen – Wang 1975); (2) pronunciation improvements are first seen in 'new' words, while 'older' words may remain conservative in the child – though frequency may also play a role; (3) our picture
of the child's vocabulary may be blurred by his systematic avoidance of
words containing segments so far 'difficult' for him (Drachman 1973b); (4)
conversely, the expansion of word classes may be influenced by a deliberate
choice of words containing 'favored' segments (Ferguson – Farwell 1975)
and (5) it is also relevant to consider whether Wang's (1969) theory on
residues is sustained for child language, viz., that a given change, though
implemented abruptly, may not reach all the relevant morphemes as it dif-
fuses across the lexicon if another change competes for part of that lexicon.

I cite one set of cases, that of Velten (1943), where we see a spectrum for
diffusion, though with no indication that residues are being caused by competing processes. Thus, (1) suppression of C.S. word-initial voicing and word-
final unvoicing of consonants were very fast, with no residues; (2) on the
other hand, suppression of intervocalic voicing of consonants took three
months to reach 'most' of the vocabulary; while (3) early and frequent words
sometimes retained primitive shapes for some time – thus, *bang* → [ba] , and
remained so for many months after later CVC words were rendered as CVC.[26]
Cf. the case (Smith 1973) of labial harmony, which swept the vocabulary
immediately, as against that of velar harmony, which took six weeks to do so.
It remains to be investigated whether there are processes uniformly showing
instantaneous modification and others whose modification often or always
leaves residues in child language development.

It is not clear what status to assign to family-specific baby-talk words or other very early shapes surviving into the adult language of individuals, in this debate.

7. Suprasegmentals

Intonation and stress are probably the very first language-like elements to be noted in the vocalization of infants. By contrast to the segmentals, these elements are also (with reservations) correctly produced very early.

Thus, at a stage when the child produces no inflections whatever, placement of primary stress in isolated words shows only very sporadic errors. And indeed, stress (with the caveat in II.1 above) seems largely to determine the word-shapes that can be reproduced, or even (Waterson 1971) perceived and stored. Retardates, including mongoloids, acquire normal word-stress (Drachman 1975b). Not surprisingly, word-stress seems less resistant to disintegration under pathologies like motor aphasia or pure dysarthria.[27]

Stress alternations, however, whether phonologically or grammatically controlled, are mastered much later; in Greek, for some alternations not before 5 years of age, for others even later (Malikouti-Drachman – Drachman 1976). Similarly, the elements of compounds may at first carry level stress (Leopold 1939–49), while contrastive compound stress may be acquired as late as 12 years (Atkinson-King 1973).

In turn, tones within isolated words may be acquired very early, e.g., by 28 months for Chinese (Chao 1951); though again, tone-sandhi is mastered rather later. And intonation, though perhaps the earliest of these mechanisms to appear, is not mastered contrastively (i.e., in association with grammar) until several years have passed (Weir 1962).

The dichotomies sketched, i.e., early first use, but much later full mastery under syntagmatic and grammatical control, make it difficult to speculate on the role of primary acquisition in language change for stress, tone and intonation systems. It would seem, however, that system changes such as reversals in Scandinavian pitch patterns (Öhman 1967) or Japanese tones (McCawley, this volume) as also perhaps stress-shifts like that from Proto-Slavic to Old Czech, are to be associated with later acquisition stages if with child language at all.

8. 'Common' processes

The 'coherency hypothesis' set out above (I.2) is seriously brought into question by data such as those in II. 1–7. But as already pointed out, this does not mean that children do not in principle change language at all. Comparing distant assimilation (as in consonant harmonies) with contact assimilation, it is clear that the former presupposes the latter, which is to say that the latter is of course the more powerful process type. It stands to reason then, and it is also a fact, that contact assimilations "survive" primary acquisition and are thus processes common to all modalities. But it also follows (as Jespersen 1922 points out) that such processes in language change could as easily be attributed to children as to adults. Much the same point applies equally to historical cluster simplification (though perhaps not to cluster resolution by vowel epenthesis, as already mentioned).

What requires clarification, however, is whether *all* contact assimilation (and dissimilation?) sub-types apply across all modalities, for frequency, motivation, and hierarchies.

It remains to add that it is to such processes par excellence that the problem of the basis of articulation (Drachman 1973c) may in the end relate, while the "distant" processes discussed above are perhaps attributable more to higher level programming problems.

III. Conclusions

Stampe assumed without question that the processes are 'the same' across modalities, and by a brilliant conceptual leap concluded that the child thus causes historical sound change by failure to limit, suppress or order the relevant ones for his language. Stampe thus achieved what I have called a 'coherent' hypothesis. But of course neither he nor anyone else has ever examined longitudinal acquisition data to check the obviousness of the conclusion.

But what if the process sets across modalities are not "the same"? I have shown that certain processes have quite different motivations, that others show a different distribution of subtypes across modalities, and that many are 'common' and hence ambiguous to the problem of child versus adult in sound change. It is not clear whether there are any types of phonetic change which must be attributed to primary acquisition. Crucially, some processes very early suppressed by children are commoner in adult language than others later suppressed. Since, then, there are processes seen in adult language and history not attributable to learning failure in primary acquisition, the coherent hypothesis is an insufficient one.

And what if the processes in fact survive primary acquisition? Now Stampe of course supposes that many must, to enable casual speech outputs to occur. But he overlooks the fact that the more 'primitive' processes may in fact also be de-inhibited later, as is seen for instance in speech to young children, not to mention drunkenness or aphasia. On such a view, linguistically mature persons could as easily as children be responsible for sound change (cf. also II.8 on common processes), so that the coherent hypothesis is also an unnecessary one.

Thus the role of primary acquisition in language change seems to have been exaggerated. In particular, the conjecture we set out to examine, that the child's failure to limit universal processes in primary acquisition *is* sound change, is partly disconfirmed and partly not establishable.

Could a weaker 'coherent hypothesis' be sustained? One strategy might be to assert 'coherency' for the processes of adult language and those of language-change, dismissing the vexing child-language processes as mere 'development problems'. I should, however, personally wish to claim that the full set of phonetic processes is indeed universal, and accounts for all the data in all three modalities. But this presupposes more precision in the auxiliary hypotheses by which we account for the modality-specific nature of some processes, e.g., the doomed nature of some child-language processes I have discussed.[28]

Notes

1. Earlier versions of this paper were read at the Technische Universität Berlin, and at the Universities of München and Salzburg. For valuable written or oral comments I thank especially C. J. Bailey, W. U. Dressler, H. W. Eroms, A. Malikouti-Drachman, W. Mayerthaler, O. Panagl, H. J. Sasse and Th. Vennemann. Further acknowledgments are made at appropriate places in later footnotes. Exculpations go without saying.
2. For the proposition see, e.g., Schleicher (1861–62), Paul (1886:31), Ament (1899), Herzog (1904), Sturtevant (1917), de Saussure (1916), Baudouin de Courtenay (in Stankiewicz 1972), Sweet (1889), Halle (1962), Kiparsky (1971). Against, e.g., see the later Sweet (1900), Meringer (1908), and Jespersen (1922). Compare the complex version in Andersen (1973).
3. My sub-title is naturally adapted from Popper's book title.
4. Jakobson's (1941) powerful thesis of course antedates Stampe's by many years, but does not concern itself with phonetic processes as such. Stampe's conjecture is the first on phonetic process to be formulated precisely enough to be subject to refutation.
5. For a further point of probable non-overlap involving the vexed question of hierarchies, see my paper for the 3rd Phonology Meeting, Vienna, Sept. 1976, forthcoming
6. Yaaku is Eastern Cushitic, but is today spoken in a language area in which the obstruent systems have a single (marginal) dental spirant /s/ (e.g. South Nilotic). (Private communication, Sasse).
7. For $p \to f$, cf. Dressler (1974).
8. I do not here discuss syncope of medial syllables, a phenomenon common to all three 'modalities'. Greek data (Drachman 1975a) suggest syllable-loss is sometimes by process-succession, of V-loss and cluster reduction: but it is not clear how far

such processes are quantal in Lass' sense (this volume). A Greek example is /kapélo/ 'hat', rendered by one child (aged 2.6 years) as [pélo ~ papélo], but once also rendered [ʔpélo]. Clearly, we may postulate *kapélo, with (1) labial harmony or (2) syllable-loss. For (2), we further reasonably postulate kapélo→ [kpélo] → [pélo]. But should we also postulate, as first stages, [kəpelo] → [kəpélo]? Or even [kəpélo] → [kupélo] by assimilation, → [kupélo], etc.?

9. It is unclear whether 'last syllable is longer' plays a role.
10. Stable-stress languages are, on this hypothesis, the ones most likely to show the effect discussed: for languages with alternating stress, the habituation effect will be complexly bound to paradigms and sub-paradigms.
11. The alternative ("CV" program) theory predicts total reduplication, but says nothing of development to "only consonant harmony". For the present view, total reduplication simply results from total immaturity of tract control. Grammatical reduplication in adult language can hardly rest on such a primitive stage as first cause (i.e., in Stampe's sense). And assonance and rhyme in poetry (not to mention nursery rhymes, etc.) are further evidence for the 'survival' of such processes in adult intuition – see part III. The higher-level unifying power of such rhythmic processes in poetry constitutes, as it were, "the right-hemisphere's revenge". There is hardly space to do more than mention the fascinating discussion on child vs. adult rhyming that followed the presentation of this paper.
12. For the child at least (Vincent, this volume) the hypothesis that phonetics is the least 'accessible' part of language is hardly borne out.
13. See Stern (1928, Ch. 8) for a dramatic collapse: between 1.11 and 2.7 years, initial consonants are largely (but hierarchically) replaced by [x~h~∅]. I describe this case elsewhere.
14. McCawley points out that [prɪti] might be extra-systemic, and the later form a fresh acquisition. These are of course two quite separate claims: the first is (as they say) a notational variant of my own claim, while the second seems ad-hoc and unconfirmable, if also unfalsifiable!
15. Though Turkish is said to have expanded its harmony so. But cf. Hooper (1973): Vowel-harmony is morphologized in Granadese Spanish, where it partly distinguishes number in Noun and Adjectives and persons in the Verb. Lass points to South Dravidian, Swedish, and even Scots.
16. Contra Kim (this volume); though child data show very occasional dominance of unstressed vowels.
17. Bailey (1970) offers a pious hope, while Hjelmslev's (1970) 'order of expiration' theory is simply wrong, as Silva (1973) points out.
18. While French (Roussey 1899, 1900) shows agreement in élastique → [sakit], ma toque → [ma kot]; the two solitary cases in Norwegian (Vanvik, 1971) contradict Bailey: thus buksa → [buska], and seks → [sesk].
19. Contra Hjelmslev, cf. fn. 7. But cf. Menn (1973) for a counter-case.
20. In Korean, Greek, and Twana, glides metathesize across resonants; in Zoque, even across stops – e.g., pama 'clothes' m-bama 'my clothes', but p-y-ama 'his clothes'.
21. Vowel-epenthesis as a cluster-resolving mechanism is rather uncommon in early child-language, though it is common enough in the other modalities, as well as in dysarthria.
22. W. Winter reminds me of cluster-resolving metathesis in Armenian.
23. The metathesis [dz] → [zd] postulated between very early (Mycenean) and early (sub-Mycenean) Greek may belong here (Heubeck 1971): but cf. Bailey's interpretation (1968).
24. But cf. glottalization before plosives in English (Roach 1973).
25. Cf. Nadoleczny's case of Duten Ta Herr Dotta, for 'guten Tag, Herr Doktor' cited in Jakobson (1941) as hypercorrection, but more reasonably accounted for by distant assimilation (see II.3).

Dressler's child Elizabeth had *t*-epenthesis (a kind of harmony?) in 'Donau-*t*' and 'Tante Nova-*t*' from 2–3 years (personal communication Dressler). Lass reminds me of forms such as *drownde*d; Traugott of *whilst, among*st and '*gain*st; and Andersen of *thum*b.

26. Contrariwise, adult and historical lexical diffusion seems to be strongly affected by frequency.

27. Some pathologies in fact result in syllable-by-syllable pronunciation, which of course wipes out stress distinctions.

28. I have characterized the notion that "the full set of phonetic processes does (with suitable auxiliary hypotheses) account for the data in all modalities" as a weaker hypothesis. But this is so only in the face of Stampe's account of sound-change. If the processes are in fact in some sense always available, then my claim constitutes a competing strong coherency theory of process phonology: and this paper constitutes a first tentative statement of the required auxiliary hypotheses, at least so far as child language is concerned.

References

Ament, W.
   1899   *Die Entwicklung von Sprechen und Denken beim Kinde* (Leipzig).
Andersen, H.
   1973   "Abductive and deductive change", *Language* 49: 765–793.
Anttila, R.
   1972   *An introduction to historical and comparative linguistics* (New York: Macmillan).
Atkinson-King, K.
   1973   *Children's acquisition of phonological stress contrasts* (= *UCLA Working Papers in Phonetics* 25). [Ph.D. dissertation, UCLA.]
Bailey, C. J. N.
   1968   "The pronunciation of zeta in Ancient Greek", in: *Papers from the Fourth Regional Meeting, Chicago Linguistic Society*, pp. 177–193.
   1970   "Towards specifying constraints on phonological metathesis", *Linguistic Inquiry* 1.3: 347–349.
Bar-Adon, A.
   1971   "Primary syntactic structures in Hebrew child language", in: Bar-Adon – Leopold 1971, pp. 433–472.
Bar-Adon, A. – W. F. Leopold (eds.)
   1971   *Child language: A book of readings* (Englewood Cliffs, N.J.: Prentice-Hall).
Baudouin de Courtenay, J.
   1897   "Statement of linguistic principles", in: *A Baudouin de Courtenay anthology* (Ed.: E. Stankiewicz) (Bloomington, London: Indiana University Press, 1972), pp. 213–215.
Beeler, M. S.
   1970   "Sibilant harmony in Chumash", *IJAL* 36: 14–17.
Blasdell, R. C. – D. Jensen
   1970   "Stress and word position as determinants of imitation in first-language learners", *Journal of Speech and Hearing Research* 13: 193–202.
Bloomfield, L.
   1933   *Language* (New York: Holt).
Bond, Z.
   1971   *Units in speech perception* (= *Ohio State University Working Papers in Linguistics* 9) (Columbus, Ohio). [Ph.D. dissertation.]

Broadbent, S.
    1964   *The Southern Sierra Miwok language* (= *University of California Publications in Linguistics* 38) (Berkeley, Los Angeles: University of California Press).
Chao, Y. R.
    1951   "The Cantian idiolect: An analysis of the Chinese spoken by a 28-month-old child", in Bar-Adon – Leopold 1971, pp. 116–130.
Chen, M. Y. – W. S.-Y. Wang
    1975   "Sound change: Activation and implementation", *Language* 51: 255–281.
Drachman, G.
    1969   *Twana phonology* (= *Ohio State University Working Papers in Linguistics* 5) (Columbus, Ohio).
    1973a   "Baby talk in Greek", in: *Ohio State University Working Papers in Linguistics* 15, pp. 174–189.
    1973b   "Some strategies in the acquisition of phonology", in: *Issues in phonological theory* (Eds.: M. J. Kenstowicz, C. W. Kisseberth) (The Hague: Mouton), pp. 145–159.
    1973c   "Phonology and the basis of articulation", *Die Sprache* 19: 1–19.
    1975a   "Generative phonology and child language acquisition", in: *Phonologica 1972* (Eds.: W. U. Dressler, F. B. Mareš) (München: Fink), pp. 235–251.
    1975b   *Linguistic aspects of mongolism.* [Paper read at the Vienna meeting of Deutsche Gesellschaft für Aphasieforschung und –therapie.]
Dressler, W. U.
    1974   "Some diachronic puzzles for natural phonology", in: *Chicago Linguistic Society Parasession on natural phonology*, pp. 95–102.
Elson, B. – V. Pickett
    1967   *An introduction to morphology and syntax* (Santa Ana, California: Summer Institute of Linguistics).
Ferguson, C. A. – C. B. Farwell
    1975   "Words and sounds in early language acquisition", *Language* 51: 419–439.
Grammont, M.
    1902   "Observations sur le langage des enfants", in: *Mélanges linguistiques offerts à M. A. Meillet* (Paris: Klincksieck), pp. 61–82.
    1956   *Traité de phonétique* (Paris: Delagrave).
Grégoire, A.
    1937   *L'apprentissage du langage* (Paris: Droz).
Guile, T.
    1972   *On constraining the assimilation and dissimilation of place of articulation features.* [Paper read at the Christmas meeting of the Linguistic Society of America.]
Hall, R. A., Jr.
    1966   *Pidgin and Creole languages* (Ithaca, N.Y.: Cornell University Press).
Halle, M.
    1962   "Phonology in generative grammar", *Word* 18: 54–72.
Hashimoto, M. J.
    1970   "Internal evidence for Ancient Chinese palatal endings", *Language* 46: 336–365.
Herzog, E.
    1904   *Streitfragen der romanischen Philologie* (Madison, Wis.: University of Wisconsin Press).
Heubeck, A.
    1971   "Zur *s*- und *z*-Reihe in Linear B", *Kadmos* 10: 113–124.
Hjelmslev, L.
    1970   *Language* (Madison: University of Wisconsin Press).
Hooper, J. B.
    1973   *Aspects of natural generative phonology.* [Ph.D. dissertation, UCLA.]

Ingram, D.
1974   "Fronting in child phonology", *Journal of Child Language* 1: 233–241.
Jakobson, R.
1941   *Kindersprache, Aphasie und allgemeine Lautgesetze* (Uppsala: Almqvist & Wiksell).
Jensen, J. T.
1974   "A constraint on variables in phonology" [to appear in *Language*].
Jespersen, O.
1922   *Language. Its nature, development and origin* (London: George Allen and Unwin).
Karek, A.
1975   *The 'sonority hierarchy' in child phonology*. [Paper read at the Eighth International Congress of Phonetic Sciences.]
Kaufman, T.
1969   "Teco – a new Mayan language", *IJAL* 35: 154–174.
Kelkar, A.
1964   "Marathi baby talk", *Word* 20: 40–54.
Kinkade, M. D.
1973   "The alveopalatal shift in Cowlitz Salish", *IJAL* 39: 224–231.
Kiparsky, P.
1967   "Sonorant clusters in Greek", *Language* 43: 619–635.
1971   "Historical linguistics", in: *A survey of linguistic science* (Ed.: W. Dingwall) (College Park: University of Maryland), pp. 576–649.
Koutsoudas, A.
1966   *Writing transformational grammars: An introduction* (New York: McGraw-Hill).
Leopold, W. F.
1939-   *Speech development of a bilingual child: A linguist's record*. Vols. 1–4
49   (Evanston, Ill.: Northwestern University Press).
Lovins, J.
1972   "Southern Paiute /s/ and /c/", *IJAL* 38: 136–142.
Malikouti-Drachman, A. – G. Drachman
1976   "The acquisition of stress in Greek", in: *Salzburger Beiträge zur Linguistik* 2 (Ed.: G. Drachman) (Tübingen: Narr), pp. 277–289.
Malone, J. L.
1971   "Systematic metathesis in Mandaic", *Language* 47: 394–415.
Menn, L.
1971   "Phonotactic rules in beginning speech", *Lingua* 26: 225–251.
1973   "On the origin and growth of phonological and syntactic rules", in: *Papers from the Ninth Regional Meeting, Chicago Linguistic Society*, pp. 378–385.
1974   *A theoretical framework for child phonology*. [Paper read at the Summer Meeting of the Linguistic Society of America.]
Meringer, R.
1908   *Aus dem Leben der Sprache* (Berlin:Behr).
Moskowitz, A. I.
1970   *The acquisition of phonology* (= *Working Paper* 34, *Language Behavior Research Laboratory*).
Neisser, U.
1967   *Cognitive psychology* (New York: Appleton-Century-Crofts, Meredith).
Nida, E. A.
1949   *Morphology. The descriptive analysis of words*[2] (Ann Arbor: University of Michigan Press).
Öhman, S. E. G.
1967   "Word and sentence intonation: a quantitative model", in: *Quarterly Progress*

and *Status Report* 2–3, *Speech Transmission Laboratory* (Stockholm: Royal Institute of Technology), pp. 20–54.

Ohnesorg, K.
1959   *Another study in pedophonetics* (Brno: Universita).
Pačesová, J.
1968   *The development of vocabulary in the child* (Brno: Universita v Brně).
Paul, H.
1886   *Principien der Sprachgeschichte*² (Halle: Niemeyer).
Perkell, J. S.
1969   *Physiology of speech production* (Cambridge, Mass.: MIT Press).
Pernot, H.
1907   *Phonétique des parlers de Chio* (Paris).
Popper, K.
1963   *Conjectures and refutations* (London: Routledge and Kegan Paul).
Pyle, C.
1971   "West Greenlandic Eskimo and the representation of vowel length", *Papers in Linguistics* 3: 115–146.
Ramge, H.
1975   *Spracherwerb*² (Tübingen: Niemeyer).
Roach, P. R.
1973   "Glottalization of English /p/, /t/, /k/ and /tʃ/, a reexamination", *Journal of the International Phonetic Association* 1973: 10–21.
Roussey, C.
1899-   "Notes sur l'apprentissage de la parole chez un enfant", *La parole* 1899,
1900   11: 791–799, 12: 870–888; 1900, 1: 23–40, 2: 86–98.
de Saussure, F.
1916   *Cours de linguistique générale* (Paris: Payot).
Schleicher, A.
1861-   "Some observations made on children", in Bar-Adon – Leopold 1971,
62   pp. 19–20. [Translated from a note in *Beiträge zur vergleichenden Sprachforschung*.]
Schourrup, L.
1973   *The sources of phonetic segments in child language*. [Paper read at the Seventh Meeting of the South Eastern Conference of Linguists.]
Semiloff-Zelasko, H.
1973   "Glide metathesis", in: *Ohio State University Working Papers in Linguistics* 14, pp. 66–76.
Sigurd, B.
1975   "Linearization in phonology", in: *Phonologica 1972* (Eds.: W. U. Dressler – F. B. Mareš) (München: Fink), pp. 185–208.
Silva, C. M.
1973   "Metathesis of obstruent clusters", in: *Ohio State University Working Papers in Linguistics* 14, pp. 77–84.
Smith, N.
1973   *The acquisition of phonology* (Cambridge: Cambridge University Press).
Stampe, D. L.
1969   "The acquisition of phonetic representation", in: *Papers from the Fifth Regional Meeting, Chicago Linguistic Society*, pp. 443–454.
Stern, C. – W. Stern
1928   *Die Kindersprache*⁴ (Leipzig: Barth). [Reproduced 1975 by Wissenschaftliche Buchgesellschaft, Darmstadt.]
Sturtevant, E. H.
1917   *Linguistic change* (Chicago: University of Chicago Press).

Sundén, K.
    1904   *Elliptical words in modern English* (Uppsala).
Sweet, H.
    1899   *The practical study of languages* (London: Dent). [Reprinted in 1964 by
            Oxford University Press, London.]
    1900   *The history of language* (London: Dent).
Trager, F. H.
    1971   "The phonology of Picuris", *IJAL* 37: 29–33.
Trimingham, J.
    1946   *Sudan Colloquial Arabic* (London: Oxford University Press).
Ultan, R.
    1971   "A typological view of metathesis", in: *Stanford University Working Papers
            on Language Universals* 7, pp. 1–44.
Vanvik, A.
    1971   "The phonetic-phonemic development of a Norwegian child", *Norsk Tids-
            skrift for Sprogvidenskap* 24: 270–325.
Velten, H. V.
    1943   "The growth of phonemic and lexical patterns in infant language", *Language*
            19: 281–292.
Vihman, M. M.
    1971   "On the acquisition of Estonian", in: *Stanford Papers and Reports on Child
            Language Development* 3: 51–94.
Wang, W. S.-Y.
    1969   "Competing changes as a cause of residue", *Language* 45: 9–25.
Waterson, N.
    1971   "Some speech forms of an English child – a phonological study", *Transac-
            tions of the Philological Society of 1970*, pp. 1–24.
Weir, R.
    1962   *Language in the crib* (The Hague: Mouton).

WOLFGANG DRESSLER

How much does performance contribute to phonological change?

1.1. In opposition to traditional views that language change starts in performance (parole), generative grammarians have equated linguistic change with change in competence[1]. Due to the speculative character of argumentations and due to lack of historically documented phonetic details most of the claims and counterclaims made consisted in untestable ideas.

From phonological change I try to exclude detailed phonetic change (involving intrinsic allophones only, if a separation from extrinsic allophones is possible at all), and I definitely exclude — for my purpose — morphonological change, morphologization, restructuring, rule loss (all of these changes referring only or more to morphology rather than to phonology, and belonging undoubtedly to change in competence)[2]. Moreover, I concentrate on the origin, not on the spread of phonological change.

1.2. According to Anttila (1972:128 and in later studies) "most changes seem to be triggered by performance". Performance[3] contains variation due to imperfect control, to imperfect articulatory organs, to memory restrictions, slips of the tongue or of the ear, other errors such as involuntary contaminations, variation due to fluctuations in attention and to inadvertence[4], to confusions, to playfulness, etc., and individual "biophonetic" characteristics (see Trojan 1975), which can not be described by rules.

Of course it is very difficult to ascertain what various authors mean by competence and performance (cf. Linell 1974:19ff); moreover competence and performance, for most authors, are inseparable from one another. Therefore I must stick to cases which are generally thought of as performance deviations from competence, i.e., the above-mentioned deviations from correct performance (as intended by competence and as described by rules of the grammar). Therefore my question really is whether and how many types of sound changes can be attributed to performance changes which anticipate correlated changes of competence in such a way that this "anticipation" could be (possibly) observed or at least inferred. Only after having answered this question can one try to grapple with the question which came first: the chicken or the egg, i.e., whether, in general, sound change originates in competence or in performance or in both.

In performance hypotheses sound change is said to be (always or most of the time) the result of random vacillations and gradual fluctuations, to be imperceptible, to be due to ease of articulation or to individual tendencies, to result from the inability of the individual to produce exactly the sounds which he hears, to be due to stylistic fluctuations, to be of a statistical nature, etc.

1.3. As is well known, generative grammarians have claimed that sound change originates in competence. Their arguments have been of a theoretical and/or speculative nature. Empirical evidence against performance hypotheses of sound change have been rarely advanced, e.g., the abruptness of many types of sound change — but also slips of the tongue and other mere performance substitutions can be abrupt; grammatical conditions of sound change; the describability of sound change by means of abstract rule change.

As the exact origin of sound change can never be observed or captured in a direct way[5], I want to discuss in an indirect, but at least partially empirical, way the amount of sound change types that have been or may be attributed to origins lying in performance, and that seem not to have attracted enough empirical discussion in the literature.

2. Sound change due to **loans** (from a substratum, superstratum, or adstratum) is probably the case where possible origins of phonological change can be most easily ascertained. Imperfect application of phonological rules of the target language by speakers of a source language (cf. Fasching 1973) is often seen as due to lack of competence in the target language, or more precisely performance errors. However, we must distinguish between confusion errors which can not be directly traced back to a model in the source language on the one hand, and transpositions of parts of the competence in the source language into the target language on the other.

The former errors are performance errors — often of a random nature — which seem not to have any chance to survive in future generations of speakers of the target language; the latter ones represent a deviant, calqued competence which can be described as rule or segment borrowing. Thus sound change (in the sense of rules or laws) originating in language interference is not based on performance (as distinct from competence).

A striking example of diachronic rule interference can be seen in the Poitevinian dialect of Galloromance (Gamillscheg 1937:80—92): French (and

Provençal) transformed *t* to *d* between sonorants, the langue d'oc *d* to *z*; the transition dialect of Poitevinian telescoped both changes to t > z.

3. Many authors — especially in the 19th and early 20th centuries — have derived much of sound change from speech errors (slips of the tongue, including non-analogical contaminations). This view seems to go back to the very origins of methodical, systematic work done in comparative philology, where language change has been described in analogy to the history of texts: here philologists have to deal with manuscript copying and have to reconstruct stemmata according to common errors (= shared innovations) of manuscripts (cf. Hoenigswald 1973:25 ff). A related root is the 19th-century equation of language change with corruption.

Both views are completely outdated today. Moreover performance errors cannot have the necessary prestige for spreading and becoming institutionalized innovations or rules[6]. This (speculative) reasoning can be backed up by empirical evidence.

3.1. (Non-analogical) **contaminations** in speech errors are rather different from blends in language diachrony (see Dressler 1976a): e.g., the well-known case of the Latin genitives *jecinis* and *jecoris* "of the liver"resulting in *jecinoris* shows a resulting form which is longer than both source forms, and which has a different stress pattern, whereas contaminatory errors result in forms which retain the length of the source forms, if they have already identical length; moreover they retain their stress patterns most of the time.

According to Paul (1920:160–2) diachronic contamination nearly always occurs between words which are either etymologically related or suppletive or antonymous, which is not the case at all in speech errors (see Dressler 1976a § 13). Cases of institutionalized blends which fit the statistical tendencies in speech errors are rather rare (cf. Wood 1911:1973 ff), e.g., *br/unch* from *br/eakfast* and *lunch*.

Most, if not (nearly) all historical blends are either of an analogical nature (and not phonological contaminations such as many errors) or are consciously coined or are due to interference between two dialects, e.g. *g/alancer* (Geneva, Savoy) from *gangaler* and *b/alancer* "to balance" (cf. Goebl 1976), i.e., they exhibit an interference of two competences (see 2). Finally blends never result in phonological change, as it is commonly understood.

3.2. Non-contaminatory **slips** of the tongue (cf. Meringer — Mayer 1895, Meringer 1908, Fromkin 1973) are generated by syntagmatic influences, mostly at a distance ("Fernwirkungen"), such as assimilatory (more rarely dissimilatory) anticipation and preservation, assimilatory increment, and

dissimilatory loss. Parallels in diachronic change are sporadic word deformations such as Italian *cocodrillo* "crocodile" from Ancient Greek *krokódilos*.
Thus there are sporadic cases of vocabulary change (of a phonological nature)
that probably originated in performance.

Sporadic distant processes which were applied in isolated words either
optionally or obligatorily (with restructuring in general) seem to be due to
the same psychological factors of performance (Schopf 1919:35 ff) as
parallel slips. Thus here we may have a good case of sound change originating
in performance, being later sanctioned by competence (first of isolated
speakers, then socially accepted)[7]; but this holds only for very few words of
a language, e.g. Italian *albero* "tree" from late Latin *arbore(m)*.

However, many slips such as *lawfully joined* → *jawfully loined* (Fromkin
1973:245 C.9) violate (also as in aphasic errors) the relevancy condition (or
crossover constraint; cf. Howard 1975:112 ff), which holds in distant assimilations, dissimilations, and metatheses of natural languages. The example *Kathy
can type* → *tathy can type* shows, in addition, a distant process between non-
neighboring words (cf. Schopf 1919:51), whereas in natural language grammars
distant processes occur only within the same word or, very rarely, between
closely connected neighboring words, e.g. Latin *aulam extarem* (Plautus,
Rudens) from *aulam extalem*, if this is not an error itself. As with violations
of the relevancy condition, slips go with recorded substitutions in aphasia
and child language.

Among speech errors there occur distant metatheses where single distinctive features are moved (as in aphasia), e.g. *Lebanon* → *Lemadon, pedestrian*
→ *tebestrian* (cf. Fromkin 1973:17, 223 ff, 252 ff), a type of metathesis
which so far has been cited in historical linguistics only for the feature [voiced],
and even here only as a very rare phenomenon, i.e. Span. *gritar < cridar,
gretar* < Lat. *crepitare* (via *credar*, see Schopf 1919:190 f).

3.3. **Perceptual errors**[8] are very complex and cannot possibly give rise to
"sound laws"[9]. If J. Ohala (in the abstract for this conference) claims that
"sound change originates not as 'grammar change', but as a misapprehension
of the speech signal"[10], then he seems to refer, if I understand him correctly,
either to systematic substitutions in child language acquisition (i.e. competence, cf. 4 for abductive change) or to perception experiments with
isolated sounds, logatoms or words, or to word pairs in identical sentence
frames that rarely occur outside the experimental situation. But these
experiments are hardly comparable to conditions in actual speech situations
where phonological change of adults would originate. Systematic mis-perception of phonemes of allophones either occur as contact phenomena (i.e.
interferences of competences, see 2) or in language disturbances such as

aphasia (i.e., disturbance or loss of competence). If isolated words or names
are restructured due to misperception, this does not constitute a sound change.

3.4. Rogger and Hermann (1931:88) hypothesized that **popular etymologies**
(paretymologies) are due to perceptual reinterpretation. These involve, however, semantics and derivational morphology or lexical analysis, and are thus
neither theoretically nor empirically the source of phonological change.
Bredsdorff (1821:12) tried to explain them rather by restrictions of memory
reliability.

3.5. Reimold (1974:42—4) has proposed a type of natural phonological
processes which he calls "sloppy timing rules": they would explain the inter-
change between *prints* and *prince* in casual speech, i.e. [ns~nts]. In addition
to casual speech, such changes occur both in slips (also in disturbances) and
in optional or obligatory phonological change. Barnitz (1974) attributes the
genesis of all these substitutions to performance. In slips (and in puns) these
substitutions are quite optional whereas in diachronic change we find often
obligatory, regular or lexically diffused change, which might be generalizations by competence. I do not know of any specific studies of such substitutions in casual speech. Due to the rather anecdotal state of evidence in this
area (with the exception of diachrony), I cannot judge the hypothesis that
this is a sound-change originating in performance (cp. Ohala 1974a:357—359).

3.6. I do not want to give the impression of grossly undervaluing the importance of articulatory, acoustic, and perceptual phonetics for phonological
change. Literature, rightly, abounds with notes on sound changes involving
only small articulatory changes. And Jonasson (1971:38) may be quite right
in saying that "the probability of a phonological change is inversely correlated
with the perceptual distance between segments".
    But I maintain that it is not the organs themselves that are responsible for
the change, e.g., by sloppiness or erroneous functioning, but that it is the
brain, which is quite aware of the articulatory and perceptual possibilities
and restrictions of the speech and hearing apparatus. Therefore it is in order
to avoid mis-perception[11] that some sounds are changed to more readily
perceivable ones. Or, another type of change, phonological processes of
casual speech where certain perceptual distinctions are blurred and less
attention is paid to preserving articulatory distinctions, are generalized to
formal speech[12].
    Thus even sound changes which have a very clear relation to general
articulatory and acoustic constraints, can be said to be mentalistic and to
reflect change in competence[13]. The same holds for language specific con-

straints: e.g. German does not tolerate the vocalic sequence [iø] ; therefore the learned word *Diözese* "diocesis" (of Greek origin) is metathesized in ordinary speech (at least in Austria) to [die'cφ:zə] . Although this metathesis is unconscious (and no adult acquainted with this word would dream of writing *Diezöse*), it is not a performance error, but (for most speakers) a split between language competence and orthographic competence.

4. Child-language acquisition is thought to be the principal source of phonological change by most linguists nowadays[14] . If a process of child language (such as A. Meillet's French example of [λ] → [i̯] (or final devoicing of obstruents)) is said to initiate phonological change, then it is a question of general and systematic substitutions, reflecting the (older) child's competence, and this even in the case of incipient lexical diffusion.

To my knowledge there are no systematic studies of performance aspects of child language (with the partial exception of Hsieh 1972; Chen – Wang 1975:263 ff), though it is recognized, e.g., "that the sound fluctuations in children's spontaneous speech are sometimes due to imperfect control ˑnd slips of the tongue or playfulness" (Bodine 1974:5). A prominent type of possible performance processes of the child are distant processes (e.g., distant assimilations), which Drachman (1975:242) compares with slip processes. But since such distant processes are more and more restricted and finally nearly suppressed in later stages of child language, chances of their survival as diachronic changes are slim (cf. Drachman, this volume).

Besides (primary) articulatory substitutions, perceptual reinterpretations have been put forward as sources of phonological change, particularly in connection with Andersen's (1973) notion of abductive change and with experimental perceptual (and acoustic) phonetics. But perceptual theories of child substitutions (if they differ from perceptual theories of adult substitutions) hinge on the maturational development of perception and thus refer to physiological restrictions of competence. If one calls them a part of performance (to the exclusion of competence), then one could not avoid the absurd consequence (exposed for aphasia by H. Whitaker), that even the elimination of the physiological basis of competence (e.g., by lobectomy) would not affect competence itself, but only performance. Therefore I follow those (e.g., Troike 1969) who postulate the existence of receptive competence as part of general linguistic competence. Performance related misapprehensions are hardly the source of phonological change (see above III.3)[15] .

5.1. Another performance-based source of phonological change is said to be stylistic fluctuations and style change (cf. Samuels 1972:177). The performance character of such variation seems to be corroborated by its frequent psychological induction (cf. Vanecek — Dressler 1975), its statistical character, and its random phonetic zones of dispersion (cf. Labov — Yaeger — Steiner 1972).

However Labov's pioneering studies concern spread rather than origin of sound-change (e.g., of vowel raising in American English)[16]. The ultimate causes of such finely graded stylistic or sociolinguistic changes are social changes, as Labov and other sociolinguists have shown, i.e., they reflect changes in sociolinguistic competence and undoubtedly not sociologically unmotivated changes in psychological factors such as attention and emotion[17]. Here the idealized, purely linguistic Chomskyan notion of competence must be extended to the notion of sociolinguistic competence, as has been widely argued in recent literature (cf. the discussion in Dittmar 1973:200—95).

5.2. Also the influence of the frequency of occurrence of words (cf. Mańczak, this volume)[18], which might be called a performance factor, can be explained only by means of sociolinguistic reasoning which includes parts of sociolinguistic competence (cf. Dressler 1973:137—138). One incentive to choose a more casual style is greater familiarity or acquaintance with parts of the speech situation[19]; high frequency is one factor of familiarity; words used belong to the speech situation; casual styles show more generalized processes of weakening and deletion than more formal styles. Thus, it is explainable that the speaker may choose for frequent words or morphemes more casual (= weakened, mutilated) forms. But such choices appertain to sociolinguistic competence as well as generalizations of more casual style forms in general; they do occur also in accordance with natural process hierarchies as permitted in the style ranges of a language.

5.3. Also phenomena of drift, such as parallel innovations in distant, but cognate dialects (e.g., umlaut and fortition in different Germanic dialects) cannot be considered as good evidence for slow, random phonetic changes in performance. We can hypothesize (cf. Dressler 1973:144 f., 1975:230) that these innovations existed already in casual styles before the dialect split, only the generalization from casual to formal styles (that usually are the only attested styles in historic documents) would then be an independent parallel innovation in those separated dialects. This hypothesis, a hypothesis based on the basis of articulation, and a performance-hypothesis would now have to be compared and checked.

5.4. Lexical diffusion (Chen — Wang 1975, Hsieh 1972, Chen 1972) seems to propagate in a random fashion, and this random character might be attributed to performance.

However, there seem to exist cases where this random character is severely restricted by grammatical constraints. In Scottish Gaelic[20] original *ē* has been broken (diphthongized) to *ia, eu*, etc. (according to the specific dialect), in various degrees in the dialects. It occurred first and in most dialects in the ordinal number *a'chiad* "the first", then in the cardinal numbers *diag* "ten" and *sia* "six", then in various lexical items; the last and least frequent item to undergo breaking has been the proper name *Siamas* "James". Here lexical diffusion has been governed by grammatical classes, with sound change occurring first in number names, where sound changes are often anticipated (cf. Dressler 1973:135); the conservative character of proper names is equally well-known. The lexicon proper (common nouns, etc.) is much less organized and does not exhibit such clear-cut compartmentalizations, therefore lexical diffusion may be implemented in a rather random fashion.

Secondly, lexical diffusion belongs to spread, not to the origin of sound changes, such as the changes in 5.1—3.

Thirdly, with the exception of early child language (Hsieh 1972, cf. Drachman, this volume) lexical diffusion generally seems to apply to specific lexical items in a categorical way, not in an optional one. Such categorical choices cannot belong to performance only.

6. Among the phenomena of *language death* or language decay (cf. Dressler 1972) one finds instances of confusion and random behavior, e.g. some young Bretons (Dressler 1972:454) vary freely between apical [r] (the original dialect pronunciation), uvular [R] (their French pronunciation), approximant [ɹ] and fricative [ř], which both have no model or antecedent in Breton or French. These sounds then may be new allophonic realizations which belong to performance only. But the cause of their genesis is decay or loss of competence (comparable to aphasia). Further stages of such advanced language decay are a new competence calqued from the competence of the victorious language or language death, i.e., complete loss of competence in one language. Thus such phenomena are totally different from phonological change in the sense of innovations in the development of a vigorous language.

In language decay we find the unique case of competence without performance, e.g., the last native speakers of Manx were (and still are?) competent speakers of Manx (at least in the restricted sense of semi-speakers, cf. N. Dorian, forthcoming), but lately they have never spoken to each other (except on the rare occasions brought about by linguists or celtophiles), thus there was no Manx performance (I do not know whether they still dreamt or monologued in Manx). In language disturbances and in child language we find cases of both competence without performance and of performance without competence.

7. Finally, there is one very delicate type of sound change which is very different from the discrete quanta of rule change in the sense of generative grammar: changes in the **basis of articulation**[21] (cf. already Passy 1890:244 f). That this may be a possible primary source of sound change, is indicated by the existence of different bases of articulation within the area of the same language, e.g., North German and South German dialects diverge markedly in their respective bases of articulation.

But as Drachman (1973) has convincingly stated, a language-specific basis of articulation is a unifying force of high complexity that children have to learn in order to speak their respective language properly. Thus it must be part of their competence, and we may speculate, that also changes in the basis of articulation are subject to mental control (competence).

It is questionable whether sound-change might originate directly as a basis change at all, for in this case all members of a sound-class (be it phonemes or allophones) would have to be subject to the process at the same time. There would be no place for lexical diffusion, as it seems to be absurd to postulate that any adult (or older child that has settled for a definite basis of articulation) would use different bases for identical segments of different words. Therefore adherents of the theory of lexical diffusion (and of sound-change originating as style change, 5.2—4) could allow primary changes in the basis only in two cases: (1) if a language is taken over by a new population with a different basis of articulation, (2) if children "decide" to learn a new basis of articulation which differs from the basis of their parents and (older) siblings. Then lexical diffusion would have taken place before they would have decided about their definite basis of articulation. Otherwise changes in the basis of articulation would be secondary, i.e., reorganizations of the basis in view of new processes having entered (i.e., being allowed or "accepted" by) the language.

8. My tentative conclusions are these. We know little about how and where phonological change originates, but insofar as we can argue about it and use empirical arguments (at least *per analogiam*), the outlook is very bleak that much of phonological change may originate in performance, with competence trying to catch up with previous changes in performance (Kiparsky 1970:305, pace Koch 1970). The primary cause of nearly all of sound-change seems to be change in competence or simultaneous change in competence and performance. Most of the time, changes and variations in performance are only, very trivially, the (Aristotelian) **causa materialis** of sound-change.

Notes

1. E.g., Postal (1968). The mentalistic character of sound change has been well articulated already by Bréal (1897:7, cf. 10): "C'est donc dans l'intelligence, dans le cerveau, qu'il faut chercher la cause première des changements phoniques" and "La volonté cessant de surveiller les organes, ceux-ci obéissent à leurs propensions. Mais de ces propensions il y a si loin à des nécessités, qu'un peu d'attention, un léger retour de volonté suffit pour remettre les choses au point".
2. Anttila (1974:63 ff, 83, 137 ff) and others (cited there) think that analogy rather starts in performance.
3. Beyond normal (and institutionalized) correct actualization of competence, where competence and performance cannot be well distinguished *for our purposes.*
4. For our purposes, only insofar as they are induced by psychological factors, with the exclusion of sociopsychological factors (cp. Vanecek-Dressler 1975).
5. E.g., if sound change starts with an individual innovator of the change ("Sprachschöpfer", cf., e.g., Schuchardt 1971:137), this particular innovator is irretrievable.
6. Pound (1914:21, 58) reports about the nonce blend *sweedle* ← *swindle* and *wheedle* that has subsisted in the speech of one Nebraskan family, and about the contamination *trinkle* ← *trickle* and *twinkle* that was "in occasional use by adults and children" in his time.
7. Unfortunately neither Schopf (1919) nor Grammont (1895) distinguish systematically between errors (either oral slips as in Meringer-Mayer 1895 or written errors in inscriptions and manuscripts) and definite changes of word forms in a language or a dialect.
8. As far as one can tell from the very rare studies on misperception of words in actual speech situations, see Meringer – Mayer (1895:157–59), Meringer (1908:142–43), Garnes – Bond (1975): e.g. *Cupid → Cuban, dental → dinner* etc. In my opinion such cases of mishearing should be separated from the principle of acoustically printed monitoring.
9. One of the earliest claims about sound change being due to erroneous hearing and understanding is to be found in Bredsdorff (1821:9). Later Kruszewski (1883:71) speaks of inaccuracy of perception ("Ungenauigkeit der Auffassung").
10. Ohala (1974a:378) even thinks that "The origin of velar softening may have involved the misperception of a [ki] sequence as [tʃi] or [si] ". But this is highly unlikely, as the palatalization rules of the type [ki → či] (not to speak of [ki → si]) seem to have been telescoped from at least two processes: [k → kʲ, kʲ → č] (cf. Dressler 1976b § 3.4.2.3).
11. This holds also for the arguments in Chen – Wang (1975:270, 274 ff.).
12. Ohala (1974a:368) passingly dismisses "ease of articulation" and "perceptual needs" without any in-depth discussion of the various explanatory possibilities that lie in these and related notions, and which could supplement Ohala's own line of research without contradicting it.
13. If I interpret Andersen's (1974) system correctly, "perceptually induced sound changes" correspond to his abductive changes, and they are innovations due to specific decisions of the speakers as to how to interpret perceptually ambiguous or unclear sound productions.
14. I do not accept the highly divergent view of G. Drachman (this volume) although I have myself exposed discrepancies between child language acquisition and diachrony in Dressler (1974a), and although our views coincide enough elsewhere.
15. There are other problems with perceptual hypotheses of phonological change: (1) Often they do not predict the directionality of sound change: e.g. $t > w, k^W > p$, but never $*w > t, *p > k^W$. It is true though, that in recent literature the unidirectionality of some alternations is made clear, see Ohala (1974b), Thurgood – Javkin (1975).

16. Labov (like many others nowadays) sees not much point in distinguishing origin and spread of sound change. Nevertheless in studying explicitly "sound changes in progress" he indicates clearly that he is primarily interested in propagation, not in origin.
17. E.g. Germanic tribes supposedly having got more emotionally aggressive during the Great Migrations, thus, have been thought of provoking therefore the 2nd Sound Shift — and even that would constitute a certain sociopsychological motivation!
18. Already proposed by H. Schuchardt (see Vennemann-Wilbur 1971:25) and by Bréal (1897:4), cf. Malmberg (1971:285).
19. Malmberg (1971:285) relates this to information theory: more frequent, i.e., predictable, words can be reduced more easily.
20. Jackson (1968). This article has been brought to my attention by David Clement (Edinburgh); more research is needed in this subject.
21. And possibly basis of perception?

References

Andersen, H.
   1973   "Abductive and deductive change", *Language* 49: 765–793.
   1974   "Towards a typology of change: Bifurcating changes and binary relations", in: *Proceedings of the First International Conference on Historical Linguistics* 2 (Eds.: J. M. Anderson – C. Jones) (Amsterdam: North-Holland), pp. 17–60.
Anttila, R.
   1972   *Introduction to historical and comparative linguistics* (New York: Macmillan).
   1974   *Analogy* (= *Dress Rehearsals* 1) (University of Helsinki, Department of Linguistics).
Barnitz, J.
   1974   "Bloom-p-field, Chom-p-sky, and phonetic epen-t-thesis", *Studies in the Linguistic Sciences* 4, 2: 1–13.
Bodine, A.
   1974   "A phonological analysis of the speech of two mongoloid (Down's syndrome) boys", *Anthropological Linguistics* 16: 1–24.
Bréal, M.
   1897   "Des lois phoniques", *Mémoires de la Société de Linguistique de Paris* 10: 1–11.
Bredsdorff, J. H.
   1821   *Über die Ursachen der Sprachveränderungen* (Trsl.: U. Petersen) (Tübingen: Narr, 1975).
Chen, M.
   1972   "The time dimension: Contributions toward a theory of sound change", *Foundations of Language* 8: 457–498.
Chen, M. – W. S.-Y. Wang
   1975   "Sound change: Actuation and implementation", *Language* 51: 255–281.
Dittmar, N.
   1973   *Soziolinguistik* (Frankfurt: Fischer Athenäum).
Dorian, N.
   forthcoming "The problem of the semi-speaker in language death", in: *Special issue of the International Journal of the Sociology of Language on 'language death'* (Eds.: W. Dressler – R. Leodolter).
Drachman, G.
   1973   "Phonology and the basis of articulation", *Die Sprache* 19:1–19.
   1975   "Generative phonology and child language acquisition", in: Dressler – Mareš, pp. 235–251.

Dressler, W.
1972   "On the phonology of language death", in: *Papers of the Eighth Regional Meeting of the Chicago Linguistic Society*, pp. 448–457.
1973   "Pour une stylistique phonologique du latin", *BSL* 68: 129–145.
1974   "Diachronic puzzles for natural phonology", in: *Parasession on natural phonology of the Chicago Linguistic Society*, pp. 95–102.
1975   "Methodisches zu Allegro-Regeln", in: Dressler – Mareš, pp. 219–231.
1976a   "Tendenzen in kontaminatorischen Fehlbildungen (und ihre Beziehung zur Sprachgeschichte)", *Die Sprache* 22: 1–10.
1976b   "Morphologization of phonological processes", in: *Linguistic studies presented to Joseph H. Greenberg* (Ed.: A. Juilland) 2: 313–337.
Dressler, W. – F. Mareš (eds.)
1975   *Phonologica 1972* (München: Fink).
Fasching, P.
1973   "Phonologische Adaptionsprozesse beim Zweitspracherwerb", *Wiener linguistische Gazette* 3: 3–24.
Fromkin, V. (ed.)
1973   *Speech errors as linguistic evidence* (The Hague: Mouton).
Gamilscheg, E.
1937   *Romanisches. Ausgewählte Aufsätze* (= *Zeitschrift für Romanische Sprachwissenschaft*, Supplement 15).
Garnes, S. – Z. S. Bond
1975   "Slips of the ear: Errors in perception of casual speech", in: *Papers of the Eleventh Regional Meeting of the Chicago Linguistic Society*, pp. 214–225.
Goebl, H.
1976   "Wortkontamination und Diasystem", in: *Innsbrucker Beiträge zur Sprachwissenschaft* (Ed.: W. Meid), 18: 93–129.
Golick, M.
1974   "Phonological development: Does misperception play a role in children's misarticulations?", in: *Montreal Working Papers in Linguistics* 1, pp. 109–122.
Grammont, M.
1895   *La dissimilation consonantique dans les langues indo-européennes et dans les langues romanes* (Dijon: Darantière).
Hermann, E.
1931   *Lautgesetz und Analogie* (Berlin: Weidmann).
Hoenigswald, H. M.
1973   *Studies in formal historical linguistics* (Dordrecht: Reidel).
Howard, I.
1975   "Can the 'elsewhere condition' get anywhere?", *Language* 51: 109–127.
Hsieh, H.
1972   "Lexical diffusion: Evidence from child language acquisition", *Glossa* 6: 89–104.
Jackson, K.
1968   "The breaking of original long ē in Scottish Gaelic", in: *Celtic studies for A. Matheson* (Eds.: J. Carney – D. Greene) (London: Routledge), pp. 65–71.
Jonasson, J.
1971   "Perceptual similarity and articulatory reinterpretation as a source of phonological innovation", in: *Papers of the Institute of Linguistics, University of Stockholm* 8, pp. 30–42.
Kiparsky, P.
1970   "Historical linguistics", in: *New horizons in linguistics* (Ed.: J. Lyons) (Harmondsworth: Penguin), pp. 302–315.
Koch, W. A.
1970   *Zur Theorie des Lautwandels* (Hildesheim: Olms).

Kruszewski, M.
1883   "Prinzipien der Sprachentwicklung", in: *Sprachwandel* (Ed.: D. Cherubim)
        (Berlin: de Gruyter, 1975), pp. 62–77.
Labov, W. – M. Yaeger – R. Steiner
1972   *A quantitative study of sound change in progress* (NSF Report) (Philadelphia:
        University of Pennsylvania).
Linell, P.
1974   "Problems of psychological reality in generative phonology", in: *Reports
        from Uppsala University, Department of Linguistics* 4.
Malmberg, B.
1971   "La notion de 'force' et les changements phonétiques", in: B. Malmberg,
        Phonétique générale et romane (The Hague: Mouton), pp. 281–286.
        [Originally published in 1962.]
Meringer, R.
1908   *Aus dem Leben der Sprache (Versprechen, Kindersprache, Nachahmungstrieb)*
        (Berlin: Behr).
Meringer, R. – K. Mayer
1895   *Versprechen und Verlesen* (Stuttgart: Göschen).
Ohala, J.
1974a   "Experimental historical phonology", in: *Proceedings of the First Inter-
        national Conference on Historical Linguistics* 2, pp. 353–389.
1974b   "Phonetic explanation in phonology", in: *Parasession on natural phonology
        of the Chicago Linguistic Society*, pp. 251–274.
Passy, P.
1890   *Études sur les changements phonétiques et leurs caractères généraux* (Paris:
        Firmin-Didot).
Paul, H.
1920   *Prinzipien der Sprachgeschichte*[5] (Halle: Niemeyer).
Postal, P.
1968   *Aspects of phonological theory* (New York: Harper and Row).
Pound, L.
1914   *Blends. Their relation to English word formation* (Heidelberg: Winter).
Reimold, P.
1974   "Phonologische Feature-Systeme und die strukturelle Definition natürlicher
        phonologischer Regeln", *Linguistische Berichte* 33: 27–46.
Samuels, M. L.
1972   *Linguistic evolution with special reference to English* (Cambridge: Cambridge
        University Press).
Schopf, E.
1919   *Die konsonantischen Fernwirkungen* (Göttingen: Vandenhoeck und Ruprecht
Thurgood, G. – H. Javkin
1975   "An acoustic explanation of a sound change: *-ap* to *-o*, *-at* to *-e*, and *-ak*
        to *-æ*", *Journal of Phonetics* 3: 161–166.
Troike, R. C.
1969   "Receptive competence, productive competence, and performance", in:
        *Linguistics and the teaching of Standard English to speakers of other
        languages or dialects* (Ed.: J. E. Alatis) (= *Monograph Series on Languages
        and Linguistics* 22) (Washington, D.C.: Georgetown University Press),
        pp. 63–74.
Trojan, F.
1975   *Biophonetik* (Mannheim: Bibliographisches Institut).
Vanecek, E. – W. Dressler
1975   "Bericht über psycholinguistische Experimente zur Sprechvariation",
        Wiener linguistische Gazette 9: 17–38.

Vennemann, T. – T. Wilbur
    1971   *Schuchardt, the neogrammarians, and the transformational theory of phono-
            logical change* (Frankfurt: Athenäum).
Wood, F.
    1911   "Iteratives, blends, and 'Streckformen' ", *Modern Philology* 9: 157–194.

MARTIN B. HARRIS

The inter-relationship between phonological and grammatical change

Although the concept of syntactic drift dates back at least to the writings of
Sapir (1921), recent work in the field seems to have needed a catalyst in the
shape of the clear and systematic presentation of a number of 'syntactic
universals', above all by Joseph Greenberg (Greenberg 1966[1]). Largely on
the basis of these insights, we have seen the rapid development of an extremely
convincing language typology based on the observed fact that there is a clear
correlation between the relative ordering of a variety of different constituents,
and between these patterns of ordering and a number of other important
morphosyntactic characteristics such as for example the degree of reliance
placed on suffixed case-endings. In general, one of these features, namely the
relative ordering in simple sentences of the verb and its direct object, is,
implicitly or explicitly, accorded priority — a point which we shall take up
below — and languages are said to be of either VO or OV type (with, of
course, a greater or lesser degree of consistency). The juxtaposition of such a
typology with the original concept of drift, by such scholars as Lehmann
and Vennemann, leads inevitably to the conclusion that morphosyntactic
changes will almost invariably be in accord with a tendency for a particular
language to become 'typologically consistent', that is to admit changes which
further the 'drift' of that language towards an 'ideal' VO or OV type. This
much more sophisticated concept of drift has of course been best demonstrated with regard to the Indo-European languages, which — with relatively
few exceptions, of which modern German is perhaps the most significant
(cf. Lehmann 1971) — show an over-riding tendency to become consistently
VO in type; we should bear in mind, however, that similar evidence is now
available from a very wide variety of languages on a world-wide basis. The
purpose of the present paper is to investigate in the light of conflicting claims
the interrelationship between syntactic drift, thus defined, and phonological
change, with particular reference to three well-documented grammatical
changes in Romance.

The clearest stance on this particular issue is probably that taken up consistently by Theo Vennemann, for whom the cause of drift as a whole is without doubt phonological reduction. The following quotation (Vennemann 1975:301) will serve to illustrate this view which appears widely in his writings: "Sapir was moving in the right direction when he ... viewed phonological change as the ultimate cause of drift. We are now, half a century after Sapir's exposition of the problem, in a position to make deeper and more comprehensive generalizations about the nature of phonological and syntactic change". As Koch points out (1974:63), in saying this, Vennemann is the latest of a long series of scholars who have explained most, if not all, of the specific changes which are now grouped together within the 'drift' from OV to VO typology by reference to the erosive effect of phonological change.

Other scholars, such as Koch, reverse this view completely (cf.: "It is clear that inflections cannot be eroded away if they are still functional – or if they are still harmonious with the basic word-order of the language" [Koch 1974:101]), while yet others (such as R. Lakoff) regard any discussion of a cause-effect relationship between phonological and syntactic change as 'ridiculous', in that the two are inextricably linked. Her claim with regard to one of the specific instances that we shall be examining below is that "the phonological changes could not have occurred, with preservation of intelligibility, unless prepositions had developed beyond their functions in Classical Latin, and the syntactic changes in the case system would not have flourished, had not changes in the phonology rendered them essential" and that therefore "one needs to look simultaneously at two levels of grammar: the syntactic and phonological components" (Lakoff 1969:86). These three conflicting claims will be scrutinized carefully in the light of three specific instances of historical change in Romance: the drastic reduction of the case system in Vulgar Latin, the effacement of final [-s] in Old and Middle French, and the increased use of subject personal pronouns in French to the point where they are now mandatory.

Let us look first at the progressive elimination of the affixed case-morphemes of Latin and their replacement by other devices, in particular by a 'grammaticalized' SVO word-order and by prepositional phrases. There is general agreement today, of course, that both developments are very much in accord with those which would be predicted for a language in transition between OV and VO type, such as Latin most certainly was. We need to consider two main approaches to the explanation of this phenomenon: (i) a fundamental change in the order of the major sentence constituents from OV to VO rendered the loss of case endings and the more widespread use of prepositions inevitable (i.e., a change in the basic sentential elements has logical and chronological priority); and (ii) reductive phonological change inevitably destroyed the efficacy of the case system, and was thus ultimately responsible for the whole set of changes associated with the passage from OV to VO.

The first of these views is very much along the lines proposed, in a more general sense, by Lehmann. For Lehmann "the verb is distinguished as a central element in language – the element fundamental in the ordering of the grammatical elements and markers" (1973:65), a view repeated frequently elsewhere in his various treatments of this topic. It would follow, then, as Vennemann had observed (1974:354), that typological change could occur only when the basic verb position changes. It is beyond the scope of the present paper to ask what might cause such a change in the basic verb position: suffice it to say that Lehmann does have proposals to make on this matter (for example 1974:242). What we need to ask is: can we in fact, on the data available, attribute primacy to this particular change within the general typological shift in Latin, especially with regard to the specific morphological changes under consideration?

The answer is clearly no. Of the two changes under consideration here "the change from postpositions to prepositions (already in the earliest literature) long antedated the change of the verb from final to 'medial' position". So says Miller (1975:45), with evidence not only from Linde (1923) for the literary language (and Marouzeau, 1938:106–107), but also from his own personal investigations of *graffiti*. While, therefore, the evidence of the co-occurrence of certain syntactic changes is strengthened by the situation in Latin, the claim that verb-movement 'entails' the other restructurings is not supported by the facts, at least in this instance.

So now we may turn to the central issue: are such changes to be attributed, solely or primarily, to reductive phonological change? While it would be rash indeed to eliminate it as a contributory factor, a scenario whereby phonetic erosion reduced the efficacy of the S-O morphological opposition, thereby necessarily inducing a verb-position shift which in turn disfavors postposed morphology which is not in harmony with the new VX typology of the language (cf. Vennemann 1973:10; 1974:356) is, as we saw in the preceding paragraph, simply not in accord with the data, in that many of the typological changes associated with an OV–VO shift long preceded that of the verb shift.

What alternative explanation could be offered? I should like to suggest tentatively here that two apparently unconnected factors may be at work. Firstly, as is well known, the classification of nouns into such purely formal categories as declensions, genders and the like leads inevitably to a great deal of unmotivated variation; but, as Anttila puts it (1972:181), "the mind shuns purposeless variety". Languages adopt a whole variety of analogical procedures to reduce this difficulty in surface structure, even though such

changes may reduce the efficacy of the system as a whole from a communicative point of view. Further, however, and more seriously, the selection of
the actual cases themselves (i.e., the realizations of underlying 'case functions')
also becomes progressively more problematic by virtue of an ongoing tendency to increase surface-structure regularity at the expense of greater
opacity in respect of the relationship between underlying structure and its
actual exponents. (See Harris 1972:273 and 1975a:191 for details of this
process operating in Latin and French.) We thus have, as I have shown elsewhere (and cf. Koch 1974:64), a system which becomes increasingly unmotivated and inconsistent, scarcely in accord therefore with the dictum of
Anttila cited above. Alternative structures — which we now know will usually
be harmonious with the general drift of the language — are gradually developed
and there normally comes a time when these new, more consistent and more
motivated, structures oust their earlier rivals from the language.[1] (Harris
1975b describes the period of overlap and the eventual prevalence of the
innovating structure in more detail.) It goes without saying that the new
structures then become liable to exactly the same processes as their predecessors; hence the cyclical nature of change in this area. Note finally that such an
explanation can account in principle not only for the stage when a suffixed
morphology is lost — particularly amenable to the 'phonetic erosion' hypothesis — but also for example for the decline of a prefixed morphology as
part of a return from VX to XV at another point in the cycle (cf.
Vennemann 1974:371).

Many syntactic changes — e.g., the development of a new S-O morphology
(cf. Vennemann 1974:359) — cannot be attributed to reductive phonological
change; they must be viewed as part of an ongoing cyclical process. The
question is: what keeps the wheel turning? I have tried to suggest a possible
reason here, and the point is taken up once more in the final paragraph of
this paper.

One final note is necessary before we pass on to our next specific example.
Our claim that phonetic erosion was not the primary cause of the loss of the
Latin case system does not mean that such endings could not subsequently
be eroded; but neither does it mean that they necessarily would be. (This
point is taken up again in note 9 and in the concluding paragraph, and is
accordingly not elaborated upon further here.) As a matter of fact, in early
French final vowels and consonants were heavily reduced, to the point that,
in effect, only the final [-s] which is discussed in the next section survived;
and yet that language retained a two-case system of sorts for some fifteen
hundred years. In Spanish, however, apart from final [-m], already effaced
in Latin, the majority of the vowels and consonants employed to mark cases
survive in final position to this day. The loss of the case-system was, however,

far more rapid and more absolute in Spanish than in French. In this instance, therefore, we have yet further evidence that phonetic erosion is not the major cause of this particular change.

Let us now turn our attention from a situation where phonetic erosion does not seem to be the primary cause of morphosyntactic change to one where the Sapir/Vennemann view of reductive phonological change as the ultimate cause of 'drift' seems to be better supported. In Old French, largely owing to the persistence of final [-s] in positions where it had been found in Latin, the majority of masculine nouns retained a two-case system, with nominative forms being opposed to oblique[2] forms in both the singular and the plural. The position was complicated by the fact that this one suffix, [-s], normally served to mark both the nominative singular and the oblique plural of masculine nouns, while serving simply as a marker of plurality in the case of feminine nouns. Typical "declensions" were thus

	m.		f.	
	s.	pl.	s.	pl.
nom.	*murs*	*mur*	*rose*	*roses*
obl.	*mur*	*murs*	*rose*	*roses*

Clearly, the effacement of [-s] would totally destroy the inter-connected systems used in Old French for the marking of case and number; and we indeed find — with reference from now on exclusively to the spoken language — that these systems have been radically reorganized and [-s] has been virtually eliminated. To what extent is the latter development the cause of the former?

As this question is one which I have examined more fully elsewhere (cf. Harris, forthcoming), the more salient points only will be repeated here. We must distinguish carefully between the loss of the case-markers and the loss of the plural marker. The former change — which, in the written language at least, took place between the twelfth and fourteenth centuries (cf. Foulet 1968:32—36) — is one which traditional descriptivists and modern students of typological change are at one in predicting. A case system which was marked at all on only about half of the nouns in use in the language, which used the same suffix as was used elsewhere to mark plurality, and which was in any event redundant given the increasing use of word-order to distinguish subject and object was bound to be lost in time, and the generalization of the oblique form ($\emptyset$ singular, -s plural) was inevitable, given the numerical superiority of oblique forms and their clear morphological parallelism with feminine nouns; such is a succinct representation of the traditional explanation of this change (cf. Foulet 1968:32—36; Price 1971:96—98). Scholars might today 'explain' the change even more simply by saying that, given the shift from an XV to a VX language, by this time drawing near to completion in French, the residual traces of the earlier suffixed case-markers were bound to be eliminated. This, of course, begs the question as to why the case system survived as long as it did; nevertheless, its ultimate loss successfully restored the 'typological purity' of French at least in this particular respect.

Interestingly, the effacement of final [-s] is rarely if ever mentioned in discussions on the loss of the residual case-system; it all seems so 'obvious' that no appeal is made outside the morphosyntactic area in question. (That such a development had been equally 'obvious' for over 1000 years is ignored, or else the earlier retention of the system is attributed to the influence of Frankish or to conservative socio-historical forces; see, for example, Ewert 1966: § 176.) This may well be correct; and, furthermore, the case-system may well have been lost in the spoken language well before its disintegration in our written texts. Nevertheless, at the same period that the case-system was being progressively eliminated, so [-s], on which the system exclusively depended[3], was being effaced from the spoken language (cf. Pope 1952: §§ 613, 621).

My own view is that the loss of [-s] in this instance did no more than, at most, accelerate an inevitable process in the language, whether we see it as an analogical restructuring on the basis of the commonest morphological pattern or as the inescapable concomitant of the ongoing typological shift from XV to VX. What is clear, however, is that this same instance of phonetic erosion did have marked consequences elsewhere within the grammatical structure of French, in that the identical suffix, [-s], as we have seen, served also to mark plurality in French. The loss of this consonant, then, presented the spoken language with two options only: to cease to mark the distinction of number at all (in all but a handful of cases), or to find some alternative method of marking it, either by creating some new device or by extending another system already available at certain points in the language.

French, of course, has adopted this last solution. Although nouns them-selves are not now generally marked for plurality in the spoken language, number as a grammatical category is normally — though not invariably — marked within the noun phrase by means of one of a variety of determiners. (These same pre-nominal particles serve to mark gender in the singular, which distinction is neutralized in the plural.) It is my contention, argued in detail elsewhere (Harris, forthcoming), that the radical restructuring of the 'article' and 'demonstrative' system in French, and specifically the increased use of the 'definite article' solely and simply as a marker of gender or number, (i.e., without the original semantic connotations of specificity: cf. *l'eau bout à 100°*, *la haine provoque les guerres*, and the like), which in turn led to the restructuring of the 'partitive' system, and which was facilitated by a parallel change within the demonstrative system, is to be attributed, in part at least, to the increasing inadequacy of the original suffixed marker of plurality, namely -s. In other words, where a category still felt to be important in the language is threatened — in this case, by phonetic erosion — then remedial action may well be taken, even where, as here, the resultant morphosyntactic change appears at first sight to be quite distinct from the point of structure apparently under pressure. We may say, therefore, that reductive phonological change threatened a meaningful category, plurality, still felt — unlike case, also marked by -s — to be necessary within the language, and this caused a major restructuring elsewhere in that language. We may observe that a similar restructuring of the determiner system has not occurred in English, where plurality is still clearly marked suffixally and where gender has been discarded cf. *hatred provokes wars.*

One last point on this topic. Given that the suffixed marker of plurality ceased — gradually, over a long period, cf. Bourciez (1967: § 554d) — to be adequate, and that — gradually, over the same long period, cf. Foulet (1968:49) — a reorganized determiner system comes to fill this role, we can say without hesitation that such a change is in accord with the ongoing typological shift of French. Prefixed morphology is very much a feature of SVO languages (cf. Vennemann 1974:365), a type to which, as we shall see in the next section, French now almost wholly belongs. The relationship of preposed prepositions and determiners to nouns is similar to that of preposed personal pronouns and auxiliaries to verbs. It could conceivably be, therefore, (cf. Lakoff 1969:174) that even this change in the determiner system, which we have so confidently attributed to phonetic erosion, is in fact a necessary concomitant of typological change, which simply has not yet happened in (say) English. The arguments in favor of the causal status of phonetic erosion in this instance, however, are strong indeed.

Let us now turn our attention finally to the much described phenomenon in French whereby subject personal pronouns, largely used as markers of emphasis in Classical Latin, come to be used ever more frequently, to the extent that in the modern language they are mandatory in all but a few residual phrases (*advienne que pourra*, for instance). The conventional view of this change[4] in the language is simple: phonetic erosion destroyed the distinctive person suffixes inherited from Latin, which made the use of subject pronouns essential if intolerable ambiguity were to be avoided. A representative statement might be that of Ewert (1966: § 240): speaking of the subject pronoun category, he says: "the gradual breakdown of flexional distinctions makes its use necessary: it ceases to be used for emphasis and becomes an adjunct of the verb". At first sight, therefore, this is a clear example of a grammatical change caused by reductive phonological change;

the facts, however, seem on closer inspection not to accord with such an analysis.

Detailed inspection of Old French texts reveals that, as far as the basic order of elements within sentences is concerned, there are two favored patterns: SVX and TVX (where T equals any complement, including adjectives or adverbs). In other words, Old French is a clear instance of a "verb second" language: for Vennemann, both these patterns are within the same TVX verb-second category. (The picture is set out in detail in Foulet (1968: 306–329) and well summarized in Price (1971:146–147); it is interesting to reflect that such data have been readily available at least since the first edition of Foulet's admirable book, which dates from 1919; for a full set of references to even earlier descriptive works, see Haiman (1974:121–123).) What is significant from our point of view is that, from the earliest texts, the subject pronoun is almost invariably present if the verb would otherwise appear in first place. Put in other words, if topicalization or any other factor led to the appearance of some element other than the subject in initial position, then the subject pronoun could be – and normally was – omitted; but otherwise the subject pronoun appeared. In a sample of a representative prose text of the early 13th Century, Price has shown (1971:146–147) that all but 20 of nearly 800 cases where the subject of the verb is – or could be – a personal pronoun confirm either to the pattern SpnVX (with the pronoun initial, and present) or to the pattern TVØ (where the pronoun would be postposed, but is in fact absent). Of these two structures which are so overwhelmingly more popular than their rivals, the former – with the pronoun present – occurs twice as often as the latter. The statistics in Foulet (1968:326), drawn from a wide range of texts, show that initial subject pronouns are never omitted in more than 6.32% of relevant instances, and generally far less often.

We have then a situation very different from that usually described, in which subject pronouns were supposedly inserted primarily to mark emphasis. We find, on the contrary, that subject pronouns were inserted, almost invariably, in the large number of instances where the absence of any special topicalization rule left the subject in initial position, and where the typological characteristics of the language at that time then required an overt subject in surface structure, whether or not this was a personal pronoun, to ensure that the verb could occupy its preferred second position. Typological criteria alone, then, are sufficient to explain the presence of the subject pronouns in these instances. Price observes (1971:147): "It seems probable that the construction SpnV was already well-established in the preliterary period ...", in other words long before the phonetic changes occurred which were to reduce the distinctiveness of the personal suffixes on verbs. Subject pronouns did not occur, however, in post-verbal position (i.e., where they were not required by virtue of the principle outlined above); even in the popular drama *Le Jeu de la Feuillee*, only 32.24% of relevent TV structures show a subject pronoun postverbally (Foulet 1968:326–327).[5]

Reference is made to this same change by Haiman (1974) in the course of an examination of the strategies used by languages to conform to their current word-order typology. Haiman is primarily concerned with *es*-insertion in German, and comparable structures such as the use of impersonal *il* in French. He advances very convincingly a view directly analogous to that put forward here, namely that French 'conspires' to achieve the 'target' of obeying its 'verb-second' constraint. In order to do this, subject pronouns – whether personal or impersonal – would be necessary (quite regardless of any considerations of stress, or of phonetic erosion) in instances where no fronting rule had operated (whether for reasons of topicalization, anaphora, or whatever), but were clearly not felt to be necessary when the fronting of some other constituent enabled the verb in any case to occupy its preferred second slot (cf. especially Haiman 1974:123). For Haiman, then, subject pronouns clearly come to be virtually mandatory in Old French in pre-verbal position precisely in order to satisfy the constraints operating in the language at that time.

The role of phonetic change, therefore, in this particular syntactic change must be re-evaluated. Subject pronouns occurred very often from the earliest times in situations where the verb might otherwise appear in initial position. On discovering further that, in Old French, conjunctions "don't count" as elements permitted to fill the 'initial' slot (Foulet 1968:309), we are not surprised to learn (Foulet 1968:311–315) that subordinate clauses also frequently reveal the SpnV syntagm. At no time do we need to appeal to phonetic factors to explain the widespread introduction of subject pronouns, given what we now know of the strong tendency of languages to conform to their current typology. Furthermore, the dating of the loss of distinctiveness among verbal suffixes is illuminating.[6] Two (-*ons* [ɔ̃] and -*ez* [e]) are still distinct today; one (*ent*) passed, via [ɔ̃t] and [ət], to [ə] between the fourteenth and sixteenth centuries (Pope 1952: § § 615,897), whereas the second person singular suffix gradually came to be the same as that of the first and third persons singular (which merged early) over a long period between the twelfth and sixteenth centuries (Pope 1952: § § 613, 617) and its pronunciation was still controversial in the seventeenth century (Pope 1952: § 621). And yet we have seen that in Price's early 13th century prose example, two thirds of the relevant instances already show the SpnV structure! One final piece of evidence, again drawn from Haiman (1974:84) is that Romansh, which has a full system of verbal desinences, does not allow subject-pronoun deletion – and it too is a "verb second" language! (Haiman 1974:68).

We cannot, therefore, accept the view put forward by Vennemann
(1975:298), that "As s (= suffixed person/number morpheme) is rendered
non-dependable by phonological change ..., once-"emphatic" S pronouns
become obligatory". On the contrary, it is precisely — and solely — the need
for a specific surface-structure constituent to fill initial position when no particular topicalization rule had operated that led to the widespread presence
of subject pronouns in Old French. (That the topicalization of subjects may be
regarded as 'normal' or 'unmarked' is widely accepted and will not be discussed further here: cf. Miller 1975:48—49, and the references cited there;
also Vennemann 1974:340.)

But what of the second phase of the development we are considering here,
whereby non-initial subject pronouns become mandatory also in the inverted
structure (i.e., TVX > TVSpnX)? Surely, we may feel that here the erosion
of the personal verb-suffixes is a decisive factor? Possibly, although even
here there are certain difficulties. For example, TVX structures resisted
pronoun insertion until well into the sixteenth century (cf. Gougenheim
1951:68), but then the pattern changed abruptly between the mid-sixteenth
and the seventeenth century (cf. Haase 1969: § 153), in other words, well
after any ambiguity caused by the erosion of verbal endings must have arisen.
(This may, of course, simply reflect the greater conservatism of the written
language.) An argument based solely on a surface analogy ('if the pronoun
is present in the major PnV structure, it will gradually extend to the minor
VPn order') is also less than wholly convincing, since such an analogical
change could have operated at any time during the preceding four or five
hundred years. Ideally, we need to find some significant factor that changed
in the language at roughly the same time as the process we are concerned with
here.

I suggest that just such a factor is the typological change which French has
certainly undergone, whereby it has passed from being a 'verb-second' language
to an orthodox SVO language. (In the terminology of Vennemann 1974:
esp. 360—361, French has passed from 'TVX verb second' status to SVX.[7])
This development seems to have begun in the popular language in the sixteenth
century and has now become so deeply rooted that, in *français populaire*,
even such former strongholds of inversion as interrogation now almost
invariably exhibit alternative structures (cf. Price 1971:270[8]). As a consequence of such a change, patterns of the TVX type, where T ≠ S, with the
subject omitted if a pronoun — a structure which, as we have seen, was without any doubt whatever a thriving structure in Old French, quite independent
of the alternative SVX structure — ceased to be in accord with the new
typology of the language, but became residual survivors of an earlier period.
The passage from TVX to SVX is not at all unexpected; on the contrary,

given that the subject is the primary topic case, TVX will in fact be SVX in the majority of instances. As Vennemann clearly indicates (1974:361), the generalization of this favored pattern is a wholly natural development; SVX prevails and, as we know, pronoun subjects had long been mandatory in this construction.

The earlier TVX structure, then, is now isolated. In such circumstances, one or both of two things may happen. Either the construction may be modified to resemble as closely as possible the newly favored pattern (i.e., in this case, by the insertion of subject pronouns; for a more formal presentation of similar conclusions, cf. Haiman 1974:144), or it may be abandoned altogether by the language (and this, of course, is what has largely happened in *français populaire*).

So here too phonetic factors seem to have been at most only minimally relevant. In the ultimately triumphant SVX structure, subject pronouns were introduced, for syntactic reasons, well before the relevant phonetic erosion occurred[9]; whereas in the case of the TVX pattern, pronoun insertion was resisted strongly while the construction was still 'in harmony' with a 'TVX verb second' typology, with pronouns coming to be generally used after the structure had become 'residual' within the spoken language, which is now exclusively SVX in structure, and form which the TVX pattern as a whole has ultimately been almost entirely excluded. Only syntactic factors need to be taken into account to explain this particular change.

We are now in a position to pull together certain general conclusions from the specific examples discussed above. We are obliged to reject the view that reductive phonological change is necessarily the ultimate cause of syntactic drift, partly because it does not always accord with the data — the development of personal pronouns in French is a particularly clear example — but mainly because, as Vennemann rightly indicates, syntactic drift is cyclical, and only one phase of this development — the elimination of suffixed morphology — can be attributed with any plausibility to phonetic erosion. We have also, in passing, cast further doubt on the claim that the change in the order of the basic sentence constituents is logically — or chronologically — prior to the other features associated with drift in any given direction. Conversely, the claim that reductive phonological change can never affect an element still bearing functional load — in other words, that phonetic erosion can only be a consequence, never a cause, of syntactic drift — is demonstrated to be untrue, specifically with respect to the marking of plurality in French, where the development of a systematic alternative to the use of suffixed -s was certainly a reaction to rather than a cause of the effacement of that suffix, at least in certain positions. Finally, the view of Lakoff that the causal link between phonological and syntactic change is

always reciprocal seems also to be untenable, in that syntactic changes do
flourish when not rendered essential by phonological change, and phonological changes do occur before a wholly satisfactory alternative is necessarily
available. (Recall our quotation above from Lakoff 1969:189.)

We would wish to argue in fact that phonetic erosion and typological
change are, in principle, unconnected (cf. Harris 1975b). Of course, because
reductive change is the dominant type of phonological change (Vennemann
1974:359), then, when the drift is from XV to VX and suffixal morphology
is being discarded, there will clearly be two forces operating in the same
direction; this fact may well underly the attribution to phonetic erosion of
the role of ultimate cause of syntactic drift, a role which we cannot accept.
Phonetic erosion operates in general regardless of the syntactic typology of a
particular language and quite independently of the ongoing process of drift;
to give just one example, the fact that a final phoneme has been rendered
redundant by morphosyntactic change does not necessarily lead to its elimination (cf. the persistence of case or person endings in languages such as German
which use both prepositions and obligatory personal pronouns.) We therefore
conclude that there is no necessary connection between phonological reduction and syntactic drift, whether causal, as suggested by Vennemann, or
inherent, as suggested by Lakoff.

Our overall view of the cause of syntactic drift is more complex than any
of those considered at the outset of this paper. We accept, as far as it goes,
the view of Miller (1975:45): "it seems evident that typological change can
be motivated by either reductive phonological change [as with plurality marking in French – MH] or syntactic considerations [as with subject personal
pronouns in French – MH] or a combination of these two factors working
together [as with the loss of the two-case system in French – MH]". Specific
manifestations of syntactic drift are clearly to be attributed to a variety of
causes, as Miller rightly indicates. To this, however, we would wish to add
our claim, discussed in some detail above, that underlying these specific
causes is a conflict between the principle whereby languages tend to avoid
purposeless variety, and the demonstrable ongoing tendency of language, by
surface restructurings, to obscure the motivation for, and the transparency of,
its realization rules, and thereby to increase such purposeless variety. This
leads inevitably to the creation of new, consistently motivated structures –
which must themselves be in accord with the current 'target' typology of the
language – but these new structures are themselves thereafter liable to the
very same pressures as their ousted precursors. And so the pendulum swings
back. In this way, we can explain, in part at least, the incidence and cyclical
nature of syntactic drift, regardless of the direction of the typological change
at any given moment. These factors can, as we have seen, be supplemented in

certain circumstances (essentially, during the passage from XV to VX) by phonetic erosion. Overall, an approach such as the one I have outlined here seems to account best for the attested data, which is not always true, as we have seen, of alternative, more limited proposals.

Notes

1. Such a tendency cannot be caused, but may well be accelerated, by contact with some language exhibiting the target structure (cf. Lehmann 1973, for various possible instances; for a comment on this view, cf. Vennemann 1974:353). Another relevant situation is when large numbers of people come to acquire the language in question as 'second' language; Meillet (1965:201) writes: "il va de soi qu'une population qui acquiert une langue nouvelle a peine à assimiler une morphologie complexe et délicate". To these adjectives, one might add 'inconsistent in respect of both case assignment rules and surface case realizations'.
2. So called because such forms could function not only as 'accusatives' but also, in certain circumstances, as 'genitives', 'datives', or 'absolutes'; in other words, a complex case-system survives the loss of distinctive suffixes! Foulet (1968:14–32) treats such uses very fully.
3. As Bourciez (1967: § 302a) puts it succinctly "Le système de declinaison en ancien français ... reposait ... essentiellement sur l'emploi de s".
4. The status of the subject pronouns is in fact continuing to evolve, particularly in *français populaire* (cf. Harris 1975a:193).
5. It is, of course, fair to point out that pronouns thus already appear in one third of the possible post-verbal contexts. The conclusion drawn by Foulet is that "en parlant. on employait plus de pronoms personnels qu'en écrivant". He continues "Résultat qui n'est pas pour nous surprendre, car il annonce déjà le triomphe futur de cet emploi dans la langue moderne".
6. Recall that in Old French there was a completely unambiguous paradigm of personal suffixes for many verbs (cf. Pope 1952: § 887).
7. Note how well Vennemann's own description (1974:366–369) of the development of the French negative structure from *ne* to *ne ... pas* to *pas* fits, both typologically and chronologically, with the change from SOV to TVX and SVX.
8. There has been some reaction to this development in the literary language which need not concern us here (see Price 1971:263, and the references cited on p. 261).
9. We must not conclude either that this syntactic change necessarily led to phonetic erosion: such a development has not happened in German, for example, where subject pronouns are also obligatory. In this instance, as elsewhere, phonological and syntactic change seem in principle to be unconnected.

References

Anttila, R.
    1972   *An introduction to historical and comparative linguistics* (London, New York: Macmillan).
Bourciez, E.
    1967   *Éléments de linguistique romane*[5] (Paris: Klincksieck).
Ewert, A.
    1966   *The French language* (London: Faber).

Foulet, L.
    1968   *Petite syntaxe de l'ancien français* (Paris: Champion).
Gougenheim, G.
    1951   *Grammaire de la langue française du seizième siècle* (Lyon, Paris: IAC).
Greenberg, J. H. (ed.)
    1966   *Universals of language*[2] (Cambridge, Mass.: MIT Press).
Haase, A.
    1969   *Syntaxe française du XVIIe siècle*[7] (Paris: Delagrave).
Haiman, J.
    1974   *Targets and syntactic change* (The Hague: Mouton).
Harris, M. B.
    1972   "Problems of deep and surface structure, as reflected in a diachronic analysis
            of the French verbal system", *Journal of Linguistics* 8: 267–281.
    1975a   "Some problems for a case grammar of Latin and early Romance", *Journal
            of Linguistics* 11: 183–194.
    1975b   "A note on Monica Koch's 'Demystification of syntactic drift' ", in:
            Montreal Working Papers in Linguistics 5, pp. 57–72.
    forthcoming " 'Demonstratives', 'articles', and 'third person pronouns' in French:
            Changes in progress", *Zeitschrift für Romanische Philologie*.
Koch, M.
    1974   "A demystification of syntactic drift", in: *Montreal Working Papers in
            Linguistics* 3, pp. 63–114.
Lakoff, R.
    1969   "Another look at drift", in: *Linguistic change and generative theory* (Eds.:
            R. P. Stockwell, R. K. S. Macauley) (Bloomington: Indiana University Press,
            1972), pp. 172–198.
Lehmann, W. P.
    1971   "On the rise of SOV patterns in New High German", in: *Grammatik, Kyber-
            netik, Kommunikation* (Ed.: K. G. Schweisthal) (Bonn: Dümmler), pp. 19–24.
    1973   "A structural principle of language and its implications", *Language* 49: 47–66.
    1974   *Proto-Indo-European syntax* (Austin: Texas University Press).
Linde, P.
    1923   "Die Stellung des Verbs in der lateinischen Prosa", *Glotta* 12: 153–178.
Marouzeau, J.
    1938   *L'ordre des mots dans la phrase latine*, 2: *Le verbe* (Paris: Belles Lettres).
Meillet, A.
    1965   *Linguistique historique et linguistique générale* (Paris: Champion).
Miller, D. G.
    1975   "Indo-European: VSO, SOV, SVO, or all three?", *Lingua* 37: 31–52.
Pope, M. K.
    1952   *From Latin to Modern French, with especial consideration of Anglo-Norman*[2]
            (Manchester: Manchester University Press).
Price, G.
    1971   *The French language: Present and past* (London: Edward Arnold).
Sapir, E.
    1921   *Language: An introduction to the study of speech* (New York: Harcourt Brace).
Vennemann, T.
    1973   "Explanation in syntax", in: *Syntax and semantics* 2 (Ed.: J. Kimball)
            (New York: Seminar Press), pp. 1–50.
    1974   "Topics, subjects and word order: From SVX to SVX via TVX", in: *His-
            torical linguistics: Proceedings of the First International Conference on
            Historical Linguistics* (Eds. J. M. Anderson, C. Jones) (The Hague: North
            Holland), pp. 339–376.
    1975   "An explanation of drift", in: *Word order and word order change* (Ed.: C. Li)
            (Austin: Texas University Press), pp. 269–305.

HENRY M. HOENIGSWALD

Secondary split, typology, and universals

For reasons that run deep sound change has persistently been at the center
of interest in historical linguistics. All the major issues have a way of coming
to a head in connection with sound change in particular. There is the matter
of delimitation: What 'is' sound change, or rather: what is meant by 'sound'
change when it is distinguished from other varieties of linguistic change
(surely not just 'alteration in sound' — a label which, directly or indirectly
would fit them all)? In sound change reducible to some other change category as a special case, and what would be gained if it were? How does synchronic variation become diachronic change (if this is indeed what happens);
how can a line of ancestry and descent between two languages be established
on the basis of sound change; and what is the standing of the old motif of
separating 'internal' from 'externally caused' sound changes? Are changes,
or sound laws, discrete and countable? How can they be classified? According
to useful phonetic labels, into palatalizations, unvoicings, epentheses, dissimilations, etc.? According to whether they destroy, preserve, or create contrast? What are the relations between such classifications? How are sound
laws related to phonological rules? What is involved in the business of 'explaining' a sound change? Universals (including, perhaps, properties like markedness)? The typology of a target structure? Specific explanation in terms of
the vicissitudes undergone by the speech community? This is only enumerating
the factors, or some of them; what counts is their mutual logical dependence,
the overriding question being which of them are material, which circular and
definitional, and which merely speculative.

On the problem of interdependence there are hints in the literature. When
Meillet (1925:95–96) distinguishes two kinds of change (including sound
change), one according to les formules générales, and the other introducing
innovations spécifiques, he argues as follows:

Tant qu'il n'intervient pas de tendances caractéristiques nouvelles, le système linguistique ne change pas essentiellement. Les modifications qu'amènent les tendances générales au changement ne provoquent pas d'ordinaire la création de phonèmes nouveaux. Ainsi quand un phonème perd par dissimilation l'un de ses éléments, la langue ne garde pas le phonème singulier qui résulterait purement et simplement de la dissimilation. Si, dans un ancien *veneno*, la première des deux *n* perd l'abaissement du voile du palais, le résultat n'est pas une occlusive très faible sans nasalisation, comme on l'attendrait; ce phonème dont l'articulation serait trop peu marquée a été aussitôt remplacé par un phonème de type voisin existant dans la langue, et l'on a *veleno*; l'*n* denasalisée n'a eu qu'une existence virtuelle. Le changement une fois accompli, il y a eu dans la langue une *l* dans un mot de plus, mais non pas un type phonique de plus.

The example is the Latin word for 'poison' in Italian. It was used in the preceding chapter of Meillet's book to illustrate the generality of Grammont's work on dissimilation. Note, incidentally, that when Meillet speaks of 'phoneme', he often means 'phone' or 'sound type'.

Meillet (1925:96) goes on to give another example of the same kind: the transformation, in relatively recent French, of palatal or palatalized (mouillé) laterals into *y*:

Après l'innovation, le français a eu beaucoup plus de *y* qu'il n'en avait précédemment; mais le système phonique n'a pas ete modifié.

By contrast, Germanic umlaut with its creation of rounded front vowels is fundamentally different:

Il en est résulté des complications extrêmes, etc. (Meillet 1925:98).

This passage contains elements of great interest. First, let us observe that the use of dissimilation as a standard example of change by formule générale (rather than as an innovation spécifique) is no accident. It reflects Grammont's (1933:270) emphatic declaration that dissimilation does not create new sounds 'such as would be out of place in the system of the language' (just what he means with his added remark, 'si les éléments qui subsistent [after the dissimilatory action as such] ne sont pas suffisants pour constituer un phonème, ils sont éliminés, **avec ou sans compensation**' [emphasis supplied] is no clearer than it is in Meillet's paraphrase)[1]. Brugmann (1909:150) says the same: dissimilations do not seem to add 'entirely new sounds'.[2]

It is not often that a statement of such uncompromising directness appears in the classical record. In this case a phonetic category – dissimilation – is correlated with a matter of contrast – no addition to the system. Naturally we would like to know how the generalization was justified: as empirical and inductive, as self-evident, or as speculative and a priori. It does not seem to have been **meant** empirically; at least there appears to have been no effort – certainly not by the thorough Grammont – to make it so, though the reader, on going through Grammont's exhibit on his own, does not find counter-evidence, either. To be sure, there is a more extensive task ahead, namely that of applying the test to more varied material than Grammont had. Like so many investigations of alleged or potential universals this cannot be done in a hurry, if it can be done at all with our present resources.

Is the generalization intended as self-evident? Let us see whether its negation would strike us as absurd; let us, in other words, ask in what kind of 'new phoneme' a dissimilatory process **could** result. Unfortunately it is not altogether clear how to tell 'new' phonemes. If one were to take a Saussurian view of diachrony, its consequence would be to consider the phonologies of any two languages, even if they happen to be, by some valid criterion, two stages linked in lineage, as incommensurate; they would be seen as connected only by replacement relations (sound laws, like OE $p >$ NE p, IE $d >$ Gmc t, IE $_{s]}$ $\emptyset_{[r} >$ Gmc t) but not in such a way as to permit judgments on sameness and difference between phonemic entities from stage to stage (in which case OE p could have been siad to 'remain' p, while IE d would have been 'changed to' t); and all the phonemes of the later stage are 'new'. If, on the other hand, some permanent framework (perhaps in terms of distinctive features) **is** imposed, then two possibilities for the rise of 'new' units may be discerned. **First**, such a sound change may consist in replacement by an entity which simply calls for a different phonetic description. For all that is known, a proto-Semitic p was replaced, without merger, by f (or: 'stop' in the environment 'labial', where 'spirant' has not theretofore occurred, by 'spirant') in Arabic. Though subphonemic in a sense, the innovation could be considered important in some typological context.[3] Or take the contraction, in some ancient Greek dialects, of ee (from ese, etc.) into a 'new' long higher-mid front vowel $\bar{e}$ which takes its place between the old $\bar{\imath}$ and the old $\bar{\varepsilon}$. As we recall, however, that Meillet's example for a sound change that does create something new is neither of these, but rather Germanic umlaut, we are led to attach greater importance to the **second** variety of addition to the system, namely that in which former positional variants come to stand in mutual contrast, precisely because they do **not** necessarily undergo physical alteration when the conditioning differences in the environment are merged. The fronted allophones of u, as they are, become distinctive upon mergers in the syllables that follow, without needing polarization. We usually refer to this process as Phonologisierung[4] or secondary split.

The upshot is that dissimilatory changes are declared to figure only in primary split processes; that is, in such a way that the dissimilated phoneme itself undergoes merger — the sequence which results exists already; it is not 'new' — and never in such a way as to gain independence as the dissimilating phoneme loses its separate identity. This is interesting because the latter development is by no means impossible to imagine. Suppose, for instance, that a language has these words, *veleno, veneno, venedo*, and that the first *n* in *veneno* is subphonemically dissimilated into Meillet's 'denasalized *n*' — apparently something other than a *d*. Suppose, further, that at this point a sound change does away with all word-final syllables, but that the denasalized *n* — let us write '*N*' — persists nevertheless: the result would be *vele, veNe, vene*, with secondary split of *n*, or Phonologisierung of *N*, or, in other words, a dissimilation which will indeed have created a new phoneme. What Brugmann, Grammont, and Meillet are telling us is that these things are not known to happen, perhaps because while there were situations in known history where typological pressure existed in favor of the establishment of front rounded vowels as a going concern, no such forces were ever observed to work for intermediate degrees of nasality and such. This is probably so, although the matter is still one of typological or universal fact to be verified empirically, and not one of self-evidence. However this may be, we find that Meillet formulates his judgment by decreeing that the sound type 'which we would expect' as the result of dissimilation and which disappeared 'immediately' did so because it had been insufficiently equipped ('trop peu marquée') for survival.'[5]

There is another turn of phrase to give us pause. When Meillet says, in effect, that dissimilations have been found to function in primary, but not in secondary, split[6], he at first puts this very naturally by explaining that the language has not, in the process, acquired an additional phonemic counter. But the second time (apropos of *l* mouillée) he goes further and declares (Meillet 1925:96) that 'the phonemic system has not changed' (merely by giving more lexical incidence to the already existing *y*). This strikes us as an extraordinary thing to say since we would argue that the creation of a gap is as serious a modification of a sound system as is the addition of a unit. It is also a matter of some weight, considering that the prototype of phonemically relevant change is precisely merger,[7] and merger, by definition, causes gaps. The prototypical **innovation** in language history, with all that this implies for the technique of subclassification and tree construction is, therefore, not some 'new' object, but, paradoxically, the disappearance of an old one. There is, to be sure, nothing novel or startling about this, but it is instructive to observe how our formulations differ from those made only a few decades ago, especially when we claim to be dealing with the obvious. With greater justice (though with some sophistry as well) we might, in fact, wish to say that it is in the case of secondary split that the system has been preserved more faithfully inasmuch as the emergence of fresh contrast (e.g., the front rounded vowels) compensates for the loss.

The pronouncement on dissimilation not leading to new elements must, we repeat, be taken as typological in nature and hence as subject to empirical confirmation, especially as its claim to universal validity goes. Whether it was intended this way is another question. In part it no doubt was; but there was a speculative thought present also. Ever since E. Sievers (1901) and probably longer, a connection had been made not only between phonetic classifications like dissimilation on the one hand, and phonemic effect on the other, but also between these classifications and the category of graduality. There was a belief, and it has persisted ever since, that ordinary sound change depends for its functioning on physical graduality, that is, on a condition such that each speaker goes through a succession of infinitesimally different articulations until the endpoint of the collective change is reached; but that there are, however, other, 'minor' changes (dissimilations being characteristic examples) such that they are neither gradual, nor, for that matter, 'regular' after the general manner of sound change in the neogrammarian view, but sudden.[8] The implication is that here existing phonological units are exchanged in discrete fashion, much as morphs are exchanged in the processes to which we refer as analogic change, borrowing, and the like. Whatever the merit of these views, there is no doubt that they have played their role in making it plausible that dissimilations and other so-called minor sound changes will not introduce hitherto unknown types.

Generalizations are, however, not always offered as absolute and universal. Sometimes their scope is less sweeping: contingent, specific, and historically concrete, with the idea of summarizing the essence of a particular body of change events. This restraint is productive — there is sometimes more to be learned from a less ambitious, but more carefully circumscribed investigation.

In the course of the history of Latin, short vowels in word-interior open syllables have been reduced to zero, or syncopated, possibly in connection with an accent on the first syllables of words. The exact terms for this syncope to have occurred are notoriously difficult to discover, partly because of an overlay of analogical remakings, partly because the process competed with other accentual effects (vowel 'weakening'), and partly because it was chronologically and stylistically complex. Still, where it did take place, it was by and large subject to the same rules as are, according to our authorities, dissimilations: it added incidence to sequences already current but did not, with insignificant exceptions, create new sequences.[9] Only, this time we may hardly speak of a universal, since very similar developments elsewhere often **have** given rise to such new sequences — sometimes (as, say, in the case of the Slavic *jers*) to a spectacular extent. In the Romance languages, where further syncopations took place, these were also no longer constrained in the classical Latin way. In classical Latin, however, the constraint holds good and constitutes a characteristic systematic trait.

The material has been collected many times: by Lindsay, by Leumann, and by Kent, to mention just a few of the standard sources; more recently it has been discussed by Rix and by Hoenigswald.[10] It may be helpful to arrange it as follows:

(1) $C_1 \check{V} C_2$ merges with $C_1 C_2$ into what is, at the later stage, also best represented as '$C_1 C_2$'; example: *prop(V)ter* 'because of', *captus* 'seized'.

(2) $C_1 \check{V} C_2$ merges with an entity X (Y ...)Z (including, e.g., $C_1 C_3 C_2$, $C_1 C_4$, $C_5 C_2$, $C_6 C_7$, ..., but not including $C_1 C_2$) into '$C_1 C_2$'; example: *ol(V)nā>ulna* 'elbow, arm', *alsnos>alnus* 'alder'.

(3) $C_1 V C_2$ merges with an entity XZ (including, e.g., $C_1 C_3$, $C_4 C_2$, $C_5 C_6$ ..., but not including $C_1 C_2$) into 'XZ'; example: *host(V)pot(i)s>hospes* 'host, guest', *vesper* 'evening'.

(4) $C_1 V C_2$ merges with an entity $X(Y$ ...)Z (including, e.g., $C_1 C_2 C_3$, $C_1 C_4$, $C_5 C_2$, $C_6 C_7$, ..., but not including $C_1 C_2$) into 'UW', where UW is different from both $C_1 C_2$ and XZ; example: *dwen(V)los>bellus* 'pretty', *welse > velle* 'wish (inf.)' (other examples: *walnis > vallis* 'valley' with XZ metathetically $= C_2 C_1$; *saldō > sallō* 'salt (v.)', see below).[11]

In sum:	syncopated		non-syncopated	
(1)	*p (V) t*	*(propter)*	*pt*	*(captus)*
(2)	*l (V) n*	*(ulna)*	*lsn > ln*	*(alnus)*
(3)	*st (V) p*	*(hospes)*	*sp*	*(vesper)*
(4)	*n (V) l*	*(bellus)*	*ls > ll*	*(velle).*

The vagueness reflected in the use of inverted commas around the merger results above corresponds to two well-known and real indeterminacies: sameness from stage to stage being definable only in terms of some universal notation but not in Saussurian terms, and redundancy being expressed incompletely in most accepted notations, whether autonomous or systematic. For this reason the notion that (3) and (4) describe effective intermediate stages (*hostpe(t)s, dwenlos*) must be taken with the requisite skepticism. The essence of the matter is, after all, that a state of neutralization exists between zero and t, after s and before p, during the time interval concerned.[12] Meillet (1925:95, 99) uses the term 'aussitôt' in the very similar circumstance discussed earlier, and Rix, too, tells us that it is, after all, conceivable that those alien clusters did come into existence, only to be changed immediately.[13] This self-conscious terminology implies that we are dealing here with rules rather than with sound laws, and with derivation rather than with reconstruction.

The idea of an intermediate stage has a more natural and more solid foundation in those situations in which it is typologically reasonable to equate it with the $X(Y...)Z$ of class (4) so as to obtain $(C_1 VC_2 >)X(Y...)Z > UW$. An example is $par(V)s\bar{a} > pars\bar{a} > parra$ 'owl or woodpecker' alongside $ters\bar{a} > terra$ 'land', where there is not only a feeding rule order but also a good likelyhood that the syncope actually took place before the change from rs to rr.

Other points of relative chronology are worth clearing up, too, whenever possible. Thus, we might ask whether $alsnos$ had already gone to $alnos$ when $ol(V)n\bar{a}$ was syncopated. If the answer were yes, the step from the intermediate language state (exhibiting $alnos$ but a still trisyllabic $olVn\bar{a}$) to the later stage, taken by itself, would simply fall into class (1).

The various sound sequences of which examples are given above are numerous.[14] In contrast with this, there is only one instance of a syncopation result that is clearly 'new': the ld of $vald\bar{e}$ 'very' (compare $validus$ 'strong'). This cluster has no other antecedents, since an earlier ld has gone to ll (see on $sall\bar{o}$ above) and no other old cluster yields ld either.[15] To explain this away by deciding that ld is only accidentally missing before the time of syncope but is nevertheless 'grammatical' would be precarious, considering that it was a solid sound law which led to the elimination of the inherited ld. It would have to be shown that the framework had truly changed in the direction of making a new ld once again welcome. — Aside from ld, the verdict must be that the only alteration which syncopation brought to the Latin sound system was syncopation itself, that is, the reduction of the privileges of occurrence for word-internal short vowels, mostly in open syllables; and even this was to some extent offset by anaptyxes of the type $p\bar{o}tlom > p\bar{o}culum$ 'cup'.[16]

The foregoing discussion should also show that any attempt to explain why syncope occurred, with some regularity, in some sequences but not in others, by a direct appeal to the phonemic system, as it was at the time, is doomed. After all, the absence of a cluster stp as such (assuming that this were the clear-cut fact which it is, in fact, not; see above note 12) did not prevent the syncopation of $host\breve{V}potis$. The process simply ended at the 'nearest existing' phoneme.

Notes

1. See, in particular, the discussion in Posner (1961:15).
2. See note 14.
3. There is a significant isogloss linking Arabic with South Arabian and Ethiopic.
4. Following Jakobson.
5. How is it possible to know that a subphonemic dissimilation occurred at some time or other rather than that the dissimilated allophone was 'always' there? Perhaps it is implied that such allophones are indeed as old as the morphological constructs (words with particular affixes, etc.) and the particular morphs in which the sequences figure. But there is also the particular vacillation in the use of the term 'change': it may refer to the operation of a low-level rule ('such-and-such a segment is rewritten x in the environment y'), or else to an event in time.
6. What is being 'split' here is the total population of the n's: some are dissimilated, others are not.
7. Merger and split are linked by Polivanov's law which states, in effect, that split presupposes merger but merger may occur without split.
8. As well as conditioned across a distance in the flow of speech rather than by an immediately following, immediately preceding, or co-occurring articulation. H. Andersen wants internally caused ('evolutive' – the term goes back to Grammont) changes, unlike externally caused ('adaptive') ones to be necessarily gradual in a physical sense. It is, however, remarkable that both those changes which are likely to occur gradually and those which are not (mainly because of the uncomfortable typological consequences of the contrary assumption) lead to the same kind of end result so that the need to distinguish between them is not strongly felt by the historian. As for the difference between internal and external causation, it is of course difficult to find a diagnostic property except, perhaps, where there is an indisputable, gross substratum visibly at work; besides, our growing insight into the mechanics of variation at a given time calls the whole distinction into question. – Note, in addition, that graduality has no clearly defined place in secondary split, where the alteration may occur outside the segment in question.
9. See Rix (especially 48) where credit is given to Lindsay. – If this formulation ('new sequences') had not been sedulously avoided up to this point, the above statements by Grammont and Meillet (see note 5) would have revealed their dependence on a redundant notation. In fact, Grassmann's famous dissimilatory laws may not create new '**sounds**' either in Greek (t from dh before, say, bh in the next syllable) or in Indic (d from dh under the same condition); Greek t's and Indic d's are in the inventory anyway. But while in Indic d . . bh is also an already existing sequence so that, at least ideally, homonyms could have arisen (but see Hoenigswald 1965), there is, in Greek, nothing (such as say, a former t . . bh) for the new t . . ph to merge with: the entire **sequence** is 'new'. However, just for this reason, the replacement of the old dh . . bh by the new t . . ph, could be dismissed, under a sophisticated notation, as subphonemic. This is of course only what the well-known compensatory nature of secondary split amounts to.
10. For a slightly fuller list of examples, arranged in a somewhat different fashion, see Hoenigswald (forthcoming).
11. As always, care must be taken to keep the stages apart. The *ln* of *walnis* and that of *ulna* are unrelated in the Saussurian sense, and are in a bleeding relation if the appropriate permanent framework is considered.
12. If we were to write *hostpes, vestper* for the actual Latin forms, we would of course be flying in the face of realistic segmentation, and be quite arbitrary. But to the extent of indicating that *stp* and *sp* do not contrast (so that it makes no difference which we use) this notation is free from contradiction; note that its choice eliminates the intermediate stage. In more favorable cases – that is, in cases where the

preference is phonetically less grotesque – of this general sort we would, therefore, have reason to say that the intermediate stage is 'only' notational.
13. Existence virtuelle!
14. See the list in Rix.
15. There is a question of how much environment to take into account. It seems possible that the sequence $\bar{V}nd$ (unlike $\breve{V}nd$) is only found in syncopated material ($\bar{u}ndecim$ 'eleven')
16. Rix.

References

Andersen, H.
   1972   "Diphthongization", *Language* 48: 11–50.
Brugmann, K.
   1909   *Das Wesen der lautlichen Dissimilation* (Leipzig: Teubner).
Grammont, M.
   1895   *La dissimilation consonantique* (Dijon: Darantière).
   1933   *Traite de phonétique* (Paris: Delagrave).
Hoenigswald, H. M.
   1965   "A property of Grassmann's law in Indic", *Journal of the American Oriental Society* 85: 59–60.
   forthcoming "On the impact of vowel syncope in Latin".
Jakobson, R.
   1931   "Prinzipien der historischen Phonologie", *Travaux du Cercle Linguistique de Prague* 4: 247–267.
Kent, R. G.
   1940   *The sounds of Latin*[2] (Philadelphia).
Leumann, M.
   1926   *Lateinische Laut- und Formenlehre* (München).
Lindsay, W. M.
   1894   *The Latin language* (Oxford: Clarendon).
Meillet, A.
   1925   *La méthode comparative en linguistique historique* (Paris: Champion).
Posner, R.
   1961   *Consonantal dissimilation in the Romance languages* (Oxford: Blackwell).
Rix, H.
   1973   "Die lateinische Synkope als historisches und phonologischen Problem", in: *Probleme der lateinischen Grammatik* (Ed.: K. Strunk) (Darmstadt Wissenschaftliche Buchgemeinschaft) pp. 90–102.
Sievers, E.
   1901   *Grundzüge der Phonetik*[3] (Leipzig: Breitkopf und Härtel).

JOAN B. HOOPER

Constraints on schwa-deletion in American English

0. Introduction

Schwa-deletion processes observable in present day American English provide
a fruitful basis for a detailed study of the type of sound change that leads to
vowel loss. Diachronic correspondences yield information only about the
results of sound change; changes in progress supply the data necessary for the
study of the implementation of a sound change, which will eventually lead
to an understanding of the various factors that encourage or inhibit a sound
change. The processes under consideration here could be studied from
several points of view: we could examine aspects of the lexical diffusion of
schwa-deletion, as I have done elsewhere (Hooper 1976a); we could study the
gradualness of vowel loss changes; or we could study the phonological environments that allow or inhibit schwa-deletion. The present paper concentrates
only on the last point, and attempts to relate the phonological environments
for schwa-deletion to a general theory of syllable structure.

The schwa-deletion processes discussed here are not necessarily limited to
casual speech, but are found in their most advanced form in casual speech. I
am assuming that reductive sound change begins in casual speech, and initially
marks off the casual style from the more formal style, where reduction is suppressed. The phonetic changes work their way into formal speech as the language
is transmitted to new learners. The new learners take the casual speech forms to
be basic, and eventually the formal style, which lacked certain reductions, is
replaced by a new formal style (based on the old casual forms), which contains
the reductions. Another dimension to this process concerns the lexical diffusion
of a sound change. It appears, especially in the case of schwa-deletion in American
English, that lexical items may be affected one by one or in small classes. One
factor influencing the course of lexical diffusion is word frequency. Thus a very
frequent item such as *every* has long since been restructured so that even in
formal speech, for most speakers, *every* contains no schwa.

The particular aspect of schwa-deletion to be examined here was first discussed by Arnold Zwicky in an article called "Note on a phonological hierarchy in English". Zwicky examines a number of phonological processes occurring in casual speech in American English and discovers a hierarchy of segments functioning in these processes. He (Zwicky 1972:277) states the hierarchy as follows:

(1) Vowels Glides [r] [l] [n] [m] [ŋ] Fricatives Stops

This hierarchy is practically identical to the strength hierarchy of Foley (1970 and 1972), which is used in Vennemann (1972) and Hooper (1973) in developing a theory of syllable structure. The purpose of the present paper is to show that Zwicky's hierarchy is indeed the same hierarchy that functions in syllable structure. I will argue in addition that the English data support the general relation between this hierarchy and syllable structure, and further that the English data give clear evidence for the universality of the theory of syllable structure developed in Hooper (1973). Before going into an examination of the data, I will briefly present the theory that relates the consonantal hierarchy to syllable structure, and make a few general remarks about English syllable structure.

1. The universal syllable-structure condition

The syllable-structure theory I will employ here is similar to that proposed by Saussure (1939 [1915]). First we assume that segments may be ranked along a scale, similar to that in (1), but more applicable universally, when stated as in (2):

(2)					fricatives		stops	
glides	r	l	nasals	voiced	voiceless	vd.	vl.
1	2	3	4	5	6	7	8

Strength

Saussure ranked the segments by degree of aperture. Foley (1970) does not look for a phonetic correlate, but merely presents phonological evidence for the hierarchy, and calls it a strength hierarchy. (This evidence is from the Romance and Germanic consonant shifts, and is totally independent of syllable structure.) Hankamer and Aissen (1974) cite evidence for a reverse hierarchy, which they call the sonority hierarchy. (In this case most of the evidence cited is also independent of syllable structure.)

The hierarchy can be characterized in various ways: as degree of opening or closure, or degree of sonority. One can think of it in this way: if we assume that a voiceless stop is the optimal consonant, and a full vowel, /a/, is the optimal vowel, then the hierarchy is the ranking of all other segments between these two. Strictly speaking, no phonetic correlate for the hierarchy has been found. However, I am confident that a phonetic correlate or set of correlates is involved. That is, the hierarchy exists for phonetic reasons, not just for phonological reasons.

I will usually refer to the hierarchy as stated in (2), although we could just as well run the numbers from right to left and call it a sonority hierarchy. A sonority hierarchy would include vowels, but a strength hierarchy does not, because "strength" by definition refers only to non-syllabic segments. No theoretical significance should be associated with my choice to "strength" over "sonority". I use "strength" merely because I am accustomed to thinking of consonant positions as being strong and weak.

The hierarchy (as noted by Saussure) relates to syllable structure in the following way. The nucleus of the syllable is the most open or sonorous part of the syllable; the consonant positions closer to the nucleus are also more open or sonorous than the consonant positions at the edges of the syllable. Or, to state the principle in terms of strength, the outer consonant positions are typically the strongest, and the closer the consonant is to the nucleus, the weaker it must be. Translating this principle into formal notation, a universal syllable structure condition would have the following form (Hooper 1973):[1]

$$(3) \quad {}^{\$}C_m C_n C_p \quad V \quad C_q C_r C_s{}^{\$}$$

$$m > n > p \qquad\qquad q < r < s$$

The subscripts refer to numbers along the strength scale. Every language will have a syllable structure condition (SSC) which is governed by the conditions in (3). That is, given a hierarchy such as (2) (which may be in part language specific), L will have a SSC in which the highest strength value allowed in syllable-initial position, C_m, will be higher than the highest value allowed in the second or C_n position. Thus for L, $m > n$. A typical situation is the following: L allows any consonant in C_m position, i.e. $m \leqslant 8$, but in second position only liquids and glides are allowed, i.e. $n \leqslant 3$. The mirror image usually holds for syllable-final consonants.

In Hooper 1973 the conditions represented in (3) are taken to be universal conditions on the form of language specific SSCs. It has become apparent, as recognized in Hooper 1976b, that the conditions in (3) must be regarded as universal tendencies. Violations of (3) do exist in particular languages; in fact, some examples from English will follow. However, these violations are ordinarily short-lived. They develop through processes such as vowel-deletions, e.g. French *journalisme*/ẑurnalizm/ and *ministre* /ministr/, but eventually yield to further processes that bring them back into line with the conditions in (3), e.g. Montreal French [minis] and [ẑurnalis] (Tranel 1974). Thus while we will see that the condition in (3) may not be regarded as absolute, we will also see evidence that (3) expresses a very powerful universal tendency.

Some apparent violations of (3) are probably not violations at all, but are due to the phonetic realizations of the particular consonant. For instance, a strongly trilled [r] will be more likely to function as a strong consonant than as a liquid. If the hierarchy has a phonetic basis, then the ranking of any consonant will have to be based on the phonetic properties of that consonant.[2] It should also be observed that the hierarchy in (2) could be worked out in greater detail, and could perhaps include rankings according to place of articulation. I have not attempted this, and at present I am not sure if such rankings would be language-specific or universal.

Condition (3) and the associated hierarchy account for certain universals of consonant clustering discovered by Greenberg (1965). For instance, Greenberg found that the existence of $CNV implies the existence of $CLV (where C = obstruent, N = nasal consonant, and L = liquid). This implicational relation follows from the fact that nasals are stronger than liquids, and a language will have an upper limit placed on each consonant position. Thus if a language allows nasal consonants in second position, liquids must also be allowed. Similarly, the condition (3) predicts that $CCV implies $CNV; this implication is not mentioned by Greenberg, but should be checked. Predictions are also made for syllable-final clusters. Many of these have been verified, according to Guile (1973). (See Hooper [1976b] for details.)

Language specific SSCs will also need a condition specifying the minimal strength difference allowed between the syllable-initial consonant and the second consonant. It is not enough that the first be stronger than the second, but for most languages, the first must be considerably stronger than the second. Thus, a language (such as Spanish or English) may allow any consonant in first position, and only liquids and glides in second position, but when second position is occupied by a liquid, the first position must be occupied by an obstruent. No clusters of nasal plus liquid are allowed. Such a restriction will be stated for each language. Given that such restrictions are necessary, and given the strength hierarchy, it follows that the existence of $NLV implies the existence of $CLV as found by Greenberg. Thus if a language allows as little difference in strength between the first and second consonant as between N and L, then it must also allow clusters of C and L, where there

is a greater difference in strength. Similarly, Greenberg found that clusters of
$LLV are universally disallowed; this is because there would not be a differ-
ence, or not a sufficient difference, in strength between two liquids.

One final condition needs to be mentioned. Syllable-initial position in any
language is stronger than syllable-final position. This difference is manifested
in several ways: (i) syllable-initial position usually allows the full range of
consonants, while syllable-final position may be restricted, usually to the
weaker consonants; (ii) weakening in the form of neutralization or assimilation
is much more frequent in syllable-final position than in syllable-initial position;
and (iii) weakening in the form of sonorization or deletion is common in
syllable-final position, but almost non-existent in syllable-initial position. Thus
syllable-final weakness is manifested on the contrastive level by restricted
distribution for syllable-final position, and on the phonetic level by phonetic
processes which produce a weaker articulation. Examples of these processes
abound (see Hooper 1973 and 1976b).

2. English syllable structure

Stress affects syllabification to varying degrees, according to the strength of
the stress; English has a very strong stress, and thus English syllable structure
is heavily influenced by the presence or absence of stress. Differences between
stressed and unstressed syllables occur both in the consonants and vowels. It
is well known that unstressed vowels reduce in English, and as we shall see
below are eventually lost entirely, while stressed vowels tend to retain their
full quality. A similar difference exists between initial consonants in stressed
versus unstressed syllables. Hoard (1971) describes the difference between
the medial consonants in columns (a) and (b) of (4) as a difference in tenseness, manifested as aspiration in voiceless stops and length in fricatives. The
consonants occurring before a stressed vowel are tense and those occurring
before an unstressed vowel are less tense:[3] (Hoard 1971:134)

(4) (a) Tense medial C	(b) Lax medial C
abíde	ábbey
redéem	cáddy
acadámic	acádemy
aghást	ágate
begín	béggar
appéar	úpper
attáck	áttic
pecán	péccary

(a) Tense medial C
   affórd
   assáult
   avówed
   resíde
   allów
   arríve

(b) Lax medial C
   éffort
   éssay
   ávid
   éasy
   álloy
   áiry

The most obvious manifestation of the difference between consonants in stressed and unstressed syllables in the neutralization of /t/ and /d/ after a stressed syllabic, resulting in the flap of words such as *butter* and *caddy*.

Another phenomenon plays a role here also. A stressed syllable in English attracts consonants into its coda. Hoard (1971) and Pulgram (1970) have different interpretations of this phenomenon, neither of which is entirely correct. The phenomenon is well illustrated by the pair of words *télegràph, telégraphy*. In *télegràph* the primary stressed syllable is very similar, if not identical to the word *tell*; the /l/ is dark, which is characteristic of a word-final (and hence syllable-final) /l/, even though it is released onto the following vowel. The final syllable is virtually identical to the word *graph*. In *telégraphy*, on the other hand, the stressed syllable is like the word *leg*. Here the /l/ has the characteristics of a syllable-initial /l/, while the /g/ is more like a syllable-final consonant than a syllable-initial one, despite its release onto the following syllable.

Hoard's syllabification rules overplay the extent of the attraction of consonants into the coda. According to his rule, all unstressed, non-initial syllables begin in vowels, while stressed syllables begin in the maximal initial cluster. Syllabifications such as the following result:

(5) *potato*   /pə\$téyt\$ow/
   incomplete   /in\$kəm\$plíyt/
   congress   /kángr\$əs/
   congressional /kən\$gréš\$ən\$əl/
   telegraph   /tél\$ə\$græf/
   telegraphy   /t ə\$légr\$ə\$f̄i/

Phonetically it is often difficult to determine the exact location of a syllable boundary. Nevertheless, I think Hoard's syllabifications can be improved.

It is not entirely accurate to consider medial consonants preceding unstressed syllables to be completely syllable-final. Such consonants are syllable-initial in the sense that they release onto a syllabic element, but syllable-final, as I mentioned before, in that their phonetic characteristics resemble true syllable-final consonants. It seems, in fact, that they must be considered both syllable-final and syllable-initial; they will thus be referred to as ambisyllabic. I will represent ambisyllabic consonants with a $ directly above the alphabetic symbol for the consonant; thus *potato* will be syllabified as in (6).

(6) /pə$téyto/

The status of medial consonants between two unstressed syllables is less clear; e.g. is the /m/ in *animal* syllable-initial or interlude? This problem deserves further attention, but for present purposes I will consider the /m/ in *animal* as fully syllable-initial. This would accord with universal tendencies for intervocalic consonants to be syllable-initial. Thus in English only medial consonants following stress will be considered interlude consonants.

A second problem with Hoard's syllabifications is that he relies on a "law of initials" (as named in Vennemann 1972), but ignores entirely the "law of finals". The latter is certainly weaker, since greater freedom of clustering is allowed in the coda than in the onset, but there are some constraints. Hoard's syllabifications of *congress* as /káŋgr$ɛs/ and *telegraphy* as /tə$légr$əf i/ yield unpronounceable final clusters. As I pointed out above, the stressed syllable in *telegraphy* is phonetically the same as the word *leg*, but the /g/ is released onto the following syllable, suggesting a syllabification /tə$légrə fi/. If *congress* is considered in terms of a pronounceable coda and onset, the only possible syllabification is /kaŋ$grɛs/, since /ŋg/ is not a possible coda.[4] In some cases it is not easy to tell which consonants are in which syllable; e.g. *transitive* may be /trǽnzə tɪv/, with an interlude /z/, but *sister* is /sɪsto/ or /sɪs$to/, but not /sɪsto/, even though /st/ is a possible final cluster. The goal seems to be to ensure that all stressed syllables are closed by a consonant, even if that consonant is shared with the following syllable.

My purpose here is not to propose a general principle that handles syllabification in English, for there are a number of problem cases. These are irrelevant for our present purposes. For the discussion that follows, it is only important to remember the following:

(1) Stressed syllables are strong; they attract a maximal initial cluster.
(2) A stressed syllable attracts at least one consonant into its coda; if this consonant must initiate the following syllable, the two syllables share the consonant.

Pulgram (1970) comes to a similar conclusion. He claims that all English stressed syllables must be closed, either by a consonant or a glide. He considers

English tense vowel or diphthong nuclei to represent closed syllables: thus *bee, bay, buy, boy, bow* are all closed syllables. The monosyllables [bɪ], [bɛ], [ba] , etc. do not occur in English, Pulgram claims, because of this restriction. In syllabifying medial consonants, Pulgram makes a distinction between syllables with tense and lax vowels. If a tense vowel in a stressed syllable is followed by a medial consonant, that consonant is considered to be in the next syllable, *filing* [fay$lɪŋ] . A stressed lax vowel followed by a medial consonant, however, attracts the consonant, which is then considered to be shared by the two syllables, *filling* [fɪɫ$lɪ ŋ] .

This is the point at which I disagree with Pulgram. If there were a differ- ence in syllabification of *filing* and *filling*, we would expect a different phonetic quality for the two medial consonants. Yet the two consonants are the same. This is even more clearly illustrated with pairs which have medial /t/, because a flap for orthographic /t/ (and /d/) appears wherever the /t/ straddles two syllables, *kitty* [kɪɾi] , but *serenity* [sərɛ́nɪ$tʰi] . Thus if *fitting*

and *fighting*, were syllabified as /fɪ́tɪŋ/ and /fay$tɪ ŋ/ respectively, we would expect a flap in *fitting* but not in *fighting*. Both, in fact, have a flap, suggesting an identical syllabification. I conclude, then, that the tenseness of a stressed vowel does not influence syllabification.

3. Post-stress schwa-deletion

We are finally ready now to examine schwa-deletion processes in American English. The processes to be discussed are in a variable state. A few words seem to have lost their schwas entirely, e.g. *every, camera, family, general, chocolate* (Zwicky 1972:283); some words can be pronounced with or without schwas, e.g. *elaborate, happening, leveling*; while still others seem to resist schwa-deletion, e.g. *infirmary, mockery, perjury*. There is a great deal of variation among individual speakers, and variation for a single speaker depend- ing upon the syntactic position of a word, the style of speech being used, and the speed of speech. The number of words affected by schwa-deletion makes systematic testing of the corpus out of the question. However, I have run a test on 112 words ending in *V́Cəry*, and in this test three phonological con- straints turned up. These will be discussed below. This test also showed that speakers are more likely to delete the schwa in frequent words than in in- frequent words. These results are reported in Hooper (1976a). Except for this test, the data discussed here are based on Zwicky's data, which represent his own judgments as a speaker, and on my judgments, which largely agree with Zwicky's. Thus the nature of the data is not the best one could hope for; yet the phonological patterns I will be discussing are unmistakeable. In the few cases where an apparent counter-example shows up, i.e., a schwa in a phonological environment conducive to deletion, which does not delete, it is always in a very infrequent word.

Post-stress schwa-deletion (Zwicky's 'slur') refers to the deletion of a schwa following a stressed syllable. This deletion always produces a syllable-initial cluster, although the initial consonant may be ambisyllabic as in *separate* [séprət], *family* [fǽmli], *reasoning* [ríyznɪṇ], or fully syllable-initial where it is preceded by consonant, as in *factory* [fǽktri] and *chancellor* [čǽnslər]. In words in which the deletion of the schwa leaves a cluster with /n/ as the second number, two pronunciations are possible, one with a syllable-initial cluster, *happening* [hǽpnɪŋ], and one in which the cluster is divided between the two syllables, [hǽpnɪŋ].

The deletion in question should not be confused with another schwa-deletion process which is restricted to certain regional dialects (particularly of the southern and south-western United States, see Zwicky 1972:298 footnote 13). This other deletion process creates a new syllable-final consonant in *America* [əmɛ́r$kə], *imperative* [ɪmpɛ́r$tɪv], *Carolina, guarantee, skeleton, Europe,* etc. Such pronunciations are stigmatized as substandard regional pronunciations, while deletions of the type to be discussed here are well accepted in American English. The difference, again, is that the post-stress schwa deletion of concern here creates a syllable-initial cluster, while the other creates a syllable-final plus syllable-initial series.

Zwicky's observation about post-stress schwa deletion is that it is conditioned by the following consonantal hierarchy: deletion occurs readily before /r/, /l/ and /n/, rarely before/m/ and never before obstruents. Zwicky gives no explanation for this fact, but the explanation is very obvious once syllable-structure is taken into account, and viewed in terms of a universal hierarchy. If deletion goes through, a syllable-initial cluster will be created. The consonant originally occurring after the schwa will be the second member of the syllable-initial cluster. Therefore, it must be a weak consonant, and, indeed, the weaker the better. According to the universal hierarchy (2), deletion before liquids will be favored over deletion before nasals, and deletion before nasals will be favored over deletions before obstruents. And this is precisely what the data show.

Further refinements in the hierarchy will explain further intricacies in the data. First, as Zwicky notes, /r/ is lower on the hierarchy than /l/. The same relation is observed to hold in Spanish (Hooper 1973:133–134),

Icelandic (Vennemann 1972:6), and Pali (Hankamer and Aissen 1974:132); in each case /r/ is weaker than /l/. There is independent evidence for the weakness of /r/ in English, since in syllable-final position /r/ is lost in many dialects, but /l/ is not disturbed. Second, to understand the data, we must assume that /m/ is stronger than /n/, for Zwicky finds a difference between /m/ and /n/. However, I cannot argue for this relation because general strength relations for point of articulation have not been established, and furthermore, it is not clear that point of articulation relations will be universal. We will merely assume that /m/ is stronger than /n/.

The following words all allow pronunciations without the post-stress schwa. They are categorized according to the types of clusters that result. Note especially that the resulting clusters in the left-hand columns (a) are clusters that ordinarily occur in English in syllable-initial position, but the resulting clusters in the right-hand columns (b) do *not* ordinarily occur in English, but are considered possible clusters universally.

(7) before *r*

(a) obstruent + *r*	(b) obstruent + *r*	sonorant + *r*
separate, temperature	*misery, nursery*	*scenery, general*
elaborate, laboratory	*every*	*memory, camera*
factory, adultery	*treasury*	*celery*
hindering, boundary	*dangerous, surgery*	
hickory, licorise	*century*	
reference		
mystery, factory		
authoring		

(8) before *l*

(a) obstruent + *l*	(b) obstruent + *l*	sonorant + *l*
stapling	*leveling, javelin*	*finally*
gambling	*easily*	*family, Emily*
mentally	*especially*	
pedaling		
erratically, chocolate		
boggling		
awfully		
desolate, excellent		

(9) before *n*

(a) obstruent + *n*	(b) obstruent + *n*	sonorant + *n*
personal	*happening, opener*	*?effeminate*

arsenal	*reckoning*
	definite, infinite
	prisoner, seasoning
	rational, national
	marginal, progeny

Since deletion is currently taking place before *r, l* and *n*, the next candidate would be *m*. Zwicky (1972:285) notes that for most words deletion does not occur before *m*. The following are some examples:

(10) *monogamy*   *consummate* (adj.)
      ultimate   *gossamer*

However, in more frequent words, a tendency to delete can be detected, especially after *s: handsomer, blossoming, decimal,* and *specimen* are acceptable in very rapid speech without a schwa before the *m*. Post-stress schwa-deletion may perhaps be encroaching on environments before *m*.

The process, however, has not touched schwas which occur before obstruents, even if the resulting cluster is an actually occurring syllable-initial cluster in English, e.g. clusters of *s* plus a voiceless stop. Note the following words, where schwa-deletion is not possible:

(11) *picketing*   *balloting*   *candidate*   *voracity*
      rocketing   *panicking*   *monitor*   *pomposity*
                                              opacity
                                              capacity
                                              gossiping

A deleted schwa in the more frequent words, *capacity* and *gossiping* may perhaps be possible in very rapid speech, but deletion in these words, in which a possible English cluster is created, is lagging far behind deletion before *r, l,* and *n* which produce non-English clusters, e.g. *century* [čr] , *family* [ml] , *every* [vr] . These facts suggest that the constraints on schwa-deletion are not governed by language-specific syllable-structure conditions, but are governed by universal constraints by which sonorants in second position are favored over obstruents.

Other contexts in which schwa-deletion is blocked also reveal the workings of a universal syllable-structure condition, since contexts constraining deletion are just those where deletion would produce a syllable-initial cluster that violates the universal conditions outlined in section 1. The contexts that block deletion are those in which: (a) the consonant preceding the post-stress schwa is weaker than, or the same strength as, the consonant following the schwa; (b) a cluster follows the schwa; (c) a syllable-initial cluster precedes the schwa.

There are several different examples of the conditions described in (a). One is the case where a sonorant precedes the schwa, and is weaker than the sonorant following the schwa, as in the following words:

(12)   *rl*   *ln*   *rn*
         quarreling   *felony*   *paranoic*
         barreling   *colony*   *irony*

A deletion in these words would produce the unacceptable syllable-initial clusters, *rl, ln, rn*. Observe that sonorant clusters in which the first sonorant is stronger than the second are allowed as the result of schwa-deletion in *scenery, memory, celery, finally, family* and so on. Again, let me emphasize that the clusters created in this latter set of words, *nr, mr, lr, nl* and *ml* are not ordinarily found in syllable-initial position in English, although they are universally possible syllable-initial clusters.

Post-stress schwa-deletion between *m* and *n* is less acceptable than deletion between a nasal and a liquid, but more acceptable than in the examples in (12). Zwicky gives the following examples:

(13) *feminine*   *stamina*   *nominal*
     geminate (adj.)   *phenomenal*   *dominant*
     hominy   *aluminum*   *voluminous*
     prominent   *Germany*

The reason is the small difference in strength between *m* and *n*. The labial is slightly stronger than the alveolar, which makes *mn* clusters acceptable on universal principles as syllable-initials, but the difference in strength is so slight that such clusters do not form as freely as clusters with greater strength differences.

The failure of post-stress schwa deletion after orthographic /t/ in some cases is due to a prior process weakening /t/ to a flap. This weakening, as we mentioned above, occurs when the alveolar stop is an ambisyllabic consonant, i.e., when it is preceded by a stressed syllabic, as in *watery, buttery,* and even when the stressed syllabic has an *r*-quality, as in *artery*, and followed by an unstressed syllabic other than [n]. (Before [n], /t/ has become [ʔ], as in *button.*) A *t* preceded by a consonant does not flap, e.g. *factory, adultery, mystery.*[5] A schwa following a flap tends to remain undeleted, e.g. *artery, watery, buttery, flattery*, etc., although a schwa following a

non-flapped *t*, as in *factory, adultery* and *mystery*, tends to delete. The test
I mentioned earlier revealed this tendency rather clearly.

In this test, eight subjects classified 112 words ending in *Vry*, according
to whether they *Usually* leave out the unstressed schwa, *Sometimes* leave it
out, or *Rarely* leave it out. There were eight words in the corpus containing
flaps; of the 63 responses for these words, 86% were classified into the
Rarely delete category, 9% in the Sometimes category, and 5% in the Usually
category.

On the other hand, there were 16 words that have a full /t/, which occurs
after a consonant, e.g. *mystery, factory*, etc. Of the 125 responses for these
items, 44% were in the Usually category, 32% in the Sometimes category,
and 24% in the Rarely category. Thus there is a clear difference between
deletion after a flap and after a non-flapped /t/.[6]

My explanation for the failure of deletion after a flap is that the flap is
too weak to be the first member of a syllable-initial cluster. A schwa-less
pronunciation of any of the flap words requires a full voiceless stop
before the *r*. This is shown clearly in words that have *n* preceding *t*. For
example *elementary* has two pronunciations in my own speech. In one pronunciation the flap occurs, and the schwa must be present [ɛləmɛ́ɾəri] . In
the other pronunciation, the schwa is absent, and the *t* is voiceless aspirated:
[ɛləmɛ́ntʰri] . Since flapping is obligatory in my speech, there is no pronunciation (except a hyper-correct pronunciation) with a schwa and without
a flap: *[ɛləmɛ́ntʰəri] .

In another case, Zwicky noted that schwa-deletion is blocked if a cluster
follows the schwa. The following are his examples of words that never have
schwa-deletion.

(14) *development*   *honestly*
     graciously   *earnestly*

The reason the deletion is blocked here is that the resulting cluster would be
too complex, i.e., would not be a possible syllable-initial cluster. Similarly,
deletion is blocked if a cluster precedes the schwa. On the test mentioned
above, the words *burglary, contrary* and *penury* (with a [ny] cluster) where
judged consistently as non-deleting. Again the reason is that the cluster
resulting from deletion, e.g. /glr/, /trr/ and /nyr/ would all be impossible
syllable-initial clusters. For schwa-deletion to take place in such words, the
cluster would have to be reduced also. This is probably what has occurred in
the pronunciation [mɤkri] for *mercury* (a pronunciation used for the make
of automobile, but rarely for the element or planet), and [laybri] for *library*
which is heard occasionally in very sloppy speech. Only the most frequent
words would undergo such a radical reduction.

One further constraint on post-stress schwa deletion discussed by Zwicky seems to be quite independent of syllable-structure. If the schwa occurs between a primary and secondary stress, no deletion may occur, even if all other conditions favor deletion.

(15) *degéneràte* (vb) (cf. *degénerate*, adj.)
imáginàry (cf. *imágining*)
mémorìze (cf. *mémory*)
hýphenàte
vócalìsm

The failure of deletion here is probably due to the strong tendency found in English to alternate stressed and unstressed syllables. This same tendency gives us *markedness* and *ashamedly* which have schwas where the words they are formed from (i.e. *marked, ashamed*) do not. This same tendency is probably the major factor behind the deletions we are discussing here, since post-stress schwa-deletion always occurs between a stressed syllable and an unstressed syllable, reducing a sequence of two unstressed syllables to a single unstressed syllable.

To summarize the discussion of post-stress schwa-deletion, we find that all the segmental contexts that favor or disfavor schwa-deletion can be explained by universal principles of syllable structure, which have been developed completely independently of the data discussed here. The data we find here, however, shed some light on the metatheoretical status of the universal syllable-structure condition, since the constraints on deletion follow universal syllable-structure conditions rather than language-specific conditions. The difference is summarized in general terms in the chart in (16). Post-stress schwa-deletion is producing clusters with a weak second member, i.e. *r, l* and *n*, in that order, and the only restriction on these clusters is that the first member be stronger than the second. Because the deletion is conditioned by the weakness of the second consonant, obstruent plus obstruent clusters have not been created as yet.

(16) Deletion produces

English has

obstruent[7]
nasal } + r
l

stop
voiceless fricative | + liquid

obstruent
nasal | + l
obstruent + n
*obstruent + obstruent

s + { liquid
{ nasal
{ stop

However, English already has obstruent plus obstruent clusters, where the first obstruent is /s/, but does not have many of the clusters produced by deletion. These facts suggest that universal constraints, which could not be abstracted merely from the surface forms of English and are not a part of the language-specific grammar of English, are nonetheless operating to constrain the creation of new clusters in English. These universal syllable-structure conditions are a part of the speakers' linguistic apparatus, presumably his inheritance, whether they are phonetically-based constraints or psychologically-based constraints. Furthermore, since schwa-deletion is a casual speech process which takes place among adult speakers (see Hooper 1976a), these universal constraints must be "known" to adults. These are not merely constraints which operate in language acquisition, and then become inoperative, once language specific constraints are learned.[8]

We should ask also why the constraints operating in the case of schwa-deletion are the universal conditions rather than the language-specific conditions of English. There are two directions we could follow in seeking an answer to this question. In one direction we could reason that it is merely a peculiarity of post-stress schwa-deletion that it follows this particular pattern based on universal constraints. Or, we could investigate the possibility that the synchronic language-specific constraints are partially arbitrary in the sense that they may have come about under the influence of factors unrelated to syllable structure. Under this view we would expect deletion rules to be constrained by universal patterns rather than the partially arbitrary synchronic constraints. In the next section we will see evidence of a different type to show that synchronic language-specific syllable-structure conditions may be partially arbitrary.

4. Pre-stress schwa-deletion

Zwicky mentions pre-stress schwa-deletion only in passing. His comments are that it "seems to have no relationship to the hierarchy in (5)" (i.e., the hierarchy governing post-stress schwa-deletion), and that its failure to apply in some words is "presumably for phonetic reasons" (p. 284), although he does not specify what these phonetic reasons are. I have examined pre-stress schwa-deletion in greater detail, and I will show here that while there are major differences between the two deletions, the pre-stress deletion is governed by universal principles of syllable structure, much as post-stress deletion is.

The major difference between post-stress and pre-stress schwa-deletion is that pre-stress schwa-deletion operates very freely, creating clusters that violate English syllable-structure, and even creating some clusters that violate universal syllable-structure conditions. The particular deletion I am discussing here occurs in the initial syllable of words that have stress on the second syllable. Thus, in effect, a new word-initial, pre-stress cluster is created. As I mentioned above, stressed syllables are stronger in English than unstressed syllables; therefore we might expect that stressed syllables would tolerate freer clustering in initial position than unstressed syllables.

The second difference between pre-stress and post-stress schwa-deletion involves the extent to which each process is developed in American English. Post-stress schwa-deletion is quite well-developed; it occurs in all styles of speech (although it is certainly more pervasive in the more casual styles), and has permanently affected a number of lexical items. Pre-stress schwa-deletion on the other hand is restricted to very rapid and casual speech styles. The only lexical items I know of that have been permanently affected by pre-stress deletion are *tata* (from *potato*) or *tater*, *'cause* (from *because*) and *'member* (from *remember*) which exist as casual or colloquial variants of the still-existing full forms. (I assume that the loss of schwa in these forms led to the loss of the initial consonant as well.) Because pre-stress schwa-deletion has not made much head-way in the language, this section will be much more speculative than the last. It is extremely difficult to make judgments about rapid-speech forms; therefore, the judgments presented here are rather gross approximations, but they have been informally verified by several other speakers.

In considering the examples to be presented, bear in mind that the pronunciation in which the first vowel is deleted is a very rapid pronunciation. This pronunciation will seem natural only for the most frequent words, but I have listed less frequent items along with more frequent items in order to present the full range of possible consonant clustering. Notice further that the deletions occur more readily if the word occurs in a position of low sentence stress.

In the schwa-less pronunciation of the examples in (17), an initial stop obstruent (as in (17a–17e)) will be reduced to a stop gesture at the appropriate point of articulation, and this gesture will not be accompanied by voicing. However, original voiceless stops retain aspiration, while original voiced stops are unaspirated. A fricative in initial position, e.g. *fatigue* [ftíyg] is similarly reduced to a brief gesture, and it may also be voiceless, as in *vicinity* [fsínəti].

The examples in (17) are of the type that allow pre-stress schwa-deletion. The resulting clusters in these cases are sequences of two obstruents, (a) – (g), or sequences of obstruent plus nasal, (h). Such clusters do not occur in initial position in careful speech forms, and would presumably not be allowed by English syllable-structure conditions based on careful speech.

(17) Pre-stress schwa-deletion

Stop – stop

(a) voiceless + voiceless
capacity
catastrophe
capricious
petition
pecan
potato
toponymy
topography
Topanga

(b) voiceless + voiced
cadaverous
pedestrian
pedantic
tobacco
together
today

(c) voiced + voiceless
become
because
botanical
batallion
depend
depressed
deposit
Dakota
Japan

(d) voiced + voiced
beginning
bedazzle
begonia
debate
degrade
degree
digest
debilitate

(e) stop + fricative
defeat
default
decision
deceive
development
divisible
beside
buffoon
cassette
pacific
discuss
discover
discover
dissolve
guffaw
pastrami

(f) fricative + stop
fatigue
fatality

(g) fricative + fricative
vicinity
façade

(h) obstruent + nasal
Canadian
Chamelian
commercial
committee
beneath
demand
diminish
tomorrow
tonight
tenacious
fanatical
thermometer[9]

The relative strength of obstruents is not clearly established, especially with regard to stops relative to fricatives. (See Hooper (1976b) for a discussion of this problem.) Still, it seems clear that the universal constraints discussed in section 1 are violated by the clusters resulting from pre-stress schwa-deletion, because the initial obstruent is weaker than the second obstruent. The reason for this is that the second obstruent originally (and still in normal speech) begins a stressed syllable, and thus is strong, while the initial consonant begins an unstressed syllable, and thus is weaker. This is clear from the descriptions given just above of the articulation of these clusters. At the present, then, these rapid speech forms violate the universal syllable-structure conditions. There are two paths that could be taken to bring the forms back into conformance with the universals: (1) the weak initial consonant could drop, as in *tater* and *'cause*, or (2) the initial consonant could strengthen enough to reinstate the proper strength relations. For obstruent-obstruent clusters, (1) seems to be the favored course, since this has already occurred in some words. We will see below that for obstruent-liquid clusters, (2) is also a possibility.

There is one clear universal concerning obstruent clusters that is not violated by the reduction of these forms. This universal states that in initial clusters a voiced consonant cannot be followed by a voiceless consonant (Greenberg 1965). We have already observed that the initial consonant lacks voicing if the schwa is totally absent, so this universal law is not violated.

Another constraint emerges from an examination of the forms in (17): homorganicity of the resulting cluster impedes deletion. This is especially true of words such as *familiar, bemoan, deny* and *detach*, and may also be true of the more frequent words such as *tonight*.

In the examples in (18) and (19), pre-stress schwa-deletion would create initial clusters of the type that occur in careful speech forms in English. The forms in (18) have initial /s/. In initial position, /s/ occurs before /p, t, k, m, n, l/. But pre-stress schwa-deletion in the forms in (18) does not create true clusters. *Sonority* cannot be said with a clusters like that of *snore; superior* cannot have the initial cluster of *spear*, etc. Of all the examples in (18), the only one that can even marginally be reduced to a true cluster is *suppose*, in its parenthetical reading. The normal reduction in all of these forms is from [sə] to a long or syllabic pronunciation of the /s/.

(18) | s + obstruent | s + nasal | s + l | s + r |
|---|---|---|---|
| *security* | *sonority* | *cylindrical* | *serenity* |
| *secretion* | *semantic* | *salinity* | *cerebral* |
| *satanical* | *senility* | *saliva* | *sorority* |
| *support* | | *solarium* | |

s + obstruent

suppose
superior
supremacy
sophisticated
subordinate
sagacious

Compare these words with other words beginning in fricatives that undergo deletion; *fatigue* may have a very short /f/, much shorter than the acceptable /s/ of, e.g. *security*. It might be that deletion after /s/ lags behind other deletions precisely because clusters with initial /s/ already exist in English; that is, some tendency to avoid merger may be delaying reduction in these cases.

The forms in (19) will begin in obstruent-liquid clusters when the first vowel is deleted. There seem to be two stages in the reduction. In the first, the vowel is lost and the initial consonant exists only as a voiceless gesture preceding the stressed syllable. This pronunciation is analogous to that found in the reduction of obstruent-obstruent clusters discussed above. In another pronunciation, which I take to represent a second stage, the initial consonant is drawn fully into the stressed syllable; the obstruent is strengthened and takes on the characteristics of a pre-stress, syllable-initial obstruent, and the liquid takes on the phonetic characteristics of a second consonant. For instance, if the first consonant is voiceless, then the liquid is produced as partially voiceless.

(19) *parade*   *police*
      parenthesis   *polite*
      correct   *Columbus*
      corrupt   *collapse*
      terrific   *balloon*
      Toronto   *believe*
      ferocious   *galoshes*
      direction
      garage

The reason I take the pronunciation in which the obstruent is strengthened, and fully syllable-initial, to be a second stage is that this pronunciation seems less acceptable, less standard, or sloppier, to me. This is merely impressionistic, and thus speculative. However, it is clear that there are two types of pronunciation.

Notice again that the reduction is more natural in frequent items, e.g.

[pliys] is often heard for *police*; people who live in Toronto say [tračǝ]. One further comment on (19): examples of words in which deletion of the first vowel would produce clusters not occurring in English have not been included. Such examples would be alveolar stops plus /l/, affricates plus liquid, e.g. *delay, telepathy, jalopy*, etc. Whatever the differences are between such forms and the forms in (19), they are too slight to be distinguished on the basis of intuition, and must be distinguished experimentally before any conclusions are drawn.

Let us turn now to a discussion of forms in which schwa-deletion leaves clusters beginning with sonorants. There are two categories: (i) clusters in which the first consonant is stronger than the second, and (ii) clusters in which the first consonant is weaker than the second. According to the strength hierarchy discussed above, the following clusters of category (i) are possible: *mr, ml, nr, nl* and *lr*. These are listed in descending order, according to the difference in strength between the two members. Pre-stress schwa-deletion produces clusters of *mr* in the following words:

(20)   *marine*   *mirage*   *morale*
       Marie   *miraculous*   *moronic*

These are judged as acceptable (by the speakers I consulted), and are most natural for the more frequent words *marine* and *Marie*.

However, the speakers I consulted judged *ml* sequences to be less acceptable, as in the following words:

(21)   *melodic*   *millennium*
       malicious   *molecular*

The difference between (20) and (21) would follow from the theory of syllable structure presented in section one, since *l* is stronger than *r*, and the greater the strength difference between the first and second consonant, the better. However, the difference may also be due to a difference in frequency, since there are no very common words which would yield an *ml* cluster under deletion.

Next we should consider words yielding clusters of *nr* and *nl*. However, there is a gap in the data at this point; I was unable to find any appropriate words of the form *nǝr*, and the only possible candidated for *nǝl* are *nilometer* and *Nilotic*. Even if these words contain a first-syllable schwa, applicable data would have to come from speakers who use such words.

The last possible strong-weak cluster is *lr*, which is a universally impossible cluster according to Greenberg. The theory employed here would predict a low acceptability for such a cluster, since the difference in strength is so slight. These predictions are borne out; deletion in the forms of (22) is less acceptable (though not totally unacceptable) than in the forms of (21).

(22) *Lorraine*
      laryngeal

However, the conclusions we might want to draw concerning clusters of strong plus weak sonorants are severely weakened by the gaps in the data.

Let us examine now deletion that produces clusters of sonorants followed by stronger consonants. We will consider clusters whose initial member is *m, n, l* or *r*, in that order, and we will find that pre-stress schwa-deletion produces violations of the universal syllable structure condition, but at the same time, the functioning of the universal syllable-structure condition is clearly discernible.

First, consider words in initial *m* where deletion will produce a cluster of *m* plus an obstruent.

(23) *mechanic*   *massage*
      metallic   *methodical*
      magician   *metropolis*

In these forms the initial *m* may be reduced to a bilabial closure, with open velum, and with or without a short period of vocal-cord vibration. This pronunciation is similar to the pronunciation described above for obstruent-obstruent clusters. This pronunciation is easily accepted by the speakers I consulted. Note, however, that initial clusters of sonorant plus obstruent violate the universal conditions presented earlier. Notice further that the violations may be ranked according to the strength of the first sonorant; a violation with *m* is less serious than with a weaker sonorant. And, as expected, the weaker the sonorant, the less acceptable the deletion. Thus deletions between *n* and an obstruent are less acceptable than between *m* and an obstruent.

(24) *neglect*   *notorious*   *nativity*
      negociate   *necessity*

In this case the permitted pronunciation is analogous to that described above for *m* plus obstruent.

Deletions after *l* and *r*, as in (25) and (26) are increasingly less acceptable, as predicted.

(25) *laborious*
latrine
legitimate
logician
linoleum
lament

(26) *remarkable*   *republican*   *relax*
revision   *record*   *refrigerator*
rhetorical   *reciprocal*   *remember*
                    religious

A deletion after *l* is marginally possible but it leaves the *l* unsupported and reduced to a weak gesture. A deletion after *r* is simply not possible; the loss of the vowel is accompanied by the loss of the consonant, as in *'member* for *remember*.

With all these facts now presented, we can formulate some general statements concerning pre-stress schwa-deletion. Pre-stress schwa-deletion is a general weakening or reduction of unstressed initial syllables leading to the deletion of the vowel. (Note that this occurs in vowel-initial words as well, *'bout, 'round, 'nuf* for *about, around* and *enough*.) The deletion of the vowel, which occurs only in very rapid speech, produces a consonant cluster. Further, the deletion is constrained by the type of cluster that is created. The deletion is constrained by universal syllable-structure constraints, but in a relative manner, and not absolutely. Deletion is constrained on a relative scale according to the extent to which the universal conditions are violated. We have suggested that deletion leaving an *mr* cluster is acceptable, while deletion leaving an *ml* or *lr* cluster is less acceptable. More striking, however, are the deletions leaving weak-strong clusters: *m*-obstruent clusters, which are disallowed theoretically, may occur, but *n*-obstruent clusters are less acceptable, and *l*-obstruent and *r*-obstruent clusters are unacceptable.

Pre-stress schwa-deletion illustrates an important point concerning the metatheoretical status of syllable-structure conditions. The universal syllable-structure conditions are not absolute, inviolable constraints. They are rather relative conditions expressing relations among segment types. Whether the conditions hold for a given language at a given synchronic stage will depend on the history of the language, and in particular upon the relative power of competing tendencies in a language. That is, the tendency to delete unstressed vowels must compete with the tendency to maintain universal constraints on syllable structure. In the case of post-stress schwa-deletion we observe that the universal conditions are keeping schwa-deletion in line; no universally

unacceptable clusters are created. Pre-stress schwa-deletion is to some extent
overpowering the syllable structure conditions, but only in rapid speech.
Should the latter deletion ever become a general and pervasive process in the
language, as the former deletion has, there are two possibilities for subsequent
developments of the clusters created (especially the universally unacceptable
ones). The loss of the vowel may be followed by the loss of the initial consonant, as in *tater*, *'cause*, and *'member*. This seems to be the favored possibility, in view of the reduced words just cited, and the phonetic weakness of
the initial consonants, as described above. But the alternate possibility is
worth considering because of its theoretical consequences. The alternate
possibility is the stabilization of the new clusters. This may require the
strengthening of the initial consonant, as we observed as one possibility for
the obstruent-liquid clusters in (19). This development would lead to a synchronic state in which existing syllable-initial clusters violate the proposed
universals. I would expect such a state to be possible, but temporary, since
there are always forces acting to reinstate preferred syllable structure. The
hypothetical synchronic state described here would be arbitrary in the sense
mentioned in the conclusion in section 3. That is, if universal conditions on
syllable structure were allowed to work on language unopposed by other
forces, then all languages would conform to the universal conditions. Since
these conditions are seldom unopposed, synchronic states could exist in
which syllable structure is less than optimal. Of course, total violation is not
possible and the type and extent of possible violations remain to be determined. This view implies that universal syllable-structure conditions cannot
be determined solely from the study of language-specific, synchronic syllable
structure, but such studies must be supplemented by a study of changes, such
as those discussed here.

Let me emphasize that while these deletion processes point to the relational character of universal syllable-structure conditions, they also strongly
support the *universal* character of syllable-structure conditions, as I pointed
out before. The conditions functioning in both pre-stress and post-stress
schwa-deletion are not English-specific conditions. They could not be learned
by speakers as a part of the grammar of English. Since these conditions are
also seen operating in other languages, they must be considered universal.
The phonetic and psychological bases of such universals, however, remain to
be determined.

Notes

1. The condition in (3) is meant only to illustrate the general form of the universal
   syllable structure condition; there are probably more consonant positions allowable
   universally. But see the discussion in sections 3 and 4 of the metatheoretical status of
   the universal condition.

2. A problem for which I have not found a totally satisfactory solution, however, is the problem of /s/, which functions as a very strong consonant in English, where syllable-initial clusters of /sp/, /st/ and /sk/ are allowed, but as a very weak consonant in Spanish, where /s/ cannot figure in syllable-initial clusters.
3. Hoard's examples contrast words with a tertiary stress on the final syllable with words which have an unstressed final syllable. To illustrate the maximal difference between the consonants, the examples in (4) contrast stressed with unstressed syllables. The different degrees of stress probably correlate with degrees of tenseness if secondary and tertiary stress are taken into consideration.
4. This syllabification makes it impossible to account for the [ŋ] in *congress* versus the [n] in *congressional* on the basis of syllabification, as Hoard proposes. His rule assimilates /n/ to a tautosyllabic velar. However, this rule does not work, since *increment* would be syllabified by Hoard as /ínkr$əm$ənt/, but no assimilation takes place.
5. After /n/ the situation is variable; see below.
6. Of course, given the way I conducted the test, asking speakers directly for their judgments, I did not obtain data on the actual phonetic status of deletion, but rather on the speakers' notions about deletion. I do not consider the two to be substantially different in this case.
7. There is one restriction on the initial obstruent for some speakers: it cannot be an affricate. On the test discussed earlier, several (but not all) speakers very consistently put words which would have affricate-liquid clusters if deletion applied, into the Rarely delete category. Examples are: *century, injury, surgery*, etc.
8. Pertz and Bever (1975) have shown experimentally the mono-lingual adolescent English speakers can demonstrate sensitivity to universal clustering constraints.
9. The pronunciation of this form which allows schwa-deletion is r-less in the first syllable, [θəmámə ʃ] .

References

Foley, James
    1970   "Phonological distinctive features", *Folia Linguistica* 4: 87–92.
    1972   "Rule precursors and phonological change by metarule", in: Stockwell – Macaulay 1972, pp. 96–100.
Greenberg, Joseph H.
    1965   "Some generalizations concerning initial and final consonant sequences", *Linguistics* 18: 5–34.
Guile, Timothy
    1973   "Glide-obstruentization and the syllable coda hierarchy", in: *Papers from the Ninth Regional Meeting of the Chicago Linguistic Society*, pp. 39–56.
Hankamer, Jorge – Judith Aissen
    1974   "The sonority hierarchy", in: *Natural Phonology Parasession of the Chicago Linguistic Society*, pp. 131–145.
Hoard, James E.
    1971   "Aspiration, tenseness, and syllabication in English", *Language* 47: 133–140.
Hooper, Joan B.
    1973   *Aspects of natural generative phonology*. [Unpublished Ph.D. dissertation, UCLA.]
    1976a   *Word frequency in lexical diffusion and the source of morpho-phonological change,* in: *Current progress in historical linguistics* (Ed.: W. Christie, jr.) (Amsterdam: North-Holland), pp. 95–105.
    1976b   *Introduction to natural generative phonology* (New York: Academic Press).

Pertz, D. L. – T. G. Bever
    1975   "Sensitivity to phonological universals in children and adolescents", *Language*
            51: 149–162.
Pulgram, Ernst
    1970   *Syllable, word, nexus, cursus* (The Hague: Mouton).
Saussure, Ferdinand de
    1959   *Course in general linguistics* (Trsl.: Wade Baskin) (New York: Philosophical
            Library). [Original edition: 1915.]
Stockwell, Robert P. – Ronald K. S. Macaulay (eds.)
    1972   *Linguistic change and generative theory* (Bloomington: Indiana University
            Press).
Tranel, Bernard
    1974   "A note on final consonant deletion, the pronunciation of cardinal numbers,
            and linguistic changes in progress in Modern French", in: *Montreal Working
            Papers in Linguistics* 3, pp. 173–189.
Vennemann, Theo
    1972   "On the theory of syllabic phonology", *Linguistische Berichte* 18: 1–18.
Zwicky, Arnold
    1972   "A note on a phonological hierarchy in English", in: Stockwell – Macaulay,
            pp. 275–301.

DAVID HUNTLEY

Phonological models and Slavic palatalizations

The purpose of the present paper is to examine the way in which certain palatalizations that have occurred in the history of Slavic throw light upon the adequacy of three types of phonological model: (1) an autonomous phonemic model; (2) a strong generative model which includes the principle of absolute neutralization, i.e., the principle that segments that do not occur in surface representation may be allowed to occur in underlying representation; (3) a weak generative model which excludes absolute neutralization.

In early Common Slavic, velar stops became assibilated palatals before front vowels, e.g.:

*bēgīte > *bēȝīte 2pl. pres. 'flee'
*krīkēs > *krīčēs 2sg. aor. 'shout'

This change did not occur before back vowels, e.g. *mogām lsg. pres. 'be able', roikā nom. sg. 'river'. The results of this change can be adequately accounted for within an autonomous phonemic level, since velars and palatals were in complementary distribution. (It can be shown that the change ē > a after palatals took place only much later).

At a later period, Common Slavic diphthongs became monophthongs, in particular oi > ē, ī, but by this time the above-mentioned palatalization ceased to be productive. Instead, velars now became assibilated dentals before these new front vowels, e.g.:

*mogois > *mogīs > *moȝīs 2sg. imperative-optative 'be able'
*roikai > *rēkē > *rēcē dat.-loc. sg. 'river'

Within an autonomous phonemic model, velars, palatals, and dental affricates now have to be separate phonemes, since both palatals and dental affricates can occur before front vowels. At the morphophonemic level, however, the palatals and the dental affricates are alternants of velars. Such a model forces one to separate at the phonemic level, segments which in many lexical items are connected one with the other at the morphophonemic level.

Considerations of this kind have led generative phonologists to abandon the autonomous phonemic level. However, accounts given by generative phonologists of the Slavic *k:c* alternations, or their reflexes, are also not adequate synchronic models. In Contemporary Standard Russian, the reflexes of the dental palatalization of velars are palatalized velars in the locative and dative of nouns and in the imperative (here the velars have been re-established analogically), but elsewhere remain as dentals. Lightner (1972a: 139–140) states that velars become palatals before an underlying front vowel. He claims that velars become dentals or palatalized velars before an underlying diphthong *ai* (265–266). The evidence for this diphthong is said to be the verb *pet'* inf., *poju̇* lsg. pres. 'sing'. After the rule changing velars to palatals before front vowels is applied, a later rule shifts *ai* > *ē* when not before a vowel. Before this derived *ē*, a still later rule shifts word-initial velar to dental and causes non-initial velar to become palatalized.

A similar analysis of velar: dental alternations in Old Church Slavonic is given by Lunt (1974:152). The evidence for deriving *oi* → *ě* is in Lunt's words, 'In an isolated verb, *oj* occurs before vowel but *ě* before consonant: *pojǫtъ pěti.*' In my view this is not an adequate synchronic argument, for one knows only on diachronic grounds that OCS *ě* in *pěti* is in fact connected with *ě* in, for example, *rěčě*.

I now hold the view that in instances where no alternation appears on the surface both palatals and dental affricates must be included in the underlying representation of certain forms in Old Church Slavonic and in late Common Slavic. This is a modification of the view expressed in Huntley 1975:361. Where the alternations are present in the surface structure, the underlying form has the velar. The dental alternant occurs before declensional desinences and before imperative desinences that begin with *ě* or *i*. e.g., *rěčě, mozi*. The palatal alternation, e.g., *kričě* → *kriča, možete, bože,* occurs before all other front vowels. In such a model, an underlying representation would have the same stock of segments as would the surface representation in Old Church Slavonic and in late Common Slavic. Such a model would have a large number of morphologically conditioned rules and would be less elegant and less powerful than a model which included the principle of absolute neutralization. Nevertheless, in the absolute-neutralization model one is forced to have recourse either to diachronic information or to arbitrary procedures, so that the weaker and less elegant model is the more adequate one from a synchronic point of view.

In the absolute-neutralization model morphologically conditioned rules are allowed in order to account for phonological irregularities. It would appear that the very concept of phonological irregularity is not even admissible in the autonomous phonemic model. The history of the verb *tkat'* 'weave' in Russian is instructive in this respect. According to Jakobson (1949:17), when present tense 2sg., etc. of this verb changed analogically from *tčoš* to *tk'oš*, there was introduced a 'new phoneme, the soft *k*', which formerly was a mere positional variant of the phoneme *k*.' The corollary of this statement, however, is that in Contemporary Standard Russian the highly marginal *k*' is assigned equal paradigmatic status along with the regularly occurring palatalized labials and dentals. On the other hand, Lightner (1972b:427–428) states, 'It is clear that the grammar must contain a rule which shifts velars to palatals, rule (K → Č), and it is likewise clear that the root in *tku/tket* is an exception to rule (K → Č).' However, in Lightner 1972a, rule (K → Č) is not applicable to sets of quite regular nouns whose stems end in a palatal. These nouns, along with nouns whose stems end in palatalized labials and dentals are merely marked as [-hard]. In other words, palatals and palatalized consonants, contrary to Lightner's claim, do occur in the underlying representation of Contemporary Standard Russian. In the kind of model advocated in this paper, the palatalized velar in *tk'oš* would be generated by a morphologically-conditioned rule shifting plain velar to palatalized velar before *o* in the present tense. Thus the weak generative model would reduce the stock of phonemes in Contemporary Standard Russian, as compared with the autonomous-level model, by one item, namely *k*'.

There are now strong indications that generative phonologists in their treatment of Slavic data are beginning to move towards the position advocated in this paper. Lightner (1972b:428, fn. 6) states that the transformational cycle must be abandoned and that to explain the shift *e → o* in Russian 'at worst one will have to refer to the relevant morphological categories.' In a review of Lunt 1974 (Huntley 1975:361), I state that if Lunt's modifications of TG phonology were carried further, 'one would end up with something like a more highly formalized model of the type found in Jakobson's 1948 description of Russian conjugation, but without an autonomous phonemic level.' After this review was sent to the press, but before it was published, further confirmation of this view came to light. Coats and Lightner (1975:339) stated that in order to derive present tense *pišet* versus infinitive *pisat'* 'write', it is necessary to set up a minor rule for which verbs of this type are marked. They claim that the stem of such verbs is *pisáj-*, but that they are marked to drop *-a-* in the present, whence *pisj → piš-*. They add (340), 'It is also interesting that the proposed analysis brings us back much closer to Jakobson's original analysis.' The same point is made much more strongly in Lightner 1975:630, where DM = derivational morphology. 'After

Jakobson's ground-breaking analysis of 1948, Halle 1963 noted several inadequacies which seemed best handled by introduction of the transforma-tional cycle. A brief review of these (and other) analyses is given in Lightner 1972, in which yet another transformational-cycle analysis is proposed. But Coats and Lightner 1975 refer to DM, and show not only that what have been for years considered crucial questions in the analysis of Russian conjugation are not even well-formed questions, but also that the correct solution in fact strikingly resembles Jakobson's original analysis.'

The Coats and Lightner analysis, however, is much more complex than Jakobson's. Setting up a stem *pisáj-*, dropping -*a*-; claiming that substitutive softening is triggered by the jod, and then dropping the jod is merely a roundabout way of saying that the stem-final consonant undergoes substitu-tive softening in the present tense, and is thus inferior to Jakobson's more direct formulation. Once again, Lightner has used the technique of absolute neutralization. Here, though, diachronic information is not used; instead we have a quite arbitrary procedure. It would seem that if we remove the arbitrary procedures from Coats and Lightner's recent paper, we do indeed end up with the kind of model advocated in this paper; a model that closely resembles Jakobson 1948 except for the fact that it lacks an autonomous phonemic level.

References

Coats, Herbert S. – Theodore M. Lightner
    1975   "Transitive softening in Russian conjugation", *Language* 51: 338–341.
Halle, Morris
    1963   "O pravilax russkogo sprjaženija", in: *American contributions to the Fifth International Congress of Slavists* (The Hague: Mouton), pp. 113–132.
Huntley, David
    1975   Review of Lunt 1974, *Slavic and East European Journal* 19: 357–361.
Jakobson, Roman
    1948   "Russian conjugation", *Word* 4: 155–167.
    1949   "The phonetic and grammatical aspects of language in their interrelations", in: Actes du Sixième Congrès international des linguistes (Paris: Klincksieck), pp. 5–18.
Lightner, Theodore, M.
    1972a   *Problems in the theory of phonology* (Edmonton: Linguistic Research, Inc.).
    1972b   "Some remarks on exceptions and on coexistent systems in phonology", in: *The Slavic word* (Ed.: Dean S. Worth) (The Hague: Mouton), pp. 426–436.
Lunt, Horace G.
    1974   *Old Church Slavonic grammar*[6] (The Hague: Mouton).

ROBERT J. JEFFERS

Restructuring, relexicalization, and reversion in historical phonology

0. One of the major insights of early linguistic investigation was the recognition that the phonetic segments which speakers use in the oral production of their language are organized into a highly structured system, and that the design of this *phonological system* is determined by the way in which various phonetic features function to establish distinctive oppositions, and by a set of 'rules' which relate phonetically distinct, but morphologically unique forms. Since the establishment of the notion *phoneme*, historical linguists have been concerned not simply with a descriptive typology of phonetic change, but also with a complementary typology of phonological changes. The best known of such descriptive typologies are associated with American structuralism (e.g. H. Hoenigswald, 1960), Prague school structuralism (e.g., R. Jakobson, 1931), and generative grammar (e.g., R. D. King, 1969).

While the various theoretical biases which are associated with these three approaches to phonology have each served to highlight important aspects of phonological change, it is notable that these same biases have resulted in accounts of phonological change which are descriptively inadequate. In the first part of this paper I will consider some of the failures of the treatments of phonological change offered by the above-mentioned schools of phonological theory, and I will attempt to integrate the valuable contributions which have come from these three sources, looking toward a descriptive account of phonological change which will attend to all interesting and relevant issues.

1. As students of American structural linguistics turned their attention to linguistic change in general, and sound change in particular, interest understandably centered around the ways in which the inventory of phonemes might come to be reorganized. How and when are new oppositions introduced, or old ones lost? How and when does a realignment in the system of phonological contrasts take place, i.e., under what circumstances do the phonological (i.e., phonemic) representations of given morphemes change without con-

comitant change in the phonemic stock? Based largely on the work of Henry Hoenigswald (1960) a system of classification for phonological change was developed. (I begin with this system only because the terminology introduced with American structuralism appear to me to be the most widely used in descriptions of phonological change and phonological changes.)

The basic premise of the structuralist system for classifying phonological change is that all forms of phonological restructuring begin with phonetic split or merger. A complete merger results when two (or more) sounds fall together in all environments where they formerly contrasted. This may reflect a phonetic alteration in either or both of the phonemes involved. An unconditioned merger always results in a change in the phonological system, and that change is assumed to be irreversible. Where there were once two (or more) phonemes, after merger there is one, and its subsequent history will in no way reflect its multiple origins.

Conditioned merger necessarily coincides with phonetic split. If some tokens (allophones) of a phoneme $/x/$ merge with $/y/$, a conditioned split in $/x/$ has occurred. This phenomenon is termed primary split. Latin rhotacism is a well-known example.

Pre-Latin s and r remain distinct in Classical Latin with the exception that the s coalesces with r (probably via z) in intervocalic position.

I.   i. $\boxed{s}$ . . . . . . .s (except as in ii)
       ii. $\boxed{s}$ . . . . . . $\boxed{r}$ / V___V
       iii. r - - - - - - - - $\boxed{r}$

(The dotted and broken lines in I represent the concomitant split in s and merger of r and s, respectively.)

The phonological consequence of primary split is a realignment in the system of phonological contrasts. The phonological representation of the Old Latin personal name *Valesius*, for example, includes a medial $/s/$, whereas its Classical Latin correspondent shows medial $/r/$. As a result of primary split the phonological representation of certain morphemes changes without any alteration in the inventory of phonemes.

It is often the case that a phonetic split results in a change in the phonemic inventory only after a later change has taken place. In one type of secondary split, the term which describes such developments, the segment(s) which served to condition the original split themselves undergo change. Secondary split may also occur when some development subsequent to a change which introduces a phonetic alternation results in an expansion of the types of phonetic contexts in which one of the alternants may occur. In situations of this type, it is common that the secondary development is not a sound change.

Paradigmatic levelling is often the source for this type of phonological change. An expansion of the context in which a given segment occurs may also arise when tokens of that segment are introduced from some secondary source.

A similar categorization of phonological change, which was developed by Roman Jakobson (1931:247–261), is associated with the Prague school of structural phonology. In this system, the two principal categories of phonological change are *dephonologization* and *phonologization*, which correspond roughly to merger and split respectively. However, these two types of phonological change differ from merger and split in that they are not restricted to the system of phonological oppositions. Prague School phonology distinguishes between *phonological contrast*, i.e., the system of distinctive phonological oppositions, and *phonological correlation*, i.e., the system of relationships which hold between features that characterize classes of sounds. Hence, dephonologization may refer to the loss of a contrast and/or the loss of a correlation. For the most part phonologization corresponds to secondary splits in the system developed by American structuralism.

A third type of phonological change, *rephonologization*, is also defined in the Prague School system. Rephonologization occurs when a change creates a reorganization in the old system of correlations without any decrease or increase in the number of distinctive oppositions. The unconditioned change from proto-Indo-European *ǵ* > Slavic *z* is an example. The correlation *voiced/voiceless* which was probably only distinctive for non-continuants in Proto-Indo-European has become distinctive for sibilants, as well, in Slavic.

Before proceeding to a discussion of phonological change as it is viewed in generative phonology, let us contrast the two similar classifications of phonological change just described. The Prague-school system is deficient in that it incorporates no way to characterize the kinds of changes which leave the system of phonological oppositions intact, but which result in a reorganization of the tokens of occurrence of given phonemes in specific morphemes. Such changes do affect the system of phonological structure in a language, altering the phonemic representation of forms, sometimes resulting in a general readjustment of the system of morpheme structure.

Considering its preoccupation with the issue of phonemic opposition (contrast), it is not surprising that this type of change represents an important type for the American Structuralist school. Primary split is a change which results in a realignment in the system of phonemic oppositions, and is hence a type of change which is considered to affect the phonemic system. However, it is this same preoccupation with the system of oppositions which permits the American Structuralist school to neglect changes which affect the system of correlations.

A system restricted to the notions merger and split cannot characterize, e.g., the unconditioned change from pre-Greek *u* to Attic *ü* as a genuine phonological change. Certainly, the phonological representation of the sound in question is different for a speaker of pre-Greek and for his Athenian descendent. Moreover, the feature [round] has a status in the phonological system of the Attic speaker which it did not have in the earlier system. The Prague School concerns with matters of phonological correlation highlight this important type of phonological change which is missed in a system concerned essentially with contrasting segmental entities, and with changes in that system of contrasts.

The account of phonological change which has been developed by the generative school of phonology is similarly a product of a particular theoretical veiwpoint. The generative school assumes that grammars are rule-governed systems, and that phonological systems consist of a set of underlying representations which incorporate all the idiosyncratic information concerning any given linguistic form, and a set of surface representations which are derived from underlying forms by rules of grammar which are the formal devices which speakers use to make generalizations about their language.

Due to the special concern with the synchronic rules of grammar, generative discussions of linguistic change have centered on those developments which are associated with the introduction and loss of alternations. Little regard has been accorded to other types of change which alter the phonological system and phonological structure. In R. D. King's (1969) book, which has become the standard reference for generative historical linguistics, three major types of rule change are discussed: rule addition, rule loss, rule reordering[1]. Rule insertion, a special case of rule addition, whereby a rule is added at a point in the cycle of extrinsically ordered rules other than at the end[2], has been shown to be an unlikely candidate for a possible change type (see, e.g., Watkins 1970; King 1973). Recently, a fourth type of rule change, rule inversion, has been described by Vennemann (1972). In a rule inversion, surface representations come to be reinterpreted as underlying representations, and forms which are consistent with the 'old' underlying representation come to be derived by rule[3].

As a descriptive device rule addition and phonetic split are equivalent notions; both refer to situations whereby morphophonemic alternations are introduced into a language. Rule loss, reordering, and inversion classify a variety of different phonological changes which result from instances of non-phonological or phonetic plus non-phonological changes. Consequently, the explication of these phenomena represent a significant contribution both to our understanding of the ways in which synchronic phonological systems are organized and of the range of and limitations on possible phonological changes. In the Prague School and American structuralist taxonomies, the

account of phonological restructuring resulting from non-phonological changes
is restricted largely to phonemic splits (secondary split/phonologization).
Clearly, the facts of language history merit a more complex and informative
classification.

However, many instances of change cannot be described as rule change,
and such changes are not dealt with in any detail in the generative literature.
Complete mergers, for example, have no effect on the system of phonological
rules. Such changes are categorized as 'primary changes', and are said simply
to result from 'innovation.' In fact, any account of the effect of historical
changes on the make-up of the system of phonological oppositions appears
outside the scope of generative historical phonology as it currently approaches
issues of phonological change. This is especially distressing in light of the fact
that there exists considerable evidence for the psychological reality of the
system of distinctive phonological contrasts, and it is quite likely that this
system may, indeed, play an important role in the motivation of, at least,
certain sound changes. Consider, e.g., Martinet's work (e.g., 1952) on the
functional explanations for sound change[4]. Moreover, reference to changes in
the system of contrasts is accorded an important role in the establishment of
genetic relationship, language split, and other facts concerning the internal
histories of language families. The failure to offer any enlightening account
of this type of change is an important deficiency in the generative taxonomy
of phonological change.

It is desirable and necessary that a descriptive account of phonological
change attend both to changes in the phonological structure of morphemes,
for which we might use the term *relexicalization*, and to changes in the make-
up of the phonological system, for which we might restrict the use of the
term *restructuring*. In the case of restructuring, we might distinguish between
those types which affect only the phonemic inventory, such as merger, and
those which affect the system of rules. The former necessarily coincides
with widespread relexicalization, while the latter may or may not. Relexicalization may occur with or, as is the case in primary split, without concomitant
change in the phonemic inventory.

Such a distinction is appropriate within any framework for phonological
structure. For example, in the case of a change such as Latin rhotacism
(discussed above), the nature of the restructuring will be different for the
structural/taxonomic phonemicist and for the generative phonologist. For
the structuralist, there will be a change in the phonemic shape of every form
(morph) which undergoes rhotacism, hence, introducing multiple lexical
representations for all forms affected by the sound change. For the generativist
the innovation will affect the system of rules (hence, a restructuring has
taken place), but there will be no change in the lexical representation of

forms which show the innovating alternation $s \sim r$. However, it is usual that innovations which result in a change in the system of alternations will also affect segments occurring in morphemes, or in positions within morphemes where no alternation arises. Such is the case in a form like *Valesius > Valerius* after Latin rhotacism. A structural change in the phonological shape of morphemes has occurred and might well be classified with other such changes of the same type. As has been noted, the term relexicalization seems appropriate.

2. In the second section of this paper I would like to consider phonological restructuring (of whatever type), as it is used to make specific claims about synchronic phonological structure. However, it will first be necessary to consider the issue of phonological reversion.

Most historical linguists believe that a change or series of changes which result in a restructured phonological system cannot be undone, that such changes are irreversible (Hoenigswald 1960. 117 et passim; 1966). The assumption that phonological reversion is impossible is at the foundation of the establishment of language splits, and consequently, it permits the reconstruction of the histories of language families (Hoenigswald 1966). With the recognition that levels of phonological structure more abstract than the traditional taxonomic phoneme might exist, the question arises: At what level of phonological structure does reversion, indeed, become impossible? Is it at some systematic level, at the taxonomic level, or at some sub-phonemic level? Moreover, can evidence concerning the potential reversibility of phonological change be used to argue for or against the psychological reality of particular systems of phonological description?

Let us consider for the purpose of reference another well-known change which, like Latin rhotacism, might be classified as a primary split. In Germanic PIE $*dh > *d$[5]. PIE $*t$ falls together with $*d$ or develops as $*\theta$ under the conditions of Verner's Law[6]. Most generative accounts of Early Germanic phonology would distinguish $*d < *dh$ (i.e., d_1) from many of the occurrences of $d < (*t)$ (i.e., d_2) at a systematic phonemic level because d_2 is in alternation with θ in many forms. d_2 is, in large part, synchronically derivable. An historical argument for this particular synchronic analysis would present itself if d_1 and d_2 had different histories within Germanic. They do not. This is no surprise to the phonemicist since d_1 and d_2 would be identified phonologically at the taxonomic level. I think most linguists who have worked in the area of historical phonology would agree that a systematic distinction will not affect the development of segments with different prehistories if those segments have coalesced at the level of surface contrast. Hence the claim that phonemic merger is irreversible appears to stand despite the possibility that tokens of a given phoneme may have different synchronic derivational histories[7]. However, while the facts concerning sound change do not argue *for* a systematic phonemic analysis, they do not, in any significant way argue *against* such as synchronic analysis. There is no *a priori* reason to assume that all aspects of synchronic structural organization need play a role in linguistic change[8].

To pursue this point a step further, the fact that d_1 and d_2 show identical historical development does not *per se* argue even for the existence of a 'phonemic level' of phonological structure. It may simply reflect that 'regular' sound change affects phones (some sub-phonemic phonetic entities) which speakers perceive as phonetically identical. No one would or could argue that sound change affects phonemes in a uniform way. If such were the case phonetic split would never occur. It is likely that the so-called 'unconditioned sound changes' are the fortuitous result of the fact that all tokens (allophones) of a particular phoneme are perceived to be identical by language users. While phonological restructuring (including phonemic change) is often the result of sound change, despite Bloomfield's famous dictum 'Phonemes change' (1933:357), phonological change is certainly not equivalent to sound change.

To conclude, then, in part 1 of this paper I considered certain deficiencies to be noted among various taxonomies of phonological change, and noted the variety of phenomena which must be taken into account in every discussion of phonological change. In part 2, it was pointed out that, although phonological restructurings which alter the system of surface contrasts indeed, preclude phonological reversion. The establishment of this kind of fact is an issue separate from that concerning the use of evidence from phonological change to argue for or against the validity of any particular synchronic analysis of phonological structure.

Notes

1. I am concerned here with rule change as a device by which we might characterize instances of phonological change. No claim is advanced that the rule change 'explains' language change in any significant way.
2. Of course the position that rules of grammar are intrinsically ordered would render this issue irrelevant.
3. It has been shown recently (Sag 1974), e.g., that Grassmann's Law has undergone rule inversion in the course of the history of Sanskrit. It is clear that Grassmann's Law operated at one point in Indic prehistory to dissimilate sequences of 'aspirate' consonants in adjacent syllables. However, for Classical Sanskrit it would be simpler and more reasonable to assume that no underlying diaspirate roots occur (i.e., e.g., /bhodh/ > /bodh/) and that instances of root initial aspirate consonants (e.g., *bhot-*) reflect the introduction of a new rule which introduces the root initial aspirate at the surface.

4. Martinet suggests, for example, that assymetries in the system of phonological opposition may serve as a motivating force in the operation of historical sound shifts.
5. The Germanic developments discussed affect the whole system of obstruents (Grimm's Law). I refer only to dentals for simplicity of presentation.
6. I.e., Proto-Indo-European voiceless stops become voiced continuants (subsequently developing as voiced stops in most dialects) in voiced surroundings when not immediately preceded by accent. Otherwise they develop as voiceless continuants.
7. That a level of structure corresponding to the taxonomic phoneme be incorporated into the generative model is currently being discussed in the literature (e.g., Schane 1971).
8. Similarly, the fact that syntactic change cannot be motivated in the system of transformations does not preclude the existence of transformations or the fact that most syntactic change can be described in terms of a reorganization in the system of transformations. (See Jeffers 1976).

References

Bloomfield, Leonard
    1933   *Language* (New York: Henry Holt).
Hoenigswald, Henry M.
    1960   *Language change and linguistic reconstruction* (Chicago: University of Chicago Press).
    1966   "Criteria for the subgrouping of languages", in: *Ancient Indo-European dialects* (Eds.: H. Birnbaum, J. Puhvel) (Berkeley, Los Angeles: University of California Press), pp. 1–12.
Jakobson, Roman
    1931   "Prinzipien der historischen Phonologie", *TCLP* 4: 247–267.
Jeffers, Robert J.
    1976   "Syntactic change and syntactic reconstruction", in: *Proceedings of the Second International Conference on Historical Linguistics* [Tucson, Arizona, January, 1976] (Ed.: W. Christie) (Amsterdam: North-Holland), pp. 1–10.
King, Robert D.
    1969   *Historical linguistics and generative grammar* (Englewood Cliffs, N.J.: Prentice Hall).
    1973   "Rule insertion", *Language* 49: 551–576.
Martinet, André
    1952   "Function, structure, and sound change", *Word* 8: 1–32.
Sag, Ivan A.
    1974   "The Grassmann's Law ordering paradox", *Linguistic Inquiry* 5: 591–607.
Schane, Sanford
    1971   "The phoneme revisited", *Language* 47: 503–521.
Vennemann, Theo
    1972   "Rule inversion", *Lingua* 29: 209–242.
Watkins, Calvert
    1970   "A further remark on Lachmann's Law", *Harvard Studies in Classical Philology* 74: 55–65.

CHIN-W. KIM

"Diagonal" vowel harmony?: Some implications for historical phonology*

Typology of vowel harmony (cf. Aoki 1968) can be divided into two major types: horizontal vowel harmony and vertical vowel harmony. The latter which is often called palatal vocal harmony is characterized by the dichotomy of harmonic vowel classes into front (palatal) and back (velar). Finnish (Kiparsky 1968, Rardin 1969), Hungarian (Makkai 1972), Mongolian (Poppe 1965), Turkish (Lightner 1972), etc. exhibit this type of vowel harmony. For example, in Turkish, 4 front vowels (*i, e, ü, ö*) harmonize together against 4 back vowels (*ï, a, u, o*). In horizontal vowel harmony, the harmonic classes are grouped in terms of vowel height, e.g., high vs. low, raised vs. lowered, or tense vs. lax. Vowel harmony wholly in terms of high vs. low is rare, but is reported to be found in Tibetan (Miller 1966, Sprigg 1957) and Coeur d'Alene (Sloat 1972). The phenomenon found in many Bantu languages in which mid vowels and peripheral (i.e., high and low) vowels behave distinctively (cf. Kim 1973a) may be closer to a case of vowel metaphony rather than vowel harmony. What is called a vowel harmony in tongue-root advancement (cf. Berry 1957 and Stewart 1967 for Akan, Carnochan 1960 for Igbo, and Ladefoged 1971:78 for Igbirra) can be said to belong to the horizontal vowel harmony group, as the vowels are paired raised vs. lowered, i.e., *i/e*, *ɛ/a*, *o/ɔ*, and *u/ɷ̈*.

A third type, although rare, is found in such languages as Korean, Nez Perce (Aoki 1966, Zwicky 1970), Chukchi (Kiparsky 1968:36–42), Washo (Jacobsen 1968:822), etc. This type can be called "diagonal" because the line dividing the harmonic classes runs diagonally in the vowel chart, e.g.,

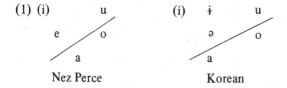

(1) (i)   u   (i)   ɨ   u

      e   o   ə   o

         a   a

   Nez Perce   Korean

Aoki (1966) calls *e* and *u* in Nez Perce "Recessive," and *a* and *o*, "Dominant." *i* is ambivalent. In Korean, *i̵*, *u*, and *ə* are generally called "Dark" or "Feminine," and *a* and *o*, 'Light" or "Masculine," *i* is neutral.

Some examples:

(2) Nez Perce:
  to:t 'father', *na̱? to:t* 'my father'
  meq 'uncle', *ne̱? me̱q* 'my uncle'
  qitti 'place firmly' (recessive)
  cik?il 'destroy' (dominant)
  tu̱le:qittine 'I am putting my foot down firmly'
  to̱la:cik?ilsa 'I am destroying with my foot'
Korean:

ka-a 'go', **ka-ə*	*cu-ə* 'give', **cu-a*
po-a 'see', **po-ə*	*kər-ə* 'walk', **kər-a*
non-a 'divide', **non-ə*	*pu-ə* 'pour', **pu-a*
tʰodak-tʰodak 'toddle'	*tʰudək-tʰudək* 'thump'
čʰolang-čʰolang 'light waves'	*čʰuləng-čʰuləng* 'heavy waves'

(The last two pairs of examples are mimetic words.)

 Given the two classes of harmonic vowels such as those found in Nez Perce and Korean, how shall we describe the vowel harmony? Here, no single parameter or distinctive feature of vowels can distinguish the two harmonic classes. This fact alone is such an unusual phonological phenomenon that it merits further investigation. Yet previous works on the subject (e.g., Aoki 1966, Rigsby and Silverstein 1969, Zimmer 1967, Zwicky 1970) were primarily concerned with the problem of how to describe this peculiar vowel harmony, and paid little attention as to why such an unnatural phonological phenomenon exists and what might be its implications for phonology. I will return to this topic after reviewing some possible ways to describe the diagonal vowel harmony, for if it can be proven that the diagonal vowel harmony can be described simply and straightforwardly without posing any problem to phonological theory, then we might be building a straw man. On the other hand, if it turns out that no simple and natural solution exists, then it is warranted to seek an explanation for the aberrant phonological behavior.

 What looks attractive initially is the so-called ROOT-MARKER solution (à la Lightner 1965). In this solution, lexical items are specified with a diacritic morphemic marker, say +GRAVE or DOMINANT, or −GRAVE or RECESSIVE.

 Then, vowels in a word marked +GRAVE are converted to [+grave] vowels, and those in a word whose lexical marker is −GRAVE, to [−grave] vowels. For this solution to operate properly in Nez Perce, however, a look-up table of the following kind is necessary:

(3)

DOMINANT	RECESSIVE (= –DOM)	
o	u	Higher
a	e	Lower

Taking *u* and *e* as unmarked vowels for lexical entry, the derivation will look like:

(4) [ne?-tu:t] $_{+\text{DOM}}$ → *na? to:t* 'my father'
    [ne?-meq] $_{-\text{DOM}}$ → *ne? meq* 'my uncle'

As has been pointed out by many, however, this solution is highly abstract and arbitrary. If there is a straightforward and natural mapping relation between a lexical feature GRAVE and a phonological feature [grave], then the lexical marking is redundant. If on the other hand there is no natural mapping relation between the two as in Nez Perce and a look-up table is necessary for mapping, then the apparent elegance disappears, for it is but a complex form donning a disguise of simplicity.

Related to the above solution is the "prosodic" approach such as the one applied to Turkish by Lyons (1962). In this approach, a given prosodeme associated with a word is distributed to every vowel in the prosodic group, converting it to an appropriate form in the process. For example, taking A as Dominant prosodeme, and E as Recessive prosodeme, and taking *e* and *u* as unmarked vowels, one may have the following derivation:

(5) A[ne?-tu:t] → *na? to:t*
    E[ne?-meq] → *me? meq*

Parallelism between (4) and (5) is apparent. +DOM to the right of the brackets in (4) is merely replaced by A to their left in (5). The same criticism therefore applies. Whatever the independent advantages of the prosodic approach over the traditional phonemic approach may be, its application to Nez Perce vowel harmony does not produce a better solution than the ROOT MARKER device as long as there is no simple and natural way to distribute the prosodeme to the segments except via an arbitrary correspondence formula: A = (a, o), E = (e, u).

A distinctive feature solution has been proposed by Aoki (1966) for Nez Perce:

(6) $\begin{bmatrix} \alpha\,\text{diff} \\ \alpha\,\text{grav} \end{bmatrix} \rightarrow \begin{bmatrix} -\text{diff} \\ -\alpha\text{comp} \\ +\text{grav} \end{bmatrix} / [\ldots \underline{\quad} \ldots]$ +DOMINANT

By this rule, if the word is DOMINANT, *e* becomes *a*, and *u* becomes *o*.

This is however another form of ROOT MARKER solution. Notice that the morpheme or the word must have a specification +DOMINANT for the rule to apply. This is equivalent to +GRAVE in the root-marker solution. The rest is nothing but a distinctive feature specification of the change involved, i.e., $e/u \to a/o$. Furthermore, the form of the rule is at best clumsy and there is no elegance or simplicity that makes it a better solution, nor does it make the diagonal vocal harmony look like a more natural phonological phenomenon. The fact that the $e/u \to a/o$ change could be specified with variables involving three different distinctive features is an accident or at best a spurious generalization and does not capture any significant and natural phonological process. For example, a rule of the parallel form

$$(7) \quad \begin{bmatrix} \alpha \, \text{ant} \\ \alpha \, \text{nas} \end{bmatrix} \to \begin{bmatrix} -\text{aspir} \\ -\alpha\text{tense} \\ +\text{voice} \end{bmatrix}$$

whereby m and n become lax (whatever that may mean) and g and j become tense does not really state a plausible unitary phonological process, but merely represents a case in which two or more isolated processes happen to be coalesceable by a cleverly devised rule.[1]

More recently, Moon (1974), being aware of the problem and recognizing that the vowel-harmony process should be specifiable with a single distinctive feature whose polar values distinguish the two harmonic classes, proposed to classify the Korean vowels in the following way, adopting the vowel feature system proposed by Wang (1968):

(8)

	−back	+back		
−mid	i	ɨ	u	+ high
+mid		ə		
		ɐ	o	−high
−mid		a		
	−round	+ round		

ɐ is a now extinct Middle Korean vowel which then paired with ɨ, and is irrelevant to our discussion for the moment.

In this system of vowels then, the vowel harmony in Korean operates neatly, +high vs. −high, and meets the formal requirement that the vowel-harmony process be specifiable with a single distinctive feature. In this vowel system, a diagonal disappears and an elegant pattern symmetry is achieved.

Evidence available from textual analyses, however, does not give the

Middle Korean vowel system that Moon reconstructs, especially with respect to the position of the extinct ʀ. Scholars place ʀ below *o*, i.e., as a low back and probably rounded vowel (cf. K-M. Lee 1972:111) rather than as a mid central unrounded vowel that Moon conveniently posits. Furthermore, there is much evidence to indicate that at the time when the Korean vowel harmony was fully operative (in the early Middle Korean and/or Old Korean period), the vowel system was rather quite different from the late Middle Korean system which is more or less the same as the present-day Korean (cf. W-J. Kim 1963).

Zwicky (1970), in the last of a series of articles on vowel harmony and vowel systems in Sahaptian languages, of which Nez Perce is one, argues that Jacobsen's (1968) postulation of six vowels (*i, e, u; ə, a, o*) for prehistoric Nez Perce is the most preferable of all alternative treatments on the ground that the palatalization process in Sahaptin is describable in a phonetically more natural way in Jacobsen's analysis than in others, e.g., Rigsby and Silverstein (1969). Jacobsen posits *ə* as the Dominant counterpart of Recessive *i* (the two merging to *i* later). This presumably gives a phonetically natural explanation why palatalization does not take place in front of Dominant *i* (= historical *ə*). Jacobsen didn't symbolize this sixth vowel as *ɨ*, an equally valid choice, "in order to give more homogeneity to the class of dominant vowels" (Jacobsen 1968:822). This contrasts with Rigsby and Silverstein (1969) that postulates a six-vowel system of *i, a, o* (Dominant) and *e, æ, u* (Recessive). Zwicky points out that this arrangement would make palatalization occur, counterintuitively, before *i* and *æ*, but not before *e*. Zwicky, however, leaves unresolved the naturalness question of the harmonic classes themselves and the historicity of an obviously odd "diagonal" vowel harmony phenomenon.

A decade ago, when I was working on Korean phonology, especially on the vowel system, I was unable to come up with a satisfactory solution to the problem of vowel harmony in Korean and had to settle with a promise of "forthcoming" in a footnote in a subsequently published article (Kim 1968:520, fn. 20). It took me five years and a framework in Chomsky and Halle (1968) to propose a tentative solution (Kim 1973b).

In a desire to give a coherent and compact description of Korean vowel harmony which looked like operating on a diffuse vowel system, I borrowed the concept of "adjustment rules" from Chomsky — Halle (1968) which has basically the function of adjusting the output of the syntactic component so that it may take an appropriate form for phonological rules to apply.

To give an example from Chomsky — Halle (1968:372), the following sentence has the phrase structure as is indicated:

(9) This is [$_{NP_1}$ the cat/that caught [$_{NP_2}$ the rat/that stole [$_{NP_3}$ the cheese/] $_{NP_3}$] $_{NP_2}$] $_{NP_1}$

There is overwhelming evidence in stress rules in Chomsky – Halle (1968) and elsewhere that syntactic bracketings which are motivated internally play a major role in determining the phonetic representation of the utterance. This being the case, one would expect a close correlation between the phrase structure (9) and its phonetic shape. But when one examines the intonational contour of the sentence, the breaks in breath group seem to occur not at the noun-phrase boundaries but at the places marked with slashes. Since intonation assignment rules generally refer to the node S (cf. Stockwell 1960), it is reasonable to assume that some such nodes must occur at the intonational breaks, and in fact, each part divided by the slashes corresponds to an elementary sentence in surface structure. Thus, a normal operation of intonation rules will necessitate the adjustment of the original syntactic bracketings before the utterance enters into the phonological component.

A good example of adjustment in segmental phonology is provided by what is called Rounding Adjustment in English (Chomsky – Halle 1968:194). In English, the underlying $\bar{u}$ comes out phonetically as [aw] after going through Diphthongization and Vowel Shift rules, e.g., *pronounce, profound, loud*, etc. But in words like *ambiguity, Neptune, cube*, etc., the underlying $\bar{u}$ does not become [aw] but [yuw]. The solution proposed is that in the latter case the underlying $\bar{u}$ be unrounded to $\bar{ɨ}$ by the Rounding Adjustment rule. Then, the Diphthongization and Vowel Shift rules will not apply to $ɨ$, but the Glide Insertion rule applies, and later $\bar{ɨ}$ is converted back to $\bar{u}$

What I did for Korean almost parallels Rounding Adjustment in English. I changed u to $ɨ$ by an adjustment rule prior to operation of vowel harmony rule, thereby creating a vowel system in which the line dividing the two harmonic classes now runs vertically separating back vowels from non-back (front and mid) vowels as in:

(10) i   ɨ ⊣ u
           ə | o
              | a

An ordered set of rules to derive the proper linking vowel in *ku-* 'to roast' is as follows:

(11) Lexical representation: ku-V
      Adjustment: u → ɨ   kɨ-V
      Vowel harmony: kɨ-ə
      Readjustment: ɨ → u   ku-ə

Arbitrary as it may seem, this solution is actually akin to an "abstract" approach that has been more readily accepted, e.g., a case in which a phonetically identical [i] is given two different underlying segments /i/ and /ɨ/ in order to describe different behavior with respect to, say, palatalization or vowel harmony, later converting the abstract /ɨ/ to phonetically more realistic *i* by a "patch-up" rule, i.e., readjustment. Much has been said on this topic (cf. Kiparsky 1968, Hyman 1970), and this is not the place to go into it. I later return briefly to justify the Adjustment solution I proposed.

All of the above solutions, however, are makeshifts. All of them contain an element of arbitrariness and forcefulness, and even if one of them may be simpler in some sense and less cumbersome than the others, none explains the "oddity" of the diagonal vowel harmony phenomenon.

Ten years ago when I was working on Korean vowels, I predicted purely on theoretical grounds that there must have been a historical vowel shift in Korean if the pattern of Korean vowel harmony was to be explained in a plausible and logical way.[2]

There are several indications that are suggestive of some sort of historical vowel shift in Korean. They are:

(a) Pairs of vowels that participate in vowel harmony assume neither the same height nor the same font/back dimension. Thus, compared to Turkish whose vowels are paired *i/i, ö/o, ü/u,* and *ä/a,* the pairing in Korean, *o/u, a/ə,* is highly irregular and may be the result of a historical vowel deformation. Furthermore,

(b) The counterparts of *i* and *ɨ* are missing in modern Korean. The loss may have been due to the merger with their "spouses," which may have contributed to the vowel deformation.

(c) All the other languages in the Altaic family to which Korean is supposed to belong possess fairly regular palatal (vertical) vowel harmony. If the palatal vowel harmony is assumed to be a common Altaic feature, shouldn't Korean have had the same in an earlier period? The present system could be the result of a "decay" of an earlier harmonically ideal system.

(d) Vowel harmony in Korean is in the process of disruption. Historical texts show that it was much more regular and systematic in 15th century Korean. In modern Korean it operates primarily between verb roots and certain suffixes and in mimetic words (phonetic symbolism). The vowel deformation must be directly responsible for the disruptive process of vowel harmony.

These indications seemed to warrant a search for elegance, for that original state when the vowel system was optimally ideal for the operation of vowel harmony. The earlier vowel system that I reconstructed was the following. In this theoretical reconstruction, I kept in mind that not only the changes that individual vowels underwent must be plausible, not wild, ones, but also that the path of the shift as a whole must form a link or a chain conforming to the known theory of sound change, avoiding direct permutations, zigzags, and other unpredictable directions.

(12) modern K	i	$\dot{\textbf{i}}$	u	o	a	ə	ϕ
*early K	i	ə	$\dot{\textbf{i}}$	u	ɔ	a	o

Diagrammatically,

$$
\begin{array}{lll}
(13)\ \ i \quad \dot{\textbf{i}} \leftarrow u & \quad i \quad \dot{\textbf{i}}\,(u) & u\,(o) \\
\qquad\ \downarrow \quad \uparrow & & \\
\qquad\ \ \ \ ə \quad o \quad \rightarrow & \quad ə\,(\dot{\textbf{i}}) & o\,(\phi) \\
\qquad\ \ \ \ \downarrow & & \\
\qquad\ \ \ \ a \rightarrow & \quad a\,(ə) & ɔ\,(a)
\end{array}
$$

$$\qquad\qquad \text{modern Korean} \qquad\qquad \text{*early Korean reconstructed}$$

The arrows on the left-hand side of the diagram do NOT indicate the direction of the historical shift but the DIRECTION OF RECONSTRUCTION. On the right, the modern reflexes of the reconstructed vowels are given in parentheses. What the diagrams in (13) show is that I could achieve a harmonically optimal vowel system of a hypothetically earlier period by shifting non-front vowels in modern Korean by one position in the COUNTERCLOCKWISE direction. Since a "hole" appeared in the mid back position, I placed the extinct vowel (Moon's ɐ in (8)) there. Not incidentally, this is precisely the place where it SHOULD be if it is to be the missing harmonic counterpart of $\dot{\textbf{i}}$.

The above theoretical reconstruction was made at the time when I was not well acquainted with the literature in Korean historical linguistics. Later, I was only too delighted and surprised to find that it matched remarkably well with the reconstruction made by native scholars on textual evidence (cf. W-J. Kim 1963, K-M Lee 1968). I was however a little too greedy for pattern symmetry, for according to K-M. Lee (1972:114), the early Middle Korean system (12th/13th century) was more probably like:

$$
\begin{array}{lll}
(14)\ \ i\,(i) & \dot{\textbf{i}}\,(u) & u\,(o) \\
\quad\ \ e\,(ə) & ə\,(\dot{\textbf{i}}) & o\,(\phi) \\
& a\,(a) &
\end{array}
$$

although Lee himself envisages the system like (13b) as a possible vowel system in Old Korean. In (14) modern reflexes are again given in parentheses. To be noted is that in (14) *a* remains invariant and that *e* (ə) is more front and higher than *a* (ə) in (13b). Incidentally, Lee thinks that *e* (ə) started a "push-chain" reaction by retracting to the mid-central area occupied by ∂ ($\dot{i}$), which was then raised to $\dot{i}$(u), which was then pushed back to u (o), which then went to o (ϕ) pushing it down to $\mathfrak{o}$, which was later lost.

Textual evidence for this sort of vowel shift includes the following kind. It is well to keep in mind in this regard that the Korean script as we know it today was invented in the 15th century, and that therefore the construction of a system of an earlier period takes the form of comparison between the pre-15th-century Chinese and Mongolian texts that contain transcriptions of contemporary Korean words with their (post-) 15th-century reflexes. This of course assumes that the sound system of the 15th-century Korean is well-established. Indeed, with a few exceptions (e.g., extinct letters, diphthongs, double consonants, etc.), modern historical and comparative linguistics has firmly established that there has been little change in the sound values of the Korean script since its invention.

(a) The original vowel u in early Chinese loan-characters is transcribed as o in post-15th-century Korean texts, indicating that there was an $u \rightarrow o$ change sometime before the 15th century.

(b) Mongolian loan-words that came into Korean during the 13th century but were written down in Korean script in the 15th-century show the following correspondences (K-M. Lee 1972:112):

(15) Mongolian (13c)	a	o	u	e	ö	ü	i
Korean (15c)	a	o	o	ə	wə	u	i

(c) The 12th-century Chinese texts transcribe the now extinct Korean vowel with the characters whose vowels were either o or a, indicating that this extinct vowel may have had the range of $o \sim a$, if not outright $\mathfrak{o}$, in the 12th century.

The above shows then that there was indeed a (Great!) Vowel Shift in Korean and that this vowel shift is directly responsible for the oddity of the "diagonal" vowel harmony in modern Korean on the one hand and for the gradual disruption of vowel harmony on the other.

If we accept this conclusion, its implications for historical phonology are the following:

(a) There is no such thing as a "diagonal" vowel harmony. It is not a system; it is a transitional phenomenon; a deformation and a historical vestige of an ideal vowel-harmony system.

(b) When we find a diagonal vowel harmony, we can reconstruct an earlier vowel system in which the harmonic classes are ideally arranged according to a natural phonological class, i.e., we can predict that an earlier vowel system had a regular vowel harmony. We can also predict that vowel harmony will eventually disappear from the diagonal vowel system.

(c) Since a diagonal vowel harmony is a historically later development from an ideal vowel harmony, it can be said that if a language has a diagonal vowel harmony while other genetically related languages display regular vowel harmony, then the language with a diagonal vowel harmony must be the most innovated of all languages in the group. In the case of the Altaic language family, this assumption means that Korean is the most innovated of them all. This in fact seems to be the case. Scholars posit a stage of Common Mongolian-Turkic-Chuvash, while connecting Korean directly to Proto-Altaic (cf. Poppe 1965, K-M. Lee 1967).

Appendix: Some further speculations on vowel harmony

(A) What is the origin of cause of vowel harmony? Is it *morphemic* in the sense that each word is associated with a semantic marker which is in turn associated with a vowel "color"? Or is it *phonological* in the sense that, as L. Anderson (1975) recently speculated, it is an attempt to keep the number of vowel oppositions intact in the face of a threat to neutralize them in unstressed positions? Or is it *phonetic* in the sense that it is nothing but a form of vowel assimilation?

In the absence of contrary evidence, I tend to think that vowel harmony begins as a purely phonetic process. Such assimilatory processes as vowel euphony, mutation (umlaut), and metaphony (cf. Bright 1966 for Dravidian) should be precursors of vowel harmony.

In view of what we know about the processes of speech production (namely, articulation is in general anticipatory), a vowel metaphony is most likely to occur in $V C \acute{V}$. In modern Persian, for example, unstressed prefix vowels have begun to be attracted to the stem vowels, e.g.,

(16) *bo-xor* 'eat!'   cf. *be-gir* 'take!'
      bo-ro 'go!'   *be-deh* 'give!'
      bo-gu 'say!'   *be-bin* 'see!'
      bo-kon 'do!'   *be-baxšid* 'excuse!' (standard
                              Persian)

      ne-mi-kon-am 'I don't do'   *na-kon-id* 'don't do!'

In Tibetan where a suffix vowel is in general assimilated to a high base vowel, the base vowel becomes high if the suffix vowel is high and *stressed*.

The Mashad dialect of Persian gives a good example of a vowel harmony in the making.[3] In this dialect, the vowel of the present-tense affix *mi-* which is invariant in Standard Persian assimilates to the stem vowel, e.g.,

(17) *mi-riz-om*   'I pour'   *mi-bin-om*   'I see'
      me-zen-om   'I hit'   *me-reqs-om*   'I dance'
      mo-bor-om   'I carry'   *mo-xor-om*   'I eat'
      mu-kuš-om   'I kill'   *mu-duš-om*   'I squeeze'
      me-mān-om 'I remain'   *me-rān-om*   'I drive'

In the last examples, the prefix vowel *i* becomes *e* due to the attraction of the stem vowel *a*. If the assimilation goes one step further and *e* becomes *a* or *o*, and if the suffix vowels also assimilate to the stem vowel in the like manner, then a palatal vowel harmony would be born. Note that while both prefix and suffix vowels are unstressed, the vowel most susceptible to metaphony is the one that precedes the stressed syllable (the stem).

(B) The decay of vowel harmony on the other hand should begin in the environment $\acute{V} C V$, as the unstressed vowels will tend to centralize (reduce). In Korean, for example, the loss of the "extinct" vowel which played a major role in the deformation of vowel harmony occurred first in the non-initial unstressed syllables and only later spread to the initial syllable.

It is interesting to note in this regard that the Altaic languages that maintain stress in non-initial or final syllables, Turkic, South-Eastern Tungusic (Nanaj, Olcha), reveal much more regular vowel harmony than those in which the stress falls on the initial syllable, Mongolian,[4] North-Western Tungusic (Evenki, Lamut), and Korean.

Some further observations on the vowel harmony decay:

(a) The vowel-harmony deformation will occur first with the merger of *i* and *ï* to *i*. This is probably due to a highly marked character of *ï*.

(b) The Recessive or "unmarked" harmonic vowels are *ï, ə, u*, not *a, o, ɔ*. That is, a neutral stem vowel takes a recessive affixal vowel, and when vowel harmony is eventually disrupted, *i, ə, u* replace *a, o, ɔ*, not vice versa.[5] Why? It may be because of the fact that *ï, ə, u* are more central and neutral than *a, o, ɔ*. *u* does not appear to be any more neutral/central than any of the latter group, but it is phonetically weaker, and remember that, at least in the case of Korean, it *used to be* a central vowel.

(c) Is there a diagonal vowel harmony in which the diagonal line runs at the right angle to the one we find in Korean and Nez Perce? If there isn't such a diagonal vowel harmony, is it an accidental gap or is there a natural and logical explanation for it?

(C) An interesting picture emerges from the foregoing discussions. That is, if we trace the historical path of a vowel system, in particular the Korean vowel systems, we have the following lineage:

(18) PROTO-VOWEL SYSTEM → ⟨vowel metaphony⟩ → VOWEL
      HARMONY → ⟨vowel shift⟩ → DIAGONAL VOWEL HARMONY
      → ⟨monophthongization⟩ → MODERN KOREAN VOWEL
      SYSTEM →?

Those in capitals denote states, and those in angled brackets, processes.

In following this path, one notices that the size of the vowel system increases and decreases alternately. That is, if one may envisage a proto-vowel system as consisting of 3 optimum vowels *i, a, u*, it grows into a 5-vowel (*i, e, a, o, u*) system during metaphony, finally developing into a 6-, more probably 8-vowel system with 4 harmonic pairs. This maximum size is reduced via vowel loss and vowel reduction brought about by the deformation of vowel harmony. A new equilibrium is then sought. In Korean a new series of front vowels have merged through the monophthongization process of back diphthongs, i.e., *uy → ü, oy → ö, ay → ä, əy → e*, etc. Already, a new simplification process is in progress, with gradual loss of *ü* and *ö* (or segmentalization into *wi* and *we* respectively) and a tendency to merge *ä* with *e*, giving us back an Early Middle Korean vowel system reconstructed in (14)! Such is the life of language.

In Korean, from the beginning of the vowel-harmony deformation (15th-century) until the emergence of a new vowel system, it took about 500 years. If one could determine the approximate duration from the beginning of metaphony to the appearance of a full-fledged vowel-harmony system, and furthermore, if one can generalize this chronology and extend it to other languages, then it may have further implications in historical phonology, in particular, in determining the approximate date of split of subbranches of a language family, and in determining the direction of internal reconstruction.

Let me illustrate with a small example.

Aoki (1966) and Rigsby (1965:310–311) derive the five-vowel system of Palouse (*i, e, a, o, u*) from the three-vowel proto-Sahaptian system *\/i, a, u/*. If the present Palouse vowel system represents a vowel metaphony (the rule Rigsby proposes does), then I agree with their description. On the other hand, however, if the Palouse vowel system represents a "diagonal" vowel harmony as it does in Nez Perce, then I would argue that the earlier (proto-) system must be richer than the present one,[6] for a diagonal vowel harmony is a transit from a full vowel-harmony system to a reduced vowel system.

It is interesting to note again in this regard that in Nez Perce *i* is ambivalent, e.g., *ne?i:c* 'my mother': *na?ci:c* 'my aunt', and that palatalization of *k* to *c* in Sahaptin occurs before vowels corresponding to Nez Perce *e* and Recessive *i*, but not before Dominant *i* (cf. Rigsby and Silverstein 1969:49). This indicates that the two i's in Nez Perce must have been segmentally distinctive in an earlier period, and that this pre-diagonal vowel system was richer at least to that extent. I agree in this regard with Aoki (1962) and Jacobsen (1968).

(d) Finally, how shall we describe a "diagonal" vowel harmony in a synchronic grammar? To the extent that a diagonal vowel harmony is a historical vestige and operates on the historically earlier vowel system, it may be argued that the most reasonable description has to restore, at least partially, this earlier system via a sort of adjustment rules (à la Kim 1973b). Notwithstanding disclaimers by many, I do not think that recapitulation of a historical process in a synchronic grammar is a sin, for how else can one account for the fact that in Evenki and Buriat *e* and *ö* behave as if they are back vowels (e.g., *ög-or* 'with the forest', Poppe 1965:184), or that in Evenki the vowel in *dil* 'head' acts like a back vowel although it is phonetically identical to the vowels in *irgi* 'tail' which are full-blooded front vowels, except by way of saying that *e* and *ö* in Evenki and Buriat were historically derived from *ay* and *oy*, respectively, and that *dil* in Evenki was historically *dïl*?[7] Of course, when they finally behave like front vowels as they do in Kalmuk (e.g., *ög-äs* 'from the forest', *ibid*.), then we can say that a restructuralization has been completed and that the past has indeed passed.

Notes

* My debt to Prof. Ki-Moon Lee (1972) is obvious in the text. I have also benefited from correspondences and discussions with Dr M. R. Bateni of Tehran University, Dr Y-K Kim-Renaud of Virginia, Dr Han Sohn of the University of Illinois, and Prof. Su-Hi To of Chungnam University, Korea. To all the above, I express my sincere thanks.

1. Rigsby and Silverstein's (1969:53) rearrangement of Nez Perce vowels enable them to express the harmonic classes in terms of two distinctive features [α diff, -α grave]. While this is an improvement over Aoki's three-feature specification, the problem still remains, for, ideally, the two vowel harmony classes should differ in only one distinctive feature. Furthermore, the posited split of *i* to *i* and *e*, while persuasive in principle, is not supported by any proof that the lost phoneme was *e*, not, say, *ɨ* or *ə*.

2. A few of my colleagues who received copies of my working paper that eventually became Kim (1968) without the section on vowel harmony can attest to this.

3. I owe the examples to Dr M. R. Bateni of Tehran University.

4. Good preservation of vowel harmony in Mongolian despite the dominant word-initial stress may be due to what is called musical accents that occur on long vowels in non-initial syllables. Still, the Mongolian vowel harmony is not as perfect as the Turkish one.

5. However, a statistical study of vowel harmony violations in the 15th- and 16th-century Korean texts by To (1964) shows inexplicably that violations were more frequent for the dominant (masculine) vowels than those for the recessive (feminine) vowels until the end of the 15th-century, when the situation reversed itself.

6. Unless Palouse acquired the diagonal vowel harmony through a diffusion from Nez Perce (cf. Aoki 1966:767). Aoki's earlier article (1962) posits a six-vowel proto-

Sahaptian system. Rigsby and Silverstein (1969) reconstruct a five-vowel proto-Sahaptian system from which they derive a six-vowel Nez Perce system as a case of vowel metaphony, regarding vowel harmony, not present in the proto-system, as arising in the process in some daughter languages.
7. For an argument for "abstract" description of vowel harmony in several Uralic and Altaic languages, see Vago (1973).

References

Anderson, L.
  1975   *Theory and typology of vowel harmony*. [Unpublished Ph.D. dissertation, University of Chicago.]
Aoki, H.
  1966   "Nez Perce vowel harmony and Proto-Sahaptian vowels", *Language* 42: 759–767.
  1968   "Toward a typology of vowel harmony", *IJAL* 34: 142–145.
Berry, J.
  1957   "Vowel harmony in Twi", *BSOAS* 19: 124–130.
Binnick, R. I.
  1969   "Non-high neutral vowels in Modern Mongolism vowel harmony", in: *Papers from the Fifth Regional Meeting of the Chicago Linguistic Society*, pp. 295–301.
Boadi, L. A.
  1963   "Palatality as a factor in Twi vowel harmony", *Journal of African Languages* 2: 133–139.
Bright, W.
  1966   "Dravidian metaphony", *Language* 42: 311–322.
Carnochan, J.
  1960   "Vowel harmony in Igbo", *African Language Studies* 1: 155–163.
Chomsky, N. – M. Halle
  1968   *The sound pattern of English* (New York: Harper and Row).
Hyman, L.
  1970   "How concrete is phonology?", *Language* 46: 58–76.
Jacobsen, W. H., Jr.
  1968   "On the prehistory of the Nez Perce vowel harmony", *Language* 44: 819–829.
Kim, C.-W.
  1968   "The vowel system of Korean", *Language* 44: 516–527.
  1973a   "Opposition and complement in phonology", in: *Issues in linguistics* (Eds.: B. B. Kachru et al.) (Urbana: University of Illinois Press), pp. 409–417.
  1973b   "Adjustment rules in phonology", in: *Issues in phonological theory* (Eds.: M. J. Kenstowicz – C. W. Kisseberth) (The Hague: Mouton), pp. 130–144.
Kim, W.-J.
  1963   "New observations on the Korean vowel system", *Cintan-hakpo* 23. [In Korean.]
Kiparsky, P.
  1968   *How abstract is phonology?* [Manuscript, MIT.]
Ladefoged, P.
  1971   *Preliminaries to linguistic phonetics* (Chicago: University of Chicago Press).
Lee, K.-M.
  1967   "The formation of the Korean language", *Hankwuk-munhwa-sa taykyey* 5 (Seoul). [In Korean.]

1968   "Vowel harmony and the vowel system", in: *Festschrift for Lee Swung-nyeng* (Seoul). [In Korean.]
1972   *Studies in the phonological history of Korean* (Seoul). [In Korean.]
Lee, S.-N.
1947   "Study of vowel harmony", *Cintan-hakpo* 16. [In Korean.]
Lightner, T. M.
1965   "On the description of vowel and consonant harmony", *Word* 21: 244–250.
1972   *Problems in the theory of phonology* 1 (Edmonton, Alberta/Champaign, Ill.: Linguistic Research Inc.). [Pp. 343–355: "Vowel harmony in Turkish".]
Lyons, J.
1962   "Phonemic and non-phonemic phonology", *IJAL* 28: 127–134.
Makkai, V. B.
1972   "Vowel harmony in Hungarian", in: *Phonological theory* (Ed.: V. B. Makkai) (New York: Holt, Rinehart, Winston), pp. 634–647.
Miller, R. A.
1966   "Early evidence for vowel harmony in Tibetan", *Language* 42: 252–277.
Moon, Y.-S.
1974   *A phonological history of Korean.* [Unpublished Ph.D. dissertation, University of Texas.]
Poppe, N.
1965   *Introduction to Altaic linguistics* (Wiesbaden: Harrassowitz).
Rardin, R. B., II
1972   "On Finnish vowel harmony", *MIT Quarterly Progress Report* 94: 226–231.
Rigsby, B.
1965   "Continuity and change in Sahaptian vowel systems", *IJAL* 31: 306–311.
Rigsby, B. – M. Silverstein
1969   "Nez Perce vowels and Proto-Sahaptian vowel harmony", *Language* 45: 45–59.
Sloat, C.
1973   "Vowel harmony in Coeur d'Alene", *IJAL* 38: 234–239.
Sprigg, R. K.
1957   "Vowel harmony in Lhasa Tibetan", *BSOAS* 24: 116–138.
Stewart, J. M.
1967   "Tongue root position in Akan vowel harmony", *Phonetica* 16: 185–204.
Stockwell, R. P.
1960   "The place of intonation in a generative grammar of English", *Language* 36: 360–364.
To, S.-H.
1964   *A study of vowel harmony* (Traejon).
Vago, R. M.
1973   "Abstract vowel harmony systems in Uralic and Altaic languages", *Language* 49:579–605.
Wang, W. S.-Y.
1968   "Vowel features, paired variables, and the English vowel shift", *Language* 44: 695–708.
Zimmer, K. E.
1967   "A note on vowel harmony", *IJAL* 33: 166–171.
Zwicky, A.
1970   "More on Nez Perce: Alternative analyses", in: *Ohio State University Working Papers in Linguistics* 4, pp. 115–126.

FREDERIK KORTLANDT

I.-E. palatovelars before resonants in Balto-Slavic

1. Two recent publications once again draw the comparativist's attention to the classical problem of the velar series in Proto-Indo-European. Steensland shows in his monograph on the subject (1973) that the so-called 'pure velars' are largely in complementary distribution with the other series. Čekman lists 70 instances of "Gutturalwechsel" in Baltic and Slavic, not counting the onomatopoeic cases (1974). Both investigations support the conclusion that there were no more than two velar series in Proto-Indo-European.

2. What were the phonetic characteristics of these two series? The immediate comparative evidence points to a palatovelar and a labiovelar series. Steensland's rash rejection of such a reconstruction as "von Kuryłowicz ... ein für allemal als typologisch undenkbar abgestempelt" (1973:120) is not in conformity with the author's serious analytical work elsewhere in the book. The simultaneous presence of palatovelars and labiovelars and absence of 'pure velars' is well attested in the languages of the world, e.g. in the Caucasus (Circassian, Ubykh) and on the Canadian Pacific coast (Kwakiutl, Heiltsuk).* A wider acquaintance with less privileged languages would save Indo-European linguists a lot of unwarranted generalizations.

3. Čekman attributes the large number of doublets in Baltic and Slavic to the previous existence of a Proto-Balto-Slavic *centum* dialect (1974:133). Unfortunately, such an assumption can be neither proved nor disproved because it cannot be co-ordinated with any other linguistically relevant fact. In particular, the *centum* words in the Balto-Slavic area do not in any way deviate semantically from the regular inherited lexicon. Čekman's assumption must be considered an *ultimum refugium* and should only be resorted to if every other line of investigation fails to explain the facts.

---

* The presence of uvular series in these languages is not relevant in this connection.

4. For the time being I think that we must look for a phonetic explanation. Re-examining the existing literature, I find no substantial progress in this part of Indo-European linguistics since Meillet's 1894 article on the subject. As far as I can see, his conclusions remain valid and unsurpassed. In the following I shall continue this line of thought and indicate how a further specification of the conditions only corroborates Meillet's results and demonstrates the fruitfulness of his approach.

5. I find two positions of neutralization between palatovelars and labiovelars for the Indo-European proto-language, viz. after *u and after initial *s. The neutralization after *u was established by Brugmann (1881:307n.) and de Saussure (1889:161f.), e.g., Gk. *leukós, zugón, boukólos, thugátēr*, Arm. *loys, dustr*. The neutralization after initial *s is discussed by Meillet (1894: 294ff.) and Steensland (1973:30ff.) and can hardly be doubted. It accounts for such correspondences as OCS *skopiti*, Lith. *kapóti*, Gk. *kóptō*; Lith. *skìrti, kiȓsti*, OCS *(s)kora*, Gk. *keírō*; Lith. *(s)keȓdžius*, OCS *čředa*, Goth. *haírda*; Lith. *(s)keȓsas*, OCS *črěšъ*, Gk. *egkársios*; Skt. *kavíḥ*, Gk. *koéō, thuoskóos*; Lith. *skélti, kálti*, OCS *klati*, Gr. *kláō*, and possibly for a number of cases where an initial *s has been lost in the historically attested material, as may have been the case with OCS *kosa*, Skt. *śắsti*; OCS *kotora*, Skt. *śātáyati*; Russ. *cévka*, Lith. *šeivà*; Russ. *kopýto*, Skt. *śapháh* (cf. Martynov 1968: 149ff.).

6. In the Western languages (Italic, Celtic, Germanic) the labial feature of the labiovelars was lost before rounded vowels and before obstruents (cf. Meillet 1894:279ff.), e.g., Goth. *haidus*, Skt. *ketúḥ*; Goth. *hails*, OCS *cělъ*; Lat. *cottīdiē, incola, stercus, secus*; OIr. *guidiu*, Gk. *pothéō*; OIr. *gorn*, Skt. *gharmáḥ*. This rule accounts for the correspondence between OCS *gostь* and Lat. *hostis*, Goth. *gasts*.

7. The palatal feature of the palatovelars was lost before a following *r in Indo-Iranian. This development was established by Weise (1881:115f.), e.g., Skt. *kravíḥ*, Gk. *kréas*; Skt. *krátuḥ*, Gk. *krátos*; Av. *xrū-*, Gk. *krúos*; Skt. *grásate*, Gk. *gráō*. It also accounts for the correspondence between Skt. *grháḥ* and Gk. *khórtos*, Lith. *žárdas*. The palatal feature was restored whenever there was a model for its restoration, e.g., Skt. *śvaśrūḥ (śváśurah), śmáśru (hári-śmaśāru-), áśru* (Lith. *ašarà*), *ájrah (ájati)*.

8. The same development can be established for Balto-Slavic (cf. Meillet 1894:297), e.g. OCS *kryti*, Gk. *krúptō*; Lith. *krõkti*, Gk. *krõzō*; Lith. *krùšti*, OCS *krъxa*, Gk. *kroúō*; OCS *grъměti, gromъ*, Gk. *khremizō, khrómos*; Lith.

griēti, Gk. *khriō*; OCS *grędǫ*, OIr. *adgrennim*. Other examples: OCS *krovъ*, Welsh *craw*; Lith. *krākė*, Gk. *króssai*; Lith. *kraūjas*, Skt. *kravyám*, Welsh *crau*; Lith. *kirnis*, Gk. *kránon*; OCS *črъnъ*, Skt. *kṛsnáh*; OCS *svekry*, Skt. *śvaśrūḥ*; Lith. *smākras*, Skt. *śmáśru*; OCS *žrъdъ*, Lith. *žárdas*.

9. Here too, the palatal feature was restored in a number of cases, e.g. OCS *zrъno*, Lith. *žìrnis*, Goth. *kaúrn*, cf. OHG *kerno*, OCS *zьrěti*, Skt. *járati*; OCS *srъdьce*, Lith. *širdis*, Gk. *kardia*, cf. OPr. *seyr*, Arm. *sirt*, Gk. *kēr*, OCS *srěda*, Lith. *šerdis*; ORuss. *sьrstь*, OHG *hursti*, cf. ORuss. *serexъkъ*, Lith. *šerȳs*; ORuss. *sьrna*, OPr. *sirwis*, cf. Lat. *cervus*, Gk. *keraós*. If OCS *pьstrъ*, *ostrъ* are identical with Gr. *pikrós*, *ákros*, which is not necessarily the case, the palatal feature has been restored on the basis of other derivatives of the same root, cf. Lith. *paĩšas*, *ašerȳs*, Skt. *péśaḥ*, *aśániḥ*.

10. The similarity between the Indo-Iranian and Balto-Slavic developments suggests that they arose from a common innovation. This is not necessarily the case. Since most examples from Indo-Iranian involve a word-initial palato-velar, the development was possibly limited to this position. It had a much wider range in Balto-Slavic, where the palatal feature was also lost before other resonants under certain conditions. There is positive evidence against the development having occurred in Armenian, cf. *srunkᶜ*, Lat. *crūs*, and *merj*, Gr. *mékhri*. The palatal feature cannot have been restored in these cases because there was no model for such a restoration. The metathesis in the latter word was posterior to the Armenian palatalization (cf. Kortlandt 1975, section 5), which was in turn posterior to the assibilation of the palatovelars in this language (cf. Kortlandt 1976, section 3).

11. In contradistinction to Indo-Iranian, the depalatalized velar often spread to related forms in Balto-Slavic, e.g., Lith. *gaŕdas*, Russ. *górod* next to *žerd'*, cf. *zoród*, Lith. *žárdas*, *žaŕdis*; Russ. *čerëmuxa*, *čeremšá*, Lith. *kermùšė*, cf. *šermùkšnis*, Gk. *króm(m)uon*, Welsh *craf*; Lith. *kárvė*, Russ. *koróva* next to Polish dial. *karw*, OPr. *curwis*, cf. Gk. *keraós*, Welsh *carw*; OCS *žeravь*, Lith. *gérvė*, *garnȳs*, cf. Gk. *géranos*, Lat. *grūs*, Welsh *garan*. If the Armenian word *kṙunk* is related to the latter family, it must be a borrowing, not only because the initial *k* cannot represent a palatovelar and because the initial cluster has not undergone metathesis, but especially because *-ṙ-* would require PIE *-sr- or *-rs- according to the sound laws of this language. Words like OPr. *kērdan*, *kērmens* do not belong in this paragraph because the initial velar must be attributed to the presence of a mobile *s, not to the influence of the following *r*.

12. Burrow has suggested that the distinction between velars and labiovelars before *r* was preserved in Sanskrit if the resonant was syllabic and long (1957:143), e.g. *kīrtíḥ, gurúḥ*, Gk. *kēruks, barús*. I think that a similar rule can be formulated for Balto-Slavic. Unfortunately, the original distribution is blurred by subsequent developments. As was pointed out by Trautmann (1923:3), the choice between the reflexes *-ir-* and *-ur-* of the syllabic resonant is largely dependent on apophonic relationships in Baltic and Slavic. Thus, the original qualitative alternation which is still extant in OCS *gъnati, ženǫ* has disappeared both in Lith. *giñti, genù* and in OPr. *guntwei, gunnimai*, cf. Hitt. *kuenzi, kunanzi*. Similarly, we find the original reflex in ORuss. *gъrlo*, Lith. *gurklỹs*, OPr. *gurcle*, cf. Gk. *bárathron*, not in Lith. *gìrtas*, OChSl. *žъrq*, where the vowel quality is based on Lith. *gérti*, OChSl. *žrěti*. There is a secondary back vowel in the noun Russ. *korm*, which is undoubtedly related to the verb Lith. *šérti*. I am unable to explain the front vowel in Lith. *kirmis*, OCS *črъvь*, Skt. *kṛ́miḥ*, where Welsh *pryf* points to an original labiovelar.

13. The loss of the palatal feature was not limited to the position before a following **r* in Balto-Slavic. Meillet suggested that the development of the palatovelars before **l* was determined by the following vowel (1894:298), e.g., OCS *slovo*, Gk. *kléos*, but Lith. *klausýti*, Arm. *luay*. Other examples: Lith. *šliēti, šliñti, šlitìs*, Gk. *klī́nō, klísis*, Lat. *clīnō*; Lith. *žlėjà*, OIr. *glé*; OCS *poklopъ*, Gr. *kléptō*; OCS *glěnъ*, Russ. *glev*, Gk. *gloiós*; OCS *glogъ*, Gk. *glōkhī́s*; Lith. *miglá*, OCS *mьgla*, Gk. *omíkhlē*. The correspondence between OCS *klětъ* and Lith. *šlitė* is perfect, except for the existence of Lith. *klětis*: the latter must be an older borrowing from Slavic.

14. Analogical levellings led to the introduction of the depalatalized velar before **l* plus front vowel, e.g. OCS *glina*, Lith. *glitùs*, Gr. *gloiós*; OCS *zaklepe*, OPr. *auklipts*, Gk. *kléptō*. They also re-introduced the palatal feature before **l* plus back vowel, e.g. Lith. *šlúoti*, Lat. *cluō*; Lith. *šlaunis*, Skt. *śróṇiḥ*; Lith. *šlainùs*, OIr. *clóin*; OCS *sluti*, Lat. *clueō*. The coexistence of forms with and without the palatal feature gave rise to a large number of doublets, e.g. OCS *kloniti, sloniti*, Lith. *klãnas, šliēti*; Lith. *klausýti*, OCS *slušati*; Lith. *kleĩvas, šleĩvas*; Lith. *glibti, žlìbti, kliaũkti, šliaũkti, glēgžnas, žlēgžnas*. This type of alternation became productive in Lithuanian at a certain stage (cf. Čekman 1974:128).

15. The palatal feature was also lost before a syllabic **l*, e.g. Russ. *žëltyj* next to *zóloto, zelënyj*, Lith. *geĩtas* (with secondary vocalism), *žélti, žãlias*, Skt. *háriḥ*, Gk. *kholē*. The feature was restored in Lith. *šiĩtas*, cf. *šáltas*, Welsh *clyd*, Lat. *calidus*. Words like Lith. *kálti, kélmas* do not belong here

because the initial velar is due to the influence of a preceding mobile *s, not to the following resonant.

16. I think that the same rule which Meillet established for the development of the Proto-Indo-European palatovelars before *l in Balto-Slavic can be formulated for their development before *w: the palatal feature was retained if the resonant was followed by a front vowel and lost if the following vowel was back, e.g. Polish *zwierz*, Lith. *žvėris*, Gk. *thḗr*, Lat. *ferus*; Polish *święty*, Lith. *šveñtas*, Latv. *svinêt*, Av. *spǝnta-*; Polish *świtać*, Lith. *švitėti*, *švìtras*, Skt. *śvitráḥ*; Polish *gwiazda*, Czech *hvězda*, Gk. *phoîbos*; Polish *kwiat*, Czech *květ*, Skt. *śvetáḥ*. The development before a syllabic *u was the same as before other vowels, not as before other syllabic resonants, e.g. Polish *język*, OPr. *insuwis* from PIE *-uH-.

17. The palatal feature was largely restored analogically, e.g., Polish *dzwon*, Arm. *jayn*, next to Polish *dźwięk*, Russ. *zvenét'*; Polish *świat*, *świeca*, Lith. *švaitýti*, Skt. *śvetáḥ*, next to Polish *świt*, Lith. *švisti*, *šviẽsti*, *šviesùs*; Lith. *zvaigždè*, *žvaĩnas*, Latv. *zvàigzne*, *zvaidrît* next to Lith. *žvygulỹs*, Latv. *zvidzêt*; Lith. *žvalgýti* next to *žvel̃gti*, Gk. *thélgō*; Lith. *žvangéti* next to *žvéngti*, Arm. *jayn*; Lith. *ašvà* next to *ašvíenis*, OPr. *aswinan*, Skt. *áśvaḥ*. The depalatilized velar was extended in a few cases only, e.g. Polish *gwizdać*, cf. Lith *žviẽgti*; Polish *kwitnąć*, Latv. *kvitêt*, cf. Polish *kwiat*, Lith. *švitéti*. The velar in Lith. *pēkus*, OPr. *pecku* stems from the oblique cases because Skt. *paśúḥ* belongs to the hysterodynamic paradigm, as the gen.sg. *paśváḥ* shows (cf. Kuiper 1942: 51f.). Latv. *kuṇa* has nothing to do with Lith. *šuõ*, etc. (cf. Būga 1922:196).

18. The palatal feature was also lost before nasal resonants in Balto-Slavic, e.g., Lith. *akmuõ*, Skt. *áśmā*; OCS *gniti*, OHG. *gnītan*; OPr. *balgnan* next to *balsinis*. The feature was restored in Lith. *ašmuõ*, cf. *aštrùs*, and in the family of Latv. *znuõts*, Russ. *znat'*, *známja*, Gk. *gnōtós*, *gnōsis*, *gnõma*, cf. Lith. *žénklas*, Goth. *kannjan*. The palatal in Lith. *iẽšmas* is regular because it goes back to a cluster containing *s, as is clear from the aspirate in Gk. *aikhmḗ* (cf. de Saussure 1892:90f.).

19. There are a few indications that the palatal feature was lost before a syllabic *n, e.g., OPr. *cucan* (i.e., *kunkan*), Gk. *knēkos*, and Lith. *gentìs* (with secondary vocalism) next to *žéntas*, OCS *zętъ*, Skt. *jñātíḥ*. This might also provide an explanation for the coexistence of Lith. *žąsìs* and Russ. *gus'* if we assume an earlier alternation in the root of this old consonant stem. The vocalism of Gk. *khḗn* and Lat. *ānser* can hardly go back to the Indo-European proto-language. I think that it is an old European word which was differently

adapted to existing patterns in various languages. Alternatively, the velar in the Slavic word must be attributed to Germanic influence.

20. Indications that the palatal feature was lost before a syllabic *m are very scarce, e.g., Lith. *kum̃pis* next to *šum̃pis*. This pair of words is probably not old. Some counter-examples cannot easily be explained in terms of analogical levelling. Though the palatal feature might have been restored in Lith. *dešimt*, *dešim̃tas* on the basis of forms comparable to Skt. *daśamáḥ*, Lat. *decimus*, such an explanation is hardly possible in the case of Lith. *šim̃tas*, Skt. *śatám*. It seems more probable that the syllabic *m received a svarabhakti vowel at an earlier stage than the other syllabic resonants in Balto-Slavic so that the depalatalization rule did not apply.

21. As far as I can see, the Albanian material agrees with the rules put forward for Balto-Slavic, e.g., *ka, gardh, vjéhërrë, mjégullë*, Russ. *koróva, górod, svekróv', mgla*. Other examples: *quhem, qanj, grua, gju* (from *$glun$- from *$gnun$-), Gk. *klutós, klaĩō, graũs, gónu* (cf. Hamp 1956:128 and 1960:275f.). Elsewhere I have suggested that the initial velar in Alb. *gjënj* is the regular reflex of a palatovelar before a syllabic *n, cf. Gk. *ékhadon* (1976, section 2). The Albanian development before *w cannot be compared with that in Balto-Slavic because in the former language the resonant turned into a feature of the preceding obstruent at an early stage (cf. Kortlandt 1976, section 3).

22. The following conclusions about the chronology can be drawn. The loss of the palatal feature before *r may have been a common Indo-Baltic development, which Armenian did not share. Indo-Iranian did not share the Balto-Slavic depalatalization before other resonants, whereas Albanian did. The restoration of the palatal feature took place independently in Indo-Iranian and Balto-Slavic, in the latter dialect group partly after the split into a Baltic and a Slavic branch. The material shows that the loss of the palatal feature was anterior to the rise of an epenthetic vowel before syllabic *r, *l, *n, but probably posterior to the same development before syllabic *m. The agreement with Albanian suggests that this language was still a transitional dialect between Balto-Slavic and Armenian at the time under consideration.

References

Brugman[n], K.
    1881   "Griechische Etymologien", *KZ* 25: 298–307.
Būga, K.
    1922   *Kalba ir senovė* (Kaunas: Švietimo Ministerijos Leidynis).

Burrow, T.
1957   "Sanskrit gr̄-/gur- 'to welcome'", *BSOAS* 20: 133–144.
Čekman, V. N.
1974   "O refleksax indoevropejskix *k̑, *g̑ v balto-slavjanskom jazykovom areale",
         in: *Balto-slavjanskie issledovanija* (Moskva: Nauka), pp. 116–135.
Hamp, E. P.
1956   "OPruss. *soye* 'rain'", *KZ* 74: 127–128.
1960   "Palatal before resonant in Albanian", *KZ* 76: 275–280.
Kortlandt, F. H. H.
1975   "Notes on Armenian historical phonology I", *Studia Caucasica* 3: 91–100.
1976   "Albanian and Armenian", *KZ* [forthcoming].
Kuiper, F. B. J.
1942   *Notes on Vedic noun-inflexion* (Amsterdam: North-Holland).
Martynov, V. V.
1968   *Slavjanskaja i indoevropejskaja akkomodacija* (Minsk: Nauka i Texnika).
Meillet, A.
1894   "De quelques difficultés de la théorie des gutturales indo-européenes",
         Mémoires de la Société de Linguistique de Paris 8: 277–304.
Saussure, F. de
1889   "[Gr.] Boukólos", *Mémoires de la Société de Linguistique de Paris* 6: 161–
         162. [= *Recueil*, pp. 417–418.]
1892   "[Gr.] *kh, ph* pour *ks, ps*", *Mémoires de la Société de Linguistique de
         Paris* 7: 90–91. [= *Recueil*, p. 459.]
Steensland, L.
1973   *Die Distribution der urindogermanischen sogenannten Gutturale* (Uppsala:
         Universitetsforlaget).
Trautmann, R.
1923   "Ein Kapitel aus der Lautlehre der baltisch-slavischen Sprachen", *Slavia*
         2: 1–4.
Weise, O.
1881   "Ist anlautendes [gr.] *g* vor [gr.] *l* abgefallen?", *Beiträge zur Kunde der
         indogermanischen Sprachen* 6: 105–118.

ROGER LASS

Mapping constraints in phonological reconstruction: on climbing down trees without falling out of them[1]

1. 'Projection' and 'mapping'

It is often said that linguistic reconstruction (e.g., comparative method) is basically a matter of 'extrapolation': 'working back' from attested forms to their ancestors. Thus Lehmann (1962:92) in a textbook statement says that 'in normal use of the comparative method we proceed backwards by triangulation'. More elaborately, Haas (1969:32–3) says:

> ... in the beginning of the work, what is reconstructed reflects what can be discovered by working backwards in those cases where ... the daughter languages point to the same conclusion.

Scholars of this persuasion also assume that the establishment of the changes by which the protocategory reconstructed by 'triangulation' differentiates into the attested reflexes is achieved simply by inverting the original process. Haas again (1969:3):

> If we turn the whole thing round and look at it from the other direction we see that the daughter languages are not only different from each other but from the proto-language. We describe this differentiation by calling it 'linguistic change'.

Others express similar views. Thus Anttila (1972:256):

> The formulation of ... rules ... is not superior in theoretical terms to the establishment of the starting points. Both are by-products of each other, that is, complementary. Regular sound change makes comparison possible, and comparison then establishes the starting points, at the same time giving the mapping rules, that is, the sound changes that made it work.

I suggest that this is not the case. It is an oversimplification to assume that comparison both establishes protoforms and 'at the same time' provides the 'mapping rules'. It seems to me that there are two operations involved: one 'comparative' only, the other (strictly) 'historical', which differ greatly at least from the point of view of heuristics and controls.

One operation establishes the mother-nodes of genetic trees; the second takes the mother as a starting point and establishes the daughters. I will claim that the construction of originating nodes is quite different (both in theory and practice) from the construction of pathways down the tree. This is not of course apparent from the completed tree itself, since it can be read in either direction.

I will call these two processes respectively *projection* and *mapping*, and de-fine them as follows:

(i) *Projection*. Given a set of reflexes, establish a mother node for the tree of which they are terminal symbols. (The set may consist of equivalent segments in cognate items in comparative reconstruction, or a set of differing segments in a pair or n-tuple of allomorphs in internal recon-struction, etc.)

(ii) *Mapping*. Given a mother node and a set of terminal symbols, con-struct the appropriate pathways between them.

The bulk of this paper will be an attempt to define the notion 'appropriate', and to discuss its theoretical implications. Regardless of the apparent sym-metry of a completed tree, these two operations are methodologically sepa-rate, and have rather different consequences: it is not really possible to 'work up' to a protosegment, but only to 'work down' to a reflex.

Let me take a microcosmic illustration, which will serve as an introduction to the problem (more details in § 2). Consider the following Dravidian forms:

(1) Tamil	Todu	Telugu	Kannaḍa	
pōku	pïˑx	pōgu	hōgu	'go'
pāl	poˑs	pālu	hālu	'milk'
pal	pas̲	pallu	hallu	'tooth'

(Cf. Emeneau 1970: §§ 2, 16.4, 37, 46, 49; Burrow–Emeneau 1961: items 3734, 3370, 3288; Lass 1976: ch. 6).

This set of data, which could easily be expanded, suggests a regular equiva-lence-class, i.e., we have what looks like *prima facie* evidence for cognateness. Simply, Ta., To., Te. /p/ 'corresponds to' Ka. /h/ before back vowels. For-mally, we can express this relation as an equivalence class like this:

(2) E (Ta. *p*, To. *p*, Te. *p*, Ka. *h*)

(With the context 'before back vowels' omitted for simplicity). That is, there is a relation E(quivalence) holding among the members of the parenthesized set. Obviously, this class, as represented, is in fact a 'proper bracketing': it is equivalent to the tree (3):

(3)

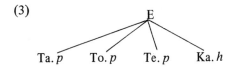

(I assume that equivalence-classes like (2) and trees like (3) are natural expressions of cognateness).

More precisely, the relation or bracketing 'E' presupposes the existence of some rule *R* which is a mapping function; formally, in this case, a PS-type rewrite rule. Genetic trees of the comparative variety, it seems, are in general specifiable by rather simple rules of the string-replacement type.[2] The real problem that any theory of historical phonology must deal with, as we will see, is one of vocabulary: what are the appropriate symbols for successive lines of historical derivations? But I anticipate: I haven't yet shown that there is a real problem here.

The task of projection, strictly speaking, is merely to supply a 'value' for 'E' (phonetic, phonemic, or whatever: see below): since the equivalence-class presupposes at least a mnemonic 'content' for the mother node of the tree. (At least this is the case for any metatheory that makes genuinely *historical* comparative reconstruction possible: and I am not calling this possibility into question. I shall in fact insist on it as a necessity in § 2 below, and discuss this further in § 6.) In this example, if we look at more data, it becomes clear that the rest of Dravidian has /p/ in this position: only Kannaḍa has /h/. Therefore we (confidently) project a P(roto)- D(ravidian) */p/ rather than */h/, producing the tree (4):[3]

(4)

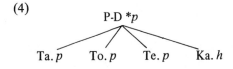

This is a 'projection' in the sense defined above: but it is in no way a 'working back' up the branches of the tree (though it is, in the properly static sense of the term, a 'triangulation'). The act of projection here is logically and methodologically independent of any 'downward' mapping or 'derivation'. The historian as projector may wish to have nothing to do with the latter once the projection has been made; it is then up to the historian as mapper (who may be someone else) to decide how — or even if — to get down the tree. The projection, governed by familiar projection-centered criteria like 'simplicity', etc., stands relatively unassailable at the top. I will clarify this in the following section.

2. The implications of historicity

The division of labor between projector and mapper is not arbitrary, though it is undesirable and probably indefensible. There are theories of comparative linguistics which in effect absolve the linguist of the responsibility for mapping in any meaningful detail. A good example is the 'formulaic' (or 'non-ontological' definition of reconstruction typified by Meillet's statement (1922:42) that "les 'restitutions' ne sont que les signes par lesquels on exprime en abrégé les correspondances". What comparative linguists have produced through their work on Indo-European, he says (47), 'n'est pas une restitution de l'indo-européen tel qu'il a été parlé; *c'est un système défini de correspondances entre les langues historiquement attestées'*. (Emphasis Meillet's). On the face of it, this is surely too black-and-white a view: one can believe that reconstructions are more than empty cover-symbols for sets of correspondences without accepting the absurd proposition that they represent a protolanguage 'tel qu'il a été parlé'. That view has been a dead horse since Schleicher.[4]

There is at least a methodological distinction between setting up 'content-less' protoforms as cover-symbols, and investing them with some kind of 'phonetic' (as opposed to merely algebraically generative) content. Thus even rather cautious writers like Hoenigswald, who maintains that 'in a literal sense reconstruction procedures serve only to identify the number of contrasting entities in the proto-language' (1960:134), allow that there is room for content: continuing, Hoenigswald says that they may 'give us information on the physical nature of the proto-phones and proto-phonemes'. And the procedures for getting this information depend 'to some extent on the physical consensus between the daughter languages (as distinct from the recurrence of correlations in sets) and on certain considerations of phonetic and typological plausibility'.[5] I will return in some detail to the matter of 'plausibility' below.

But there is more to the problem of 'content'. A view like Meillet's is not only essentially non-linguistic, but is clearly not historical. The whole mapping

issue of course disappears, because in this kind of framework genetic trees
are static, not 'derivational'. They are simply topological networks in an
abstract space, not graphs whose ordinate is time. A view of the function of
comparative method like Meillet's omits time altogether; though a certain
amount of 'reconstruction' is done, it is not historical.[6]

I take it that if a theory is truly 'genetic' or historical, this means that its
trees are drawn (or we believe they are drawn: see § 7) against a time-axis.
The points in the space defined by such a tree are not 'geometrical' points in
an abstract space, but content-full points in real time. (The very admission of
'real time' would seem to presuppose content anyhow: there are no 'empty
events' in history.) This means that any configuration in a graph in which a
symbol appears that is different from the one that dominates it must represent
an event in real time, i.e. a 'sound change'.[7]

Let us consider this now in relation to our Dravidian example. According
to my loosely defined 'historicity' requirement, we can now say that the
tree (4) implies a mapping rule '$*p \rightarrow h$' to produce its rightmost path:

(5)

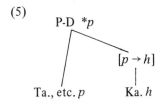

P-D $*p$

$[p \rightarrow h]$

Ta., etc. p Ka. h

Here projection and mapping coincide nicely, and the comments cited earlier
about their being inverses seem to hold. But I will now show that only the
simplicity of the data produces this effect: the projection of a mother node
is half (or less than half) the job. The **historical** part of reconstruction (to
which the purely 'comparative' one is only a prelude) involves climbing
down the tree without falling out of it. In what follows I will attempt to outline the rudiments of a theory of how you can tell if you do fall out.

The asymmetry between projection and mapping is not yet apparent, but
it will be. Given a case like this Dravidian one, where there are no attested
'intermediate stages' between /p/ and /h/, the simplest mapping is obviously
the direct one: mother to daughter with no way-stations. We can take the
(static) 'diachronic correspondence' /p/:/h/ and change the colon into an
arrow: '/p/→/h/'. Thus we turn a 'correspondence' into 'change' by notation,
and apparently confirm Anttila's claim that comparison both establishes
the mother node and provides the mapping rules. The innovation that separates Kannada from the rest of Dravidian is simply a direct change /p/→/h/.

But things aren't this simple: we can question the legitimacy of this inference. Let us imagine (as it happens, counterfactually but not impossibly) that there is a Dravidian dialect with /f/ corresponding to Ta. /p/, Ka. /h/, i.e. that 'milk' is *fālu, etc. We are still justified in reconstructing P-D */p/: but should the tree now be (6)?

(6)

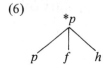

Most linguists, I imagine, would be unwilling to accept the purely pro-jection-centered tree (6), with its three independent lines of descent mirroring the three-way equivalence /p/:/f/:/h/. Everything we know about language change, synchronic allophony, usual sources of /h/, etc., plus simplicity considerations, tells us that /f/ is a 'natural intermediate stage' between /p/ and /h/. The existence of a dialect with /f/ for Proto-*/p/ tells us in effect that Ka. /h/ **must have come from** /f/. Given the correspondence shown in the terminal symbols of (6), and taking '*/p/' to have the content 'roughly [p]', the necessary tree is not (6) but (7) below (in the absence of hard counterevidence):

(7)

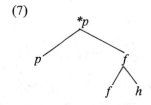

We have a leniting vs. a non-leniting group, and Ka. has gone 'one step further' than the /f/-dialect. (This suggests, incidentally, that genetic trees have **phonet-ic** content as a minimal property: though they may have 'phonemic' content as well. Unless the input level for reconstruction is 'broad' surface-phonetic, virtually all arguments of this familiar type are unintelligible.)

This example shows, I think, that if reconstructions have phonetic content projection and mapping can't be simple inverses. Mapping must have its own independent principles. We reach this conclusion, if in no other way, on methodological grounds: in the two reconstructions, the nature of the paths between /p/ and /h/ depended on whether or not /f/ was attested. Our re-constructions were determined, not by general theory, but by the accidents of survival. What are we to make of the notion that in the absence of /f/, /p/ to /h/ is an acceptable path, but in the presence of /f/ we must have /p/ → /f/

→ /h/? Do we in fact have any warrant for **not** positing an intervening /f/ even in the /p/:/h/ case, where there is no direct evidence for it? If we have no such warrant, then mapping is a separate operation, with its own theory.[8]

3. Constraints on mappings, 1: Well-formed outputs

Projection up trees and mapping down them are not apparently governed by the same constraints, and projection is not necessarily strictly speaking 'linguistie'. And here is the problem: it is clear that reconstruction *can* be done so that no choice of a protoform will have any but purely methodological consequences (if those) for the shape of a tree. This will always be the case unless mapping can be constrained in a sufficiently rigorous way. It seems clear (judging by the Dravidian material, for instance) that if any correspondence $X:Y$ can be converted into a 'change' $X \to Y$ by notation alone, then all that counts in establishing a tree is that the correspondences be regular. (Consider the implications of this for a pair like Latin /du-/: Armenian /erk-/.) Obviously we need something better: few linguists would deny this, and fewer still would actually do without such 'plausibility' or 'naturalness' considerations, however inchoate, in their actual work. But there is still very little consensus on how to introduce such considerations, and what form they should take, or what precise content they should have. There is precious little agreement on, or specification of, such matters as whether plausibility considerations are 'universal' or language-specific; how large a 'quantum jump' is permitted between two segments; or how to distinguish 'genuine' (i.e. internal) change from substitution through borrowing.[9] If I do nothing else here, I will try to deal with these points, at least to the extent of establishing some criteria for decisions.

Back to Dravidian /h/. The problem is that we have two possible mappings of /p/ into /h/, one direct and one via /f/; plus an intuitive feeling (we can hardly yet call it more than that) that the longer path was preferable for /h/-dialects given the existence of /f/-dialects. But if this couldn't be extended to cases without /f/, we had the unsatisfactory situation of a method dependent on the accidents of survival.

Formally, the problem is this: given a mother node A and a terminal symbol a, there is in fact an infinite set $M = \{m_1, m_2, \ldots m_n\}$ of possible mappings $m_k (A \to a)$, where $m_k \in M$. This set also involves, obviously, an infinity of intervening symbols. In terms of trees, the number of graphs that can connect any pair of points is infinite. A straight line may be the (geometrical) shortest distance between two points, but there is no reason to expect geometrical optimalness in the course of linguistic change.

Our job is to reduce this set to a finite one: preferably the smallest possible. What this means is that, if the reduction is not to be arbitrary, we must be able to define the notion 'shortest well-formed derivation of *a* from *A*.' (There is no reason to believe, as we will see, that this will be the same or even similar for all pairs (*A*, *a*): and all I will try to do here is to define 'shortest paths' for a few selected derivations, to set up a framework on which we might begin to erect a theory.)

So far this is merely a mathematical (or pseudo-mathematical) problem. But since all nodes have phonetic content, the eventual solution must be cast in phonetic terms. Let us assume that in some given case either (a) the projection problem has been reasonably solved, or (b) that there is good independent evidence (orthoëpic, inferential, or whatever) for the mother node. The question is, what is a well-formed sound change, and how do we find out? That is, the mapping between *A* and *a* consists, for the reconstructing historian, in the invention of sound changes.[10]

So the task is to restrict the membership of M for any pair (*A*, *a*). But there are two extra problems. One is that it will be, as we will see, impossible to set up a universal theory of constraints, except in very broad outline: the set M for a given pair (*A*, *a*) will not be the same, once we have constructed it, even for the same pair in different languages. And second, we must develop a theory not only controlling the appropriateness of **paths** between successive nodes, but the specific appropriateness of all the **nonterminal nodes** themselves. In other words, the general theory of mapping constraints ('control of the size of quantum jumps') must be complemented by a largely language-specific theory of output constraints. I shall now try to justify this assertion.

Let us first look at this notion of double well-formedness (paths and nodes) from a universal point of view. The first step is to distinguish (as is often not done) between successive lines in say a synchronic generative phonological derivation and successive lines in a historical derivation. If in a generative phonology, only the input and output ('systematic' phonemic and phonetic) levels are 'theoretically significant', there is no control (or any need for one) on the amount and type of preterminal garbage that gets generated. There are no 'canonical' constraints on intermediate levels (at least in the 'standard' model; but cf. Harms 1973).

Historians should not enjoy this dubious freedom (though many 're-constructed' forms in the literature suggest that they often do). Each stage in a history represents a phonetic event in real time; and each successive line in a historical derivation (or node in the descent of a tree) represents therefore some object, and a rather superficial one at that (cf. § § 5, 7 below) in a natural language. This is not the case in the usual sort of synchronic derivation, where all kinds of 'crazy rules' (Bach – Harms 1972) and malformed intermediate output are allowed, subject only to pre-terminal 'rescue' operations.[11] So we have at least the rather trivial constraint that every line in a historical derivation must represent a 'pronounceable' entity. This is especially clear when we are dealing with larger entities like clusters, syllables, etc.; the problem of ill-formed **segments** (in the sense of phonetically impossible ones) doesn't usually arise, because most reconstructions are carried out against phonetic grids sufficiently sophisticated to prevent gross howlers like voiced ejectives or simultaneously spread and rounded vowels.

But the temptation to reconstruct impossible sequences can arise when one is working over large stretches of elapsed time, and trying to pack as much as possible into a protoform: cf. Lehmann's liquid+nonsyllabic vowel+ laryngeal sequences like OHG *scirun* from */skryX-/, where /y/ = [i̯] (1952: 60). This is simply confusing a formal derivation with a genuine historical sequence: though this kind of thing too can be avoided through reasonable care with one's phonetic theory. The problem can often be solved synchronically, too, by means of rather obvious constraints (if it's intelligible to talk of 'phonetic' constraints on 'mental' derivations).

But even with these rather trivial universal constraints out of the way, there are still difficulties which must be taken care of before we even get to the larger problem of optimal mappings. These hinge on the distinction between 'general' and 'specific' constraints. Say that a segment is itself well-formed; and say that the mapping that produces it is also (in some sense to be defined) well-formed; does it follow that reconstruction of this segment is *ipso facto* justified? I.e., can all well-formed segments be allowed in histories if the paths that produce them are (universally speaking) well-formed — regardless of the language involved?

A theory like this is too powerful: our original aim of reducing the set of acceptable mappings is surely not furthered by this kind of permissiveness. The question now is whether there is any non-arbitrary way of reducing the inventory of outputs allowable in reconstructions in a given language. I suggest that there is at least one: utilizing a general typological overview of the language in question.[12] There are both weaker and stronger versions of such typological constraints on segment well-formedness; I will give an example of each, with some discussion. When I have outlined some possible constraints on path well-formedness, I will try to put both sets of conditions together in a case study of systemic evolution, and finally deal with some of the epistemological issues involved (§ § 4–5; 6; 7).

The weakest condition I can imagine is (i) below:

(i) No segment in a reconstruction is well-formed if it does not appear in surface-phonetic forms in some present-day dialect of the language in question.[13]

By this criterion we do not allow [ɯ] in reconstructions of the history of any Germanic language, [y] in Dravidian, [ɦ] in Bantu, etc.

This rather weak requirement is all right when we are dealing with a single language; but as time-depth and geographical range increase it becomes difficult. Given the range in, e.g., Indo-European, the constraints on what could have occurred in just about any category are minimal. There is no known vowel type that can be ruled out, and very few consonant types: probably pharyngeals alone as far as place of articulation goes. Among the airstreams we can rule out the velaric (which is of very limited distribution anyhow); and we can also disallow (phonemic) laryngealized voicing (unless the Danish *stød* is a 'segment'). Among the secondary articulations we can rule out phonemic pharyngealization.[14] (I suspect that this array is unusual: other families, like Bantu and Dravidian, show a rather more restricted range.)

But there is a stronger version of (i), which might have a good deal of heuristic potential:

(i') No segment is well-formed if it does not appear in surface-phonetic representations **in the same etymological category that is being reconstructed**, in the language in question.[15]

This is obviously more problematical than (i): but it is also much stronger, and if justified will give us a much richer theory of change than we had before. It may also be wishful thinking, as many of the best 'strong' hypotheses are.

Quite simply, if (i') is valid, it drastically reduces the inventory of segments available for any complex mapping operation. It also claims, by implication, that the notion 'etymological category' is a theoretical prime. The idea behind (i') is that it might serve eventually to help define something like 'well-formed history for category X in L', for any given L. I will produce evidence later to show that this is not as absurd as it sounds (§ 6); and that in fact we can often construct satisfyingly plausible histories by adhering to this restriction. Another possible use for (i') might be that if in general it is well taken, then any case where adherence to it is impossible is *prima facie* evidence for (relatively) massive typological change.

I hope at least that I have shown that the problems of well-formed segments and well-formed mappings are distinct; even though of course their consequences interpenetrate in any discussion of real data. So for now I will abandon this line of argument — and especially the strong constraint (i') — and look at some more general aspects of mapping.

4. Is sound change 'gradual' or 'discrete' (or both)?

A reading of Postal's discussion of the Neogrammarians, Bloomfield, Hockett, etc. on sound change (1968: pt. II) would lead one to believe that the old 'gradualness' problem is another one of those dead horses whose corpses litter the field of rational inquiry. This is confirmed by King's later textbook treatment (1969: ch. 5). Sound change is 'mentalistic', and takes place strictly in terms of the 'higher-level' primitives given us by the theory of generative phonology. The old ghosts of 'local frequency maxima', 'allophonic drift' and the like have been exorcized.

This is grossly oversimple, and embodies a number of typical confusions (as do most all-or-nothing answers to complex problems). The real question is: if you can show that **some** sound changes are non-gradual, does this mean that **all** are? King constructs an elaborate (and in places misinformed) argument purporting to give a positive answer: but he ends up with a negative one as well. In a sense he is right on both counts, but righter on one than on the other. Let us look at his argument, and see where it leads.[15 a]

He begins (1969:107) by attempting to discredit a basically statistical view of 'allophonic drift' as a mechanism for change: e.g. the view that when PIE /b d g/ became /p t k/ by Grimm's Law, 'gradually during many generations the allophones of /b d g/ came to resemble those of ... /p t k/, resulting in a new phonetic series'. He takes Hockett's theory of the drift of 'local frequency maxima' as paradigm for this view, and tries to show (a) that the notion of a change from say /d/ to /t/ by a series of 'infinitesimal' shifts of the maximum from greater to lesser voicing is untenable; and (b) that any attempt to break up the 'continuum' between phones like this is arbitrary. Then, if (a) and (b) are true, there is no principled restriction against changes like /d/ → /t/.

His arguments for (a) run like this (108): first, the 'strong gradualist' view elevates 'performance' to the status of a primary causal mechanism: the shifts of maxima are brought about solely by 'external' factors like the state of the vocal tract, etc., not by 'competence'. (This is in essence an argument from revealed truth, as we will see.) He attributes to Hockett (1958:443) the view that is is **solely** these external variables that determine allophonic drift; but Hockett says later in the same passage that King cites that the 'speaker's intention' is one of the determinants of performance (thus admitting, if not 'competence', at least something 'mental'). And on the next page Hockett adds the rider that every one of the long list of external factors he cites 'bears indirectly on sound change'. And, he adds, 'the situation is so complex that it is hard to imagine how sound change could *not* go on all the time'. Hockett in fact distinguishes clearly, here and elsewhere, between phonetic drift and

its systematic effects; King oversimplifies his position to the point of caricature, as well as introducing the non-argument (which we will meet again)
that this account is faulty because it neglects competence.

King ends this section of his argument with an assertion that is even less
amenable to examination than Hockett's rather common-sensical and intui-
tively plausible view (108): 'First and foremost ... change is change in competence reflected by alterations in the grammar. The role of performance
remains the same, causing the same kinds of fluctuations after the change in
competence as before'. (As if the 'change in competence' were an observable
like the fluctuations).

King then tells us what the change /d/ → /t/ 'really' is:

> ... we assume that a rule $d > t$ has been added to the speaker's grammar.
> Where he previously said d he now says t ... Before the innovation, realiza-
> tions of /d/ doubtless did fluctuate in various ways ... but precisely the
> same performance factors are active after the innovation as before.

(But does the speaker necessarily respond to them in the same way?) He concludes: 'Their relation to the change in competence is one of complete
neutrality – they neither caused it, contributed to it, abetted it, nor slowed it
down'.

This view is, on the evidence, untenable: there is an extensive literature
suggesting, to take one example, that a speaker's monitoring of his own output can have significant effects on changes in the phonological system (cf.
Ohala 1974; Lass 1976: ch. 7). In any case, King counters his caricature of
Hockett with nothing but a set of 'canonical' assertions.

On point (b), the arbitrariness of splitting up continua, King says (109):

> The statistical model of gradual sound change ... assumed that change was
> infinitesimal over a continuum. This strong version of gradualness can be
> weakened by dropping the requirement of infinitesimal change; rather we
> posit 'small' changes, where 'small' is understood as ... 'within the limits
> set by a given phonetic alphabet and its associated diacritic marks.'

King disapproves of this as 'arbitrary': but note that it is really the view ad-
hered to in practice by generative phonologists. They seem to use a criterion
like this: if the primitives of competence are binary features of a certain type,
and if certain kinds of rules are allowed, than anything that can be represented in those features and rules is a 'change'. Since certain kinds of change
can't be so expressed, they don't belong to competence, and we are free to
disregard them.[16]

King then goes on to show that gradualness is 'not a necessary condition for sound change'; and further, that in any case, 'grammars, not sounds, change' (109). One wonders how a theory like this can even talk about 'devoicing'. But the supporting arguments are, to say the least, weak. The main one is 'the indisputable existence of cases such as loss, metathesis, and epenthesis in which any kind of gradual process strains the imaginative faculties' (109). These cases are important, because they are the main ones cited in support of 'categorial' or 'discrete' change. I will show that in general, only one of the three types cited by King as being unimaginable in gradual terms is really likely to be so.

First, deletion. King cites the undoubted fact that languages lose segments. If, e.g., '*t* is lost word finally, we account for this simply by assuming that a rule ... was added to the grammar of one or more speakers' (109). He then says that in a case like the loss of /t/ 'it is true that one can postulate some sort of undeniably gradual process', like [t] to 'lax' [t] to [θ] to 'lax' [θ] to zero: 'But in cases ... like this there is never unambiguous evidence in the form of scribal testimony or dialectal variations that would clinch the argument for a gradual process. What we find is that a consonant was in full force in one stage of the language and gone later.'

This is simply untrue, given a reasonable time-scale. Intermediate stages (though not generally as fine as 'lax' vs. 'tense' [t]) are easily observable in such changes, and the literature is full of them.[17] In fact there are enough of them so that we can say that a sound change involving direct loss at least of an obstruent is extremely suspect.[18] Some typical cases involving obstruent loss are:

(i) Latin /f/ → Old Spanish /h/ → ∅: *filius* → *hijo*, etc.
(ii) PIE */s/ → Greek /h/ → ∅ ('psilosis').
(iii) PIE */k/ → PGmc /x/ → OE zero intervocalically ('loss of *h*': cf. Lass & Anderson 1975:ch. III); later loss of /x/ in all dialects except Scots.
(iv) Proto-Uralic */-k-/ → (/-g-/?) → /-γ-/ → /-h-/ → ∅: Finnish *joki* 'river', Ostyak *jogəñ* (g = [γ]), Yurak *jæha*, Vogul *jŏŏ*, Hungarian *jó-* (Collinder 1960:§ 108).
(v) PU */-t-/ → (/-d-/?) → /-ð-/ or /-z-/ →∅: Fi. *käte-* 'hand', Cheremis *kidə* (d = [ð]), Hu. *kéz*, Votyak *ki* (Collinder § 113).
(vi) PU */-s-/ → /-z-/ → /-r-/ →∅: Fi. *kuusi* 'Norway Spruce', Mordvin *kuz*, Yenisei Samoyed *kari*, Tavgi *kua* (Collinder § 156).
(vii) ME /kn-/ → ENE /tn-/ → /hn/ → /n/ (*know*, etc.): cf. Kökeritz (1945).

I submit that examples of this kind represent the 'rule' rather than the 'exception': when segments are lost, it is typically by way of a stadial lenition, not a simple vanishing.[19]

Let us turn to King's next 'unimaginable' case: metathesis. He cites such well known cases as E. *third, horse* < OE *ðridda, hros*, and asks: 'What kind of gradual change by allophones can be imagined here or in any case of metathesis?' (III). This example is badly chosen because there is orthographic evidence to suggest that while it may not have come about by 'allophonic drift' (and change doesn't have to qualify as gradual), it certainly happened by stages.

The earliest examples of *r*-metathesis are in Old English: they illustrate the opposite metathesis to King's (CVrC → CrVC rather than CrVC → CVrC), but we will see that the same explanation can be invoked for the latter. The metathesized forms frequently show doublets (and triplets) of an interesting kind: thus *geberehtniga* ~ *gebrehtniga* 'to shine', *berht* ~ *breht* 'bright', *fyrhto* ~ *fyrihto*~*fryht* 'fright', *forhtiga*~*forohtiga* ~ *frohtiga* 'frighten' (Brunner 1965: § 166). The CVrC forms are older types (cf. Go. *baírhts, faúrhts, faúrhtjan*). We see a progression: CV́rC → CV́rVC → CVrV́C → CrV́C. As Brunner says, after svarabhakti insertion, 'der ursprüngliche Tonvokal fehlt und damit Methasese des *r* erscheint' (ibid.; cf. also Jordan 1934: § 165, Anm. 1). In other words, we have vowel epenthesis after /r/, transfer of stress to the inserted vowel, and deletion of the original stressed vowel.[20]

This is (at least indirectly) supported by two parallels. First, in Northern Middle English (c. 1300) there is frequent epenthesis of a vowel in /r/ + dental clusters: *wirid* 'fate', *erid* 'earth', *bered* 'beard', *erel* 'earl', etc. (OE *wyrd, eorðe, beard, eorl*: Jordan 1934: § 148). And in Modern Scots, epenthesis of [ə] between /r/ and another sonorant is extremely common: *farm, arm, furl* are often [farəm arəm fʌrəł], and so on. Neither of these processes apparently led to metathesis: but the frequency of this kind of process in /r/-environments supports the standard analysis of the OE phenomenon.[21] Given the Old English material, the obvious history for *horse* is /hrós/ → /horós/ → /hóros/ → /hórs/.

This argument does not hold for all kinds of metathesis: certainly not for obstruents, like /ps/ → /sp/ in *wasp, lisp, hasp* (OE *wæps, wlips, hæpse*: for more examples cf. Campbell 1959: § 460). There is evidence here for 'parasiting', and given an obstruent cluster, no reason for it. I am not arguing that all metathesis is stepwise; only that apparent 'immediate' metathesis, due to a complex sequence of other kinds of change, is imaginable, and actually attested. Just because some changes seem to be irreducibly nongradual doesn't mean that all (or most) are. Quite the reverse: as far as I can tell there is only one out of King's list that is uniformly non-gradual, and this is (virtually by definition) epenthesis. It would be hard to challenge this one even if I wanted to. Clearly the epenthesis that gave rise to French *école* from L. *schola* etc. can only be considered a change from zero to a full-fledged vowel.[22]

Other changes too seem often (or usually) non-gradual: typically point of articulation assimilation (King, 112), and articulatory shifts of consonants like that of Proto-Romance velars to labials in Rumanian (*opt, lemn, limbă* < L. *octo, lignum, lingua*: cf. King 115).[23] But changes like this are a special and fairly restricted class; and anyhow, even the most rigorous demonstration of non-gradualness for them doesn't admit extension to other cases where gradualness is plausible (and of course where it is attested). In any case point of articulation changes for consonants are rather different from manner changes, which seem virtually always to proceed stepwise; and both are different again from vowel changes.

To sum up so far: there is no case to be made for the 'strong gradualist' assumption that all sound change proceeds by infinitesimal steps. But there is a strong case for the claim that most (all?) sound changes **of certain kinds** proceed by quite small discrete increments, and that changes like 'obstruent loss' are typically loss of weaker categories produced by lenition sequences; and that at least some forms of 'metathesis' are the result of sequences of other changes. Certainly a 'weak gradualist' assumption for most changes seems in order; though there is admittedly a problem in coming up with a set of primitives explicit enough and responsive enough to the data to allow us to define what a 'step' in a sequence of changes is (more on this on 259–273). But we must remember that no one theory of change (and because of this no one set of primitives) will work for all types: it is not a 'simplification' of a theory to force all change under one rubric, simply because this **can** (with some violence to the facts) be done.[24] We need a view that is both pluralist and strongly constrained, and (if possible) data-based, rather than based only on (meta)theory.[25]

5. Constraints, 2: Synchronic evidence for well-formed mappings

Despite the assertions of convinced anti-gradualists, it seems clear that one primary mechanism of sound change is the utilization of variability – capitalizing on the allophonic variation (however motivated: socially, phonetically, etc.) present at any given time in a language. (For detailed examples of this now familiar type of variability cf. Labov 1963, 1966, 1972: Labov *et al.* 1972; Trudgill 1974). That is, the 'local frequency maximum', whatever motivates it, has a part to play. Judging from the well-documented examples of change in progress produced by Labov and his colleagues and followers, one way in which fairly massive alterations can occur over not too long periods of time is by speakers gradually coming to favor variants of a particular type (or better, variants in a particular **direction**). The raising of long /a/ and /ɔː/

in New York, and of long /æ/ in Philadelphia are familiar examples of this kind of process, where the range of variants moves gradually higher and higher (Labov 1966, 1972; Labov *et al.* 1972). Crucially, it is the **range** of realizations that moves, as is clear from the shifting clusterings of F_1/F_2 values that Labov and others have shown (cf. the displays in Labov *et al.* 1972: vol. 2). This data also shows – significantly in the light of King's criticisms of the 'arbitrariness' of gradualism – not 'infinitesimal' change but rather change by small 'quanta', which are essentially discontinuous.

Given this as one (certainly not the only) mechanism, we might utilize this and similar phenomena as sources of evidence about the size of sound changes, as follows. Clearly the one kind of solid information we have about the extent to which speakers can 'change one sound into another' is precisely the coexistence of variants between which they can shift. If a speaker can, for instance, have [y:] and [ʉ:] as variants of /y/ in the same context (a Scots example, in forms like *you, smooth*), then a direct change [y] → [ʉ] or [ʉ] → [y] is possible, etc. (I will refine this a bit below.) That is, we can begin to erect a theory of possible changes (as opposed to correspondences, which can be much further apart; cf. /du/ : /erk/). And we can do this on the basis of capacities that speakers actually seem to possess and utilize. If I can shift from one phone to another as a realization of some phoneme in some context, then I can 'change' completely from one to the other by simply ceasing to use one of them (cf. Hoenigswald's interpretation of change as essentially 'substitution').

'Drifts' of the kind studied by Labov are one source of information: here we can see change occurring over stretches of (at least 'apparent') time, i.e. in something like the dimension we normally consider 'historical'. But along with such movements over time (or over 'generations', anyhow) we get (often coterminous) movements from style to style, and perhaps more importantly, from **tempo to tempo**. Variation between tempi can be a vital source of information on direct assimilations, lenitions, and other kinds of 'simplification' (haplology, deletion, restriction of 'segmentalization': cf. Linell 1974). The theoretical importance of 'allegro' styles (both synchronically and historically) becomes greater the more we know about them (cf. Zwicky 1972, Dressler *et al.* 1972, Dressler 1975). The basic importance is that '*Schnellsprechprozesse*' (Dressler *et al.* 1972) can help us to define hierarchies of 'strength' and the like, as well as defining possible mappings of certain types on the basis of direct synchronic attestation. For any change that a speaker can effect in moving from one tempo to another is literally a sound change (whether or not it has, in the end, historical effects). This latter choice is contingent: variation becomes change through loss of an input.

I suspect that in most cases we can safely say that **sound change is change**

of sounds, not change of grammars. The latter, when and if it occurs, is by no means a primary determinant. Even if the notion 'grammar' is coherent,[26] the types of (phonological) phenomena called 'grammar change' are by and large effects, not causes: when the sounds have changed far enough, the grammar is restructured (cf. Anttila 1972:121). I see nothing in the standard generative arguments to compel us to abandon the kind of relationship between phonetic and phonological change postulated for the Old High German umlaut in Twaddell's pioneering paper of nearly forty years ago (1938): certainly none of the discussion of King, Postal, etc. amounts to a 'refutation'. The analytical style that prefers to postpone change of underlying representations as long as possible is just that: a style, an artefact of a notational apparatus with the power to do it. (Cf. the alternative treatments of OE umlaut in Lass – Anderson 1975: ch. IV, VI.)

There is a lot we don't know about this kind of change; I will give some examples below from Dressler's work that might suggest what sort of things we ought to look for. But there is one point that ought to be made clear at the outset: contrary to the usual practice, the data we need to establish 'change' will not come from 'phonological rules' in the usual sense (cf. note 18), or from any kind of 'abstract' grammatical analysis. Rather the reverse: we should look at the lowest-level phonetic detail that can be fruitfully examined (not that there are no problems in agreeing what this is). It is here alone that the actual 'changes' begin at least to verge on the observable.[27]

Note 'observable': I stress this because most study of sound change until recently has lacked a basis in detailed phonetic observation (with notable exceptions like some of Labov's work, and especially that of Trudgill). All too often the linguists most concerned with phonological change are not phoneticians, and not too many phoneticians are interested in change (but for a good example of one who is, cf. Gimson's 1964 study of change in RP). I am now suggesting a rather primitive notion of what constitutes a 'change', but one that is accessible to some sort of intersubjectively agreed-upon observation procedures (precisely in the sense that the stages intervening between the poles of correspondences, or 'deep' and 'surface' forms in a synchronic phonology, are not).

If we want to say that 'a change has been observed', we should meet some specified conditions. I suggest the following as a beginning:

(i) Both the 'early' and 'late' forms must be observable in phonetic output from the same speaker; preferably from more than one speaker in a given language community.
(ii) The change must be observable as a regularity: i.e., speech errors are ruled out.[28]

(iii) 'Intermediate stages' must be scrupulously observed. If a speaker has both [ts] and [s] (as well as [t]) as allophones of /t/ in the same context, this does not allow a change [t] → [s], but only a sequence [t] → [ts] → [s].[29]

I think it is observation constrained by notions like these that may allow us to begin groping our way to an answer to the question: 'What is a phonological "quantum"?' We will look later at some types of historical evidence that also bear on the question.

But before we get to this, there is a vital (and not too easy) distinction to make. If we are going to erect a theory of allowable changes based partly on the size of alternations that speakers can control, we have to distinguish between true alternations (where speakers 'change one sound into another') and borrowings, where speakers may substitute one (unrelated) element for another. This is hard to do: in many cases it is undoubtedly impossible, but these, mercifully, are the ones we will never know about. It can however be done unambiguously in some cases, and these are instructive.

Consider the phenomenon, quite common in Scotland, of speakers who for members of certain etymological categories have quite (phonologically) distinct stylistic variants. Given 'broad' and 'less broad' styles, we find patterns like these:[30]

(8)	Lexeme	Source	Broad	Less Broad
	HOME	OE $\bar{a}$	hem	hom
	STONE	OE $\bar{a}$	sten	ston
	MORE	OE $\bar{a}$	me:r	mu:r
	NO	OE $\bar{a}$	ne:	no:
	DO	OE $\bar{o}$	de:	dy:
	TOO	OE $\bar{o}$	te:	ty:

([u:] in *more* is the usual allophone of /o/ before /r/.)

If speakers (apparently) control changes of the seize [e] → [o], [e] → [y], should these be admitted under the criteria I have been suggesting as possible sound changes? The answer would appear to be no, as we will see.

First, one of the striking features of these interchanges is their disjunctiveness: there are no 'intermediate stages' either in single speakers or in the dialects. One could imagine a sequence [e] → [ø] → [ɵ] → [o], or something of the sort: but this doesn't occur. At this point it might be objected that I am stacking the cards in my favor: the notion that there should be sequences seems to be based solely on my unwillingness to accept e.g. [e] → [o] as well-formed. But we will see in the next section that in cases where we have good independent evidence for a genuine process of internal evolution, the pattern is quite different. In evolutive changes we usually get a finely graded continuum in the available dialect material, whereas abrupt leaps, with no continuum, are typical of cases of known borrowing.

And this is in fact such a case. The [o]- and [y]- forms are borrowed from another dialect,[31] and occur precisely in the styles where some 'shifting' toward the norms of that dialect is to be expected. Given what we know of the history here, as well as the lexically sporadic character of the interchanges, the variation would appear not to represent 'sound change', but choices of lexical alternants. In these dialects, they are entirely parallel to alternations like *thole* ~ *bear, thrapple* ~ *throat, howk* ~ *dig* (potatoes), etc.: the domain is lexemic, not phonological.

But to return to actual 'synchronic sound change'. Much of the available data focusses on what we would call 'simplification': this is only one type of attested change, but an important one, and any evidence on the limitations that exist will be helpful. The work of Dressler *et al.* (1972) on allegro-rules in colloquial Viennese German is a fruitful source: a great number of individual rules or varying types appears in one corpus. The point of these phenomena is that each one is **by definition** a candidate for a possible sound change, since speakers perform them in going from one style or tempo to another. And the basic observational condition (i) above is met, since both input and output are observable.

A few examples from this work will make the point.[32] From an overall methodological and heuristic point of view, Dressler's material illustrates nicely the distinction I have been making between 'correspondences' and 'changes'. Consider the two 'extreme' realizations of the sentence '*Wir haben alle ein Auto gehabt, aber trotzdem sind wir mit der Straßenbahn nach Hause gefahren*'. Let us take the most 'careful' and formal version, and compare it with the most relaxed (Dressler *et al.* 1972:14–15):

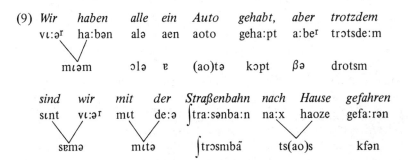

(9) *Wir   haben   alle   ein   Auto   gehabt,   aber   trotzdem*
    vɪːəʳ   haːbən   alə   aen   aoto   gehaːpt   aːbeʳ   trɔtsdeːm

        mɪəm   ɔlə   ɐ   (ao)tə kɔpt   βə   drotsm

    sind   wir   mit   der   Straßenbahn   nach   Hause   gefahren
    sɪnt   vɪːəʳ mɪt   deːə   ʃtraːsənbaːn   naːx   haoze   gefaːrən

         sɛmə   mɪtə   ʃtrɔsmbã̄   ts(ao)s   kfən

If the two styles were set up as poles of a correspondence, some of the

changes would be immense: e.g. [gefa:rən] → [kfən] , [sɪnt vɪ:əʳ] → [sɐmə] .
But if we look at the whole graded series of style changes, the individual steps
are much smaller. In the last case we actually have (pp. 14–15):

(10) sɪnt vɪ:əʳ → sɪnt vɪ:ɐ → sɪnt vɪə→ sɪn vɪə → sɪmə → sɐmə

Rather than [ntv] → [m] , we have [ntv] → [nv] → [m] ; rather than [ɪ:əʳ] →
[ə] we have [ɪ:əʳ] → [ɪ:ɐ] → [ɪə] → [ə] . The attested intermediate stages
show much smaller increments of change than a comparison of the extremes
would suggest. And the analysis given by Dressler and his colleagues suggests
that in many places the sequence of changes is strictly ordered: *sind wir* as
[sɐmə] presupposes loss of final /t/ (see below); the assimilation and coalescence will not take place across an obstruent.

The general rule types that emerge from this study are familiar: vowel-
lowering by one height (16, 18); centralization of unstressed vowels ([e] →
[ɪ]: 18); loss of unstressed vowels (16–19); vocalization of /r/ (19); shortening of long vowels (19–20); monophthongization (20); place-assimilation for
nasals (22–3); syllabification of nasals and laterals following loss of a preceding unstressed vowel (22–3); 'fortisness' assimilation (24); degemination
(24); lenition (24); spirantization of intervocalic /b/ to [β] (25); palatalization of /s/ after apical /r/ (25); lenition of intervocalic voiceless stops (25,
26); loss of /h/ before unstressed vowels (26).

All these changes could be called 'categorially minimal' (a point I will
return to in the next section): vowels move 'one place' along a given parameter, obstruents change one feature at a time, and the only relatively massive
changes are nasal assimilation (expectable), deletion of vowels and /h/ (also
expected on grounds of 'strength': Lass – Anderson 1975: ch. V; Lass 1976:
ch. 6). Aside from these, there are only a few that involve larger steps:
unstressed [e] (which is probably pretty central) → [ɐ] before /r/ plus a
stressed vowel (19); and three cases of obstruent loss: dental elision before
boundaries (24: cf. *sind wir* above); loss of dentals before syllabified /l/; and
loss of velars before [ɬ] (25). Note that in the last two cases the obstruent-
sonorant sequence is at least partly homorganic. Homorganic loss and degemination are probably the only types of direct obstruent loss that are reasonably
widely attested: even deletion before boundaries (when it occurs) is often
categorially homorganic (if boundaries are in fact to be taken as obstruents
in certain languages: cf. Lass 1971; Lass – Anderson 1975; ch. V).

If this material is characteristic – as I think it is – it bears out what I have
been suggesting: that the synchronically attested change types are nearly all
gradual, in the sense of moving by small steps along given parameters. Not
'infinitesimal' ones, but of a size more or less constrained by the existing set

of categories in the language. The theoretical importance of this last point
will be clarified in the next section.

This exposition is not intended, of course, to provide an 'inventory' of
possible changes: rather to give an example of the kind of data likely to bear
on speakers' capabilities. This is surely the primary empirical problem in
establishing the governing conditions for sound change: it may even be about
the only genuinely empirical issue in this area.

But now a *caveat*: argument from allegro forms may have limited validity
for types of change other than 'natural' rules like assimilations and the like.
For here we are concerned primarily with change in the spoken chain, not in
isolated forms. And it is arguable that the chain itself is not a major domain
for changes other than 'simplifications', or those that are 'natural' in the
Stampean sense. Certainly (despite the arguments of Horn & Lehnert 1954
and Samuels 1972) there is no strong evidence that changes like vowel shifts
and the like have their sources in the spoken chain, rather than in a combination of systemic factors and pure arbitrariness. And it is precisely such
changes that are my main concern here (though the others are included).[33]
Whatever the evidential value of examples of this kind (and I think it is great),
we cannot make a general claim that in all cases yesterday's allegro is tomorrow's lento.[34]

6. Constraints, 3: Diachronic evidence for well formed mappings

I suggested above that poles like [e] and [o], for example, are typical not of
the results of internal sound change, but of situations where we have reason
to believe that interdialectal borrowing is involved.[35] In this section I will
look at the kind of patterns we typically get where we have known internal
historical evolutions of some magnitude. The picture in borrowing is dis-
junctive; but evolutive change, where comparative evidence will often give us
poles at least as far apart as those found in borrowing, will give us an **overall**
set of attested reflexes showing a rather finely graded continuum. A continuum, in fact, whose various points can be taken as 'intermediate' stages
between the poles: virtually a static picture of the evolution, laid out like a
fossil record.[36] And we can see that this can also be supported by independent historical evidence. The goal of this section will be to produce a case
study in justification of a particular set of mapping constraints, with some
comments on the general theoretical problems raised by them, and their
particular mode of response to evidence.

The continuum I will look at — which I maintain illustrates the normal
pattern in large-scale evolution — is the reflexes of ME /u:/ in the North and

North Midlands of England. As is well known, one of the striking features of
the northern dialects (including Scots) is that by and large ME /u:/ did not
diphthongize parallel to /i:/ in the Great Vowel Shift (giving patterns of the
type: [u:]/[aɪ] in *mouse/mice* rather that [aɔ]/[aɪ], etc.) Thus we get a
North/North Midland isogloss with [u:] or something of the sort in *mouse,
about, cow* etc. north of the line and [aɔ] or other diphthongal types south of
it.[37] It is also clear that [u:] represents the original nucleus, and the diphthongal forms the output of a long series of historical changes, possibly ranging
over as much as half a milennium.

But what were the individual stages in this development, and how large
were they? Some of the early stages (e.g. those in the 16th–17th centuries) are
familiar; but the picture in the northern parts of Britain has not been well
studied, and the range of developments is much larger and more complex
than the 'histories of English' usually tell us about. I will present below some
data for the North and North Midlands, taken from the relevant *Survey of
English Dialects* volumes (Orton – Halliday 1962 for the North, and Orton –
Barry 1969 for the North Midlands). The development I will be concerned
with is that of ME /u:/ in closed syllables under stress (SED Questionnaire
item VII.2.8, *about*).[38] For each county I have listed the major reflexes, with
the SED network number after each type showing at least one area where it
occurs. Types occurring more than once are listed for one occurrence only in
each county: my concern is the range of types, not the density of distribution. (Scots is omitted, as there are no 'native' diphthongal nuclei in this category, and the loss of phonemic length has distorted the picture considerably;
cf. Lass 1974.)

Table I: Reflexes of ME /u:/ in the North and North Midlands

1. Northumberland: [u:] all areas.
2. Cumberland: [u:] 2.1; [aɔ] 2.6.
3. Durham: [u:] 3.1; [ᵊu:] 3.3; [ᵓu:] 3.5.
4. Westmoreland: [u:] 4.1; [ɵu:] ~ [ᵊu:] 4.2.
5. Lancashire: [aɔ] 5.1; [a:] 5.6; [æˑə] 5.9; [ɛ:] 5.12.
6. Yorkshire: [ʌɔ] 6.1; [u:] 6.2; [aɔ] 6.5; [ᵊu:] 6.6;
    [ʌɒ̨] ~ [ǝɔ] ~ [ǝu:] 6.8; [a:] 6.14; [ɵu:] 6.15;
    [æɔ] 6.21; [a:] 6.26; [ɛǝ] 6.29; [ɛa] ~ [ɛä]
    6.30; [æˈǝ] ~ [æǝ] ~ [ᶐa] 6.31; [æ:] 6.32.
7. Isle of Man: [ou], [oɔ] ~ [oɒ̨], [oˑ] 1; [u:], [ʉ:] 1;
    [æu:] 1; [ǽü] 2; [ǝü] ~ [ᵊü] 2.
8. Cheshire: [aɪ] 7.1; [æɔ] 7.2; [aɪ] 7.3; [aɔ] 7.4; [ɛ̨ɔ] 7.6.
9. Derbyshire: [ɛ̨ɔ] 8.1; [a:] 8.2; [ɛ:] 8.3; [ɛ̨:] 8.4; [ą:] 8.4.

10. Shropshire: [aɷ] 11.1; [æɷ] 11.2; [εɷ] 11.4; [uː] 11.7;
                       [əuː] 11.11.

This data is not complete; it does not indicate relative frequency of different reflex types (except insofar as they occur in more than one county). Nor
have I made any attempt at setting up geographical subgroupings. But this is
not important for my particular argument here: what counts is the actual inventory, and the relative coherence (if any) of the picture it presents.

Let us start from the uncontroversial assumption that all these dialects
started out in late Middle English with [uː]. And let us assume further that
changes do not necessarily travel along geographical lines (though of course
they may). I.e., dialect developments are largely autonomous: once a change
has begun, the 'decision' as to whether or not to go on with it (and how to go
on) is more or less up to the dialect in question.[39] So with respect to a starting point [uː], what counts is the degree of innovation: dialects with [uː]
are obviously maximally conservative, those with [ᵊuː] or [ɷu] marginally
innovating, those with [aɷ] still more so, and (if we follow the history) those
with [εɷ], [ɛː], [aː] or [aɩ] the most innovating.

Table I is not so chaotic as it looks. Given what we know independently
about some points of the history, we can see quite an interesting pattern
emerging. First let us recall that the information we have from early witnesses
(say Hart 1569 to Cooper 1687) suggests that the early history of the vowel
shift of ME /uː/ followed this simple pattern:

(11)   uː → ou → ʌu

In other words, the first stage of this chain of vowel changes was a descent
down the back series of the first element of /uː/.[40] Once we know this, we
can sort out the major reflexes in a rough order of novelty, as follows:

Table II: Major reflexes of ME /uː/ in order of increasing 'novelty'

1.   Unchanged: [uː]
2.   Minimal diphthong: [ᵊuː], [ɷuː], [ᵓuː]
3.   Diphthong with (relatively) close back second member: [ou], [oɷ],
      [əu], [aɷ], [æɷ], [εɷ], [əü], [ʌɷ]
4.   Diphthong with nonback second member: [æˑə], [ɛə], [ɛa], [ɛä],
      [aɩ], [aɩ]
5.   Nonback monophthong: [aː], [æː], [ɛː]

This ordering reflects the history: type (3), as [ou] or [oɷ], was present in the 16th century (Hart 1569), and the [ʌ ω], [aω] types show up a good deal later (the latter probably not until the late 18th or early 19th century). Types (4–5) can be taken as the latest: they clearly presuppose the general type (3) if the development is to make any sense at all. I will return to this later.

Now if we assume relatively small stages for internal sound change, this material sorts itself out quite rationally, in a way that also accords with the history. In the exposition that follows, I will simplify things a bit: I will for the moment disregard diacritics, half-length, and the like, and equate (post-vocalic) [ι ω] with [i u] respectively. With this framework we can extract from the data (Table I) and the restricted taxonomy (Table II) the following historical sequence:

(12)

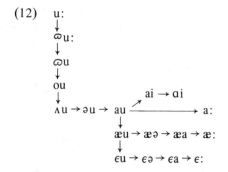

(There are a number of possible alternative paths: e.g. [a:] → [æ:] → [ɛ:], or [əu] → [ɛ:]. The first is more or less ruled out by the unlikelihood of a second Great Vowel Shift chain of this type restricted to one category; the choices for the others are controlled by methodological considerations I will discuss below).

I ordered this material rather simply, according to a number of more or less empirical principles. The first control, obviously, was the known history: the sequence from [u:] to [ʌu] is virtually a matter of record, as is the position of the [ʌu], [əu] types as sources of the modern and widespread [au].[41] Given the developments in the [u:] → [ʌu] column as fixed, and [ʌu] → [əu] as nearly as well fixed, the rest arranges itself naturally: changes in the second elements of the diphthongs seem to be in the direction back peripheral to central to front open, and then up the front, with the monophthongizations following; the first element changes also follow this pattern. It looks as if this aspect of the vowel shift is a matter of the two elements being out of phase with each other, but following basically the same direction in the vowel space.

If comparative evidence gives us, as I have claimed, and as most historical linguists seem to accept, a view of the stages of an evolution set out as it were achronically, then this argues in general for quite small steps. Indeed, it is difficult to imagine a picture like this emerging except through incremental change. And this is a typical picture — given the alphabet of distinctions that the data was captured in (the Cardinal Vowel scale plus diacritics). Similar pictures using finer tools produce tighter networks, with finer (but still dialectally criterial) distinctions.

But the significant point is that even given the relative crudeness of the representing alphabet, and given further my expository reduction of it, we still come out with no reason to postulate any massive changes, with the possible exception of three: the sequences [au] → [aː], [au] → [ai], and [ai] → [ɑi]. The first represents one of the few vowel changes of this size that there is any good evidence for: monophthongization by assimilation of one member of a divocalic nucleus to the other. The [u] → [i], [a] → [ɑ] changes (front to back direct) are as far as I know unattested in any convincing form: a similar space may have been covered by the *i*-umlaut of PGmc */u/, but there is no reason not to assume at least an intermediate stage [ʉ] for this.

The front-to-back shift [a] → [ɑ] is of a type whose inverse is supposed to be attested in English in the 'Anglo-Frisian Brightening' (cf. Lass & Anderson 1976: ch. II). The actual change itself has been assumed to have occurred in the lengthening and retraction of ENE /æ/ to [ɑː] in *path, grass*, etc.; but this probably was gradual, as the dialect material shows at least the stages [æː] → [aː] → [äː] → [ɑ̈ː] → [ɑ̇ː] → [ɑː] (evidence in Lass 1976: ch. 4).

So of the whole set of changes attested in this complex development, very few are of a larger size than (at most) what could reasonably be represented as a movement of one symbol in a given direction on the IPA grid. The [u] → [i] shift remains difficult, and I will return to it later.

But, leaving aside the few problem cases, the general situation seems to be: the more evidence we have, the smaller the attested changes. Thus ongoing changes of the Labovian type are very small indeed; the really massive changes seem (not surprisingly) to show up mainly when we get back far enough so that all or nearly all our evidence is orthographic.

This fact alone should have made historical phonologists in general more suspicious than it has: certainly the elements of this information have been around for more than a decade (Labov 1963). While I would not go so far as to accuse historical generativists, as Bluhme in another connection has the synchronic ones, of a 'heillose Verwechslung von Laut und Buchstabe' (1975: 44), the problem is not unknown. The danger is constant for those whose main preoccupation is with written records.

Let us make the tentative conclusions reached so far a bit more specific.

This English data, plus the material in Labov, Trudgill, etc., suggests that vowel changes in particular can be constrained in a particular way for reconstructive purposes: at least in terms of maximal distances for single changes. I will make some concrete proposals shortly. But let us remember that historically what we can recover is much less finely specifiable that what we can get synchronically. Modern dialect evidence shows areal differentiations maintained consistently at vocalic distances as small as 'one quarter of a Cardinal Vowel': e.g. one area will have consistent [ɛ] against another's [ɛ̞]. So distances this small are perceptible and potentially significant (in a way that say a rise of .005 Hz in F_1 would not be); and therefore the units of change can be at least this small.

But let us propose an alphabet coarse enough to be historically useful, and try to frame a set of constraints on vowel change in its terms. (Remember that a 'constraint on change' is really a constraint on reconstruction.) If we keep in mind the typological conditions I suggested earlier (§ 3), then there is no 'universal' grid we can use. Rather we must cut our cloth according to our language (to some extent): at least with respect to what categories we admit.

To take an example: present-day English dialects allow, as far as I know, for the construction of vocalic nuclei (simple of complex) out of a limited inventory, which contains the following basic distinctive types:[42]

(13)

i y		ɨ ʉ		u
e ø	ɪ Y		ɷ	ɣo
ɛ œ		ə		ʌ ɔ
a				ɒ ɑ

The grid (13) defines a **trajectory-space** for vowel change in English. On the basis of structural properties of attested systems, and what is known about historically 'completed' change and change in progress, we allow it to define the **maxima** for permitted changes. In other words, a set of operations defined on (13), plus a set of other constraints I will suggest, give us a set of well-formed vowel changes for English.

First: adhering to the typological appropriateness principle, no segments which **might** occur in the blank cells are allowed to appear in the course of a change (e.g. [ɯ] or [ɘ]). So although the provisional constraints to be given below will operate on a principle of preferred (rectilinear or diagonal) adjacency, violations of adjacency are allowed just in case the adjacent cell is unfilled. Thus [u] → [ʉ], [ə] → [a] are allowed, because only blank cells intervene. (I suspect that in general the phonological histories of languages consist largely of moves about partly blank grids like (13), and that creation of new cells is rare: there are not too many episodes in Indo-European like the *i*-umlaut or the development of implosives in Sindhi. Cf. Hoenigswald in this volume.)

The interpretive conventions for (13) are:

> (14) i. A well-formed vowel change is *ceteris paribus* no larger than a move from one cell to an adjacent one (vertically, horizontally, diagonally).[43]
> ii. A change may cross a blank cell to the nearest nonempty one.

This gives us — overall — the permitted maximal units of change (here in historical perspective, but probably synchronically as well). Minimal movements may or may not be constrained in principle: but the alphabet here will simply not notice them.

The hedging *ceteris paribus* in (14.i) has two main glosses, one formal and the other (at first sight anyhow) rather fishy. The more formal one is:

> (15) In a cluster V_iV_j, where $i \neq j$, $V_j \rightarrow V_i$ is well-formed.

(I.e., we allow total assimilation of the rightmost member of a divocalic cluster to the leftmost. This seems to be the English pattern: anticipatory assimilations are normally less than total: cf. OE [eo] → [ɸ:] in the Southwest and Southwest Midlands, [iu] (orthographic *ie*) → [y:] , etc. For details Lass & Anderson 1975: ch. 3, § 8; ch. 4, § 3.)

The second gloss of *ceteris paribus* is:

> (16) Things are not equal if there is overwhelming evidence that a violation of (14) actually occurred.

This needs discussion. The purpose is to take care of notable violations like the [au] → [ai] change mentioned above. But before we invoke something so 'weak', could we get rid of this unpleasant change in some way that might avoid *ad hoc* strategies like (16)? This massive shift might be an exception and just that (a possibility I will discuss below); or it may simply be that the intermediate stages between [u] and [i] are missing. This is doubtful, however: (a) because the wealth of material and its fine-grainedness elsewhere makes it unlikely that so much should be missing; and (b) because the intermediate output types that (13–14) would produce are not acceptable. That is, a sequence like [au] → [aɨ] → [ai] can be rejected on typological grounds ([aɨ] is not a well-formed English diphthong, as far as I know). Another series in accord with (13) would be [au] → [aʉ] → [ay] → [ai] ; this is less peculiar in general English terms, since we get [aʉ], [ay] types in the Southwest and Southwest Midlands: but it is areally odd. English, yes, but not northern enough. It looks as if the general constraint won't work here.

The obvious conclusion is that imposition of my restrictions is misguided: the [au] → [ai] change is a counterexample. But this would be to misunderstand both my proposal and the role of counter-examples. Actually, (16) is not as brazen a piece of face-saving as it looks.

First, I am not proposing a 'universal' theory, or even a totally 'predictive' (or postdictive) one. As far as I can see (and cf. § 7 below and Scriven 1959), total ('nomological') prediction in history of any kind is possible only on a scale so broad as to make the results trivial. I am proposing a set of essentially **methodological** constraints, keyed to a theory of the role of method as an 'information source' or 'truth-defining algorithm' in historical investigation (more on this below). The principle is clear: if you don't have hard evidence to the contrary, the best-attested change type is what happened. Invoking unusual or poorly-attested changes without specific compelling evidence violates elementary canons of simplicity and plausibility. But a theory of the 'natural' doesn't preclude the 'unnatural' (cf. Lass 1972) – even (within bounds) the wildly unnatural: it just makes it harder to justify. I am not saying that nothing surprises me: only that I need more conviction the greater the surprise.

Further, a counterexample no more 'refutes' an otherwise serviceable theory than an exceptional lexical item 'refutes' an otherwise valid phonological or morpheme-structure rule. Thus physicists from Newton to Einstein lived with a theory in which the perihelion of Mercury was an 'anomaly': but they didn't scrap the Newtonian framework because of this, they simply worried and waited around for someone to get rid of it. We must weigh up the consequences carefully before we allow anomalies or counterexamples to get too upsetting. At its best, a collection of anomalies can be a heuristic leading to a better theory or new rules of procedure (cf. Verner); at its worst, it can produce a healthy uneasiness, without calling for wholesale revision. (All theories, like all grammars, leak.) Constraints of the type I am proposing simply maximize the probable changes, and make it harder to justify the improbable ones.

Let us now add to our armory the 'etymological condition' on well-formed outputs (§ 3, i'): any stage in change-sequence must be attested as a current reflex of the same etymological category. (We could even strengthen this, and add 'in the same typological/regional dialect area'.) Let us see how this would affect one of the problematical areas in the development of ME /uː/, i.e. the sequence leading to [ɛː]. According to the remarks in note 40

above, I will take the two poles of this development as [uu], [ɛɛ].
The first part can be represented in terms of (13–14) as:

(17) uu → ou → ʌu → əu

From here, there are two obvious shorter paths, shown as (18.i, ii):

(18) i. əu → eu → ɛu → ɛɛ
      ii. əu → au → ɛu → ɛɛ

There are also two possible longer paths:

(19) i. əu → au → ɛu → ɛə → ɛɛ
      ii. əu → au → ɛu → ɛə → ɛa → ɛɛ

(cf. (12) above: I am still equating [ɷ] with [u].)

Of these four choices, one is immediately ruled out by the etymological constraints: (18.i). There is no attestation in the corpus (or anywhere else, as far as I know) of [eu] as a reflex of this category. The etymological condition thus says that (a) we may not reconstruct an unattested intermediate stage; and (b) that this is a rational restriction; because if we follow other paths, we in fact get the whole set of attested reflexes as part of our sequence – provided we also follow (13) and its conventions.

If we want to decide among the remaining alternatives, we can couple the desire to get the whole set of reflexes (or as much as possible) with the empirically-based constraint that lies at the heart of the whole exercise. If when we look at typical chartings of change in progress, the stages by which vowels move are certainly no bigger than (13–14) suggest; and if we rely on statistical probability as a guide to reconstruction, then the 'simplest' account of a change (i.e. the one requiring least auxiliary justification) is the one where the steps are smallest. Since the evidence tells us that this is to be expected, even relatively well attested changes like [ɛu] → [ɛɛ] are less preferable than smaller ones.

Therefore the simplest evolution leading to [ɛ:] is (19.ii), which is also the longest. But given the comparative picture, the history, and what we can learn from progress-studies, this is the most likely.

So a combination of the trajectory-space (13), the constraints (14), and the etymological condition virtually dictates a solution. And the notion of 'simplicity' that comes out here (like the same notion elsewhere in linguistic theory) is far from obvious: the longest derivation, moving by the smallest steps, is theoretically 'cheaper' than any of the shorter ones.[44]

7. Epilogue: Methodology as a source of truth

I have been trying to clarify some of the ways in which evidence of one kind or another can serve, in combination with methodological principles, to constrain the excessive power of reconstructive technique. And I have been arguing from a specific metaphysical position, which is that historical linguistics is necessarily and incurably 'realist' in a way that synchronic linguistics is not. At least this is the case with reconstruction, if not (necessarily) with non-reconstructive explanation. Or perhaps better, since all historical explanation is 'reconstructive' of something, the realist imperative applies to the reconstruction of entities and their changes, if not to that of 'causes' and the like.

This is because the reconstruction of entities is rather superficial: as I have emphasized throughout, we necessarily reconstruct something pretty close to (very crude and idealized) phonetic output. This is both because the data that reconstruction works on represents this level, and because nothing else is reconstructible with even the minimal 'certainty' we have about this material. If we adopt a 'uniformitarian' view of language history (more on this below), then what we can reconstruct is further limited by our empirical knowledge of things that occur in present-day languages.

This is where the main difference from synchronic linguistics comes in: in the current climate, anyhow, synchronic descriptions are always trying to transcend the 'merely empirical'. Our attention is turned toward the 'underlying', away from the surface. Therefore we are not constrained by public empirical knowledge in the same way as we are (or should be) in reconstruction. What we are after in history is minimally precisely the same as our **superficial empirical knowledge** of present-day languages: not our deeper **theoretical knowledge** (though some historical inquiries may lead to this as well). It may in fact be a category mistake to allow empirically-based notions like 'phonetic naturalness', for instance, to dictate the shape of what are supposed to be 'mental' derivations: sound change must be constrained by observation, but subsurface derivational processes exist by definition in a different universe. To attempt to constrain them by surface empirical knowledge, much of it about very peripheral characteristics of the speech tract, may be merely to give descriptions a false and inappropriate aura of 'empirical justification'. But having raised this contentious matter to frame the discussion, I will drop it: for discussion cf. Linell (1974), Lass – Anderson (1975: ch. VI), and Lass (1977).

Reconstruction is an attempt to bring into the present as an object of contemplation some past surface conditions. If this is so, then it raises an epistemological problem: in what sense is 'knowledge' of previous language states gained through reconstruction to be trusted? What is the status of a form of

knowledge that is gained through minimal (often absent) observation procedures, and maximal deployment of an armory of methodological dictates?
For we tend to act (perhaps myself more than many others) as if such dictates are **direct sources of knowledge.**

And so they are; or have to be, anyhow, if we are going to do any rational
history at all. I shall give a short and inadequate account of why this is so, as
a coda to the previous discussion: some day, as we say, I shall write a book
about it. Basically, the informative power of methodological choices is a consequence of a uniformitarian philosophy; and without such a philosophy (or
better, metaphysics) there is no history.

The past as a coherent entity exists only because of some 'constitutive' act
we perform on the data that we take to represent it: it is only through intel-
lectual effort that history (even in its lowest form, which is chronicle, hopefully *vera narratio*) comes into being. All the characteristics of sequence,
coherence, etc., are due to theories interacting with objects that we take (on
whatever grounds) to be 'records'. Simply by virtue of the 'directionality' and
'irreversibility' of time, the past can never be independently known; our reconstructions can't be compared with the object itself they purport to
reconstruct. Therefore we need principles of comparison, so that alternative
accounts of a missing past can be evaluated; and the only way I can see to
make such judgements is to base them on what we know, i.e., the present.
(This is why in the 19th century the post-Lyell 'uniformitarianism' influenced
Darwin and everybody else so strongly: 'catastrophism' and the like simply
have no empirical content, but allow unrestrained *ad-hoc* hypotheses whenever things get difficult.) Thus if we interpret theoretical 'strength' in the
Popperian sense as the power to 'forbid' states of affairs in nature, uniformitarianism of a rather strong kind is automatically preferable to an unconstrained theory. And not only this: uniformitarian principles can themselves
be sources of 'new' information about the past.

Let me give a brief example from evolutionary biology, which may clarify
things. Consider the statement: '*Smilodon*, a "sabretooth tiger" of the Pleistocene, was a carnivore'. There are two kinds of assertions here: one is a
matter of historical record (i.e. an identifiable cat-like animal that lived at a
specifiable point in geological time). The second is not a matter of record at
all: that it was carnivorous. Yet we are as certain of this as we are of the
other, despite the absence of people who saw it eat, etc. How do we get such
'moral certainties'? Presumably, by a process like this:

i. Smilodon had huge canine teeth, small incisors, no true molars, massive
attachment points for the jaw muscles, and long sharp curved claws.

ii. Among present-day mammals, the set of predicates (i) is found only in obligatory carnivores.

iii. The 'laws of nature' are constant over time.

iv. Smilodon was an obligatory carnivore. Q.E.D.

This is a characteristic kind of historical argument. In addition to the record (i), we employ a present-day predicate (ii), which is legitimized by the uniformitarian axiom (iii). This gives us (iv).

Note the fruitfulness of this strategy: the argument from the 'old' historical record (i) gives us a 'new' record (iv). Witnesses of the past plus a uniformitarian axiom give us new witnesses of the past. We could now go on to explore 'unobservables' like Pleistocene ecology: we could figure out (again, on the basis of present-day mammals as close to *smilodon* as possible) what it probably ate. This illustrates the important point that the techniques of historical argument can produce new 'facts' that produce still more.

But we could raise a question of validity: what gives us the right to invoke the uniformitarian principle? How does (ii) being true 'make' (iv) true? The answer is of course that it doesn't: it's not that because (ii) is true there is an empirical certainty that (iv) is: rather the basic shape of the argument is one we feel at home with, one which seems a guarantor of validity. For we have here in essence the familiar *modus ponens*: if p then q; p; therefore q (where p = dentition, etc., q = 'is a carnivore'.)

Not all historical argument can be reduced to entailment relations (either like these or like *modus tollens*); in many cases (most?) the information is insufficient to allow 'law-like' statements. But at least some forms of historical argument do have this pleasing shape; enough of them so that if we can build this general structure into the overall framework, we feel a certain confidence in the results.

This is in its own way as 'irrational' as Humean induction: if (cf. Popper 1968) it is not rational (though it may be useful) to believe that constant co-occurrences in the past will repeat themselves in the future, then why should we believe that the present is in some sense a 'repetition' of the past? But either we do this or we give up.

The example I gave above was excessively neat and rather trivial: but the principle is not trivial. In one form or another it is the axiomatic foundation of all history. Basically it is:

(20) Nothing (no event, sequence of events, conjunction of properties, 'general law') was ever the case only in the past.

I.e., the general principles that govern the world in the present hold for the past as well. Without this control, nothing can stop us from reconstructing anything at all, and justifying it by *ad hoc* auxiliary hypotheses ('*smilodon* was the only herbivore that ever had carnivore's teeth'). The corollary of this is that historical inference can only take us back to the furthest-past point when the governing principles were the same as they are now: anything beyond that is by definition not reconstructible, i.e., not part of history.

But let us remember that this doesn't mean that the past must have been identical to the present in detail: only the 'immanent' principles are the same; the contingent or 'configurational' ones (cf. Simpson 1964: ch. vii) change. **History is an infinite sequence of unique, nonrepeatable events, each of which at some level is a token of one of a finite set of repeatable types.** There is thus a necessary nonhistorical background to history, and it is this that makes the purely historical (spatiotemporally bound) available at all.

There are very few absolute universals, of course. Most of what we deal with in history (and historical linguistics as a special case) is 'trends', 'tendencies', 'naturalness', and the like. But these come under the same methodological heading, if in a weaker version. If the strong form of the uniformitarian axiom says that nothing impossible ever happened, the weaker form says:

(21) The distribution of probabilities in cases where a choice is available from a set of alternatives has always been the same as it is now.

(Cf. Lass – Anderson 1975: ch. V; Lass 1976: ch. 3). In cases of indeterminacy, the probable happened. Like the strong axiom, this is both a constraint on reconstruction, and a source of new information about the past.

There are two kinds of historical knowledge: relatively direct, gained from the record by the application of theoretical principles, and indirect, derived from theory in conjunction with the present state of things, and a minimal or severely gapped record. If the principles of inference are valid (or at least if *we* believe them to be) then the second type of knowledge is just as useful as the first. And in fact an important part (perhaps a major part) of the 'historical record' as linguists utilize it consists of second-order (purely theoretical) inferential knowledge.

Whether we like it or not, we can't reject it: the game cannot be played except within some such structure. If we reject the binding force of uniformitarian principles on the content of history, then we reject all interesting history. If we do not accept that a constraint can be a source of knowledge, then we reject historical knowledge. Historians must operate on a rather restricted notion of 'truth': something approaching a procedural definition. 'True knowledge' of historical matters is **what our methodological principles tell us is true.** I do not think it has a much more 'objective' definition.[45] But insofar as our methodological principles and the constraints and procedural dictates arising from them have some kind of empirical substance, and insofar as some of our reconstructive techniques are subject to testing, our knowledge has some sort of claim to reliability.

Notes

1. A preliminary version of part of this paper was presented to the Scottish Philological Society in Edinburgh. I am grateful to the members for comments. I am also indebted to John Anderson and Jim Miller for reading a draft of the whole thing, and commenting.

    Many participants in this conference pointed out problems: Mary Taylor suggested that my strategy for identifying borrowings in § 5 is rather crude, which I agree is the case; and Bob Stockwell provided many comments on and criticisms of my account of the evolution of ME /u:/ and the conventions for interpreting the phonetic grid in § 6, which are probably well taken; but these things will have to be ironed out in future. I have nothing better at the moment.

    The usual disclaimer about errors being mine, though not very informative, is presented as part of the ritual.

2. I specify comparative trees, because not all genetic stemmata are 'trees' (in the graph-theoretical sense), and therefore some cannot be specified by (well-formed) Phrase-Structure rules. A simple case is any stemma that represents a merger, since this requires rules of the form AB → C.

3. On the content of */p/ see below. The methodology governing the choice of proto-segments in cases like this (recall that '*/p/' is still only a symbol for the bracketing of an equivalence-class) is familiar: see any textbook account of comparative method.

4. Bloomfield seems to have held a similar view: 'The comparative method tells us ... nothing about the acoustic shape of reconstructed forms; it identifies the phonemes in reconstructed forms merely as recurrent units' (1933: 309). For a much more extreme version, in effect stigmatizing reconstruction of phonetic content as 'unscientific' see Allen (1953). Allen gives a very full discussion of the literature on this matter ('ontological' vs. 'algebraic' theories).

5. Cf. also Pike (1957: 2). Some writers however do make a hard-and-fast distinction between establishing correspondences and protoforms, and investing the latter with content. Thus Collinge (1970: 71): ' ... "phonetic speculation" [here characterization of PIE '*H': RL] applied to phoneme-sequences – and not merely the stating of such PIE sequences – is the business of comparative reconstruction when it relates its findings to constructs – when it shunts forward, in fact.' I gather that the 'findings' are formulaic; the 'constructs' involve history in some sense (though not precisely mine, I think). For a more radically content-full view of protoforms, cf. Haas (1969: 44–45) and Ellis (1958). Ellis' answer to Allen's (1953) strictures on 'realist' comparative method (152–158) is particularly to the point; I take his defense of reconstructing phonetic content as definitive.

6. For Katičić (1970: 99) it is 'not correct to classify the comparative method as a diachronic procedure'. It is 'descriptive and achronic'. For Allen (1953) this lack of historicity is a plus: it enables comparative method to be 'descriptive', and not make ontological commitments. He goes so far as to say that 'historical' linguistics in an 'evolutionary' sense is suspect, because it necessarily involves teleology, which he assumes without comment is to be avoided (cf. especially 104). Even if it were true that a genuinely historical linguistics had to be teleological (which it isn't),

there is no reason to bar teleology from linguistic theory, and a good deal of solid motivation for including it (Lass 1974, Anttila 1975). In any case, Allen's objections are based on a positivist stance which I do not accept; it is not necessary in any case to apologize for not accepting a particular epistemology (epistemologies being above all metaphysical commitments). My own will perhaps becomes clearer later on.

7. This ontological insistence may be a bit simple-minded. I have argued elsewhere (Lass 1976: ch. 1, *Epilogue*; Lass 1977) that purely nonontological descriptions can be insightful, i.e., ones with no truth-value claims attached to them or the objects in them (the 'Harrisian' mode). But this is possible only in synchronic linguistics, whose subject matter is pattern and (perceived) structure (cf. § 7 below).

8. Cf. the not dissimilar loss of PIE */p-/ in Goidelic Celtic (Lat. *porcus*, OE *fearh*, OIr. *orc*, etc.) The evidence from Grimm's Law would suggest /p/ → /f/ → ∅ as a minimal path (though there is no Irish attestation of /f/). And changes like Lat. /f/ → OSpan. /h/ → ∅ (cf. Menéndez Pidal 1918: 101-102; Lass, forthcoming a: ch. 6) suggest a further intermediate /h/ as likely. It so happens that some mutations in Old Irish, as well as scattered forms like Old Cornish *hethen* (= Lat. *penna*) confirm at least some /h/ < */p/ (Lewis & Pedersen 1961: § 24.1). But if these were missing, wouldn't we still want to posit /h/? After all, this is a very sporadic case of accidental survival, probably via aborted lexical diffusion. I suspect that in practice 'realist' historical linguists wouldn't worry about the absence of *hethen*, etc.

9. Every change is in some sense a 'substitution' (cf. Hoenigswald 1960: ch. 1); but there is a difference between the two kinds, as we will see later (§ § 5–6).

10. 'Invention' either in the English sense or that of L. *inveniō*: if these are in fact different.

11. For some constraints see Harms (1973). On the general problem of 'false steps' and 'rescue rules' see Zwicky (1974).

12. For some remarks on this from a somewhat different point of view, see my critique of markedness theory (1972).

13. This should probably be changed to specify that the segment be a regularly occurring phone: I don't include accidental variants like [β] for /b/ produced by English speakers talking during meals. But by the same token we cannot rule out ejectives in English, since they are quite regular for final /p t k/ in some dialects. But we could rule out **distinctive** ejectives in Germanic (and probably western Indo-European generally: but not eastern, since Armenian has them). Similarly we can probably rule out implosives except in Indic (Sindhi).

14. I specify 'phonemic' since in many dialects of English, for instance, open vowels are pharyngealized. Velarization at a distinctive level might appear to be out as well: certainly the best known occurrences are in things like postvocalic 'dark' [ɫ] in some forms of English, or the less well-known velarization of all coronals in many dialects including RP and most East Coast U.S. (I owe this observation to Betsy Uldall). But in fact Albanian and some dialects of Yiddish have contrasting velarized and palatalized laterals, so we have to allow this for Indo-European.

15. For a preliminary discussion of the issues raised by this constraint, see Lass (1976: ch. 3). Some of the discussion here is partially based on this.

15a. In all fairness, the King I am attacking in what follows is historically a partial straw man (cf. King 1975). But the importance of the book, and the number of people who still adhere to ideas like this, makes the argument useful.

16. Even in the change '/d/ → /t/' there is a certain latitude that must be a function of 'competence'. King assumes that if [± voice] is the only 'categorial' distinction, variations in voicing must be 'performance phenomena'. This is surely false: the **degree** of voice (even within English, say) is criterial for dialect distinctions (e.g. obstruents in Scots vs. RP). And even though [± voice] can characterize phonemic oppositions adequately (maybe), if the speakers of a language habitually use a partic-

ular degree of voicing in voiced stops, then this must be a function of their 'know-ledge of the language', and therefore subject to change by the same mechanisms as any other part of it.

17. King does admit later (117) that 'rejecting the gradualness assumption does not force one to exclude a priori ... intermediate steps', and that 'in certain cases incre-ments may be more expected ... than great leaps'. But he fails to show that in **any** case of internal change of this kind we are forced to assume 'leaps': all he shows is that in certain cases we can't find e.g. strictly age-graded sequences from a segment to zero. But the kind of dialect-differentiation that typically occurs has precisely this sort of evidential value, as we will see.

18. We do 'find' such rules in synchronic grammars, in the form of segment ~ zero **alternations** that can be expressed as deletion rules. But there is no particular evi-dence that such rules reflect the form of the sound changes they are relics of (if they are). Nor of course is there any evidence (other than the theory's insistence that certain alternations must be so described) that synchronic mutation-rules exist anywhere outside of grammatical descriptions. They are convenient, and even 'in-sightful': but a synchronic feature-chainging rule cannot be evidential for anything, since its existence is more strictly theory-dependent than (in general) the existence of a sound change *qua* historical event. In any gradual loss there does come a point when it becomes 'abrupt': but the likelihood of abruptness is inversely proportional to the 'strength' of the segment (in articulatory, not Foleyan terms: Lass 1971; Lass – Anderson 1975: ch. V). In a progressive lenition, loss is the final stage: the two 'pre-final' (i.e. most eminently loseable) segment types are vowels and [h ɦ]. It seems rather rare for obstruents (probably also nasals and liquids) to be subject to immediate loss.

19. I make the usual comparativist assumption that I made in § 2: the existence of a graded series (in a fairly obvious sense) between two segments in dialect material suggests that the 'intermediate' stages are frozen historical events (cf. § 6 below). King (on no particular evidence) refuses to accept this: he apparently takes the mere ability of a notation to write 'segment → zero' as a guiding principle in recon-struction (cf. his discussion of the loss of postvocalic /r/ in non-rhotic dialects of English, 110).

20. Vowel loss as a direct change is plausible, and requires no special justification: cf. note 18.

21. This analysis is not unchallenged, but there are no cogent arguments that I know of. But cf. Campbell (1959: 184, n.2).

22. John Taylor in the discussion of my paper suggested that epentheses of this type may also be gradual: e.g. a sequence from syllabic /s/ to a voiceless vowel to a voiced one. Certainly the opposite is well attested, e.g. syllabic obstruents deriving from vowel deletion, as in RP allegro [juːnɪ́vɜːʂtɪ] 'university', etc. (Cf. also Hooper in this volume). The French loss of /s/ in *école, être*, etc. plausibly involved a stage /h/ (cf. loss of /h̄/ < */s̄/ in Greek, /h/ < /f/ in Spanish, and the sequence /s/ → /h/ → ∅ as a variable in Modern Spanish (on this last see Cedergren 1973: 14ff.)

23. A final change type that King cites as *ex definitione* nongradual is change by alpha-switching rules: and it would be if it existed. These cannot be taken as 'data', but are probably notational artifacts (cf. Stockwell 1966).

24. Many generative phonologists (*inter alia*) have adopted Procrustes as a culture hero. Cf. my discussion of reductivism as a form of theoretical imperialism (1976: ch. 7).

25. There is nothing wrong with purely theoretical constraints: only their necessity decreases when the data furnishes a source in a fairly direct way.

26. And this may be conceding a lot. Cf. Hockett's arguments against the generative notion 'grammar' (1970: ch. 3).

27. Not that impressionistic (or acoustic) phonetics gives us a 'theory-free observation language' (which is an absurdity). But there are some low-level 'public' or 'inter-

subjective' criteria in phonetics, while there are only purely theory-internal (and totally nonobservational) ones in any non-surface phonology. E.g., two phoneticians with similar training but different theoretical preoccupations (say a doctrinaire transformationalist and a doctrinaire taxonomic surfacist) could agree that an alternation in some language was [a] ~ [ɑ]. But they could not agree on properties of (pre-phonetic) rules or representations, because only the transformationalist, for whom these things have been relegated from theory to 'background knowledge' can possibly have any 'knowledge' of them.

28. Despite the frequently 'non-anomalous' nature of speech errors (Fromkin 1971) there is no evidence I know of that they are implicated in change: probably because they are by definition 'unsystematic' in the sense not of lacking linguistic structure, but of not being repeated (I except the Rev. Dr. Spooner, who is atypical). Cf. also Householder (1971: 308).

29. For the beginnings of a phonetically grounded theory of 'intermediate stages' see Lass – Anderson (1975: ch. V). For criticism of this theory, much of it well taken, cf. Dekeyser in this volume.

30. Based on data from Aberdour Parish (Fife) speakers; but the patterns are common throughout Scots-speaking Scotland. For the history of OE /o:/ and the length distributions see Lass (1974).

31. The [y] - forms are Scots 'versions' of [u:] or [ɔu] types in other dialects, 'nativized' borrowings. These Scots dialects typically lack high back rounded vowels except before /r/. Given the history we know, [y:] in *do* cannot be native: it must come from a dialect that had late ME /o:/ here, since the Scots dialects had lME /φ:/ which must give a mid front vowel (still [φ:] in some areas).

32. I omit the few cases discussed where the input to a rule is a 'remote' representation of any kind, i.e. anything other than an observable phonetic form (e.g. *Auslautverhärtung*, 24). For a discussion of the synchronic implications of this work, see Linell (1974: ch. 7). In the data I have omitted boundary symbols, and adjusted the transcription to conform with IPA conventions.

33. Though certainly **exceptions** to general changes have been claimed to be due to 'low sentence stress', 'inherent unstressability', etc. Cf. Luick (1964: § 268.2) on failure of an early Middle English lengthening rule in 'Wörtern mit geringerem Ton, wie *and ... under*'.

34. If this were a general principle, it would lead to an infinite regress of simplifications (cf. Linell 1974: ch. 7 on the limits of such processes). But there is no doubt that many changes of a simplifying type are general in allegro and appear only sporadically in lento, which distorts the historical picture (Dressler 1975).

35. Other examples: 'native' vs. 'borrowed' [φ:] for ME /ɔ:/ in Durham (Orton 1933); [ʁ] vs. [ɹ] in Tyneside (Hepher 1954). In these and other cases the contact origins are transparent.

36. At least where a lot of evidence is available. I have argued elsewhere (1976: ch. 3–4) for the importance of extensive comparative evidence from synchronic dialectology in establishing the overall shapes of major sound changes.

37. For a map, see Wakelin (1972: 103). There are many more nuclear types than [u:] [aɔ] involved, as we will see, but the essential division is [u:] vs. everything else. For some discussion of ME /u:/ in the north, see Lass (1969; 1976: ch. 2). The scholarship on possible paths from [u:] to [aɔ] is critically discussed in Wolfe (1972), from a rather different point of view.

38. Open-syllable environments give a less clear picture, as there is a tendency here toward secondary diphthongization and other changes. Thus many dialects that are really '[u:]-dialects' will show [əu] etc. in *cow*. The same for other categories: Haltwhistle, Northumberland (SED 1.7) shows [u:] in *about* but [əu:] in *cow*, [ɣɪ] in *white* but [aɪ] in *sky* (ME /i:/), and [i:] in *sheep* but [eɪ] in *see* (ME /e:/).

39. For the general irrelevance of areal links to 'progress' along the stages of a change

look at the distribution of palatalized and nonpalatalized reflexes of Gmc */sk/ before back vowels: [sk] in Danish and Swedish, [sx] in Dutch, [ʃ] in German and English. If as seems likely this began with spirantization of /k/ and then palatalization of the cluster and loss of /k/ (or 'fusion' in the sense of Sigurd 1975), each of the three reflexes has gone a different number of steps along the path. But the two [ʃ] languages are separated by the North Sea, and one [sk] language (Danish) is contiguous to German.

40. I.e., '/u:/' = /uu/ (Lass – Anderson 1975: ch. I, VI; Lass 1976: ch. 1, 3). It seems reasonable to take long vowels in general as divocalic identical clusters: certainly this pays off nicely for the history of English, as the material cited above argues. But even if there is a progression [u:] → [uu] (whatever that means), the series [u-] → [o-] → [ʌ-] is obvious. (On the controversial view – held e.g. by Stockwell – that the shift began with a chain like [uu] → [ɨu] → [ʌu] see Wolfe 1972).

41. It seems clear that the [əɑ͡], [əɩ] nuclei in Canadian and Northern U.S. *house, white* do not represent an innovation (the so-called 'Canadian Raising'), but are older than the [aɑ͡], [aɩ] types (cf. Gregg 1975, where the history of these nuclei is discussed: /u:/ is parallel to /i:/). There have been changes of the opposite type: e.g. from [aɑ͡] to [ɐɑ͡] to [əɑ͡] : but these are secondary developments in certain areas (e.g. Martha's Vineyard: Labov 1963). The directionality in the diagram seems nearly beyond dispute.

42. The symbol [ə] covers the difficult range [ə–ɜ] . I omit [æ], as I take it for diasystemic purposes to be a 'kind of [a]'. That is, no dialect I know of has an [a] :[æ] contrast, though many of course have [ɛ] :[æ]. I don't know why this is: many dialects show equally small contrasts among closer vowels, like [i] :[e̞] :[e] in some Scots (cf. Catford 1957). Perhaps there are perceptual reasons for small contrasts being clustered at the top. It is certainly not unusual for Scots dialects anyway to have very crowded systems (four contrasts) in the [i] –[ɛ] range, and then nothing between there and [ɑ] .

43. Perhaps in (14.i) I should add 'with the same roundness value'. I would not like [a] → [œ] or [ɨ] → [Y], whereas a spatially larger move like [u] → [ʉ] seems plausible. But the evidence for [o] → [ʌ] in the vowel shift is very strong. A shift [ɑ͡] to [ʌ] for ME /u/ (*but, come*) is not needed: the intermediate stages [o], [ɔ] are attested (e.g. in Western Yorkshire).

44. This is not a historical argument for – or even an analogue of – the 'free ride' principle. The reason long derivations are preferred here has nothing to do with 'maximum rule utilization' or any formal principle: it is a probability (= plausibility) judgement based on the evidence.

45. This and some of what follows may sound like a plug for a 'coherence theory' of truth. Maybe it is. Certainly there is no doubt that even in the natural sciences the beauty of a framework has very strong effects on the acceptability of a theory (cf. Polanyi 1958).

References

Abercrombie, D. – D. B. Fry – P. A. D. MacCarthy – N. C. Scott – J. L. M. Trim (eds.)
    1964   *In honour of Daniel Jones. Papers contributed on the occasion of his eightieth birthday, 12 September 1961* (London: Longmans).
Allen, W. S.
    1953   "Relationship in comparative linguistics", *Transactions of the Philological Society* 1953: 52–108.
Anderson, J. M. – C. Jones (eds.)
    1974   *Historical linguistics. Proceedings of the First International Conference on Historical Linguistics, Edinburgh 2nd–7th September 1973* (Amsterdam: North-Holland).

Anttila, R.
1972   *An introduction to historical and comparative linguistics* (New York: Macmillan).
1975   "Exception as regularity in phonology", in: Dressler – Mareš 1975, pp. 91–100.
Bach, E. – R. T. Harms
1972   "How do languages get crazy rules?", in: Stockwell – Macaulay 1972, pp. 1–21.
Bailey, C.-J. N. – R. Shuy (eds.)
1973   *New ways of analyzing variation in English* (Washington: Georgetown University Press).
Bloomfield, L.
1933   *Language* (New York: Henry Holt).
Bluhme, H.
1975   "Distinktive Eigenschaft, Laut und Phonem", in: Dressler – Mareš 1975, pp. 43–48.
Brunner, K.
1965   *Altenglische Grammatik, nach der Angelsächsischen Grammatik von Eduard Sievers³* (Tübingen: Niemeyer).
Burrow, T. – M. B. Emeneau
1961   *A Dravidian etymological dictionary* (Oxford: Oxford University Press).
Campbell, A.
1959   *Old English grammar* (Oxford: Oxford University Press).
Catford, J. C.
1957   "Vowel systems of Scots dialects", *Transactions of the Philological Society* 1957: 107–117.
Cedergren, H. J.
1973   "On the nature of variable constraints", in: Bailey – Shuy 1973, pp. 13–22.
Collinder, Bj.
1960   *Comparative grammar of the Uralic languages* (Stockholm: Almqvist & Wiksell).
Collinge, N. E.
1970   *Collectanea linguistica* (The Hague: Mouton).
Cooper, C.
1687   [See Sundby 1953.]
Dressler, W.
1975   "Methodisches zu Allegro-Regeln", in: Dressler – Mareš 1975, pp. 219–234.
Dressler, W. – P. Fasching – E. Chromec – W. Wintersberger – R. Leodolter – H. Stark – G. Groll – J. Reinhart – H. D. Pohl
1972   "Phonologische Schnellsprechregeln in der Wiener Umgangssprache", *Wiener Linguistische Gazette* 1: 1–29.
Dressler, W. – F. V. Mareš (eds.)
1975   *Phonologica 1972. Akten der Zweiten Internationalen Phonologie-Tagung, Wien, 5. – 8. September 1972* (München/Salzburg: Fink)
Ellis, J.
1958   "General linguistics and comparative philology", *Lingua* 7: 134–174.
Emeneau, M. B.
1970   *Comparative Dravidian phonology: A sketch* (Annamalainagar: Annamalainagar University).
Fromkin, V.
1971   "The non-anomalous nature of anomalous utterances", *Language* 47: 27–52.
Gimson, A. C.
1964   "Phonetic change and the RP vowel system", in: Abercrombie *et al.* 1964, 131–136.

Gregg, R. J.
    1975   "The distribution of raised and lowered diphthongs as reflexes of M.E. in
            two Scotch-Irish (SI) dialects", in: Dressler – Mareš 1975, pp. 101–106.
Haas, M. R.
    1969   The prehistory of languages (The Hague: Mouton).
Harms, R. T.
    1973   "Some non-rules of English" (Bloomington: Indiana University Linguistics Club).
Hart, J.
    1569   An orthographie. [Facsimile reprint: Menston: The Scholar Press, 1969.]
Hepher, S. J.
    1954   The phonology of the dialect of Scotswood, Newcastle-on-Tyne. [Unpublished
            B.A. thesis, University of Leeds.]
Hockett, C. F.
    1958   A course in modern linguistics (New York: Macmillan).
    1970   The state of the art (The Hague: Mouton).
Hoenigswald, H. M.
    1960   Language change and linguistic reconstruction (Chicago: Chicago University
            Press).
Horn, W. – M. Lehnert
    1954   Laut und Leben 1 – 2 (Berlin: Deutscher Verlag der Wissenschaften).
Householder, F. W.
    1971   Linguistic speculations (Cambridge: Cambridge University Press).
Jordan R.
    1934   Handbuch der mittelenglischen Grammatik I: Lautlehre [Revised by H. Ch.
            Matthes] (Heidelberg: Winter). [Translation of third edition (Heidelberg:
            Winter, 1968) by E. J. Crook: Handbook of Middle English grammar: Phono-
            logy (The Hague: Mouton, 1974).]
Katičić, R.
    1970   A contribution to the general theory of comparative linguistics (The Hague:
            Mouton).
King, R. D.
    1969   Historical linguistics and generative grammar (Englewood Cliffs, N.J.: Prentice-
            Hall).
    1975   "Integrating linguistic change", in: The Nordic Languages and Modern Linguis-
            tics 2 (Proceedings of the Second International Conference of Nordic and
            General Linguistics, University of Umeå, June 14–19, 1973) (Ed.: K.-H.
            Dahlstedt) (Stockholm: Almqvist & Wiksell International), pp. 47–69.
Kökeritz, H.
    1945   "The reduction of initial kn and gn in English", Language 21: 77–86.
Labov, W.
    1963   "The social motivation of a sound change", Word 19: 273–309.
    1966   The social stratification of English in New York City (Washington: Center for
            Applied Linguistics).
    1972   "The internal evolution of linguistic rules", in: Stockwell – Macaulay 1972,
            pp. 101–171.
Labov, W. – M. Yeager – R. Steiner
    1972   A quantitative study of sound change in progress 1–2 (Philadelphia, Pa.: The
            U.S. Regional Survey).
Lass, R.
    1969   On the derivative status of phonological rules: The function of metarules in
            sound change (Bloomington: Indiana University Linguistics Club).
    1971   "Boundaries as obstruents: Old English voicing assimilation and universal
            strength hierarchies", Journal of Linguistics 7: 15–30.
    1972   "How intrinsic is context? Markedness, sound change, and 'family uni-
            versals' " in: Edinburgh Working Papers in Linguistics 1, pp. 42–67. [Revised

version in: D. L. Goyvaerts – G. K. Pullum (eds.), *Essays on the sound pattern of English* (Ghent: E. Story – Scientia), pp. 475–504.]
1974   "Linguistic orthogenesis? Scots vowel quantity and the English length conspiracy", in: Anderson – Jones 1974, vol. 2, pp. 311–352.
1976   *English phonology and phonological theory: Synchronic and diachronic studies* (Cambridge: Cambridge University Press).
1977   "Internal reconstruction and generative phonology", *Transactions of the Philological Society*: 1–26.
Lass, R. – J. M. Anderson
1975   *Old English phonology* (Cambridge: Cambridge University Press).
Lehmann, W. P.
1952   *Proto-Indo-European phonology* (Austin: University of Texas Press).
1962   *Historical linguistics: An introduction* (New York: Holt, Rinehart, Winston).
Lewis, H. – H. Pedersen
1961   *A concise comparative Celtic grammar* (Göttingen: Vandenhoeck & Ruprecht).
Linell, P.
1974   *Problems of psychological reality in generative phonology: a critical assessment* (Uppsala: University of Uppsala).
Luick, K.
1964   *Historische Grammatik der englischen Sprache* 1–2 (Oxford: Basil Blackwell). [Reprint.]
Meillet, A.
1922   *Introduction à l'étude comparative des langues indo-européennes*[5] (Paris: Librairie Hachette).
Menéndez Pidal, R.
1918   *Manual de gramática historica española*[4] (Madrid: Suarez).
Ohala, J.
1974   "Phonetic explanation in phonology", in: *Papers from the parasession on natural phonology of the Chicago Linguistic Society*, pp. 251–274.
Orton, H.
1933   *The phonology of a South Durham dialect* (London: Kegan Paul, Trench & Trübner).
Orton, H. – M. V. Barry
1969   *Survey of English dialects. B: The basic material, 1: The West Midland counties* (Leeds: Arnold).
Orton, H. – W. Halliday
1962   *Survey of English dialects. B: The basic material, 1: The six Northern counties and the Isle of Man* (Leeds: Arnold).
Pike, K. L.
1957   *Axioms and procedures for reconstruction in comparative linguistics: An experimental syllabus* (Santa Ana, Calif.: Summer Institute of Linguistics).
Polanyi, M.
1958   *Personal knowledge* (London: Routledge & Kegan Paul).
Popper, K. R.
1968   *Conjectures and refutations: The growth of scientific knowledge* (New York: Harper).
Postal, P. M.
1968   *Aspects of phonological theory* (New York: Harper).
Samuels, M.
1972   *Linguistic evolution* (Cambridge: Cambridge University Press).
Scriven, M.
1959   "Explanation and prediction in evolutionary theory", *Science* 130: 477–482.
Sigurd, B.
1975   "Linearization in phonology", in: Dressler – Mareš 1975, pp. 185–208.

Simpson, G. G.
  1964   *This view of life: The world of an evolutionist* (New York: Harcourt, Brace
          & World).
Stockwell, R. P.
  1966   *Problems in the interpretation of the great English vowel shift.* [Unpublished
          manuscript.]
Stockwell, R. P. – R. K. S. Macaulay (eds.)
  1972   *Linguistic change and generative theory. Essays from the UCLA Conference
          on Historical Linguistics in the Perspective of Transformational Theory,
          February 1969* (Bloomington: Indiana University Press).
Sundby, B.
  1953   *Christopher Cooper's English Teacher (1687)* (Lund: Gleerup).
Trudgill, P.
  1974   *The social differentiation of English in Norwich* (Cambridge: Cambridge
          University Press).
Twaddell, W. F.
  1938   "A note on Old High German umlaut", *Monatshefte für deutschen Unterricht*
          30: 177–181.
Wakelin, M. F.
  1972   *English dialects: an introduction* (London: Athlone Press).
Wolfe, P. M.
  1972   *Linguistic change and the great vowel shift in English* (Berkeley: University of
          California Press).
Zwicky, A.
  1972   "Note on a phonological hierarchy in English", in: Stockwell – Macaulay
          1972, pp. 275–301.
  1974   "Taking a false step", *Language* 50: 215–224.

JAMES D. McCAWLEY

Notes on the history of accent in Japanese

1. Accent in the modern standard language

Standard Japanese is a particularly clear example of a pitch-accent system. Phrases differ from each other accentually only as regards the place where pitch falls; that is, leaving out the effects of intonational contours which may be superimposed on a sentence, the pitches on a phrase are predictable from its segmental composition plus information as to where (if anywhere) the pitch falls. For example, among phrases consisting of four short syllables (illustrated here by phrases consisting of a 3-syllable noun followed by a 1-syllable case marker), there are only the following four distinct melodies[1]:

(1) $\overline{ma}$kura ga   'pillow' (nominative case)
    ko$\overline{ko}$ro ga   'heart'
    $\overline{atama}$ ga   'head'
    sa$\overline{kana}$ $\overline{ga}$ 'fish'

These can be characterised as exhibiting (respectively) fall in pitch after the first syllable, after the second, after the third, and nowhere, and can be represented as follows, using ' to mark the place where pitch falls:

(2) ma'kura ga
    koko'ro ga
    atama' ga
    sakana ga

The pitch on a phrase can be predicted from the accent mark as follows: everything is high before the accent mark and low after it, except that if the second syllable is high (i.e., if there is no accent on the first syllable) the first is low.

Consideration of long syllables necessitates some revision of this last rule. Japanese exhibits both short syllables (consisting of consonant plus short vowel, or of just short vowel) and long syllables (consisting of (C)VV or of (C)VC, where long vowels are represented as geminate). The distinction between long syllable and short syllable is a distinction between syllables that 'count as two units' and syllables that 'count as one unit' for certain purposes, as in the scansion of Japanese poetry, which typically involves lines alternately of 5 and 7 units, as in the 5-7-5 pattern of haiku. The units just referred to are called **moras**. The only reasonable definition of 'mora' that I am aware of is: 'something of which a long syllable consists of two and a short syllable consists of one'. Since a long syllable consists of what would make up a short syllable, plus additional material, one can take the initial (C)V- of a long syllable to be its first mora and the remaining -V or -C to be its second mora. For example, *gakkoo* 'school' divides into the two syllables *gak-koo* and the four moras *ga-k-ko-o*.

Among speakers of standard Japanese, there is variation as to whether an unaccented CVV or CVn first syllable is pronounced all on a high pitch or with its first mora low pitched. Pitch may fall after the first mora but not after the second mora of a long syllable. Thus, while the a-forms in (3) are real phrases, the b-forms are phonologically inadmissable:

(3) a. *se'ika ga* 'floral arrangement'
     sense'i ga 'teacher'
     si'nnen ga 'New Year'

   b. **sei'ka ga*
     *sensei' ga
     *sin'nen ga

Each syllable thus affords only one possible place for the pitch to fall: at the end of its first mora. One may thus take the accent to be borne by the syllable: specifying the accent of a phrase amounts to specifying the syllable, if any, where (= after the first mora of which) pitch falls. The rule for predicting pitch from accent marks must thus be revised as follows:

(4) i. Everything is high-pitched up to the first mora of the accented syllable and low-pitched thereafter, except that
   ii. The first mora is low-pitched if
   a. (for some speakers) the second mora is high-pitched.
   b. (for other speakers) the second mora is high-pitched and is in the following syllable.

Regardless of whether *sakana ga* is treated as unaccented or as having an accent on *ga*, (4) will assign the same pitches to it, namely LHHH. It is in fact essential that the rules work this way, since the distinction between underlying accent on a final short syllable and underlying accentless is neutralized. Since the accents manifested in (1) are obviously contributed by the four nouns, the nouns require the underlying forms in (5a); when pronounced in isolation, they exhibit the pitches (5b) that are predicted by (4), and the accentual distinction between *atama* and *sakana* is neutralized:

(5) a. /ma'kura/   b. *ma̅kura*
     /koko'ro/   *koko̅ro*
     /atama'/   *atama̅*
     /sakana/   *saka̅na*

The discussion in the last paragraph suggests that for any positive integer *n*, nouns of *n* syllables divide into *n* + 1 underlying accentual types: 1st syllable accent, 2nd syllable accent, . . . , *n*-th syllable accent, and unaccented. This is in fact the case. The following examples illustrate the possibilities for nouns of one through four syllables:

(6) 1-syllable: *e̅ ga* 'picture' /e'/
                  e ḡa 'handle' /e/
     2-syllable: *ka̅ki ga* 'oyster'   /ka'ki/
                  kaki̅ ga 'fence'   /kaki'/
                  kaki̅ ḡa 'persimmon'   /kaki/
     3-syllable: (see (1) and (5))
     4-syllable: *ka̅makiri ga* 'praying mantis' /ka'makiri/
                  kuda̅mono ga 'fruit' /kuda'mono/
                  kagi̅ribi ga 'campfire' /kagari'bi/
                  kami̅sori ga 'razor' /kamisori'/
                  kamaboko̅ ḡa 'fish pudding' /kamaboko/

Case-markers and other postpositions also have underlying accents, e.g. /kara'/ 'from', /ma'de/ 'to', and /śika/ 'only', though these accents are manifested only when the preceding noun is unaccented:

(7)   'from . . .'   'to . . .'   'only . . .'

'the pillow'   *ma'kura kara*   *ma'kura made*   *ma'kura sika*
'the heart'   *koko'ro kara*   *koko'ro made*   *koko'ro sika*
'the head'   *atama' kara*   *atama' made*   *atama' sika*
'the fish'   *sakana kara'*   *sakana ma'de*   *sakana' sika*

'From the fish' must be treated as final-accented rather than unaccented (and 'from' thus represented as /kara$'$/ rather than /kara/) since a fall in pitch appears when the topic marker *wa* is added:

(8) *sakana k̄ara wa*

There are in fact no unambiguously unaccented postpositions in standard Japanese: those which could be analyzed as unaccented (*wa* 'topic', *ga* 'nominative', and *mo* 'even, also') could equally well be analysed as final-accented, since they occur only phrase-finally and thus do not contrast with unambiguously final-accented postpositions such as the dative marker *ni*. The data in (7) call for a rule that deletes all but the first of the underlying accents in a phrase.

See McCawley (1968, forthcoming) for details of accent in verbs and adjectives. Verbs and adjectives differ from nouns and postpositions in that only a two-way underlying distinction of 'accented' vs. 'unaccented' is maintained, with the place of accent in accented verbs and adjectives predictable.

2. Accent in Japanese dialects

The general outlines of the accentual system of standard Japanese also apply to the accentual systems of the dialects of Hokkaidō, Eastern Honshū (except for a large area running from Chiba prefecture to Miyagi prefecture, in which all accentual distinctions have been lost), Western Honshū, the western tip of Shikoku, and eastern Kyūshū. In all of these dialects, only the place of fall in pitch is distinctive[2], and the place where pitch falls more often than not agrees with the standard language (but see § 3 for some systematic differences in place of fall in pitch), though the various dialects differ quite a bit as regards how the pitch on the various moras is related to the place where pitch falls, a point that will be taken up in § 4.

In two large areas, however, significantly different accentual systems are found: the area (traditionally called 'Kansai') encompassing central Honshū and most of Shikoku, and the area encompassing western Kyūshū, the Amami Islands, and the Ryūkyū islands (see map on facing page).

2.1 Kansai dialects
In the dialects of the Kansai area (including Kyōto, Ōsaka, Wakayama, and most of Shikoku), not only the location of fall in pitch (if any) is distinctive but also the pitch level (high or low) on which the phrase starts. In the dialect of Befu, Hyōgo prefecture (data from Hirayama 1960), one of the more

Accent in the Japanese dialects

conservative Kansai districts as regards accent, the following accentual types occur in 1-, 2-, and 3-syllable nouns:

(9) $\overline{ka}$, $\overline{ka}$ ga 'fly' $\overline{kaki}$, $\overline{kaki}$ ga 'persimmon' sakana, sakana $\overline{ga}$ 'fish'
    hà, $\overline{ha}$ ga 'leaf' $\overline{hasi}$, $\overline{hasi}$ ga 'bridge'   azuki, $\overline{azuki}$ ga 'red bean'
    tá, ta $\overline{ga}$ 'field'   hasí, hasi $\overline{ga}$ 'chopsticks' $\overline{awabi}$, $\overline{awabi}$ ga 'abalone'
             madò, mad$\overline{o}$ ga 'window'   usagí, usagi $\overline{ga}$ 'rabbit'
                                   kab$\overline{u}$to, kab$\overline{u}$to ga 'helmet'

In each case there are more distinct accentual types than could be distinguished in terms of just location of fall in pitch. Since there are pairs of words that do not differ as regards place of fall in pitch but do differ as regards whether the word starts on a high or on a low pitch (e.g. 'persimmon' vs 'chopsticks', 'red bean' vs. 'helmet'), the distinction between low-initial and high-initial is an obvious choice for an additional characteristic to take as one of the distinctive differences among phrases in dialects of this type.

It is reasonable to use the symbol for 'fall in pitch' also to stand for 'low initial' when written at the beginning of a phrase, since there in fact is a fall in pitch if something ending on a high occurs before the word in question, e.g.

(10) *a̅n̅o̅ u̅s̅a̅g̅i̅* 'that rabbit'   cf. *a̅n̅o̅ a̅w̅a̅b̅i* 'that abalone'
a̅n̅o̅ k̅a̅b̅u̅to 'that helmet'

I will thus transcribe the nouns in (9) as

(11) *ka   kaki   sakana*
      ha'   ha'si   azu'ki
      'ta   'hasi   a'wabi
            'mado'   'usagi
                     'kabu'to

The relationship between accent marks and pitches in this dialect is given by the following rule:

(12) i. After a ', all moras are low-pitched up to either a mora marked
         with a ' or, if the ' preceded the phrase, the last mora of the phrase,
      ii. All other moras (i.e. a mora marked with a ', or the last mora of a
          phrase that is preceded by a ' and contains no other ', and any moras
          not preceded by a ') are high pitched.

The identification of low-initial and fall in pitch in Kansai dialects is supported by some facts about accent in adjectives in Kyōto dialect. In Kyōto, the distinction between what in standard Japanese are accented and unaccented adjectives has been lost[3]. In the present tense, monosyllabic adjectives are low-initial and longer adjectives are high-initial:

(13) *'ee*   'good'   (< *'yo* + *i*)
      a'kai   'red'
      suru'doi   'sharp'

The identification of low-initial with fall in pitch makes it possible to state a single generalization covering both the monosyllabic case and the polysyllabic case: accent goes one mora before the present tense ending /-i/. There is also an alternation between low-initial and high-initial in monosyllabic and disyllabic adjectives:

(14) Present   Adverbial

    'ee   *yo'o (= yo + 'u < 'yo + 'u)*
    a'kai   *'ako'o (= 'aka + 'u)*
    (cf. *kana'sii, kana'syuu* 'sad')

Evidently, one of the two accents in *'ako'o* is contributed by the adjective stem and one by the ending. Facts about compounds provide evidence that the low-initial allomorph of disyllabic adjectives is more basic than the high-initial allomorph. In Kansai dialects, a compound starts high or low, depending of whether its first member starts high or low[4], and in Kyōto, almost all compounds beginning with a disyllabic adjective stem are low-initial:

(15) *'aka-hata* 'red flag'   *'taka-i'biki* 'loud snore'
      'aka-si'ngoo 'red traffic light'   *'taka-go'e* 'shrill voice'
      'aka-to'nbo 'red dragonfly'   *'taka-'hiku* 'high and low'

This means that the present tense of a disyllabic adjective exhibits attraction of accent from the stem (where it would be realized as low-initial) to the first-syllable of the stem (which is then realized as high-initial):[5]

(16) *'aka + i → a'ka + i.*

Combinations of noun plus postposition are subject to the same rule of accent deletion as in the standard language, with the qualification that the preposed accent signifying low-initial causes no loss of the underlying accent of the postposition:

(17) | | Noun | 'than . . .' | 'even . . .' | 'from . . .' |
|---|---|---|---|---|
| 'cow' | *usi* | *usi'yori* | *uside'mo* | *usikara* |
| 'horse' | *u'ma* | *u'mayori* | *u'mademo* | *u'makara* |
| 'toad' | *'gama* | *'gama'yori* | *'gamade'mo* | *'gamakara* |
| 'monkey' | *saru'* | *'saru'yori* | *'saru'demo* | *'saru'kara* |

The presumable underlying forms for 'than' and 'even' are /'yori, de'mo/. Since *kara* in 'from the cow' does not have a fall on its final syllable, nor is it followed by a fall when the topic marker *wa* is added (i.e. *usi kara wa* is

pronounced on a level high pitch), *kara* requires an unaccented underlying
form in Kansai dialects: /kara/. (18) illustrates the action of the accent deletion rule:

(18) *u'ma* + *'yori* *'saru'* + *de'mo* *'hasi* + *de'mo* *usi* + *'demo* *'saru'* + *kara*
   → *u'ma* + *yori* *'saru'* + *demo*   —   —   —

2.2 Western Kyūshū and the Ryūkyū Islands

In western Kyūshū and parts of the Amami and Ryūkyū Islands, not only
verbs and adjectives but also nouns exhibit only a two-way accentual opposition, regardless of length. The details as to which moras or syllables are pronounced high and which ones low varies considerably from one locality to
another.[6] The simplest variant of this type of accentual system is found in
Kuma (Fujitsugun, Sage prefecture). Using the terms 'falling' and 'level' for
the two accentual types, a phrase beginning with a falling morpheme has its
first mora high-pitched and all subsequent moras low-pitched; a phrase beginning with a level morpheme is on a level low pitch:

(19) a. Falling nouns   b. Level nouns

   h̄i, h̄i ga 'day'   hi, hi ga 'fire'
   h̄ana, h̄ana ga 'nose'   hana, hana ga 'flower'
   k̄uruma, k̄uruma ga 'vehicle'   abura, abura ga 'oil'
   k̄amaboko, k̄amaboko ga   yomikata, yomikata ga
      'fish pudding'   'pronunciation'

Other localities in Western Kyūshū have accentual systems that appear to have
developed from this system via spread or shift of the high pitch to the right,
as in the following illustrations of 'falling' nouns:

(20) Higashi-
      Kawanobori (Saga)   Nagasaki   Kagoshima

   h̄i, h̄i ga ___   hì, h̄i ga ___   hì, h̄i ga ___
   hana, hana ga   h̄ana, hana ga   h̄ana, hana ga ___
   k̄uruma, k̄uruma ga   kur̄uma, kur̄uma ga   kur̄uma, kur̄uma ga ___
   kam̄aboko,   kam̄aboko,   kamaboko,
      k̄amaboko ga   kam̄aboko ga   kamabok̄o ga

In Nagasaki, the high pitch has shifted to the second mora (syllable?) of the
phrase, provided that the phrase has at least three moras (syllables?). In
Kagoshima, the accent has shifted to the next-to-last syllable of the phrase. In
Koshikijishima (Kagoshima pref.), it has shifted to the next-to-last mora:

(21) Kagoshima (syllable-counting)   Koshikijima (mora-counting)

$\overline{mei}rei$ 'order' $mei\overline{rei}$
$\overline{hoo}tai$ 'bandage' $hoo\overline{tai}$
$\overline{kyuu}syuu$ 'Kyūshū' $kyuu\overline{syuu}$

The references to 'next-to-last syllable/mora' must be qualified in that certain morphemes do not count as part of the phrase for the purpose of accent
shift. For example, when the above falling nouns are combined with the
copula *da* in Kagoshima, the result is:

(22) *hi da*
      $\overline{ha}na\ da$
      $ku\overline{ru}ma\ da$
      $kama\overline{bo}ko\ da$

There thus is a surface distinction between phrases with high-pitched penultimate syllable and phrases with high-pitched ante-penultimate syllable.

Except for a locality discussed in § 4, in western Kyūshū the only variation in the pronunciation of phrases beginning with a level morpheme is
whether the phrase is pronounced on a low-level pitch, or low with a high
pitch on the final syllable or mora. The placement of this final high involves
the same qualification about morphemes that 'do not count'. Thus, in Kagoshima a phrase ending . . . LHL can be either a falling phrase whose final
syllable 'counts' (e.g. *hanā ga* 'nose (Nom.)') or a level phrase whose final
syllable 'does not count' (e.g. *hanā da* 'it's a flower').

Most of the dialects of the Amami and Ryūkyū Islands also exhibit only a
two-way accent contrast, with the same kind of variation from one locality to
another as to the details of the contrast: in Miyako-Ōura, the second mora of
'falling' phrases is high, except when there are only two moras, in which case
the first is high (cf. Nagasaki); In Miyako-Karimata, the penultimate mora
of a falling phrase is high-pitched (cf. Koshikijima); in Miyako-Shimoji, the
second mora of a falling phrase is high pitched even if there are only two
moras.[7]

3. History

The principal correspondences for 2-syllable nouns between Kansai Japanese
and Tōkyō Japanese (which for present purposes can be identified with the
standard language) are illustrated by the four words

(23)   Kansai Tōkyō

'cow'   *usi*   *usi*
'bridge'   *ha'si*   *hasi'*
'chopsticks' *'hasi*   *ha'si*
'window'   *'mado'* *ma'do*

Since there is no segmental characteristic from which the difference between
the 'chopsticks' type and the 'window' type is predictable, the parent accentual system must have had an accentual distinction between the two which
was lost in the development of Tōkyō Japanese. The data in (23) are in fact
consistent with the hypothesis that the parent system is identical to the
modern Kansai system and that the Tōkyō system developed by a shift of
accent one mora to the right.

   A consideration of additional dialects makes it necessary to set up an additional accentual type in the parent language. The 'bridge' type divides into
two distinct sets of reflexes on western Kyūshū, eastern Kyūshū (e.g. Ōita),
and in northern Honshū (e.g. Akita):

(24)   Kansai Tōkyō Akita/Ōita W. Ky. Reconstruction

   1. *usi* 'cow'   OO   OO   OO   F   OO
   2. *hasi* 'bridge'   O'O   OO'   OO   F   O'O
   3. *hana* 'flower'   O'O   OO'   OO'   L   'O'O
   4. *hasi* 'chopsticks' 'OO O'O   O'O   L   'OO
   5. *mado* 'window'   'OO' O'O   O'O   L   'OO'

In sets 1, 2, 4, and 5, Kansai high-initial corresponds to Western Kyūshū F
(= 'falling') and Kansai low-initial corresponds to Western Kyūshū L (=
'level'). Set 3, which is not distinct from set 2 in Kansai and Tōkyō, deviates
from this correspondence by virtue of having L instead of F in Western
Kyūshū. The obvious difference to posit between set 2 and set 3 in the reconstructed parent system is that of high-initial (set 2) vs. low-initial (set 3). The
identification of Western Kyūshū falling and level with reconstructed high-
initial and low-initial which are generally but not always so realized in Kansai
is supported by a parallelism between the accent rules for compounds in the
two areas. In Kyōto, as noted above, and indeed in the Kansai area in general,
the high-initial or low-initial character of a compound is that of the first
member of the compound. (However, any fall in pitch in the compound is
determined by the second member of the compound). In Western Kyūshū,
the first member of the compound provides the falling or level character of
the entire compound, as illustrated by the following examples (quoted from
Hirayama 1960):

(25) *hà* 'leaf' + *sakura* 'cherry tree' → *hazakura* 'post-blossom foliage of
 cherry tree' (F + F > F)
isi 'stone' + *kat* 'fence' → *isigat* 'stone fence' (F + L > F)
yama 'mountain' + *sakura* 'cherry tree' → *yamazakura* 'wild cherry
 tree' (L + F > L)
iro 'color' + *siro* 'white' → *iroziro* 'fair-skinned person' (L + L > L)

Under the proposed reconstruction, these two rules are reflexes of the same
rule of accent in proto-Japanese.

Northern Honshū and eastern Kyūshū largely agree with Tōkyō in accent
but have unaccented rather than final accented reflexes for set 2. The agreement between northern Honshū and eastern Kyūshū in distinguishing set 2
(about 20 nouns) from set 3 (about 40 nouns) is striking, since the two areas
are separated by a 1000 km stretch of Honshū in which they are not distinguished.[8]

It is not obvious how to interpret the accentual formula reconstructed for
set 3. How would a form like /'ha'na/ be pronounced? A low-pitched syllable
followed by a still lower one? A rising pitched syllable followed by a low? Or
would perhaps the first   make the first syllable low and the other one make
subsequent syllables low, thus making the word level low? The last possibility seems the best bet, since it makes the reconstruction conform very well
to the pitches recorded in the Ruijumyōgishō, a thesaurus compiled in Kyōto
about 1100 A.D.:

(26)   Reconstruction   Ruijumyōgishō

1.	OO	HH(H)
2.	O'O	HL(H)
3.	'O'O	LL(H)
4.	'OO	LH(H)
5.	'OO'	LH(L)

(The parenthesized pitches are those of a following postposition.) If this reconstruction is correct, then the following historical developments have
occurred:

i. (W. Kyūshū) Syllables past the first became L; thus, only the pitch on
the first syllable remains distinctive.
ii. (E. Kyūshū [Ōita] and N. Honshū [Akita]) Accent is lost in high-initial
words.
iii. (All Japan)[9] 'O 'O > O'O.

298   James D. McCawley

iv. (E. Honshū [incl. Tōkyō, Akita] , W. Honshū [Hiroshima] , E. Kyūshū [Ōita]). Accent shifts one mora to the right.

The rightward accent shifts in Eastern and Western Japan are evidently independent developments (iv).

The correspondences for three-syllable nouns are much less neat than those for two-syllable nouns. In the following table, I have listed the seven distinct pitch forms recorded in the Ruijumyōgishō, with the most common manifestations of those types in the modern dialects. In many cases, here indicated by parentheses, there are so few representatives of a particular type and their modern reflexes so diverse that it is rather arbitrary to pick a particular modern reflex as the 'regular correspondence'. Kansai dialects are represented here by Befu (Hyōgo Pref.), which is more conservative than Kyōto or Ōsaka.

(27)	Ruijumyōgishō	Kansai	Tōkyō	Akita	Ōita	W. Kyūshū
1. *sakana* 'fish'	HHH(H)	OOO	OOO	OOO	OOO	F
2. *tokage* 'lizard'	HHL(L)	('OO'O)	(OOO)	(OOO)	(OOO)	F
3. *awabi* 'abalone'	HLL(L)	O'OO	(O'OO <OO'O)[10]	(OO'O)	(OOO')	F
4. *atama* 'head'	LLL(H)	OO'O	OOO'	OOO'	OOO'	L
5. *namida* 'tear'	LLH(L)	O'OO	(O'OO <OO'O)	(OO'O)	(OO'O)	L
6. *nezumi* 'mouse'	LHH(H)	'OOO	OOO	OO'O	O'OO	L
7. *kabuto* 'helmet'	LHL(L)	'OO'O	O'OO OOO	(OO'O)	(O'OO)	L

The correspondences between western Kyushū and the Ruijumyōgishō work out perfectly, but nothing else does. Moreover, while representations in terms of accent marks suggest themselves for the Ruijumyōgishō pronunciations of types 1–3 and 6–7, there is no obvious assignment of accentual formulas to types 4 and 5. One of them would have to be represented as 'O'OO and the other as 'OOO', but which would be which? The similarity in pronunciation between type 4 and the two-syllable type 3 (both all-low, followed by a high postposition) suggests assigning the former formula to type 4. However, that assignment gives no clue as to why the Kansai and Tōkyō reflexes of type 4 are what they are (e.g. if *atama* and *hana* were parallel, the Kansai reflex should be *a'tama*, not *ata'ma*), though the reverse assignment is no better on this score.

Hayata (1973) argues that proto-Japanese had more accentual distinctions than were recorded in the Ruijumyōgishō. He points out that certain accentual types not found there could be hypothesized to exist in proto-Japanese to account for some otherwise exceptional correspondences. Specifically, the Ruijumyōgishō dialect, like most modern Kansai dialects, has no nouns of the accentual shapes OO' or OOO'. Such accentual types, if subject to the rightward accent shift (iv, above) would yield unaccented words in Tōkyō and Hiroshima. Hayata proposes that these accentual types gave rise to the following correspondences:

(28)

	Kansai	Tōkyō	W. Ky.	Proto-Jap.
'person'	hi'to	hito	F	*OO'
'lizard'	'toka'ge[11]	tokage	F	*OOO'
Cf.				
'bridge'	ha'si	hasi'	F	*O'O
'red bean'	azu'ki	azuki'	F	*OO'O

He proposes that Kansai Japanese underwent a retraction of final accent by one mora, except when there is not enough room for such a retraction to take place, as in na' 'name' and 'mado' 'window'.

There is an additional class of words to which Hayata's proposal is applicable. The three-syllable nouns of class 7 divide evenly as regards whether they are unaccented or initial-accented in Tōkyō:

(29) Tōkyō unaccented

| Tōkyō accented

itigo 'strawberry'   ka'iko 'silkworm'
usiro 'rear'   ka'buto 'helmet'
kuzira 'whale'   ta'yori 'news'
kusuri 'medicine'   tu'baki 'camelia'
tarai 'tub'   ya'mai 'illness'

Suppose that the words in the first column were assigned a proto form 'OOO' and those in the second column a proto form 'OO'O. The hypothesized Kansai accent retraction would obliterate the difference between the two types in Kansai dialects. In both Tōkyō and Hiroshima, type-6 nouns (with presumable proto form 'OOO) are unaccented. While it is not clear what steps are involved in getting from proto 'OOO to unaccented reflexes in Tōkyō and Hiroshima, the same steps would presumably yield unaccented reflexes for the hypothetical 'OOO', since accent shift would obliterate the difference between 'OOO and 'OOO'.

Hayata's proposal leads to a hypothetical proto-language in which there are six accentual possibilities for two-syllable nouns and nine for three-syllable nouns:

(30) 1. HH(H)   1. HHH(H)
      2a. HH(L)   2a. HHH(L)
      2b. HL(L)   2b. HHL(L)
      3. LL(H)   3. HLL(L)
      4. LH(H)   4. LLL(H)
      5. LH(L)   5. LLH(L)
                            6. LHH(H)
                            7a. LHH(L)
                            7b. LHL(L)

Hattori (1951) conjectures that there was yet an additional proto-Japanese accentual type, to account for the distinction between nouns of type 5 which are accented in Eastern and Western Honshū (*nami'da*, > *na'mida* in Tōkyō) and those which are unaccented there (*abura*):

5′. LLH(H) e.g *abura* 'oil'

If these reconstructions are correct, however, then it is impossible to represent accentual distinctions in proto Japanese in terms of just high- vs. low-initial plus place of fall in pitch: there are nine, perhaps ten distinct accentual types for three-syllable nouns in the reconstruction under consideration here, whereas there are only 8 (= 2 × 4) possible combinations of high vs. low initial, plus accent on first, second, third, or no syllable.

An alternative mode of representing accentual distinctions in proto Japanese is suggested by Okuda (1971), namely in terms of place of rise in pitch (written ⌐) and place of fall (written ¬), where both are in principle distinctive. Suppose, to modify Okuda's notation slightly, high-initial words are written with a preceding 'rise', so that every word will have a rise, and somewhere after the rise there may (but need not) be a fall. The above accentual types would then be represented as:

(31) 1. ⌐OO   1. ⌐OOO
      2a. ⌐OO¬   2a. ⌐OOO¬
      2b. ⌐O¬O   2b. ⌐OO¬O
      3. OO⌐   3. ⌐O¬OO
      4. O⌐O   4. OOO⌐
      5. O⌐O¬   5. OO⌐O¬
                          (5′. OO⌐O)
                            6. O⌐OO
                            7a. O⌐OO¬
                            7b. O⌐O¬O

This would make complete use of the combinatory possibilities for 'rise' and 'fall': if every word must have a rise and if a fall can only follow a rise, then there are six possibilities for two-syllable nouns and ten possibilities for three-syllable nouns.

4. Speculations on mechanisms of change

I know of no clear case of a language in which what is distinctive accentually is precisely the location of a rise *and* the location of a fall in pitch.[12] However, there is a common type of tone system, namely that in which every syllable has a contrastive high or low pitch, which could turn into the system of the reconstruction indicated in (31) via a 'natural' change, namely the assimilation of L's that are sandwiched between H's to the pitch of the H's: $HL_1 H > HH_1 H$. Such an assimilation persists as a synchronic rule in certain Bantu languages (e.g. Ganda [see Stevick 1969] and Tonga [see McCawley 1973]), though the underlying forms in these languages exhibit the same system as in standard Japanese (in the case of Ganda) or Kyōto Japanese (in the case of Tonga), and their surface forms involve more distinctions than could be expressed just in terms of the place of a rise and of a fall, as a result of additional phonological rules. I thus conjecture that the proto-Japanese accentual system that I have reconstructed arose from a true tonal system with distinctive high or low pitch on each syllable, by means of some change which would eliminate $HL_1 H$ sequences, such as an assimilation of the L up to H.

This conjecture does not completely fit my proposed reconstruction, since the reconstruction involves a contrast betwen fall after the final syllable and no fall at all, both of which would presumably correspond to a high pitch on the final syllable (since if the final syllable were L, there would have to be a fall somewhere earlier in the word). However, this point may not prove a fatal objection to the conjecture, in view of the fact that the most detailed reconstruction of the vowel system of proto-Japanese of which I am aware, that of Unger (1975), derives many of the vowels of ancient Japanese from sequences of two vowels. Thus, many Japanese words will have evolved from antecedents with a greater number of syllables. However, I have not yet determined whether the words that have final accent in the reconstructed accent system proposed here generally have an extra vowel (not necessarily an extra vowel in the final syllable, since monophthongization of a non-final vowel-sequence might be accompanied by rightward shift of pitch off of the lost vowel) according to Unger's reconstruction.

The sketch given above of how the different dialects could have evolved from the proposed proto-Japanese accentual system involves at least three independent shifts of accent to the right: (i) in the dialects of Eastern and northern Honshū, (ii) in the dialects of western Honshū and Eastern Kyūshū, and (iii) in some of the dialects of western Kyūshū, with (iii) encompassing at least two independent shifts if, as I conjecture, the dialects of the Kagoshima area (high pitch on the penultimate syllable/mora in 'falling' phrases) evolved through an intermediate stage like that of modern Nagasaki, in which high pitch had shifted from the first mora to the second if that was non-final. A second shift of accent in the area indicated by (ii) has been discussed by Smith (1968) and Okuda (1971), namely the dialect of Izumo (Shimane pref.). The data cited in Hirayama (1966b) suggest that a rightward shift of accent took place independently in most of Amami-Tokunoshima, where two-syllable nouns exhibit the same pitches as in Akita except that unaccented phrases (sets 1 and 2) have a low followed by highs rather than the level low of Akita. Thus, shift of accent to the right appears to be a relatively common phenomenon in the history of Japanese, and there is presumably something about Japanese accent which makes such a change 'natural'. I will conclude this paper with some speculation on this point.

There are at least two dialects in which an inversion of pitch has taken place. A comparison with Kagoshima forms makes clear that Makurazaki (Kagoshima prefecture) has undergone a pitch inversion[13]:

(32) a. Falling   b. Level

Kagoshima	Makurazaki	Kagoshima	Makurazaki
hì, hī ga 'day'	hī, hi ga	hī, hi ga 'fire'	hì, hī ga
hāna, hanā ga 'nose'	hana, hāna ga	hana, hana ga 'flower'	hana, hana ga
asōbu 'play'	asobū	inorū 'pray'	inoru

The only Makurazaki forms which are not exact tonal inversions of the corresponding Kagoshima forms are the isolation forms of monosyllables. The falling pitch of Kagoshima 'day' and Makurazaki 'fire' is a compression onto a single syllable of the melody that is manifested when ga follows.

In Narada (Yamanashi Prefecture), the pitch shapes are what one would get by replacing the high pitches of neighboring dialects by lows and lows by highs and in addition making low all moras that follow a rise in pitch, or to put it slightly differently, pitches in Narada are the opposite of what they are in the neighboring dialects, except that when a phrase ends in a sequence of low-pitched moras in the neighboring dialects, all but the first of those moras are also low in Narada; the accent system of the neighboring dialects is identical to that of the standard language except for some details of the rules for compounds, and thus standard forms are given for comparison:

(33) standard   Narada

u̅sa̅gi ga   u̅sagi ga
ka̅bu̅to ga   kabu̅to ga
ko̅ko̅ro ga   ko̅koro̅ ga
a̅ta̅ma̅ ga   a̅tama ga̅
ka̅nsai ga   kan̅sai ga

Note that the change that Narada has undergone has had an effect rather similar to that of a shift of accent one mora to the right: where standard Japanese has a fall in pitch, Narada has a fall in pitch one mora further to the right; in addition, where the standard Japanese word begins on a low pitch, Narada exhibits a fall in pitch after the first mora. It is not appropriate to treat Narada morphemes as having an underlying 'accent' in the places where pitch falls, since (i) fall in pitch on the first mora is completely predictable, and (ii) morphemes corresponding to those which in the standard language have a final-mora accent contribute a fall in pitch on the first mora of the next morpheme, and thus, assuming that underlying accents have to be on actual syllables or moras of the underlying form, that fall in pitch must be represented on a mora earlier than the one where it is manifested:

(34)   standard   Narada
     'from the head'   a̅ta̅ma kara   a̅tama ka̅ra
     'from the fish'   sakana kara   sakana kara

However, it wouldn't take much of a change to turn the Narada accentual system into one that demands underlying forms with falls in pitch where they occur in surface phonology. For example, if the second of two falls in pitch in the same phrase were uniformly lost, then there would be no obstacle to analysing Narada morphemes as having accent one mora to the right of where it is in the standard language, except (note that the distinction between 'from the head' and 'from the fish' would have been wiped out) that morphemes that are unaccented or final-accented in the standard language would have a first-mora accent in Narada.

Note that the actual Narada changes plus the hypothetical loss of a second fall in pitch would have the effect of a shift in accent if it were applied to Kansai forms:[14]

(35)   with Narada   plus loss of   new underlying
      Kōchi / /   Kochi [ ]   accent change   second fall   forms

     usi ga   u̅si̅ ga   u̅si ga   –   /usi/
     ha'si ga   ha̅si ga   hasi̅ ga   –   /hasi'/
     'hasi ga   ha̅si̅ ga   ha̅si ga   –   /ha'si/
     'mado' ga   mado̅ ga   ma̅do ga̅   ma̅do ga   /ma'do/

What appears in the last column are, of course, the Tōkyō underlying forms.

I have no clear feeling as to whether pitch inversion is a natural change. I would maintain, though that it is vastly more plausible as a phonological change than are the 'exchange rules' that figure in Chomsky and Halle's (1968) analysis of English. I maintain that perception of a pitch movement is more basic than perception of the direction of pitch movement (i.e., people will frequently misidentify the direction in which pitch has moved, but will hardly ever hear a pitch movement where there is none or hear a level pitch where there is a significant change in pitch). This claim is supported by such impressionistic observations as (1) that people more readily perceive that another language or dialect has rises or falls that their own dialect does not than that it has a preponderance of one type of pitch contour, e.g., they will notice that Norwegian has a 'sing-song' sound to it but not that Norwegian sentences all end with a rising pitch; and (2) that foreign learners of Mandarin Chinese more easily confuse the rising pitch and the falling pitch than any other pair of tones (or at least, that's the confusion that *I* most often make). Furthermore, if only the place where some pitch phenomenon occurs is distinctive, rather than each syllable or mora having a distinctive pitch, communication between speakers that had undergone a pitch inversion and speakers that had not would not be materially impaired: if the perceiver is not identifying individual pitches but merely identifying the place where something 'happens', he can adjust easily to speakers for whom something different happens in that place. In addition, Luba and some closely related Bantu languages appear to have undergone pitch inversion; see the references cited in Spaandonck (1967:26) for details. I thus tentatively conclude that pitch inversion can be expected to occur sporadically in a language in which pitch is used accentually, and that pitch inversion is not at an adaptive disadvantage, i.e. it has at least a fighting chance of spreading.

The Narada accent changes involved not merely pitch inversion, but also the realization as low pitches of what would otherwise have been the tail-end of a phrase-final sequence of high pitches. I conjecture that this exemplifies a more general tendency to avoid stretches on a level pitch, particularly on a level high pitch. In this connection, it is worthwhile looking at the non-distinctive pitches on moras preceding the accented mora in Japanese dialects. In dialects of the Tōkyō type, in which the place of fall in pitch (if any) is all that is accentually distinctive in a phrase, there are three principal treatments of the moras before the accented mora: (i) they are all L (as in Aomori), (ii) the first is L and the rest are H (as in the standard language), and (iii) the first (if there is more than one) is H and the rest are L (as in Tarō, Iwate prefecture, and in Nakamura, Kōchi prefecture):

(36) standard   Aomori   Tarō

　　　a̅t̅a̅m̅a̅ ga   *ada̅m̅a̅ ga*   *a̅d̅a̅ma̅ ga*

Note that in types (ii) and (iii), a sequence of pitches on the same level is avoided, in that the first and second moras are guaranteed to differ in pitch. Moreover, there is at least one locality in the Kansai area, namely Katsuura, Wakayama prefecture, which has undergone a change whereby the first mora of an initial sequence of two or more high-pitched moras has become low, and where thus the distinction between 'high-initial' and 'low-initial' is maintained as a distinction as to whether at most the first mora is low-pitched or all moras before the accented or last mora are low-pitched:

(37) Kyōto   Katsuura

　　　u̅s̅i̅ ga   *u̅s̅i ga*

　　　h̅asi ga   *h̅asi ga*

　　　hasi g̅a̅   *hasi g̅a̅*

　　　mad̅o̅ ga   *mad̅o̅ ga*

The following developments from the Ruijumyōgishō dialect to modern Kyōto are widely held by Japanese linguists to represent a change in which high pitch was imposed on all but the last of a sequence of initial lows:

(38) *atama g̅a̅ > a̅t̅a̅ma g̅a̅ (> a̅t̅a̅ma ga)*

　　　namid̅a̅ ga > n̅a̅m̅i̅d̅a̅ ga (> n̅a̅mida ga)

If this apparent tendency to avoid sequences of highs at the beginning of a phrase extends also to sequences of highs at the end of a phrase, then accent shift can be interpreted as the end effect of three relatively natural changes: pitch inversion, then lowering of non-distinctive high pitches after a high pitch, then elimination of all but the first fall in pitch in a phrase.

Notes

1. The overline indicates high pitch: unmarked segments are low pitched. Rising and falling pitch will be indicated by ′ and ‵.
2. One possible exception to this statement, namely the dialect of Narada (Yamanashi prefecture), will be discussed in § 4.
3. The distinction is preserved in some Kansai dialects, for example, that of Kōchi (southern Shikoku):

Unaccented in standard language	Accented in standard language
atuˈi 'thick'	*aˈtui* 'hot'
osoˈi 'late'	*naˈgai* 'long'
kuraˈi 'dark'	*kuˈroi* 'black'

306   James D. McCawley

However, even in Kōchi, the distinction is lost in longer adjectives.
4. See McCawley (forthcoming) for ample illustration of this point.
5. The deletion exhibited in the adverbial form of 'good' (*'yo* + *'u* →*yo'u*) plays a role in a number of other forms, details of which are given in McCawley (forthcoming). Of course, some rule would have to eliminate the combination *'O'O*, which is not permitted in modern Kansai dialects. In § 3 I will argue that *'O'O* occurred as a distinct accentual type in an ancestor of the Kansai dialects.
6. The data given here are taken from Wada (1962) and Tōjō (1961, vol. 4).
7. The data cited here are from Hirayama (1966a, 1967).
8. A distinction between sets 2 and 3 is also found in a portion of Shizuoka prefecture, in one locality in the Noto peninsula, and in much of Shikoku and some islands in the Inland Sea. See Tokugawa (1962) for details.
9. Except for a couple of localities where sets 1, 2, and 3 remain mutually distinct: Togi (Noto peninsula) and Ibuki Island (Kagawa pref.). (iii) is a gross oversimplification. See Tokugawa (1962) for reasons why the coalescence of sets 2 and 3 was an independent development in several different regions.
10. In most 'Tōkyō-type' dialects (e.g. Numazu and Hiroshima, which otherwise agree closely with Tōkyō in accent), these words have OO'O. In Tōkyō, OO'O is comparatively rare in 3-syllable nouns: aside from compound and derived nouns, only *koko'ro* has that accentuation. Tōkyō thus appears to have undergone a shift OO'O > O'OO. The same change has occurred in Kyōto, though since Kyōto has not undergone the general rightward shift, it affects different nouns, namely types 2 and 4.
11. Though high-initial words in the Ruijumyōgishō are generally high-initial in modern Hyōgo and Kyōto, those type 2 nouns which are unaccented in Tōkyō are mainly low-initial in Hyōgo and Kyōto.
12. I know of one language that may demand an analysis in terms of underlying forms in which both distinctive rises and distinctive falls occur, namely Maasai. However, my attempt to reanalyse the copious data on Maasai given in Tucker and Mpaayei 1955 is as yet sufficiently tentative as to preclude my presenting it here.
13. Data from Tōjō 1961, vol. 4, 277–8.
14. I have used Kōchi rather than Kyōto, because in Kōchi the 'low-initial' forms have only the first mora low. Kōchi is in fact more conservative than Kyōto in this respect.

References

Chomsky, Noam A. – Morris Halle
    1968   *The sound pattern of English* (New York: Harper and Row).
Hattori Shirō
    1951   "Gensi nihongo no akusento" [The accent of Proto-Japanese], in: *Kokugo akusento ronsō* [Symposium on Japanese accent] (Eds.: Terakawa *et al.*) (Tōkyō: Hōsei-daigaku), pp. 45–65.
Hayata Teruhiro
    1973   "Accent in Old Kyōto and some modern Japanese dialects", *Sciences of Language* (Journal of the Tōkyō Institute for Advanced Studies on Language) 4: 139–180.
Hirayama Teruo
    1960   *Zenkoku akusento zietn* [All-Japan accent dictionary] (Tōkyō: Tōkyōdō).
    1966a   "Ryūkyū sentō hōgen no akusento-taikei" [The accentual system of the outer Ryuku Islands], *Kokugogaku* 67: 11–117.
    1966b   *Ryūkyū hōgen no sōgōteki kenkyū* [Compendium of research on Ryukyu dialects] (Tōkyō: Meiji-shoin).

1967   *Ryūkyū sentō syohōgen no sōgōteki kenkyū* [Compendium of research on the dialects of the outer Ryukyu Islands] (Tōkyō: Meiji-shoin).
McCawley, James D.
1968   *The phonological component of a grammar of Japanese* (The Hague: Mouton).
1973   "Some Tonga tone rules", in: *A festschrift for Morris Halle* (Eds.: S. Anderson – P. Kiparsky) (New York: Holt, Rinehart, and Winston), pp. 140–152.
forthcoming "Accent in Japanese", in: *Proceedings of the 1976 USC Symposium on Tone* (Ed.: L. Hyman).
Okuda Kunio
1971   *Accentual systems in the Japanese dialects.* [Dissertation, UCLA.]
Smith, Donald L.
1968   *Some observations concerning the similarities of the accentual systems of Eastern and Western Japan.* [Unpublished.]
Spaandonck, Marcel van
1967   *Morphotonologische analyse in Bantu-talen* (Leiden: Brill).
Stevick, Earl, W.
1969   "Tone in Bantu", *IJAL* 35: 330–341.
Tōjō Misao
1961   *Hōgengaku kōza* [A course in dialectology] 1–4 (Tōkyō: Tōkyōdō).
Tokugawa Munemasa
1962   "Nihon syohōgen akusento no keifu shiron" [Towards a family tree for accent in Japanese dialects], *Kokugo-kokubun gakkaishi* 6. [English translation by J. D. McCawley in *Papers in Japanese Linguistics* 1: 301–320.]
Tucker, A. N. – J. Tompo Ole Mpaayei
1955   *A Maasai grammar* (London: Longmans).
Unger, J. M.
1975   *Studies in Early Japanese morphophonemics.* [Dissertation, Yale University.]
Wada Minoru
1962   "Akusento" [Accent], in: *Hōgengaku-gaisetu* [Introduction to dialectology] (Tōkyō: Musashino-shoin).

WITOLD MAŃCZAK

Irregular sound change due to frequency in German

The notion of irregular sound change due to frequency is not new[1]. It would be difficult for me to say who was the first to use this term, but in any case it was used as early as 1846 by Diez (1846:12), the founder of the comparative grammar of the Romance languages, who considered Fr. *sire* < Lat. *senior* as 'durch häufigen Gebrauch verkürzt'. Some years later, the famous etymologist Pott (1852:315) stated that It. *andare*, Sp. *andar*, and Fr. *aller* derive from Lat. *ambulāre* 'mit zwar ungewöhnlichen, aber durch Häufigkeit des Gebrauchs von diesem Worte gerechtfertigten Buchstaben-wechseln'. Other linguists followed them. There is, however, an essential difference between the opinions of my predecessors and mine on this subject. Until now, irregular sound change due to frequency has been considered as something sporadic, affecting only the vocabulary, whereas, to my mind, irregular sound change due to frequency, which concerns also reductions in morphemes, especially in inflectional ones (which are even more frequently used than words), is the third essential factor of linguistic evolution, in addition to regular sound change and analogical development: in any text of any language, more or less one third of the words show an irregular sound change due to frequency.

In brief, the theory of irregular sound change due to frequency can be presented as follows. There is a synchronic law according to which the linguistic elements which are more often used are smaller than those which are less often used. There is a kind of balance between the size of linguistic elements and their frequency. Anyhow, the size of linguistic elements is not stable. As a result of regular sound change, the size of words may change considerably as the comparison of some Old and New High German words shows:

OHG *ūf* (2 phonemes) > NHG *auf* (3 phonemes) – increase of 50%;

lēra (4)	>	*Lehre* (4) – no change;
hros (4)	>	*Ross* (3) – decrease of 25%;
skōni (5)	>	*schön* (3) – decrease of 40%.

Since frequency of words is not stable either, it may happen that the balance between the size of a word, or of a morpheme, and its frequency is disturbed. If a word or a morpheme becomes too short in relation to its frequency, it is replaced by a longer one. But if a linguistic element (i.e., a morpheme, word, or group of words) becomes too long in relation to its frequency, it must be shortened, and then there are two possibilities: either a mechanical shortening (*Universität* > *Uni*) or an irregular sound change due to frequency (OHG *hēriro* > *hērro*, *dū* > *du*, MHG *bist du* > *biste*).

If irregular sound change due to frequency is far advanced, it consists of the decay of one or more phonemes, e.g. **hiu tagu* has been reduced to *heute*. However, if the development due to frequency has just started, it may only consist in a partial reduction of a phoneme, e.g.

(a) the long vowel undergoes a reduction: OHG *sun* shows a short vocalism, although the vowel was long in Proto-Indo-European, cf. OI *sūnú-*, Lith. *sūnùs*, OCS *synъ*;

(b) the degree of the vowel opening is subject to a reduction ($a > e > i$ or $a > o > u$), e.g., in OHG *nëmamēs* > *nëmumēs*, the vowel *a* narrowed to *u*, in OHG *stān* > *stēn*, to *e*;

(c) the full vowel is changed into a reduced one: E *shall* may be pronounced with an [ə];

(d) the nasal vowel is subject to denasalization: Pol. *będzie* 'will be' may be pronounced with *e* instead of *ę*;

(e) the palatal consonant undergoes a depalatalization: the Russian reflexive pronoun *-sja* may be pronounced as [sa];

(f) the voiced consonant loses its voicedness, e.g. Lat. *vicem* developed into Fr. *fois* instead of **vois*.

There are four criteria which allow us to recognize that irregular sound change due to frequency is involved:

(1) If a frequency dictionary for a given language and for a given epoch exists, we may use it, since the majority of words showing an irregular change due to frequency (about 90%) belong to the thousand words most frequently used in the given language.

(2) In addition to irregular sound change due to frequency, there are other irregular sound changes, namely assimilations, dissimilations, metatheses, and expressive and overcorrect forms. These irregular sound changes are characterized by the fact that they occur in different words in different languages, e.g. a dissimilation took place in *Fibel* < *Bibel*, a metathesis in *Born* < *Bronn*; however, in another Indo-European language, it would not be easy to find a word meaning 'primer' with a dissimilation or a word meaning 'a well' with a metathesis. In other words, there is no parallelism between the words showing irregular changes such as assimilations, dissimilations, etc., in different lang-

uages, whereas the irregular sound change due to frequency occurs in various languages more or less in parallel, which is explained by the fact that the most frequently used words are nearly the same in all languages. Here are some examples.

Ger. *Herr* shows an irregular reduction. The same is true for E *mister* < *master* or *sir* (which derives from Fr. *sire*, also irregularly developed from Lat. *senior*), Fr. *monsieur* < *monseigneur*, or Sp. *don*, being used alongside the more regular *dueño*. Although the opinions on the etymology of Pol. *pan* or Czech *pán* are not unanimous, it is unquestionable that these words derive from a longer form, as is the case with R *barin*, which has developed from *bojarin*.

The fact that a whole mosaic of Old High German forms *anti, ande, enti, endi, indi, inti, inde, inte, int, in, unta, unte, unti, un* correspond to NHG *und* shows explicitly that we face here an irregular sound change due to frequency. Similarly, in none of the Romance languages, Lat. *et* has developed normally, cf. Fr. *et*, It. *e*, or Sp. *y*. The conjunction *a*, attested in many Slavic languages, also shows a reduced form.

OHG *gangan* is irregularly reduced to *gān, gēn*, whence modern *gehen*. Similarly, reduced forms occur in other Germanic languages, cf. E *go*, Dutch *gaan*, Dan. *gå*, etc. Also, Lat. *ambulāre* undergoes a reduction in the Romance languages, cf. Fr. *aller*, It. *andare*, Sp. *andar*, Prov. *ana*, etc. In the same way, Common Slavic *šьdlъ* (> Pol. *szedł*, R *šël*, etc.) exhibits an irregular reduction, namely the occurrence of *ь* instead of *e* (alternating with *o* in **choditi*).

(3) If in a given language, a morpheme, word, or group of words occurs in a double form (regular and irregular), irregular sound change due to frequency is characterized by the fact that the irregular form is usually used more often than the regular one, e.g., the suffix *-isk* developed in German regularly into *-isch* and irregularly into *-sch*, and *deut-sch* is used more frequently than *französ-isch, italien-isch*, or *ungar-isch*. This is similar in other West Germanic languages, cf. E *Wel-sh, Scot-ch, Fren-ch, Dut-ch* but *Swed-ish, Dan-ish*, or Dutch *Vlaam-s, Fran-s* but *Macedon-isch* or *Arab-isch*. An identical situation is found in the Scandinavian languages, cf. Sw. *sven-sk, ty-sk* but *jon-isk, arab-isk*, Dan. *dan-sk, nor-sk* but *arab-isk, bulgar-isk*, or Norw. *nor-sk, ty-sk* but *polit-isk*. It is interesting that the Germanic *-isk* also reached French, where, similarly, it had a double development: the irregular one in more frequently used forms of the type *franç-ais, angl-ais* and the regular one in less common forms of the type *Franç-ois*.

The situation is similar if there are not double suffixes, but double words, e.g., the irregular *hübsch, Herr* are more often used than the regular *höfisch, hehrer*. The same observation concerns groups of words, e.g., the irregular *zwar* is more frequently used than the regular *zu wahr*.

(4) If the irregular sound change due to frequency occurs within a paradigm, it may be recognized by the fact that only the more commonly used forms are subject to it, whereas the forms used less frequently remain regular; e.g., the Old High German verb *stantan, standan* is reduced to *stān, stēn* (> *stehen*). That this development is due to frequency is proved by the fact that the change concerns the more frequently used present tense and does not apply to the less frequently used preterite (*stand*). Besides, it should be pointed out that in Old High German texts collected in Braune's chrestomathy, the reduction takes place in the simple forms (*stantan* > *stān, stēn*), whereas, in the majority of the compound forms such as *gistantan, aʒstantan, intstantan, ūfstantan, ūfarstantan, umbistantan, widarstantan*, it does not occur (except in *farstantan* and *arstantan*). Obviously, the simple forms are generally used more often than the compounds.

The same applies in the case of the Old High German verb *gangan*, which is reduced to *gān, gēn* in the present tense, which explains today's difference between the irregular *gehen* and the regular *ging*. Claiming our attention also is the fact that among the compound forms of this verb mentioned in Braune, 14 do not show any reduction (*ar-, bi-, fer-, ful-, fram-, in-, int-, missi-, ubar-, ūf-, untar-, ūʒ-, ūʒar-, zigangan*).

When we consider Ger. *haben*, it appears that the forms in the singular present indicative, which are more often used, are shortened (*hast, hat*), whereas the plural forms *haben, habt* are regular. As far as the relation of this verb to its compound forms is concerned, it is worth comparing the irregular E *has, have, had* to the regular *behaves, behave, behaved*. Anyway, a similar phenomenon occurred in Old High German: *habēn* was shortened to *hān* but the compound forms *anthabēn, bihabēn* did not exhibit any reduction.

Towards the end of the fifties, I realized that irregular sound change due to frequency was the third essential factor of linguistic evolution and since then I have been concerned with this phenomenon both in the Romance and in the Slavic languages (Mańczak 1969, 1974, 1975). At the moment, I would like to concentrate upon this phenomenon in the Germanic languages, beginning with German. In German, as in other languages, irregular sound change due to frequency occurs in frequently used word-groups, words, and morphemes. This may be illustrated by the following examples.

The frequent Old High German phrase *sō eigi ih guot* 'so habe ich Gutes, so wahr es mir gut gehen möge' was reduced to *s'ēg ih guot*. If a group of words is very frequently used, it may merge into one word, e.g., *sintemal* < MHG *sint dem māle* or OHG *swër* < *sō hwër, swelīh* < *so hwelīh*. *Heute, heint, heuer* developed in a similar manner. The following table demonstrates that the frequency of occurrence plays an important role here:

zu dem Vater > zum Vater   *zu den Vätern*
zu der Mutter > zur Mutter   *zu den Müttern*
an dem Tisch > am Tisch   *an den Tischen*
von dem Tisch > vom Tisch   *von den Tischen*
in das Feld > ins Feld   *in die Felder*

As the above examples suggest, the merging of a preposition and an article
into one word occurs only in the singular, which is more often used than
the plural.

As far as irregular sound change of words due to frequency is concerned,
it has often been explained as being caused by the lack of stress. This seems
false, since some words, which are subject to reductions, may in no terms be
called unaccented, e.g. *Morgen* 'guten Morgen', whose pronunciation is sometimes reduced. These changes are explained elsewhere in terms of a certain
syntactic function, which is also not a valid explanation, since the words
belonging to all parts of speech are reduced, which may be illustrated by the
following examples.

(1) Nouns. The names of kinship are among the frequently used nouns
and are sometimes reduced irregularly, e.g. *Oheim > Ohm*. The word for
'man' is subject to an irregular shortening in different languages (cf. Sp. *hombre*
without a diphthong as contrasted with OSp. *huembre* or Pol. *człek <
człowiek*). Therefore, the development of OHG *mennisco > Mensch* is not
surprising; nor is the fact that Ger. *Mann* (like Gr. *ánthrōpos* or OCS *člověkъ*)
has no clear etymology.

(2) Articles. The indefinite (cf. dialectal *'n Vogel < ein Vogel*) as well as
the definite articles exhibit many reductions (e.g., the fact that nowadays
der is pronounced both with a long and with a short vowel). It is to reveal a
misunderstanding to assert that the simplification of a geminate in OHG
dëmu (against Goth. *þamma*) occurred "in unbetonter Satzstellung", since,
if we disregard Verner's rule, the accentuation had no influence on the
development of consonants in German.

(3) Pronouns. Pronouns present many reduced forms, e.g., *ich, mich, dich,
sich, du, wir, ihm, kein, nichts*. It should be emphasized that the average
frequency of pronouns is very high. Besides, if there are double forms of the
type of E *mine/my*, the reduced form is used more often than the regular one.

(4) Adjectives. In the superlative degree of adjectives *e* is preserved after
s, ss, and *z*, e.g. *weiseste, süsseste, kürzeste*. In contrast to these words, the
reduced form is shown by the most frequently used adjectives *grösste, beste,
letzte*. A similar relation occurs between the rarely used *mannigfaltig,
mannigfach*, and *manch*.

(5) Numerals. Many numerals show irregular reductions, e.g. OHG *sibun*

< *septm (an irregular disappearance of *t) or elf < OHG einlif (stressed on the second part of the compound, cf. E eleven).

(6) Verbs. Among the several thousands of verbs which exist in German, only a few of them exhibit irregular reductions: first of all, the most frequently used verb sein (bin, bist, ist) and some other verbs which very often occur: haben (hast, hat, hatte), gehen, stehen, sollen (whereas the words Schuld, schuldig, which are used less frequently, exhibit a regular development of the initial sk), müssen (< OHG muoʒan but the less common words Musse, müssig have preserved a regular vocalism). Also it is a result of frequency that o is short in kommen, which, deriving from OHG quëman, belongs to the same ablaut series as nehmen < nëman. In the past, some other verbs showed the change due to frequency, namely OHG lāʒen > lān or some verbs denoting the act of speech: OHG quidis > quis̄, quidit > quīt, MHG seite, geseit (cf. the irregular E says, said), or OHG sprëhhan > spëhhan. As a parallel to the disappearance of r in OHG spëhhan or E speak, we may quote the irregular development of R govorit 'speaks', which, in dialects, is reduced to gryt > gyt.

(7) Adverbs. In Old High German, the regular adverbs end in -o, e.g. gërno (> gern). Against this background, the most frequent Old High German adverb wola, wëla, wël has an exceptional form, which has never been explained. In my opinion, it is the question of an irregular sound change due to frequency, which, in a preliterary period, was responsible for an irregular shortening of *-ō to *-o, and this normally developed into -a. In order to support this assertion, it is possible to cite the fact that Latin adverbs usually end in -ē, and only the most frequently used benĕ and malĕ show an irregular shortening of the final vowel. The development of OHG wëla > wël is similarly caused by frequency of occurrence, as is the development of bene in the Romance languages: in French, the regular bien appears beside the reduced ben, and in Italian, there exists only the irregular form, without a diphthong, bene. Other adverbs also exhibit an irregular change due to their frequency, e.g. da, nicht, nur.

(8) Prepositions. Similarly to pronouns, prepositions constitute a class of words which are very often used. Therefore, it is not surprising that prepositions often show irregular reductions, e.g., OHG gegini has developed not only as gegen but also as gen.

(9) Conjunctions. The same applies as far as conjunctions are concerned, e.g., weil derives ultimately from OHG dia wīla sō.

(10) Interjections. Among interjections, reduced forms appear also, like herrje or herrjemine.

If we consider all these words showing reductions, we must state that the feature which links all of them is not a syntactic function, but only frequency.

Besides, irregular sound change due to frequency takes place in formative morphemes; e.g., the suffix *-lich*, which occurs in many adjectives, is subject to a reduction only in the two most frequently occurring derivatives of this type, namely *welch* and *solch*. However, irregular sound change due to frequency occurs in inflectional morphemes considerably more often. This is due to the fact that inflectional morphemes are more frequently used than derivative ones. Here are some examples.

Opinions on the origin of the weak preterite in the Germanic languages are not unanimous: some consider it to be derived from the 2nd person aorist of the middle voice, others, from the verb corresponding to Ger. *tat*. In the light of the theory of irregular sound change due to frequency, the latter hypothesis should be considered the correct one. In Gothic, the conjugation of the preterite indicative and optative was the following:

	Indicative	Optative
Singular	*nasida*	*nasidēdjau*
	nasidēs	*nasidēdeis*
	nasida	*nasidēdi*
Plural	*nasidēdum*	*nasidēdeima*
	nasidēduþ	*nasidēdeiþ*
	nasidēdun	*nasidēdeina*
Dual	*nasidēdu*	*nasidēdeiwa*
	nasidēduts	*nasidēdeits*

The distribution of forms with and without reduplication is the following: (1) the less frequent optative displays reduplication in all its attested forms, whereas the more frequent indicative does not show it in all the attested forms; (2) within the indicative forms, the less frequent plural and dual exhibit reduplication, but the more common singular does not. Thus, everything suggests that, originally, the reduplication existed in the singular preterite indicative, and its disappearance is accounted for by an irregular sound change due to frequency, which first attacked the forms used most often and only then the forms used less commonly. This resulted in the state known from the Germanic languages attested later than Gothic, where there is no trace of any reduplication in the forms of the weak preterite. It is understood that the weak preterite exhibits other unclear points, but this often happens when irregular sound change due to frequency operates. If they had not known Latin, the comparativists would have maintained that the forms of the perfect Fr. *chant-a*, It. *cant-ò*, and Roum. *cînt-ă* derive from three different forms with asterisks. However, it is known that all these forms derive from one form *cant-āvit*, and the variation *chant-a, cant-ò, cînt-ă* is explained by the fact that the reductions due to frequency may manifest themselves in different ways, cf. the Old High German counterparts of the modern *und*, quoted above.

A different example. In Old High German, there exist simultaneously forms of the type *nëmamēs, nëmumēs*, and *nëmēm* in the 1st pers. plur. pres. ind. The views on the relations between these forms are varied. In the light of the theory of irregular sound change due to frequency, the problem is solved in the following manner. The ending *-mēs* (< *-mēsi*), which resembles Vedic *-masi* and Avestic *-mahi*, is the oldest one, whereas *-m* (< *-mes*) constitutes an ending reduced because of frequent use. This is not surprising, if we compare these facts to the state known from the Slavic languages, where, for example, there is an ending of the 1st pers. plur. *-mo* (<* -mos*) in Serbo-Croatian, *-me* (<*-mes*) in Czech, and *-mъ* in Old Church Slavic (as well as in Old Russian). The last ending shows a reduction in relation to *-mo, -me*. Moreover, in German, the ending *-m*, which later is regularly changed into *-n*, is subject to a reduction, namely in Middle High German, there occur not only forms of the type *nëmen wir*, but also irregular ones of the type *nëme wir*. Also, it is worth adding that the Gothic ending *-m* exhibits still another reduction, namely the irregular disappearance of the final *s*, which is also known in some Romance languages, cf. OProv. *cantam* < *cantāmus*.

From an Indo-European point of view, *nëmamēs* and *nëmumēs* have the ending *-mēs* but from the Old High German point of view, they have the ending *-amēs, -umēs*. Contrary to what von Kienle, for instance, writes in his grammar, it should be stated that, in these endings, not *u* but *a* is regular (*a* exactly corresponds to the vowel in Goth. *nimam* or Gr. φέρομεν), whereas *u* in *-umēs* is to be explained by an irregular sound change due to frequency, which often consists in the reduction of the vowel opening. As a parallel, it is possible to quote an irregular reduction of *a* to *o* in Fr. *chant-ons* < *cant-āmus* or the irregular reduction *a* > *o* > *u* which occurs in different Italian dialects, cf. Piedmontese *kantuma* < *cant-āmus*.

Another example: in Middle High German in some dialects, the *-n* of the infinitive disappears, e.g., *nëmen* > *nëme*. A similar change has taken place in English, where a difference exists between, e.g., *to give* and the participle *given*. This change is also due to frequency, which is proved by the fact that infinitives without *n* (typical both of strong and of weak verbs) are more often used than participles with *n* (only typical of strong verbs). In the same way, frequency accounts for the irregular simplification of a geminate in the Old High German gerunds of the type *nëmanne* 'zu nehmen' > *nëmane*.

Further example. In Gothic and in Old High German, the declension of the *ā*-stem nouns was of the following shape:

			Gothic	Old High German
Sing.	Nom.	*-ā	giba +	geba +
	Acc.	*-ām	giba +	geba +
	Gen.	*-ās	gibōs	geba, gebu +
	Dat.	*-āi	gibái	geba, gebu +
Plur.	Nom.	*-ās	gibōs	· gebā +
	Acc.	*-āns	gibōs	gebā +
	Gen.	*-ōm	gibō	gebōno
	Dat.	*-āmis	gibōm	gebōm

As is known, the Indo-European *ā and *ō result in *ō in Proto-Germanic. Therefore, the development of the forms not marked by crosses is regular. In historical grammars, this double development is accounted for by the existence of the acute and the circumflex intonations in Proto-Indo-European. This explanation gives an impression of an *ad hoc* explanation for two reasons: (1) the distribution of regular and irregular endings in Gothic differs considerably from that of regular and irregular endings in Old High German; (2) everything indicates that the Balto-Slavic intonation arose independently of Greek; therefore there is no proof that any intonation existed in Proto-Indo-European. For these reasons, the irregular endings of the Gothic and OHG ā-stem nouns are to be accounted for on the basis of their frequency, which is proved by the fact that, both in Gothic and in Old High German, the irregular development occurs in the more frequently used endings, since it is known that (1) the singular is used more often than the plural, (2) the nominative and the accusative are used more often than the dative and the genitive. As a parallel, we may cite the fact that, in the frequently used Latin nominative singular of the type *tabul-ă*, the final vowel underwent an irregular shortening, whereas, in the less frequently used ablative singular *tabul-ā*, the old length was preserved.

Still another example. It has been asserted that, in Old High German, in the final syllable, Proto-Germanic *a disappeared earlier than Proto-Germanic *i and *u, which means that e.g. OHG *tag* is as regular as OHG *wini* or *sunu*. In my opinion, this assertion should be doubted for two reasons:

(1) The disappearance of final unstressed vowels occurs in various languages, but I do not know a language where the final unstressed a (which is considerably wider than i, u) disappeared earlier than i, u (whereas the disappearance of i, u prior to the disappearance of a is often found).

(2) In Old High German, there are some words which are not o-stem nouns, and which end in a, e.g. *ana* (> *an*), *aba* (> *ab*), *unta* (> *und*), *fona* (> *von*). The majority of these words derive from words ending in *a or *o in Proto-Indo-European: *ana* < *ana, *aba* < *apo, *unta* < *nta. Since it is

known that Proto-Indo-European *a and *o merge into *a in Proto-Germanic, the question arises of how to reconcile the fact that the Proto-Indo-European *a, *o were preserved in OHG *ana, aba*, or *unta*, and the fact that the ending *-o-s in the nominative singular of the o-stems disappeared in Old High German, which resulted in the nouns of the type *tag*.

In my view, Old High German words of the type *ana, aba, unta* show a regular change of the final unstressed Proto-Germanic *a (< Proto-Indo-European *a, *o), whereas the disappearance of *-o-s in the nominative singular of the o-stem nouns is to be accounted for by an irregular sound change. To put it differently, the final vowel disappeared irregularly in the frequently used o-stem nouns (OHG *tag*), whereas it was regularly preserved in the less often used i- or u-stems (OHG *wini, sunu*). Such an interpretation of these phenomena in Old High German is supported by parallels drawn from outside the Germanic languages. In Old Church Slavic, the i- and u-stems show a regular development (*gost-ь, syn-ъ*), but the masculine o-stem nouns show an irregular reduction (*grad-ъ*), whereas the less frequently used o-stem neuters exhibit a nearly regular development (*lět-o*). A similar situation occurs in Lithuanian. Although no difference exists between the o-, i-, and u-stem nouns (*vilk-as, ánt-is, tuřg-us*) in the literary language, there are dialects where the reduction takes place in the o-stems (*vilk-s*), whereas the development is regular in the i- and u-stems. An analogous case occurred in Old Prussian, where the more frequently used o-stem masculines exhibited both the full and the reduced endings (*deiw-as* and *deiw-s*), whereas the ending is always regular in the o-stem neuters (*assar-an*).

Finally, I would like to emphasize two things:

(1) The above remarks do not deal with all the problems of irregular sound change due to frequency in German.

(2) If the theory of irregular sound change due to frequency is true, the historical grammar of the Germanic languages will have to be revised in many respects.

Note

1. I am indebted to Professor A. Szulc, who discussed these problems with me.

References

Diez, Friedrich
    1846   *Altromanische Sprachdenkmale* (Bonn).

Mańczak, Witold
  1969   *Le développement phonétique des langues romanes et la fréquence* (Kraków: Nakładem Uniwersytetu Jagiellońskiego).
  1974   *Phonétique et morphologie historiques du français*[3] (Warszawa: PWN).
  1975   *Polska fonetyka i morfologia historyczna*[2] (Warszawa: PWN).
Pott, August Friedrich
  1852   "Plattlateinisch und Romanisch", *KZ* 1: 309–350.

JERZY RUBACH

Phonostylistics and sound change

As has been recently emphasized by Labov (cf. esp. 1972) the notion of sound change need not be limited to describing diachronic analyses. It may also be applied synchronically and then we talk about sound changes in progress.

A good synchronic source, if one looks for sound changes in progress, is an analysis of casual and/or rapid speech phenomena. It is especially interesting to look at the relationships which hold between obligatory rules and phonostylistic (i.e. casual and/or rapid speech) rules. A careful inspection of these relationships may, as we shall try to point out, provide grounds for the formation of hypotheses concerning sound changes which are likely to occur as future developments in the language.

I have discussed in another paper the implications of phonostylistic rule overlap for changes in underlying representations (Rubach 1976). I shall here examine the opacity and transparency of some obligatory and phonostylistic processes in British English and Polish. Thus the paper will illustrate the principles originally formulated in Kiparsky (1971) and revised in Kiparsky (1973). In particular, we shall look at palatalizations in British English and later at two rules of stop deletion in Polish. The data come from the available literature both theoretical and practical (such as transcriptions in *Le Maître Phonétique*) and from experiments and observations which I carried out for my dissertation (Rubach 1974).

For British English[1], the words in (a) below have obligatorily undergone palatalization while those in (b) have not:

(a) *intonation, partition, partial, artificial, partiality, musician;*
(b) *factual, sensual, Christian, associate, association, Asian, issue.*

All the instances quoted in (b) may undergo palatalization but not in careful, monitored style where they appear with sequences of a coronal obstruent plus a nonback glide or [i].

Thus one of the major issues in the grammar of palatalizations for British English is the formulation of obligatory phonological rules in such a way that these would apply to the items in (a) but not to those in (b) which would be handled by phonostylistic rules.

Notice that in the Chomsky — Halle (1968) account all the cases where /jV/ follows, the appropriate consonants undergo palatalization obligatorily. Therefore we have to look first at the rule which turns /i/ to /j/, i.e., Chomsky — Halle's rule 118b. For our purposes we can restrict the rule to the context of obstruent plus /i/ ignoring other cases (*companion, rebellious* etc.):

(1)
$$
\begin{bmatrix} +\text{high} \\ -\text{back} \\ +\text{syll} \end{bmatrix} \rightarrow [-\text{syll}] \Big/ \begin{bmatrix} +\text{obstr} \\ +\text{coron} \\ \langle -\text{contin} \rangle \\ \langle -\text{voiced} \rangle \end{bmatrix} + - \begin{bmatrix} V \\ -\text{stress} \end{bmatrix} \langle N \rangle
$$

This is a slightly modified version of rule 118b: the following vowel has been restricted to [−stress] and the context of /di/ in nonnouns has been excluded. Chomsky and Halle suggest (1968:227) that the latter should be done by a [−Rule 1] feature. We have incorporated this restriction into the rule itself. Thus now rule (1) will not apply to: *cardial, invidious* (Chomsky — Halle), *Canadian, cordial* etc. However, (1) will handle *division* /divīd+iV̌n/, *invasion* /invǣd+iV̌n/, *persuation, decision, conclusion, explosion* (cf. the evidence for an underlying stop in these words: *divide, invade, persuade, decide, conclude, explode*) etc. because they are nouns, i.e. they take the /+iV̌n/ ending. On the other hand, words like *cordiality* are excluded since the following vowel is stressed. By the same token we exclude *negotiȧte, associȧte, negotiȧtion, associȧtion.*
Rule (1) applies therefore to the following cases:

(a) *Egyptian* /t+i+æn/ (cf. *Egypt*), *partial* /t+i+æl/ (cf. *part*), *expeditious* /t+i+os/ (cf. *expedite*), and also *beneficial* (cf. *benefit*), *facial* (cf. *face*), *financial* (cf. *finance*), *officious* (cf. *office*);

(b) /+t+iV̌n/: *production* (cf. *produce*, /t/ is an augment), *description* (cf. *describe*), *absorption* (cf. absorb);

(c) /+iV̌n/: *fusion* (cf. *fuse*), *confusion* (cf. *confuse*), *television* (cf. *televise*), *tension* (cf. *tense*), *confession* (cf. *confess*), *mission* (cf. *missive*), *intonation* (cf. *intonate*), *appreciation* (cf. *appreciate*), *nation* (cf. *native*), *definition* (cf. *definitive*), *constitution* (cf. *constitute*), *postulation* (cf. *postulate*), *delegation* (cf. *delegate*), *reaction* (cf. *react*), *permission* (cf. *permit*), *attention* (cf. *attentive*).

There are, however, many words for which it is impossible to adduce any phonological evidence pointing to the fact that they have a coronal obstruent followed by a two-vowel ending, e.g., *pension* (*pense), *mention*. In other words, we do not have any phonological evidence that they undergo (1), they may just as well have an underlying final sequence of /šVn/. If this is the case one may probably resort to some morphological considerations, such as finding parallels in the morphological productivity between the words for which we do have phonological evidence and those for which we do not. For example, *reaction – reactionary* is a parallel formation to *pension – pensionary*. To what extent such considerations are valid and legitimate is a matter of further investigation. Similarly, we can use paradigmatic evidence in the absence of phonological support; the forms *caution, cautionary, cautious* are sufficient to establish that their underlying representation meets the environment of (1).

Recall that (1) is in part morphologically conditioned: it depends on the presence of a formative boundary before /i/. If this boundary is not present the rule does not apply: *frontier, Pontius, otiose, brasier, Silesia, osier, Rhodesia, India, aphasia, physiological*, etc. Sometimes there is a formative boundary but it follows and does not precede (as is required by (1)) the /i/ vowel: *Silesi+an, Polynesi+an, Asi+an, pite+ous, plente+ous, medi+al, associ+able*[2] etc. Words such as *Silesian* are derived from the underlying /silēsiV̆+æn/ where the final vowel of the noun (the surface [ə] in *Silesia*) is deleted by a phonological rule before the suffix /æn/. Although rule (1) seems to capture the basic regularity it still leaves a large number of cases which have to be treated as exceptions. Many words have to be marked [–Rule 1] in the lexicon, for example, *Parisian* (which does have "+" before /i/, cf. *Paris*), *Venetian, Christian, courtier* etc.

Now many words undergo Spirantization – SPE Chomsky – Halle (1968:229), rule 120. Thus the /t/ of *partial, partiality, investigation, provocation, Egyptian* (but not in, e.g., *Christian* which has to be marked as an exception) is changed to /s/. In this form they are further inputs to Palatalization.

Before we proceed to the Palatalization rule itself let us consider still another group of cases. Standard British is different from many other dialects of English in that it does not require palatalization in *factual, issue, fluctuate* etc. It might appear that we should simply exclude all words with /ū/ from palatalization. However, upon further inspection we discover that this is not entirely true. In *future, creature, pressure* the only possible pronunciation is that with [č] or [š]. It is clear (cf. Chomsky – Halle) that the /j/ glide in *factual* and also in *future* (cf. *futurity*) is not underlying but comes from an insertion rule. Thus if we want to prevent *sensual, sexual* from undergoing Palatalization we should order *j*-insertion after Palatalization. The situation is very complicated. For *future*, etc., /j/ must be inserted before Palatalization so as to get the appropriate phonetic forms. Thus we have not one but two *j*-insertion rules: one applying before Palatalization and the other after it.

Informally, the rule applying before Palatalization has the following shape:

(2) $\phi \rightarrow j \: / \: - \bar{u}r$

It inserts /j/ before /ūr/, viz., *mature, maturity, future, futurity, endure, endurance, moisture, mixture, exposure, closure, pressure, creature, texture, scripture, expediture, seizure* etc. In these words it is clear that underlyingly we have a dental obstruent preceding /ūr/ since it surfaces phonetically in alternative forms which undergo or do not undergo (2), viz. *futurity* and *moist, expose, press, create*, respectively. In some words there is no direct evidence for an underlying dental obstruent /t, d, s, z/ but the underlying form can be established on the basis of paradigmatic comparison of stems: *structure – con=struct – con=struct+ion*. As previously, there are some words for which we do not have any obvious evidence at all. Thus it is not certain whether *torture, lecture* end in /tūr/ which goes to /tjūr/ and /čūr/ (ultimately to [čə(r)] by other rules) or whether they should be represented underlyingly with /čVr/. Again, there might be morphological considerations which make disambiguation possible.

Furthermore, there are words which undergo (2), but which must be exempted from Palatalization. At least for some speakers the following are pronounced with [tjuə(r)] in slow speech: *literature, candidature, caricature, aperture, armature, tablature, curvature*, etc. Clearly the number of exceptions to Palatalization in the above list will vary considerably because of the tendency to suppress this exceptionality particularly among the younger generation. Thus *literature*, being a very common word, will be much less likely to have the [tjuə(r)] pronunciation (rather [čə(r)], i.e. Palatalization applies regularly) while *curvature*, being a rare word, will normally be pronounced with [tjuə(r)].

Now we can proceed to the discussion of the obligatory phonological Palatalization rule. This is a considerably modified version of SPE (121) (p. 230):

(3) $\begin{bmatrix} -\text{sonor} \\ +\text{coron} \\ \langle +\text{contin} \rangle \\ \langle -\text{voiced} \rangle \end{bmatrix} \rightarrow \begin{bmatrix} -\text{anter} \\ +\text{strid} \end{bmatrix} \: / \: - \begin{bmatrix} +\text{high} \\ -\text{back} \\ -\text{cons} \\ \langle +\text{syll} \rangle \end{bmatrix} \begin{bmatrix} -\text{cons} \\ \left\{ \begin{bmatrix} -\text{stress} \end{bmatrix} \right\} \\ \left\{ \begin{bmatrix} -\text{tense} \end{bmatrix} \right\} \end{bmatrix}$

This rule turns dental obstruents /s, z, t, d/ to nonanterior stridents [š, ž, č, ǰ], respectively. It differs from SPE (121) in that we have allowed /s/ to palatalize not only before /j/ but also before /i/. As the context has been extended to vowels we have had to introduce the [+high] restriction to guarantee that (3) will not apply before front vowels such as /e/.

The part of the rule not embraced by angle brackets says that dental obstruents are always palatalized before /j/ if they are followed by an unstressed nonconsonantal segment. Thus we have palato-alveolars in:

> *innovation, intonation, provocation, nation, attention, description, invasion, division, decision, precision; official, racial, facial, substantial, financial, artificial, potential, officious, expeditious, malicious; Egyptian, future, scripture, pressure, moisture.*

Rule (3) does not apply to *endure, mature, futurity* etc. because the vowel which follows /j/ is stressed. The angle bracket specification allows (3) to apply if /s/ is followed by /i/ and a nontense vowel, be it stressed or unstressed. Thus we get phonetic [š] in *partiality, potentiality, artificiality, negotiability, sociable*. The restriction to nontense vowels correctly excludes *associate, association, negotiate, negotiation, emaciate, pronunciation, enunciative, associative* etc. Incorrectly, however, (3) does not apply to *differentiate, substantiate, insatiate, appreciative* and a few other similar words. As we have noted, palatalization before /i/ will not take place in the preceding obstruent is a stop or /z/. Consequently, the following are correctly excluded: *hideous, piteous, invidious, cordial, cordiality, Christian, Christianism, Christianity, osier, brasier, Polynesia, Silesia, Rhodesia, Asian* if the latter have /z/ and not /s/. There are cases where we might suspect that a nonanterior strident obstruent is present underlyingly. Some of these can be presumably disambiguated by morphological considerations which would allow us to establish an underlying dental obstruent in *initial, rational, motion* (*motive*?) but there are also some for which there is no evidence whatsoever that they undergo (3), e.g., *ration*. Even though considerably restricted, (3) wrongly applies to some words which may have nonpalatalized pronunciations in slow speech: *omniscient, enunciable* etc. Consequently, these have to be marked [−Rule 3].

Now let us look at some phonological derivations:

Egyptian	*division*	*partial*	
/−t+i+æn/	/−d+iV̆n/	/−t+i+æl/	
t+j+æn	d+jV̆n	t+j+æl	Rule (1)
s+j+æn	z+jV̆n	s+j+æl	Spirantiz.
š+j+æn	ž+jV̆n	š+j+æl	Rule (3)

Egyptian	*division*	*partial*	
š+æn	ž+V̆n	š+æl	*j*-deletion
š+ən	ž+ən	š+əl	other rules

partiality	*future*	*pressure*	
/–t+i+æl+i+ti/	/–tūr/	/–s+tūr/	
–	tjūr	sj+ūr	Rule (2)
s+i+æl+i+ti	–	–	Spirantiz.
š+i+æl+i+ti	čjūr	šj+ūr	Rule (3)
–	čūr	š+ūr	*j*-deletion
–	čə(r)	š+ə(r)	other rules

We have already noted that there is a group of words which systematically do not undergo Palatalization:

(a) *sensual, sexual, usual, sensuous, issue, tissue*;
(b) *factual, habitual, eventual, conceptual, ritual, contextual, residual, gradual, tumultuous, actuate, accentuate, graduate, Portugal.*

These words are excluded from Palatalization because /j/ has not yet been inserted, hence they do not meet the environment of (3). The glide is inserted by a later rule which could be stated informally thus:

(4) $\phi \rightarrow j \ / \ – \bar{u}$ in some contexts

In the Chomsky – Halle theory this /ū/ is previously turned to /i̶/ by another rule (cf. rules 49–51, Chomsky – Halle 1968:194). Since the Chomsky – Halle analysis of vowel shift with back vowels is not very well motivated, hence highly controversial, we shall not go into the exact formulation of (4). In fact, whatever the correct formulation is, it is not essential for the point which we are making here. The important thing is to recognize two different *j*-insertion rules. It is clear that (4) will also apply to *titular* etc. where /ū/ comes from insertion (Chomsky – Halle 1968:196, rule 56) since obviously the slow speech output has [tj] and not [č]. On the other hand, *tune, dew, dune, tutor* etc. may get /j/ either by (2) or by (4) since the presence of a stressed vowel will correctly exclude them from Palatalization.

After Palatalization has applied we still need a rule which could delete the /j/ which has caused palatalization. Thus *division* does not end in [žjən] but in [žən]. The *j*-drop is given as rule 122 in Chomsky – Halle (1968:231). The rule, as it stands, deletes all instances of /j/ after /š, ž, č, ǰ/. This is in-

correct for words like [reĵšĵ̇ow] . Thus we have to restrict rule 122 to the
context before an unstressed vowel (note *ratio* has [3stress] on the final
vowel). Consequently, the *j*-drop takes the following shape:

(5) $\begin{bmatrix} -\text{cons} \\ -\text{syll} \\ -\text{back} \end{bmatrix} \rightarrow \phi \, / \quad \begin{bmatrix} -\text{anter} \\ +\text{strid} \end{bmatrix} \quad - \quad \begin{bmatrix} V \\ -\text{stress} \end{bmatrix}$

Rule (5) will delete /j/ in *partial, Egyptian, decision, attention, intonation,
future, pressure*, etc. It is precisely for this reason that *partial* /–t+i+æl/
→ /s+i+æl/ (Spirantization) had to undergo (1). Notice that Palatalization
would apply anyway since the vowel following /i/ is neither stressed nor
tense. We would end up, however, with [šiəl] and there would be no way of
deleting /i/ since there is no rule deleting /i/ before an unstressed vowel and
after a nonanterior coronal obstruent. Actually, although this statement seems
to be true the matter is not entirely clear: /i/ does delete after /š/ in *sociable*
(the /ī/ of *society*). However, this seems to be exceptional. Regularly, /i/ does
not delete in such contexts (cf. *appreciable*) or, more precisely, the deletion
may take place but is a phonostylistic and not an obligatory process. Similarly,
side by side with *official*, which undergoes (5), we have *facial* and *racial*,
where /j/ may surface phonetically.

The above presented complications in the analysis seem to be unavoidable
if one aims at accounting for obligatory palatalizations in English. The lack
of clarity in the situation described is a corollary of the fact that we are
facing a sound change in progress. Some items have and some have not undergone palatalization. As a result of this we have opacity by Kiparsky's cases
(i) and (iib) (cf. 1973:79). The clearest exemplification here is the process of
j-insertion. We have postulated two separate rules thus making the process
opaque by (iib) (a process P of the form A → B/C − D is opaque to the
extent that there are forms in the language having B not derived by the process
P in env. C − D; Kiparsky 1973:79). Since the second *j*-insertion rule applies
after Palatalization, we have managed to account for phonetic [tj] , [sj] etc.
in *factual, sensual*. However, as noted above, not all the items having /j/ by
virtue of applying the first *j*-insertion rule undergo Palatalization: *candidature,
aperture* etc. have to be marked as exceptions. Consequently, we have opacity
by case (i) (there are phonetic forms having A in env. C − D; Kiparsky
1973:79).

This opacity makes a prediction that sound change will proceed in the
direction of eliminating the unnatural situation of having two *j*-insertion
rules and costly lexical markings for exceptionality. Changes in casual and/or
rapid speech fully confirm this expectation. Let us look at some details of
phonostylistic palatalization in English.

The first rule to be considered is a phonostylistic reflex (counterpart) of rule (1). As is typical, phonostylistic reflexes of obligatory phonological rules are broader and less restricted in their environments (and inputs). Unlike in (1), in the rule below the nature of the preceding consonant is irrelevant:

$$(6) \quad \begin{bmatrix} +\text{high} \\ -\text{back} \\ +\text{syll} \\ -\text{stress} \end{bmatrix} \quad \rightarrow \quad [-\text{syll}] \quad \Big/ - \begin{bmatrix} V \\ -\text{stress} \end{bmatrix}$$

Rule (6) changes [i] to [j] [3] in, e.g., *Asian, Andalusian, gladiatorial, tedious, immediately, courtier, frontier, Christian, cordial, brasier, Parisian*. As we can see, it now applies to all those words which for one reason or another have not undergone (1) or have had to be quoted as exceptions to (1). Rule (6) does not apply if [i] is stressed or if it is followed by a stressed vowel (whatever degree of stress it might carry): *tear, here, merely, associate* (verb), *cordiality, sociology, pronunciation, differentiation, gladiator, Indiana, radio* [4] .

The phonological Palatalization rule manifests itself phonostylistically as rules (7) and (8) which are basically two subparts of the same rule.

$$(7) \quad \begin{bmatrix} +\text{coron} \\ +\text{obstr} \\ +\text{contin} \end{bmatrix} \quad \rightarrow \quad \begin{bmatrix} -\text{anter} \\ +\text{strid} \end{bmatrix} \quad \Big/ - \begin{bmatrix} +\text{syll} \\ +\text{high} \\ -\text{back} \\ -\text{stress} \end{bmatrix} \quad V$$

Rule (7) turns [s, z] to [š, ž] before unstressed [i] and another vowel: *associate, association, appreciate, appreciative, appreciation, differentiation, Asiatic, sociology, emaciate, denunciate, negotiate.*

The requirement for the [i] to be unstressed correctly excludes *seer, Sears*, etc., but even then there are some exceptions to (7), which is unusual, since phonostylistic rules are by and large exceptionless: *pronunciation, Seattle*. The last example points to the fact that we should probably restrict the rule not to apply in word-initial position, which is not uncommon for phono-stylistic rules (cf. Rubach 1974). Rule (7) is further restricted not to apply to stops. This restriction seems to be correct in view of the fact that *cordiality, Indiana, gladiator, radio, mediation, Christianity* etc. do not have [č, ǰ] even in rapid speech (our recordings).

So far we have talked about [i] as the conditioning segment for palatalization. Quite obviously, if [j] follows a dental obstruent, palatalization is still more likely:

$$(8) \quad \begin{bmatrix} +\text{obstr} \\ +\text{coron} \\ \langle +\text{contin}\rangle_a \end{bmatrix} \rightarrow \begin{bmatrix} -\text{anter} \\ +\text{strid} \end{bmatrix} \Big/ \langle\#\rangle_b - (\#)\langle\#\rangle_a \begin{bmatrix} -\text{back} \\ -\text{syll} \\ -\text{cons} \end{bmatrix} \Big\langle \begin{bmatrix} V \\ -1\text{stress} \end{bmatrix} \Big\rangle_b$$

Let us analyse the conditions of the rule. In the first place whenever a dental obstruent is followed by [j] within the word palatalization may take place: *sensual, issue, tissue, individualism, factual, gradual, mutual, graduation, mutuality, sensuality, Christian, Christianism, Parisian, brasier, frontier, media, Silesian, Rhodesian, overture, cordial, tedious, India, education, latitude, multitude, Neptune, situation, constituent, postulate, substitute, constitute, immediately* etc. Within words even the context of a following stressed vowel does not inhibit palatalization: *luxurious, azure, produce, introduce, mature, maturity*. However, if the dental obstruent is word-initial ('angle brackets "b"') then the following vowel must not have a primary stress: thus (8) applies to *duration*[5], *tutorial* but not to *tune, tutor, sewer*[6]. Across single #(8) applies freely to all dental obstruents: *don't you, wouldn't you, would you, but you, not yet, as you, had you, told you, gives you, mind you, helps you, miss you*, where in the latter examples the original ## has been readjusted to # by Selkirk's convention (1972). If there is ## between the obstruent and [j] (8) applies only if the obstruent is a continuant. Thus we may have [š, ž] in *six years, Mrs. Young, miss your turn, what's your weight, miss young people*, but there is no [č, ǰ] in *meet young people, read yellow pages*. The phrase *last year* stands apart since it may have [č] but clearly the whole expression exhibits a fairly advanced process of lexicalization (hence the boundary may be very well # and not ##, as the boundary assignment convention would predict).

There is one group of words to which (8) cannot apply. We never get [š] in *supreme, consume, consumate, consulate* etc. Rather, instead there is a rule of *j*-deletion which operates roughly in the environment $\begin{Bmatrix} \mathtt{\theta} \\ u \end{Bmatrix} C$ and precedes (8) so that *consulate* can never meet the environment of (8). Instead, it reduces ultimately to [ə]: [sju] → [sjə] → [sə]. Since we have not investigated this rule in detail let us leave this question open[7].

Finally, there is a rule of *j*-deletion which is a phonostylistic reflex of (5):

$$(9) \quad \begin{bmatrix} -\text{cons} \\ -\text{syll} \\ -\text{back} \end{bmatrix} \rightarrow \phi \Big/ \begin{bmatrix} -\text{anter} \\ +\text{strid} \end{bmatrix} (\#) - \begin{bmatrix} V \\ \langle -\text{high}\rangle \end{bmatrix} \langle C\rangle$$

Rule (9) applies not only within words but also across a single word boundary:

factual, sensual, Silesian, Parisian, postulate, constitute, Christian;
wouldn't you, told you, what's your ..., lets you[8] .

There is no requirement for the following vowel to be unstressed since side
by side with *graduate* we get [ǰu] in *produce, reduce*, [čʰu] in *statue* as well
as in *mature*. There is some other conditioning: if the vowel is nonhigh then
[j] deletes only if a consonant follows. Thus we have: *Asian, omniscient,
immediately, Indian, Andalusian* vs. *ratio, Andalusia, Silesia, Felicia, India*,
etc. If the vowel is high then [j] may delete also word-finally before this
vowel: *tissue, issue*. The conditioning of a high vowel is not accidental. Notice
that [j] is also [+high] so it is natural that there is more reduction when
two adjacent segments have more features in common.

To illustrate the above described processes let us look at some phonostylistic derivations:

	Christian	*associate*	*don't you*	
Slow speech		3.		
forms:	−stiən	−siejt	−t ju	
	stjən	−	−	Rule (6)
	−	šiejt	−	Rule (7)
	sčjən	−	čju	Rule (8)
	sčən	−	ču	Rule (9)
	ščən	−	−	Assimil.

Our analysis of phonostylistic changes points to a very strong tendency to
reduce opacity produced by obligatory phonological rules. Nearly all the items
marked as exceptions to obligatory Palatalization are regularized in casual
and/or rapid speech. Notice that certain patterns are repeated: dental stops
undergo phonostylistic palatalizations less readily than dental continuants (cf.
the restrictions in rule (8)); recall that the exceptions to obligatory palatalizations *caricature, candidature* etc. all ended in dental stops.

Assuming that in sound change rules are first variable and only later become
obligatory (according to Labov, confirmed in Kiparsky 1971:603) we may
further hypothesize that today's transparency of phonostylistic palatalizations will be true of obligatory processes in the future. One may expect that
first words like *candidature* will assume the [čə(r)] pronunciation as the only
possibility, later the same change will take place in words like *mutual*. The
reason for such a gradation is that *candidature, caricature*, etc., show what one
might describe as a higher opacity in the sense that they are true exceptions
to phonological rules while *mutual, sensual*, etc., do not undergo obligatory
Palatalization due to the existence of a second *j*-insertion rule, i.e., it is not

the words themselves but the rule which is opaque. Our informal observations seem to confirm this hypothesis: for many speakers *literature, candidature*, etc., are not exceptions at all (i.e., they can only have the palatalized pronunciations) while *mutual, sensual*, etc., still show palatalized — nonpalatalized variability. These latter examples will have obligatorily palatalized pronunciations after the two glide insertion rules have merged into one. This unified Gliding will apply before Palatalization in accordance with the natural tendency to have feeding relationships between rules.

In connection with the above hypothetical statements it is interesting to bring to attention the rule of *d*-deletion in Polish. Benni (1964:43) in his book published originally in 1915 notes phonostylistic variability of [ndn] ∼ [nn] in *porządny* 'orderly', *względny* 'relative', etc. Sixty years later, Biedrzycki (1974:99) regards [ndn] in these words as an example of "spelling pronunciation", i.e., he believes that [d] has to be deleted obligatorily. Thus a former phonostylistic rule has now become obligatory:

$$(10) \quad \begin{bmatrix} -\text{contin} \\ -\text{del rel} \\ +\text{coron} \\ +\text{anter} \\ +\text{voiced} \end{bmatrix} \rightarrow \phi \quad / \quad \begin{bmatrix} +\text{nas} \\ +\text{coron} \\ +\text{anter} \end{bmatrix} \quad - \quad \begin{bmatrix} +\text{nas} \\ +\text{coron} \\ +\text{anter} \end{bmatrix}$$

Undoubtedly, *względny* 'relative', *porządny* 'orderly', *błędny* 'mistaken' have to be analysed as cases of *d*-deletion. Although not attested phonetically in these words (confirmed by our observations), the dental stop must be postulated as underlying: it surfaces in cognates like *wzgląd* 'reason', *porządek* 'order', *błąd* 'mistake' where there is no *-ny* suffix. Notice by the way, that the change has a very clear articulatory motivation (it is a supporting case for Ohala's hypothesis, cf. Ohala 1974): [d] is deleted between homorganic nasals. If there is no homorganity, as in *urzędnik* 'office-worker', *względnie* 'relatively' — [ndń], *nędzny* 'miserable' — [ndzn] (an affricate, not a stop), or no agreement in voice as in *ponętny* 'tempting', *wstrętny* 'abominable' — [n̥tn], then the deletion (or replacement of [t] by a voiceless nasal) may occur only in casual and/or rapid speech.

Finally let us look at some other contexts in which dental stops delete in Polish. As found by Gussmann (1973), there are obligatory phonological deletions of /t, d/ in the environment: fricative — /n/ or /ń/:

$$(11) \quad \begin{bmatrix} +\text{obstr} \\ +\text{coron} \end{bmatrix} \rightarrow \phi \quad / \quad \begin{bmatrix} +\text{obstr} \\ +\text{contin} \end{bmatrix} \quad - \quad \begin{bmatrix} +\text{nas} \\ +\text{coron} \end{bmatrix}$$

This rule[9] (quoting after Gussmann) applies to: *świsnąć* 'to whistle', *chlusnąć* 'splash', *bolesny* 'painful', *szczęsny* 'lucky', *radosny* 'joyful', *żalosny* 'miserable', *miłosny* 'love' (adj.), *litosny* 'pitiful' vs. *świstać* 'to whistle' (imperf.) etc.; *gwiezdny* 'starry', *przyjezdny* 'visiting', *kostny* 'bone' (adj.), *ustny* 'oral' are given as exceptions to (11), *szastnąć* 'spend lavishly', *zachłystnąć* 'choke', *bezszelestny* 'without a noise', *gwizdnąć* 'to whistle' – as fluctuating forms. The same deletions are true if the nasal which follows is /ń/: *świśnie* 'he will whistle', *chluśnie* 'he will splash', etc.

Notice, however, that there are many more exceptions to (11): *korzystny* 'advantageous', *zawistny* 'jealous', *nienawistny* 'hateful', *napastnik* 'agressor', *uczestnik* 'participant', *postny* 'meatless', *rozpustny* 'immoral', *istny* 'real', *przepastny* 'precipitous', *chrzestny* 'god-' as in 'god-father'. In fact there are more exceptions than regular cases. In this situation one may wonder whether there is sufficient reason to posit a rule like (11) at all. Or perhaps having postulated (11) we should assign it the status of a minor rule.

Both alternatives are wrong. The evidence comes from phonostylistics. All the words which have to be marked [-Rule 11] in the lexicon are regularized without exception in casual and/or rapid speech[10] (cf. Biedrzycki 1974:99). Thus *przyjezdny* is very frequently realized with [zn], *postny, zawistny, korzystny* have [sn], *uczestnik, rozpustnie* – [sń].

As is typical, the rapid speech rule is much broader: the nasal need not be coronal – the [t] of *astma* 'asthma' – [stm] disappears just as easily, even more, the right environment need not contain a nasal at all: the rule applies to *napastliwy* 'aggressive' – [stl'] and (after Biedrzycki 1974:99) to *ciekawostka* 'peculiarity', *artystka* 'artist' (fem.), *dentystka* 'dentist' (fem.), *wyrostków* 'teen-agers' (pejorative, gen.) – [stk], *maszynistki* 'typists', *królewskie miłostki* 'king's love-affairs' – [stk']. Notice that from the examples just given it follows that the right environment is any noncontinuant segment (nasal, lateral, or stop). This is correct: there are no simplifications in *bóstwo* 'idol', *mnóstwo* 'many', *województwo* 'district', *państwo* 'state', *musztra* 'military training' where a continuant follows. However, the statement is not entirely precise: [t] may also delete in *warstwa* 'stratum', *głupstwo* 'nonsense', *przestępstwo* 'crime', *lekarstwo* 'medicine', *kłamstwo* 'a lie', *czerstwy* 'stale', *braterstwo* 'brotherhood'. Consequently, the rule reads: dental stops may delete in the environment – obstruent and a noncontinuant, or a continuant but then the proceeding obstruent must be clustered with another consonant, be it an obstruent (*głupstwo*) or a sonorant (*kłamstwo, czerstwy*). The preceding segment must be an obstruent as there is no deletion in *partner* 'partner', *pośmiertny* 'post-mortal' – [rtn], *klątwa* 'excommunication' – [ntf], *popędliwy* 'hot-tempered' – [ndl'], *pogardliwy* 'scornful' – [rdl'], *kształtny* 'well-proportioned' – [wtn], *mdlić* 'feel sick' – [mdl'].

In comparison with (11) the rule is so broad now that we must check
whether there are no restrictions on what type of obstruent must precede
the dental stop: the phonotactic constraints operative if the right environment
is limited to coronal nasals (as is the case in (11)) are not operative any longer:
along with *wszystko* 'everything', which may become [fšisko], we get *haftka*
'hook and eye'. This, however, does not simplify: *[xafka] is not a possible
pronunciation. Thus the conditioning obstruent has to be limited to coronal
continuants.

In short, the phonostylistic dental stop deletion is the following:

$$(12) \quad \begin{bmatrix} -\text{contin} \\ -\text{del rel} \\ +\text{coron} \\ +\text{anter} \end{bmatrix} \rightarrow \phi \quad / \quad \langle C \rangle \quad \begin{bmatrix} +\text{obstr} \\ +\text{coron} \end{bmatrix} \quad - \quad \begin{bmatrix} +\text{cons} \\ \langle +\text{contin} \rangle \end{bmatrix}$$

The rule correctly excludes words like *strona* 'page', *zdrajca* 'traitor' ([r] is a
continuant, hence the extended specification with angle brackets is considered
– the environment is not met), *wdmuchnąć* 'blow in', *stlić się* 'burn down
slowly' – here the segmental environment is met but the rule does not apply
due to the presence of an internal word boundary (cf. Rubach 1974).

A few derivations sum up our discussion of rules (11) and (12):

	chlusnąć	*przyjezdny*	*wszystko*	
	'splash'	'visiting'	'everything'	
	/-st+n–/	/–zd+n–/	/–stk–/	
	s+n	–	–	Rule (11)
Slow speech				
forms:	sn	zdn	stk	
	–	zn	sk	Rule (12)

In sum, the only correct solution is to postulate a rule like (11) as a
legitimate rule of Polish phonology. The fact that the rule is heavily opaque
(case (i) of Kiparsky's principle) is a virtue rather than a drawback in the
analysis. Opacity makes a prediction that the exceptions to (11) will be
regularized and this is actually attested in casual and/or rapid speech. We can
make further hypotheses about sound change in the diachronic sense. One
may expect that all the items which are now regularized only phonostylistically
will tend to become regular with respect to the obligatory phonological rule,
i.e. the /stn/, /zdn/ clusters will be simplified by rule (11) in all cases. Costly
markings for exceptionality will be pushed out of the lexicon.

In this connection it is worth mentioning that in the diachronic sense rule

(11) has already produced some changes in underlying representations. Ułaszyn (1956:43) quotes *Gniezno* (a name) — [zn], *poczesny* 'honorary', *rosnę* 'I grow' — [sn] as coming originally from *Gniezdno* — [zdn], *poczestny, rostnę* — [stn]. These items do not have cognate words where the dental stop would surface phonetically[11]. Consequently, /t, d/ cannot be postulated as underlying. This is not true for other examples in rule (11). For them we do have alternations, viz. *chlusnąć* 'splash' (perf.) — *chlustać* 'splash' (imperf.), *bolesny* 'painful' — *boleść* 'pain' (cf. Gussmann 1973). If we assume that obligatory phonological rules may originate from phonostylistic rules then rules (11) and (12) are an interesting case. A part of the environment of (12) has separated out and has given rise to the obligatory phonological rule (11).

In conclusion, let us once more draw attention to some of the more important theoretical issues discussed in this paper. It has been shown that Kiparsky's principles of opacity and transparency make correct predictions with respect to sound changes which take place in casual and/or rapid speech. Whenever phonostylistic processes eliminate opacity produced by obligatory phonological rules it seems reasonable to expect that a sound change in the diachronic sense will ensue. If, however, there are items which remain as exceptions with respect to phonostylistic rules when their opacity is not likely to be soon eliminated (*pronunciation* in our discussion of palatalizations, *Irenka* 'Irene', *panienka* 'miss' (dimin.), *tkanka* 'tissue', *wanienka* 'bath-tub' (dimin.) — all having [n] instead of the expected [ŋ], which is exceptional with respect to both obligatory and phonostylistic nasal assimilations in Polish (cf. Rubach 1977)). In other words, opacity makes predictions with respect to phonostylistic changes; if these turn out to be transparent then one may further hypothesize about diachronic changes. The attested changes in *Gniezno, rosnę*, etc., give plausibility to such hypotheses. There seems to exist evidence (see our discussion of /ndn/ simplifications in Polish) that obligatory phonological rules may originate from phonostylistic rules through the separating out of some portion of the environment of a phonostylistic rule which then becomes established as the environment of an obligatory rule. Casual and/or rapid speech changes may be used in cases of heavy opacity as an argument for or against positing a minor rule or admitting a phonologically productive rule with a very large number of exceptions. In sum, it is not only necessary from the descriptive point of view but also revealing from the point of view of linguistic theory to clearly distinguish between obligatory and phonostylistic processes in language. The latter have received attention in phonological considerations only very recently (the works of Zwicky, Stampe, Dressler) and certainly deserve further exploration.

Notes

1. There are considerable differences between British and American English with respect to palatalizations. Thus Chomsky – Halle (1968:228) quote *emaciate* as typically having only [š] phonetically. British sources (cf. the *English Pronouncing Dictionary*) allow [si], i.e., [ši] is a phonostylistic variant in this word.
2. As argued in Rubach (1974) *prettier, easier* etc. have a word- rather than a plus-boundary. This excludes them from the domain of both obligatory and phonostylistic gliding rules.
3. In the Chomsky – Halle analysis (6) should be interpreted as /i/ deletion since, for example, *tedious* is represented phonetically with final [ɨyəs]. We shall leave this problem open since it is not clear to what extent such representations would be accurate for British English (cf. *English Pronouncing Dictionary*).
4. In this case and in many others (cf. *associative, associate, easier*) a later rule will change [i] to [j].
5. Rule (8) may also apply to *during* if it appears in a sentence in a relatively unstressed position.
6. According to Dobson (1968:707) palatalization was possible in this position in the 17th century: for some people *due* was homophonous with *Jew, duel* with *jewel*. Apparently a later change reintroduced nonpalatalized pronunciations, hence the restrictions in the present-day rule. See also footnote 7.
7. According to Lehmann (1970:350) ater the 17th century palatalization [s] was reintroduced in these words as a result of "spelling pronunciation". Perhaps it is generally true that the reintroduction of an earlier pronunciation seriously inhibits tendencies for a natural development in the items concerned.
8. Clearly the rule also applies in the context of the original nonanterior coronal obstruents as in *catch you, push you, oblige you* (cf. Sweet 1890:62).
9. In fact we have quoted only one part of Gussmann's rule. The other part refers to deletions of velar stops but these will be omitted as the situation with both obligatory and phonostylistic rules is parallel to the one which we present in our discussion of dental stops.
10. If we were dealing with a minor rule such as plural fricative voicing in English (cf. Schane 1973:109) this would not be true.
11. This may not be true about *poczesny*, since we have the word *cześć* 'honor'. It is not clear whether these items should be related by a via rule or by productive morphological processes. I consider the first alternative to be better.

References

Benni, T.
    1964   *Fonetyka opisowa języka polskiego*[4] [Descriptive phonetics of Polish] (Warszawa: Ossolineum).
Biedrzycki, L.
    1974   *Abriss der polnischen Phonetik* (Warszawa: Wiedza Powszechna).
Chomsky, N. – M. Halle
    1968   *The sound pattern of English* (New York: Harper and Row).
Jones, D.
    1969   *English pronouncing dictionary*[13] (Ed.: A. C. Gimson) (London: Dent).
Dobson, E. J.
    1968   *English pronunciation 1500–1700*[2] (Oxford: Clarendon Press).

336   Jerzy Rubach

Gussmann, E.
    1973   A phonology of consonantal alternations in English and Polish. [Unpublished Ph.D. dissertation, M. Curie-Skłodowska University, Lublin.]
Kiparsky, P.
    1971   "Historical linguistics", in: A survey of linguistic science (Ed.: W. O. Dingwall) (College Park, Md.: University of Maryland), pp. 577–649.
    1973   "Abstractness, opacity and global rules", in: Three dimensions of linguistic theory (Ed.: O. Fujimura) (Tokyo: TEC Company), pp. 57–86.
Labov, W.
    1972   Sociolinguistic patterns (Philadelphia: University of Pennsylvania Press).
Lehmann, W. P.
    1970   "Change in phonological systems", in: English linguistics (Eds.: H. Hungerford et al.) (Glenview: Scott, Foresman and Co.), pp. 338–360.
Ohala, J. J.
    1974   "Experimental historical phonology", in: Historical phonology 2 (Eds.: J. M. Anderson – C. Jones) (Amsterdam -North-Holland), pp. 353–390.
Rubach, J.
    1974   Variability of consonants in English and Polish. [Unpublished Ph.D. dissertation, Warszawa.]
    1976   "Overkill in phonology", in: Papers and studies in contrastive linguistics 5 (Ed.: J. Fisiak) (Poznań: Uniwersytet im. A. Mickiewicza), pp. 39–46.
    1977   "Rule ordering and concrete derivations in phonology", in: Linguistica Silesiana 2 (Katowice: Uniwersytet Śląski), pp. 77–90.
Schane, S. A.
    1973   Generative phonology (Englewood Cliffs, N.J.: Prentice-Hall).
Selkirk, E. O.
    1972   The phrase phonology of English and French. [Unpublished dissertation, MIT.]
Sweet, H.
    1890   A primer of spoken English (Oxford: Clarendon Press).
Ułaszyn, H.
    1956   Ze studiów nad grupami spółgłoskowymi [Investigations of consonant groups] (Wrocław: Ossolineum).

ROBERT P. STOCKWELL

Perseverance in the English vowel shift

Foreword. There are those who will think I am beating a dead horse. 'What?!
The vowel shift again? Surely if Chomsky and Halle didn't settle it, then
Labov must have!' But I don't think it is settled. I don't think this paper will
settle it either, so I want to do something that is a bit outside the regularly
accepted style of academic argumentation. I want to try to establish a different kind of **feel** about what it means to be a vowel shift. No flip-flop rules,
no variable rules, no statistics — just typological characterization of the
varieties of pronunciation that the system allows, hopefully thereby defining
properties that are the unique medium within which this kind of vowel
shifting is possible or at least natural. In the sense that one can then say something about why **these** kinds of changes occur rather than other imaginable
ones, it is explanatory, though, of course, not in the sense of being able to
say why a particular variant is chosen over other system-available variants at
a particular time.

My thesis is that the changes in the pronunciation of stressed English
syllabic nuclei usually summarized as 'the vowel shift' and considered to have
occurred between the death of Chaucer and the birth of Shakespeare are
described incorrectly in all standard sources in three respects:

I. Chronology. The vowel shift occurred no more at the usually cited dates
than at any other date in the documented history of English. That is, it
did occur then, and also (equally, I believe) over the past 200 years, or
over the 200 years between the birth of Alfred and the death of Aelfric,
or any other period of that length. This kind of vowel shifting is a
pervasive and persevering characteristic of vowel systems of a certain type.
II. Typology. Though I bow to the standard wisdom that we cannot recapture
the phonetic shape of history, I am not certain that I believe it, really,
and I think maybe an educated guess at the phonetics of history is likely

to be more accurate than certain other guesses that contemporary
scholars are willing to hazard (e.g., the speculation of Labov *et al.* [1972]
that speakers maintained systematic surface distinctions even where no
evidence exists to support these contrasts and where among living
speakers all perceptual tests fail to reveal the existence of similar distinctions; or the converse speculation of Halle [1962], and of Lass — Anderson
[1975], that speakers maintained systematic abstract distinctions even
where the surface forms were identical). We know an enormous amount
about contemporary phonetic facts of English. Without overwhelming
evidence to the contrary — which then boils down to an argument about
the point at which you're willing to be overwhelmed by certain interpretations of orthography and orthoepistic evidence (my own position
is spelled out in Stockwell — Barritt [1955, 1961]) — we must assume
that typological characteristics of contemporary pronunciation are the
best guide to historical pronunciation, and that vowel shifts now in
progress are the most informative evidence about the nature of vowel
shifts in history. The standard wisdom, claiming that there was a long/
short dichotomy as well as a full complement of diphthongs, and that the
vowel shift was restricted to a subset of long vowels, flies in the face of
probabilities based on observation of contemporary typological facts.

III. Causation. There is no standard wisdom on this point, though many
explanations have been offered. I have offered mini-versions of my own
explanation in various publications (in particular 1961 and 1964). Mine
is close enough to that of Labov *et al.* (1972) about chain-shifting that
perhaps I can relate theirs to mine now in a useful way. I will confine
my claims to the specifically English chain-shifts. I believe these claims
also cover the similar phenomena of other Germanic dialects. I do not
think most of the non-Germanic shifts to which Labov *et al.* refer are of
the same type at all: I believe they require different explanations and
do not yield to the generalizations that are correct for English and
much of Germanic. In essence, my hypothesis is that vowel shifting of
the English type occurs only in vowel systems where there is a fundamental opposition between in-gliding diphthongs and out-gliding diphthongs, with a ceaseless conflict between glide maximization (the **perceptual** ideal) and glide minimization (the **productive** ideal).[1] That is, the
two perceptually optimal in-gliding types [ia] and [ua], and the two
perceptually optimal out-gliding types [ai] and [au], cause concentric
forces of movement to be set up: e.g., [æə] moves upward in its
first element, to approximate [ia], while [ii] moves downward in its
first element, to approximate [ai]; and correspondingly in the back [ɔə]
→ [ua] and [uu] → [au]. Under the conflicting productive motivation of

glide minimization, a diphthong may shift from one set to the other: e.g., [æ̯u̯], with shortening in the production of the glide and loss of rounding, will be perceived as in-gliding (i.e., → [æə]). I claim that all stages of shifting in the 'tense' vowel system of English are motivated by one of these ideals (the tense vowel system is exactly the system of diphthongs, under my interpretation). A vowel can 'drop out' of the flow, so to speak, only by losing its glide (and becoming a member of the non-shifting set of simple vowels);[2] the system can change (as it has in some Germanic dialects, apparently including the Modern High German school standard but not most of the local dialects) by stabilizing minimal diphthongs as long vowels – at which point vowel shifting of this type ceases; and new diphthongs may be created, and become a part of the flow, by various processes of 'lengthening' (= in-glide accretion) and 'vocalization' (= development of out-glides from consonants).

I. Chronology

Consider the most conspicuous feature of the shift, the putative 'diphthongization' and lowering of ME $\bar{\imath}$ and $\bar{u}$ to [əy] and [əw] respectively.[3] The evidence of the 17th- and 18th-century orthoepists[4] unambiguously indicates that the shift was no further along than, say, [ʌy] and [ʌw], possibly only [əy] and [əw].[5] In Southern and South Midland American dialects of Modern English, ME $\bar{u}$[6] turns up most commonly as [æw]; in Cockney (Sivertsen 1960) as [æw] or [ɛw]. In Cockney and its Australian relatives, ME $\bar{\imath}$ turns up as [ɔy], where most dialects have [ay], a few [ʌy]. Now, at what point is it 'the' vowel shift? At the chronologically later end of the shift, it is simply not possible to say when the shift had finished occurring. It occurred, and occurred, and it's still occurring.

At the earlier end of the shift, suppose we assume that the first stage was diphthongization of [i:] to [iy]. That would involve a typological shift which I will argue against below: but even allowing it, for the sake of argument, there was certainly a still earlier change which was either [iy] → [i:] or its converse, namely [i:] → [iy], in words like OE *stig* 'sty', *tigl* 'tile', *twiges* 'twice', *nigon* 'nine'. This change is never considered to be part of 'the' vowel shift. Why not? Presumably the answer is that the change is considered an 'isolated' merger to [i:] rather than to [iy]. (There was a corresponding merger in the back to which this whole discussion applies equally: OE *fugol* 'fowl', *sugu* 'sow', *bugan* 'bow', etc.) If, on the other hand, the merger was to [iy], it was quite literally the first stage of the vowel shift, even as traditionally formulated. We could then more readily see why the inherited OE *ī* became out-gliding (either on my assumption that it had been previously in-gliding [ih], or on the traditional view that it had been [i:]) – namely it merged with a pre-existing out-glide.

The source of most Middle English diphthongs was the 'vocalization' of *-g* (= [-y] or [-w] depending on the front/back dimension of the preceding vowel) and of *-w*:

OE *wæg, weg*	ME *wei, wai, way, wey*
dæg, deg	*dei, dai, day, dey*
bugan	*bowe*
bōga	*bough*
āgan	*owne*
snāwan	*snowe*
grōwan	*growe*
fēawe	*few, fiw*
nīwe	*new, niw*

Why should diphthongization be the natural outcome of vocalization with mid and low vowels but not with high? It is at least plausible that 'vocalization' in late Old English had already created high front and back out-gliding diphthongs and that what came to be noticed as the vowel shift of the 15th century (i.e., when we began to get spellings like *ei/ey* occasionally, and *ou/ow*, or the testimony of Hart in the 16th century) was the next step – regardless of whether that next step is to be correctly analysed as lowering or as centralizing or both. It seems quite likely to me that when the invention of printing 'froze' (relatively, at least) the spelling system, subsequent commentary about the divergence of phonetics from orthography singled out a change that is not in fact distinguishable from the identical change occurring at other periods.

Another example, this one arguing for perseverance of raising among English in-gliding vowels, is the exact parallel between what has happened to [æh] and [ɔh] in New York, and what happened to OE *ǣ/ēa* and *ā* well before the 15th century. The Old English vowels raised from low to mid between Old and Middle English times:

OE *lǣdan* 'to lead'	ME *lēden* ('long open e')
cēap 'cheap'	*cheep*
stān 'stone'	*stōn* ('long open o')

It doesn't matter much, at this stage of the argument, whether we think of these Old English vowels as 'long' or as 'in-gliding': those two characterizations are probably real variants of each other at the extremes of the vocalic space anyway. What matters is that we do **not** think of them as **out**-gliding, for two reasons: (1) there were already out-gliding diphthongs in existence, mainly from the vocalization source noted above, but also some originals like *grow* and some borrowings like *they* – the Old English 'long' vowels did not merge with these; and (2) if the glide is homorganic (i.e., [y] with front vowels, [w] with back vowels), out-gliding diphthongs do not characteristically have their vocalic element raised. This second point is not a circular argument, but simply an observation of what is manifestly true of those diphthongs that we know for sure were out-gliding in Old English and later (such as *grow, they*). Rather than raising the first segment, as in-gliding diphthongs do, these tend to **lower** and/or centralize the first element to exaggerate their diphthongal quality.

This Old English raising of *ǣ* and *ā* is surely not different in typology or motivation from the later stage which raises ME *ē* and *ō* to Early Modern English high vowels (there are only some differences of detail: see Stockwell (1961). Therefore we must conclude that an early stage of 'the' vowel shift occurred between Old and Middle English times. As Labov (1966) and Hubbell (1950) have persuasively documented, New York speech, beginning toward the end of the 19th century and continuing into this century, underwent such raising of the low front and low back in-gliding vowels in words like *grass, man, loss,* and *off,* with the result that the high extreme of the (æh) variable is [ɪh] and that of (ɔh) is [ʊh]. The phenomenon is, of course, not restricted to New York City. It was documented in the New England Atlas and has been widely noted along the entire Middle Atlantic seaboard. It is my impression that the educated upper-middle class norms at both formal and casual style levels for that area are now [eh] and [oh], precisely the stage that was reached by Middle English times for the Old English low front and low back 'long' vowels.

One does not need to restrict himself to recorded Old English for examples of early vowel shifting. The development of WGmc *au* to OE *ēa* (i.e., in my interpretation, [aw] → [æw], later [æw] → [æh] collapsing with inherited [æh] *ǣ*) was an instance of the same change that typically occurs to non-homorganic out-gliding diphthongs in the Germanic system – one that has occurred again in various parts of the English-speaking world (Cockney, southern England, southern and South Midland United States). This particular argument requires that Old English diphthongal spellings not be taken too literally, but it provides a natural interpretation of their history:

WGmc *iu* → OE *īe, īo*
[iw]   [iw], later [ih]

$$eu \rightarrow \quad \bar{e}o, \bar{i}o$$
$$[ew] \quad [ew], later [eh]$$

$$au \rightarrow \quad \bar{e}a$$
$$[aw] \quad [æw], later [æh]$$

The development of [aw] is quite like the later history of [aw] (from ME $\bar{u}$) in some parts of the deep South of the United States where words like *house* are pronounced [hæhs]. These typically are dialects where a maximum reduction in nonhomorganic out-glides has taken place, resulting in pronunciations like [bɔh] for *boy*, [ah] for *eye*, and the like.

The notion that there was a unified set of changes in the English 'long vowels' that can be specified for a beginning and end point in time is, then, misleading. **Much closer to the truth would be a characterization of a set of variable nuclei for any given period and dialect area, plus a summary of the range over which those variables operate for that period and dialect, and a route that specifies directionality between each period and its predecessor/ successor.**

II. Typology

What, then, are the properties of a vowel system that will be characterized by the English sort of vowel shift? Labov *et al.* (1972) correlate up-drift with a feature of 'peripherality' and down-drift with a feature of 'nonperipherality'. This feature is one I invented (Stockwell 1966) to explain the naturalness of systems containing front-unround and back-round vowels as the unmarked members of which parallel behavior is to be taken as natural. Labov *et al.*'s use of the feature for the shiftable nuclei of English, however, turns out to be entirely redundant. Their principles say:

I'. In chain shifts, peripheral vowels rise.
II'. In chain shifts, nonperipheral vowels usually fall.

But if we examine the entities to which they assign the positive value of this feature in their primary data — the data which was collected by phonetic observation, not historical inference, and therefore the only data relevant to making historical inferences — they are, without exception, in-gliding diphthongs. The nonperipheral ones are out-gliding diphthongs or short vowels.[7] Labov *et al.*'s principle IV, which allows tense or long vowels to develop in-glides as they rise from mid to high position, and its converse principles V and VI allowing diphthongs at the extremes of vocalic space to become monophthongs, simply have the effect of specifying the conditions under which we're allowed to count long monophthongs as legal variants of diphthongs. **The single perceptual principle that optimal glides tend to maximize the distance of the glide**[8] **predicts that Labov** *et al.*'s **principles I′ and II′ will be characteristic of a language with a vowel system of the English type.**[9] Given the optimal productive principle (the 'ease of articulation' principle that has been a standby of every theory of linguistic change since the early 19th century, in spite of the difficulties that exist in stating the limits on its operation) that gliding articulations tend to minimize the distance of the glide, their principles V and VI also have a natural explanation. Principle IV is probably incorrect as it stands: I think in-glides simply become more evident, not actually generated, as the nucleus starts from a higher point in the mouth. Principle III, that back vowels move to the front, is not involved in the standard English vowel shift except for unrounding. Indeed it is counter-indicated within diphthongs by the development of diphthongs like [oy] from ME *ī*, which surely must be predicted by the same principle that operates to give [ew] from ME *ū*. So while [ew] from [uw] illustrates back vowels moving to the front, [oy] from [iy] illustrates a counterflow of front vowels moving to the back. Principle III cannot be involved, nor is it needed, to express the regularity of these shifts (principles I′ and II′, as modified below, are sufficient):

Other instances like ME *ū* becoming Scots [üw], which is certainly a fronting, do support principle III, in the very same dialects where [ɪ] becoming [ʌ] would seem to counter it. It is not obvious how principle III is related to the others, which all have a clear typological unity and a plausible explanation for their existence.[10]

There is a typological point that I have made repeatedly since my first foray into the vowel-shift jungle (Stockwell – Barritt 1951), and few scholars ever seem to have been persuaded by it. Unfortunately, Lass – Anderson (1975), who are exceptions to the preceding acknowledgment of failure, conclude that while my typological principle was right, the consequences I drew from it were wrong. My principle is that Old English cannot have been a language with contrasts between both long and short vowels and long and short diphthongs, since no language is known to exist which has that set of contrasts. It's against the rules of historical linguistics, I trust, to reconstruct systems of types that are not attested among the languages we can observe at first hand. Chomsky – Halle (1968) also violate this principle, since their reconstruction of Hart's vowel system requires [e], [ey], [e:], and [e:y] and correspondingly the mid-back vowels (p. 263). This typological conclusion has little bearing on the vowel shift (unless you think it happened as described by Chomsky – Halle), since the entities in question are the 'short diphthongs' which had, by everyone's view, dropped out of contention before the relevant vowel shifts took place. But this particular principle has a corollary: not only do you not reconstruct systems that are now unattested, you also don't reconstruct systems that are different from the type a language now has unless you can show both how the system changed and very strong evidence to support the claim that in fact it did change. I am talking, of course, about surface or near-surface phonologies: with the unconstrained imagination that freely reigns in the abstract phonologies of recent years, there is no basis for comparison between systems except at something like the taxonomic phonemic level (or, equivalently, that level within a derivation where only phonetically-motivated exceptionless rules remain to be applied).

Given this corollary, and the perceptual/productive conflict outlined above, it is possible to make typological generalizations about what types of variation are to be expected for a given norm (i.e., what the range is over which each type of variable can be expected to operate); and about what the natural routes are toward new norms (i.e., to what extent the direction of change is predictable). In particular, given a phonological system containing V, Vh, and Vy/w, we expect these variants to exist and to be favored in the directions indicated:

1. The V of Vh and nonhomorganic Vy/w drifts upward. (Note that this subsumes principle I' of Labov et al. [1972], but goes beyond it to include the nonhomorganic Vy/w which constitute behavior contradictory to their principle. They try to handle it by establishing a hierarchy of principles [p. 159], with the feature of tenseness overriding peripherality. But the correct interaction is between perceptual and productive principles. In effect, to explain the upward drift of [ɔy] and [æw], they must consider them to be [+PERIPH] along with [ɔh] and [æh], though [ay], [ey], etc. are [−PERIPH]. Such juggling makes the peripherality feature vacuous, like the tensity feature in reference to in-glides vs. out-glides [both should be tense relative to the 'short' or 'lax' vowels].)
2. The V of homorganic Vy/w drifts downward. (This is equivalent to Labov et al.'s principle II' minus the lax vowel claim of that principle.)
3. Homorganic glides at the extremes of the vowel quadrilateral alternate

with and may come to be stabilized as nongliding long vowels ([iy uw æh ah ɔh]. Minimization of in-glides coincides in these same vowels (this explains why sets like [ih], [iy], and [i:] are co-existing variants that initiate new downdrifts, since they are perceptually ill-sorted).

4. Minimization of out-glides produces new in-glides (e.g., [æw] → [æh]), resulting in variation between *Vy/w* and *Vh*. There is never unconditioned variation between *Vy* and *Vw* without intermediate *Vh* (transition, historically).

III. Causation

I do not propose to make any claim whatever about causation in the sense of what the social setting might be for a particular favoring of variant X or variant Y. This will rarely if ever be recoverable from the past, even though it can, because of Labov's extraordinarily insightful efforts and methods, be tagged with considerable precision for those on-going changes that we have the time and manpower to investigate currently. Neither do I have anything to say about the phonetic environments that favor, and that lead the way, in the raising of *Vh*. I am persuaded that Labov *et al.*'s characterization of the favoring environments indeed has a purely phonetic basis of the type that recently Ohala (1974, 1975) and much earlier Schuchardt (Vennemann – Wilbur 1972) argue for, with secondary change (i.e., spread) coming about by borrowing and analogy.

But it strikes me as highly interesting that so much of the same sort of change and even the very same changes should have occurred and recurred in English (and in most of the Germanic languages) for such a long time; what is the nature of their perseverance? Somehow they must be 'natural' changes in the same sense that assimilation and other 'conditioned' changes are natural. The perseverance must be a function of coherence within the vowel system itself, with the essential properties of the system having changed little or not at all. The possibilities of vowel change in general are very rich, and when we find that a language has strongly favored, over a huge geographic area and long time span, a very small subset of these theoretical possibilities, and has used them over and over again, we want to know why. My explanation, as is known from my earliest publications on this subject, is that the vowel system of Old English – I would say, in fact, of Proto-Germanic – was not at all a system of long–short oppositions, with a set of long–short diphthongs, all out-gliding (in fact, all to [-w] under a conservative interpretation of the *io, eo* spellings), but rather a system of simple vowels with both in-gliding and out-gliding diphthongs. What has been added to that view in this presentation is coherence in the explanation of the possible shifts through generalizing Labov *et al.*'s principles of chain-shifting under competing principles of diphthong optimization, namely perceptual and productive principles. Both are often cited in the literature on sound change but not, so far as I know, united elsewhere to account for these particular constraints on variation within vowel systems of this specific type. Nor, so far as I know, have other students of historical Germanic tried to explain the perseverance of these sound changes (if they perceived perseverance as existing at all) as being guaranteed and predicted by the typological properties of the system. The scholars who saw it first and most clearly were George L. Trager and Henry Lee Smith, Jr., though they published the historical consequences of their views very fragmentarily (the only item I know is Trager – Smith 1950). The kind of phonological theory they espoused is unfashionable these days. Because of the variable-rule feature-notation Labov has adopted, his views may appear to be closer to more recent kinds of phonology: but the substance of his claims about chain-shifting, at least, and the kinds of phonetic realities his chain-shifts operate on, are quite close to Trager-Smith views and to their development in the history of English that I continue to pursue. It seems to me that abstract phonologies have a great deal to say about morphophonemic alternations but that they tend to obscure the surface system that is the residence of regularity in and motivation of sound change.

Notes

1. It is the interaction between these two that Labov *et al.* (1972) fail to capture, as I understand their explanation. See below, sections II and III, for further discussion. I mean my remarks to be supportive, not critical, of Labov's position, though in the effort to clarify and generalize my position I may appear to be more critical than I intend to be about his.
2. It only appears superficially that ME *ŭ* and ME *ŏ* have 'shifted' rather like the diphthongs. They merely unround, with some adjustments thereafter toward pre-existing or universally less marked norms. The simple nuclei do not remain absolutely stable, but the changes are differently motivated and differently activated. And they are in any case much more stable than the diphthongs, in the history of all the Germanic languages.
3. For convenience, I will hereafter write [y] for [i̦] and [w] for [u̦]. I think they also represent the best phonemicization of the data, but that conclusion is neither necessary to nor entailed by my argument. Also for convenience, I will write [h] for [ə].
4. Wolfe (1972) finds no orthoepistic support for my view that a central diphthong [ɨy]/[əy] is the stage that follows [iy]. That leaves any analysis stuck with the necessity to explain why [ey] from numerous sources did not collapse with the putative [ey] from ME *ī*. Several possibilities are more likely than the Labov *et al.* (1972) use of the peripherality feature: e.g., assign [ɛy] to *day* in contrast with [ey] in *die*. This question, though both unsettled and unsettling, does not affect the remainder of my argument.

5. I use [ʌ] to represent the vowel of MnAmerE *but, putt, mud*, which I would characterize as tense mid central unround. I use [ə] to represent a somewhat higher vowel than [ʌ], approximately [ɨ].

6. I refer to a historical vowel by its standard philological identification. This serves only the purpose of identification; it does not represent what is in my opinion the most informative symbolization of the best phonetic/phonemic reconstruction we can devise.

7. Labov *et al.* (1972) consider [o] → [ɔ] → [a] to be an instance of II′, which I find mysterious since I see no phonetic feature shared by these vowels and the usual down-drifting nonperipheral diphthongs like [ʌw], [ʌy]. One can make a case that ME *ŭ* → MnE [ʌ] in *but, cut, rub* is a 'falling', but more reasonably it is simply unrounding with subsequent normalization of the universally highly-marked high-central or high-back-unround vowel.

8. This principle, called 'functional nucleus-glide differentiation' by Labov *et al.* (1972), is very old in the metatheory of linguistic change. I am not yet sure who first enunciated it clearly, but at least Vendryes had it clear in 1902 (Keiler 1972:113).

9. Principles I′ and II′ are not in fact 'translations' (p. 106) of their first-stated I and II. The latter don't work at all, as far as I can see, whereas I′ and II′ **do** work because they correlate with in-gliding and out-gliding. That correlation does not exist for tense/lax, in any consistent way.

10. Principle III seems correct, nevertheless, given French [u] going to [ü] and the Scots example above. If it is correct, it would in principle support my view that the stage following OE/ME [uw] was a high-central diphthong rather than the orthoepistically supported [ow].

References

Chomsky, Noam A. – Morris Halle
  1968   *The sound pattern of English* (New York: Harper and Row).
Goyvaerts, D. L. – Geoffrey Pullum
  1974   *Essays on The sound pattern of English* (Ghent: E. Story – Scientia).
Halle, Morris
  1962   "Phonology in a generative grammar", *Word* 18: 54–72.
Hubbell, Alan F.
  1950   *The pronunciation of English in New York City: Consonants and vowels* (New York: King's Crown Press).
Keiler, Alan R.
  1972   *A reader in historical and comparative linguistics* (New York: Holt, Rinehart and Winston).
Labov, William
  1966   *The social stratification of English in New York City* (Washington, D.C: Center for Applied Linguistics).
Labov, William – Malcah Yaeger – Richard Steiner
  1972   *A quantitative study of sound change in progress* (Philadelphia: U.S. Regional Survey).
Lass, Roger – John M. Anderson
  1975   *Old English phonology* (Cambridge: Cambridge University Press).
Ohala, J. J.
  1974   "Experimental historical phonology", in: *Historical linguistics* 2: *Theory and description in phonology* (Eds.: J. M. Anderson – C. Jones) (Amsterdam: North-Holland).
  1975   "Phonetic explanations for nasal sound patterns", in: *Nasalfest: Papers*

from a Symposium on Nasals and Nasalization (Eds.: C. A. Ferguson –
L. M. Hyman – J. J. Ohala) (Stanford, California).
Sivertsen, Eva
    1960   *Cockney phonology* (Oslo: Oslo University Press).
Smith, M. E. (ed.)
    1973   *Studies in linguistics: Studies in honor of George L. Trager* (The Hague:
           Mouton).
Stockwell, Robert P.
    1961   "The Middle English 'long close' and 'long open' mid vowels", in: *Studies in*
           language and literature (Austin: University of Texas Press).
    1964   "On the utility of an overall pattern in historical English phonology", in:
           Proceedings of the Ninth International Congress of Linguists, Cambridge,
           Mass., August 27–31, 1962 (Ed.: H. C. Lunt) (The Hague: Mouton),
           pp. 663–671.
    1966   "Problems in the interpretation of the Great English Vowel Shift". [Presented
           at the 1966 Texas Conference on English Phonology. Published with revisions
           in Smith (1973: 344–362); reprinted with addendum in Goyvaerts – Pullum
           (1974: 331–353).]
Stockwell, R. P. – C. W. Barritt
    1951   *Some Old English graphemic-phonemic correspondences*: æ, ea, *and* a
           (= *Studies in Linguistics, Occasional Papers* 4).
    1955   "The Old English short digraphs: Some considerations", *Language* 31:
           372–389.
    1961   "Scribal practice: Some assumptions", *Language* 37: 75–82.
Trager, George L. – Henry Lee Smith, Jr.
    1950   "A chronology of Indo-Hittite", *Studies in Linguistics* 8: 61–70.
Vendryes, J.
    1902   "Réflexions sur les lois phonétiques", in: *Mélanges linguistiques offerts à*
           Antoine Meillet (Paris), pp. 115–131. [Translated in Keiler (1972: 109–120).]
Vennemann, Theo – T. H. Wilbur
    1972   *Schuchardt, the Neogrammarians, and the transformational theory of phono-*
           logical change (Frankfurt: Athenäum).
Wolfe, Patricia
    1972   *Linguistic change and the Great Vowel Shift in English* (Berkeley/Los Angeles:
           University of California Press).

GUY A. J. TOPS

The origin of the Germanic dental preterit: Von Friesen revisited

1. Preliminaries

1.0. *Introduction*[1]

Historical linguistics always involves a certain amount of guesswork. When the available data are insufficient to solve a particular problem, one can of course throw in the sponge and accept total defeat. But this is not very attractive. It is also possible to acknowledge frankly that one is guessing, and to minimize the chance of guessing wrong by imposing a number of restrictions upon oneself.

The insoluble problem (Penzl 1972:35) I will be dealing with in this paper is that of the origin of the Germanic dental preterit. There are three restrictions I want to impose upon myself. First, I have tried to propose a formally correct solution that is neither contradicted by itself nor by known facts. This may seem obvious, but I have shown elsewhere (Tops 1974) that most if not all solutions presented thus far are contradictory. In this paper I will refrain from dealing in detail with other theories, except in the appendix, where I will, for reasons explained there, discuss Rauch's (1972) article. Secondly, I have attempted a solution which is simple and straightforward in that it requires little or no analogy and only a very limited mixture of forms, which, I hope, is not controversial. It is also simple in that only one origin of the Germanic dental preterit is posited rather than a multiple origin in the different Germanic languages. Incidentally, positing that the formation began in one language (viz., Proto-Germanic) entails at least the probability that the dental form has but a single origin. (For the disadvantages of assuming an Indo-European origin, see § 1.3.) Thirdly, I have tried to please linguists of different persuasions. It seems to me that a solution which is acceptable to a great many people, who may have very different notions about the nature of language and language change, has a better chance than one that is acceptable only to the orthodox generativist or the diehard taxonomist.

To be honest, however, I hereby give advance warning to those who refuse
to recognize all and any form of grammatical conditioning that they will
not find my solution to their liking. But before they turn away from this
paper, I would advise them to let themselves be convinced by Anttila
(1972:77f.), who establishes beyond reasonable doubt that grammatically
conditioned sound change does occur.

If all this sounds very promising, it remains necessary to stress once again
that the problem is indeed ultimately insoluble for lack of data, and that the
"solution" I offer remains to a large extent guesswork. I do not think that it
is worse than some of the previous solutions, which were often presented with
much more self-confidence than I would venture to show. That it has actually
a better chance of being correct is something I can merely hope.

1.1. *The dilemma*

The dental of the Germanic "weak" preterit appears in the Germanic languages
as *d* (Go. *nasida* 'I saved'), *t* (Go. *mahta* 'I could' — formally *I might*), *þ* (Go.
kunþa 'I could') and *ss* (Go. *wissa* 'I knew'). The first, *d*, points back to IE *dh*,
via Grimm's law, or to IE *t*, via Grimm's and Verner's laws. The others all point
unambiguously to IE *t*: IE *t* normally becomes PGmc. *þ* (Grimm's law), but
remains *t* under certain circumstances; as for *ss*, it is derived from IE *dt* or *tt*.
All this is generally accepted.

The next point to be made is that the long Gothic forms of the dual and
plural indicative and of the optative *somehow* contain the preterit of the verb
*dōn 'to do'. Thus the ending of Go. 1 pl. ind. *nasi-dēdum* 'we saved' is to be
compared with OS *dēdun, dādun*, OE *dǣdon* and OHG *tātum* 'we did'. This
is not generally accepted; yet all other explanations of the long Gothic endings are so intricate and tortuous that they must be rejected, especially in
view of the remarkable coincidence that Gothic has short forms (of the type
1 sg. *nasida*) where Old Saxon and Old High German have short stem vowels
in their past paradigms of *dōn* and *tuon* (1 sg. OS *deda*, OHG *teta*). Even if
it is not immediately clear how these two facts are connected, I find it hard
to believe that they are not connected at all.

The Proto-Germanic verb **dōn* is derived from the Indo-European root
*dhē-/dhō-. This, then, is the dilemma: there are forms that require us to go
back to IE *t* and others which we can derive only from IE *dh*.

1.2. *Conceivable solutions*[2]

Theoretically, such a dilemma can be solved in two ways: by invoking a
mixture of *t* and *dh*-forms and by reducing one of these to the other by
means of a sound law. The latter alternative has been attempted only by
Collitz (1912), who later seems to have abandoned his sound law (see Tops

1974:51–53), and by Rosén (1957) and Wisniewski (1963), who both admit that their solutions are only partial.

Several kinds of mixtures could be proposed. (a) It may be assumed that an Indo-European *t*-formation lies at the basis of the dental preterit and that this formation was subsequently influenced by PGmc. *dōn* (<IE *dhō-). This is currently the most popular solution, defended by, among others, Wagner (1960), Watkins (1962), Bech (1963), Ball (1968), Hiersche (1968), Meid (1971) and Rauch (1972), although these authors differ widely as to the details. (b) Conversely, one may assume that the verb *dōn* lies at the origin of the endings and that *t*-formations later intruded. This is the position of most supporters of the classical composition theory, which seems somewhat discredited nowadays. The latest paper to take this position was that of Hermann (1948), but in the nineteenth and in the beginning of the twentieth century some of the greatest names in the history of historical linguistics held this view (see Collitz 1912). Two fairly recent Gothic handbooks also continue to uphold it, Hempel (1966) timidly, Krahe (1967) boldly.

Whereas (a) and (b) are secondary mixtures (that is to say, they suppose either *t* or *dh* to be original, and subsequently add the other), (c) through (e) are true mixtures. (c) It can be supposed that some forms are derived from Indo-European *t*-forms and others from Indo-European *dh*-forms. The best known, most recent, and perhaps most notorious defender of this position seems to have been Hirt (1932). (d) It is also conceivable that all dental preterits go back to formations containing IE *t* and that some of these also contained IE *dh*, but nobody has ever proposed anything like this. (e) The last conceivable solution would be to derive all preterits from a formation containing IE *dh* and to allow for some of these to contain IE *t* as well. This idea, in a way the converse of (d), was proposed by von Friesen (1925).

A survey of all these conceivable solutions is given in the following table.

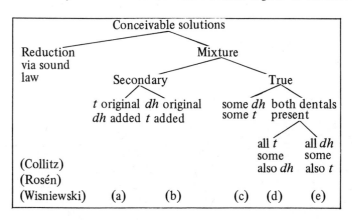

1.3. *Methodological evaluation of the conceivable solutions*

Methodologically, the reduction via a sound law would be the most attractive solution. Unfortunately, Rosén's accounts for a very limited number of forms only. Wisniewski claims to be able to solve all problems except for three forms (Go. *wissa, bauhta* 'I bought' and OHG *tohta* '(me) thought'). Even if we accept all her solutions — and Hiersche (1968) and I (Tops 1974) are of the opinion that one should not — we must notice that she is forced to posit an Indo-European sound change and hence that the Germanic dental preterit is an Indo-European formation. In the absence of other dental preterits in Indo-European languages, corresponding to the Germanic one, this is such a methodological disadvantage that it surely cancels whatever advantage the reduction via a sound law might have.

True mixtures are obviously preferable to secondary ones, as the latter must explain how the introduction of *dh* (in solution (a)) or of *t* (in solution (b)) came about.[3] Among the true mixtures, solution (c) will have a very hard time explaining such forms as Go. *kunþēdum* 'we could', which has two dentals, *þ* pointing to IE *t* and *d* (presumably) to IE *dh*. This leaves us with alternative (e).

Of the four mixtures proposed this is, on the face of it, the most attractive one. It becomes even more attractive when we notice that the forms with and without *t* are for von Friesen forms of very much the same kind.

2. An outline of von Friesen's theory

2.0. *Introduction*

In this section I will present an outline of von Friesen's theory. I will not enter into details; instead, I will concentrate on a number of objections which have been raised to it but which I think to be invalid. This will, I hope, salvage a number of essential points of von Friesen's theory, which I will need later on in presenting my own.

2.1. *Starting point*

The starting point of von Friesen's theory is that of the classical composition theory: the dental preterit was originally a Proto-Germanic compound consisting of a verbal noun plus the perfect tense of **dōn.*

In a way this very starting point is doubtful, for it seems to be the general view that in the Germanic languages compounds consisting of a noun and a verb are very late.[4] Meid (1967:35—36) makes a possible exception precisely for the dental preterit. Lowe (1972:216) bluntly says that this sort of compounds was a development in the dialects. Voyles (1974:169) reconstructs but one type of noun-verb compound in West Germanic, but it is one expressing an S-V relation, and of course West Germanic is not Proto-Germanic.

Yet this objection cannot weigh very heavily. In the first place, periphrasis is already an Indo-European device. Secondly, periphrasis by means of the verb *do* occurs all over Germanic (Hiersche 1968:404). These two arguments are largely sufficient to allow *do*-periphrasis in Proto-Germanic, even if the actually attested forms can be shown to be independent of each other. For it can then be argued that the tendency to periphrastic formation was always present, in Indo-European, in Proto-Germanic, and in the attested daughter languages, and that it rose to the surface at different times and in different places, among others in the dental preterit.

The step from periphrasis to compounding is not very great.[5] It must be borne in mind that the bound between the verbal noun and the periphrastic verb was very tight, the periphrasis serving to mark past tense. Indeed, the construction occurred with preterit-present and derived verbs, which could not be inflected for past tense.

2.2. The compound

Von Friesen made an original contribution to the composition theory in that he allowed two kinds of verbal nouns to appear as the first element of the compound. Before him, all the adherents of the composition theory had reconstructed the first element of the compound as related in some way to the verbal noun in IE *-onom*, which lies at the base of the Germanic infinitives. But to account for the dental preterits containing IE *t*, von Friesen invoked verbal nouns in IE *-ti* and *-tu*. The formal similarity between these verbal nouns and some dental preterits had already been noticed by Collitz (1912, chapter 2).

For von Friesen the second element of the compound was furnished by what used to be the Indo-European perfect. This is not exactly an uncontroversial point: several people have argued for invoking aorist forms, and Bech (1963: § 53) has posited an Indo-European imperfect to explain the endings of the dental preterit. I do not want to enter this polemic here.[6] Instead, I consider it sufficient to point out (a) with von Friesen, that all unassailable explanations of Germanic preterit endings involve Indo-European perfect forms; (b) that there is a large minority, if not a majority, of current scholarship that agrees with this position; and (c) that, keeping Occam's razor in mind, it is preferable to start from perfect forms if this can be done without too much inconvenience; I think this is quite possible.

2.3. The reduction of the compound

The reduction of the formidable compounds thus posited (e.g., **panhti-dedā^x*, **bruhtu-d̃edā^x*, **fullejo-d̃edā^x*, to use von Friesen's transcriptions) was von

Friesen's major problem. He tried to solve it by means of haplology and an accent attraction rule. As I will not retain any of these arguments, there is no need to present them here.[7]

2.4. *The endings*

The reconstruction of the endings and their development is a matter of detailed study and I think no two scholars will agree about each and every point. I deviate from von Friesen in a number of what I would call minor issues, but, as already indicated, I follow him in deriving the endings from what used to be the Indo-European perfect of *dhē-/dhō-*. Precisely this point has called forth a fundamental objection from Sverdrup (1929:28f.), which must here be rejected.

It is obvious that in the old Germanic languages the endings of the dental preterit differ a great deal from the past paradigm of the verb *do*. According to Sverdrup, the association between the forms of this independent paradigm and the endings of the Germanic dental preterit (if we derive the latter from the former) would have been so strong as to prevent the formal divergence we actually find.

But this point is not well taken. The transition from compounding to derivation may very well cause a weakening of the morpheme which loses its independent status. Lowe (1972:213, 222) makes this quite clear. As an example he uses PGmc. *līka-* 'body', which obtains the meaning 'having the body of' when it functions as a suffix. The development in the modern languages is obviously even more conclusive than in the older ones, adduced by Lowe. As an independent word, *līka-* developed into Du. *lijk* [lɛ.ˡk] 'corpse', Southern German *Leiche* 'burial' and English *like*. It is still a recognizable suffix in Du. *vrese-lijk* [lək] 'terrible' (lit. 'fear-like'), Ger. *bitter-lich* and English *bitter-ly*. In Du. *zulk*, Ger. *solch* and Eng. *such* the suffix has been reduced beyond recognition.

An example that is an even better contradiction of Sverdrup's objection can be found outside Germanic, viz., in the French conditional.[8] This paradigm is a development from an original compound consisting of the infinitive plus the imperfect of Lat. *habēre*, Fre. *avoir* 'to have'. Most forms of the French paradigm of *avoir* are direct continuations of the full forms of the Latin paradigm, but the endings of the conditional go back to reduced forms of this paradigm; compare

	Latin full forms	French full forms	Latin reduced forms	French reduced forms
Sg. 1	*habēbam*	*avais*	*-ēam*	*chanter-ais*
2	*habēbās*	*avais*	*-ēas*	*chanter-ais*

	Latin full forms	French full forms	Latin reduced forms	French reduced forms
Sg. 3	*habēbat*	*avait*	*-ēat*	*chanter-ait*
Pl. 1	*habēbāmus*	*avions*	*-eamus, -iamus*	*chanter-ions*
2	*habēbātis*	*aviez*	*-eatis, -iatis*	*chanter-iez*
3	*habēbant*	*avaient*	*-ēant*	*chanter-aient*

It is interesting that these reduced forms are described as regular phonetic developments (Fouché 1967:411) and that the reduction of the full form *habēbat to habēat* (the stage between the full Latin forms and the full French ones) is ascribed to "un phénomène de dissimilation dans les imparfaits dont le radical se terminait par la même consonne" (Fouché 1967:236).

3. Other arguments in favor of von Friesen's theory

3.0. *Introduction*
In § 1.3 I have stressed the methodological advantage of von Friesen's theory; § 2 was devoted to discarding basic objections to it. In this section I will discuss a number of arguments that should further recommend this theory to us.

3.1. *Formal arguments*
The formal argument that favors all variants of the composition theory has already been mentioned on p. 350: where the West Germanic past paradigm of **dōn* has a short stem vowel[9], the endings of the Gothic dental preterit are also short (cp. OS *deda*, Go. *nasida*); where this paradigm has a long stem vowel, the endings of the Gothic dental preterit are also long (cp. OS *dādun*, Go. *nasidēdum*).

Von Friesen's theory also has the advantage of accounting for the different ablaut gradations to be found in the stem of the dental preterit. As a general rule, verbal nouns in *-ti* had zero grade in the root, those in *-tu* had full grade and those in *-onom* also had full grade. But already in Indo-European times this rule had many exceptions (Meid 1967:151) so that it is impossible to trace for each individual word which root one should expect. Nor is this necessary for our purpose: it is sufficient to establish the general principle that these different verbal nouns can account for the different stem vowels in the dental preterit. The credit for this argument must go to von Friesen, although I have modified it somewhat.

3.2. *A semantic argument*
One of the major problems of the composition theory has always been the elucidation of the relation between the two elements of the compound. (This remained a problem for Hermann as late as 1948.) In von Friesen's theory

there is no such problem: it is a straightforward O-V relation, semantically transparent and uniform for all dental preterits.

3.3. *A confirmation?*

One of the most convincing and impressive arguments an historical linguist can ever encounter is a reconstruction that is subsequently confirmed by an attested form. I venture to suggest that three Gothic forms von Friesen was apparently unaware of may actually confirm his reconstructions. They are *faurhtidēdun* (Codex Argenteus, Luke 9:34; regular **faurhtēdun), usbauh-tidēdi* (Ambrosianus A, Gal. 4:5; regular **usbauhtēdi*) and *mahtēdēdeina* (Ambrosianus B, 2 Cor. 3:7; Ambrosianus A has the regular *mahtēdeina* here). I put forward this suggestion with considerable trepidation, since I am well aware that these three forms can be interpreted in several ways.

The form *faurhtidēdun* can be considered a regularization. The original infinitive of the verb meaning 'to fear' had no dental suffix, but forms like *faurhteiþ* (Matt. 8:26, Mark 16:6) and *faurhtjaina* (John 14:27) allows us to safely reconstruct a new infinitive **faurhtjan*, interpreted presumably as a denominal infinitive and containing the suffix *t*. *Faurhtidēdun* is then a regularization, according to this new infinitive, of the third person plural of the past.

This way of reasoning is unassailable. But it cannot be applied without further ado to *usbauhtidēdi* and *mahtēdēdeina*, since there are no forms that could lead us to set up secondary infinitives **bauhtjan* and **mahtjan*.[10]

An attempt could be made to explain *usbauhtidēdi* and *mahtēdēdeina* as regularizations of another type. As a general rule the preterit of weak verbs should be derived from the present. But, one could argue, *mahta* and *bauhta* are so irregular that they contain what are really preterit stems in their own right. *Usbauhtidēdi* and *mahtēdēdeina*, then, are regularizations in that they consist of the preterit stems plus the most frequent endings of the dental preterit, viz., those of the *jan*-verbs (*nas-idēdi* : *bauht-idēdi*). This requires us to read *mahtēdēdeina* as **mahtidēdeina*, but that is no problem in view of the frequent scribal alternation *i ~ ē*. In the first version of this paper I was willing to allow this reasoning as possibly valid; now, however, I think it is spurious. The flaw is that it compares two stems of very different kinds, viz., a dental stem (*bauht-, maht-*) and a non-dental stem (*nas-*). It should be borne in mind that the dental is the primary characteristic of the feature past. The only comparison of stems which is sensible, therefore, is that of *bauht-* and *maht-* with *nasid-*.[11]

Finally, it is obvious that *mahtēdēdeina* can be a simple scribal error of a very frequent type, namely the repetition of the identical segment *ēd* or *dē*. But the same cannot be claimed for the other two forms.[12]

It is acceptable to give separate explanations of these three forms. But it is preferable to explain them in a uniform way, as archaisms corresponding to von Friesen's reconstructions. (But see also § 4.4.) Also, it seems that this is the only way to account for *usbauhtidēdi*.

4. Von Friesen revisited

4.1. *The beginnings*
I put the beginnings of the dental preterit (that is, the intensive use of the periphrastic construction) very early, perhaps in the earliest period of Proto-Germanic, and certainly at a time before Proto-Germanic began to systematically use the verbal noun in IE *-onom*, PGmc. *-anam*, as an infinitive. That this was a fairly late development has recently been shown by Jeffers (1975). At that time all sorts of verbal nouns could be used in the periphrasis and there are good reasons to believe that the verbal nouns in *-ti* and *-tu* were so used. It is certain that the Germanic dental preterits whose dental goes back unambiguously to IE *t* are very old. They are irregular in that they have no medial vowel and often *t, þ* or *ss* instead of the far more frequent *d*. They occur with great frequency in all the Germanic languages. Finally, *t*'s typically occur in preterit-present verbs, a notoriously old category, whose Germanic infinitives are not direct continuations of Indo-European verbal nouns in *-onom*, but secondary infinitives formed in later times and modeled on Germanic infnitives in *-an(am)*. For all these reasons I claim that the oldest dental preterits were formed from verbal nouns in *-ti* and *-tu* plus the perfect tense of **dōn*.[13]

The reconstruction of this paradigm is problematic. I will not attempt an Indo-European construction since this is unnecessary, the dental preterit being a Germanic innovation. The Proto-Germanic forms I would like to propose are the following:

Sg. 1	**dedōm/dedēm*	Pl. 1	**dedōm-*
2	**dedōs/dedēs*	2	**dedōþ-*
3	**dedōþ/dedēþ*	3	**dedōn-*

This paradigm is very similar to that proposed by Knapp (1968:311). The following points require further discussion. (a) I accept, with Knapp and others, both *ē* and *ō* gradations; cp. Go. *slēpan/saislēp* and *lētan/lailōt*. (I omit the *ē* grade in the plural because I do not need it.) I grant that this is irregular. But then the verb **dōn* was irregular, whichever way it is looked at; witness the *ō* grade in the present.[14] (b) In the plural Watkins (1969: § 22) wants to reconstruct a reduplication with a long vowel, comparing Go. *dēdun* and OS *dādun* with Gatha-Av. *dādarə*, and in this he is followed by Meid (1971:86). I cannot evaluate his argumentation from the Indo-European point of view. But if one considers the consequences, within the Germanic languages, of positing an original 3 pl. PGmc. *dē¹dun* in combination with an original 2 sg. *dedōs* or *dedēs*, it will be seen that this combination causes immense problems for the explanation of certain later forms, notably 2 sg. OS *dādi* (OHG *tāti*) and 3 pl. OS *dedun*. Either it can be argued that the Old Saxon verb was reduplicating and then *dedun* is readily explained as containing a generalization of the short reduplicating vowel; but *dādi* stands unexplained. Or one could argue that the Old Saxon verb was strong and, given the general tendency of all the North West Germanic languages to give up reduplicating in favor of strong or weak preterits, this could be the wiser solution. In this view *dādi* presents no problems: in the strong verbs of the fourth and fifth classes the second person singular always has a long vowel. But now *dedun* cannot be explained. The reconstruction I am proposing offers no such problems: *dedōs* and *dedun* are considered old, reduplicating forms; *dādi* and *dādun* innovations, which occurred when the verb went from reduplicating to strong.[15] (See also below, § 4.3.)

4.2. The reduction of the t-forms, stage 1

4.2.0. Introduction
The next step required is a first reduction of the compounds of the type *banxtidedōm*. This cannot be justified phonologically; hence we must have recourse to morphological, grammatical conditioning.[15a]

4.2.1. Orthodox generativism
This is no problem for some generativists, who allow reference to be made "to the morphophonemic and/or superficial grammatical structure of relevant strings." The quote is from Postal (1968:233–34), who argues very forcefully for this possibility. Scholars who accept his argumentation will think it sufficient to state that the medial vowels of compounds consisting of a noun and a verb were dropped early in Proto-Germanic.

4.2.2. Functionalism
But this way of reasoning is not acceptable to many scholars. Campbell (1974), besides questioning the validity of Postal's examples (in his footnote 2), imposes a formal constraint on the morphological conditioning of sound change: "Morphological conditioning of sound change happens only in cases where an unrestricted sound change would eliminate important morphological

distinctions" (Campbell 1974:89). The examples in Anttila (1972:77f.) seem to corroborate this constraint.

The drop of the medial vowel I am proposing in the compound N + V can without any great trouble be described within this constraint. An unlimited drop of the medial vowel in compounds would tend to obscure the first element of that compound. This would be very awkward in a compound consisting, e.g., of $N_1 + N_2$ or of Adj. + N. Dropping the medial vowel in such a compound would formally separate N_1 or Adj. in that compound from uncompounded N_1 or Adj.; yet one would still want to perceive compounded N_1 or Adj. as identical to uncompounded N_1 or Adj. In our case, however, a formal separation of compounded *þanxt(i)- from the uncompounded noun was not so bad, because the entire compound was beginning to function as part of the inflection of a verb. It was far more important for the first part of *þanxt(i)dedōm to become associated with the verb *think* (I do not venture a Proto-Germanic reconstruction) than to remain associated with the uncompounded noun *þanxtiz.

4.2.3. Natural generative phonology

Insofar as the reduction I am proposing requires direct grammatical conditioning, it is unacceptable to the variant of natural generative phonology defended by Hooper (1973). She claims that any new rule that enters the language should be strictly phonetically motivated − that is, it should be statable in purely phonetic features −and therefore exceptionless. In order to explain the counter-examples to this strong regularity hypothesis, she makes the following claims: (a) It is necessary to distinguish between the result of a sound change, which may show irregularities, and a sound change in progress, which must not. (b) A new rule (which is always purely phonological, as stated above) enters the language as an optional rule. (c) (I quote:) "Very soon, the new rule runs headlong into the established morphophonological processes in the language and a conflict sometimes results, particularly if the output of the new rule obscures some morphological distinctions, or violates some other phonological constraints active in the grammar. When the new rule stabilizes as an obligatory process, the conflict must be resolved." (Hooper 1973:126)

Whether Hooper is right or wrong is something I do not want to discuss here. But it is possible to state the reduction I am proposing in terms that meet her claims. It would be easy to formulate a general rule in purely phonetic terms; roughly

$$\begin{matrix} \breve{V} \\ [- \text{stress}] \end{matrix} \Rightarrow \phi \; / \; \# \; [+ \text{stress}] \; \underline{\hspace{1cm}} (X) \; [+ \text{stress}] \; (Y) \; \#$$

(A short unstressed vowel is dropped when it is immediately preceded by a stressed syllable and followed (not necessarily immediately) by a stressed syllable.)

This rule, if applied, would precisely have the two results which Hooper claims will prevent its absolute generalization. It would blur morphological distinctions, viz., the structure of the first element of the compound (see the previous section). And its result would contain all sorts of medial consonant clusters which did not occur in Proto-Germanic.[16]

4.3. The reduction of the t-forms, stage 2

4.3.0. Introduction
After the first reduction *panxtidedōm has become *panxtdedōm, which one may safely assume to have been simplified, via *panxttedōm, to *panxtedōm.[17]

The status of this form is interesting. Functionally it is becoming a preterit, on a par with the ablauting preterits of the strong verbs; but its accentuation, which has two main stresses, suggests it is still a compound. It is from this ambiguous status that we must start when describing subsequent developments.

But before that, I must devote some attention to two phenomena whose role we must not lose sight of: the re-interpretation of *dedōm and the accentuation of the posited compounds.

4.3.1. *dedōm re-interpreted
The re-interpretation of *dedōm, originally reduplicating, as a strong verb of the fifth class [17a] poses no problems for North West Germanic. Because there the entire class of reduplicating verbs disappeared except for a few traces.

But in Gothic the reduplicating verbs constituted a viable class; so why should *dedōm have been re-interpreted there? Would it not be better to accept Watkins' view and assume an original long vowel in the preterit from the start? But as I have already explained (§ 4.1), this hypothesis creates problems for the explanation of other forms. Moreover, the problem posed by this transition is not exactly insurmountable. Parallel cases, that is to say, transitions of verbs from one viable class to another, perhaps even less viable, do occur. In certain Dutch dialects, for instance, the past tense of the verb maken 'to make', originally and regularly maakte (dental preterit) has become mīk (new ablaut, class VII), although obviously the dental preterits are the far more numerous and viable class. A better-known example is snuck used as the past of sneak by many Americans. No good "reason" for such transitions can be given; they can only be stated.

A second problem pertaining to this re-interpretation is its date, or better, its chronology relative to the second contraction (to be discussed in § 4.3.3). I place it before that second contraction in (pre-)Gothic, but after it in (pre-) North West Germanic. It might be objected that I am thereby putting the separation of the Germanic languages far too early, perhaps even before the Germanic accent shift (see below), and that, moreover, I am really positing two origins of the Germanic dental preterit.

However, van Coetsem (1970:15) has pointed out that the first differentiation between the Germanic languages must be placed before the Germanic accent shift. I think I am therefore justified in putting a relatively minor change such as the re-interpretation of one verb fairly early in one dialect and somewhat later in another.

As for the second objection, I am positing a single **origin** of the formation. It cannot be denied that at one point the Gothic and North West Germanic dental preterits diverged, and I see no fundamental objection to putting this **divergence** fairly early.

4.3.2. Accentuation of the compound
I have so far avoided marking the accents on my reconstructions. Von Friesen silently assumed that the first syllable of each element of the compound was stressed, and thus transcribed *ϕánhti-ðéðā^x. However, I put the origin of the formation in the earliest period of Proto-Germanic, that is, before Proto-Germanic shifted all its accents to the first syllables. In reduplicated forms the accent was originally on the root and not on the reduplicating syllable (Meid 1971:97f.), and thus I reconstruct *ϕánxtidedõm, later *ϕánxtedõm.[18]

4.3.3. The reduction proper
A form like *ϕánxtedõm was subject to the tendency to drop its medial vowel. Prokosch (1939:135) is clearly right when, discussing the developments in medial syllables, he writes: "In *Medial Syllables* conditions are so irregular that a general rule working with uniform consistency can hardly be established." However, one may cite a number of reasons why forms like *ϕánxtedõm were particularly hard pressed to drop their medial vowels. (a) The first syllables of forms of this type were always long, as they ended in the final root consonant plus *t*, belonging to the original suffix. It is generally accepted that medial vowels were dropped sooner after long stems. (b) The unstressed syllable stood between two fully stressed syllables. This is a very different situation from a non-compound word such as Go. *auþida* 'desert', in which the last syllable did not have primary stress.[19] (c) A form like *ϕánxtedõm may provoke haplology. Whereas Sverdrup (1929:24–31) may be right in claiming that haplology all by itself cannot lie at the basis of a sound law, it may in this case have been a contributing factor. And we must

not forget what happened to the French forms discussed in § 2.4. (d)
While the root *þanx- was recognizable as such, the endings (whichever
their shape at that time) were also recognizable as past endings.[20] But the
extra syllable containing e belonged neither to the stem nor to the ending.

For all these reasons we may assume that *þánxtedōm in its turn was
shortened and that the resulting consonant cluster was again simplified,
yielding *þanxtōm.[21] This shortening occurred in all forms in North West
Germanic and in the singular indicative in Gothic. The Gothic optative and
plural indicative, however, had a long ē, which was not dropped. The long
Gothic forms were thus to retain their semi-compound character, and it is
noteworthy that Bennett (1970:466–67) also describes these forms as
"quasi-compounds", albeit for very different reasons.

4.4. The overlong Gothic forms

The overlong Gothic forms already discussed in § 3.3 present a problem in
that an explanation for the absence of the syncopation must be given. I
could solve this problem most neatly by invoking the theory of lexical diffusion, for which it seems to me Chen and Wang (1975) offer convincing
arguments. In this view the overlong Gothic forms could be lexical items
left unsyncopated after the first syncopation had petered out.

But this theory is fairly novel, has not been received without criticism,[22]
and may therefore not seem convincing to everybody. For those that remain
sceptical about it, I would point out that the long Gothic forms never
underwent the second syncopation. Thus they retained the ambiguous state
discussed in § 4.3.0. If they could still be perceived as compounds, it is
conceivable that the unsyncopated, full form of the compound could again
emerge to the surface when the first syncopation rule disappeared from the
language. The "quasi-compound" intonation which they kept may have
helped here.

I am well aware that this is a fairly weak argumentation. Yet those three
overlong Gothic forms so tantalizingly reflect von Friesen's reconstructions
that I cannot but advance it, for all its weakness.

4.5. The regular forms

Having accounted for the t-forms[23], I still have to explain the forms containing d. In particular I must answer an obvious objection, voiced first and from
a slightly different viewpoint, by Sverdrup (1929:23) against von Friesen:
how can one drop the i of *þanxtidedōm, yet find the i preserved in nasida?
There are two possible solutions. The simplest is to assert that the rule
dropping i was preserved in Proto-Germanic only as long as Proto-Germanic
used nouns in -ti and -tu to form its dental preterits; when it started to use

the forms later to become infinitives, this rule was dropped. This solution, although very simple, is also very much ad hoc. It is better to point out that the forms which were to develop into infinitives had two suffixes (IE *-on-om*, PGmc. *-an-am*), unlike the nomina actionis in *-ti* and *-tu* discussed so far. It is impossible to trace exactly what portion of a Proto-Germanic infinitive like **nasjanam* would enter into a compound. The only sure ground we can tread on here is the certainty that the original shape of a later form containing a medial vowel was a lot longer than the original shape of a later form without such a vowel.

If one is willing to assume that the "regular" weak verbs formed their dental preterits very late, that is, at the time the "irregular" dental preterits had already gone through both stages of their syncopation, one may assume an analogy along the proportions outlined in the first paragraphs of Bech (1963):

Go. *þaht-a* = dental stem + ending = *nasid-a*,

in which the dental stem could be obtained from the participle.

This analogical proportion may well be needed anyhow, even for those who prefer to put the origin of the "regular"dental preterits early, to account for the second stage of the reduction; unless they are prepared to have haplology play an exceedingly important role in bearing the brunt of that syncopation (see above, pp. 361–362).

If this last page has sounded somewhat fuzzy, it is because I am not quite certain myself which possibility I should choose. Certainly the analogical solution is by far the simplest, but I doubt whether the "regular" dental preterits were formed so late, and also, if I apply it, I lose the methodological advantages discussed in § § 1.0 and 1.3.[24]

4.6. *OS* habda, *etc.*

Whatever the precise history of the Old Saxon forms without medial vowel (*habda* 'I had', *hogda* 'I thought', *lagda* 'I laid', *libda* 'I lived' and *sagda* 'I said') they are not problematic for my theory, since they contain *d*, which is my starting point. The consonant clusters *bd* and *gd* they show are highly unusual. Bennett's (1966) discussion of Go. *gahugds* 'conscience' seems to suggest that they are not original formations. Bammesberger (1969) assumes a zero grade *ə* for the suffix of class III weak verbs,[25] which then presupposes as the origin of this formation **habədedōm*, etc.

5. The endings proper

There is little that remains to be said about the endings. If one starts from
the double paradigm proposed in § 4.1, almost all the actually attested
endings can be derived in a straightforward manner. For an outline, see
Bech (1963:5–6) and Tops (1974). Again, this presupposes a timely divergence of the dialects (see above, pp. 360–361).

Except for Alemannic and a few Franconian dialects, whose plural endings
are direct continuations of the proposed paradigm, the plural endings of the
dental preterit must be derived analogically from the endings of the strong
verbs.

A final problem concerns the Alemannic optative ending $-\bar{i}$, for which I
accept Bech's (1963:29–30) explanation. I have summarized this before in
Tops (1974:81), where I also signalled Hammerich's (1964:16) criticism.
However, I unaccountably forgot to include the rejection of this criticism
which I had in the unpublished version of my thesis. I am therefore obliged
to take up all of this here. Briefly, Bech assumes for the weak verbs an
indicative paradigm with endings containing $\bar{o}$ throughout, versus an optative
paradigm containing $\bar{i}$ endings. This distinction was preserved even where
auslautgesetze would otherwise require a reduction of $-\bar{i}$ to $-i$. Hammerich
objected that the indicative first and third person singular had the ending $-a$.
But I would point out that this $-a$ is derived from an ending containing $\bar{o}$.
At one point, therefore, the conditions proposed by Bech did prevail. One
must only suppose that the auslautgesetz normally reducing $-\bar{i}$ to $-i$ occurred
before the qualitative reduction of the $\bar{o}$ ending to $-a$. Since the $\bar{o}$ was protected in both first and third person by a following consonant, this supposition
is quite reasonable.

6. Summing up

The following points sum up the revised version of von Friesen's theory I
have proposed. (= vF: elements taken over from von Friesen; ≠ vF: changes
in his theory).

All Germanic dental preterits go back to Proto-Germanic compounds
consisting of a nomen actionis plus the perfect tense of *$d\bar{o}n$ (= vF). In
preterits whose dental points to IE t the nomen actionis goes back to an Indo-
European noun containing the suffix $-ti$ or $-tu$ (= vF). Such preterits are
older than the others (≠ vF), which contain the Proto-Germanic verbal noun
in $-anam$ (= vF). This mixture explains the variation both in the stem vowel
and in the dental (= vF). The reduction of the forms is due to a combination

of morphological, phonological, and perhaps also analogical factors ($\neq$ vF). The difference between the long Gothic forms and the others is explained by the different ordering of two rules occurring somewhere in Germanic: in pre-Gothic the re-interpretation of *$ded\bar{o}m$ as a class V verb comes before the second reduction of the compound dental preterit; in pre-North West Germanic it is the other way round (= vF, but very differently formulated). The endings proper are derived straightforwardly ($\neq$ vF), except for the plural endings (= vF) and Alemannic $\bar{i}$ ($\neq$ vF).

Appendix

Rauch's argumentation is based on the following premises: (a) Aspect is primary, tense is secondary. This is true for Indo-European, but also in general: there is evidence from child language and from European-based pidgin languages that tense distinctions develop subsequently to aspectual modifications. (b) The parent Indo-European language construct is considered "advanced", containing "adult" features; the daughter language Pre-Germanic is postulated "with a view to language origin" and is accorded a fairly autochthonous development. (c) Overt periphrasis consisting of verbal strings is considered a relatively sophisticated device, which had better not be assumed for the early genesis of Pre-Germanic.

With these premises in mind Rauch reconstructs Pre-Germanic as an initially tenseless language with imperfective and perfective stems. The former had perfective counterparts by ablaut, which developed into nascent past-tense paradigms; the latter utilized suffixed verbal nouns for tense distinctions, in our case the to-participle.

I can accept neither the premises of this argument nor its consequences. Unless it is argued that Pre-Germanic was a pidgin language, one cannot postulate it "with a view to language origin". Pre- or Proto-Germanic is simply one of the continuations of Indo-European, neither more nor less capable of sophisticated devices than its parent language. Since periphrastic tense forms occur all over Indo-European, it is a methodological necessity to consider periphrasis an Indo-European feature and to allow its possibility for Germanic.

It is by no means certain that Indo-European had a system which distinguished aspect rather than tense. Szemerényi (1970:286f.) argues forcefully against this view. But even if it did, it cannot be denied that Germanic at one point replaced it by a system distinguishing tense. When this replacement took place is anybody's guess.

The consequences of Rauch's theory are equally unacceptable. She proceeds on the "semitacit assumption that the dental preterites are historically derivable both phonologically and syntactically from participles" (Rauch 1972:226) and admits herself that her solution for the long Gothic forms (reduplication) is "a matter of controversy" (Rauch 1972:229). For objections to all this, see fn. 3 of this paper and Tops (1974:62–63 and 73–74).

By way of conclusion I would like to stress that, in spite of my disagreement, I consider Rauch's article highly interesting and inspiring. The only reason I did not discuss it in my book is that it came too late for inclusion, its actual publication date being much later than 1972. Especially her call for a combination of "methods which exploit the theoretical insight of the generativist with the historical perspective of the traditionalist" (Rauch 1972:232) should be heeded by all well-wishers of both historical linguistics and linguistic theory.

Notes

1. This paper is a thoroughly revised version of the sixth chapter of my Cornell Ph.D. thesis. The first five chapters of this thesis have been published elsewhere (Tops 1974).

   It is a pleasure to again acknowledge V. T. Bjarnar and G. M. Messing, Members, and especially F. van Coetsem, Chairman, of my Special Committee at Cornell. Their criticism contributed substantially to my thesis. X. Dekeyser and G. J. Steenbergen, both of the University of Antwerp (UFSIA), and F. de Tollenaere, of the Instituut voor Nederlandse Lexicologie at Leiden, have given valuable comments on a draft of this version. The help they all gave me does not necessarily imply that they agree with the contents of this paper, and of course I alone am responsible for the imperfections it undoubtedly contains.

   This work was supported by a grant from the Department Taal- en Letterkunde of the UFSIA. My participation in this conference was made possible by a grant from the Ministerie van Nationale Opvoeding.

2. The names listed in this section are not intended as a complete survey of the scholarship on the problem; for such a survey, see Collitz (1912) and Tops (1974). For the period after 1912, add especially Hiersche (1968) and Rauch (1972).

3. Given the number and reputation of the scholars who currently defend alternative (a), it seems advisable to repeat here why I am not convinced. I will limit myself to answering the most popular solution, according to which the participle in IE -to plus the endings of the verb *dōn constitute the basis of the Germanic dental preterit.

   It is certainly acceptable to propose that a past participle may come to act as a preterit. This has happened, for instance, in Russian. Notice, however, that there it retains its nominal endings (*ja, ty, on čital* 'I, thou, he read', masc.; *ja, ty, ona čitala* 'I, thou, she read', fem.; *my, vy, oni čitali* 'we, you, they read', pl.), whereas for Germanic it is alleged to have taken on verbal endings. But let us accept that it did so. We are then told that it took on, not the most frequent endings (viz. those of the strong verbs of classes I through VI), but of a reduplicating verb, and an irregular one at that. This comes near to being unbelievable. But again let us follow. The result is that all verbs have the same past endings in the plural. And then, it is said, this ideal situation is disturbed, for in Gothic not only the endings but even the stem of the past tense of *dōn is taken on: *nasid-um (parallel to *stig-um, bud-um, lailōt-um*, etc.) becomes *nasidēdum*. The third step all by itself is to my mind totally unbelievable; taken together, the three assumptions must be rejected.

4. For Rauch's objections, see the appendix.
5. An obvious condition is that the order of the Proto-Germanic periphrasis was noun + periphrastic verb (unlike in Modern English). But the status of Proto-Germanic as an SOV language is well established; see sepecially Lehmann (1972).
6. For details, see Tops (1974). It is noteworthy that Watkins, who once defended a theory that necessitates the use of aorist forms (Watkins 1962), later agreed with Polomé (1964) that the entire Germanic preterit must be derived from Indo-European perfect forms (Watkins 1969:44).
7. The argumentation and the criticism are summarized in Tops (1974:17f.).
8. I do not discuss the future, which has a similar formation, because four of its six endings are the same as the full forms of the present tense of *avoir*, and in the other two analogical developments have occurred.
9. As for the claim that this is a stem vowel and not a reduplicating vowel, see fn. 15.
10. Against Jellinek (1926:156).
11. This objection could also be argued from the opposite viewpoint: *-idēdi* is not an ending at all, but an ill-founded composite of the vowel *i*, which properly belongs to the stem, plus the ending *-dēdi*. The result is the same.
12. A remarkable explanation of these three forms can be found in Krause (1968:225). It is conditioned by Krause's derivation of the entire dental preterit from the verbal ending IE *-t(h)ēs*, PGmc. *-tēs* or *-þēs*. Generalizing the dental and the vowel *ē* throughout the paradigm we obtain an element *dē/tē/þē*. In North West Germanic this ending was replaced by the endings of the strong verbs; in Gothic it was felt to be functionally strong ("als funktionsstark empfunden"). It was therefore introduced, in front of the strong endings, into the plural and dual indicative and optative paradigms, and doubled in the overlong forms *mahtēdēdeina* and **usbauhtēdēdi*, and perhaps also in **faurhtēdēdun*. I have shown elsewhere that this reasoning is untenable (Tops 1974:68).
13. Von Friesen assumed that the dental preterit occurred first with secondary verbs and only later with preterit-presents. But since both categories go back to Indo-European and since both were in equal need of a (new) preterit once the original perfect of the so-called preterit-presents had assumed a present meaning, I see no reason to follow him in this. Apparently he considered the preterit-presents a later development than I do: "Vi måste tänka oss att då vi finna det svaga preteritum även hos preteritopresentiska verb dessa svaga preteritibildningar successive tillkommit efter mönstret av avledda verbs preteritum, i samma mån som præterito-præsentia uppstodo och behovet att uttrycka förfluten tid till den nya betydelsen gjorde sig gällande." (von Friesen 1925:12)
14. In a fairly hesitant manner Meid (1971:86) proposes a paradigm containing originally only *ē* forms, but he does so merely on the basis of the prevalence of *ē* forms over *ō* forms.
15. For Knapp, *deda* is a weak form. But then, presumably, the plural should also be weak, and this cannot be; cp. the strong endings in Alemannic *tātum, tātut, tātun* (weak endings *-ōm, -ōt, -ōn*; see § 5).
15a. In this volume Mańczak suggests still another solution: he assumes that the phonologically inexplicable shortenings the compound forms underwent may have been due to their frequent use. I welcome this suggestion. In fact, there does not have to be a conflict between his solution and mine. To put it succinctly, he claims that the endings *-dedōm*, etc., were shortened because they were used so frequently; I claim that *dedōm*, etc., were shortened when they were used as auxiliaries attached to main verbs — and that, of course, is a frequent occurrence. We must notice that neither Mańczak's hypothesis nor mine has the power of prediction: both the shortening after frequent use and in certain syntactic environments can only be ascertained post factum.
16. For a list of medial consonant clusters in Proto-Germanic, see Moulton (1972, esp. 168–69).

17. It may be defended in several ways. Von Friesen (1925:18) accepts assimilation without further explanation. Foley (1973) would presumably argue for the greater strength of the voiceless obstruents. The simplification of the double consonant is explained analogically by von Friesen (ibid.): "de sålunda uppkomna långa konsonantljuden förkortas efter föregående konsonant enligt välkända analogier inom nord- och västgermanska språkgrenarna." One may also assume that Proto-Germanic had no geminate obstruents other than *ss* (see van Coetsem 1972:194; against Moulton 1972:143). In view of the blurred morphological boundaries, one might perhaps also invoke van Coetsem's (1972:178–79) Morpheme Length Restriction.

17a. Naturally 1 and 3 ind.sg. *deda* remained and must therefore be regarded as synchronic irregularities; see above § 4.1 and Tops (1974:80).

18. This does not necessarily conflict with Bennett (1970:465), whose reconstruction PGmc. *xé-xàjte* (> Go. *haíhàit*, OE *heht*) may be valid for late Proto-Germanic, i.e., Proto-Germanic after the Germanic consonant shift.

19. Sverdrup (1929:21f.), who equalled the accentuation of **þanxtedōm* with that of Go. *auþida*, had a good case against von Friesen, who assumed a different intonation than I. His argument is of course not valid against my reconstruction, not even if I assume an accentuation **þánxtedòm*. For even then the secondary stress on *-dōm* is different from whatever "stress" might be supposed on the final syllable of *auþida*.

20. It is interesting to observe that Knapp (1968:301) considers ON *sera*, ON *rera* and WGmc. *deda* to have been weak forms.

21. Both **þanxtdōm* and **þanxtōm* are or may be inaccurate forms in that no change in the ending is shown. The precise shape of the endings will be dealt with briefly in § 5.

22. See King (1969:138). This outright criticism was not swallowed by Robinson and van Coetsem, who in their (1973) review of King's book merely called for more research on this hypothesis.

23. It may be necessary to account explicitly for the *ss* in *wissa*. The spirantization rule converting (*dt*>) *tt* to *ss* may be very old, but there are good reasons to assume that it was preserved in Germanic for a long time after its beginnings (Tops 1974:82–84). Thus I would posit

    underlying representation   **wittidedōm* > **wittdedōm* > **wittdōm*
    surface representation   **wissidedōm*   **wissedōm*   **wissōm*

24. An argument against this analogy which is bound to come up and which at first blush seems obvious could be: am I not rejecting the participial theory through the front door only to again drag in the participial stem through the back door? In other words, am I not, via a highly circuitous and controversial route, putting forward the same participial theory I have so strongly opposed (see esp. fn. 3)? The answer must be no, for two reasons. One, none of the steps I have taken seems entirely impossible to me, even if it is undeniable that some must seem more plausible than others; whereas some steps required by the participial theory are to my mind indefensible. Two, I am in entire agreement with Ball (1968:172) where he argues for "the principle of textual criticism according to which, other things being equal, the more difficult reading is preferred." Obviously the long Gothic forms are the more difficult reading; equally obviously I must disagree with Meid (1971:113) when he writes: "Jedenfalls ist das teilweise Eindringen von **dō-n* in got. *-dēdum* usw. leichter zu begründen als sein Verlust ausserhalb des Gotischen (ahd. *-tum*) und das *t, þ, s* der athematischen Bildungen."

25. OS *lagda*, belonging to the more frequent class I verbs, seems to have gone over to class III. For a defense of such a possibility, see § 4.3.1.

References

Anttila, R.
1972   An introduction to historical and comparative linguistics (New York: Macmillan; London: Collier – Macmillan).
Ball, C. J. E.
1968   "The Germanic dental preterite", Transactions of the Philological Society 1968: 162–188.
Bammesberger, A.
1969   "Germanic *-hug-di-z", Language 45: 532–537.
Bech, Gunnar
1963   Die Entstehung des schwachen Präteritums (= Historisk-filosofiske Meddelelser, Det Kongelige Danske Videnskabernes Selskab 40, 4) (København: Munksgaard).
Bennett, W. H.
1966   "The Germanic evidence for Bartholomae's Law", Language 42: 733–737.
1970   "The stress patterns of Gothic", PMLA 85: 463–472.
Campbell, L.
1974   "On conditions on sound change", in: Historical linguistics 2 (Eds.: J. M. Anderson – C. Jones) (Amsterdam/Oxford: North-Holland; New York: Elsevier), pp. 89–97.
Chen, M. Y. – W. S-Y. Wang
1975   "Sound change: Actuation and implementation", Language 51: 255–281.
van Coetsem, F.
1970   "Zur Entwicklung der germanischen Grundsprache", in: Kurzer Grundriss der germanischen Philologie bis 1500, 1: Sprachgeschichte (Ed.: L. E. Schmitt) (Berlin: de Gruyter), pp. 1–93.
1972   "Proto-Germanic morphophonemics", in: van Coetsem – Kufner 1972: 175–209.
van Coetsem, F. – H. L. Kufner (eds.)
1972   Toward a grammar of Proto-Germanic (Tübingen: Niemeyer).
Collitz, H.
1912   Das schwache Präteritum und seine Vorgeschichte (= Hesperia 1) (Göttingen: Vandenhoeck & Ruprecht).
Foley, J.
1973   "Assimilation of phonological strength in Germanic", in: A festschrift for Morris Halle (Eds.: S. R. Anderson – P. Kiparsky) (New York: Holt, Rinehart and Winston), pp. 51–58.
Fouché, P.
1967   Le verbe français: Etude morphologique² (Paris: Klincksieck).
Friesen, O. von
1925   Om det svaga preteritum i germanska språk (= Skrifter utgivna av kung. humanistiska vetenskapssamfundet 2, 5) (Uppsala).
Hammerich, L. L.
1964   "Eine neue Hypothese vom schwachen Präteritum", in: Taylor Starck festschrift (Eds.: W. Betz – E. S. Coleman – K. Northcott) (London/The Hague/Paris: Mouton), pp. 12–18.
Hempel, H.
1966   Gotisches Elementarbuch⁴ (Sammlung Göschen 79–79a) (Berlin: de Gruyter).
Hermann, E.
1948   "Zusammengewachsene Präteritum- und Futurum-Umschreibungen in mehreren indogermanischen Sprachzweigen", KZ 69: 31–75.

Hiersche, R.
1968   "Neuere Theorien zur Entstehung des germanischen schwachen Präteritums",
        Zeitschrift für deutsche Philologie 37: 391–404.
Hirt, H.
1932   *Handbuch des Urgermanischen* 2: *Stammbildungs- und Flexionslehre*
        (Heidelberg: Winter).
Hooper, J. B.
1973   *Aspects of natural generative phonology.* [Unpublished Ph.D. dissertation,
        UCLA. Quoted from the 1974 reproduction by the Indiana University
        Linguistics Club.]
Jeffers, R. J.
1975   "Remarks on Indo-European infinitives", *Language* 51: 133–148.
Jellinek, M. H.
1926   *Geschichte der gotischen Sprache* (= *Grundriss der germanischen Philologie*
        1, 1) (Berlin/Leipzig: de Gruyter).
King, R. D.
1969   *Historical linguistics and generative grammar* (Englewood Cliffs, N.J.:
        Prentice-Hall).
Knapp, F. P.
1968   "Ahd *teta – tatum*", in: *Festschrift für O. Höfler zum 65. Geburtstag* (Eds.:
        H. Birkhan – O. Geschwantler) (Wien: Notring), pp. 301–314.
Krahe, H.
1967   *Historische Laut- und Formenlehre des Gotischen, zugleich eine Einführung
        in die germanische Sprachwissenschaft*[2] (Ed.: E. Seebold) (Heidelberg:
        Winter).
Krause, W.
1968   *Handbuch des Gotischen*[3] (München: Beck).
Lehmann, W. P.
1972   "Proto-Germanic syntax", in: van Coetsem – Kufner 1972, pp. 239–268.
Lowe, P., Jr.
1972   "Germanic word formation", in: van Coetsem – Kufner 1972, pp. 211–237.
Meid, W.
1967   *Germanische Sprachwissenschaft* 3: *Wortbildungslehre* (Göschen 1218–1218a–
        1218b) (Berlin: de Gruyter).
1971   *Das germanische Präteritum* (= *Innsbrucker Beiträge zur Sprachwissenschaft*
        3) (Innsbruck: Institut für Vergleichende Sprachwissenschaft, Universität).
Moulton, W. G.
1972   "The Proto-Germanic non-syllabics (consonants)", in: van Coetsem – Kufner
        1972: 141–173.
Penzl, H.
1972   "Methods of comparative Germanic linguistics", in: van Coetsem – Kufner
        1972:1–42.
Polomé, E. C. G.
1964   "Diachronic development of structural patterns in the Germanic conjugation
        system", in: *Proceedings of the Ninth International Congress of Linguists,
        Cambridge, Mass., August 27–31, 1962* (Ed. H. G. Lunt) (The Hague:
        Mouton), pp. 870–880.
Postal, P. M.
1968   *Aspects of phonological theory* (New York/Evanston/London: Harper & Row).
Prokosch, E.
1939   *A comparative Germanic grammar* (Philadelphia: Linguistic Society of
        America and University of Pennsylvania).
Rauch, I.
1972   "The Germanic dental preterite, language origin and linguistic attitude", *IF*
        77: 215–233.

Robinson, O. W., III — F. van Coetsem
1973   Review of King (1969), *Lingua* 31: 331–369.
Rosén, H. B.
1957   "Laryngalreflexe und das indogermanische 'schwache' Perfektum", *Lingua*
        6: 354–374.
Sverdrup, J.
1929   "Das germanische Dentalpräteritum", *NTS* 2: 5–96.
Szemerényi, O.
1970   *Einführung in die vergleichende Sprachwissenschaft* (Darmstadt: Wissenschaft-
        liche Buchgesellschaft).
Tops, G. A. J.
1974   *The origin of the Germanic dental preterit: A critical research history since
        1912* (Leiden: Brill).
Voyles, J. B.
1974   *West Germanic inflection, derivation, and compounding* (The Hague: Mouton).
Wagner, H.
1960   "Keltisches *t*-Praeteritum, slavischer Wurzelaorist und germanisches schwaches
        Praeteritum", *ZCPh* 28: 1–18.
Watkins, C.
1962   "The origin of the t-preterite", *Ériu* 19: 25–46.
1969   *Geschichte der indogermanischen Verbalflexion* (- *Indogermanische Gram-
        matik* 3: *Formenlehre* 1 [Ed.: J. Kuryłowicz]) (Heidelberg:Winter).
Wisniewski, R.
1963   "Die Bildung des schwachen Präteritums und die primären Berührungseffekte",
        PBB(T) 85: 1–17.

PAUL VALENTIN

The simplification of the unstressed vowel systems in Old High German

1. Introduction

1.1. The question to be examined can be formulated in a very simple way: how come that the wide spectrum of different vowels which appear in unstressed syllables at the beginning of the Old High German period is replaced 250 years later in most cases by much simpler systems? But if some kind of explanation along structural lines can be found for the evolution observed in the texts, it leads to other questions: Which is, if any, the influence of morphological patterns upon the history of the vowels of inflectional syllables? And how do the subsystems of phonemes established for each position relate with one another and with the more differentiated system to be found in stressed syllables?

1.2. This paper is based on the results of two previous studies, published in French (Valentin 1969, 1972; see also Valentin 1975), other recent publications in this field being Lawson (1961), Lloyd (1961, 1964), McLintock (1961). Only texts of a certain length can be used for the purpose of a graphemic and phonological analysis, which means that we can resort only to the six following works:

(1) the translation of Isidor of Sevilla's *De fide catholica contra Iudaeos*, henceforth called 'Isidor': some sort of Western or Southern Franconian, last decades of the 8th century;
(2) the translation of the Benedictine Rule: Alemannic, beginning of the 9th century;
(3) the translation of Tatian's *Diatessaron*, henceforth called 'Tatian': Eastern Franconian, c. 830;
(4) the poem after the Gospels by Otfrid of Weissenburg, henceforth called 'Otfrid': Southern Franconian (mss. V and P), c. 870;

(5) the commented translation of Boethius' *De consolatione philosophiae* by
     Notker of St. Gall, henceforth called 'Notker': Alemannic, beginning of
     the 11th century;
(6) the commented translation of the Song of Songs by Williram of Ebersberg,
     henceforth called 'Williram': Eastern Franconian, c. 1060.

1.3. Each of these texts has been closely studied with the means of graphemics,
helped by prosodic and orthoepic methods where feasible (Penzl 1970). Only
the results will interest us here, expressed within the theoretical frame of
'classical' phonemics (Trubetzkoy 1939; Martinet 1955, 1960). The phonological systems are of course established for each text separately, which means
that the point of view is strictly synchronic and syntopic at first; then systems
are compared and hypotheses about their evolutions are formulated. Although
in none of the texts the language used can be viewed as the continuation of
the language used in any other text, it is still possible to consider two groups
of texts with strong affinities which offer a rather consistent history: a
Franconian group with texts (1), (3), (4), (6) and an Alemannic group with
texts (2), (5).

1.4. The list of the contrasting vowels found differs for each position in the
word. So we will set up different systems reflecting the corresponding oppositions for the vowels in pretonic position, in posttonic but nonfinal (medial)
position, in checked final position, and in unchecked final position. The
relevant units whose oppositions constitute these systems shall be called
briefly 'phonemes' and the corresponding symbols shall be written between
slant lines, although their exact status and their role in the overall phonological pattern will be discussed later.
     As in most Germanic languages, the syllable bearing the principal stress can
be exactly determined. There is no evidence of an emphatic stress and of the
role it could have played in otherwise unaccented syllables.

2. Pretonic syllables

2.1. With the exception of some loan words, not frequent in Old High German,
and of the negative particle, pretonic syllables are only the so-called inseparable prefixes to be found in verbs and in verbal derivatives. As the graphic
material concerned can be easily summarized, we describe it. Only statistically
normal forms are cited; less frequent ones are given between brackets; very
rare ones are omitted.

2.2. *Isidor.* The prefixes are written as follows:

bi gi zi
fir (fyr): ar
ant, in

The structural conclusion is obvious: there are two vowels in this position, i.e. two relevant units or 'phonemes', /i/ and /a/, which contrast before /r/ and perhaps before /n/; yet some philological difficulties in this last case prevent us from being positive. But when there is no homosyllabic consonant after the vowels, only /i/ is possible, i.e. the opposition is neutralized.

2.3. *Tatian.* The manuscript has been copied by a number of scribes, each with a different writing system. But there is a very strong consistency in their work as they have

either *ar: for,* or *ar: fur,* or *er: for*
and all *bi gi zi int*

The phonological situation is the same as in Isidor, i.e. there is a system of two phonemes, probably in an opposition open: close. But this contrast functions only before /r/; it is neutralized elsewhere.

2.4. *Otfrid* yields different data:

bi gi zi int
ir, er, yr, ar
fir (far, fer, for)

There is only one phoneme, that can be noted /I/ for the sake of convenience. But as it does not contrast with another one its value cannot be ascertained, and it is likely that its realizations do not matter very much; this could account for the varying forms before /r/, unless they represent an attempt at noting a [ə] type allophone of /i/.

2.5. *Williram* has a system similar to that of Otfrid:

be ge ver zer
er (ir)
int

The one phoneme may be noted /e/, as its allophones seem to be rather open, with the exception of the position before /nt/.

2.6. The *Benedictine Rule*, the older text of the Alemannic group, offers a somewhat intricate situation, as a series of scribes were at work here. As for the unchecked vowels, they use one of these possibilities:

pi: ke ze
pi ki: ze
pi ki zi
pi ki, ka zi

In other positions they all write

er: far
int

with the exception of one who has *int* (*ent*).

So they all have a two vowel system, say /a/: /e/, realized as such before /r/, but neutralized under a more closed form before /nt/. In unchecked position, some have the same neutralization, whereas others seem to retain an opposition, but with more closed allophones for /a/ and /e/.

2.7. *Notker's* usage is very simple:

be ge ze
er (*ir*) *fer*
int (*ent*)

i.e. one phoneme with slight allophonic variations.

2.8. *Proclitic elements other than verb prefixes.* The only element which is always proclitic is the negative particle, placed before the verb and under the dominance of its stress. It behaves exactly like *bi, gi, zi* and appears either as *ni* or *ne*, in keeping with the usage in each particular text.

The prepositions *bī* and *zuo* have unstressed variants *bi, be* and *zi, ze*, which are treated in the same manner as the particles. They must be considered as proclitic to the noun phrase before which they stand.

The only loan word with a proclitic syllable which recurs in nearly all our texts is *corōna*. The vowel of its first syllable did not fit into the system; so it is very instructive to observe that it was finally lost (MHG *krōne*) by means of a syncope similar to that of *gilouben* > *glouben*.

2.9. *Conclusion*. If we now compare the succeeding systems in both dialect groups, we find the same line of evolution. At the beginning of the written tradition, there is an opposition between two phonemes, which is already neutralized in certain environments. The history consists in the extension of this neutralization, which finally leads to a single phoneme with more or less distinguishable allophones.

This simple evolution is classically explained by the concentration of the stress on the stem syllable; the proclitic element would have been then phonetically neglected in anticipation of the more powerful nucleus of the word. This explanation, which resorts to 'Lautmechanik', is quite possible, but we feel that another fact should be taken into consideration. Strictly speaking, the vowels in the proclitic elements never stand in pure phonemic contrast, as the consonantic environment is never the same: there is no such pair as *be: *ba*. The functional load of the opposition between vowels is nil, as these vowels do not in fact convey any difference in meaning. So they could easily be reduced to a very neutral value, if other conditions — such as stress — were favorable: both explanations may be suitable at the same time and complement each other. That this vowel was very unimportant seems to be proved by some cases where our texts go as far as syncopating it, from Tatian onwards. In this new sense only could it retain its old label of 'Indifferenzvokal'.

3. Medial syllables

3.1. *Long vs. short*. In keeping with the tradition we use these terms to describe an opposition which may equally well have been tense vs. lax; what really matters here is whether an opposition does exist between two series of vowels, or not. This question has to be answered for every of the three remaining positions.

Direct proof of the existence of 'long' vowels may be derived from double graphemes (Benedictine Rule and Isidor) or from circumflexes (Notker and Williram). Semidirect proof can be elicited from the prosodic treatment in verse (Otfrid only). Indirect proof is given when graphic treatment obviously differentiates two sets of vowels: consistent notation of a historically long vowel as opposed to more or less erratic allographs for a historically short vowel certainly indicates that both have remained different, and there is a strong probability that the former one either is long (or tense), or bears a secondary stress, or both, while the other one does not.

3.2. *Isidor* probably has a ternary short vowel system, which can be represented as

$$/i/ \qquad /u/$$
$$/a/$$

There are open allophones of /i/ before /r/, like [e], while /a/ shows a wide range of allophonic variations, from [e] to [o] and [a] : even some sort of [ə] value is not impossible, as phonetic influence of the surrounding vowels can be detected. Most important is the coalescence of former */e/ and */a/ in /a/, as it corresponds to the levelling of a number of morphological differences between strong verbs and first-class weak verbs.

Apart from /ī/ in the suffix -liih-, which seems to bear a secondary stress and could have been treated as a stem syllable, only two long phonemes can be detected: /ē/ and /ō/, most instances being in second- and third-class weak verbs.

3.3. *Tatian* looks very much like Isidor. For most environments we may posit this system:

$$/i/ \qquad /u/$$
$$/a/$$

But there certainly still is an opposition /i/: /e/ before nasal + consonant, along with /e/: /a/, which means that the analogical levelling in the verb morphology is not as advanced as it is in Isidor. In other cases /i/ and /u/ conversely show open allophones, and there are even graphic confusions with /a/. One has the impression that a rather elaborate system is on the verge of a sudden, total collapse, which should result in some sort of 'Indifferenzvokal'.

The evidence for long vocalic phonemes is even weaker than in Isidor. Only /ī/, /ō/ and /ē/ could be considered; /ī/ would be found only in some adjective suffixes, /ō/ and /ē/ in second- and third-class weak verbs, and /ō/ in comparative and superlative suffixes.

Furthermore it should be noted that for both Tatian and Isidor we come to no satisfactory, i.e. clear and regular, opposition between long and short vowels in medial syllables. Long vowels remain in inflectional and suffixal syllables only, as if they were better protected by their belonging to grammatical patterns than by their integration into a phonemic system.

3.4. *Otfrid.* Like Tatian, this text has four short vowels:

$$/i/$$
$$/e/ \qquad /o/$$
$$/a/$$

But /e/ appears before /r/, /nn/, /nt/ only and is possibly on its way to a merger with /a/ even there. /a/ has a number of allophones, depending on the surrounding vowels, which seems to indicate that it has already come very near to [ə].

As for the long vowels, there is richer and better evidence, due to the length of this text and to the possibility of a prosodic analysis. There certainly is an elaborate phonemic system:

$$/\bar{\imath}/$$
$$/\bar{e}/ \qquad /\bar{o}/$$
$$/\bar{a}/$$

At first sight it looks very much symmetrical to the short vowel system; but in reality it does not function accordingly. Most important is the fact that these long vowels are possible after a long or polysyllabic stem only: thus *beitōta*, *bredigōta*, but *korăti*, with a short medial vowel typically written with an *a*, although this weak verb belongs to the second (*ō*) class. The etymologically long vowels which clearly become short after a short stem do not appear under the form of the corresponding short phoneme; rather, /ō/, /ē/ and /ā/ are all replaced by the probably fairly central /a/; only /ī/ appears as a short /i/, but its case is not as clear as that of the other three phonemes. At any rate, it is obvious that there no longer is a regular correspondence between the long and short vowel system.

The conditions under which length is lost may be called rhythmic. But the evidence provided by Otfrid is not sufficient to give an exhaustive picture of these conditions, as we notice considerable differences in the treatment of the old long vowels, for which no explanation can be offered. The adjective suffixes *-ig-* and *-in-* seem to have no long vowel at all, whereas *-lih-* probably retains it in some rather obscure cases. Weak verbs of the second and third class behave as described, which means that the two types have merged in the case of a short stem; but the comparative and superlative suffixes, **-ōr-* and **-ōst-* have already become /-ar-/ and /-ast-/ without exception; the plural genitive ending **-ōno* seems to be on its way to lose the /ō/ altogether. Finally, Otfrid seems to have two different suffixes of the *-ari* type, one with /a/ and one with /ā/, the latter behaving according to the rhythmic conditions described.

3.5. *Williram* uses circumflexes obviously to denote long vowels, which enables us to posit the following system:

$$/\bar{\imath}/$$
$$/\bar{e}/ \qquad /\bar{o}/$$
$$/\bar{a}/$$

As in Otfrid, length is possible after long or polysyllabic stem only; after short stem there appears in all cases the short /ə/ to be discussed later on. *-lich-* and *-in-*, but not *-ig-*, account for the /ī/, weak verbs for /ō/ and /ē/, *-are* for /ā/, but irregularly. On the whole, length is used less frequently than in Otfrid, although the long phonemes are the same.

Short vowels are:

$$/i/ \qquad /u/$$
$$/ə/$$

The wide range of allophonic variation for the lower phoneme, along with the fact that it catches all the abridged long vowels, lets us posit it as /ə/. /i/: /u/ is possible before /ng/ only, and /i/: /ə/ before /n/ and /d/ only. In fact, there remains in most cases only one short vowel. So there is only one suffix left for comparative (/-ər-/) and superlative /-əst-/), and all three weak verb classes have merged in case of a short stem, as well as the former adjective suffixes *-ag-* and *-īg-*, etc.

3.6. The *Benedictine Rule* has three short vowels

$$/i/ \qquad /u/$$
$$/a/$$

with /a/ covering a wide range of phonetic variation under the influence of context. This is a situation comparable to that in Isidor.

Difference in graphic treatment gives indirect proof that there are at least three long phonemes /ā ō ē/, attested in the usual suffixes. Although no proof, either direct or indirect, is possible, an /ī/ is highly probable, while an /ū/ can be supposed in the forms of one word only. The absence of circumflexes and the almost total lack of double letters are a hindrance.

3.7. *Notker* seems to have a very simple system of short vowels. A single unit corresponds to most of the short phonemes in previous texts: /e/, with an [i] allophone before /ng/, /sk/, /st/; before /ng/ it contrasts with /u/, which is unattested in other environments. There is a slight possibility that an /i/ and an /a/ exist, but the functional load of their oppositions with /e/ would be extremely low; the probability for an /o/ is even more remote.

The very systematic and regular use of circumflexes in this text permits us to formulate a precise rule for the treatment of the long vowels: length is preserved solely between a long or polysyllabic stem and an inflectional ending which has a short vowel and does not bear a secondary stress (this excludes an

/i/ to be discussed in section 4). Typical examples in Notker's graphic system are: *ládota, áhtotîn: áhtôta*. There are at least four phonemes that function in this way, i.e. have a long and a short allophone according to their environment:

$$/\bar{\imath}/$$
$$/\bar{e}/ \qquad /\bar{o}/$$
$$/\bar{a}/$$

An /ū/ is unlikely. But it could well be that, even under the conditions described, length is not equally preserved in all grammatical series: only second-class weak verbs follow the rule closely, whereas their third-class counterparts, comparatives, superlatives, and the various adjectival suffixes seem to have the short allophone more often.

3.8. *Conclusion.* The history of the short vowel system is very much the same in Franconian and in Alemannic. The general trend is toward a single, more or less central, phoneme. By the mid-eleventh century, the final point of this evolution has not yet been reached, but the remaining oppositions have a very low functional load.

Long vowels can be thoroughly studied in the later texts only. The systems established and their functioning are quite comparable, although Notker seems to have more refined shortening rules (but this could be due to the more refined graphic rules of the text). But a trend toward simplification cannot go unnoticed: from text to text, there are less words or suffixes with a phoneme of this type. The lack of continuity in the tradition as well as the small number of words attested prevents us from describing this process exactly.

But as there is no symmetry between the two vowel systems, the appearance of a short allophone does not result in the neutralization of an opposition; e.g. a short [o] allophone stands alone, as there is no short /o/ phoneme. Only when there are no long allophones left in a specific context (phonemic or, probably, also morphological) does the now short phoneme have to be placed in the short vowel system. It seems then that /ī/ merges with /i/ (as long as the latter exist) and that the other phonemes are absorbed by /a/ or /ə/. This must have yielded very intricate situations which we cannot reconstruct, and might well be one of the reasons for the further simplification and destruction of the long vowel system.

4. Unchecked vowels in final syllables

4.1. *Isidor.* In this text there are certainly five short vowels:

$$/i/ \qquad\qquad /u/$$
$$/e/ \qquad\quad /o/$$
$$/a/$$

There is a very slight possibility that an open /ȩ/ and a closed /e̩/ should be distinguished. Nothing points to neutralizations, but there is some morphological levelling under way, which primarily affects the functional load of the opposition /e/: /a/.

Due to the lack of any evidence, direct or indirect, nothing can be said of the existence of long vowels in this position.

4.2. *Tatian.* This text is equally silent as far as long vowels are concerned.

Most scribes have a short vowel system with five elements, as in Isidor. One scribe could have had two /e/. Morphological levelling is active, especially in the nominal declension; but beyond this, true neutralization is beginning in the case of the opposition /u/: /o/; it is in favor of /o/.

4.3. *Otfrid* has a short vowel system very much similar to that of Tatian, and with the same beginning neutralization. A few scribal facts could indicate either that /o/: /a/ and /e/: /a/ are somewhat less resistent, or, more likely, that /a/ may have central, not very low allophones.

Historically long vowels seem to have merged with their short counterparts at an earlier date. But there is evidence to suggest that there exists a /i/ phoneme which behaves differently; it is likely that it bears some sort of secondary stress — it is less probable that it is long.

4.4. In *Williram*, there are only three short vowels left:

$$/e/ \qquad\quad /o/$$
$$/a/$$

The opposition /e/: /a/ is even on the verge of neutralization, and /a/: /o/ shows some signs of weakening.

There certainly are no long vowels. But an element written *íu, íu, iu* has to be considered. It does not seem to mean [y] or [y:]; it could be some diphthong, the value of which we cannot ascertain. Obviously, it is the continuation of an ending *-iu* found in previous texts, but which probably is biphonematic there and is being replaced by *-u.* So for Williram we must content ourselves with positing a phoneme /iu/.

4.5. The *Benedictine Rule* probably has neutralized the opposition /u/: /o/, so that its short vowel system looks like

/i/
/e/   /o/
/a/

As for long vowels, there is satisfactory evidence for a /ī/ and scant evidence
for a /ō/. A /iu/ is possible.

4.6. *Notker* has a simple system of short vowels, written with astonishing
regularity:

/e/   /o/
/a/

The /ī/ already found in previous texts undoubtedly exists here, as well as
/ā/; but the latter is weakened by a strong analogical levelling in favor of /a/.
And there is a /iu/, which certainly is not a diphthong; it could be [y:]. In
this case, we might write a ternary system which could to a certain extent be
compared with the short vowel one:

/ī/   /iu/
/ā/

4.7. *Conclusion.* This integration of /iu/ into the long vowel system is something new: it permitted this unit to survive, and conversely it helped the whole
system resist the menacing destruction. This is a typical Alemannic fact,
which goes along with the rather swift simplification of the short vowel
system in this area. One has the impression that both evolutions compensate
each other, in order to maintain a minimum of phonemic — and morphological — distinctions.

    In Franconian, evolution follows another pattern. Long vowels were pre-
sumably lost very early, with the exception of one /ī/ or /i/, whereas the short
vowel system was simplified more slowly. But Williram shows that the final
reduction was to come soon.

5. Checked vowels in final syllables

5.1. *Isidor* has a short vowel system with five elements:

/i/   /u/
/e/   /o/
/a/

There are no noticeable neutralizations. But it must be remarked that /o/ is attested only as the product of a previous */ō/; otherwise there would be a gap in the system.

Evidence for long vowels is scant. There probably are /ī ē ō/, but it could well be that their length is associated with a secondary stress.

5.2. *Tatian* has the same system of short vowels as Isidor. But /u/: /o/ does not function with the same regularity as /i/: /e/. Before /n/, which is by far the most frequent environment here, there is a lot of morphological levelling going on, the situation being very different from one grammatical category to the other; but isolated words do not follow suit. This seems to be an instance of neutralization induced by morphology rather than by pure phonetic evolution.

There is no evidence to suggest that long vowels exist in Tatian. The only probability is that the suffix -*lih* had a long vowel under secondary stress.

5.3. As for the short vowels, the situation is very much like the one in Tatian, with the same phenomenon of morphological levelling in the case of /u/: /o/, which in effect weakens /u/ and helps bring about conditions favorable to the neutralization of this opposition.

We cannot detect any long vowels, even in the case of the suffix -*lih*. But the prosodic treatment perhaps suggests a secondary stress on /i/, /o/ and /e/ in subjunctive endings.

5.4 On the other hand, *Williram* does have a /ī/ in -*lih*, but only after a long stem. There is a comparable /ā/ in -*sam*. Other suffixes usually prone to have a long vowel (at least when medial) certainly have a short one here.

There are four short vowels:

/i/
/e/   /o/
/a/

But /i/: /e/ is already neutralized before /t/, and there even are some environments where one vowel only is possible.

5.5. In the *Benedictine Rule* five short vowels form a well-balanced system:

/i/   /u/
/e/   /o/
/a/

Like in other texts, analogy interferes with the functioning of /u/: /o/, but here also with that of /e/: /a/.

One scribe uses double letters for long vowels, which enables us to describe the corresponding system:

$$/ī/ \qquad /ū/$$
$$/ē/ \qquad /ō/$$
$$/ā/$$

Only /ē/ and /ō/ are attested in a great number of forms; the suffix -*lih* does not seem to have a long vowel.

5.6. *Notker* has a very simple short vowel system. In most cases it is reduced to /ə/; only before /n/ + consonant it is

$$/u/$$
$$/ə/$$
$$/a/$$

/ə/ appearing then under the form of a [i] allophone.

Vowel length is marked with a circumflex; the system is

$$/ī/ \qquad /ū/$$
$$/ē/ \qquad /ō/$$
$$/ā/$$

These phonemes can have a short allophone after short stem, but apparently in the following cases only: suffixes -*lih* and -*ig*, superlative -*ost* and perhaps comparative -*or*; there is no evidence for such allophones in the nominal or verbal flection. This is very puzzling, as analogy can hardly be made responsible for it: one might think that analogy works at the phonemic, not at the allophonic level.

5.7. *Conclusion.* Franconian loses its long vowels very early; it is quite possible that it has a secondary stress on some endings, which could then protect their vowels for some time. On the other hand, Franconian short-vowel systems resist simplification very well; one reason is that the functional load of the corresponding oppositions was high, as the whole burden of morphological distinctions lay upon them.

Alemannic, on the contrary, simplifies its short vowel system earlier, but retains a rich long-vowel system until well into the eleventh century. The reason adduced to explain the history of Franconian can obviously be used for Alemannic, in reverse direction.

6. Phonological and morphological change

6.1. Two main factors play a part in the history of the unstressed vowels of Old High German as these vowels belong to phonological systems and to grammatical systems at the same time. Stressed vowels, that is, in German, stem vowels, do not belong to grammatical systems in the same manner; there are only 'word families', that seem not to interfere very often with the phonological evolution: facts such as the replacement of *gülden* by *golden* or the semantic estrangement of *hübsch* and *Hof* are rather isolated in the history of German.

Most unstressed vowels are to be found either in prefixes and suffixes or in inflectional endings: as in one given prefix, suffix or ending the environment is constant, any phonetic change automatically affects all the individual words with this element, and it so has far-reaching consequences for communication. But all morphological changes are not of a phonetic nature: beside the neutralization of oppositions (when, e.g. /i/: /e/ is neutralized, the endings *-in* and *-en* merge), there is analogical levelling, i.e. the replacement of an ending (or prefix or suffix) by another one taken from the existing stock: an infinitive ending of strong verbs, *-an*, may thus be replaced by the corresponding ending of weak verbs, *-en*. But as long as there are other endings which distinguish /a/ and /e/, for instance *-ar* and *-er*, the opposition between the two phonemes exists; it is neutralized only in the context before /n/, and only if there are no other *-an* endings in the morphology of the language. Yet it is obvious that such levellings impair an opposition, as they weaken its functional load; thus they may in fact induce neutralizations, if they do not produce them.

It is not always easy to ascertain whether analogical actions have come first and are to be made responsible for the final loss of an opposition, or the neutralization of an opposition, due to non-morphological reasons, has had one or more levellings as a consequence. The Old High German texts offer examples of both.

6.2. *Which comes first?* Take for instance the loss of length in medial and final syllables under certain rhythmical conditions that we have described. As this change does not affect one specific vowel, but the whole systems, it may be considered certain that it has not been triggered by some analogical action, but that it has a purely phonetic origin. We are not in a position to understand this phenomenon; but we suspect that alternances in secondary stress have played a part. It must also be noticed that the new short phonemes, as there were no satisfactory correspondences between the two sets, did not merge with the short phonemes. In fact, a rather long period of time elapsed before neutralization was really achieved. And only then did morphological levelling become possible. */ladōta/ had become /ladəta/, */ahtōtīn/ had become /ahtətin/: in such forms second-class weak verbs and third-class weak verbs were no longer distinguishable, and could even merge with first-class weak verbs where the previous */-i-/ was, if present, /-ə-/. But an /ō/ was still possible, as in /ahtōta/. Then a second wave of levelling arrived, later than our texts: it generalized /ə/ in all forms, and from now on there was only one type of weak verbs.

The same applies to the superlative and comparative suffixes */ōst/ and */ōr/, which finally merged with */ist/ and */ir/, respectively, under the forms /əst/, /ər/. It applies also to any isolated word with a possible */ō/. When all these mergers had taken place, there was no /ō/ phoneme left. But this final neutralization had in turn been caused by morphological levelling, while what triggered the whole evolution first may well have been the fixation of stress on the stem syllable a thousand years before.

6.3. *Chicken and egg.* This proves once more that the main question is not to know whether the chicken or the egg comes first, as this eludes our knowledge, but to observe and describe how the egg follows after the chicken and the chicken after the egg. We could discuss one Old High German instance only, but we feel that such facts should be studied in detail whenever possible: this would give us interesting insights into the history both of German phonology and of German morphology.

7. The overall system

7.1. The relevance of a unit can be determined by substitution only, which means that relevant units can be defined and described for a given position only. In fact, we have come to different lists of relevant units for each position, and observed that these lists have each a different history. It is of course possible to unify the two lists of checked and unchecked final vowels, the vowels of one list being considered the combinatory allophones of the ones of the other list in specific contexts. On the other hand, medial and final vowels could be combined into a single system on the grounds that a great number of them appear now as medial (*ahtōta*), now as final (*ahtōt*), and that the identity of inflectional syllables has to be preserved throughout the paradigms.

But no similar considerations may permit us to combine these vowels and the proclitic ones with the relevant units found in stressed syllables. The only reason to do so probably is economy and simplicity of description. But if we may find some common relevance in the /ō/ of *ahtōta* and in the /ō/ of *ahtōt*, it seems difficult to say that this /ō/ is the same *relevant* unit as the /ō/ in *hōh*.

7.2. But let us take a concrete example, the vowels of Notker, to see how it works. In stressed syllables, we assume the following subsystems of relevant units, without discussing details or difficulties (such as short /ø/):

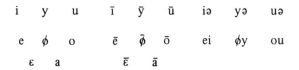

i	y	u		ī	ȳ	ū		iə	yə	uə
e	ø	o		ē	ø̄	ō		ei	øy	ou
	ε	a			ε̄	ā				

Subsystems for other positions are, as we know:

medial

i		u		ī		
e				ē		ō
	a				ā	

checked final

		u		ī		ū
	ə			ē		ō
	a				ā	

unchecked final

e		o		ī	ȳ
	a				ā

proclitic

ə

As the subsystem in stressed syllable is the most elaborate, we may take its units as the principal allophones of the phonemes of the overall system and describe the other subsystems as variations thereof under the influence of context. There are no special difficulties as far as the long phonemes are concerned; gaps in unstressed positions can be accounted for by the neutralization of the corresponding oppositions existing in accented syllable. The same is possible for short vowels.

But there is some difficulty with /ə/. It seems that we have to consider it as the result of the neutralization of /i/: /e/ and /o/: /e/ in checked final position, and of all oppositions in proclitic position. In fact, this is a general problem, which has to be solved for Modern German as well. As for Notker, there would be no difficulty at all if we took the rising diphthongs in stressed position as biphonematic; but this solution is unlikely, as [ə] has no contrasting role in these syllables, i.e., is by itself not relevant.

Is it legitimate to establish a single overall system in this manner?

References

Lawson, Richard H.
    1961   "The alternation of first and second class weak verbs in Otfrid and Tatian",
            JEGP 60: 491–497.
Lloyd, A. L.
    1961   "Vowel shortening and stress in the Old High German of Notker Labeo",
            JEGP 60: 79–101.
    1964   "Vowel shortening and stress in Old High German. 2: Otfrid", *JEGP* 63:
            679–695.
Martinet, André
    1960   *Éléments de linguistique générale* (Paris: Colin).
    1955   *Économie des changements phonétiques. Traité de phonologie diachronique*
            (Bern: Francke).
McLintock, D. R.
    1961   "Medial vowels in the dialect of Otfrid von Weissenburg", *Archivum Lin-
            guisticum* 13: 1–32.
Penzl, Herbert
    1970   *Lautsystem und Lautwandel in den althochdeutschen Dialekten* (München:
            Hueber).
Trubetzkoy, N. S.
    1939   *Grundzüge der Phonologie* (= *Travaux du Cercle Linguistique de Prague* 7)
            (Prague).
Valentin, Paul
    1969   *Phonologie de l'allemand ancien. Les systèmes vocaliques* (Paris: Klincksieck).
    1972   "Les voyelles inaccentuées de Williram", In: *Hommage à Maurice Marache*
            (Paris: Les Belles Lettres), pp. 107–118.
    1975   "Graphematik und Phonologie. ⟨y⟩ bei Otfrid", in: *Phonologica 1972* (Eds.:
            W. Dressler – F. Mareš) (München/Salzburg: Fink), pp. 123–130.

THEO VENNEMANN

Rule inversion and lexical storage:
The case of Sanskrit visarga[1]

1. The phonological form of words in the lexicon: An hypothesis and a strategy for its confirmation

In my paper "Words and syllables in natural generative grammar" (Vennemann 1974c) I have shown that one consequence of the principles of natural generative grammar is the assumption that the minimal unit of lexical storage is not the morpheme but the word, and I have given evidence from natural languages that this assumption is correct and is, thus, a desirable consequence of the principles. I have suggested in the same paper that the phonological form in which lexical material is stored is the "pronunciation in isolation" form, rather than some abstract form or contextual variant.

In the present paper I provide evidence in support of this additional assumption. What is required are specimens of linguistic behavior that can be explained only on the assumption under discussion. Following the methodological suggestion made in Kiparsky (1968), one place to look for records of such behavior is language change. The most forceful evidence for the assumption coming from this area would be a series of changes of the following structure. (Letters A, B, C represent classes of segments or zero, P a position "in pausa" [i.e., either at the beginning or at the end of a "pronunciation in isolation"], $\#$ a position at the word boundary on the same side as in the case of P; a bar on a letter indicates the complementary class of environments.)

(1) First change(s):

$A > C/P$
$B > C/P$
where C is not a previously existing class of segments of the language.

(2) Second change:

$B > A/\#K$

where K is either $\bar{P}$ (i.e. the class of all non-pausal, i.e., segmental environments) or a subset of $\bar{P}$, and the change is not (part of) a phonological change.

Such a series of changes would constitute evidence of the required kind because it permits only the following interpretation.

(3) Situation after the first change: A and B in pausa are relexicalized as C. Where such A and B were not in pausa but in the environment $\#\bar{P}$, and thus not changed to C, they are now interpreted as derived from C by the inverse rules

$C \rightarrow A/\#\bar{P}/M$
$C \rightarrow B/\#\bar{P}/N$

where M and N represent the sets of forms in which C historically developed from A and B, respectively.

(4) Nature of the second change: The language now has, in particular, the rule:

$C \rightarrow A/\#K/M$

This rule is generalized to the form

$C \rightarrow A/\#K$

by which the rule for B is curtailed accordingly as B disappears in the environment $\#K$.

The crucial assumption in this interpretation is that of rule inversion, i.e., relexicalization with rule-derived residue;[2] and the evidential step in the series of changes is the non-phonological merger of the residues.

I will show in this paper that the development of Sanskrit visarga sandhi provides instances of change that follow precisely this pattern. These changes thus constitute evidence for the hypothesis that words are stored in their "pronunciation in isolation" form. Conversely, the hypothesis permits a unified description of all relevant aspects of visarga sandhi.

2. The pre-pausal merger of *s* and *r*

Consider the following abbreviated singular noun paradigms, cited as they appear "in isolation":

(5)   'race'   'light'   'eye'
    Nom.   *jánah*   *jyótih*   *cáksuh*
    Dat.   *jánase*   *jyótise*   *cáksuse*
    Gen.   *jánasah*   *jyótisah*   *cáksusah*

Since these paradigms look like a textbook exercise in internal reconstruction (or transformational phonology, for that matter), I need not say much about them. All the stems once ended in **s*. There is no case suffix in the nominative, but there are in the dative and genitive. Before the suffixes, *s* is preserved as a sibilant, but changed to a retroflex after *i* and *u* by the so-called *ruki* rule.[3] In pre-pausal position, exemplified by the nominative, **s* (actually **s* and **ṣ*, but I will often omit the reference to **ṣ*) has changed to visarga, *ḥ*.[4] Comparative evidence confirms this reconstruction:

(6)   Skt.   Lat.   PIE
    Nom.   *jánah*   *genus*   **génos*
    Dat.   *jánase*   *generī*   **génesei*
    Gen.   *jánasah*   *generis*   **génesos/-es*

Indeed, the genitive suffix *-ah* and its source **-os* (or the allomorph **-es* of **-os*) exemplify once again the pre-pausal change of **s* into *ḥ*.

Consider further the abbreviated singular noun paradigms, again cited in their "isolation" forms:

(7)   'mother'   'voice'   'city'
    Nom.   *mātā*   *gíh*   *púh*
    Acc.   *mātáram*   *gíram*   *púram*
    Voc.   *mātah*   –   –

While the paradigms are not quite as textbook-like as the set (5), it is still easy to see that a pre-pausal **r* has changed to *ḥ* (except, of course, where it had been lost after a lengthened vowel at the end of polysyllables, as in *mātā*).[5] Again there is comparative evidence to confirm this guess:

(8)   Skt.   Greek   PIE
    Nom.   *mātā*   *mḗtēr*   **mātē(r)*
    Acc.   *mātáram*   *mētéra*   **mātérm*
    Voc.   *mātah*   *mḗter*   **mā́ter*

The changes so far exemplified can be summarized as follows:

(9) $s > h/\underline{\quad}P$
     $r > h/\underline{\quad}P$
where h did not exist in the language prior to these changes.

They are thus of the kind required in (1) of § 1.

3. Visarga before voiceless frontal stops

Consider the following pairs of forms. The left column shows "isolation" forms of words reconstructed with final *s, cf. (5) and (6), while the right column shows the same words as they appear before a word beginning with a voiceless frontal stop, here abbreviated as F.[6]

(10) $\underline{\quad}P$	$\underline{\quad}\#F$	gloss
jánaḥ	jánas tuṣyati	'the race rejoices'
	jánaś ca	'and the race'
jyótiḥ	jyótis táthā	'the light therefore'
	jyótiś ca	'and the light'
cákṣuḥ	cákṣus tátra	'the eye there'
	cákṣuś cakāra	'he has made an eye'

These examples[7] illustrate the following regularity: Word-final s has been preserved as a sibilant before frontal stops, but assimilates its place of articulation to that of the stop.[8]

Consider next a set of forms which differ from (10) in that the words in the left column have been reconstructed with final *r rather than *s, cf. (7) and (8).[9]

(11) $\underline{\quad}P$	$\underline{\quad}\#F$	gloss
mā́taḥ	mā́tas tṛpnuhí	'mother, be pleased'
	mā́taś cacā́ra	'mother, it has moved'
gī́ḥ	gī́s tavīti	'the voice is strong'
	gī́ś chidyate	'the voice is cut off'
pū́ḥ	pū́s tīrṇā́	'the city (has been) crossed'
	pū́ś ca	'and the city'

These examples illustrate that word-final *r, which has changed to ḥ in the
environment _____ P (before a pause), is reflected as a sibilant in the environment _____ #F (before a voiceless frontal stop at the beginning of the next
word). Since ś before palatals is merely an assimilated variant of s, as shown in
(10), the changes of *r exemplified in (11) can be represented as follows:[10]

(12) $r > s/$___ #F
    where F is a subset of P̄, i.e. a subset of the segmental cross-boundary
    environments of final *r, and the change is not a phonological change
    or part of a phonological change.

That the change is not phonological can be seen from the fact that it does not
occur generally before frontal stops, but only in the environment across the
word boundary. It does not occur inside roots; e.g., the perfect, formed with
reduplication, of the root kr̥t 'cut' is cakárta (= ca + kart + a) 'he has cut',
rather than *cakásta. The change does not occur before suffixes; e.g. from the
root kr̥ 'make' one derives, with a derivational suffix, the gerundive kártva
(= kar + tu + a) 'to be made', and, with an inflectional suffix, cakártha (= ca
+ kar + tha) 'thou hast made', rather than *kástva or *cakástha. Nor did the
change originally occur in compounds, as is shown by svàr-caksah 'brilliant as
light' and svàr-canah 'lovely as light' (svàḥ 'light'); but the change was carried
from sentence sandhi to compound sandhi in the early history of Sanskrit
(Macdonell, §49.d, fn. 3). While assibilation of r does occur in other languages,
it obviously cannot be assumed for Sanskrit. This is clearly recognized by
historians of the language. E.g. Burrow writes (1973:102): "It [i.e., r] even
becomes s before t . . . a development which is certainly analogical rather than
phonetic." (Cf. Benfey 1870:104.)

    The change (12) thus is an instance of the kind of development required in
(2); and (9) and (12) together constitute the kind of evidence required in
section 1 to support the hypothesis about lexical storage discussed there.

4. Interpretation of the described changes of visarga

The kind of change exemplified with visarga in sections 2 and 3 has been given
a general interpretation in (3) and (4). Let us see nevertheless how the general
interpretation applies to this particular instance.

    After the change of pre-pausal *s (and *s) and *r into ḥ, summarized in (9),
all forms affected by these changes were relexicalized with final ḥ. Since the
change had occurred only pre-pausally, s (and s) and r continued to occur in
the environment _____ #P̄, i.e., in syntactic nexus. But they were no longer

basic. Rather, they were now derived variants of h. Let S and R stand for the sets of forms in which h had developed from s (and s) and r, respectively. The relation of the derived s (and s) and r to the new basic h is then described by the following rules:

(13) $h \rightarrow s/\underline{\quad\quad} \#\bar{P}/S$
    $h \rightarrow r/\underline{\quad\quad} \#\bar{P}/R$

Rules (13) should be compared to (3). They comprise in particular the case where the following word begins with a voiceless frontal stop:

(14) $h \rightarrow s/\underline{\quad\quad} \#F/S$
    $h \rightarrow r/\underline{\quad\quad} \#F/R$

For reasons which we shall have to discuss, the former of these rules is generalized so as to cover not only S but also R, thus taking the form (15):

(15) $h \rightarrow s/\underline{\quad\quad} \#F$

The rule for R, viz. the second rule in (13), is curtailed accordingly as r disappears in the environment $\underline{\quad\quad} \#F$. Rules (14) and (15) should be compared to (4).

The absorption of the environment $\underline{\quad\quad} \#F/R$ by the environment $\underline{\quad\quad} \#F/S$ is reflected, in the traditional surface-oriented notation employing ">", by the formula $r > s/\underline{\quad\quad} \#F$, i.e. (12). The interpretation just given shows that such a formula is rather inappropriate in the present case because it suggests that it was actually *r that changed into s, i.e., that a rule $r \rightarrow s/\underline{\quad\quad} \#F$ was at some time in the history of Sanskrit, or even in Sanskrit itself, employed by the speakers of the language. The interpretation given here does not contain such an assumption at all and does not suggest it either. Rather, it assumes, first, phonological changes, viz., the gradual stabilization of rules of the form (16):[11]

(16) $s \rightarrow h/\underline{\quad\quad} P$
    $r \rightarrow h/\underline{\quad\quad} P$

It assumes, secondly, that this development leads to restructuring, i.e., a new grammar in which word-final h is lexical and s and r are derived from it by rules (13) which are the inverses of the original rules (16). It assumes, thirdly, that a certain change has occurred in a subsystem of the resulting system of inverse rules, (14), leading to the changed subsystem (15).

5. Further considerations on the described changes of visarga

The pre-pausal changes of *s and *r into h have occurred without any exception. In cases such as those cited in sections 2 and 3 it is easy to reconstruct the change. In others, it is less easy, or possible only on comparative grounds. E.g., the 3rd pers. plur. suffix in the active perfect is -uh, as in tutudúh (= tu + tud + uh) 'they have struck'. Here the corresponding middle form tutudré (= tu + tud + re) suggests that h in -uh may have developed from *r. This is not quite true, however, because comparative evidence suggests that -úh has developed from *-ŕs (Burrow 1973:310), so that h is actually the reflex of an *s.

The adverb bahíh 'outside' has no related forms with either s or r in Sanskrit. Were it not for comparative evidence, we would not know that the native grammarians were wrong when they gave the root as bahís (Burrow 1973:102).[12]

The noun údhah 'udder' belongs to a small irregular declension, with all forms other than the nom./acc. údhah being built on an n-stem: dat. údhane, gen. údhanah. As such it has the loc. plur. údhasu (= údha + su < *údlhn + su, Proto-Indo-European syllabic *n vocalizing into a in Sanskrit). But an alternative loc. plur. údhassu (= údhas + su) is also attested, which shows that someone once thought that údhah was just another member of the much more numerous class illustrated in (5), where, e.g., jánah does have the loc. plur. jánassu. Therefore, native grammarians assumed two roots, údhar and údhas (Burrow 1973:102). The former is etymologically justified, as, e.g., the English cognate udder shows. The latter is an innovation induced by the merger of pre-pausal *s and *r in h.

6. Visarga before non-frontal voiceless stops

So far we have considered the reflex of word-final *s and *r in pre-pausal position and before voiceless frontal consonants. Next I would like to discuss briefly their reflexes in the remaining contexts.

Before non-frontal voiceless stops, i.e., p, ph, k, kh, the oldest text (Rg Veda) often shows s (or ṣ) for h. This suggests that rule (15) was once more general, applying not only before frontal but before all voiceless stops.[13] The development before voiceless stops can be summarized as follows. The original sandhi, i.e., the relevant portion of (13), is (17):

$$(17) \quad h \rightarrow s / \_\_\_ \# \begin{bmatrix} \text{Voiceless} \\ \text{Stop} \end{bmatrix} / S$$

$$h \rightarrow r / \_\_\_ \# \begin{bmatrix} \text{Voiceless} \\ \text{Stop} \end{bmatrix} / R$$

At this stage, the generalization of s-sandhi occurred:

(18) $h \rightarrow s/\underline{\hspace{1cm}}\# \begin{bmatrix} \text{Voiceless} \\ \text{Stop} \end{bmatrix}$

Now a differentiation between two classes of consonants began: the frontal and the non-frontal ones. The pressure in a system of sandhi rules is toward elimination of the sandhi, because sandhi rules do not have a conceptual function and are therefore in conflict with Humboldt's universal, the principle of uniform symbolization or "one meaning, one form". So next we see the system being gradually reduced, the sandhi holding out longest in the case of a special phonetic cohesion of the contiguous segments, i.e., in the case of frontal stops. This leads to the system described by rule (15).

Where the sandhi described by rule (18) no longer took place, assimilation of the basic visarga may be marked:

(19) $h \rightarrow \underline{h}/\underline{\hspace{1cm}} \#K'$
      $h \rightarrow \underline{h}/\underline{\hspace{1cm}} \#P'$

Here $\underline{h}$ and $\underline{h}$ mark a configuration of the articulatory organs during voiceless aspiration as it occurs in the post-release phase of kh and ph respectively (Macdonell 1916: § 15.j), i.e. something resembling χ and φ; the former occurring before voiceless velar stops, K' (i.e., k and kh), the latter before voiceless labial stops, P' (i.e., p and ph).

7. Visarga before fricatives

Before initial fricatives, which are all voiceless sibilants in Sanskrit, viz. s, s, and s, the oldest layer shows s (or s or s) for *s, and r for *r; a middle layer shows s (or s or s) for both *s and *r; and the youngest layer shows general h for both *s and *r.[14] This development can be summarized as follows. The original sandhi, i.e., the relevant portion of (13), is (20):

(20) $h \rightarrow s/\underline{\hspace{1cm}}\#[\text{Fricative}]/S$
      $h \rightarrow r/\underline{\hspace{1cm}}\#[\text{Fricative}]/R$

At this stage, the generalization of s-sandhi occurred:

(21) $h \rightarrow s/\underline{\hspace{1cm}}\#[\text{Fricative}]$

This rule then became optional and was less and less employed, a development which is parallel to that before the non-frontal voiceless stops.

One will note that the change from (20) to (21) is parallel to that from (17) to (18). We must assume that they were really one and the same change, that from (22) to (23):

(22) $h \rightarrow s/$____#[Voiceless]/S
      $h \rightarrow r/$____#[Voiceless]/R

(23) $h \rightarrow s/$____#[Voiceless]

This very naturally leads us to the question of what happens before voiced segments.

8. Visarga before voiced segments

In the case of visarga before voiced segments, two cases must be distinguished.

In the first case, visarga is preceded by *a* or *ā*. Here *s*-sandhi and *r*-sandhi remain distinct through all stages of the language.

Where *h* continues **s*, *-ah* is reflected as *-o* (i.e. [ō]) before *a-* and before voiced consonants,[15] and as *-a* elsewhere; and *-āh* is reflected as *-ā*. E.g., *jánah* #*ajyáte* → *jáno ajyate* 'the race is driven',[16] *jánah* #*vádati* → *jáno vadati* 'the race speaks'; *jánah* #*ucitám* → *jána ucitám* 'the race (is) pleased'; *jánah* #*āste* → *jána āste* 'the race sits'; *māh* #*ápi* → *mā ápi* 'also a month';[17] *māh* #*gūrtāh* → *mā gūrtāh* 'the month (has been) greeted'.

Where word-final *h* continues **s* (rather, **ṣ*) after vowels other than *a* and *ā*, it is reflected as *r* before all voiced segments,[18] e.g., *cákṣuh* #*jyótih* #*árcati* → *cákṣur jyótir arcati* 'the eye praises the light'.

Where word-final *h* continues **r*, it is reflected as *r* before all voiced segments regardless of which vowel precedes: *mātah* #*addhi* → *mātar addhí* 'mother, eat' (**māto addhí*); *vāh* #*jagāma* → *vār jagāma* 'the protector has gone' (**vā jagāma*),[19] *gīh* #*vavāca* → *gīr vavāca* 'the voice has spoken'; *púh* #*jitā* → *púr jitā* 'the city (has been) conquered'.[20]

There exist essentially three problems, or clusters of problems, concerning the development of visarga before voiced consonants. The first is the fact that the treatment of **s* is different in external sandhi than the development inside words. Inside words, **s* and **ṣ* originally did not change to *r*. Before vowels and sonorant consonants, they are unchanged, cf. the paradigms in (5) or the entire section 2 for vowels and *ásmi* (= *as* + *mi*) 'I am' (**ómi*), *íṣyati* (= *iṣ* + *ya* + *ti*) 'he sends' (**íryati*), *uṣṇán* (= *uṣ* + *n* + *an*) 'they burned' (**urṇán*). Before voiced oral stops assimilatory voicing[21] and then divergent changes took place. Before non-homorganic consonants, *s and *ṣ (i.e., *z and *ẓ) became stops; e.g., the instrumental plural forms (suffix -bhiḥ) of māh 'month' (root mās) and viprúḥ 'drop' (root viprus, i.e. vipruṣ-) are mādbhíḥ and viprúḍbhiḥ. Before d and dh, *s and *ṣ (i.e., *z and *ẓ) are lost with compensatory lengthening of preceding vowels where applicable, *z changing a preceding *a to e and *ẓ retroflexing the following dentals: edhí 'be!' (2nd singular; root as, suffix dhi, cf. above ásmi 'I am'); ā́dhvam 'sit!' (2nd plural; root ās, suffix dhvam, cf. ā́ste, i.e., ās + te, 'he sits'); nīḍá- 'nest' (< *ni + zd + a, prefix ni 'in', root sad 'sit', cf. English nest); dūḷábha- 'difficult to deceive' (<*dūdábha- <*duzdábha-, prefix dus, root dabh).

These are not living processes in Sanskrit, however. On the contrary, the external sandhi has replaced the above kinds of treatment to a large extent: the instrumental plural forms of jánaḥ, jyótiḥ, cákṣuḥ are jánobhiḥ, jyótirbhiḥ, cákṣurbhiḥ, not *jánadbhiḥ, *jyótiḍbhiḥ, *cakṣuḍbhiḥ.[22] But the difference remained before vowels: jánase, jyótiṣe, cákṣuṣe (*jánae, *jyótire, *cákṣure). There also remains the other difference that while the sequence as developed into e before voiced dental stops inside the word, it there changed to o in external sandhi.[23]

The second problem is that the sandhi of -aḥ and -āḥ before voiced segments varies according to the origin of these sequences from either *-as, *-ās or *-ar, *-ār.

The third problem is the question of how word-final *ṣ (i.e., *s after i, u) changed into r before voiced segments.

Many attempts to solve these problems can be found in the literature, which it is impossible to discuss here. I will only report what seems to be the standard view. (See Thumb-Hauschild 1958: §186 for further references, and cf. Burrow 1973:101f.)

The main assumption is that word-final *s and *ṣ were voiced, *z and *ẓ, before voiced segments.[24] Then *-az changed to *-o (i.e. [ō]), which "shortened" to -a (there is no short [o] in Sanskrit) before vowels except a-; and *-ẓ was lost in *-āẓ. On the other hand, *ẓ changed to r.[25]

This account has the disadvantage of separating the sandhi of word-final *s and *ṣ before voiceless segments completely from that of word-final *s and *ṣ before voiced segments and from that of word-final *r. I would like to present in the following section an alternative description which gives a unified interpretation of word-final *s and *r in all positions.

9. A unified description of the history of visarga

First, pre-pausal *s and *ṣ, but not yet *r,[26] changed to ḥ, with restructuring and resulting inverse rules as described in sections 2 and 4, rules which can be combined in the schema (24).

(24) $h \rightarrow s/$____$\#\bar{P}$

Next, the subsystem of the schema that involves voiced initials was given up,[27] leaving a reduced system (25).

(25) $h \rightarrow s/$____ #[Voiceless]

At this stage, the changes summarized in (26) and (27) took place:[28]

(26) $ah > \bar{o}/$____ #[Voice]

(27) $\bar{a}h > \bar{a}/$____ #[Voice]

Next, pre-pausal r changed to h, with restructuring and resulting inverse rules, summarized in (28):

(28) $h \rightarrow r/$____ $\#\bar{P}/R$

In the environment before voiceless segments, (28) ran up against (25), a previously established rule of much more frequent application. Ideally, the rules would divide the environments S and R between them, as follows:

(29) $h \rightarrow s/$____ #[Voiceless] $/S$
      $h \rightarrow r/$____ #[Voiceless] $/R$

In reality, however, the second rule merely constituted an exception to the general (25):

(30) $$h \rightarrow \left\{ \begin{matrix} r/R \\ s \end{matrix} \right\} \Big/ \underline{\quad} \#[\text{Voiceless}]$$

As such it was eliminated, leaving the field once again to the original rule (25), whose domain expanded in this process to cover h from *r. This treatment of h from *r before voiceless segments reduced rule (28) to the environment before voiced segments:

(31) $h \rightarrow r/$____ #[Voice] $/R$

This rule now attracted the cases of h that were not taken care of by the sandhi rules developing from (26) and (27),[29] i.e., all h's from *s (i.e. *s after i, u), thus generalizing to the form (32).[30]

(32) $h \rightarrow r/$____ #[Voice]

In the later pre-history and history of the language, the gradual loss of all parts of rule (25) but that involving voiceless frontal stops took place, as outlined in sections 6 and 7.

One can see that in this interpretation there are two complementary developments: the generalization of s-sandhi before voiceless segments and the generalization of r-sandhi before voiced segments. An asymmetry is induced by the assumption that pre-pausal *s and *s changed to h earlier than *r did. This asymmetry is used to account for the non-parallel development of word-final *as, *$ās$ and *ar, *$ār$ before voiced segments. Except for this necessary asymmetry, the account of the development of visarga sandhi is uniform in that it assumes a single original cause, the weakening of pre-pausal *s (and *s) and *r to h and a single basic change involving the lexicon, viz., restructuring with rule inversion, the resulting inverse rules being subject to well-known mechanisms of grammar change, viz., rule generalization and rule loss.

10. Summary and conclusion

My goal in this paper was to provide evidence for the hypothesis that the phonological form in which lexical items are stored is the "pronunciation in isolation" form.

In section 1 I have described the nature of such data from language change as would support the hypothesis: We need to look for ad-pausal phonological mergers of segments into not previously existing segments, with subsequent non-phonological merger of the residues in some context, because such a change can only be explained on the assumption of relexicalization with the ad-pausal variants plus the development of inverse rules deriving the source segments from the ad-pausal segments in non-pausal contexts, with one of the inverse rules then generalizing at the cost of the other(s).

In section 2 a merger of the required kind is illustrated, that of pre-pausal *s (and its variant *s) and *r into visarga (h) in Sanskrit.

In section 3 the non-phonological merger of non-pausal residual *s (and *s) and *r into s (and $ś$) before voiceless frontal stops is illustrated.

In section 4 the changes described in sections 2 and 3 are interpreted as evidence of the required kind: $s, r > h/$____ P; relexicalization with h and inverse rules, in particular $h \rightarrow s/$___ #F/S, $h \rightarrow r/$___ #F/R, where F stands for voiceless frontal stops, and S and R for the sets of forms in which h developed from *s (*ṣ) and *r, respectively; generalization of the former so as to cover R: $h \rightarrow s/$___ #F. This concludes the theoretical part of the paper, as evidence of the required kind has been given.

In sections 5–8 further aspects of the development of Sanskrit visarga are discussed, leading to a unified account of its history based on the original ad-pausal change in section 9.

In conclusion, I would like to point out a specific consequence of the hypothesis discussed here. Changes such as that of pre-pausal *s and *r into h in Sanskrit have always been problematic in phonemic theory. Systems in which h would simply be a positional surface realization of phonemes s and r,[31] have the problem of assigning undecidable cases arbitrarily either to s or to r (e.g., the adverb bahíh 'outside'). Systems in which the merger of the pre-pausal variants of *s and *r has phonemic consequences are faced with a phoneme h of extremely limited distribution (it occurs only post-vocalically and, originally, only before the pause) and which in nearly a hundred percent of its occurrences can be traced unambiguously to either s or r on paradigmatic or other grounds.[32] – Other well-known problem cases of this sort are Icelandic þ, d, and ð, of which þ and d never occur intervocalically, and ð never occurs initially; and Western American English t, d, and ɾ, of which ɾ occurs only in intersonorant position after stress, where t and d never occur.

I should like to point out that in the theory discussed in this paper, this problem does not exist. This theory does not operate with the concept of a phoneme but only with that of positional contrast. Since words are stored in the lexicon in their phonetic form, rather than in some abstract, constructed, or contextual form, the question of phonologically associating a segment with some other (real or ideal) segment never arises. The theory only expresses that s and r occur and contrast in certain positions but not in others, and that h occurs in certain positions where s and r do not, and that h never contrasts with either s or r (except in a position where h is a free variant of s but not of r^{33}). The theory also expresses that Icelandic ð never contrasts with either þ or d, while þ and d form a contrast in word-initial position. And it expresses in a grammar of Western American English that ɾ never contrasts with t or d, while these form a contrast in many positions where ɾ cannot occur.[34] But this theory never needs to decide whether a given occurrence of h belongs to the "phoneme s" or to the "phoneme r", or whether a non-alternating ð must be "derived from" either þ or d, or whether a given occurrence of ɾ "actually is" a t or a d. There is no place in the grammar where "phonemes" are listed, and there is no methodological requirement that such a list has to be minimized. Therefore, no advantage is gained by representing a segment occurring in a lexical item as some other segment, or as some abstract unit. On the contrary, such identifications are ruled out by the principles of the theory. There is only a single level of representation for the phonological properties of lexical items, the systematic phonetic form in which they appear when pronounced in isolation. The phonological rules of the language determine the shape a lexical item may assume. Any modifications a lexical item may incur are brought about by rules which determine the possible shape of a sentence, i.e., the sandhi rules, rules related to the way the sentence is used (style, rate of speech, etc.), and, of course, sentence accent and intonation. This treatment of phonology in a grammar is, of course, a consequence of the principles of the theory. My study of Sanskrit visarga supports these principles by showing that only a phonological description that is in accordance with these principles can serve as a basis for an explanation of the historical development of visarga sandhi.[35]

Notes

1. Hurried readers or those not particularly interested in the details of Sanskrit phonology can skip sections 5–9, which deal with some finer points and additional aspects of Sanskrit visarga sandhi.
2. This mechanism of language change is discussed in Vennemann (1972, 1974a).
3. I take the name of this rule (it simply lists the segments after which the retroflection of s occurs) from Zwicky (1970). This peculiar change is not limited to Indo-Iranian, cf. Andersen (1968). I have proposed an explanation for the change in Vennemann (1974b).
4. Visarga (or visarjanīya; the term is variously translated as 'expiration' or 'final sound') is, according to the native grammarians, voiceless aspiration produced with the same configuration of the articulatory organs as the end of the preceding vowel (cf. Macdonell 1916: § 15.2.j). The sound, represented by a colon in devanāgarī, the principal native writing system, is transliterated as a (dotted) h, the plain h being employed for the so-called voiced aspiration. – The change of s to h is an instance of articulatory weakening: loss of the articulatory gesture that produces local turbulence in the oral cavity. A comparable change is that of s to h in many Spanish dialects, as in the pronunciation [ehtuδyánteh] of *estudiantes* 'students'.
5. One may speculate that the change from r to h occurred in two stages: (1) Pre-pausal devoicing of r; the only pre-pausal voiced segments in Sanskrit are vowels and nasals. This change may be compared to the devoicing of postvocalic r at the end of words in Icelandic: r is the only voiced segment that is fully devoiced in that position, while l, the nasals, and v, $δ$, g [γ] are "half-voiced" there (stops and s are always voiceless, and j does not occur word-finally); cf. Einarsson 1945:20, 23–25. (2) The change of voiceless r into h. This is, as in the case of pre-pausal s, an instance of articulatory weakening; cf. footnote 4.
6. The voiceless frontal stops (in the sense of an interrupted obstruent, i.e., including affricates) of Sanskrit are: dental t, th, retroflex t, th, and palatal c, ch. All the fricatives of Sanskrit are voiceless and frontal: dental s, retroflex $ṣ$, and palatal $ś$. Retroflex stops rarely occur in initial position, and only in the later language. Cf. Hiersche 1964:117 et passim.

7. They have been made up in the interest of transparency. Real examples abound. Some are given in Macdonell (1916: §43.1).

8. The assimilation is extended to retroflex stops in the later language, e.g., *paraśuḥ* 'hatchet', *ṭaṅkaḥ* 'axe', *paraśuṣ ṭankaś ca* 'hatchet and axe'; cf. Thumb-Hauschild (1958: § 183).

9. Again the examples, except for the last one, have been made up so as to relate them to those in section 2. Cf. footnote 5 about *r.*

10. If someone, for some theoretical reason, would rather separate the various cases and write *r > s/_____ #T, r > ś/_____ #C, r > ṣ/_____ #Ṭ* (with *T, C,* and *Ṭ* for the classes of voiceless dental, palatal, and retroflex stops – the third case not occurring in the older language; cf. footnotes 6, 8), he may simply consider only the case *r > s/_____ #T,* which is by far the most frequent anyway.

11. But cf. footnote 5 about *r.*

12. Their descriptive procedure required the native grammarians to construe a single stem as underlying a paradigm. As far as visarga is concerned, this is a straightforward matter in all cases of inflectional or derivational paradigms such as (5) and (7): the stems are *janas, jyotis, cakṣus; mātar* (actually, *mātṛ*), *gir, pur.* (The final sibilant is given as *s* in these artificial constructs even after *i* and *u* because of another rule by which a stem-final *s* is in pausa replaced by a stop, usually *ṭ,* as in *-dviṭ* 'hating' from *dviṣ* 'hate'; *ṣáṭ* (nom.-acc.) from *ṣaṣ* 'six', cf. *ṣaṣṭhá-* 'sixth'.) It is less straightforward but feasible in cases where there is no inflectional or derivational paradigm but where the sandhi behavior of a form in *-aḥ* or *-āḥ* shows it as agreeing with forms from either *s* or *r* paradigms; cf. section 8. It is not at all feasible in a non-arbitrary way in cases where there is neither an inflectional or derivational paradigm nor any special sandhi behavior, i.e., for all isolated forms in *-iḥ, -īḥ, -uḥ, -ūḥ,* and *-ṛḥ,* as, e.g., in the case of *bahíḥ* mentioned above. Here a representation as either *bahír* or *bahís* is forced by the procedure followed in the other cases, that is, by an arbitrary decision not to permit stems in *h.*

13. Macdonell (1916: § 43.2.a, footnote 3) says: "This treatment before gutturals and labials corresponds to that before *t* . . . and was doubtless the original one in sentence Sandhi." Here as before voiceless frontal stops, *r* originally had survived, as shown by compounds, e.g., *svàr-pati-* 'lord of light'. But in sentence sandhi *r* came to be treated in the same way as *s* (and *ṣ*), cf. *ántas-patha-* 'being on the way', where *h* in *antáḥ* 'in the middle of' is from **r* as shown by the retention of *r* before voiced initials – cf. section 8. Note also *cátuṣ-pād-* 'quadruped', *cátuṣ-kaparda-* 'having four tufts', with **r* indicated by Lat. *quattuor*, Engl. *four.* Cf. Wackernagel (1896: §284.c).

14. Macdonell (1916: § 43.3) gives examples both for *h* continuing **s* (and **ṣ*) and for *h* continuing **r.* To the example for **r, púnaḥ sám* or *púnas sám,* he adds a footnote: "This combination (in which Visarjanīya represents original *r*), though contrary to etymology, is universal in external Sandhi; but in compounds the original *r* frequently remains; e.g. *vanar-sád, dhūr-sád,* &c. This survival shows that *r* originally remained before sibilants in sentence Sandhi." Concerning the relative chronology of pairs such as *naḥ sapátnāḥ: nas sapátnāḥ, púnaḥ sám: púnas sám,* in which he labels the retention of the sibilants "assimilation", Macdonell writes: "Assimilation is undoubtedly the original Sandhi; but the MSS. usually employ Visarjanīya." – A slight complication occurs where an initial fricative is followed by a consonant: Here visarga is dropped, obligatorily if the consonant is an oral stop, optionally otherwise (cf. Macdonell 1916: § 43.3.a, b). This can be accounted for by an additional constraint and need not concern us here.

15. "Voiced consonants" here comprises all segments with glottal-cord vibration, i.e., the voiced stops *g, j, ḍ, d, b,* the so-called voiced aspirate stops *gh, jh, ḍh, dh, bh,* the so-called voiced aspiration *h,* and the sonorant consonants, i.e., nasals, liquids, and semivowels.

16. The *a-* may be dropped after *-o* (*jáno ajyate → jáno 'jyate*), a rule which develops

from non-occurrence in the oldest hymns to optional representation in the oldest written documents and further to an obligatory rule in Classical Sanskrit (Macdonell 1916: § 21.a and footnotes 4, 5, 6).

17. For *s in *māh*, cf. the accusative plural *māsáh* and Latin *mēnsis* 'month'.

18. There is one exception, here as well as in the case of *h* from *r*, discussed below: Since geminate *rr* is not tolerated in Sanskrit under any condition, special rules take care of sequences - *Vh* # *r*-. Where the sequence is -*ah* # *r*-, with -*h* from *s*, the general rule is followed, i.e., the result is -*o r*-. In all other cases, *h* is lost, lengthening the preceding vowel (if short): *cákṣuh* # *rábhate* → *cákṣū rabhate* 'it grasps the eye', *púnah* # *rámate* → *púnā ramate* 'he rejoices again', *vāh* # *rákṣati* → *vā rakṣati* 'the protector protects'.

19. For *r* in *vāh*, cf. the verbal root *vr* 'cover, protect' in *vṛṇóti* 'he protects', *vavára* 'he has protected', and Engl. *wary, beware, ward*, Goth. *warjan* 'hinder'.

20. The examples in this section have been made up from the words of section 2. Cf. Macdonell (1916: § § 44–46).

21. An intermediate stage of voicing can be reconstructed on comparative grounds (cf. Burrow 1973:94). The following examples are taken from Burrow.

22. The intrusion of external sandhi into the word can also be seen in the increasing use of visarga in -*as, -iṣ*, and -*uṣ* stems before the locative plural suffix -*su: jánassu* and *jánahsu, jyótiṣṣu* and *jyótiḥṣu, cákṣuṣṣu* and *cákṣuḥṣu* (cf. Burrow 1973:96).

23. The division is not quite that neat. The sequence *sūre duhitā* is found in the Ṛg Veda for *sūrah* # *duhitā* 'sun's daughter', rather than the expected *sūro duhitā*. This is explained by the influence of dialects in which -*e* rather than -*o* is the regular development of *-as* (cf. Burrow 1973:101).

24. Since *s and *ṣ did not change before vowels medially, one of two additional assumptions is necessary: Either one must assume that *s and *ṣ were voiced only before voiced obstruents and that final *z and *ẓ were analogically carried from there to prevocalic contexts; or one must assume that word-final *s and *ṣ were weakened variants of medial *s and *ṣ, and that only the weakened variants were susceptible to voicing. The latter assumption is very plausible in view of the precise parallel of word-final stops (cf. Vennemann 1974c: 360–367).

25. The assumption of such a change is perfectly plausible because Pre-Sanskrit *r* is reconstructed on the basis of its retroflexing effect on *n* following in the same word (cf. Macdonell 1916: § § 15.g, 65).

26. The suggestion that the pre-pausal change of *r* to *h* is later than that of *s* is first found in Bollensen (1868:628–636).

27. We may speculate that the part of the schema treating *h* before voiced segments was less uniform than that for voiceless segments, e.g., involving various degrees of voicing. But note that no particular assumptions concerning the phonetic realization of *h* before voiced segments have to be made under the present proposal.

28. It is likely that the change of *ah* into *o* [ō] occurred in stages. A plausible development is this: First, a lengthened variant of *a* [ə] developed, [ə̄]. This vowel was kept distinct from *ā*. The difference was even exaggerated to prevent merger. The vowel then became subject to the previously existing sandhi rule for long mid vowels, -*e* and -*o*, which remain intact exactly before consonants and *a*-, but change to -*a* before all other vowels (*o* to *av* except before *u, ū*). Later the vowel merged with *o* (with *e* in some dialects). – That *h* was lost more easily after vowels of great aperture than after vowels of small aperture (*i, u*) should permit a straightforward phonetic explanation. – The view that the loss of *s in *as, *ās before voiced segments may be due to the intrusion of the pre-pausal variants is expressed in Bartholomae (1888:571–573); for a recent statement with literature cf. Lazzaroni (1969).

29. Actually, as every new speaker of the language had to learn which of these sets of rules had to be applied to any given sequence -*ah* or -*āh* (which for some words such as the adverbs *púnah* 'again' and *tátah* 'thence' required just that, while for most it could be inferred from other forms in the paradigm), it is not surprising that errors

have occurred. I already mentioned the confusion about *ū́dhaḥ* 'udder' at the end of section 4. That this was an *r*-stem, a speaker of Sanskrit could find out every time a voiced segment followed. But this apparently did not occur frequently enough. So *ū́dhaḥ* was erroneously taken to be an *s*-stem, which not only became evident in new paradigm forms but also in sandhi behavior; e.g., *ū́dho romaśám* (for *ū́dhā romaśám*, cf. footnote 18), "under the influence of *aḥ* as the pausal form of neuters in *as*" (Macdonell 1916: § 47, footnote 1).

30. The view that *r* came to be used as a sandhi variant of *s* under the influence of *r*-sandhi was first expressed in M. Bloomfield (1882:31 footnote 2). Earlier, Benfey (1870:103) had asserted that *s* changed to *r* via *ḥ*, without, however, explaining the change from *ḥ* to *r*.

31. The native grammarians had such a system. Transformational grammar would undoubtedly take the same approach.

32. One system of this kind is that of L. Bloomfield (1933:189); he represents *ḥ* as basic, deriving *s* and *r* from it by rule. This position has been made explicit and supported more recently: "To sum up, the Visarga in Sanskrit may be treated as a separate phoneme rather than an allophone of /s/ or /h/" (Sharma 1968:309). Fry (1941) argues that visarga, with its positional allophones V (voiceless vowel), *ḥ, ś, s, ṣ,* and *ḥ* is "a subclass of the *s* phoneme". Unfortunately he does not consider the relation of visarga to *r*, either synchronically or diachronically; therefore it remains unclear why visarga would not be with equal right "a subclass of the *r* phoneme". Allen (1962:16 fn.) also favors the position that visarga is an allophone of *s*. Bright (1957) suggests that visarga may be considered an allophone of /h/ on distributional grounds; but Sharma points out that morphophonemically /h/ alternates with the retroflex and velar stops rather than with visarga. – Modern grammarians differ in their representation of words ending, in isolation, in visarga: Macdonell (1916) and Whitney (1896) write *-s* and *-r*; Thumb – Hauschild (1958) and Mayrhofer (1965) prefer *-ḥ*.

33. As noted in footnote 22, *ḥ* optionally substitutes for *s* before the ending *-su*. No substitution occurs in the case of *r*: *pūrṣú* (locative plural of *pur-* 'city'), but not **pūḥṣú*. Thus medially a sequence *ḥṣ* may contrast with *rṣ*.

34. I mean, of course, a spoken variety of the language, and one in which there is no difference either in the consonant or in the preceding vowel of, e.g., *latter* and *ladder* [lǽɾɾ]. Here [ráiɾɾ] could be assigned to either /rait/ or /raid/, but a decision in the case of the two words [lǽɾɾ] could only be made on extraneous grounds. One only need to ask oneself how to write down the name of some Mr. [réɾɾ] who has just been introduced.

35. D. Schlingloff (oral communication) believes that consistent application of Sandhi rules was a result of grammar training; this does not mean that these rules were not real.

References

Allen, W. Sidney
    1962   *Sandhi: The theoretical, phonetic, and historical bases of word-junction in Sanskrit* (The Hague: Mouton).
Andersen, Henning
    1968   "IE *s* after *i, u, r, k* in Baltic and Slavic", *Acta Linguistica Hafniensia* 11: 171–190.
Bartholomae, Chr.
    1888   "Die arische flexion der adjectiva und participia auf -nt-", *KZ* 29: 487–588.
Benfey, Th.
    1870   "Über die Entstehung und Verwendung der im Sanskrit mit *r* anlautenden

Personalendungen", *Abhandlungen der Königlichen Gesellschaft der Wissenschaften zu Göttingen (Historisch-Philologische Classe)* 15: 87–155.

Bloomfield, Leonard
  1933   *Language* (New York: Holt).
Bloomfield, Maurice
  1882   "Final *as* before sonants in Sanskrit", *American Journal of Philology* 3: 25–45.
Bollensen, Fr.
  1868   "Die Lieder des Parāçara", *ZDMG* 22: 569–653.
Bright, William
  1957   "A name [sic!] in [!] visarga", *Bulletin of the Deccan College Research Institute* (Poona) 18: 271–273.
Burrow, T.
  1973   *The Sanskrit language*[3] (London: Faber).
Einarsson, Stefán
  1945   *Icelandic* (Baltimore, Md.: Johns Hopkins Press).
Fry, Allan H.
  1941   "A phonemic interpretation of visarga", *Language* 17: 194–200.
Hiersche, Rolf
  1964   *Untersuchungen zur Frage des Tenues aspiratae im Indogermanischen* (Wiesbaden: Harrassowitz).
Kiparsky, Paul
  1968   "Linguistic universals and linguistic change", in: *Universals in linguistic theory* (Eds.: E. Bach – R. T. Harms) (New York: Holt, Rinehart and Winston), pp. 170–202.
Lazzaroni, Romano
  1969   "Considerazioni su *-as* > *-o* in sanscrito ed in avestico", *Studi e saggi linguistici* 9: 185–197.
Macdonell, Arthur A.
  1916   *A Vedic grammar for students* (Bombay). [Reprint: Oxford University Press, 1966.]
Mayrhofer, Manfred
  1965   *Sanskrit-Grammatik mit sprachvergleichenden Erläuterungen*[2] (Göschen 1158–1158a) (Berlin: de Gruyter). [Engl. ed. as *A Sanskrit grammar* (Transl.: Gordon B. Ford) (University of Alabama Press), 1972.]
Sharma, R. K.
  1968   "Visarga in Sanskrit", in: *Studies in Indian linguistics* [Festschrift M. B. Emeneau] (Ed.: Bh. Krishnamurti) (Poona: Centre of Advanced Study in Linguistics, Deccan College; Annamalainagar: Annamalai University), pp. 307–309.
Thumb, Albert – Richard Hauschild
  1958   *Handbuch des Sanskrit*[3] 1, 1 (Heidelberg: Winter).
Vennemann, Theo
  1972   "Rule inversion", *Lingua* 29: 209–242.
  1974a   "Restructuring", *Lingua* 33: 137–156.
  1974b   "Sanskrit *ruki* and the concept of a natural class", *Linguistics* 130: 91–97.
  1974c   "Words and syllables in natural generative grammar", in: *Papers from the parasession on natural phonology* (Eds.: A. Bruck *et al.*) (Chicago: Chicago Linguistic Society), pp. 346–374.
Wackernagel, Jakob
  1896   *Altindische Grammatik* 1 (Göttingen: Vandenhoeck & Ruprecht).
Whitney, William Dwight
  1896   *Sanskrit grammar*[3] (Cambridge, Mass: Harvard University Press).
Zwicky, Arnold M.
  1970   "Greek-letter variables and the Sanskrit *ruki* class", *Linguistic Inquiry* 1: 549–555.

NIGEL VINCENT

Is sound change teleological?*

With the recent revival of interest in linguistic change amongst theoretical linguists has come the re-posing of a number of old questions, not the least of which relates to the causality of change. One fundamental issue is whether final causes are allowable as a mode of explanation within historical linguistics. Among previous generations of historical linguists, powerful protagonists are ranged on both sides of the debate. Thus, Bloomfield (1934:35) argued:

> "Teleology cuts off investigation by providing a ready-made answer to any question we may ask."

while Jakobson (1931:136) maintained:

> "*When we consider a linguistic mutation within the context of linguistic synchrony, we bring it into the sphere of teleological problems.* It follows necessarily that the problem of finality can be applied to a chain of successive mutations, that is to diachronic linguistics." [Emphasis his.]

In an attempt to resolve such conflicts, often in no small part terminological, we shall seek to elaborate a theory of permissible teleology within language and to consider some recent work in the light of that theory.

Philosophers commonly distinguish two modes of explanation: causal (because of x) and teleological (in order that x).[1] Causal explanations in relation to sound change would be typified by the view that Latin [-kt-] becomes Italian [-tt-] *because of* phonetic assimilation of the first plosive to the point of articulation of the second. A teleological explanation of the same change might suggest that it took place *in order to* ease the articulatory effort for the speaker. One particular difficulty associated with teleological explanation which accounts for the aversion felt to it by many people, including a number of linguists, is what Braithwaite (1953:324) has called "the special puzzle of future reference". Put more explicitly, the problem is: How can an event in the future cause something which has already happened or is happening? When discussing the actions of rational beings a way out of the dilemma is available. Goal-directed activity may be regarded as goal-intended activity, and the individual's intentions may be seen as the prior cause. In cases where intention cannot easily be invoked, Braithwaite suggests two ways to eliminate the puzzle. The first is "to argue by analogy that in all cases the teleological explanation is reducible to one in which an intention, *or something analogous to an intention*, in the agent is the 'efficient cause', so that goal-directed activity is always a sort of goal-intended activity" (Braithwaite 1953:326, emphasis mine). There are obvious difficulties here, particularly in sorting out notions such as conscious vs. unconscious intent, instinct, etc. However, for our present purposes, we need not be concerned with such issues, since it is hard to see what kind of analogy would allow one to class rational beings and natural languages together, except the purely circular one that both exhibit behavior which might be referred to as goal-directed.

The second alternative involves attempting to eliminate teleological explanations "by reducing them to physico-chemical explanations of the ordinary causal sort" (Braithwaite 1953:327). This is the strategy behind Darwinian theories of evolution, where it is argued that a given genetic mutant survives because it is accidentally advantaged by its mutation. We may afterwards state, for example, that certain animals have the ability to alter the color of their coats for purposes of camouflage, but in evolutionary terms it was a question of the animal profiting from a situation arrived at by accident rather than intention. In the words of Sampson (1975:14), "Darwin has made this sort of teleology respectable, by showing that it is only a convenient abbreviation for longer-winded but non-teleological accounts." As a linguistic example of this type of elimination of teleology we may consider Martinet's theory of chain-shifts (Martinet 1952, 1955). According to Martinet, there are two types of chain-shift, which he refers to by the terms *drag-chain* and *push-chain*. A drag-chain occurs when a sound B changes to C and a sound A changes to B, moving, as it were, into the 'empty' space created by the shifting of original B. A push-chain on the other hand takes place when the effect of A shifting to B is to cause original B to move to C. As an oft-cited instance of the former type, consider the case of Romance lenition and the simplification of double consonants. It has been argued by Haudricourt and Juilland (1970) that the general Western Romance shift of intervocalic /-t-/ to /-d-/ as evidenced in (1)

(1)   Past participle ending:
       Latin: *-ata*   Provençal *-ada*
                                Spanish *-aða*, Old Fr. *-eðə*

permits the subsequent simplification of Latin geminates, e.g. /-tt-/ to /-t-/, as in Latin *mettetis*, Old Fr. *metez* (the double *tt* in Mod. Fr. *mettez* is purely orthographic). Evidence in favor of this view comes from Italian where inter-vocalic voicing does not take place and double consonants remain, e.g. *-ata*, *mettete*.[2] This, coupled with the fact that we know from other sources (see Politzer 1951) that simplification occurred after voicing, allows us to postulate a historical chain:

(2)   Stage 1   t > d
       Stage 2   tt > t

The question is whether we can accept the hint of a teleological explanation in Martinet's metaphor of a drag-chain. Do the geminates simplify as soon as they observe an empty space, as I might make for the seat in a crowded bus vacated by an alighting passenger? Surely not. Not only is such an assumption fanciful, it is unnecessary. If we grant Martinet's gradualist view that the realiza-tions of particular phonemes scatter around local frequency maxima, with their range of variation being conditioned by other phonemes in the vicinity, then under normal circumstances /tt/ and /t/ will be maintained as distinct. If, how-ever, /t/ for some independent reason shifts to /d/ then realizations of /tt/ will be able to stray unmolested, as it were, into the previous /t/ area, and the result will be a gradual shift along the chain. Thus, drag-chains may certainly occur, but their explanation is not irreducibly teleological.

Push-chains, however, provide a rather different type of situation. Here the only possible explanation does seem to be genuinely teleological. The only reason B shifts to C is to avoid clashing with the incoming A. As a case in point, Martinet (1952:151–2) cites the following changes:

(3)   Latin *kŭi* >   Italian *kwi*
         ECCU (H)IC   *qui* /kwi/
         kwi >   *ki*
         QUIS   *chi* /ki/
         ki >   *tʃi*
         CILIU   *ciglio* /tʃiλλo/

These may be summarised as:

(4)   Stage 1   *kui > kwi*
       Stage 2   *kwi > ki*
       Stage 3   *ki > tʃi*

There are a number of problems which reduce the force of this example. First, the chronology does not hold up, since available evidence suggests that palatalization starts before $kw > k$, thus converting the last part at least to a drag-chain. Indeed where $kw > k$ does take place early, the resulting /k/ is paiatalized, as in Lat. *TORQUERE* > Ital. *torcere, QUINQUE* > *cinque*, which destroys the notion of a chain altogether. Similar objections can be raised in the case of the remainder of the changes involved in the Romance lenition, viz. /d/ > /ð/, and /ð/ > /∅/, again cited by Martinet as a push-chain. Since it is the case that all intervocalic /d/ shift to /ð/, not just those that were originally /d/, e.g. *VITA, MUTARE*, Span. [biða] , [muðar] , and likewise with /ð/ > /∅/, e.g., *NUDA, VENUTA* > Fr. *nue, venue*, we have no evidence for anything other than a simple chronological rule sequence.

We are, of course, not the first to notice these problems with push-chains. Martinet himself was aware of the difficulty of keeping the two types of shift consistently apart.

"We thus probably have to reckon with pressure everywhere, so that *the suggested distinction between drag and push would often be blurred."* (Martinet 1952:151, emphasis mine)

King (1969:194), for different reasons, also rejects the notion of push-chain, and similar doubts are touched on by Anttila (1972:112). We may note in passing, and this is a point to which we shall return, that our negation of push-chains makes the question of teleology an empirical one. Since it is clear in principle what would constitute a push-chain, a solidly established case of such a change would stand as a counterexample to the theoretical position which this paper seeks to defend. To sum up, on the view taken here, drag-chains are legitimate but non-teleological, push-chains are indeed teleological but non-existent.

The discussion of Martinet is relevant to our understanding of the words of Jakobson cited in the opening paragraph, and to their reconciliation with the apparently contradictory views of Bloomfield. The point which both Jakobson and Martinet are making is that sound change cannot be viewed independently of its effects upon the structured phonological system within which it takes place, effects which are encapsulated in such terms as split and merger, phonologization and rephonologization. Most scholars would nowadays agree, I think, that from the point of view of language as an organized system, or "system of systems" (Jakobson 1971:525), primary importance should indeed be attached to these 'functional' aspects of change. It does not follow, however, that such primacy is chronological. It is not the structural pattern which initiates a series of changes, but rather the continually shifting phonetic flux.

A change, once achieved, may trigger off a series of further mutations as in the case of a drag-chain, but the initial impulse remains at the level of phonetic variation.

It may be argued that these 'functional' aspects of language are in themselves teleological and that therefore, for example, even the notion of a drag-chain involves teleological considerations, namely the structural pressures and margins of safety which lock the elements of the phonology into their respective places within the system. Such indeed seems to be the import of certain Bloomfieldian and post-Bloomfieldian criticisms of the Prague-school approach to phonology. At this point, however, the useful distinction made by Andersen (1973:789) between 'teleology of function' and 'teleology of purpose' is relevant. He writes:

"The notion of teleology has traditionally been erroneously identified with purpose in the sense of' '(conscious) intent'; and most students of linguistic change have been wary, and rightly so, of either ascribing (conscious) intent to linguistic systems or claiming that all change is the result of willful distortions of inherited patterns. However, there is no reason to think of purpose narrowly as 'intent'. It is perfectly proper to speak of some constituent element of a structured system as serving a certain purpose in the sense of 'function'. Defining the function of an element within the system of which it is part thus amounts to a teleological explanation. . . . In speaking of phonological change, it is necessary to distinguish this teleology of function from the teleology of purpose."

The existence of 'functional structure' may further be viewed as a natural consequence of the language-acquisition process, where the learning of successively finer distinctions plays an important role, as Jakobson (1968) has demonstrated. The work of David Stampe (1969) with its emphasis on the unlearning of certain universal processes in the acquisition of particular languages leads to a similar conclusion. We would maintain, however, that such acquisition in the realm of phonology at least is a largely unconscious activity, and not obviously goal-directed in the sense of involving "the special puzzle of future reference." Put another way, if we avail ourselves of Andersen's distinction, the question in the title refers to purposeful teleology, and we go along with Andersen, and many other linguists and philosophers, in the belief that such a mode of explanation is not directly relevant to the case of sound change, though, as we shall see, it certainly has a role to play in accounting for other types of linguistic change.

In the final sections of this paper we shall consider some recent work of an apparently teleological (the term will be used henceforth in the strong, purposeful sense) nature in the field of sound change, but before so doing it will be necessary to develop a general hypothesis regarding the speaker's intentional or volitional interference with the linguistic system which fulfills his communicative needs.

We have already stated more than once that the view which ascribes to language a will of its own, a sort of conscious control over its own future, seems to us gratuitous and untenable. It remains true, however, that language is a communicative tool at the disposal of its speakers, to whom the attribution of an independent will and volition is considerably less controversial. It is therefore reasonable to suppose that speakers will be capable of conscious, goal-directed activity in language-using situations just as much as at other times.

The most obvious cases of direct interference is the prescriptivism to which most languages with a cultural and literary tradition have been subjected at one time or another. Least subtle are cases such as the famous French minis-terial decree of 1901 which sought to lay down rules, among other things about the agreement of adjectives with the noun *gens* 'people' (feminine before the noun and masculine after). More sinister is the kind of linguistic purism instituted by Hitler and Mussolini in their respective countries. Although the consequences of such interference may sometimes be quite wide-ranging, the effect on the essential structure of the language is generally marginal, since the prescriptions tend to relate to individual points selected arbitrarily and atomistically. They can therefore be discounted in establishing a theory of language change as not representing a necessary part of the rela-tionship between a speaker and his language. A second type of situation is instanced by taboo words and euphemisms. Certain words may disappear from use as a result of their more or less conscious avoidance by the speakers of the language in question. Thus, most of the descendants of the Latin word *putta* 'girl' in Romance come to mean 'prostitute', with the consequent loss of the word in its original sense. As a contemporary example I would predict the loss of the word *gay* in the sense of 'happy' as a result of its use in collocations such as *Gay Liberation.* In cases like *cock* and *ass* cited by Bloomfield (1935:396) the mechanism is slightly different. Thus, *ass* 'donkey' is cognate with Latin *asinus*, whereas *ass* (often spelt *arse*) descends from a general Germanic root. In both instances, homonymic clash precipitates loss. Again, however, we may regard tabooing as a culture-specific phenomenon and therefore outside the immediate concerns of a general theory of linguistic change.

Going on from the last examples, there are nevertheless cases where homonymic clash is not due to taboo. Perhaps the most famous example is that described by Gilliéron and discussed at length by Bloomfield (1935:396–398). The case concerns the outcome of Latin *gallus* 'cock' (or 'rooster'!) and *cattus* 'cat' in an area of South Western France where independently attested sound changes predict [gat] for both. Yet [gat] only means 'cat', and a variety of other forms are used in different parts of the area for 'cock'. It seems reasonable to suppose that the lost form disappeared because it led to communicative difficulties, and furthermore speakers more or less consciously conspired in its elimination by selecting alternative designations for the same animal. Here, then, is an example of language change where genuine teleology of purpose seems relevant. A new word for 'cock' was found *in order to* avoid an inconvenient ambiguity.

A more systematic example of exactly the same phenomenon is attested in the history of Chinese. In the passage from Ancient to Modern (Mandarin) Chinese a large number of mergers have compounded to reduce considerably the number of distinct syllables available to give phonetic realization to the morphemes of the language. In particular we may cite the merging of initial palatal stops with the palatal and retroflex affricate series; the reduction in the vowel inventory and the loss of syllable-final stops and final /-m/. The precise details are too complex to go into here, but the overall effect is clear. In Ancient Chinese (see Martin 1953) the number of possible syllables (including accidental gaps) has been estimated by Geoffrey Sampson (personal communication) to be approximately 7,640. Given that every morpheme in the language is monosyllabic, and assuming an average vocabulary in the region of 5,000 to 6,000 morphemes, we have a somewhat better than 1:1 ratio between syllables and morphemes. For the modern language, however, Sampson's figure is approximately 1,770 phonetically distinct syllables (including tone), giving an average throughout the language of nearly four-way homophony for every syllable. Of course the fact that different items belong to different grammatical classes will help to reduce any potential confusion (compare English *bare* [V, Adj] /*bear* [V, N] or French *sang* [N] /*sent* [V] / *sans* [Prep] /*s'en* [Clitics] /*cent* [Numeral]), but nevertheless in the case of nouns the level of ambiguity is still too high to be tolerated in daily communication. Since the problem of homonymy here runs through the whole of the lexicon, simple replacement will not suffice, and so the following general strategy is employed. A given syllable, e.g. *yī*, is to be used in the meaning of 'clothes', though it has several other potential meanings. It is therefore coupled with *shāng*, which also includes 'clothes' as one of its possible meanings. Now the compound *yī shāng*[3] defines the intersection of the sets of meanings of the two syllables in isolation. Since this set has a unique member the needs of communication are thereby satisfied.

An important point to bear in mind in the previous two examples is the chronological sequence of events. First of all sound change operated to produce a situation of potential confusion – what Gilliéron[4] has called a 'pathological' state in language – and then a strategy was found to remedy things. In this way these cases serve not merely as examples of teleological behavior of speakers with respect to their language, but also as counter-examples to the view that sound change is itself directly teleological. If the latter had been the case, it is to be expected that the sound changes would have stopped before their destructive effect had been felt. It would be reasonable to argue in the case of the Gascon dialects that one single word was not sufficient to stand up to a general ongoing sound shift. However, such a line of defence is out of the question in the Chinese case. Whereas speakers, *qua* human beings, have the power to assess the future consequences of their actions, linguistic or otherwise, and modify their behavior accordingly, sound change can only proceed remorselessly on, leaving the speaker to do the best he can to mend any pieces of language that get broken in the process.

Alan Sommerstein (personal communication) has argued that spectacular mergers such as our Chinese example are not counterexamples to the notion of partial teleological motivation for sound change since, as he says, "in language, as in most things, there are *conflicting* teleologies, and in language it is apparently sufficient, in order for a change to spread, that it be advantageous in one way, even though it is disadvantageous in other ways" (emphasis his). Even granted the truth of these observations, notice however that in Chinese we are dealing with a series of sound changes, all of which appear to 'conspire' in the same direction. Furthermore these changes are independent to the extent that some affect the syllable initial, some the vocalic nucleus, and some the consonantal coda. Thus, there seem not to be conflicting effects but one cumulative one, which would presumably be all the more noticeable if the language, considered simply as a formal system, had the ability to monitor its own progress in time, which is precisely the kind of strong teleology of purpose which we are denying.

These considerations in turn suggest that sound change cannot be directly under the control of the speaker since otherwise he would be able to forestall its action in appropriate circumstances. Such a state of affairs, I would suggest, follows from the more general fact that speakers are not consciously aware of the detailed phonetic mechanisms of their language, and therefore *a fortiori* not aware of the minor fluctuations in these workings which are the substance out of which sound change develops. If true, what I have said so far may be taken as but one aspect of a much more general explanatory principle governing the relationship between a speaker and his language: the Principle of Speaker Control (PSC). According to this view, a language may be regarded as a hierarchically organized system, or system of systems in the terminology of Jakobson already referred to. Phonetics lies at the lower end of this hierarchy, with semantics – or more precisely the level of conceptual organization which is encoded by language – at the top. Furthermore the degree of conscious control or manipulation which the speaker exerts over his linguistic activity decreases as we descend the hierarchy. Basic syntactic patterns such as word order and subordination, as well as what traditional grammarians might call rhetorical devices such as topicalization and clefting, are near the top of the hierarchy, and enable the speaker to organize the semantic material he wishes to convey. The morphological and phonological resources of a language, on the other hand, depend essentially on such higher-level semantic and syntactic patterns and follow from them by rules which are not in general subject to the speaker's volitional intervention. Another way of looking at the same situation is to say that changes are more obvious the higher their effects reach up the hierarchy. Thus a subphonemic change such as the claimed shift from dental to alveolar articulation in English stops (Anttila 1972:57) will have less effect than a change involving alteration to the phonemic inventory as in most cases of palatalization (Penzl 1947). Even more noticeable are situations when the change has consequences not only for the phonology but also for the morphological system, as for example in the loss of Latin final /-s/ in Eastern Romance.

In addition to this 'top-to-bottom' dimension, there is considerable evidence for a deep-to-surface dimension where the speaker's awareness is of the surface outputs (syntactic or phonetic) of his grammar rather than of any more remote representations which the linguist may decide there are more or less good reasons for setting up. Thus, categories of change such as Anderson's (1973) 'abduction' or Anttila's (1972, 1974) re-espousal of analogy depend essentially on the idea of a misanalysis of the phonetic surface. In a similar vein is the idea put forward in Bever-Langendoen (1972) that syntactic change may reflect the interaction of perceptual strategies for establishing preliminary parsing of syntactic surface structure with the generative rule component. The integration of these two aspects of the problem – 'top-to-bottom' and 'deep-to-surface' – must, however, await further research.

As confirmation for the hierarchical view of linguistic change, I would adduce the phenomenon of 'hypercorrection' which typically takes place when a speaker tries to adapt his output to some externally given norm, for whatever reason. This in turn involves intervening directly at the lower end of the hierarchy, and we would predict that errors should ensue.

It is worth noting that the concept of hypercorrection figures largely in the work of Labov, which at first sight might seem to provide a fairly massive source of counterexamples to PSC since the type of variation he documents, for example in the case of the centralization of /aw/ on Martha's Vineyard is at the sub-phonemic level. However, Labov (1965:285) notes explicitly that "the changes began as generalizations of the linguistic form to all members of the subgroup; we may refer to this stage as *change from below*, that is, below the level of social awareness" (emphasis his). The dissemination of change, however, brings with it social awareness, but responses to it conflict with the speaker's unawareness of the relevant linguistic mechanisms, consequently giving rise to hypercorrection. Incidentally, Labov's work also provides a way of integrating into our theories of change the kind of purism and prescriptivism we discussed above (p. 414). Thus, Labov (1976:286–287):

> "Under extreme stigmatization, a form may become the overt topic of social comment, and may eventually-disappear. It is thus a *stereotype*, which may become increasingly divorced from the forms which are actually used in speech."

Many aspects of the particular types of sound-meaning association involved in literary creation are also readily explicable in terms of the PSC. Devices such as alliteration, assonance, onomatopoeia, and rhyme require explicit organization of those aspects of language which are least freely accessible to the untrained user of language. Other forms of specialist skill, such as phonetic training, can also be seen as enabling people to achieve greater degrees of conscious control over areas of their behavior which usually pass unnoticed. Thus it should be clear that we are not claiming that there is an absolute contrast between those areas of language which are controlled by the speaker and those which are not. Rather there is a system of relative accessibility, which is indeed what the term hierarchy implies. It is probably the case, nevertheless, that the bottom end of the hierarchy is fixed in the sense that in articulating speech sounds and perceiving them there are degrees of control which are not attainable because of the involuntary reactions which constitute part of the operation of our neuro-muscular systems.

The PSC is undoubtedly in need of considerable sharpening and refinement, but I think the intention behind it, and the kind of data relevant to its establishment (and perhaps eventual disconfirmation) are sufficiently clear for us to be able to proceed now to an examination of three areas of debate in sound-change theory where the claims implicit in the hierarchy have empirical consequences.

1. Morphological constraints on sound change

One area where final causes are sometimes adduced is when sound changes appear to be blocked by morphological conditions. In a frequently cited example (e.g., Anttila (1972:98–99), intervocalic /s/ is lost in Greek except where such an /s/ would be the only surface marker of future tense. Thus:

(5) *Present*   *Future*
   (a) *trépō*   'turn'   *trépsō*
   (b) *lúō*   'loosen'   *lū́sō*
   (c) *menō*   'remain'   *menéō*

In (5a) the /s/ remains since it is not intervocalic; in (5c) the future allomorph
is /es/, so the deletion of the /s/ still leaves the future minimally distinct from
the present. Such would not be the case in (5b) where /ū/ would be shortened
before another vowel, so that present and future would be homophonous.
Thus, it is claimed, the sound change does not operate in cases like (5b). However, in his discussion of this example, Anttila notes that the same facts are
susceptible to an alternative, and the traditional, explanation, namely that /s/
is indeed lost from *lū́sō*, but is later restored by analogy with other future
forms (e.g. *trépsō*) *in order to* avoid the homonymic clash with *lúō*. It should
be clear that this latter explanation is consistent with the hierarchy underlying
PSC, whereas the former is genuinely teleological in that it attributes to sound
change the power to evaluate the consequences of its own application and to
refrain from operation in cases where its effect would be detrimental to the
functioning of the morphology. The problem then is to find decisive evidence
one way or another.

    The mists of time have long since closed over any available evidence relating
to this particular example, but other cases are better documented. Hooper
(1974:126–130) discusses a sound change in the history of Spanish which
deletes final unstressed /e/ after a sequence of a vowel and one of a certain
group of consonants. As evidence for this compare the singular forms in (6)
with the forms in (7) which are respectively (a) the plurals of (6), (b) other
words in Spanish with different consonants or clusters, and (c) the cognate
words in Modern Italian.

(6) *pan*   'bread'   *real*   'royal'
    mar   'sea'   *sed*   'thirst'
    mes   'month'

(7) (a) *panes*   (b) *grande*   (c) *pane*
       mares   *monte*   *mare*
       meses   *arte*   *mese*
       reales   *nueve*   *reale*
       sedes   *leche*   *sete*

Thus both internal and comparative evidence motivate the sound change, but
there is an extensive and productive class of exceptions which appear to be

grammatically conditioned, viz., finite verb forms. Final unstressed /e/ realises the first person singular preterite of a number of irregular verbs (8a), the third person singular present indicative of all second and third conjugation verbs (8b), and the first and third person singular present subjunctive of all first conjugation verbs (8c).

(8) (a) *pude* 'I was able'   (b) *quiere* 'he wishes'
          puse 'I put'   *sale*   'he leaves'
          vine 'I came'   *une*   'he unites'
     (c) *pese* 'he weighs' (subj.)
          cene 'he dines' (subj.)
          dure 'he lasts' (subj.)

Hooper, following Menéndez Pidal, shows how at the beginning of this sound change (12–13 cent. A.D.) there were optional variants with or without final /e/ amongst both the verb forms and other areas of the vocabulary, i.e., both *pud, vin* and *pane, mare*, etc. She goes on therefore to distinguish the 'process' of the sound change, which may be optional in its initial application but is always phonetically conditioned in origin, and the 'result' of the sound change, which may be a rule incorporated into the grammar with a variety of more or less ad-hoc morphological and syntactic conditions which reflect the interaction of the sound change with the already established patterns and rules of the language. She writes (1974:130):

"I would claim that if all the facts were available, it would turn out that all cases of grammatically conditioned exceptions to phonological rules develop in just this way; all phonological rules have their source in universal phonetic constraints, and new rules never arrive at the door of the grammar with their grammatical exceptions in tow."

A similar explanation is available in the case of another candidate for morphologically conditioned sound change, namely the loss of final /-n/ in Estonian, except in first person singular forms (see Campbell 1974:90 and references cited there).

(9) *kanna-n* > *kanna* 'heel' (gen. sing.)
     kanna-n > *kannan* 'I carry'

As Campbell remarks:

"Seventeenth century manuscripts show that the loss of final -*n* was a variable rule in which -*n* was being lost, but was frequently retained if followed by a word beginning with a vowel."

Again, once we admit of the distinction between 'process' and 'result' in sound change, the way is open to a clearer understanding of the data in question.

Associated with the above claims are discussions such as that in Hyman (1975:173 ff.) in which it is argued that familiar phonological rules such as /k/ → [tʃ] may be synchronically 'natural' but they are not diachronically so. The leap from a velar stop to a palato-alveolar affricate is just too great for the gradual 'processes' involved in sound change, but as a synoptic statement of the 'result' of the incorporation of palatalization into the grammar it is entirely reasonable. As Hyman remarks (1975:182) there is a "great tendency for rules to become unnatural, that is, to lose their phonetic plausibility and become morphologically conditioned." Similar views have been expressed by Chafe (1968). Such tendencies reflect, of course, the movement of changes up the hierarchy we have established.

Anttila (1972) explicitly adopts the opposite position to ours, and in his defence cites an ongoing change from Russian, originally reported by Jakobson (1949) who draws the same conclusions from it as Anttila. Unstressed *ă* [ə] shifts to *i* after palatal consonants, thus *pójăs* > *pójis* 'belt', but in the 1940's this change did not affect inflectional suffixes where *ă* is "supported by analogy with *o* and *a* in the same suffixes when stressed" (Jakobson 1949:113). It is, however, also possible to argue that in the initial stages the sound change operates root-internally, but only with time expands across boundaries. Confirmation of this alternative account is found in Anttila's concluding observation that in contemporary Russian the sound change has spread to inflectional suffixes. If the sound change knew enough about the structure of Russian not to interfere with inflections in the 1940's, why should it decide to ignore this knowledge a quarter of a century later? It seems both methodologically and philosophically wiser not to ascribe it such knowledge in the first place.

Anttila (1972:78) makes a further point:

"To deny grammatical conditioning implies that only hearers are allowed to create change – not speakers, who come to sounds through the rest of grammar."

The reasoning here is not clear. Certainly it is true that many changes can be attributed to the hearer: a number of examples are dealt with in the next section. However, the point of PSC is that the lower end of the hierarchy is not normally consciously superintended by the speaker, and that it is therefore precisely at this point that changes may be initiated. Of course, such slight modifications rely for their propagation throughout the speech community on both speakers and hearers, but then this is generally true of all linguistic change. Put otherwise, the establishment of a change requires the mediation of both speakers and hearers, but the initial impetus may come from either source.

2. The interaction of sound change and phonotactics

Another apparently teleological mode of explanation which has become wide-spread in recent work in linguistics, particularly in phonology, is contained in the theory of targets and conspiracies first elaborated in Kisseberth (1970). To take a simple example from Italian, we may identify in that language two processes:

(i) vowel deletion: e.g., /kanta + o/ → [kanto]
(ii) glide formation: e.g., /'piu/ → ['pju]

The effect of these two rules taken together is to eliminate sequences of full vowels (with a few exceptions) from the surface phonetic strings of the language. Thus, although the rules are not formally collapsable according to the usual notations of generative phonology, nor by any obvious or natural extension of them, nevertheless the two processes have a certain unity, a 'functional' unity as Kisseberth calls it, in that they 'conspire' together to rid the language of certain unacceptable sequences of sounds which have arisen as a result of independently motivated operations in the phonology and mor-phology. We agree with Matthews (1972) and Sommerstein (1974) that in such situations it makes more sense to regard the phonotactic restrictions as explaining the existence of the rules, rather than vice-versa. The important question is whether such an explanation is teleological, to which we would reply in the negative. Although in terms of a formal model, the rules may in some sense appear to occur 'before' the surface phonetic level on which the phontactic constraints are defined, nevertheless from the point of view of the speaker the two parts of his phonology coexist at any given point in time.[5]

The true nature of the situation is brought out clearly where phonotactic restrictions can be adduced as explanations of certain sound changes. Consider Vulgar Latin syncope, which deletes a non-final, immediately post-tonic vowel Thus:

(10) (a) *colapu* > *colpo*   (b) *auriculu* > *orecchio*
          calidu > *caldo*   *oculu*   > *occhio*
          viride > *verde*   *lenticula* > *lenticchia*

The intervening stages involved in the historical derivation of the examples in (10b) are:

(11) V.L.   /ˈokulu/
      Syncope   ˈoklu
      l > *j*   ˈokju
      Gemination   ˈokkju
      Vowel changes   ˈokkjo
      Ital.   /ˈokkjo/

Given this set of changes, we should expect Ital. *vecchio* 'old' to go back to a Latin form **veculus*, whereas the attested form is *vetulus*, a diminutive of Classical Latin *vetus*. The usual, and most reasonable, explanation of this discrepancy is that /vetulu/ underwent syncope to give /vetlu/, and then, since /tl/ was not an acceptable cluster in Latin, nor in Italian for that matter, the /t/ shifted to /k/ to accommodate the new form to the phonotactic requirements of the language. The problem is whether the hypothesized intermediate stage /vetlu/ ever existed, or whether the change, so to speak, 'skipped' a stage, going straight from /vetulu/ to /veklu/. The latter possibility would be truly teleological since it involves ascribing to the sound change the possibility of evaluating the consequences of its own operation and taking appropriate avoiding action in situations where those consequences would be linguistically 'undesirable'. Direct evidence one way or the other is not available, but an inspection of the way phonotactic constraints work in observable situations in the present will provide the necessary clue. It is generally the case that speakers perceive foreign loan-words via the intermediary of their own phonological and phonotactic systems. Likewise, their attempts to reproduce foreign sounds move along pathways determined by the patterns of their native language. Thus vowels in English loan words with /ʌ/ – e.g. *club, budget, rugby, bluff* – are in French pronounced as /y/ or /œ/ (Fouché 1959:202). Similarly, Tuscans and Central Italians, where the native dialects have no final consonants, commonly add a paragogic /-e/ to borrowings like *gas, tram, sport* and *bar*. Indeed the whole field of foreign-accent studies provides a mine of data of this type.

Now, in the same way, the speech habits of innovating speakers count as 'foreign' with respect to the majority of the language community. In our example, [vetlu] may indeed be pronounced by the innovating speakers, but the perceptual/productive mechanisms of the imitators on whom language change relies for its diffusion (cf. Householder 1971:ch. 16) will bring about the shift to /veklu/ which we find attested in the Appendix Probi (*VETULUS non VECLUS*). Further examples of sound changes attributable to the acoustic properties of the speech signal are discussed in Andersen (1972, 1973). Jakobson makes a similar point when he writes (1961:2):

> "Since not the motor but the acoustical aspects of speech sounds, aimed at by the speaker, has a social value, the teleological conception of sound problems increases the relevance of acoustical analysis in comparison with the physiology of speech."

And it is clear that once more this use of teleology is reducible to a non-teleological formulation. A new dimension of the same question is hinted at in Labov (1965:286):

> "The linguistic variable now shows regular stylistic stratification as well as social stratification, as the motor-controlled model of casual speech competes with the audio-monitored model of more careful styles."

Looked at from the point of view of the hierarchy we have established, our account of the Vulgar Latin changes relies explicitly on the fact that the phonetic end of the scale is beyond the speaker's direct, conscious control in every-day language use. Such seems also to be Jakobson's view, to judge by the reference to "motor . . . aspects of speech sounds" in the passage just quoted. If every speaker of a human language were, and always behaved as, an expert phonetician, it is a reasonable guess that changes involving the effect of native phonotactics on unfamiliar articulatory habits would not take place at all, at least not in those cases where the phonotactics are based on language-particular and not universal, anatomically and physiologically necessary, limitations.

3. Linguistic orthogenesis

In a recent defence of a very extreme form of linguistic teleology, Lass (1974) examines a phenomenon which he christens 'orthogenesis' or 'directed evolution'. By this is meant situations where a series of historical changes have the cumulative effect of producing a particular synchronic state of affairs. Thus, in Lass' example, Proto-Germanic has free or phonemic quantity as a parameter of its vowel system, but this has been all but eliminated in Modern

Scots. The various stages in the development are taken as instantiations of "a higher-order instruction or 'meta-rule' (Lass 1969) that says: eliminate lexically dichotomous vowel systems. Or better, perhaps, maximise the predictability of vowel length." (Lass 1974:333.) Two points are crucial in Lass' argument. First, the time-span is so great that it cannot conceivably be covered by a single speaker, or even his immediate family. This rules out the continuity, if continuity there is, as residing in anything but the linguistic system itself. Second, the individual stages which go to make up this 'diachronic conspiracy' are not in themselves readily explicable, so that any significance they might have can only be discovered by envisaging the whole, which is to that extent greater than the sum of its parts.

Let me begin straightaway by admitting a problem, namely my own lack of familiarity with the data on which Lass' argument is based. This means that what follows is not so much a refutation as a methodological pondering on his claims, and a discussion of some possible lines of argument which might eventually lead to a reformulation of the data in non-teleological terms, together with the consideration of a related though not exactly parallel example from the history of Italian.

To give our discussion solid foundation, let us take the example first. One of the most notable characteristics of contemporary Italian phonology in comparison with the other Romance languages is the systematic contrast of single and double (or long and short) consonants. This opposition involves 15 out of the 21 consonant phonemes usually set up for Italian.[6] The interesting question from our point of view is how this state of affairs came about. There are four sources of Italian geminates:

(i) the retention of those geminates which were already an integral part of the Classical Latin phonological system;

(ii) various assimilation processes: e.g. *octo > otto, spat(u)la > spalla, ven(i)rò > verrò, capsa > cassa*;

(iii) gemination before semivowels and liquids: *cofea > /kofja/ > cuffia, venui > /venwi/ > venni, febre(m) > febbre, publicu(m) > pubblico*; (see Vincent (ms) for more detailed discussion);

(iv) a process of consonantal reinforcement in antepenultimately stressed words, e.g. *atomu > attimo, femina > femmina*; (see Tekavčić 1972:290–291 for details).

In view of the varied sources of Italian geminate consonants, the concept of a 'diachronic conspiracy' seems relevant. The difference between this one and the case reported by Lass is the fact that Italian inherited directly a fairly large stock of geminates from Latin which gives the conspiracy a head start, as it were. It is easy to see how, once the language has geminates, further changes which would produce yet more such sounds will be accepted. Assimilation of stop $+ \left\{ \begin{matrix} t \\ s \end{matrix} \right\}$ clusters, for instance, merely adds to the number of geminates in the language, whereas in a non-geminating dialect the same change would create a whole new order of phonemes. Despite, or indeed because of, this important difference between the two, the Italian example is instructive as showing the development of the later part of a diachronic conspiracy, once the initial change has been accepted into the language. If the phonotactics are regarded as a filter giving preference to sound changes which can be accommodated within the existing pattern of possibilities, or which exploit unfilled gaps in the system (cf. Martinet 1955), then it is clear how a new structural requirement — such as the elimination of phonemic vowel length in particular environments — can be strengthened and extended via the continual interplay of sound change and existing patterns, or more generally of opposing forces of dynamism and stasis.

Now, Lass insists on the idea that the changes he describes form a line through time, a developing progression towards a particular goal, and in this connection quotes Teilhard de Chardin's reference to "the appearance of the *line* as a natural unit distinct from the individual" (Lass 1974:312, emphasis Chardin's). However, it must be borne in mind that the observation of a line says nothing about its direction, yet it is precisely the direction of the line which is crucial to Lass' argument. The case of Italian gemination shows well the way in which the direction of a historical development may be given by its starting point, with all the subsequent changes doing no more than continuing along this path. The appropriate parallel is not with travelling along an existing road which has been established to get someone to a particular place, but with building the road as one proceeds, with no knowledge of what might lie at the end of the journey, but keeping going nevertheless in a direction roughly the same as before, unless some event or disturbance of the terrain forces one to change direction. As support for this alternative view of lines, consider Lass' remarks in the epilogue to his paper in which he denies that the direction taken by the changes he discusses has any 'adaptive' advantage in the biological sense. He writes (1974:344):

> "The point is that if teleology equals clear directionality in pre-definable paths (which is the essence of my claim), there is no necessity for the directions to be 'useful' in any way."

It seems strange that if languages do in some mysterious way have the power to orient their own future development towards particular goals, they do not also have the power to pick advantageous rather than randomly determined goals.[7]

Let me end these rather speculative remarks on Lass' paper by considering a strong methodological point in his favor. This is his objection that the phenomena relating to the history of Scots vowel length are capturable under one generalization, albeit one which requires a teleological explanation, and that to refrain from capturing it would be to refrain from doing linguistics. In other words, the issue is an empirical one, and here I would agree with Lass, and also with the philosopher Rescher, who writes (1970:72):

"... the issue of mechanism v. teleology ... is an essentially empirical, scientific question that waits upon a study of the actual facts, and is not a theoretical issue that can be settled by abstract reasoning from *a priori* premisses or by any decree or fiat on the basis of methodological or of conceptual analysis."

The only proviso I would add here is the familiar one that to accept orthogenesis, and in general teleology of purpose, in relation to sound change would so enormously extend our conception of what sort of things qualify as human languages that it is a position to which we should be pushed only under extreme pressure from the facts. I have tried to show in this paper that many of the facts discussed in the literature under the rubric of teleology will not bear this burden. The fact that, as yet, I have no adequate answer to Lass' examples indicates that the issue is still open.

Notes

* I am happy to acknowledge Geoffrey Sampson's help and advice in dealing with the Chinese material, as well as for more general discussion of the ideas presented here. I am also grateful to the following linguists for their comments: Richard Coates, Bernard Comrie, John Green, Martin Harris, Richard Hogg, Jim Hurford, Giulio Lepschy, and Alan Sommerstein. They do not, however, necessarily agree with all the views set forth, and none of them should be held responsible for any errors which remain.
1. It will be evident that this part of the paper relies heavily on the treatment of teleology in Braithwaite (1953:ch. 10).
2. For a detailed coverage of the various analyses of Romance lenition the reader is referred to Tekavčić (1972:157–158).
3. Kratochvíl (1968:75) refers to this type of word-formation as 'co-ordinate compound', and gives several further examples. The matter is undoubtedly more complex than we have indicated, but the general form of the argument seems clear enough. Note, too, Kratochvíl's (1968:141 ff.) discussion of the rise of polymorphemic words in Chinese, though his explanation (in terms of language contact) differs from ours. The essentially 'functionalist' interpretation of the situation which we adopt here is also

advocated by Forrest (1973:173–174). An English parallel might be the colloquial use of the groups *funny-peculiar* and *funny-ha-ha*.
4. A useful summary of Gilliéron's ideas and criticisms of them, together with a comprehensive bibliography, is contained in Iordan, Orr and Posner (1970:157 ff.).
5. For discussion of the nature and operation of phonotactics, see Sommerstein (1974).
6. For treatment of the synchronic situation and further references, see Muljačić (1969:427–435).
7. The view, incidentally, that language can pick useful goals towards which to aim has to be ruled out as leading into the oft-triggered trap that there is one general principle – e.g., King's simplification, or Martinet's adaptation of Zipf's principle of least effort – which governs linguistic change. The continual movement of languages back and forth along well-trodden paths should be sufficient to rob that notion of any credibility.

References

Andersen, H.
   1972   "Diphthongization", *Language* 48: 11–50.
   1973   "Abductive and deductive change", *Language* 49: 765–793.
Anderson, J. – C. Jones (eds.)
   1974   *Historical linguistics* 2 (Amsterdam: North-Holland).
Anttila, R.
   1972   *An introduction to historical and comparative linguistics* (London: Collier-Macmillan).
   1974   *Analogy* (University of Helsinki Dress Rehearsals No. 1).
Bever, T. – D. T. Langendoen
   1972   "The interaction of speech perception and grammatical structure in the evolution of language", *Linguistic change and generative theory* (Eds.: R. P. Stockwell – R. K. S. Macaulay) (Bloomington: Indiana University Press), pp. 32–95.
Bloomfield, L.
   1934   Review of Havers, *Handbuch der erklärenden Syntax, Language* 10: 32–39.
   1935   *Language* (London: Allen and Unwin).
Braithwaite, R. B.
   1953   *Scientific explanation* (Cambridge: Cambridge University Press).
Campbell, L.
   1974   "On conditions on sound change", in: Anderson – Jones 1974, pp. 89–98.
Forrest, R.
   1973   *The Chinese language*[3] (London: Faber and Faber).
Fouché, P.
   1959   *Traité de prononciation française* (Paris: Klincksieck).
Haudricourt, A. – A. Juilland
   1970   *Essai pour une histoire structurale du phonétisme français*[2] (The Hague: Mouton).
Hooper, J. B.
   1974   *Aspects of natural generative phonology* (Bloomington: Indiana University Linguistics Club).
Householder, F.
   1971   *Linguistic speculations* (Cambridge: Cambridge University Press).
Hyman, L.
   1975   *Phonology: Theory and analysis* (New York: Holt).

Iordan, I. – J. Orr – R. Posner
1970   *An introduction to Romance linguistics* (Oxford: Basil Blackwell).
Jakobson, R.
1931   "Prinzipien der historischen Phonologie", TCLP 4: 247–267; cited after: *A reader in historical and comparative linguistics* (Ed. A. R. Keiler) (New York: Holt, 1972), pp. 121–138.
1949   "The phonemic and grammatical aspects of language in their interrelations", in: Roman Jakobson, *Selected writings* 2 (The Hague: Mouton 1971), pp. 103–114.
1961   *Selected writings* 1 (The Hague: Mouton).
1968   *Child language, aphasia and phonological universals* (The Hague: Mouton).
King, R. D.
1969   *Historical linguistics and generative grammar* (Englewood Cliffs, N.J.: Prentice-Hall).
Kisseberth, C.
1970   "On the functional unity of phonological rules", *Linguistic Inquiry* 1: 291–306.
Kratochvíl, P.
1968   *The Chinese language today* (London: Hutchinson).
Labov, W.
1965   "On the mechanism of linguistic change", reprinted in *A reader in historical and comparative linguistics* (Ed.: A. R. Keder) (New York: Holt, 1972), 267–288.
Lass, R.
1969   *On the derivative status of phonological rules: The function of metarules in sound change* (Bloomington: Indiana University Linguistics Club).
1974   "Linguistic orthogenesis? Scots vowel quantity and the English length conspiracy", in: Anderson – Jones 1974, pp. 311–352.
Martin, S. E.
1953   *The phonemes of ancient Chinese*, supplement to *Journal of the American Oriental Society* 16.
Martinet, A.
1952   "Function, structure and sound change", reprinted in: *A reader in historical and comparative linguistics* (Ed.: A. R. Keiler) (New York: Holt 1972), pp. 139–174.
1955   *Économie des changements phonétiques* (Berne: Francke).
Matthews, P. H.
1972   *Inflectional morphology* (Cambridge: Cambridge University Press).
Muljačić, Z.
1969   *Fonologia generale e fonologia della lingua italiana* (Bologna: Il Mulino).
Penzl, H.
1969   "The phonetic split of Germanic *k* in Old English", in: *Approaches to English historical linguistics* (Ed.: R. Lass) (New York: Holt), pp. 97–107.
Politzer, R.
1951   "On the chronology of the simplification of geminates in Northern France", *Modern Language Notes* 66: 527–531.
Rescher, N.
1970   *Scientific explanation* (New York: The Free Press).
Sampson, G.
1975   *The form of language* (London: Weidenfeld and Nicholson).
Sommerstein, A.
1974   "On phonotactically motivated rules", *Journal of Linguistics* 10: 71–94.
Stampe, D.
1969   "The acquisition of phonetic representation", in: *Papers from the Fifth Regional Meeting of the Chicago Linguistic Society*, pp. 443–454.

Tekavčić, P.
    1972   *Grammatica storica dell'italiano* 1: *Fonematica* (Bologna: Il Mulino).
Vincent, N.
    MS   *On gemination in Italian and West Germanic.* [Unpublished paper.]

WERNER WINTER

The distribution of short and long vowels in stems of the type Lith. *ěsti* : *věsti* : *městi* and OCS *jasti* : *vesti* : *mesti* in Baltic and Slavic languages[1]

0. In his discussion of Baltic and Slavic present stems of *TeT*-verbs with long stem vowel, Calvert Watkins (1969:31–32) agrees with Jerzy Kuryłowicz (1956:305–308) in assuming that the lengthening in, e.g., Lith. *běgu*, R *begu*: Gk. *phébomai* was a special Balto-Slavic development (to be kept apart from the apparent parallel in Lat. *ēst* 'he is eating': *edere* 'eat') that occurred in root formations formerly, or still in historical times, athematic.

In his listing of forms, Kuryłowicz follows Antoine Meillet; he enumerates first items with lengthening throughout:

Lith. *běgu, běgti*, Slav. **běgǫ* (R *begu*, OCS *běžǫ*) 'run, flee': Gk. *phébomai*
Lith. *ědu, ěmi, ěsti*, OCS *jamĭ, jasti* 'eat': OInd. *átti*, Gk. *édomai*, Lat. *edere*
Lith. *sědu, sěsti*, OCS *sěsti* 'sit down': OInd. *sátsi*, Gk. *hédos*, ON *settr*
Lith. *įsěkti* 'engrave', OCS *sěkǫ, sěšti* 'cut': Lat. *secāre*

Short and lengthened forms are noted side-by-side in:

Lith. *grěbiu, grěbti* 'rake': OCS *grebǫ, greti* 'row'
Lith. *glěbiu, glěbti* 'embrace': P *głobić* 'fit together' (OCS *globiti*, as listed by Kuryłowicz, appears to be unattested)
Lith. *stiegiu, stiegti* (< **stěgti*) 'thatch': R *stog* 'haystack': Gk. *stégō*
Lith. *trěškiu, trěkšti* 'crackle', OCS *trěskati* 'strepitum edere': Lith. *treškěti* 'rattle', OCS (R) *troska* 'bolt of lightning'
OCS *strěčǫ, strěkati* 'sting': OCS *stroka, strikati*

Finally, Kuryłowicz adds:

Lith. *šóku, šókti* 'jump, dance': OCS *skočǫ, skočiti* 'jump'

and concludes (1956:307):

'Il résulte de cette liste, qui n'est probablement pas complète, que le balto-slave a allongé le vocalisme de certains verbes à racine légère en consonne. Tout porte à croire que ce sont, en accord avec l'hypothèse de Meillet, d'anciens verbes radicaux athématiques.'

He then proceeds to offer an explanation in terms of his 'law of polarization'. It appears, however, that once a systematic attempt is made to extend the list of forms showing unexpected vowel lengthening, both Meillet's initial hypothesis and Kuryłowicz's extension thereof prove to be insufficient to account for the data on hand.

1. It is a time-honored tenet of Indo-European comparative linguistics that a relatively stable correlation is to be assumed between morphological categories and ablaut grade to be found in them; disruptions do, of course, occur, but they require a special explanation, usually in terms of paradigmatic leveling.

In the present context, it is therefore unacceptable to be content with a mere statement that Baltic and Slavic languages show lengthened grade in old athematic presents, when the evidence from other Indo-European languages clearly indicates that *e*- and/or zero grade is all that can be expected. In this respect then, both Kuryłowicz and (in slight modification of Kuryłowicz's approach) Watkins are right in attempting to offer an explanatory hypothesis.

What invalidates these hypotheses, however, is that they do not take into account a number of important facts:

(1) Vowel lengthening is not limited to verb stems.
(2) Vowel lengthening in T_1eT_2 roots depends on the nature of T_2.
(3) Vowel lengthening is not limited to T_1eT_2 roots but is found equally well in T_1eRT_2 bases, again with T_2 as a conditioning factor.

The paper submitted here will discuss only points (1) and (2); data and arguments for (3) will be presented elsewhere.

2. An inspection of the materials found in Fraenkel (1962), Vasmer (1950–1958), and Vasmer – Trubačev (1964–1973) yields the lists included in the sections now following. Only items for which a plausible etymology is available have been introduced.

The first group of lists gives forms with long vowels not properly supported by evidence from outside the Baltic and Slavic domain; the second group enumerates forms without lengthening. Within the groups, the arrangement is exactly alike; this is the reason why there are a few lists with no members at all. Whenever available, both Baltic and Slavic forms are included; closely related items from other Indo-European languages are added, with an eye to maximum information as to the nature of T_2.

3. Forms with lengthening in Baltic and Slavic languages:

3.1. T_2 = Baltic *b*, Slavic *b*:
Lith. *obelìs*, Latv. *âbele* 'apple tree', Lith. *óbuolas*, Latv. *âbuols* 'apple': R *jabloko* 'apple': : OHG *aphul* 'apple'
Lith. *grĕbti* 'rake, grab', Latv. [*grebt* 'grab'], *grâbt* 'grab': [OCS *greti, grebǫ* 'row', R *gresti, grebu* 'grab'] : : OInd. *gr̥bhnā́ti* 'grabs'

3.2. T_2 = Baltic *d*, Slavic *d*:
Lith. *ė̃sti, ė́mi, ė́du*, Latv. *ễst, ḗmu, ḗdu* 'eat': OCS *jasti, jamĭ* 'eat': : OInd. *ádmi*, Lat. *edo* 'I eat'
Lith. *pėdà, pė́das* 'foot, footstep', Latv. *pę̂da, pę̂ds* 'footstep': − : : Lat. *pēs, pedis* 'foot'
Lith. *púodas*, Latv. *puôds* 'pot': − : : OHG *faz* 'container'
− : OCS *pasti, padǫ* 'fall': : OInd. *padyate* 'falls'
Lith. *sėdė́ti, sė́mi, sė́džiu*, Latv. *sêdêt* 'sit': OCS *sĕdĕti* 'sit': : Lat. *sedēre* 'sit'
Lith. *sė́sti, sė́du*, Latv. *sêst* 'sit down': OCS *sĕsti* 'sit down': : Gk. *hézomai* 'I sit down'
Lith. *úosti, úodžiu*, Latv. *uôst* 'smell': OCz. *jadati* 'explore': : Gk. *ózein* 'smell'
Lith. *vė́daras, vė́darai* 'entrails', Latv. *vê̂dars* 'belly': − : : OInd. *udáram* 'belly'
Lith. *vė́dis, vė́dȳs* [*vēdis, vedȳs*] 'suitor': OCS *nevĕsta* 'bride': : Homeric Gk. *éedna* 'bridal presents'

3.3. T_2 = Baltic *g*, Slavic *g*:
Lith. *bė́gti*, Latv. *bê̂gt* 'run': OCS *bĕžati, bĕžǫ* 'flee': : Gk. *phébomai* 'I am in flight'
Lith. *(pa)lė́gti* 'lie (lay) down': [OCS *lešti* 'lie down'] : : Gk. *lékhetai* 'lies'
Lith. *núogas*, Latv. *nuôgs* 'naked': OCS *nagŭ* 'naked': : Goth. *naqaþs* 'naked'
− : OCS *naglŭ* 'sudden': : Goth. *anaks* 'sudden'
− : OCS *agnę* 'lamb': : Gk. *amnós*, Lat. *agnus* 'lamb'
Lith. *úoga*, Latv. *uôga* 'berry': OCS *vinjaga* 'grape': : Lat. *ūva* 'grape'

3.4. T_2 = Lith. *ž*, Latv. *z*, Slavic *z*:
[Lith. *aš, eš*, Latv. *es* 'I'] : OCS *jazŭ* 'I': : Lat. *ego* 'I'
Lith. *ožkà* 'goat', *ožys*, Latv. *âzis* 'billy goat': OCS *jazī̆no* 'skin, leather': : OInd. *ajás* 'billy goat'

3.5. T_2 = Baltic p, Slavic p:
No examples found.

3.6. T_2 = Baltic t, Slavic t:
No examples found.

3.7. T_2 = Baltic k, Slavic k:
Lith. *-sěkti* 'cut, carve': OCS *sěšti, sěkǫ* 'cut', [*sekyra* 'axe'] : : Lat. *secāre* 'cut', *secūris* 'hatchet'

3.8. T_2 = Lith. *š*, Latv. *s*, Slavic *s*:
No examples found.

4. Forms without lengthening in Baltic and Slavic languages:

4.1. T_2 = Baltic b, Slavic b:
Lith. *abù*, Latv. *abi* 'both': OCS *oba* 'both': : OInd. *ubháu*, Gk. *ámphō* 'both'
OPr. *babo* 'bean': R *bob* 'beam': : Lat. *faba* 'bean'
Lith. *bēbras, bābras*, Latv. *bębrs* 'beaver': OCS *bebrŭ, bobrŭ* 'beaver': : OHG *bibar* 'beaver'
Lith. *dabà* [*dobà*], Latv. *daba* 'manner': R *doba* 'proper time': : Goth. *gadaban* 'fit'
 − : OCS *dobrŭ* 'good': : Lat. *faber* 'artisan'
Lith. *debesìs* 'cloud', Latv. *debess* 'sky': OCS *nebo* 'sky': : Gk. *néphos* 'cloud'
Lith. *gābalas*, Latv. *gabals* 'lump': [P *gabnać* 'grab'] : : Goth. *giban* 'give', OIr. *gaibim* 'I take'
[Lith. *grěbti*], Latv. *grebt* 'grab': OCS *greti, grebǫ* 'row': : OInd. *gr̥bhnā́ti* 'grabs'
 − : OCS *rebro* 'rib': : OHG *rippi* 'rib'
OPr. *sebbei* 'to oneself': OCS *sebě* 'to oneself': : Lat. *sibī* 'to oneself'
Lith. *sidābras*, Latv. *sidrabs* 'silver': OCS *sĭrebro* 'silver': : Goth. *silubr*, OHG *silabar* 'silver'
Lith. *stābas*, Latv. *stabs* 'post': OCS *stoborije* 'colonnade': : OHG *stab* 'staff'
OPr. *tebbei* 'to thee': OCS *tebě* 'to thee': : Lat. *tibī* 'to thee'
Lith. *vābalas*, Latv. *vabals* 'beetle': R *veblica* 'intestinal worm': : OHG *wivil* 'beetle'

4.2. T_2 = Baltic d, Slavic d:
Lith. *bèsti, badýti*, Latv. *best, badît* 'sting': OCS *bosti, bodǫ* 'sting': : Lat. *fodere* 'dig', OE *bedd* 'bed'

Lith. *mēdis* 'tree, woods', Latv. *mežs* 'woods': R *meža* 'border': : OInd.
mádhyas 'intermediate'

Lith. *medùs*, Latv. *medus* 'honey': OCS *medŭ* 'honey': : OInd. *mádhu* 'honey'

Lith. *pãdas* 'floor; sole', Latv. *pads* 'floor': OR *podŭ* 'foundation: : (see
section 9.1)

– : OCS *sedĭlo* 'saddle': : Goth. *sitls* 'seat' (see section 9.3)

– : OCS *voda* 'water': : Goth. *wato* 'water' (see section 9.4)

Lith. *vãdas*, Latv. *vads* 'leader': OCS *voevoda* 'commander': : OIr. *fedim* 'I
lead'

Lith. *vãdas* 'pawn', *vadúoti*, Latv. *vaduôt* 'redeem': – : : Goth. *wadi* 'pawn'

Lith. *vedȳs*, *vēdis* [*vèdȳs*] 'bridegroom': [OCS *nevěsta* 'bride'] : : OInd. *vadhūs*
'bride' (see section 10.2)

Lith. *vèsti*, *vedù*, Latv. *vest*, *vędu* 'lead': OCS *vesti*, *vedǫ* 'lead': : OIr. *fedim* 'I
lead'

– : OCS *vedrŭ* 'bright', R *vëdro* 'fine weather': : OHG *wetar* 'weather'

– : OCS *xodŭ* 'walk': : Gk. *hodós* 'way'; but see section 9.6

4.3. T_2 = Baltic *g*, Slavic *g*:

– : OCS *bogŭ* 'god': : Av. *baγa-* 'lord, god', OInd. *bhágas* 'purveyor' (see
section 9.5)

Lith. *dãgas* 'summer heat', OPr. *dagis* 'summar': – : : Goth. *dags* 'day'

Lith. *dègti*, Latv. *degt* 'burn': OCS *žešti*, *žegǫ* 'burn': : OInd. *dáhati* 'burns'

[Lith. *palëgti* 'lie (lay) down'] : OCS *ležati*, *ležǫ* 'lie': : Gk. *lékhetai* 'is lying'

– : OCS *lĭgŭkŭ* 'light': : Lat. *levis* 'light'

Lith. *nãgas*, Latv. *nags* 'nail', Lith. *nagà* 'hoof': OCS *noga* 'foot': : OInd.
nakhám 'nail', Lat. *unguis* 'nail'

Lith. *nagùtis*, OPr. *nagutis* 'nail': OCS *nogŭtĭ* 'nail': : OHG *nagal* 'nail'

Lith. *sègti* 'attack': OCS *prisęšti*, *prisęgǫ* 'touch': : OInd. *sájati* 'hangs' (see
section 9.2)

Lith. *rãgas*, Latv. *rags* 'horn': OCS *rogŭ* 'horn': : MHG *ragen* 'reach high' (?)

Lith. *vagà*, Latv. *vaga* 'furrow', Lith. *vãgis*, Latv. *vadzis* 'wedge': – : : Gk.
ophnís 'plough'

4.4. T_2 = Lith. *ž*, Latv. *z*, Slavic *z*:

Lith. *ẽžeras*, Latv. *ęzęrs* 'lake': OCS *jezero* 'lake': : Gk. *Akhérōn* (?)

Lith. *ežē̃* 'border', Latv. *eža* 'border of field': – : : Arm. *ezr* 'border'

Lith. *ežȳs* 'hedgehog': OCS *ježĭ* 'hedgehog': : Gk. *ekhînos* 'hedgehog'

Lith. *vèžti* 'transport', Latv. *vezums* 'cart': OCS *vesti*, *vezǫ* 'transport': : OInd.
váhati 'transports, leads'

4.5. T_2 = Baltic *p*, Slavic *p*:

Lith. *lèpti*, Latv. *lept* 'become spoiled': − : : Lat. *lepidus* 'delicate'

Lith. *sãpnas, sãpnis*, Latv. *sapnis* 'dream': OCS *sŭnŭ* 'sleep': : OInd. *svápnas* 'sleep, dream'

Lith. *septiñtas, sēkmas*, Latv. *septîts* 'seventh': − : : Lat. *septimus* 'seventh'

Lith. *šlapias*, Latv. *slapjš* 'wet': − : : Gk. *klépas* 'wet'

4.6. T_2 = Baltic *t*, Slavic *t*:

Lith. *at-*, Latv. *at-* 'away from': OCS *otŭ* 'away from': : OInd. *áti* 'beyond'
  − : OCS *otĭcĭ* 'father': : Gk. *átta* 'dear father'

Lith. *katràs*, Latv. *katrs* 'which one of two': OCS *kotoryi* 'who': : Goth. *hwaþar* 'which one of two'
  − : OCS *kotora* 'fight': : MHG *hader* 'quarrel'

Lith. *mãtas* 'measure', Latv. *mats* 'name of a measure': R *metit'* 'aim': : Gk. *métron* 'measure'

Lith. *mèsti, metù*, Latv. *mest* 'throw': OCS *mesti, metǫ* 'throw': : Gk. *móthos* 'turmoil' (?)

Lith. *petỹs, petìs*, OPr. *pette* 'shoulder': − : : Gk. *petánnumi* 'I spread'

Lith. *ratà* 'oath' [if not a loan word] : OR *rota* 'oath': OInd. *vratám* 'law, vow'

Lith. *rãtas*, Latv. *rats* 'wheel': − : : Lat. *rota* 'wheel'

Lith. *tetervà*, Latv. *teteris* 'grouse': OR *tetervĭ* 'grouse': : Gk. *tetráōn* name of a bird

Lith. *vĕtušas, vẽčas*, Latv. *vęcs* 'old': OCS *vetŭxŭ* 'old': : Lat. *vetus* 'old'

4.7. T_2 = Baltic *k*, Slavic *k*:

Lith: *akìs*, Latv. *acs* 'eye': OCS *oko* 'eye': : Gk. *ósse* 'eyes'

Lith. *ekĕti*, Latv. *ecèt* 'harrow': − : : OHG *egida* 'harrow'

Lith. *(j)ēknos*, Latv. *aknas* 'liver': − : : OInd. *yákṛt* 'liver'

Lith. *làkti*, Latv. *lakt* 'lap up': OCS *lokati* 'lap up': : Gk. *láptein* 'lap up'

Lith. *naktìs*, Latv. *nakts* 'night': OCS *noštĭ* 'night': : Lat. *nox* 'night'

Lith. *pēkus*, OPr. *pecku* 'livestock': − : : Lat. *pecū* 'livestock'

[Lith. *rēkti*, Latv. *rèkt* 'roar'] : OCS *rešti, rekǫ* 'say': : Toch. B *reki* 'word'

Lith. *sakaĩ*, Latv. *sakas* 'resin': OCS *sokŭ* 'sap': : Gk. *opós* 'sap', Toch. B *sekwe* 'pus'

Lith. *sèkti* 'dry up': OCS *isęknǫti* 'dry up': : OInd. *ásakras* 'inexhaustable'

Lith. *sèkti, sakýti*, Latv. *sacît* 'tell': OCS *sočiti* 'point out': : Gk. *ennépein* 'say'

Lith. *sèkti*, Latv. *sekt* 'follow': − : : Lat. *sequī* 'follow'

Lith. *-sèkti* 'cut' : OCS *sěšti, sěkǫ* 'cut': : Lat. *secāre* 'cut'
  −: OCS *sekyra* 'ax': : Lat. *secūris* 'hatchet'

Lith. *smãkras*, Latv. *smakrs* 'chin': − : : Arm. *mawrowkʻ* 'beard'

Lith. *tãkas*, Latv. *taks* 'path': OCS *tokŭ* 'course': : OInd. *takas* 'course'

Lith. *tekėti*, Latv. *tecêt* 'run, flow': OCS *tešti, tekǫ* 'run': : OInd. *tákti* 'runs'
Lith. *žvakė* 'candle': − : : Lat. *facēs* 'torch'

4.8. T_2 = Lith. *š*, Latv. *s*, Slavic *s*:
Lith. *āšara*, Latv. *asara* 'tear': − : : Toch. B *akrūna* 'tears'
Lith. *ašis*, Latv. *ass* 'axle': OCS *osĭ* 'axle': : Lat. *axis* 'axle'
Lith. *ašmuõ*, Latv. *asmens* 'edge': − : : OInd. *áśma* 'stone'
Lith. *dešim̃tas*, Latv. *desmitais* 'tenth': OCS *desętŭ* 'tenth': : Gk. *dékatos*
    'tenth'
Lith. *ešerỹs*, Latv. *asars* 'bass': P *jesiora* 'fish bone': : ON *ǫgr* 'sea bass'
Lith. *lãšis*, Latv. *lasis* 'salmon': R *lósos'* 'salmon': : OE *leax* 'salmon'
Lith. *nèšti, nešù*, Latv. *nest* 'carry': OCS *nesti, nesǫ* 'carry': : OInd. *náśati*
    'obtains'
Lith. *pèšti* 'pull out': − : : Gk. *pékein* 'shear'
Lith. *prašýti*, Latv. *prasît* 'ask': OCS *prositi* 'ask': : Lat. *precārī* 'ask'
Lith. *šéštas*, Latv. *sęsts* 'sixth': OCS *šestŭ* 'sixth': : Lat. *sextus* 'sixth'
Lith. *šẽšuras* 'wife's father-in-law': OCS *svekrŭ* 'father-in-law': : OInd.
    śváśuras 'father-in-law'
Lith. *tašýti*, Latv. *test* [*tēst*] 'hew': OCS *tesati, tešǫ* 'hew': : Av. *tašaiti*
    'shapes'

5. An inspection of the lists immediately shows two facts:
    (a) With the exception of one set of forms, the lists 3.5 through 3.8 are empty, while the parallel lists 4.5 through 4.8 include more than forty strings of items; beside the forms with long vowel in Lith. *-sėkti*, OCS *sěšti* 'cut', at least one related item with short *e* is found: OCS *sekyra* 'ax'. There is thus a high degree of regularity to be observed, to the effect that before voiceless stops and the spirant Lith. *š*, Latv. *s*, Slavic *s*, lengthening does not occur.
    (b) Before voiced stops and Lith. *ž*, Latv. *z*, Slavic *z*, both short and lengthened vowels are found. Absence of lengthening is more common; if mixed strings are disregarded, a total of 34 sets of forms can be cited from our lists. But the phenomenon of lengthening is well enough attested not to consider it a mere exception: sixteen sets show lengthening (again not counting any mixed ones).

6. There is a very striking difference in membership in the two parallel lists 4.1 and 3.1: while the former contains a total of eleven unmixed strings, the latter holds only one.
    Now it is a well-known fact that the reconstruction of Proto-Indo-European reveals a very unbalanced distribution of stops: whereas voiceless stops as well as aspirates are reasonably well attested for all points of articulation, the

voiced labial is very much less common than its counterparts. It follows that only a marginal attestation of reflexes of PIE *b* can be expected anywhere in the daughter languages.

A hypothesis suggests itself: If, in Baltic and Slavic languages, reflexes of Proto-Indo-European short vowels plus **b* differed from those of short vowels plus **bh*, then the rarer set of reflexes would have to be assigned to the sequence **Vb* and not **Vbh*. The rarer phenomenon is that of lengthening; therefore, *V:b* in Baltic and Slavic should be derivable from PIE *Vb*.

The data from related languages point to PIE *b* only in one single case, that of the word for 'apple'; it is found in list 3.1 and provides the only case of vowel lengthening.

For all unmixed strings in list 4.1, a derivation from Proto-Indo-European forms with **bh* is either undisputed or at least highly probable.

7. The phenomenon of vowel lengthening in Baltic and Slavic languages is not limited to a labial environment; the observation about separate development of PIE *Vb* and PIE *Vbh* should therefore be extended to other sequences of old short vowel plus voiced stop or aspirate, respectively, if this observation is to have any claim to validity.

Taking into consideration only unmixed strings, we find the following to be the case:

In list 3.2, there are eight strings with lengthened vowel; all of these are matched by forms from related languages that require a derivation from PIE *Vd.*

All five unmixed strings in 3.3 permit or require a reconstruction of PIE *Vg* or PIE *Vgʷ*.

The one example in 3.4 derives from PIE *Vǵ*.

There are no instances at all of unmixed strings with lengthened vowel that would require us to posit underlying PIE *Vdh*, *Vǵh*, *Vgh*, or *Vgʷh*.

An inspection of the lists 4.2 through 4.4, again limited to unmixed strings only, yields the following results:

In 4.2, the items Lith. *bèsti, mēdis, medùs*, OCS *vedrŭ* require the reconstruction of proto-forms with PIE *dh*; conventional etymologies point to PIE *d* for Lith. *pādas*, OCS *sedĭlo, voda, xodŭ*; for the remainder, no immediate decision seems possible.

In 4.3, eight of ten strings require positing an underlying Proto-Indo-European aspirate.

The same applies to all four strings in 4.4.

8. In summing up the findings from 6 and 7, it can be said that for twenty-seven unmixed strings without vowel lengthening, the reconstruction of

underlying Proto-Indo-European forms with aspirates is either mandatory or highly probable; fifteen unmixed strings with vowel lengthening are to be derived from proto-forms with voiced stop.

These observations can be restated in terms of a tentative rule:

In Baltic and Slavic languages, the Proto-Indo-European sequence of short vowel plus voiced stop was reflected by lengthened vowel plus voiced stop, while short vowel plus aspirate developed into short vowel plus voiced stop.

9. To make the claim made here fully acceptable, an attempt is called for to explain as many of the apparent exceptions as possible.

9.1. Lith. *pādas* 'Fuss-, Schuhsohle, Schienenfuss, Dreschboden, Dreschtenne, Ofen, Herd', Latv. *pads* 'Estrich', OR *podŭ* 'Grund' is usually explained (cf. Fraenkel 1962:521, Vasmer 1950–58 2: 382, Vasmer-Trubačev 1964–73 3: 295–296) as related to terms for 'foot' in other Indo-European languages; the underlying form would then be **podos*.

Two difficulties have to be noted. While *-os* nouns with *-o-* grade of the root are extremely common as deverbative formations (cf. Brugmann 1906:148–153), very few examples can be adduced for nouns derived from nouns (Brugmann 1906:156–157 lists only one further case, again from Baltic and Slavic); on morphological grounds then, the explanation of Lith. *pādas*, etc., as based on **podos* is far from being a natural one. Secondly, the meaning of the Baltic and Slavic words is not too close to 'foot'. For Lithuanian, Kurschat (1972:1660) lists: 'Sohle, Fusssohle; Schuhsohle; Boden; unterer Teil, Grundlage', for Latvian, Fraenkel (1962:521) gives 'Estrich', for the various Slavic languages enumerated, Vasmer (1950–58 2: 382) records 'Boden, Grund, Pritsche', 'unterer Teil eines Heuhaufens', 'Unterteil, Fuss eines Berges', 'Grund', 'Fussboden', 'Stockwerk', 'Fussboden', 'Grund, Boden, Basis', 'Unterteil', 'Grund, Boden'. It seems that the various meanings can be reconciled much better with a basic reference to 'floor, foundation, base' than to 'foot'.

Both difficulties can be resolved if a new approach is taken to the etymological explanation of Lith. *pādas*, etc. In Lithuanian, one finds other nouns in *-das* which have been interpreted in a quite different way: Fraenkel (1962:92) states: 'Komp[osita] mit W[ur]z[el] **dhē-* im Hinterglied sind lit. *ĩšdas, ìždas* 'Schatz, Schatzkasse, Fiskus, Ausgabe, Aufwand, Spesen' . . . vgl. aksl. *obĭdo* 'Schatz', lit. . . . *iñdas, indà* 'Gefäss', cf. abg. *sǫdŭ* 'Gefäss'.' Lith. *padėti* means 'put down, put under' (cf. Fraenkel 1962:522); it seems most natural to connect Lith. *pādas*, etc., with this verb, the more so as Lith. *padėklas*, which is clearly derived from *padėti* (cf. Fraenkel 1962:522), also refers to 'underpinning, storage rack, tray' and the like.

If *-das* in Lith. *pādas* derives from PIE *-dh(E)os*, the word clearly provides no counterexample to the rule proposed in 8.

9.2. Lith. *sègti* 'attach' is usually compared with OInd. *sájati* 'hangs' (cf. Fraenkel 1962:770) and considered to be related with OCS *prisẹšti, prisẹgọ* 'touch, reach for'. If the comparison is warranted, at least the Lithuanian form could not be accounted for by the above rule.

However, the situation is not altogether clear. The Slavic words have no diagnostic value for the present purposes: *seg-* could be the nasalized counterpart of short **seg-* as well as of lengthened **sĕg-*, cf. the forms of the first person singular nonpast *lẹgọ* and *sẹdọ* beside *lešti* 'lie down' and *sĕsti* 'sit down'. Latv. *segt* means 'to cover, roof, thatch', and while a connection with Lith. *sègti* is highly probable, some doubt does remain.

In spite of these difficulties, it seems advisable for the time being to consider Lith. *sègti* a true counterexample in need of further explanation.

9.3. OCS *sedĭlo*, R *sedló* 'saddle', OCS *osedŭlati* 'to saddle' point back to earlier Slavic **sedĭlo-* or **sedŭlo-*; no corresponding forms are found in Baltic. A connection with PIE *sed-* 'sit' is most natural; still, no trace of lengthening before Slavic *-d-* is encountered.

The closest match to the Slavic items occurs in Germanic; in particular, Goth. *sitls* 'seat, chair' shows extreme similarity to the Slavic words. What is there to prevent one from assuming that the Slavic form was borrowed from Gothic or, for that matter, another Germanic language similar to Gothic in the extreme?

The answer to this question seems all too obvious: a form **sedla-*, which one could imagine to be the source of the Slavic one, would lack all traces of the effects of the Germanic sound shift, and therefore such a form could not be Germanic.

However, it has long been noted that the sound shift was not a very sudden event and that in particular the reflexes of Proto-Indo-European voiced stops were slow in losing some of their *b-d-g*-like qualities. Hirt (1927:222) called attention to the fact that at the time of the first contacts between Goths and speakers of Greek and Latin the reflexes of the old voiced stops were still similar enough to Greek and Latin ones to have the borrowed sounds become identified with the then Gothic reflexes, so that Lat. *g* and Gk. *b* in early loan words could be subjected to the shift to Goth. *k* and *p* as found in the actual Gothic texts (cf. e.g., Goth. *Krēks* < Lat. *Graecus*, Goth. *kustus* < Lat. *gustus*, Goth. *paida* < Gk. *baitē*). It is highly probable that contacts between Goths and Slavs took place earlier than those between Goths and speakers of Latin and Greek; thus, if the reflexes of PIE *b g* were still close enough to Latin and

Greek *b* and *g* to permit an identification, there is no reason whatsoever why the reflex of PIE *d* should not have been *d*-like at the time of the encounter of Goths and Slavs.

In view of the arguments just presented, R *sedló* and related forms cannot be used as safe counterexamples to the rule given in 8. More important perhaps, it can be claimed that, if the word for 'saddle' is a loan word in Slavic, the time of the borrowing represents a *terminus post quem non* for the automatic application of the lengthening rule: if the data are correctly interpreted, lengthening had ceased to be an operating process by about the second century A.D.

9.4. More difficult than the case of OCS *sedīlo* 'saddle' is that of OCS *voda* 'water' and its corresponding forms in other Slavic languages.

From the point of view of form, the Slavic words are quite isolated in the Indo-European context. There is ample indication that the word for 'water' was a neuter *r/n*-stem; the former presence of such a stem even in Baltic and Slavic languages is made evident by the name of the otter, Lith. *ūdra*, Latv. *ūdris*, OPruss. *wudro*, OR *vydra*, SC *vidra*, Cz. *vydra*, P *wydra*, etc.: OInd. *udrás* an aquatic animal, Av. *udra-* 'otter', etc. (It should be noted in our context that all Baltic and Slavic designations of the otter show lengthening of the vowel before the reflex of PIE *d* and thus confirm the rule given in section 8 for a type of vocalism different from the one discussed in the present paper.) The word for 'water', as it is attested in the Slavic languages, is, however, an *ā*-stem. Why should that be so?

The closest match of Slavic *voda* in the entire range of Indo-European languages is Goth. *watō*, although it has to be stated right away that the Gothic form does not deviate as strongly from the Proto-Indo-European pattern as the Slavic forms do: Goth. *watō* is an *n*-stem, as are ON *vatn* and later North Germanic forms.

Now, if the early Gothic antecedent of attested *sitls* 'saddle' was **sedlaz*, it can be assumed that what became Gothic *watō* was **wadō* at the time of the early Gothic-Slavic contacts, and there seems to be no reason to reject the idea that Slavic *voda* was borrowed from Gothic — at least not if one wants to argue in terms of form only. What presents far greater difficulties than in the case of the word for 'saddle' is the semantic side of the question: while it can easily be imagined that the confrontation with a different type of saddle from the one previously used triggered the adoption of a foreign term for the object, no condition can be reconstructed under which the transfer of a term for 'water' would have seemed appropriate. To be sure, noncultural terms do get transferred occasionally, but this seems to happen too rarely to consider the explanation given here to have a high degree of probability.

It may, therefore, be appropriate to continue to list Slavic *voda* as an exception as yet unaccounted for to the rule given in section 8.

9.5. There has been very much discussion of the question whether the Slavic words for 'god' should be considered genetically related to OPers. *baga-*, Av. *baγa-* 'lord, god' (cf. Vasmer 1950—58 1: 98, Vasmer — Trubačev 1964—73 1: 181—182). So far, neither side seems to have been able to convince its opponents.

In the present context, we are confronted with a fairly simple choice: If Slavic *bogŭ* is part of the inherited vocabulary, then the absence of lengthening places the word in the very small group of counterexamples to the lengthening rule; if, on the other hand, the Slavic term was borrowed from Iranian, no problem exists, provided the lengthening rule had ceased to operate at the time of the transfer. To be sure, as the possibility for contact between Scythians and early Slavs existed for a much longer period of time than was the case for Gothic-Slavic contacts, not even an approximate dating (comparable to that proposed in section 9.3) seems possible; but such a state of affairs is not really surprising as the period concerned was strictly preliterate.

All things considered, it seems best to include Slavic *bogŭ* among the words borrowed from Iranian (as for the vocalism, R *vors* [*vórsa*] : Av. *varəsa-* 'hair' provides an instructive parallel; cf. Vasmer 1950—58 1: 230, Vasmer — Trubačev 1964—73 1: 355—356); no exception to the rule stated is therefore to be registered in the case of Slavic *bogŭ*.

9.6. The standard explanation for the initial *x-* in OCS *xodŭ* 'course' and related forms is not overly satisfactory (for literature cf. Vasmer 1950—58 3: 253—254, Vasmer — Trubačev 1964—73 4: 252—253): in order to be able to derive *x-* from PIE *s-* it is necessary to assume that the stem-initial consonant proper to compounds with prefixed *per-*, *pri-*, *u-* spread to simplex-based forms; only if this assumption is found plausible can there be any thought of identifying Slavic *xodŭ* as the genetically related equivalent of Gk. *hodós* 'way'.

As so many difficulties persist, the question of course can arise whether this Slavic word with its unusual initial consonant entered the vocabulary of the Slavic languages by way of borrowing. Greek as a source is excluded because of the wide distribution of the Slavic word; but would the same argument apply against the assumption of a transfer from Iranian? For the initial, OR *Xŭrsŭ* could be compared (apart from the discussion s.v. *Xors* in Vasmer and Vasmer — Trubačev see Abaev 1965: 115—117); for the vocalism, Slavic *bogŭ* offers a parallel, as does R *vors*.

Still, the fact that Slavic *xodŭ* enters into an ablaut relationship with OCS *šilŭ*, R *šël*, P *szedł* 'went' substantially detracts from the likelihood that *xodŭ* is a loan word. What remains an open question is whether the auxiliary hypotheses required to connect Slavic *xodŭ* with PIE *sed-* as found in Gk. *hodós* are not too complex, so that *xod-/šed-* should rather be viewed as a Slavic isolate. In this case, there would be nothing to force us to identify Slavic *-d-* with PIE *-d-*, and Slavic *xodŭ*, etc., could not be classified as an exception to the rule proposed in 8.

9.7. A brief summary of the discussion in 9. seems called for.

Six apparent exceptions to the lengthening rule were subjected to close inspection: Lith. *pãdas*, Latv. *pads*, OR *podŭ*, etc.; Lith. *sègti*; OCS *sedĭlo*, etc. OCS *voda*, etc.; OCS *bogŭ*, etc.; OCS *xodŭ*, etc. For the first of these, a new Balto-Slavic etymology was provided; OCS *sedĭlo and bogŭ* were identified as loan words from early Gothic and Iranian, respectively; for OCS *voda*, the possibility of a Gothic origin was adduced. The question of the ultimate origin of Lith. *sègti* and OCS *xodŭ* was left open.

As a result, it can be stated that the rule as proposed in section 8 appears to apply to all unmixed strings in our data except for two or three. The claim that the lengthening rule proposed in this paper accounts for the data available in an adequate way can therefore be called reasonably well supported.

10. Only a few of the mixed strings from sections 3 and 4 will be discussed here. It is only natural that disruptions of the regularity as found elsewhere will be explained as due to analogical transfer from related items; such an explanation will not always be feasible because not always has the source of an irregular development been discovered.

10.1. OCS *ležti* 'lie down' shows the vocalism which, in terms of our rule, is to be expected for a form matching Gk. *lékhetai* 'lies'; Lith. *-légti* contains an irregular long vowel. The Lithuanian verb occurs only in verbal compounds and nouns derived from the latter; the compounds are (cf. Fraenkel 1962:250–251): *nulěgti* 'become tired', *palěgti* 'put down; become feeble, sickly'. Alongside these forms, closely similar verbs with corresponding meanings are found (Fraenkel 1962:370): *nulíegti* 'become exhausted', *palíegti* 'become feeble, sickly'. The simple verb *líegti* means 'be seriously ill'; it is to be compared with Gk. *loigós* 'disaster' and to be derived from PIE *leyg-*. Before the reflex of a voiced stop, the lengthening of the diphthong in *líegti*, as indicated by the intonation, is proper; in *-lěgti*, in turn, the long vowel must be interpreted as due to transfer from *líegti*.

10.2. For 'bridegroom', Lithuanian has both *vēdis, vedỹs* and *vèdis, vèdỹs*. It appears that two competing bases, *ved-* and *vèd-*, have been used indiscriminately;

the former of these would, if the lengthening rule is valid, be derivable from
PIE *wedh-*, the latter, from PIE *wed-*. Pokorny, in his presentation of the
verbal root denoting 'lead; marry (said of the husband)' (1959 1: 115—116),
lists two variant forms, one with *-dh*, the other with *-d*, with the latter said to
be limited to a position before nasal. In view of forms like OInd. *ubhnấti* or
Gk. *éthnos*, there seems to be no basis for the assumption of a loss of aspiration before nasal, and it seems much preferable to postulate the former existence of two different roots. PIE *wed-* (or, with the laryngeal suggested by
Greek, PIE *Ewed-*) would then be reconstructed for Gk. *hédnon*, Homeric Gk.
éedna 'bridal presents', OE *weotuma, wetma* 'price for the bride', OFris.
wetma 'dowery', but also for OCS *věno* (for older **we:dno-*). Last not least,
PIE *wed-* (and not PIE *wedh-*) could be identified as underlying OCS *nevěsta*
'bride', a word which has attracted an unusual amount of attention (cf.
Vasmer 1950—58 2: 205—206, Vasmer — Trubačev 1964—73 3: 54—55): if the
original meaning of PIE *(E)wed-* was approximately 'to give presents connected with a marriage', then Slavic *nevěsta* would be 'the women for which
such presents have not been given'.

PIE *wedh-*, on the other hand, probably meant just 'lead'. If the act of
marriage involved not only the transfer of bridal presents, but also meant
leading the bride away to the husband's home (cf. Lat. *in matrimonium
ducere*), a confusion of the two roots could easily enough happen: the more
commonly used **wedh-* was introduced in items where **(E)wed* should have
been kept, and as a result forms like OInd. *vadhūṣ* 'bride', Lith. *vēdinti* 'marry
off', etc., could come into existence.

10.3. It appears that the mixed strings from our lists, to the extent that they
have been discussed here in detail, do not call for a revision of the basic
assumptions of the present paper; on the contrary, the application of the
lengthening rule to the data on hand contributes to a better understanding of
the process that brought the actually attested forms into existence.

11. As was stated in section 1, only roots of the type *TeT* were to be treated
in this paper; the discussion of bases with internal liquid, nasal, or semivowel
will be taken up elsewhere. Suffice it to say here that Baltic data in particular
lend their support to the assumption that the domain of the lengthening rule
extends beyond the *TeT* roots.

12. In conclusion, a question of a more general nature may be asked:
Is a development of the type $VD > V:D$ a natural one? Or is what we seem
to find in Baltic and Slavic languages an unusual phenomenon?
Rather than attempt to give a long list of parallels from other languages, I

will limit myself to a brief discussion of a well-known development within Polish.

In a very large number of Polish words, we find an alternation of the type *dwór, dworu*. The vocalism of the nominative-accusative is due to a change which was still operative at the time of the Christianization of Poland a millennium ago (cf. *kościół* < Cz. *kostel* – see Rospond 1973:78), but did not affect forms derived from relatively late borrowing processes (cf. *dorka* – see Brückner 1957:94). The change, which from present conditions would have to be called a vowel raising, is interpreted as vowel lengthening (cf. Rospond 1973:66). The conditions for the introduction of length seem to have been as follows: a short *o*, whether derived from older *o* or older *e*, was lengthened in a position before voiced nonnasal consonant, provided this consonant was followed (in terms of present-day Polish) by word boundary or morphonic boundary plus stop. It is interesting to note both similarities and differences between the conditions for lengthening in medieval Polish and in Balto-Slavic: For Polish, the decisive fact seems to be that a consonant have the feature [+ voiced], for Balto-Slavic, that this feature be a distinctive one – thus lengthening would occur before *r* in medieval Polish, but not in early Balto-Slavic. In Polish then, the phenomenon has a wider range as far as the immediately following phonemes are concerned; on the other hand, there is no requirement in Balto-Slavic that the phoneme triggering the lengthening process occur in a specific environment. Lengthening in medieval Polish and in early Balto-Slavic are, therefore, similar, but by no means identical, processes; there was in medieval Polish no revival, as it were, of an ancient rule but similar conditions merely led to similar results.

13. The lengthening discussed in the present paper has just been called a Balto-Slavic development. There seems indeed hardly a chance to interpret the phenomenon treated here as anything but a shared innovation over against earlier stages of Indo-European. It is inconceivable that Pre-Baltic and Pre-Slavic should have undergone independently from one another a partially limited merger of earlier voiced stops and aspirates, that is, a merger which was complete in all respects but one, namely, that the distinction survived in the shape of differing effects upon the syllable preceding the stops, and that these effects were exactly the same in both Pre-Baltic and Pre-Slavic. Rather, if the lengthening of vowels before reflexes of Proto-Indo-European voiced stops can be considered an established fact, one will want to insist that this phenomenon constitutes a powerful argument for postulating a Balto-Slavic unity prior to the development of separate Baltic and Slavic groups of languages.

Note

1. My thanks are due to A. Steponavičius for his kind comments on the Lithuanian data included in this paper.

References

Abaev, V. I.
1965   *Skifo-evropejskie izoglossy. Na styke Vostoka i Zapada* (Akademija Nauk SSSR, Institut jazykoznanija) (Moskva: Nauka, Glavnaja redakcija vostočnoj literatury).
Brugmann, K.
1906   *Grundriss der vergleichenden Grammatik der indogermanischen Sprachen.* 2: *Lehre von den Wortformen und ihrem Gebrauch,* 1: *Allgemeines. Zusammensetzung (Komposita). Nominalstämme.* Zweite Bearbeitung (Strassburg: Karl Trübner).
Brückner, A.
1957   *Słownik etymologiczny języka polskiego* [= 1927] (Warszawa: Wiedza Powszechna).
Fraenkel, E.
1962   *Litauisches etymologisches Wörterbuch* (Indogermanische Bibliothek, 2. Reihe: Wörterbücher) (Heidelberg: Carl Winter).
Hirt, H.
1927   *Indogermanische Grammatik* 1: *Einleitung. I. Etymologie. II. Konsonantismus* (Indogermanische Bibliothek 1.1.13:1) (Heidelberg: Carl Winter).
Kiparsky, V.
1934   *Die gemeinslavischen Lehnwörter aus dem Germanischen (Annales Academiae Scientiarum Fennicae* B 32:2) (Helsinki).
Kurschat, A.
1972   *Litauisch-deutsches Wörterbuch (Thesaurus Linguae Lituanicae)* 3 (Göttingen: Vandenhoeck & Ruprecht).
Kuryłowicz, J.
1956   *L'apophonie en indo-européen (Polska Akademia Nauk, Komitet języko-znawczy, Prace językoznawcze* 9) (Wrocław: Zakład im. Ossolińskich/ Wydawnictwo).
Pokorny, J.
1959   *Indogermanisches etymologisches Wörterbuch* 1 (Bern/München: Francke).
Rospond, St.
1973   *Gramatyka historyczna języka polskiego* (Warszawa: Państwowe Wydaw-nictwo Naukowe).
Shevelov, G. Y.
1964   *A prehistory of Slavic. The historical phonology of Common Slavic* (Heidelberg: Carl Winter).
Vasmer, M.
1950–   *Russisches etymologisches Wörterbuch* (Indogermanische Bibliothek, 2.
58   Reihe: Wörterbücher) (Heidelberg: Carl Winter).
Vasmer, M. – O. N. Trubačev
1964–   [M. Fasmer (– O. N. Trubačev)], *Ètimologičeskij slovar' russkogo jazyka*
73   (Moskva: Progress).
Watkins, C.
1969   *Indogermanische Grammatik* (ed.: J. Kuryłowicz) 3: *Formenlehre,* 1: *Ge-schichte der indogermanischen Verbalflexion* (Indogermanische Bibliothek, 1. Reihe: Lehr- und Handbücher) (Heidelberg: Carl Winter).

FREDERIK KORTLANDT

Comment on W. Winter's paper

Professor Winter claims that IE short vowels before voiced occlusives became
long and acute in Balto-Slavic. Elsewhere[1] I have put forward the thesis that
the Balto-Slavic acute intonation developed from a laryngeal feature.
Gamkrelidze and Ivanov have suggested on typological grounds that the
reconstructed IE voiced occlusives were actually glottalic.[2] It should be noted
that these three theories, though seemingly unconnected and formulated without regard to their interrelation, mutually support each other in the sense
that every one of them provides the missing link between the other two. If
short vowels became acute in the position before a definite set of consonants
and the acute intonation developed from a laryngeal feature, the latter
feature derives from the consonants. If short vowels became acute before
consonants which lost their glottalic feature, the acute intonation derives
from the latter feature. If the acute intonation developed from a laryngeal
feature and there was a series of glottalic consonants in the mother language,
the rise of the acute intonation before these consonants at the time when they
lost the glottalic feature becomes understandable. Combining the three
theories into one I would propose the following development. The proto-
language possessed a series of glottalic consonants which were preserved well
into the Balto-Slavic period. At a certain stage the feature was transferred
from a glottalic consonant to a preceding vowel and the two sets of voiced
consonants coalesced. The merger of the feature with the reflex of the IE
laryngeals was posterior to Hirt's law because of the broken intonation in
Latvian *pệds, nuôgs.*

Notes

1. *Slavic Accentuation*, Lisse 1975, especially chapter 3.
2. "Sprachtypologie und die Rekonstruktion der gemeinindogermanischen Verschlüsse",
   Phonetica 27 (1973), 150–156.

Index of names

Abaev, V. I., 442, 446
Abercrombie, D., 282, 284
Abrahams, H., 94
Äimä, F., 94
Aissen, J., 184, 192, 206
Alatis, J. E., 157
Albrecht, F., 33, 40
Allen, W. S., 278, 282, 407
Ament, W., 138, 140
Andersen, H., 1, 3, 9, 13, 16, 19, 21, 45,
    48, 51, 52, 53, 54, 55, 138, 140, 150,
    154, 155, 180, 181, 404, 407, 413,
    417, 424, 428
Anderson, J. M., 55, 103, 112, 113, 118,
    119, 120, 257, 261, 264, 269, 271,
    274, 277, 278, 280, 281, 282, 283,
    285, 336, 338, 343, 347, 369, 428,
    429
Anderson, L., 230, 234
Anderson, S. R., 23, 24, 28, 32, 39, 40,
    369
Anttila, R., 43, 45, 46, 47, 48, 51, 52, 53,
    54, 55, 119, 130, 131, 132, 133, 140,
    145, 154, 155, 161, 171, 245, 261,
    279, 283, 350, 359, 369, 412, 417,
    418, 421, 428
Aoki, H., 221, 222, 232, 233, 234
Ariste, P., 94
Atkinson-King, K., 136, 140
Avanesaw, R. I., 6, 7, 21

Bach, E., 252, 283
Bacon, F. 44, 46
Bailey, C-J. N., 131, 132, 138, 139, 140,
    283
van Bakel, J., 121
Ball, C. J. E., 351, 368, 369
Bammesberger, A., 363, 369

Bańczerowski, J., 94
Bar-Adon, A., 128, 140, 143
Barnitz, J., 149, 155
Barrit, C. W., 338, 343, 348
Barry, M. V., 266, 285
Bartholomae, C., 406, 407
Bateni, M. R., 233
Batóg, T., 74, 93, 94
Baudouin de Courtenay, J. N., 28, 40,
    138, 140
Beade, P., 112, 119
Bech, G., 351, 353, 363, 364, 369
Beeler, M. S., 129, 140
Belasco, S., 94
Benfey, T., 395, 407
Bennet, W. H., 104, 362, 363, 368, 369
Benni, T., 331, 335
van den Berg, B., 121
Bergsland, K., 93
Berry, J., 234
Betz, W., 369
Bever, T. G., 206, 207, 417, 428
Biedrzycki, L., 331, 332, 335
Binnick, R. I., 234
Birkhan, H., 370
Birnbaum, H., 220
Bjarnar, V. T., 366
Blasdell, R. C., 125, 140
Bleek, W. H. I., 94
Bloomfield, L., 130, 132, 140, 219, 220,
    255, 278, 283, 407, 408, 409, 412,
    414, 428
Bloomfield, M., 407, 408
Bluhme, H., 283
Boadi, L. A., 234
Bodine, A., 150, 155
Bollensen, Fr., 406, 408
Bond, Z., 131, 140, 154, 156

Bosworth, J., 119
Bourciez, E., 165, 171
Braithwaite, R. B., 409, 410, 427, 428
Braune, W., 312
Bréal, M., 154, 155
Bredsdorff, J. H., 154, 156
Bright, W., 230, 234, 407, 408
Broadbent, S., 133, 141
Brown, R., 50
Bruck, A., 408
Brugmann, K., 174, 176, 181, 238, 242, 439, 446
Brunner, K., 104, 120, 283
Brückner, A., 445, 446
Būga, K., 241, 242
Bulaxovs'kyj, L. A., 10, 21
Burrow, T., 240, 243, 246, 283, 395, 397, 400, 406, 408

Campbell, A., 102, 119, 280, 283
Campbell, L., 55, 358, 359, 369, 420, 428
Canonge, E. D., 94
Chao, Y. R., 128, 136, 141
Carney, J., 156
Carnochan, J., 234
Catford, J., 282, 283
Cedergren, H. J., 280, 283
Chafe, W. L., 24, 40, 48, 55, 421
Chen, M. Y., 135, 150, 151, 154, 156, 362, 369
Chinebuah, I. K., 95
Chomsky, N., 49, 225, 226, 234, 304, 322, 323, 326, 335, 337, 344, 347
Christie, W. M., 55, 206, 220
Chromec, E., 283
Clement, D., 155
Coates, R., 427
Coats, H. S., 211, 212
van Cœtsem, F., 361, 366, 368, 370, 371
Coleman, E. S., 369
Collier, R., 99, 114, 119
Collinder, B., 95, 257, 283
Collinge, N. E., 278, 283
Collita, H., 350, 351, 353, 366, 369
Comrie, B., 427
Cooper, C., 267, 283
Coseriu, E., 45, 53, 55
Cowan, H. K. J., 107, 120
Čekman, V. N., 237, 240, 243

Dahlstedt, K-H., 284
Darwin, C., 275
Debrock, M., 95, 99, 115, 116, 118, 119
De Coninck, R. H. B., 110, 120

Décsy, G., 93
Dekeyser, X., 281, 366
Delattre, P. C., 95
DeSoto, C. B., 33, 40
Dieth, E., 95
Diez, F., 309, 318
Dingwall, W. O., 336
Dittmar, N., 151, 155
Dobson, E. J., 104, 112, 120, 335
Dorian, N., 152
Drachman, G., 126, 128, 129, 132, 135, 136, 137, 138, 141, 150, 152, 153, 154, 155
Dressler, W., 138, 140, 141, 143, 147, 151, 152, 154, 156, 157, 260, 261, 263, 281, 283, 284, 334, 389

Ehrenstein, W., 50
Einarsson, S., 95, 404, 408
Ekman, P. R., 44, 55
Ellis, J., 278, 283
Elson, B., 132, 141
Emeneau, M. B., 246, 283
Eroms, H. W., 138
Ewert, A., 165, 171

Falc'hun, F., 95
Farwell, C. B., 135, 141
Fasching, P., 146, 156, 283
Ferguson, C. A., 135, 141, 348
Filin, F. P., 4, 6, 8, 9, 13, 21
Fischer-Jørgensen, E., 95
Fisiak, J., 336
Foley, J., 120, 184, 206, 280, 368, 369
Forrest, R., 428
Fouché, P., 355, 369, 423, 428
Foulet, L., 163, 165, 166, 167, 171, 172
Fraenkel, E., 432, 439, 440, 443, 446
Frei, H., 95
von Friesen, C., 351, 352, 353, 354, 355, 356, 357, 361, 362, 364, 367, 368, 369
Friesen, W., 44, 55
Fromkin, V., 95, 147, 148, 156, 281, 283
Fry, A. H., 407, 408
Fry, D. B., 282
Fujimura, O., 336

Gamillscheg, E., 146, 156
Garnes, S., 154, 156
Geschwantler, O., 370
Gilliéron, J., 414, 415, 428
Gimson, A. C., 261, 284, 335
van Ginneken, J., 61, 95
Goebl, H., 147, 156

Golick, M., 156
Goossens, J., 106, 107, 108, 110, 119, 120
Gougenhaim, G., 168, 172
Goyvaerts, D. L., 347
Grammont, M., 129, 130, 131, 141, 154, 156, 174, 175, 176, 180, 181
Greenberg, J., 159, 172, 186, 186, 200, 202, 206
Green, J., 427
Greene, D., 156
Gregg, R. J., 282, 284
Grégoire, A., 125, 128, 141
Groll, G., 283
Grucza, F., 93
Guile, T., 130, 141, 186, 206
Gussmann, E., 331, 334, 335, 336

Haas, M. R., 245, 278, 284
Haase, A., 168, 172
Haiman, M., 166, 167, 169, 172
Hajdú, P., 95
Hall, R. A., Jr., 125, 141
Halle, M., 113, 114, 120, 123, 138, 141, 212, 225, 226, 234, 304, 322, 323, 326, 335, 337, 344, 347
Halliday, M. A. K., 266, 285
Hammerich, L. L., 364, 369
Hamp, E. P., 242, 243
Handel, S., 34, 40
Hankamer, J., 184, 192, 206
Harms, R. T., 252, 279, 283, 284
Harris, J. W., 32, 40
Harris, M, B., 162, 163, 164, 170, 171, 172, 427
Hart, J., 267, 268, 284
Hashimoto, M. J., 131, 141
Hattori, S., 300, 306
Haudricourt, A. G., 95, 410, 428
Hauschild, R., 400, 405, 407, 408
Hayata, T., 298, 299, 306
Hempel, H., 351, 369
Henley, N. M., 33, 34, 37, 38, 40
Hentrich, K., 95
Hepher, S. J., 281, 284
Hermann, E., 149, 156, 351, 355, 369
Herzog, E., 138, 141
Heubeck, A., 139, 141
Hiersche, R., 351, 352, 353, 366, 369
Higgins, E. T., 34, 41
Hintze, F., 95
Hirayama, T., 290, 296, 302, 306, 307
Hirt, H., 351, 369, 440, 446
Hjemslev, L., 139, 141
Hoard, J., 187, 188, 206

Hockett, C. F., 255, 256, 280, 284
Hoenigswald, H., 147, 156, 178, 180, 181, 213, 214, 218, 220, 248, 271, 279, 284
Hogg, R., 427
Holman, E., 95
Hooper, J. B., 32, 40, 139, 141, 182, 184, 185, 187, 190, 191, 197, 200, 206, 359, 369, 419, 420, 428
Horn, W., 265, 284
Horsefall, R. B., 40
Householder, F. W., 281, 284, 424, 428
Howard, I., 148, 156
Hsieh, H., 150, 151, 152, 156
Hubbel, A. F., 341, 347
Hungerford, H., 336
Huntley, D., 210, 211, 212
Hurford, J., 427
Huttenlocher, J., 34, 40
Hyman, L., 227, 234, 348, 421, 428

Ingram, D., 132, 134, 142
Iordan, I., 428, 429
Itkonen, E., 49, 56, 96

Jackson, K., 155, 156
Jacobsen, W. H., Jr., 221, 225, 233, 234
Jakobson, R., 9, 13, 21, 53, 56, 61, 96, 120, 138, 139, 142, 180, 181, 211, 212, 213, 215, 220, 409, 412, 413, 416, 421, 424, 429
Javkin, H., 155, 157
Jeffers, R., 220, 357, 370
Jellinek, M. H., 367, 370
Jensen, J. T., 125, 133, 142
Jespersen, O., 96, 104, 120, 123, 126, 138, 142
Jonasson, J., 149, 156
Jones, C., 55, 285, 336, 347, 369, 428, 429
Jones, D., 335
Jordan, R., 258, 284
Juilland, A., 156, 410, 428

Kachru, B. B., 234
Karek, A., 132, 142
Karlgren, B., 96
Karskij, E. F., 14, 21
Katičić, R., 278, 284
Kaufman, T., 131, 142
Keiler, A. R., 347, 348, 429
Kelkar, A., 142
Kenstowicz, M. J., 234
Kent, R. G., 178, 181
Kert, G. M., 96
Kettunen, L., 48, 51, 56

Kim, C.-W., 139, 221, 225, 233, 234
Kim, W.-J., 225, 228, 234
King, R. D., 120, 213, 216, 220, 255, 256,
    257, 258, 259, 261, 279, 280, 284,
    368, 370, 412, 428, 429
Kinkade, D., 131, 142
Kiparsky, P., 30, 31, 32, 41, 123, 132,
    133, 138, 142, 153, 156, 221, 227,
    234, 321, 327, 330, 333, 334, 336,
    369, 391, 408
Kiparsky, V., 446
Kisseberth, C. W., 234, 422, 429
Klemensiewicz, Z., 17, 20, 21
Knapp, F. P., 357, 367, 368, 370
Koch, M., 160, 162, 172
Koch, W. A., 153, 156
Komárek, M., 46, 56
Koneczna, H., 17, 20, 21
Korhonen, M., 46, 56
Kortlandt, F., 239, 242, 243
Koutsoudas, A., 24, 41, 132, 142
Kökeritz, H., 257, 284
Krahe, H., 351, 370
Kratochvil, P., 427, 429
Krause, W., 367, 370
Kretschmer, P., 96
Krogmann, W., 96
Kruszewski, M., 154, 157
Kufner, H. L., 370, 371
Kuiper, F. B. J., 241, 243
Kurath, H., 120
Kurschat, A., 439, 446
Kuryłowicz, J., 237, 371, 431, 432, 446

Labov, W., 44, 45, 48, 56, 151, 157, 259,
    260, 261, 269, 270, 282, 284, 321,
    330, 336, 337, 338, 341, 342, 344,
    345, 346, 347, 417, 418, 424, 429
Ladefoged, P., 96, 120, 234
Lakoff, R., 160, 165, 169, 170, 172
Langendoen, T., 417, 428
Lass, R., 103, 112, 113, 118, 119, 120,
    139, 140, 246, 256, 257, 261, 264,
    266, 269, 271, 272, 274, 277, 279,
    280, 281, 282, 284, 285, 338, 343,
    347, 424, 425, 426, 427, 429
Lawson, R. H., 373, 389
Lazzaroni, R., 406, 408
Lee, K.-M., 228, 229, 230, 233, 234
Lee, S.-N., 225, 235
Lehmann, W. P., 159, 161, 171, 172, 245,
    253, 285, 335, 336, 367, 370
Lehnert, M., 265, 284
Leodolter, R., 283

Leopold, W. F., 129, 136, 140, 142, 143
Lepschy, G., 427
Leumann, M., 178, 181
Lewis, H., 279, 285
Leys, O., 99, 108, 119, 121
Lightner, T., 210, 211, 212, 221, 222, 235
Linde, P., 161, 172
Lindsay, W. M., 178, 180, 181
Linell, P., 145, 157, 260, 274, 281, 285
Lisker, L., 96
Lloyd, A. L., 373, 389
van Loey, A., 121
London, M., 40
Lovins, J., 129, 142
Lowe, P., Jr., 352, 354, 370
Luick, K., 99, 101, 102, 103, 104, 118,
    121, 281, 285
Lunt, H., 210, 212, 348, 370
Lyons, J., 223, 235

Macaulay, R. K. S., 206, 207, 283, 284,
    286, 428
MacCarthy, P. A. D., 282
Macdonell, A. A., 395, 404, 405, 406, 407,
    408
MacKinney, N. P., 96
MacNeilage, P. F., 96
Makkai, A., 48, 56
Makkai, V. B., 48, 56, 221, 235
Malécot, A., 96
Malikouti-Drachman, A., 136, 138, 142
Malmberg, B., 96, 155, 157
Malone, J. L., 132, 142
Mańczak, W., 151, 312, 319, 367
Marschak, J., 37, 41
Mareš, F. B., 143, 156, 283, 284, 389
Marouzeau, J., 161, 172
Marstrander, C., 96
Martin, S. E., 415, 429
Martinet, A., 95, 96, 217, 220, 374, 389,
    410, 411, 412, 426, 428, 429
Martynov, V. V., 243
Matthews, P. H., 422, 429
Mayer, K., 147, 154, 157
Mayerthaler, M., 138
Mayrhofer, M., 407, 408
McCawley, J. D., 136, 139, 290, 301, 306,
    307
McLintock, D. R., 373, 389
Meid, W., 156, 351, 352, 355, 358, 367,
    368, 370
Meillet, A., 150, 171, 172, 173, 174, 175,
    176, 179, 180, 181, 238, 243, 248,
    249, 285, 431, 432

Menéndez Pidal R., 279, 285
Menn, L., 128, 129, 134, 139, 142
Meringer, M., 138, 142, 147, 154, 157
Messing, G. M., 366
Mey, J., 109, 121
Milewski, T., 61, 93, 97
Miller, D. G., 161, 168, 170, 172
Miller, J., 278
Miller, R. A., 221, 235
Moon, Y.-S., 224, 225, 228, 235
Moore, S., 104, 121
Morris, C., 45
Moskowitz, A. I., 129, 142
Moulton, W. G., 102, 121, 367, 370
Mpaayei, J. Tompo Ole, 307
Muljačič, Z., 428, 429

Neisser, U., 125, 142
Newton, B., 23, 25, 26, 41
Nida, E., 133, 142
Noll, G., 24, 41
Northcott, K., 369

Ohala, J., 148, 149, 154, 157, 256, 285,
    331, 336, 345, 347, 348
Ohnesorg, K., 126, 130, 143
Okuda, K., 302, 307
Orlova, V. G., 4, 6, 22
Orr, J., 428, 429
Orton, H., 266, 281, 285
Öhman, S. E. G., 136, 142

Pačesova, J., 125, 126, 130, 143
Panagl, O., 138
Passy, P., 153, 157
Paul, H., 123, 138, 143, 147, 157
Pedersen, H., 97, 279, 285
Peirce, C. S., 45, 47, 56
Penzl, H., 349, 370, 374, 389, 417, 429
Perkell, J. S., 127, 143
Pernot, H., 130, 143
Pertz, D. L., 206, 207
Petrovici, E., 12, 22
Pickett, V., 132, 141
Pike, K., 46, 56, 278, 285
Pisowicz, A., 97
Pogonowski, J., 93
Pohl, H. D., 283
Pokorny, J., 444, 446
Polanyi, M., 282, 285
Politzer, R., 429
Polivanov, E., 180
Polomé, E., 367, 370

Pope, M. K., 164, 167, 171, 172
Poppe, N., 221, 230, 233, 235
Popper, K., 123, 138, 143, 275, 276, 285
Posner, R., 180, 181, 428, 429
Postal, P., 154, 157, 255, 261, 285, 358, 370
Posti, L., 97
Pott, A. F., 309, 319
Pound, L., 154, 157
Price, G., 163, 166, 168, 171, 172
Prokosch, E., 121, 370
Prokosch, E., 361
Puhvel, J., 220
Pulgram, E., 189, 190, 207
Pullum, G., 347
Pyle, C., 133, 143

Ramge, H., 143
Rardin, R. B., II., 221, 235
Rauch, I., 349, 351, 365, 366, 367, 370
Ravila, P., 97
Reimold, P., 149, 157
Reinhart, J., 283
Rescher, N., 427, 429
Rigsby, B., 222, 225, 232, 233, 234, 235
Rix, H., 178, 179, 180, 181
Roach, P. R., 139, 143
Robinson, C. W., III., 368, 370
Rosén, H. B., 351, 352, 370
Rosetti, A., 12, 22
Rospond, S., 445, 446
Roussey, C., 128, 129, 134, 139, 143
Rubach, J., 321, 328, 333, 334, 335, 336

Sadalska, G., 97
Sag, I. A., 219, 220
Sampson, G., 410, 415, 427, 429
Samuels, M. L., 51, 56, 150, 157, 265, 285
Sanders, G., 24, 41
Sapir, E., 46, 159, 163, 172
Sasse, H. J., 125, 138
de Saussure, F., 123, 138, 143, 184, 185,
    207, 238, 241, 243
Schane, S., 220, 335, 336
Schleicher, A., 123, 138, 143
Schönfeld, M., 106, 119, 121
Schopf, E., 148, 154, 157
Schourrup, L., 134, 143
Schuchardt, H., 154, 155
Schuchardt, H., 345
Scott, N. C., 282
Scriven, M., 272, 285
Seebold, E., 370
Selkirk, E. O., 329, 336
Similoff-Zelasko, H., 131, 143

Setälä, E. N., 97
Shapiro, M., 53, 56
Sharma, R. K., 407, 408
Shevelov, G. Y., 446
Shuy, R., 283
Sievers, E., 177, 181
Sigurd, B., 131, 143, 282, 285
Silva, C. M., 131, 133, 139, 143
Silverstein, M., 222, 225, 232, 233, 234, 235
Simpson, C. G., 277, 286
Sivertsen, E., 339, 348
Skaličková, A., 97
von Slagle, U., 49, 56
Sloat, C., 221, 235
Slotty, I., 51, 52, 56
Smith, D. L., 302, 307
Smith, H. L., Jr., 346, 348
Smith, M. E., 348
Smith, N., 128, 129, 131, 132, 134, 135, 143
Smoczyński, P., 125
Sohn, H., 233
Sommerfelt, A., 97
Sommerstein, A., 416, 422, 427, 428, 429
van Spaandonck, M., 304, 307
Spitzer, L., 52, 56
Sprigg, R. K., 221, 235
Stampe, D., 123, 137, 139, 140, 143, 265, 334, 413, 429
Stankiewicz, E., 138
Stark, H., 283
Steenbergen, G. J., 366
Steensland, L., 237, 238, 243
Steiner, R., 45, 56, 151, 157, 284, 347
Steinitz, W., 97
Steponavičius, A., 446
Stern, C., 134, 139, 143
Stern, W., 134, 139, 143
Stevens, K. N., 113, 114, 120
Stevick, E. W., 301, 307
Stewart, J., 97, 235
Stockwell, R. P., 206, 207, 226, 235, 278, 280, 282, 283, 284, 286, 338, 341, 342, 343, 348, 428
Strenger, F., 97
Strunk, K., 181
Sturtevant, E. H., 138, 143
Sundby, B., 286
Sundén, K., 126, 144
Sverdrup, J., 354, 361, 362, 368, 370
Sweet, H., 123, 138, 144, 335, 336
Szemerényi, O., 365, 371
Szulc, A., 318

Taylor, J., 280
Taylor, M., 278
Tekavčić, P., 425, 427, 430
Thumb, A., 400, 405, 407, 408
Thurgood, G., 154, 157
To, Su-Hi, 233, 235
Tōjō, J., 306, 307
Tokugawa, M., 306, 307
de Tollenaere, F., 366
Toller, T. N., 119
Tops, G., 99, 109, 121, 349, 350, 352, 364, 366, 367, 368, 371
Trager, F. H., 130, 144
Trager, G. L., 346, 348
Tranel, B., 186, 207
Traugott, E. C., 140
Trautmann, R., 243
Trim, J. L. M., 282
Trimingham, J., 133, 144
Troike, R. C., 150, 157
Trojan, F., 145, 157
Trubačev, O. N., 432, 439, 442, 444, 446
Trubetzkoy, N. S., 374, 389
Trudgill, P., 259, 261, 270, 286
Tucker, A. N., 306, 307
Twaddell, W. F., 261, 286

Uldall, B., 279
Ultan, R., 131, 144
Ulving, T., 97
Ułaszyn, H., 334, 336
Unger, J. M., 301, 307

Vago, R. M., 234, 235
Valentin, P., 373, 389
Vanecek, E., 151, 154, 157
Vanvik, A., 139, 144
Vasmer, M., 432, 439, 442, 444, 446
Velten, H. V., 134, 135, 144
Vendryes, J., 347, 348
Vennemann, T., 41, 138, 155, 158, 159, 160, 161, 162, 163, 165, 166, 168, 169, 170, 171, 172, 184, 189, 192, 207, 216, 220, 345, 348, 391, 404, 406, 408
Vergote, J., 97
Vernon, M. D., 47, 56
Vihman, M. M., 129, 144
Vincent, N., 45, 47, 48, 51, 53, 55, 139, 430
Voyles, J. B., 352, 371

Wackernagel, J., 405, 408
Wada, M., 306, 307

Wagner, H., 97, 351, 371
Wakelin, M. F., 281, 286
Walther, E., 47, 49, 56
Wandruszka, M., 47, 56
Wang, W. S.-Y., 135, 144, 150, 151, 154, 155, 224, 235, 262, 369
Waterson, N., 125, 136, 144
Watkins, C., 216, 220, 351, 357, 367, 371, 431, 432, 446
Weir, R., 136, 144
Weise, O., 238, 243
Wełna, J., 99
Werner, O., 46, 56
Whitaker, H., 150
Whitney, W. D., 407, 408
Wichmann, Y., 97
Wiklund, K. B., 98

Wilbur, T., 155, 158, 345, 348
Winter, W., 139, 447
Wintersberger, W., 283
Wisniewski, R., 351, 352, 371
Wolfe, P., 282, 286, 346, 348
Wood, F., 147, 158
Worth, D. S., 212

Yaeger, M., 45, 56, 151, 157, 284, 347

Zabrocki, L., 57, 98, 117, 118, 121
Zgółka, T., 93
Zimmer, K., 222, 235
Zipf, G. K., 428
Zwicky, A., 184, 190, 191, 193, 194, 195, 196, 197, 207, 221, 222, 225, 235, 260, 279, 286, 334, 404, 408